THE ROUGH GUIDE TO

Conspiracy Theories

ROUGH GUIDES

www.roughguides.com

Credits

The Rough Guide to Conspiracy Theories

Editor: Tracy Hopkins
Layout: Anita Singh
Design: Diana Jarvis
Proofreading: Jason Freeman
Cover: Diana Jarvis and Chloe Roberts
Production: Rebecca Short and Vicky Baldwin

Rough Guides Reference

Reference Director: Andrew Lockett
Editors: Peter Buckley, Tracy Hopkins, Sean Mahoney, Matthew Milton, Joe Staines, Ruth Tidball

Picture Credits

Cover images (clockwise, from top left): Sipa Press/Rex Features; AFP/Getty Images; Jason Reed/Reuters/Corbis; Dr. John C. Trever, Ph.D./Corbis; Getty Images; Bettmann/Corbis; Corbis; Andanson/Ruet/Cardinale/Corbis Sygma. **Internal images**: AFP/Getty Images 53; Ali Meyer/Corbis 156; Architecture Studio/Vincent Kessler/Reuters/Corbis 139; Bettmann/Corbis 13, 21, 38, 46, 50, 148, 191, 196, 212, 262, 281, 286, 344, 357, 371; Brooks Kraft/Sygma/Corbis 235; Corbis 26, 43, 105, 130, 296, 325, 362; Corbis/Sygma 245; Elio Ciol/Corbis 165; Getty Images 67, 110, 299, 409; Gianni Dagli Orti/Corbis 80; Hulton-Deutsch Collection/Corbis 35; James D. Phelan Collection/The Bancroft Library/University of California, Berkeley 207; John Sparks/Corbis 257; Kamal Kishore/Reuters/Corbis 176; Georges de Keerle/Corbis Sygma 389; Markowitz Jeffrey/Corbis Sygma 171; Matthew Mendelsohn/Corbis 222; Michael Ainsworth/Dallas Morning News/Corbis 312; NASA/Corbis 350; Pascal Lauener/Reuters/Corbis 248; Patrick Robert/Sygma/Corbis 293, 382; Peter Macdiarmid/epa/Corbis 432; Reuters/Corbis 122, 226, 339, 400, 420; Richard Baker/Corbis 269; Rob Howard/Corbis 396; Rolando Favo/ANSA/Corbis 135; Sergio Barrenechea/epa/Corbis 429; Tim Graham/Corbis 58, 115; Time & Life Pictures/Getty Images 18; Yann Arthus-Bertrand/Corbis 92.

Publishing Information

This second edition published September 2008 by
Rough Guides Ltd, 80 Strand, London WC2R 0RL
345 Hudson St, 4th Floor, New York 10014, USA
Email: mail@roughguides.com

Distributed by the Penguin Group:
Penguin Books Ltd, 80 Strand, London WC2R 0RL
Penguin Putnam, Inc., 375 Hudson Street, NY 10014, USA
Penguin Group (Australia), 250 Camberwell Road, Camberwell, Victoria 3124, Australia
Penguin Books Canada Ltd, 90 Eglinton Avenue East, Toronto, Ontario, Canada M4P 2YE
Penguin Group (New Zealand), Cnr Rosedale and Airborne Roads, Albany, Auckland, New Zealand

Printed in China

Typeset in Din, Helvetica Neue, Leicester and Minion

480 pages; includes index

A catalogue record for this book is available from the British Library

ISBN: 978-1-85828-281-7

1 3 5 7 9 8 6 4 2

THE ROUGH GUIDE TO

Conspiracy Theories

by
James McConnachie & Robin Tudge

CONTENTS

Mega-conspiracies and master plans 75

Secrets, myths and holy lies 151

INTRODUCTION

"And I began to question everything around me: the houses, the shop signs, the clouds in the sky, and the engravings in the library, asking them to tell me not their superficial story but another, deeper story, which they surely were hiding."

Umberto Eco, *Foucault's Pendulum*

To conspire once meant to "breathe together". It is an image of the most intimate and secretive complicity, perfectly conjuring smoky political backrooms, sinister whisperings and passionate plots. Today, "conspiracy" means a very particular kind of plan. It must involve more than one person – no "lone gunman" can make up a conspiracy of one. It must have goals that are either criminal, hostile or nefariously political – no one can conspire to forgive Third World debt or feed the homeless. And it must be secret – conspirators do not announce their manifestos to the world.

But this is a guide not to *conspiracies*, but to *conspiracy theories*. It doesn't freshly unveil hidden agendas or dramatically unmask sinister conspirators – though there's endless material here that you won't easily find published elsewhere. It doesn't presume to tell you who really shot JFK, whether Princess Diana's car crash was definitely an accident or if Neil Armstrong actually walked on the moon. We don't announce the Truth According to Rough Guides. Instead, this guide presents the world according to *conspiracists*, unleashing accusations, allegations and extreme explanations that are by turns brilliant, absurd, insightful, witty, nonsensical and sometimes outright insane.

Some of the authors, journalists, bloggers and whistleblowers this book cites believe their own theories passionately, while others undoubtedly have hidden reasons for claiming what they do. Some are even accused (by other conspiracy theorists) of being the public face of a conspiracy to discredit conspiracy theories. Many just revel in the sheer creative and iconoclastic energy of the conspiracist world. Either way, they are all given plenty of rope here. Some inevitably hang themselves – with others we've been delighted to give a gentle tug. But readers should beware: even where we haven't explicitly challenged or ridiculed a particular theory (after all, we can't begin every sentence with "supposedly" or "allegedly") it doesn't mean we think it's true or that we are presenting it as the truth. Of course there are a few exceptions and for the avoidance of doubt let's name them explicitly: the politically motivated plots to kill Fidel Castro, the "Iran–Contra" affair, the barely legal rigging of the US presidential election in 1876 and, most heinously, the Nazi conspiracy to murder millions of European Jews – despite the disturbingly motivated attempts of Holocaust deniers to claim that this is the world's greatest conspiracy theory, rather than an actual conspiracy. We can also add to these some conspiracies to provoke conflict and blame it on an opposing party: Hitler in Poland, and the US in respect of the Gulf of Tonkin incident in Vietnam. With all the other theories in this book, again, beware! **Though we have tried to be open-minded and judicious while seeking out the best-substantiated ac-**

counts of events, that still doesn't mean you should treat any of the other theories (or any of the "facts" related by us in our discussion of them) with anything other than complete disbelief.

But it's not always easy to stay dry and rational. Entering the world of conspiracy theories can be as disorientating as, say, underwater diving. Once you've left behind the reassuringly two-dimensional dry land of believing what the government or the media or indeed anyone else tells you, you're in a new and infinitely more complex world. It's hard to keep track of where you're heading, or even to know whether you're facing up or down. Everybody seems to have an agenda, no one can be trusted – your field of vision is constricted by the mask of ideology, and looking down into the murkier depths, it's easy to give way to panic and paranoia. And this is not the only danger: it's just as easy to be lured by the seductive intricacy of the conspiracy reef; stay down too long, and you may succumb to a fatal narcosis. As Umberto Eco puts it in *Foucault's Pendulum*, one of the great conspiracist novels, conspiracy theorists "are people lost in a maze: some choose one path, some another; some shout for help, and there's no telling if the replies they hear are other voices or the echo of their own". Calling for help underwater is still lonelier.

In a postmodern world where one version of history is supposedly as valid as another, conspiracy theories are often treated as a kind of game, or as the flowering of a fascinating but ultimately irrelevant subculture. Does it matter who believes what about JFK any more? Is it even possible to know what really happened? This book may, of course, lead you to think that to dismiss conspiracy theories is the greatest danger of all. You only have to look at the anti-Semitic "Blood Libel" (which is perhaps the longest-lived conspiracy theory of all) or the fraudulent screed known as *The Protocols of the Elders of Zion* (which is perhaps the most internationally widespread) to see how conspiracy theories can be supremely dangerous. It could be said that the Holocaust was allowed to happen only because ordinary German people had been persuaded that the Jews were a genuine threat.

Nazi Germany was, admittedly, one of history's most conspiracist regimes. But other totalitarian governments – Fascist Italy, Soviet Russia, Cuba and many contemporary Middle Eastern states, for example – have been equally conspiracist in their thinking. (In the case of Cuba, of course, this has been largely justified.) Perhaps Hitler saw the world as a conspiracy because he himself behaved like a conspirator. Perhaps whipping up fear of external (or, better still, internal) threats is simply the best way to suppress dissent: just ask Senator Joseph McCarthy or President George W. Bush.

It is curious that the majority of conspiracy theories seem to emanate from the right – notably when right-wing beliefs are combined with fundamentalist religion. Extremist Muslims and ultra-evangelical Christians share much in this respect. It seems that people with absolutist, black-and-white world-views tend to believe that the powerful operate in an equally absolutist way. People who desire patriarchal governments cannot conceive that their opponents might not act in a patriarchal way. If a political enemy is seen as basically evil – rather than, say, misguided or incompetent – then all their actions must surely be the result of sinister machinations. And all "accidents" are, therefore, the result of conspiracy, not cock-up.

Liberals or left-wingers prefer to imagine that they are above "naïve" conspiracist thinking, that they are relative sophisticates who understand the real workings of government – socialism grew out of Marx's profoundly intellectual analysis of history, after all. And yet the further left you go, the more conspiracist thinking creeps in. Anti-globalization campaigners typically caricature the workings of Western governments or multinational institutions as profoundly conspiratorial, and ultra-liberals and fascists alike share a belief in the corporate capture of politics.

Whether on the right or the left, it seems that the world's most conspiracist cultures tend to be those where the people feel most disenfranchised. Without any chance to witness the chaotic workings of the machinery of power, it's easy to believe that political affairs can be driven by sinister, implacable forces. Where there is no understanding of history, conspiracy theories are sucked in to fill the intellectual vacuum.

Ever since the Warren Commission into Kennedy's assassination, such inquiries themselves have often been seen as cover-ups or whitewashes – part of the original conspiracy. Yet all too frequently, the term "conspiracy theory" has provided those in power with a convenient way of brushing serious allegations aside, with the result that the official version of events prevails.

In these days of the Internet, however, the "official version" of events is subject to ever-increasing scrutiny. With access to a computer and a phone line making it possible for all and sundry to broadcast their opinions to the world (and without the benefit of editorial fact-checking), conspiracy theories have become an accelerating global phenomenon. Today, they stoke fear and outrage in the Middle East. They inspire homespun "patriot" movements in the US (and actual terrorist attacks in Oklahoma). They make liberal Europeans cynical and apathetic. They influence the politics of the entire Italian nation. They spawn computer games ("Deus Ex"), card-trading games ("Illuminati"), hip-hop albums (Public Enemy's *Fear of a Black Planet*), films (*Conspiracy Theory*, *JFK* and so on) and a whole sub-genre of fiction ranging from the intellectual games of Umberto Eco, Don DeLillo and Thomas Pynchon to the *Illuminatus!* trilogy and Dan Brown's *The Da Vinci Code* – a global publishing phenomenon in its own right.

Conspiracy theories have also given birth to a miniature academic industry. Whereas once serious historians avoided the word "conspiracy" like a disease, cultural critics and sociologists are now documenting conspiracism in popular culture, dissecting the politics of conspiracist thinking and analysing what is sometimes called the "paranoid style" – interestingly, a term borrowed from clinical psychology. A few historians are now willing to lash themselves, like Ulysses, to the mast and expose their ears to the siren voices of the conspiracy version of history. The idea that long ago it was great men's deeds that drove world affairs gave way to the notion that much bigger historical and social forces were at stake. Now, once again, it is being recognized that plans, projects, conspiracies and even conspiracy theories can change the world.

Note on the second edition

By unfortunate coincidence (or was it a conspiracy?), the first edition of *The Rough Guide to Conspiracy Theories* was due to be sent to the printers on July 7, 2005 – the day of the London bombings. A couple of years later, we're hoping another atrocity won't coincide with the completion of this second edition. Yet interest in conspiracies – both new theories and new complexities on existing theories – shows no sign of abating; hence the need for a new edition.

Much of the book remains the same, but in the interests of clarity we thought it worth noting which theories are new to this edition and which theories have been cut since the last one. There is, of course, no conspiracy behind the theories that have been dropped, beyond the need to keep the book at a reasonable length – but we would say that, wouldn't we? The cut theories are: the assassinations of Mozart, Harold Wilson and Archbishop Romero; Danny Casolaro and the Octopus mega-conspiracy; the Gemstone File and conspiracist Mae Brussell; Microsoft; and the capture of Saddam Hussein. The new theories are: the real identity of William Shakespeare; the assassinations of Franz Ferdinand, Alexander Litvinenko and Benazir Bhutto; sinister cities and Roosevelt's trailer parks; the two-day coup in Venezuela; the Taj Mahal; the Mormons; the John Birch Society; Bohemian Grove; climate change; Hurricane Katrina; UK floods and the Thames Gateway conspiracy; the shooting down of Korean Airlines Flight 007; the Rwandan genocide; the Tutsi–Hima world-domination mega-plot; 9/11 numerology; the 2004 Madrid train bombings; the 2005 London bombings; and extraordinary rendition. In addition, all of the existing material from the first edition has been reviewed, and corrected and updated accordingly. History keeps changing and the world keeps moving on, yet it is still recognized that conspiracies and conspiracy theories can change the world.

About the authors

James McConnachie lives in Winchester. In 2008, he was nominated for Sunday Times Young Writer of the Year for his history of the Kamasutra, *The Book of Love: In Search of the Kamasutra* (Atlantic/Metropolitan Books).

Robin Tudge is a Deptford-based journalist who has lived and worked in the US, Russia, Vietnam and China. He is the author of the pioneering *Bradt Guide to North Korea*, the West's first complete guidebook to that Stalinist state.

Acknowledgements

The authors would like to say a special thank you to Alice and Florence McConnachie, and to Colin Tudge and Ruth West. Thanks also to our indefatigable editors, Tracy Hopkins and Andrew Lockett, and to everyone at Rough Guides. For their encouragement, expert advice and those crucial tip-offs, we'd like to thank Jonathan Buckley, Ben Cairns, Jorinde Chang, Duncan Clark, Kris Dent, Mark Ellingham, Lucia Fairusa, Neil Foxlee, Dawn Holroyd, David Hunt, Terry Jones, Tobias Jones, Donald Kaye, Angus Kennedy, Charlie Marshall, Gwen and Robin McConnachie, Kate Rew, Robin Shaw, Julia Shillingford, Tobias Steed, Iain Stewart, Martin Strutt, Matthew Teller, Rosemary Tudge, Andrew Vereker and Greg Ward. All errors, of course, are our own.

The authors are eager to hear from anyone with conspiracy theories to push – or condemn. Please email Rough Guides at mail@roughguides.com

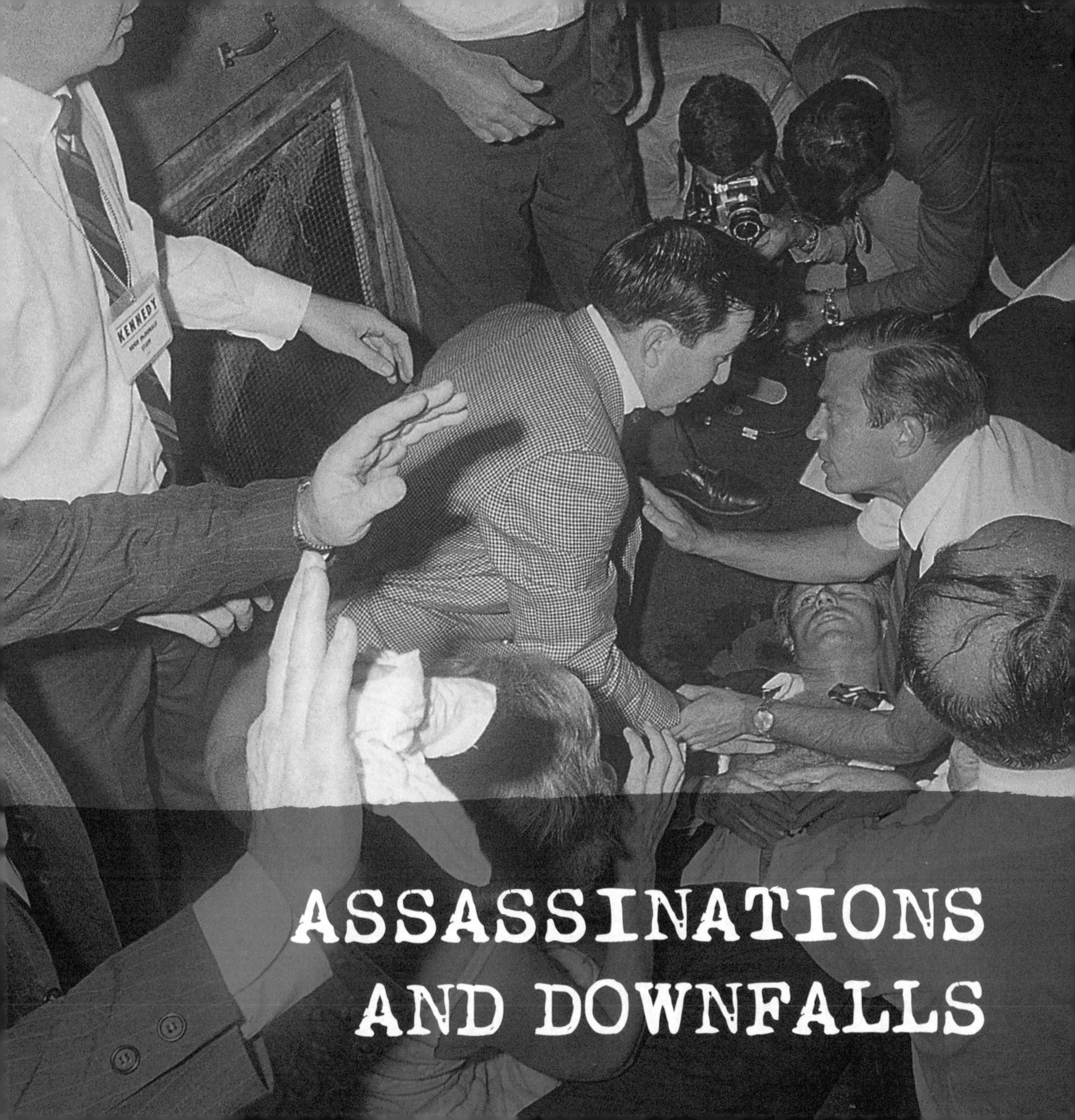

ASSASSINATIONS AND DOWNFALLS

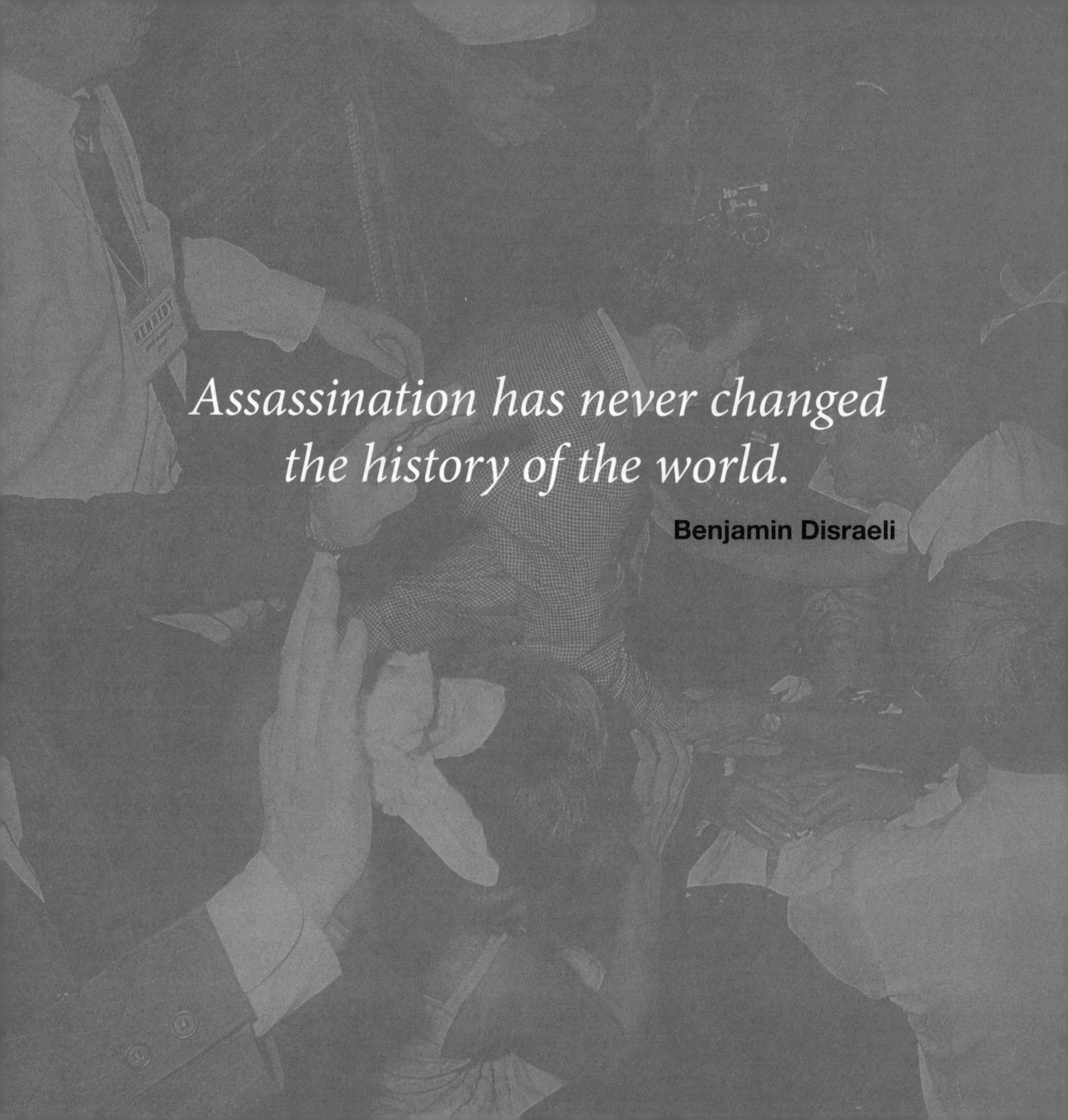

Assassination has never changed the history of the world.

Benjamin Disraeli

ASSASSINATIONS AND DOWNFALLS

Forty-five years after John F. Kennedy was shot dead in Dallas, in November 1963, his death has become more famous as a source of conspiracy theories than as an actual presidential assassination. After years of investigations and speculations, the incident has spun itself into a massive conspiracy tornado, sucking in an ever-increasing cast of suspects and spitting out an ever-mounting flow of print. JFK has become "JFK".

The maelstrom easily encompasses the other notorious assassinations of America's "Civil Rights Era": black activist Malcolm X, shot dead in February 1965; civil rights leader Martin Luther King, shot dead in April 1968; and JFK's brother, presidential hopeful Robert F. Kennedy, shot dead in June 1968. Even the 1962 "suicide" of Marilyn Monroe is dragged into the same vortex, largely thanks to her relationships with both Kennedy brothers. The names of the same mobsters and Washington insiders crop up in theory after conspiracy theory, with mantra-like repetition substituting for lack of evidence. In every case, the witnesses are said to be mistaken or lying, and the forensic evidence is supposed to have been destroyed, tampered with or misrepresented. Powerful interests were behind the killing. The truth was covered up. The gunman was not acting alone. One conspiracy theory shifts and slides smoothly into another.

The conspiracy theories of 1960s America all finger the "usual suspects": the Mafia and the CIA. Both organizations are conveniently secretive, and in the absence of reliable information, theorizing steps in. The CIA, in particular, is widely accused of orchestrating assassinations both before and after JFK's. One early victim, it is claimed, was Frank Olson, one of the CIA's own agents, who was allegedly defenestrated in murkily hallucinogenic circumstances in 1953. On the international front, practically any dead leader in the Americas has been a supposed CIA target. Chilean premier Salvador Allende, found mysteriously full of bullets after a coup in September 1973, is merely the most notorious example. Only veteran Cuban leader Fidel Castro has proved elusive – despite a baroque array of proven CIA plots against him.

Other security agencies may not attract quite as much attention as the CIA in conspiracy circles, but if two recent conspiracy theories are to be believed, their hands are far from clean. British and Russian agents, respectively, are said to have been behind the alleged suicide of WMD expert

David Kelly in 2003 and the poisoning of Russian dissident Alexander Litvinenko in 2006. Similarly, the Italian Mafia may not figure in quite as many conspiracy theories as its American grandchild, but its role in the apparent suicide of Italian banker Roberto Calvi, in 1982, is as fascinating and as hard to penetrate as any stateside scandal.

Even the death of Elvis Presley in 1977 has been linked – by some – to intelligence agents. Elvis's death is perhaps the best example of a constant in conspiracy theorizing: the refusal by fans to accept that a beloved icon could die before their time. Saints are supposed to be immortal, after all. Quasi-religious outraged disbelief was also in evidence in the wake of the deaths of Princess Diana, killed in a sordid Paris underpass crash in 1997, and ex-Beatles singer John Lennon, shot by a supposedly mind-controlled assassin in 1980. As for another popular saint, former Beatle Paul McCartney, most of the world would undoubtedly be surprised to hear that, "in fact", he died back in 1966. Why does he still appear to be alive? It is, of course, a conspiracy. A curiously reversed version of the same conspiracy has recently engulfed Elizabethan playwright Christopher Marlowe. According to some, his murder in 1593 was just a cover-up for a disappearing act: an act that allowed him to re-emerge later under a different identity – that of a certain "William Shakespeare". Some heroes, it seems, never die; others, never lived.

If someone is totemic enough, it seems that their death simply cannot have been straightforward. The shooting of Archduke Franz Ferdinand, for instance, was one of the world's most momentous events: the "starting gun" for World War I. Despite having witnesses, a motive and even a confession from the perpetrator, some historians think it must have been more complicated than a simple assassination. Reaching further back into history, some archaeologists deny that the fabled Egyptian boy king Tutankhamun could have died of something as mundane as natural causes. His mummy could surely turn up some far more interesting forensic results. Many Catholics, meanwhile, will not believe that the liberal "Smiling Pope" John Paul I could have died after just 33 days in office – unless a sinister hand was behind it. He was just too controversial to have died naturally; or, perhaps, like JFK, just too well-loved. Most recently, the assassination of Benazir Bhutto (or, some say, her bizarre death in a sunroof accident) attracted similar controversy. As Pakistan's great democratic hope, surely her death wasn't just the result of another Islamic extremist's suicide bombing? Surely the state had a hand in it too?

Tutankhamun and the curse of the pharaoh

Before Tutankhamun's dazzling tomb in Egypt's Valley of the Kings was opened by the archaeologist Howard Carter in November 1922, the pharaoh familiarly known as "King Tut" had been largely lost to history. Even today, Egyptologists remain uncertain as to exactly who he was, though most accept that he was the twelfth ruler of the eighteenth dynasty.

That would make him either the son or the half-brother of Amenhotep IV, otherwise known as Akhenaten, the "heretic pharaoh". Tutankhamun was born in around 1341 BC, and died at the age of eighteen or so, having ruled for roughly nine years. The big question is: why did the cosseted ruler of a civilized kingdom steeped in medical knowledge die so young? The first person to suggest an answer – at least, the first for some three millennia – was Ronald Harrison, a researcher at the University of Liverpool, who in 1968 took a series of x-rays of Tutankhamun's skull. He found fragments of bone dislodged within the brain cavity, and a thickening at the base of the skull that hinted at a heavy blow to the back of the head. More surprising still was the complete removal of the mummy's ribcage. Had the ribs been badly damaged? Was it murder?

Heretic pharaohs

Abnormalities about Tut's burial seem to endorse the homicide theory. Despite the presence of such amazing golden artefacts as the inner coffin and mask, his tomb was smaller than usual, and partly unfinished. Some of the artefacts that stunned the world even seemed to have been "borrowed" from other tombs – here and there, names had been painted out and replaced with "Tutankhamun". Had the young king died suddenly, before his funeral could be properly prepared? Or was his reign something of an embarrassment, to be quickly forgotten?

If Tutankhamun was indeed Akhenaten's son, he may have been tainted by association. His father has been credited with founding the world's first monotheistic religion, by turning away from the old Egyptian gods in favour of worshipping the Aten sun-disc. Indeed, Tutankhamun's name was originally Tutankhaten, "the living image of the Aten"; he changed it, or his advisers changed it for him, in what was presumably a bid to dissociate himself from the discredited "Atenist" regime of his father. As Tutankhamun, "the living image of Amun", the boy king reinstated the traditional worship of the god Amun, abandoning the new city of Akhetaten to return to the former religious and political capital at Memphis. But was that enough to establish the authority of his brief rule? Tutankhamun's name, like his father's, is glaringly absent from the "king list" in the Temple of Seti at Abydos.

Suspects – and a murdered Hittite prince

It would appear that someone set out to write Tutankhamun out of history. A leading suspect is Horemheb, a powerful courtier under Akhenaten who continued to wield influence as a military leader during Tutankhamun's minority rule. After the apparently sudden death of the boy king, Horemheb took responsibility for the restoration of the ancient temples, having his own name carved and painted over Tutankhamun's – even where the relief image obviously depicts a young man.

Even more suspicious is Ay, who was probably Tutankhamun's grandfather and acted as a kind of vizier or prime minister. Was an increasingly grown-up Tutankhamun trying to assert his authority? Did Ay and Horemheb conspire to remove him from the throne? Ay came to power after the boy king's sudden death – a wall painting in Tutankhamun's tomb shows him performing the Opening of the Mouth ceremony, a ritual traditionally carried out by the heir to the throne. Horemheb, in turn, became king after Ay. It also seems that Ay married Tutankhamun's widow, Ankhesenamun. In the aftermath of her husband's death, Ankhesenamun wrote to the Hittite king Suppiluliumas I, complaining that "they" were trying to marry her off to one of her servants, and would he please send a son as a more worthy husband. As prime minister, was this "servant" none other than Ay? Some Egyptologists argue that the letter was actually from Akhenaten's widow (perhaps the legendary beauty Nefertiti, who may have been Tut's mother), rather than Tutankhamun's, but it's hard to be sure. What is certain, however, is the fate of the Hittite bridegroom, Zannanza. He was murdered at the Egyptian border.

It is possible that Ankhesenamun herself was behind her husband's murder. Queens could inherit the throne, after all. Two mummified fetuses were found in Tutankhamun's tomb. Were these stillborn children? Had the boy king failed to provide Ankhesenamun with a child and heir?

JESUS OF NAZARETH AND THE CASE OF THE MISSING PENIS

The most baroque Tutankhamun conspiracy theory focused on his penis. Small, but clearly visible in the photographs taken in 1926, it had vanished by the time Ronald Harrison removed the mummy from the tomb again in 1968 (as had the right ear, but that's somehow less significant). Howard Carter and his crew, it turned out, had crudely hacked about the mummified body and entirely failed to replace its bandages. But had they really stolen the royal penis? Obviously, it would make a magnificent talking point on some millionaire art-collector's mantelpiece.

Some theorists believe that the mysterious castration is more ominous. Tutankhamun, they say, was the first god-king, the model for a certain Jesus of Nazareth 1300 years later. Extreme theorists even claim the two to be one and the same person – the original stories about Tutankhamun were simply displaced 1300 years into the future and a few miles down the road to Palestine. Just as Tutankhamun/Tutankhaten was "the living image of the Aten", so Jesus was "Adon", the Lord, the Son of God. Jewish circumcision is a ritual memory of the seasonal castration and rebirth of the Egyptian god Osiris – and Tutankhamun's golden coffin depicts him as Osiris, holding the royal symbols of the crook and flail. Tutankhamun's penis, therefore, is a potent ritual object representing the very wellspring of life, and its absence is a sure sign that dark forces are at work in the world. Whoever holds the penis of Tutankhamun, it appears, holds great power... Conspiracy theorists wondered what Carter's descendants knew. Unfortunately, this conspiracy line turned out to be a dead end. The CT scan of 2005 revealed that Tut's penis was, in fact, present, though not in the usual place – it was revealed to be lying in the sand tray in which the mummy rested.

Medical evidence

After 3300 years, there's more theory than substance to this conspiracy. Although wall paintings, letters and inscriptions have been used to build a serious case, the conspiracy's foundations still rest on sandy ground. Recent studies of the original X-rays – notably Richard Boyer's 2003 article "The Skull and Cervical Spine Radiographs of Tutankhamun: A Critical Appraisal" – have found no evidence of a traumatic or homicidal death, or have claimed that any injury could just as well have happened after death as before it. It was reported, however, that Tutankhamun might have suffered from Klippel Feil Syndrome, which produces abnormal curvature in the spine and fuses the upper vertebrae. It would only take a small shove to knock over and seriously injure a sufferer. As crime analyst Mike King commented for Atlantic's Discovery Channel documentary, *Mummy Autopsy*, "it was like having a bowling ball on top of a pool cue". Another study showed that he suffered from "fatty hips", which might explain the customary, bizarre depiction of Akhenaten as a deformed and androgynous-looking figure.

Serious Egyptologists tend to sniff at the x-ray story, but in early 2005, Zahi Hawass, Secretary General of the Egyptian Supreme Council for Antiquities, tried to produce more solid evidence. He subjected Tutankhamun's mummy to a CT scan, a sophisticated kind of X-ray capable of building up a three-dimensional map of the skull (the same technology had previously revealed that Oetzi, a 5200-year-old hunter-gatherer found preserved in an Alpine glacier, had been shot in the shoulder with an arrow and had a fresh gash on his hand).

Excitingly, a Photofit of Tutankhamun's face was created from the scanned images, but things didn't look quite so good for the murder theory. The boy king's left leg was found to be severely broken, which might well have caused a fatal infection. In 2007, Hawass announced that he believed the pharoah had fallen from his chariot while hunting, but the evidence was pretty thin. Spring flowers were found in the tomb, which would mean mummification began six weeks before – right in the middle of the winter hunting season. And then there were the chariots found buried alongside Tutankhamun – evidence, apparently, that he was an enthusiastic hunter. Either way, Hawass remarked, "The case is closed. We should not disturb the king any more." The bone fragments in Tutankhamun's skull were blamed on careless embalmers, or the rough handling of archaeologist Howard Carter and his team.

The curse of the press

No skull-bludgeoning, no murder. No murder, no story. If there's a real conspiracy wrapped up in Tutankhamun's bandages, it has less to do with ancient Egypt than with the modern media, which happily turned Tutankhamun into a whodunnit to boost sales. From 1922 onwards, the press conspired to concoct a better story than the mere uncovering of a tomb. The original problem was that the expedition leaders, Lord Carnarvon and Howard Carter, gave exclusive coverage to *The Times*, leaving rival newspapers with little to say. Luckily, a bright journalist – perhaps influenced by Louisa May Alcott's short story "Lost in a Pyramid: The Mummy's Curse" – came up with the "Curse of the Pharaoh".

The story usually says that Howard Carter found a clay tablet whose hieroglyphs were deciphered as reading: "Death will slay with his wings whoever disturbs the peace of the pharaoh." Fearing that panic would spread among the superstitious workers, Carter destroyed the tablet – as archaeologists are wont to do. But somehow the press got hold of the story. As you'd expect – given that the curse was entirely made up – there are scores of variations on the wording. One "curse" was borrowed from a real Anubis shrine, inscribed: "It is I who hinder the sand from choking the secret chamber. I am for the protection of the deceased." To that, some creative hack added "and I will kill all those who cross this threshold into the sacred precincts of the Royal King who lives forever".

It was a brilliant story. It pretty much eclipsed the actual tomb in fame. And it could run and run – every time an expedition member died, newspapers would speculate about the cause. It even resurfaced in 2005, when a desert wind supposedly began to blow as the mummy was being transferred from the tomb, and when the CT scanner stopped working for a couple of hours. Occultologists still swap lists of dead archaeologists, and one popular Internet conspiracy theory claims that 26 people from Carter's team died within a decade of the tomb being opened. (The true figure is six.)

Conveniently for the theorists, Lord Carnarvon died of pneumonia in April 1923. All the lights in Cairo were said to have gone out at the time of his death, while at home in England his dog Susie allegedly put up her muzzle, howled and died. Unfortunately for the curse theory, Howard Carter survived until 1939, dying at the respectable age of 64, while Alan Gardiner, the supposed translator of the curse, made it until the age of 84.

Horemheb and the foreigners

An investigation of Horemheb's tomb at Saqqara in 1975 uncovered a message from the general to his brother Egyptians. Protesting his loyalty to the dead pharaoh, he exhorted the people not to trust foreigners and "to remember what they did to Tutankhamun". Was this just misinformation? Or did it explain Tutankhamun's death? The young pharaoh is known to have conducted unsuccessful wars; perhaps he was injured on the battlefield? A lesion on his jaw is known to have begun to heal before he died, so one theory proposes that he was struck in the face in battle and fell, hitting his head and crushing his ribs, perhaps under a chariot. He then succumbed to his injuries slowly enough for his jaw to heal, but quickly enough for his tomb not to be ready. It's possible.

Unless another, near-contemporary tomb is found by a modern-day Howard Carter, it seems unlikely that the secret of Tutankhamun's death will ever be definitively unmasked, whatever the CT scans show. The vexed question of Tutankhamun's ethnicity may prove equally hard to solve. Activists have long protested that the ancient Egyptians were black Africans, not Caucasians or proto-Arabs, as they're often depicted, but the issue made headlines when the Tutankhamun exhibition was revived in Los Angeles in 2005. The show included a reconstructed bust of the boy king which showed him with light-coloured skin. Legrand H. Clegg II, attorney and producer of the documentary *When Black Men Ruled the World: Egypt During the Golden Age*, protested against the "suppression of black history" which was "conspiratorial" in nature, and demanded that the bust be removed. The truth is, well, less black and white. Contemporaries of the ancient Egyptians tended to refer to them as dark-skinned, but Egyptian tomb paintings depict skin tones more like those of modern Egyptians. Whether or not modern ideas of race have any relevance is a moot point.

SOURCES

Books

Bob Brier The Murder of Tutankhamen: A True Story (1998). A paleopathologist traces the conspiracy behind the killing of a pharaoh. Paced like a breathy thriller.

Howard Carter and A.C. Mace The Discovery of the Tomb of Tutankhamen (1933). Carter's memoirs, with some extra material. Fascinating – but there's nothing about dismembering the mummy.

Gregory M. Cooper and Michael R. King Who Killed King Tut? Using Modern Forensics to Solve a 3300-Year-Old Mystery (2004). Utah-based criminal profilers investigate the case of Tutankhamun. Reads like the TV script it is.

Christiane Desroches-Noblecourt Tutankhamen: Life and Death of a Pharaoh (1965). A classic biography.

Paul Doherty The Mysterious Death of Tutankhamun (2002). A thriller-writer's threadbare speculation that Tutankhamun died of Marfan's syndrome.

Websites

Ⓦ **www.ashmol.ox.ac.uk/gri/4tut.html** "Tutankhamun: Anatomy of an Excavation" – the complete records of Howard Carter's dig online, including his diaries and Harry Burton's original photographs.

A great reckoning in a little room: Christopher Marlowe

The handsome and preposterously talented English poet-playwright Christopher Marlowe was only 29 years old when he died, but he had already been hailed as one of the greatest writers of the age. On May 30, 1593 he went to Deptford in southeast London to drink, dine and talk with three men, Ingram Frizer, Nicholas Skeres and Robert Poley, in a house owned by the widow Eleanor Bull. The four spent the day quietly, talking and walking in the garden, but after supper a dispute broke out about the "recknynge", or bill. "Malicious words" were spoken, tempers lost, and Marlowe, who had been lying down, apparently leapt up, snatched Frizer's dagger, and slashed twice at his head, possibly with the hilt. Frizer's wounds were not serious, but in the ensuing struggle he stabbed Marlowe in the right eye, killing him outright.

Popular legend has it that the incident was nothing more than a barroom brawl – a myth that conjures up a colourful vision of Elizabethan roistering, worthy of a macho literary golden age before poets turned into daffodil-contemplating navel-gazers. Even Shakespeare was scarcely respectful of his rival's demise, punningly referring to it as "a great reckoning in a little room" in his play, *As You Like It*. The official inquest – which opened immediately, on June 1 – agreed that it was all the result of a drunken fight, and found that Frizer had indeed killed Marlowe in self-defence. Less than a month later, Queen Elizabeth I granted Marlowe a posthumous pardon for charges of blasphemy that he was on bail for at the time of his death. Was this Elizabethan efficiency or suspicious haste to close the case and any lingering questions about it? Was there something unusual about Marlowe that meant his death was unlikely to have been "just a pub fight"? Was he really an atheist? And a secret agent?

Historical detectives

With a few variations, the writings of near-contemporaries largely bear out the official story. Thomas Beard, writing in 1597, alleged that the incident took place in a London street and was because of a grudge; Francis Meres wrote in 1598 that Marlowe "was stabd to death by a bawdy Serving man, a rivall of his in his lewde love"; William Vaughan noted in 1600 that "as he meant to stab with his ponyard one named Ingram, that had invited him thither to a feast, and was then playing at tables, he quickely perceyving it, so avoyded the thrust, that withall drawing out his dagger for his defence, hee stabd this Marlow into the eye, in such sort, that his braines comming out at the daggers point, hee shortlie after dyed".

Although the seventeenth-century biographer John Aubrey accused another poet-playwright, Ben Jonson, of murdering Marlowe, it was only after 1925, when J. Leslie Hotson published *The Death of Christopher Marlowe*, that the vultures really began to circle Marlowe's corpse. A review article by a certain Eugénie de Kalb suggested that Audrey Walsingham, the wife of Marlowe's patron, had instigated the killing as part of an elaborate plot involving the succession of the Scottish king, James VI, to the English throne. In 1926, Samuel Tannenbaum's *The Assassination of Christopher Marlowe* set out to prove that Sir Walter Raleigh had bumped Marlowe off to stop him betraying the secret of Raleigh's atheism – a capital offence in those days.

An exhaustively researched, but no less involved, counter-thrust to Tannenbaum was delivered in Charles Nicholl's *The Reckoning* in 1992. This untangled the complex strands of Elizabethan espionage and court factions, only to weave together a tight web of a story in which Marlowe was killed to clear the way for a conspiracy to slander Raleigh. Nicholl originally thought the plot was the work of the powerful Earl of Essex, but later changed his mind.

Marlowe as atheist

But why should so many commentators have imagined that Marlowe's death was no accident? The answer lies in the timing. Just ten days before his death, Marlowe had been arrested and bailed by the Privy Council on charges of atheism, blasphemy and sedition. These were considered serious crimes, tantamount to treason, and a number of witnesses – or plotters and slanderers, according to the theorists – had testified against him. The most famous evidence was given by Richard Baines, who claimed that Marlowe believed "that Moyses was but a Jugler & that one Heriots, being Sir W. Raleigh's man, can do more then he … That the first beginning of Religioun was only to keep men in awe … That all protestants are Hypocriticall asses … That if he were put to write a new Religion, he would undertake both a more Exellent and Admirable methode and that all the new testament is filthily written." And, for good measure, "That all they that loue not Tobacco & Boies were fooles." If Marlowe did even think any of this, let alone say it, or persuade others it was true – as was alleged – it was staggeringly bold of him. Such beliefs risked undermining the whole structure of society, right up to the queen herself; in the right hands, however, evidence of such beliefs could bring down Marlowe and all his circle, the so-called "School of Night" and its patron, Sir Walter Raleigh.

Marlowe as secret agent

The idea of Marlowe as some kind of early-modern James Bond is widespread. He – or at least a college contemporary

TO BE WILLIAM SHAKESPEARE – OR NOT TO BE

The idea that William Shakespeare was not who he claimed to be didn't occur to anyone for a good 250 years after his death. For the last 150 years, however, book after book has claimed to hold the key to the "mystery" of the real identity of the playwright we know as Shakespeare. One count puts the number of published works on the subject at around 5000 (by authors, Bill Bryson tells us, including Messrs Looney, Silliman and Battey).

Christopher Marlowe is just one of the contenders for the title of "the real Shakespeare". The fact that he was a superb poet and dramatist in his own right lends this theory at least some plausibility. The same is true for thinker and essayist Francis Bacon, who was the first man accused of being Shakespeare. The accuser was Connecticut schoolmistress Delia Bacon (no relation, at least not outside her own mind). In the 1840s, she became obsessed with the idea that Francis was the true author of Shakespeare's plays. Wasn't St Albans (Bacon's aristocratic seat) mentioned fifteen times in Shakespeare's oeuvre, whereas Stratford-upon-Avon wasn't mentioned once? Yes, but almost always in reference to the Battle of St Albans, which plays a key role in *Henry VI*. Before Miss Bacon succumbed to mental illness she published a book detailing her theory; the fact that she didn't once mention Francis Bacon by name, but left it to her readers to guess who she was talking about, didn't stop it becoming a cult classic.

Despite the lack of any evidence, the notion that some other person was the dramatist "Shakespeare" – and that Mr William Shakespeare of Stratford was some kind of impostor or fall guy – took hold of the imagination of many literary types. The "Baconian" thesis was developed with other apparent evidence from the plays, and before too long other candidates were proposed, most notably Edward de Vere, the Earl of Oxford. The "Oxfordian" theory was sketched out in 1918 by another schoolteacher with a splendid name, J. Thomas Looney. If the poetry published under de Vere's own name was distinctly inferior to that of Marlowe or Bacon – not to mention Shakespeare – he did have some points in his favour. His daughter was engaged to the Earl of Southampton, to whom Shakespeare's great narrative poems were dedicated, and he had the aristocratic connections and education that seemed appropriate for England's greatest son. The fact that De Vere died in 1604 – five years before the shipwreck that inspired *The Tempest* – didn't seem to matter.

In all, over fifty Elizabethans have been accused of being Shakespeare, including the poet Mary Sidney (her estates were on the river Avon). The greatest theory of all posits a huge conspiracy of writers, all chipping in here and there to produce the great oeuvre. In fact, there's plenty of evidence that the plays' author was indeed William Shakespeare. The official court records of James I name him seven times; he is on the title pages of several printed works; and fellow playwrights have acknowledged him as a great talent. Why, then, would so many people claim that someone else wrote his plays? Some say it's a British obsession with class, as if a mere commoner from Stratford without a university education just couldn't have been up to it. It might also be the unfortunate lack of any significant information about Shakespeare the man. You can't write a decent biography without any personal titbits, but if you pin the authorship on someone better-documented and throw in a conspiratorial scandal, you've got a potential bestseller.

by the name of "Morley", which may be an alternative spelling of "Marlowe" – apparently went AWOL from his degree at Cambridge. While that was not uncommon in those days, what was unusual was the fact that, when he returned and found his degree in peril, he persuaded the highest powers in the land – including the Archbishop of Canterbury – to write a letter certifying that he had "done Her Majesty good service, & deserved to be rewarded for his faithful dealing". Some claim that he had gone undercover among Catholic students in exile in France, listening out for rumours of the Babington plot against the queen's life – a role certainly played by Robert Poley, one of the Deptford Four.

Curiously, Skeres and Frizer, the other two men present at Marlowe's death, had links with Sir Francis Walsingham, the queen's spymaster. Frizer had also worked for Thomas Walsingham, Francis's second cousin and a probable (but not proven) senior spy. In 2005, Professor Park Honan of Leeds University found a document revealing that James VI had given land to Thomas Walsingham's wife, perhaps in return for her husband's court-conspiring on behalf of James's claim to the English throne. Mrs Walsingham in turn leased the land to Ingram Frizer, further tying him to the controversial cause. Marlowe, meanwhile, was practically Thomas Walsingham's protégé (and any controversy he got himself into would, therefore, risk smearing his patron by association). The conclusion of the conspiracists is that Marlowe was at the tavern to meet fellow agents connected to the Walsingham ring – and that he was probably lured there to his death.

Other evidence for Marlowe being a spy is more circumstantial. The leniency with which he was treated after many of his numerous misdemeanours does seem surprising. In 1589, he got into a brawl with one William Bradley, who was stabbed by Marlowe's companion in circumstances suspiciously similar to those of Marlowe's own death. In 1592, he was caught counterfeiting Dutch shillings in Flushing, a capital offence, but was freed in a matter of months. And of course, he was arrested for sedition shortly before his death, but quickly released; by comparison, fellow dramatist and alleged atheist Thomas Kyd was tortured into confessing. Marlowe's play *The Massacre at Paris* features a non-speaking role for an "English Agent". Was he drawing on personal experience?

Marlowe as... Shakespeare

One group of conspiracists believes that Marlowe never died at Deptford. Why? Because Marlowe was Shakespeare! Propounded by the Marlowe Society, this thesis found its most articulate and committed exponents in Calvin Hoffman, who wrote *The Man Who Was Shakespeare* in 1955, and A.D. "Dolly" Wraight. Hoffman believed that Thomas Walsingham was Marlowe's lover, and that he faked the playwright's death to save him from execution. Dolly Wraight, on the other hand, works backwards, beginning with clues found in "Shakespeare's" sonnets (which, if read in the right way, apparently fit every detail of Marlowe's life – notwithstanding the fact that such sonnet sequences were rarely autobiographical) and ending with a faked death at Deptford. Marlovians have variously explained away the problem of the corpse by introducing substitute bodies or wilfully mistaken identities to the equation. Inconsistencies in the spelling of Elizabethan names provide rich soil for conspiracy theorists, who conveniently bump off the "original" William Shakespeare and allow Marlowe to slip straight into his shoes. So relentlessly have the Marlovians pushed their case, that Marlowe's memorial in Westminster Abbey's Poet's Corner actually has a question mark inscribed after his date of death.

SOURCES

Books

Bill Bryson **Shakespeare: The World as a Stage** (2007). Humourist turns his enthusiasm and wit to the topic of William Shakespeare. The competing accounts of the playwright's identity vie with the plays for Bryson's attention.

Stephen Budiansky **Her Majesty's Spymaster: Elizabeth I, Sir Francis Walsingham, and the Birth of Modern Espionage** (2005). Colourful, conspiratorial and controversial account of the Elizabethan secret state.

Park Honan **Christopher Marlowe: Poet and Spy** (2005). Suggestively shows how Marlowe's plays are fascinated by secret power, and claims that Thomas Walsingham's court status was threatened by his association with a notorious atheist.

Charles Nicholl **The Reckoning** (1992). The best book on Marlowe's life and death and a great introduction to the underbelly of Elizabethan England. Well researched and excitingly written.

David Riggs **The World of Christopher Marlowe** (2004). Worthy, detailed and excellent on the Elizabethan underworld – from hyper-talented playwrights to prostitutes and spies. Accuses Walsingham's rival (and future spymaster) Lord Burghley of being the mastermind behind the assassination (thus potentially tying the "murder" to Queen Elizabeth herself), but puts the emphasis on Marlowe's atheism, which had the potential to seriously embarrass his patrons.

Louise Welsh **Tamburlaine Must Die** (2004). Tight, intense and sexy conspiracy thriller set over the last three days of Marlowe's life.

Websites

Ⓦ **www.doubtaboutwill.org** Sign the "Declaration of Reasonable Doubt About the Identity of William Shakespeare" here.

Ⓦ **www.marlowe-society.org** The dark heart of the Marlowe-was-Shakespeare propaganda machine.

Starting gun to war: Franz Ferdinand

The assassination of Archduke Franz Ferdinand, heir to the throne of Austria-Hungary, in June 1914, was one of those rare events that was both a conspiracy and a monumental cock-up. However, the theorizing begins when you try to explore just how deep the conspiracy ran. On the surface, it appears to be the world's luckiest – because most poorly executed – assassination. But it was also the world's bloodiest. Although only two people were actually shot – Franz and his wife Sophie – their murders led inexorably, like the first two falls in a chain of dominoes, to the deaths of millions in World War I.

The Bee and the Black Hand

In the spring of 1914, Europe was turning itself into a military camp. The various nations had manoeuvred themselves into an unwieldy network of diplomatic alliances and security guarantees, meaning that the slightest provocation could set off a chain reaction of declarations of war. In the continent's most neglected corner, the kingdom of Serbia had ambitions to emulate Italy and unite all its neighbours into one Greater Serbia. Its powerful neighbour, the Austro-Hungarian Empire, was less than enthusiastic, especially as it occupied key territories in the envisaged Serb empire, notably Bosnia-Herzegovina.

The head of the Serbian Army's intelligence department, Dragutin Dimitrijevic (aka Apis, or "the Bee") had been a key player in the assassination of a former Serb king in 1903 and in the Balkan Alliance that kicked the Turks out of Europe in 1912. Since then, he had become the linchpin in a clandestine association of nationalist Serb officers known as *Ujedinjenje ili Smrt* (Unification or Death). Dedicated to the cause of Greater Serbia, the group's influence spread deep into government, and intimidated officials knew it better as the Black Hand.

When Archduke Ferdinand announced that he was going to visit his subject province of Bosnia-Herzegovina, "the Bee" saw a chance to use his sting. He contacted a small but radical group of Bosnian Serb separatists who called themselves *Mlada Bosna*, or Young Bosnia, and persuaded them to launch an assassination attempt. Each member was provided with a gun, two grenade-like bombs and a cyanide pill to swallow after the archduke was dead. The goal was to precipitate a revolt that would free Bosnia-Herzegovina to unite itself with Serbia.

Bosnian blunders

On the morning of June 28, 1914, the archduke and his wife, Sophie von Chotkovato, arrived in the Bosnian capital, Sarajevo, by train, and proceeded towards the town hall in an open car. Crowds lined the route, the seven conspirators hidden among them. The first, a Bosnian Muslim called Muhamed Mehmedbasic, lost his nerve, and let the car drive past him. The second, Nedjelko Cabrinovic, lobbed his bomb at the car, but obviously hadn't had much practice at hitting moving objects, as he missed entirely. His bomb exploded beside the next car in the cavalcade, causing serious injuries but nothing more. His credentials as an assassin didn't look any better when he took his deadly cyanide pill and jumped in the River Miljacka – the pill was a dud and the river too shallow for drowning. He was soon fished out.

The archduke sped on to the town hall, while the remaining conspirators gathered outside a café on Franz Joseph Street. That afternoon, he decided, with admirable bravado, to visit the injured in hospital. However, his driver – with breathtaking incompetence – somehow managed to turn back onto the previously planned route along Franz Joseph Street. (Oddly, no one seems to think the driver was a conspirator.) The archduke's security chief Oskar Potiorek realized what was happening, and shouted to the driver to turn back; he braked and started to turn the car around. It's

Archduke Franz Ferdinand and his wife Sophie getting into their open-top car in Sarejevo on June 28, 1914 – they were both shot dead just minutes later.

difficult to imagine what the Young Bosnian Gavrilo Princip must have thought when the archduke's car stopped right next to him. But we know what he did: he pulled out his gun and fired straight at Ferdinand, from just a few feet away. Hit in the neck, Ferdinand survived long enough to plead with his wife, who was hit in the stomach, to stay alive for the sake of their children. Both died within a few hours.

An onlooker stopped Princip shooting himself. Later, under interrogation, he and Cabrinovic revealed the names of all the other conspirators; they were arrested and charged with treason and murder (Princip was spared the death penalty, as he was under twenty years old). Meanwhile, no one in Europe was in any doubt that Serbia was behind the plot. Austria-Hungary had an excuse to impose its will on Serbia, and issued an ultimatum that led, step by irresistible step, to the Great War.

Conspiracies and counter-conspiracies

No one denies that Princip pulled the trigger, but historians disagree as to how closely involved Apis and the Black Hand actually were. One eyewitness and friend of Princip's, George Vesel, alleged in an interview in 1986 that Princip was impelled into the whole affair because his girlfriend had dumped him. Whether or not this is true, there were undoubtedy more complex factors at work.

The great conspiracy question hinges on the involvement of the Serb prime minister, Nikola Pasic. Some claim that he was part of Apis's plot, or at least privy to it. At the least, it seems certain that he had intelligence about the planned assassination – a report noting the smuggling of "six hand grenades and four revolvers" into Bosnia is annotated in Pasic's own hand. After the war, Serb minister Ljuba Jovanovic claimed that the Serbian government had known all about it. He added in 1924 that he had given a broad hint to the Austro-Hungarian minister, Dr Leon von Bilinski, that "some Serbian youth may slip a cartridge into his rifle or revolver, a loaded cartridge, not a blank, and fire it." Either Jovanovic was trying to warn the Austrians so guardedly that they would never act (though Pasic denied this) or, and this is where the main counter-conspiracy takes off, the Austrians picked up the hint and chose to do nothing about it.

It seems strange that the Austrians would allow their own crown prince to be killed, but it would actually be more surprising for the Serbs to want him dead. Serbia could ill afford war with its mighty neighbour; Austria-Hungary, on the other hand, was desperate for an excuse to start one…

SOURCES

Books

David Fromkin Europe's Last Summer: Who Started the Great War in 1914? (2004). Clear-sighted, general diplomatic history that makes Germany the key villain, using the archduke's murder to lure Russia into a war with Austria-Hungary.

W.A. Dolph Owings, Elizabeth Pribic and Nikola Pribic The Sarajevo Trial (1984). Out of print, but still a fascinating window into the documentary sources, with verbatim trial transcripts.

Clive Ponting Thirteen Days: Diplomacy and Disaster, the Countdown to the Great War (2002). This gripping day-by-day account begins with a tense dramatization of the assassination, which Ponting affirms was indeed the starting point for war.

Websites

www.firstworldwar.com/video/ferdinand.htm Streaming film footage of Franz Ferdinand's arrival at Sarajevo's town hall.

Frank Olson

On November 28, 1953, US Army scientist Dr Frank Olson hurtled through the window of his tenth-floor room in New York's Hotel Statler, and plummeted to his death. According to the inquest, it was suicide. Richard Lashbrook, a CIA colleague who was with Olson at the time, testified that he had been unable to stop Olson killing himself.

The official story stayed that way for 23 years. Then, in 1975, the Rockefeller Commission into illegal operations by the CIA uncovered "Operation Artichoke", an ultra-secret research programme investigating drugs and interrogation methods, in which both Olson and LSD were in some way involved. Olson hadn't fallen victim to his own foolhardy experimentation: the LSD had been slipped to him a few days prior to his death. The doctor had become prone to psychotic episodes, and was in New York to get treatment for shock effects induced by taking LSD.

President Ford invited the Olson family to the White House to apologize, while CIA director William Colby explained the circumstances surrounding his death over lunch, and later released numerous related CIA documents. Congress also rapidly put together a $750,000 cheque for the family. But *The New York Times* called the Colby documents "elliptical, incoherent, and contradictory", and said they contained "deletions, conflicting statements [and] unintelligible passages". Combined with the previous secrecy over the role of drugs in Olson's death, such rapid contrition from the government had a strong stench of further conspiracy to it.

The son takes up the case

After his mother's death in 1993, Frank's son Eric, who remained unsatisfied with the official explanations, began to investigate his father's death. Experts told Eric that his father would have had to run at 20mph to hurdle a radiator and smash through the hotel's heavy plate-glass windows and blinds, and he arranged for his father's body to be exhumed. Scientists from George Washington University failed to find any of the cuts or damage recorded by the first autopsy over four decades earlier, nor any traces of LSD. Instead, they noted a previously unremarked wound on his skull, consistent with his having been repeatedly struck from behind before the fall.

This sparked interest from the New York district attorney, and assistant DA Steve Saracco was assigned to reinvestigate Olson's death as homicide. Key witnesses subpoenaed from US and UK intelligence, including Lashbrook, Colby and Sidney Gottlieb, were among those to be interviewed. (Colby, however, disappeared from his Maryland holiday home on April 27, shortly after being subpoenaed. His body was found face down in a river by police eight days later; a verdict of death by accidental drowning was returned.) The investigation also revealed that the Frank Olson case was taught as a case of "perfect murder" at the assassination training unit of the Israeli secret service organization Mossad, for its success in making murder look like suicide.

Lashbrook, who was looking after Olson, was shown to have made a phone call to someone immediately after the fall, saying only "Olson's dead". Eric also uncovered a CIA manual on "dropping" people, which had parallels with his father's death. But after five years, scores of interviews and sifting through hundreds of CIA records, the case was left open. "We could never prove it was murder", says Saracco, even though he and Eric continue to believe that's exactly what it was.

From Korea with anthrax

According to the German TV documentary and book *Codename Artichoke: The Secret Human Experiments of the CIA*, Olson had worked on "Operation Artichoke", which was related to MK-ULTRA (see p.210), investigating the use of LSD in torture and interrogation. During the Korean War, Olson was based at Fort Detrick, where the US developed biological weapons such as anthrax for use against the Koreans and Chinese. Here too, ex-Korean War GIs, who had been captured and "brainwashed", were debriefed using LSD treatment, in a recklessly experimental culture that achieved mixed results, to say the least.

Olson also visited the UK's bio-research centre, Porton Down (see p.289), and elsewhere witnessed brutal interrogations based on techniques picked up from former Nazis and Soviet citizens. On his return to the US in the summer of 1953, he told a colleague that he was disgusted by the work, and informed his boss, brainwashing expert Sidney Gottlieb (head of the CIA's Technical Services Division) that he wanted to leave. According to American political magazine *Counterpunch*, Gottlieb was involved in drug experiments, backed by the Rockefeller Foundation, that were worthy of Dr Josef Mengele. Gottlieb allegedly spiked Olson's drink at a party in Maryland in mid-November, and arranged for Olson to take the ultimate high jump a few days later.

Revelations get buried

Eric Olson believes that his father had had enough of the increasingly psychotic capers that the army was paying him to work on. As he told *The New York Times* in 2001, the US biological weapons programme – and the use of such weapons in North Korea – may have been the key to his father's decision to quit the CIA, and ultimately to his murder. Eric also pointed to the simultaneous persecution of Manhattan Project scientist Robert Oppenheimer as evidence of the fate of those who turned against the military's weapons programmes.

Interestingly, both Dick Cheney and Donald Rumsfeld were young lions in President Ford's short-lived administration at the time "Operation Artichoke" came to light. Documents unearthed by California University professor Kathryn Olmstead link them to the decision not to sanction any new inquest into Olson's death at the time of the payout. A White House memo dated July 11, 1975 said that such an inquest might make it "necessary to disclose highly classified national security information", i.e. information relating to bio-warfare programmes.

In September 2001, *The New York Times* reported that the US was conducting research in violation of a 1972 treaty that prohibited the development of weapons that spread disease. When the paper reported further evidence that the US military had covertly developed anthrax and other germ bombs, interest was clouded by other events that occurred on the day of publication – September 11, 2001.

SOURCES

Books

James E. Starrs and Katherine Ramsland A Voice for the Dead: A Forensic Investigator's Pursuit of Truth in the Grave (2005). Starrs digs for dirt by literally digging up famous corpses, commenting on the smell and even sticking the bones in aircrafts' overhead lockers before he decides whether they died as reported. He also confirms the Hollywood myth that pathologists spend their time eating doughnuts over cadavers.

Websites

Ⓦ **www.counterpunch.org/gottlieb.html** A speedy, none too reverential obituary of the invidious Dr Gottlieb.

Ⓦ **www.frankolsonproject.org/Contents.html** Set up by Eric Olson, this provides a host of links to reports on Frank Olson's life and the aftermath of his untimely death.

Marilyn Monroe

Hollywood film star and all-American sex symbol Marilyn Monroe was found dead of a massive drugs overdose on the night of August 4, 1962. Her bloodstream contained enough chloral hydrate and Nembutal (a barbiturate) to kill fifteen people. Although to the world Monroe symbolized glamour and easy-going sexuality, some on Hollywood's inside circuit gossiped that she was an emotional wreck and an alcoholic. She already had a string of broken marriages and failed relationships behind her, while her career appeared recently to have stalled with her dismissal from the film *Something's Got to Give* (an ironic title in the circumstances). The Los Angeles County Coroner's court considered her sufficiently depressed to declare a verdict of suicide.

Things weren't so bad

However, some say that the suicide theory just doesn't add up. They argue that Marilyn was getting back together with her first husband, baseball star Joe DiMaggio; indeed her stepson, Joe Jr, phoned her on August 4 and said she sounded fine. She was also re-contracted to 20th Century Fox, on better money, to return to *Something's Got to Give.*

What's more, the manner of her death was odd. Although there was a police station less than three miles away, the police weren't summoned to Monroe's side until 4.30am on August 5, six hours after her publicist had been called to the house. One policeman said that Monroe's body was so neatly laid on the bed, with pill bottles tidily arranged beside it, that it was "the most obviously staged death I have ever seen". The bed linen had already been laundered by Monroe's housekeeper, and her notes and diaries were all gone. An autopsy showed that, despite all the empty pill bottles and the massive dose that killed her, her stomach was devoid of tablet residue. Nor was any explanation given about the bruising on her body. Other tissues sent for analysis mysteriously disappeared.

High life and low lives

Marilyn Monroe moved in the very highest circles. She was as glamorous as the Kennedys, the top political family she hung around with, and their glitzy circle of super-cool stars, including Rat Packers Frank Sinatra and Peter Lawford (who had married into the Kennedy family and provided Monroe with her initial entrée). According to conspiracy theorists, all this was becoming too dangerous for comfort by 1962, when Kennedy brothers Jack and Robert were enjoying public power as US president and attorney general respectively, while both privately enjoying Monroe's sexual favours. The Kennedys, therefore, unceremoniously set about ditching Monroe before the affairs could be revealed. For her part, Monroe felt shabbily treated, and was reportedly about to "blow the lid off of Washington" before she died.

So was it the Kennedys?

According to the most persistent theory, the Kennedys had Marilyn bumped off on the evening of August 4. During her final 48 hours, she was bombarded with phone calls from Robert Kennedy and from a woman telling her to "leave him alone", and she's said to have had a row with Robert at her house on the day of her death. Monroe's first husband, Joe DiMaggio, went to his grave believing that the Kennedys were responsible. However, there are different versions of precisely how the deed was done.

The first ambulance driver to arrive at Monroe's house, James Hall, subsequently wrote *Peter Lawford: The Man Who Kept the Secrets*. He contended that Robert Kennedy persuaded Monroe's psychiatrist, Dr Ralph Greenson – who arrived with the ambulance – to inject her with a lethal dose of Nembutal. "Just as Marilyn started coming around, the doctor arrived ... I believe it was Dr. Greenson. He ... pushed her breast to one side and gave her an injection." That would account for the lack of tablet residue.

According to Robert Slatzer's book *The Marilyn Files*, on the other hand, Robert Kennedy ordered CIA and Secret Service agents to kill Monroe, on the grounds that information she'd picked up from the Kennedys as pillow talk made her a threat to national security. Marilyn's phone records were then seized by the police. Frank Capell, in his 1964 book *The Strange Death of Marilyn Monroe*, blamed the communists, though he agreed they were hired on Robert Kennedy's orders. But death by communist would be ironic indeed, as FBI files released in 2005 showed that they considered the silver screen siren to be a "Red" because of her marriage to a suspected communist, playwright Arthur Miller. These suspicions were strengthened when she met with communists in Mexico in 1962 and by a rumour that she once applied for a visa to visit the USSR, as well as her questioning of atom bomb tests in the US. But then, the FBI also considered *Anne Frank: The Diary of a Young Girl* to be "left-wing".

Another twist has it that the FBI murdered Monroe on Robert Kennedy's orders, ostensibly to bail out the executive, but in reality to give FBI boss J. Edgar Hoover something he could hold over the boys in the White House. In 1973, Norman Mailer speculated in *Marilyn* that the FBI were complicit in a plot to embarrass the Kennedys. The FBI refused to comment, saying they didn't want to "feed the fires of publicity which Mailer is attempting to stoke". But the real trouble with this theory is that Hoover already knew of the Kennedys' relationship with Monroe, so why would he need to embroil himself in her murder?

The Mob did it to help the Kennedys

Joe DiMaggio's belief in the Kennedys' guilt – and his later statement of intent to kill Robert Kennedy – derived from his claim to have read Monroe's diaries after her death, diaries that then supposedly disappeared. Monroe is said to have had detailed conversations with Robert Kennedy about the CIA's plans to poison Fidel Castro with the aid of the Chicago gangster Sam Giancana, as well as ongoing investigations into union leader Jimmy Hoffa's relationship with the Mafia. She then told Frank Sinatra who, unbeknown to her, passed the details on to Giancana.

In *DiMaggio: Setting the Record Straight*, Morris Engelberg and Mary Schneider report that Monroe told Joe DiMaggio Jr on the day of her death that she was seriously considering telling all, not just about her relationships with the Kennedy brothers, but also about the other plots afoot. At that point, some theorists claim that the Kennedys called in their long-standing Mob connections to get rid

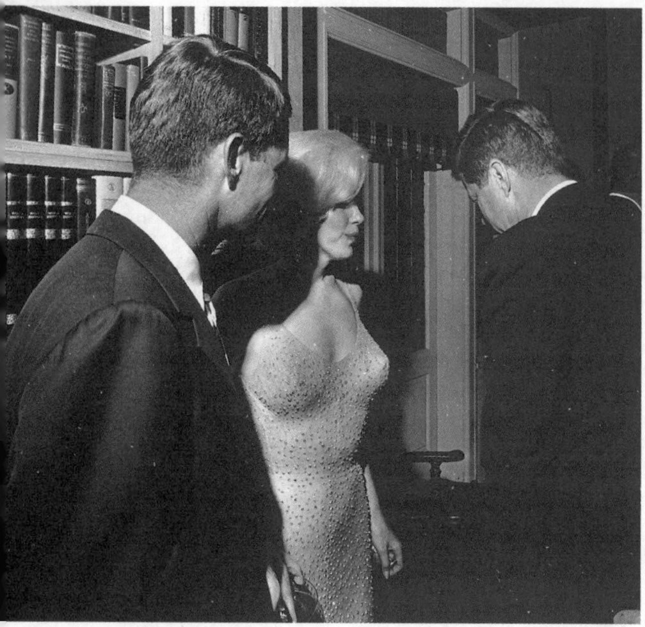

Marilyn Monroe with two of her alleged lovers: John F. Kennedy and Robert Kennedy.

of Monroe before she exposed both them and their Mafia associates. One intriguing aspect of this hypothesis is that administering chloral hydrate by enema was a known feature of Mafia-related killings, which could explain the lack of tablet residue in Monroe's stomach and the bruising on her body, indicative of a violent struggle.

The Mob did it to get the Kennedys

Or did the Mob do the deed not at the behest of the Kennedys, but in order to get at them? Family patriarch Joe Kennedy had made some of his millions as a bootlegger during the Prohibition era, allegedly thanks to connections with Mafia boss Frank Costello, while JFK's election success in 1960 has been attributed in part to Mob-assisted vote rigging. Once in office, however, the Kennedy boys bit the hand that had fed them, and Robert Kennedy's crackdown on organized crime came as a humiliating slap in the face. It's said that, as a result, besieged Chicago Mob boss Sam Giancana enlisted the aid of Teamsters' leader Jimmy Hoffa to get Robert out of office by bugging Monroe and exposing their affair. When that failed, the theory goes, they killed Monroe, hoping to implicate the Kennedys in her death; in any case, killing a Kennedy moll was satisfying in itself. The witness is a good one – Chuck Giancana, Sam Giancana's younger brother, as interviewed in the 1992 book *Double Cross*.

Monroe's mob did it with the Kennedys

In 2007, LA-based writer Philippe Mora pointed the finger back at the Kennedy boys by reporting a declassified FBI file, released under the Freedom of Information Act, that outlined a plot involving everyone from the attorney general to Monroe's housekeeper. The three-page file from October 1964 asserts that Monroe's barbiturate overdose was self-inflicted, and was just one of a string of sympathy-seeking suicide "attempts". The Kennedys sought to capitalize upon these suicide attempts to stop Monroe from making their affair public in revenge for Robert reneging on promises to divorce his wife and to save Monroe's career at 20th Century Fox. The report, titled "Robert F. Kennedy", was neither sourced nor authenticated, but it was still sent to the top of the FBI tree. In essence, the theory goes that JFK's brother-in-law Peter Lawford got psychiatrist Ralph Greenson to prescribe a whopping sixty barbiturate pills, which housekeeper Eunice Murray (hired on Greenson's advice) left by her bed. When Monroe overdosed and called Greenson, he told her to get some fresh air – visiting only after he knew she was dead. Robert apparently later phoned Lawford "to find out if Marilyn was dead yet". This astonishingly convoluted – and uncorroborated – version of events even puts Monroe's press agent in the plot, being on the federal payroll and flying to the Kennedy compound at Hyannisport, Massachusetts after her death.

However, if the Kennedys did want Monroe dead, with all the resources they had to hand, banking on her killing herself just seems a little… flimsy. Mora comments on the timing of the report, years after Monroe's death, and suggests that Hoover had the file compiled to discredit Robert Kennedy if he ever ran for president, which would likely have become a race to see who could wreck the other's career once and for all.

No more questions

Scores of books have been written about the death of Marilyn Monroe, while hundreds of websites still speculate about the possibilities. However, no reinvestigation seems imminent, and the suicide verdict still stands. Perhaps those who refuse to believe that she killed herself are simply too dazzled by Marilyn's beauty, fame and fortune. Nonetheless, lingering questions continue to surround her final hours, and there's something compellingly mysterious about the death of a woman with such murky connections to the leaders of both the free world and the criminal underworld.

SOURCES

Books

Frank Capell The Strange Death of Marilyn Monroe (1964). An anti-Red rant nailed onto Marilyn Monroe's death.

Morris Engelberg DiMaggio: Setting the Record Straight (2003). Contains some bits of interest on Monroe, but focuses mainly on the world's greatest baseball player.

James Hall Peter Lawford: The Man Who Kept the Secrets (1991). Not as enthralling as you might expect, considering Peter Lawford was both the president's brother-in-law and a Rat Packer.

Robert Slatzer The Marilyn Files (1991). The most comprehensive work on the subject.

Exploding cigars: the CIA and Castro

Were he the leader of any country but Cuba, Fidel Castro would look like the world's most paranoid premier: he believes that the US government and its CIA agents have been hellbent on the destruction of both him and his regime ever since he came to power in 1959. But Castro is right. And, for once, not only right, but proven right. A CIA report released in 1967 let slip some choice titbits; more was revealed in the Church Committee's 1975 Senate enquiry into "Alleged Assassination Plots Involving Foreign Leaders"; and in 1993, key CIA files were declassified as part of Congress's investigation into the JFK assassination by the Assassinations Record Review Board, or ARRB. A baroque array of plots and plans was revealed, aimed at destabilizing Cuba and taking out Castro. Most were subsumed under the code-name "Operation Mongoose", which was set up in late 1961 in the wake of the disastrous Bay of Pigs invasion. Conspiracy theorists were elated. If all their suspicions about the CIA and Cuba were justified, what else might not be true?

Psyops: Operation Mongoose

Operation Mongoose started out small, with plans to drop leaflets over Cuba offering a reward for Castro's murder. The CIA's ingenuity was soon put to work, however, with Operation Dirty Trick, a disinformation scheme to blame the failure of the Mercury rocket launch – if it did fail – on

Cuban electronic interference. A psyop (psychological operation) dubbed "Good Times" envisaged disseminating postcards of a fat, smug Castro living the decadent high life, which, it was noted, "should put even a Commie Dictator in the proper perspective with the underprivileged masses". Operation Free Ride would have dropped one-way tickets to Mexico City all over Cuba, though it was noted sensibly that "the validity of the tickets would have to be restricted" – there's always a catch. In 1963, the CIA envisaged creating a fictitious Cuban opposition leader to whom "humorous antics" could be credited, as well as "exploits of bravery (à la Zorro)". Even brighter were alleged plots to undermine Castro's persona as a revolutionary hero: perhaps they could spray the area around a radio studio with an hallucinogen before one of his lengthy revolutionary speeches, or lace one of his cigars with a disorienting substance, or make his famously virile beard fall out by contaminating his shoes with thallium salts.

There's something childish and slightly suspect about all of this. Even the CIA recognized as much in 1967, calling it "fruitless and, in retrospect, often unrealistic plotting". They blamed excessive pressure from the Kennedy administration. And not unreasonably so: in January 1962 Robert Kennedy publicly stated that deposing Castro was "the top priority of the US government; all else is secondary; no time, money, effort, or manpower is to be spared". Apparently, the tradition of futile machinations continues to this day. In 2003, a Miami newspaper reported that US officials had been harassed by Cuban government agents who had urinated into their homes, made nuisance phone calls in the early hours and, worst of all, retuned their car radios to pro-Castro stations. But perhaps this was just black anti-Castro propaganda…

"Devices which strain the imagination": ZR/RIFLE

In 1975, when the Church Committee published its report into "Alleged Assassination Plots Involving Foreign Leaders", it found evidence of a darker side to the CIA's plans for Cuba. It cited eight separate plans to kill Castro drawn up between 1960 and 1965 – plots that "ran the gamut from high-powered rifles to poison pills, poison pens, deadly bacterial powders, and other devices which strain the imagination".

One early scheme, before the accession of JFK, involved using the Mafia, which had its own grievance against the revolutionary regime for shutting down its casinos and prostitution rackets in Havana (as portrayed in the film *The Godfather Part II*). Conveniently, the CIA could be covered by a chain of association that would seem increasingly improbable as it became longer and apparently more tenuous. The CIA's Colonel Sheffield Edwards got in touch with ex-FBI man Robert Maheu, who contacted underworld figure Johnny Roselli, who recruited Chicago syndicate mobster Sam Giancana – Al Capone's successor, a man who had supposedly shared a girlfriend with JFK – and the Mafia boss for Cuba, Santos Trafficante. The remaining details of the operation were only exposed in 2007, when the CIA finally released its mega-dossier on illegal operations, legendarily known as the "Family Jewels". Giancana had apparently recommended using "some type of potent pill that could be placed in Castro's food or drink" and arranged for corrupt Cuban official Juan Orta to do the deed. The CIA sourced six poison pills for Orta, but after numerous failed attempts, he got scared and walked away from the deal.

After the debacle of the abortive US-backed Bay of Pigs invasion in April 1961, the Kennedy brothers upped the pressure for results. The CIA set up a top-secret assassination programme, codenamed ZR/RIFLE, and again prompted Roselli and his associates into action, supplying them with poison pills, weapons and explosives. Again, nothing happened, although the Mafia was presumably grateful for the free equipment.

Another CIA faction turned to the CIA's Medical Services Division, headed by the controversial Dr Sidney Gottlieb – also accused of testing LSD on unsuspecting US citizens as part of the MK-ULTRA programme (see p.210). The plans read like the work of a Bond villain. Castro was known to enjoy a cigar, so a box of cigars was contaminated with the botulinum toxin and delivered to "an unidentified person" in February 1961 – whereupon it vanished from the record. Castro was also known for his love of diving, so an alluring exploding conch shell was devised, the idea being to drop it at one of his favourite dive spots. Another scheme envisaged lacing the breathing apparatus of his diving suit with TB bacilli and, for good measure, dusting the whole suit with a virulent fungus that would, according to the Church Committee's report, "produce a chronic skin disease (Madura foot)". Before the plan could be put into action, however, Castro was given a good Yankee wetsuit – tragically for the CIA, minus germs and fungi – by an American lawyer.

Finally, a Cuban Army major, Roland Cubela, knocked on the CIA's door offering to kill Castro. He was promptly codenamed AM/LASH, supplied with a poison pen and promised a rifle to follow. Fortunately for Castro, Cubela's meeting with CIA agent Desmond Fitzgerald took place on the same day that JFK was shot in Dallas, and the plans were shelved.

No cigars for Fidel

At the time of writing, Fidel Castro remained alive and well – at least, so it is thought. He had intestinal surgery for an undisclosed ailment in 2006, and in the summer of 2007, he vanished from sight. There were rumours of an untreatable cancer and a Soviet-style cover-up of his death, but just as Cuban exiles in Miami got ready to break out the flags, Fidel appeared on television, blithely answering questions about current affairs. Even in his early eighties, Castro was still delivering lucid, marathon speeches, without any signs of flashbacks, and was still walking without a Madura-foot limp – so it looks as though the CIA's plans have never quite been realized. He has, however, given up cigars.

The CIA didn't come off quite so well – and neither have the Kennedys. The Church Committee hauled CIA executives and directors, including Richard Helms, over the coals. Their 1975 "Interim Report" found evidence of CIA

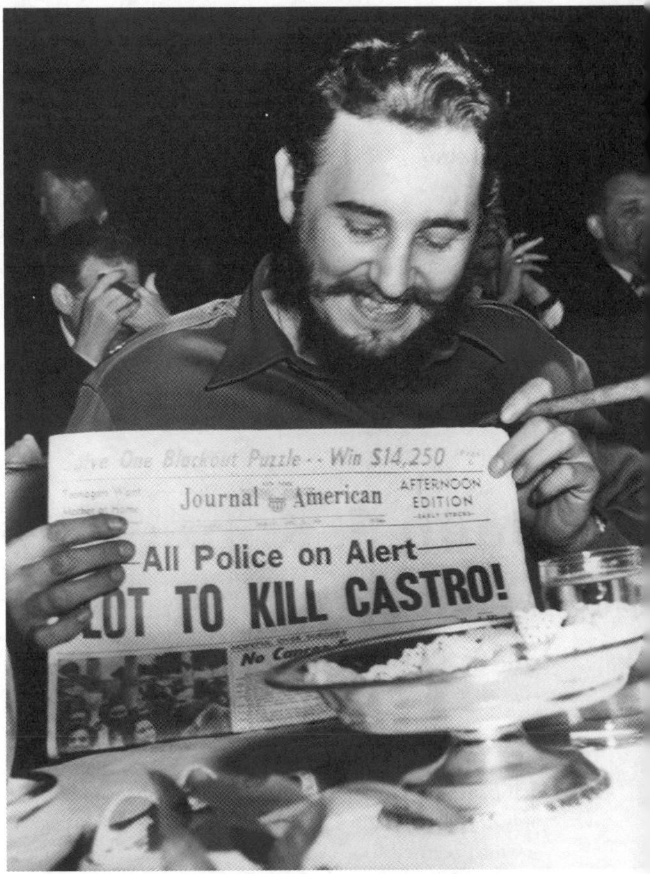

Cuban leader Fidel Castro proves that he is very much alive and well, despite assassination plots against him.

involvement in the assassinations of the Congo's Patrice Lumumba, Vietnam's Ngo Dinh Diem, the Dominican Republic's Rafael Trujillo and the Chilean leader, René Schneider, but after a lot of buck-passing and mutual accusations, its conclusions were fairly mild. The report concluded that the CIA had problems with accountability, and recommended that the US should stop trying to kill foreign leaders. President Ford's Executive Order 11905 duly declared that "no employee of the US government shall engage in, or conspire to engage in, political assassination". Ultimately, nobody's career suffered much. Least of all Castro's.

SOURCES

Books

William F. Buckley Jr Mongoose, R.I.P: A Blackford Oakes Mystery (1998). Cuba, 1963: a Yankee James Bond gets caught up in Operation Mongoose. A fair thriller.

Fabian Escalante The Cuba Project: CIA Covert Operations Against Cuba 1959–62 (1995). As the former head of Cuban counterintelligence and the director of Cuba's 1978 investigation into the Kennedy assassination, Escalante knows a thing or two.

Claudia Furiati and Maxine Shaw ZR Rifle: The Plot to Kill Kennedy and Castro (1994). This claims that the same cabal of Cuban exiles, CIA operatives and Mafioso was behind the plots to kill both JFK and Castro.

Lamar Waldron with Thom Hartmann Ultimate Sacrifice: John and Robert Kennedy, the Plan for a Coup in Cuba, and the Murder of JFK (2005). This has more on JFK's assassination than plots to bump off Castro, but it provides invaluable background on the mutual fear and hatred that existed between the US and Cuba in the 1960s.

Websites

Ⓦ **www.aarclibrary.org/publib/church/contents.htm** The full text of the Church Committee's "Interim Report: Alleged Assassination Plots Involving Foreign Leaders". Covers Patrice Lumumba, Rafael Trujillo, Ngo Dinh Diem and René Schneider, as well as Castro.

John F. Kennedy

One question defines a decisive moment for a generation: where were you when John F. Kennedy was shot? If you were in downtown Dallas, Texas, on Friday, November 22, 1963, the chances are that you either have been or will be named in some dark conspiracy to kill the president of the USA.

Had it not been for the murder of JFK, this book might never have been published. The sudden, violent death in a bright, open public space of the world's most powerful man, and the murky circumstances that surrounded not only the assassination but also the ensuing investigation – which seemed to grow murkier with every new line of enquiry – kick-started the whole modern conspiracy-theories industry. (Though, of course, that's not to say that the conspiracy theory industry wanted Kennedy dead in order to raise its public profile…)

Successive investigations into Kennedy's death in the US Congress, courts, newspapers, books, films and scientific academies have not settled, for the American public at least, the question of who killed him. In 2003, an ABC TV News poll showed that just 32 percent of Americans believed that Lee Harvey Oswald acted alone in killing Kennedy; the Discovery Channel reported just 21 percent believed it was only Oswald; and the History Channel a mere seventeen percent. So up to four out of every five Americans think there was a bigger conspiracy going on.

What's known

While almost everything about the Kennedy killing has been questioned at some point, a few hard facts remain undisputed. John Fitzgerald Kennedy and his wife Jackie arrived in Dallas on November 22, 1963, and joined Texas governor John Connally in an open-top limousine. They were driven downtown, past cheering crowds. Secret Service agents drove behind them, and a third car carried

Vice President Lyndon B. Johnson, also from Texas, and his wife Lady Bird.

At 12.30pm, the motorcade was rounding Dealey Plaza. Kennedy was in the back right-hand seat, flanked by Jackie, with Connally in front of him. In the course of a few seconds, as the president's car pulled away from the imposing Texas Book Depository, bullets drilled into both Connally and Kennedy. Connally was badly injured, while much of Kennedy's brain splattered from the back of his skull. The whole group raced to Parkland hospital. Kennedy was declared dead at 1pm, though doctors conceded that he'd died before he ever got there. As the world was informed of the killing, the presidential plane waited for Mrs Kennedy to arrive with her husband's coffin. On board, at 2.39pm, LBJ was sworn in as the 36th president of the United States. Lady Bird and the widowed Mrs Kennedy looked on.

Meanwhile, a police search of the Book Depository revealed that one employee was missing, having left minutes after the shooting. Across town, at about 1.15pm, an assailant shot and killed policeman J.D. Tippit. An hour later, Lee Harvey Oswald was traced and captured in a movie theatre and charged with Tippit's murder. The next day, he was charged with Kennedy's killing. Oswald denied both.

On November 24, as police bustled Oswald through a throng of guards and journalists at the Dallas city jail, in order to transfer him to the county jail, Dallas strip-club owner Jack Ruby stepped forward and shot Oswald. Again, the shooting was caught live on TV, and like Kennedy, Oswald was pronounced dead at Parkland hospital. Jack Ruby was convicted of his murder in 1964, but the conviction was overturned in 1966. He died while awaiting a new trial.

The Warren Commission

Just a week after the killing, President Johnson set up a commission to investigate the assassination. Headed by Chief Justice Earl Warren, the Commission included future president Gerald R. Ford; former director of the CIA, Allen Dulles; and the father of the CIA, John J. McCloy, who was also a former adviser to President Kennedy. It delivered its verdict – the so-called Warren Report – in September 1964. According to the report, Lee Harvey Oswald was the killer, and he had acted alone. He shot Kennedy from a sixth-floor window of the Book Depository, where a sniper's rifle was found among boxes that bore his handprints. Oswald fired three shots in the space of something between four and a half and seven seconds. The first shot passed through Kennedy and into Connally, the second hit Kennedy's head and the third missed. Oswald escaped and killed Tippit, before dying at Ruby's hands.

The report painted a picture of Oswald as a misfit, and a major-league one at that. A high-school dropout with strong Marxist leanings, he had been discharged from the Marines, and subsequently defected to the USSR, where he was initially refused Soviet citizenship. In 1962, he somehow managed to return to the US with his Soviet-born wife, Marina, where he set up (as the sole activist) the New Orleans branch of the Fair Play for Cuba Committee (FPCC). He stated his support for Fidel Castro in a TV interview, and in mid-1963 applied for a visa to visit Cuba. The Commission could not ascribe to Oswald "any one motive or group of motives", but noted that Oswald had "an overriding hostility to his environment", feelings of "perpetual discontentment" and a "hatred for American society"; he sought "a place in history", yet acted "without regard to the consequences" of his actions. Having considered Oswald's relations with the Russian community in Fort Worth, Texas, his life and work with the Soviets, and the idea that he may have been a government agent (the FBI interviewed him three times on his return from Moscow), and also investigated whether he already knew Ruby (the conclusion was that he didn't), "no credible evidence" of a conspiracy was found. Oswald had acted alone.

Doubts set in

Although the Warren Commission gave its verdict in 1964, it took thirty years, under a schedule instigated by LBJ, for its 26 volumes and 16,000 pages of evidence to dribble into the public domain. The painfully slow, piecemeal way in which the report was released was sufficient to arouse suspicion in itself, but the dribs and drabs that gradually emerged were found to contain more and more holes. Articles and books disparaging the report appeared with increasing frequency in the later 1960s, and titles such as *Rush to Judgement* (by attorney Mark Lane) and *Inquest* (by Edward J. Epstein) became bestsellers.

The most glaring problem was that the chief suspect, Oswald, had never reached trial. Instead, he was gunned down in public. While it seemed implausible that a lowlife like Jack Ruby could have been outraged enough to kill Oswald, it was astounding that this petty mobster, known to the police, could get within a *mile* of the chief suspect, let alone *two feet*. What were the Dallas police thinking... or plotting? Furthermore, the police at Dealey Plaza at the time of Kennedy's shooting were said to have been so "fazed" that they failed to record dozens of witness statements, and thereby left Warren to depend on FBI material.

On the other hand, no one actually *saw* Oswald shoot the president, and it's hardly surprising that his prints were found at the depository – he worked there. Then there was the supposed murder weapon, a $12 bolt-action World War II rifle with sights bought by mail order. Was it accurate enough at that range and capable of being repeatedly reloaded in the few seconds Oswald had to kill Kennedy? And was Oswald himself a good enough shot? Or was he, as he told Dallas police, "just a patsy"?

Photographs and x-rays from Kennedy's autopsy were deemed by persons unknown to be too "gruesome" even to be submitted to the men on the Commission. Instead, the investigators relied on artists' impressions, which further compromised their dubious conclusion that one single bullet had entered Kennedy's back, exited his neck and then pierced Connally's chest, hitting his wrist and entering his thigh. That "magic bullet" – exhibit 399, which was noted to be in mighty fine condition – became infamous, and helped to taint medical examinations that already appeared to be contradictory.

The Parkland doctors wrote of a big hole at the back of Kennedy's head, which would suggest a shot from the front, and thus a second assassin, as did a bullet *entry* wound on the front of Kennedy's neck. However, the autopsy said that the head wound was nearer the front, and thus the result of a shot from behind and above – Oswald's location – while the neck wound was an exit wound. Were wounds actually made to fit what became the Oswald theory, which would mean the doctors were complicit in the conspiracy – or were there perhaps two bodies, as some speculated? For that matter, were there two killers? Witnesses spoke of a man with a rifle seen leaving a "grassy knoll" just in front of the president's limo, and described the mysterious arrest of "three hoboes" who were on the scene.

The Garrison investigation

The Warren Report made a passing reference to a phone call that a lawyer received from one "Clay Bertrand" in New Orleans, during the few hours between the two killings, urging him to represent Oswald. That prompted New Orleans district attorney Jim Garrison, with the backing of a solitary US senator, Russell Long, who had doubts about the Warren Report, to launch his own investigation in 1967. Finding that Clay Bertrand didn't exist, Garrison insisted that the name was a pseudonym for homosexual businessman Clay Shaw. Shaw was arrested and charged with supposed involvement in an elaborate conspiracy with another homosexual, David Ferrie. Garrison claimed that both men were friends and conspirators with closet homosexual Oswald, as well as being CIA agents, and that Oswald's Fair Play for Cuba office was located in a building full of CIA-backed anti-Castro operatives. Over a five-week trial, Garrison portrayed a gay/CIA/FBI Johnson-backed conspiracy to kill Kennedy, with shots fired from the grassy knoll and the three hoboes as contracted killers.

The jury took 45 minutes to clear Shaw, agreeing with Garrison's chief investigator William Gurvich, as he told Robert Kennedy, that the case was "rubbish". Garrison accused Robert Kennedy of conspiring to obstruct his case, despite the fact that Robert would surely want to know who killed his brother more than anyone. Many observers saw the trial as proving that Garrison was a paranoid egotist of epic and megalomaniac proportions. Even so, it gave an "official" voice to theories blasting the government and intelligence agencies – and it also allowed the public, for the first time, to see the film of the shooting captured by Abraham Zapruder.

Zapruder

The Garrison/Shaw trial brought the Zapruder film to prominence as the most important single piece of evidence in the shooting of JFK. A short, jiggly home-movie sequence that captured the violence of Kennedy's death in horrible colour, it had been seen by the Warren Commission and used for timings and reactions, but its graphic horror had hardly been conveyed by the dry words of the Warren Report. The 1975 Rockefeller Commission's investigation into illegal activities and assassinations by the CIA, which cleared the organization of involvement in the killing, concluded from its review of the Zapruder film that the president had not been shot from the front. On the other hand, for most of the American public, who saw the movie for the first time on TV's *Goodnight America*, the footage of Kennedy's head and brain matter being projected backwards seemed to confirm the very opposite. If the bullet came from the front, Oswald could not have fired the fatal shot.

The Church Committee and the HSCA

The 1975 Senate "Church Committee" also looked into illegal activities by intelligence agencies, including the plot against Castro – something Allen Dulles, sacked by Kennedy over Cuba, had failed to mention to the Warren Commission. It was perturbed enough to order another investigation: the 1976 House of Representatives' Select Committee on Assassinations (HSCA), which reinvestigated the assassinations of JFK, his brother Robert and Martin Luther King. Its fourteen-volume report, released in 1978, concluded that Kennedy "was probably assassinated as the result of a conspiracy". Oswald fired the fatal shots, but someone else was probably involved. On a police motorcyclist's recording of events at Dealey Plaza, acoustics experts counted four gun shots: two from the Depository, and at least one from the grassy knoll. Warren Report photos of Oswald holding left-wing magazines and a rifle were also revealed as fakes.

Most of the suspicion centered on the Mafia. Among those assigned possible roles were Teamsters' boss Jimmy Hoffa and big Dons like Santos Trafficante, Johnny Roselli, New Orleans godfather Carlos Marcello and Chicago's Sam Giancana. Trafficante and Roselli were called to appear before the Committee, but they both died violent deaths before they could do so. In the end, the HSCA absolved Castro, the CIA, the FBI, the Mafia and the USSR. However, by blaming no one, their report only raised more doubts.

One consequence was that, in 1981, Oswald's body was dug up, to dispel rumours that he had never actually returned to the US and had instead been replaced by a Soviet agent. The exhumed body, however, was confirmed as Oswald's.

Further suspicions raised by the HSCA's report were allayed when its acoustics evidence was discounted by the National Academy of Sciences, and an Ohio musician got fifteen minutes of fame after he analysed a freebie recording of the tape and showed that it had been made minutes *after* the shooting.

The Communists

Among the earliest theories about the assassination, advanced by Edward J. Epstein in *Legend* and *Plot and Counterplot*, was the notion that Oswald was a KGB agent who shot Kennedy on Soviet orders. Another variation has it that Fidel Castro, livid over the Bay of Pigs incident and the Cuban Missile Crisis, but not feeling unduly threatened by Kennedy's efforts to kill him (see p.19), simply got his shot in first, hiring Oswald to do the deed. By that reckoning, Castro correctly anticipated that the CIA and FBI would sit on any evidence rather than risk another confrontation with Cuba, which was under the Soviet umbrella, and so Johnson directed the Warren Commission to pin the blame on Oswald alone.

According to Robin Ramsay in *Who Shot JFK?*, there were indeed moves to stifle investigations into the alleged Communist conspiracy, possibly in order to head off a violent reaction against the well-armed Soviets. For their part, the Soviets claimed the theory was itself a right-wing conspiracy. The strongest argument against it runs that Kennedy was considering making moves to harmonize relationships with Cuba, and it's hard to imagine Castro or Khrushchev risking such a huge provocation as shooting the US president.

The CIA and FBI

Further theories focus on the roles of the FBI and CIA. There's certainly a case for suggesting that while the FBI may not have been involved in the assassination itself, it had a strong interest in pressuring the Warren Commission to deliver a whitewash verdict. After all, the FBI had somehow

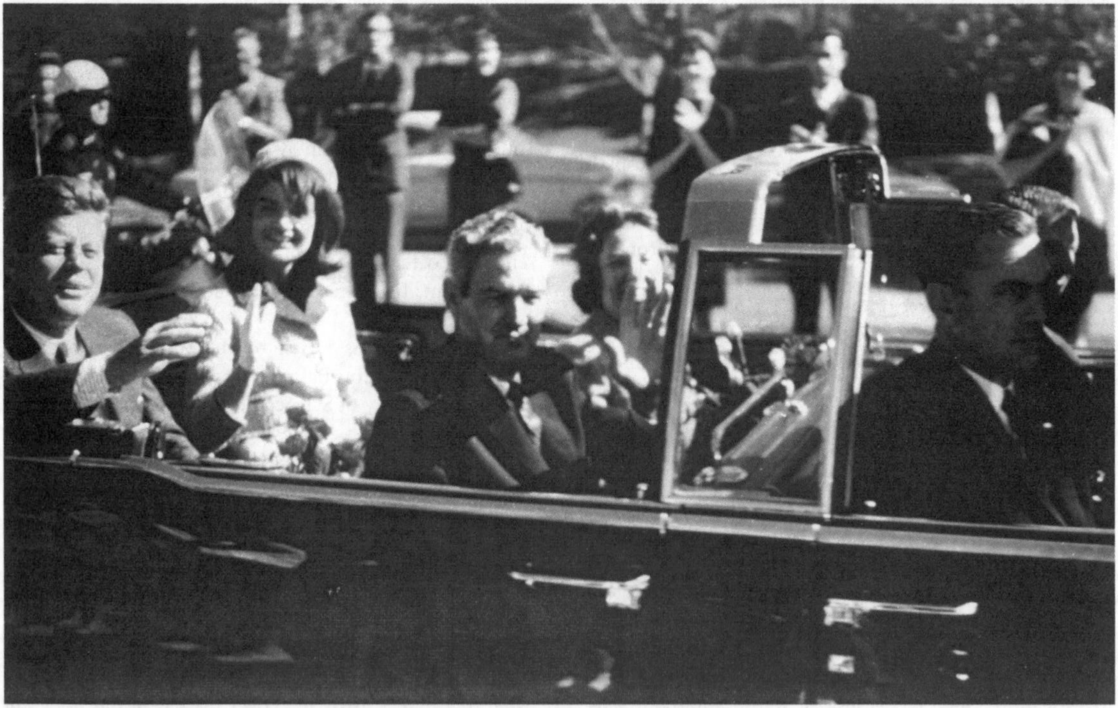

JFK, with his wife Jackie at his side, waves to the cheering crowds in Dallas shortly before his death.

allowed one of the country's most public communist agitators – Lee Harvey Oswald, whom they had been following since 1960 – to kill the president in broad daylight.

Anthony Summers, in *Official and Confidential: The Secret Life of J. Edgar Hoover*, points out that, irrespective of whether Oswald did the deed or not, Hoover showed disquieting alacrity "to protect himself and the Bureau and insist that Oswald was the lone assassin". Hoover declared himself "quite convinced they had found the right party", just four hours after the shooting, when even LBJ remarked that the evidence against Oswald was "not strong". Upon Oswald's death, Hoover hurried to have "something" issued to convince the public that Oswald was JFK's assassin, with LBJ concurring that some hasty FBI report might suffice to "get by". Summers quotes Congressman Hale Boggs, house majority leader and former Warren Commission member: "Hoover lied his eyes out to the Commission, on Oswald, on Ruby, on their friends, the bullets, the gun, you name it…"

More damning speculation has it that Oswald's New Orleans' Fair Play for Cuba Committee may have been a CIA trap to snare communist sympathizers, and that the CIA killed Kennedy using Oswald as a decoy. The CIA is said to have hated Kennedy for blaming them first for losing Cuba, and then for failing to get it back.

Questions have also been raised about the Secret Service men who were supposedly protecting Kennedy, and who seem to have been called back from doing their duty. Intriguing footage of the Kennedy cavalcade pulling off in Dallas is available on www.youtube.com. It shows two besuited Secret Service men, trotting alongside Kennedy's limo, about to hop onto the vehicle's back plate, but they are apparently told to stand aside by an agent already riding shotgun in the following car. Their confusion is visible as Kennedy's car accelerates away, now lacking a rearward human shield.

Whether the footage relates to the cavalcade leaving the airport or the later drive through downtown Dallas is disputed, but it adds to the numerous questions about the president's security. Why was Kennedy in an open-top car, with its bulletproof bubble unattached, grinding slowly past crowds of people? Why were there no marksmen overlooking the Plaza – apart from, of course, the one(s) who shot Kennedy? And why, in the seconds that followed the first shot, did the car neither accelerate nor take evasive action?

LBJ

Perhaps the most basic of all theories poses the simple question: who gained the most from the assassination? It was Vice President Lyndon B. Johnson who ascended to the presidency following JFK's death, and who, as a Texan, would have known the right people in Dallas to pull off the hit. It was also Johnson who stopped all the other investigations in favour of the unreliable Warren Commission. JFK had supposedly never liked or trusted Johnson, and may have been planning to drop him from the presidential ticket for the next election. Texas oil barons, smarting from the loss of their Cuban assets, supposedly saw Johnson as a president who wouldn't also forfeit the riches of Vietnamese oil. According to Mark North's *Act of Treason*, the plot was aided by Kennedy-hater J. Edgar Hoover and his FBI. North contends that Hoover was tipped off about possible plots on Kennedy's life, but in a murderous dereliction of duty, did nothing to prevent them, or even to warn the president.

The Vietnam connection

Shortly before his death, JFK is said to have indicated plans to withdraw US troops from Vietnam. Johnson, by contrast, scaled up American involvement in Vietnam just four days after stepping into the bloody presidential breach. According to Peter Dale Scott in *Crime and Cover-up: The CIA, the Mafia and the Dallas–Watergate Connection*, the military-industrial complex was alarmed by Kennedy's desire to cut defence expenditure, and an end to the US presence in Vietnam would have cost them dearly. The CIA were also making money from intelligence funding and drug trafficking in Southeast Asia, and, for good measure, the Mafia were profiting from the drug trade…

Richard Nixon

According to A.J. Weberman and Michael Canfield, in *Coup d'Etat in America*, convicted Watergate burglar and former Bay of Pigs operative E. Howard Hunt was one of the infamous "three hoboes" arrested on the grassy knoll at Dealey Plaza on the day JFK was shot. Hunt's presence in Dallas was apparently confirmed by a self-proclaimed co-conspirator's confession to the British *Sunday Times* in 1977. To some minds, that's enough to suggest a connection to "Tricky Dicky" himself, Richard Nixon, who was in Dallas on November 20–22, attending a Pepsi Cola convention (whereas Kennedy drank Coke). Supposedly, Nixon's motive was to gain revenge for his narrow defeat by Kennedy in the 1960 presidential election. What's more, the subsequent assassination of Robert Kennedy in 1968, just as he appeared to have secured the Democratic presidential nomination, meant that the Democrats had lost their two most charismatic leaders within five years – which paved the way for Nixon's own election as president.

The Mafia

As noted above, the 1976 House of Representatives' Select Committee on Assassinations, the HSCA, pointed a finger of suspicion at the Mafia, and the Mob's putative links with the CIA, the FBI, anti-Castro operatives, Cuba and the Kennedy family. One theory holds that Mafia bosses wanted a president who would help them get their lucrative Cuban casinos back, not one who made deals with Castro. In addition, many mobsters hated the Kennedys for their war on organized crime, especially as they had helped them attain power in the first place. The role of Jack Ruby, as a small-time gangster on the Mob payroll, was to plug Oswald before he could sing. Mark North, in *Act of Treason*, adds that J. Edgar Hoover was tipped off about an assassination plot by New Orleans mobster Carlos Marcello in 1962. He goes on to suggest that far from preventing it, the FBI boss was a racist who actively colluded in the plan – which also involved the Ku Klux Klan – to get rid of a president seen as sympathetic towards civil rights.

All aboard for Cuba

Another scenario has the CIA planning a top-secret coup in Cuba, "Operation Amworld", which was to take place on December 1, just nine days after Kennedy's death. The coup was to involve Che Guevara ousting Castro and then enlisting US help to suppress any subsequent pro-Castro insurrection. (Considering Che's later antics obliged the US to have him murdered, this particular plot would probably have been as successful as every other Washington plot against the country.) Although this was a Kennedy coup, the brothers underestimated the extent of the Mob's connection to it and other CIA operations. Sure enough, Marcello, Trafficante and Roselli apparently got wind of Amworld and used it as a cover to kill JFK, reasoning that a subsequent government investigation into his death would not lead to their doors for fear of exposing the plot and provoking another Cuban Missile Crisis-style showdown with the USSR. Oswald himself was, in fact, an anti-Communist CIA asset said to be involved in Amworld. This plot was detailed by Lamar Waldron and Thom Hartmann in 2005, in *Ultimate Sacrifice: John and Robert Kennedy; the Plan for a Coup in Cuba, and the Murder of JFK*, a tome seventeen years in the making.

Dynasties

Or perhaps the killing was the result of a dynastical fight between the Kennedys, the Rockefellers and the rising stars of the Bush family? In this "northeastern elite" scenario, George H.W. Bush, who was busy making money in Texas oil in 1963, was already working as a CIA agent, and fringe theorists have speculated that he carried out the hit, together with the CIA and Secret Service, at the behest of the Rockefellers, the first family of oil and politics. The CIA then framed Oswald as a Castro operative, allowing them to shut down the Fair Play for Cuba Committee group that was working to stop CIA-backed terrorism in Cuba. And the Rockefeller clique warned Johnson that he had better declare Oswald to be a lone nut or they would use their media influence to assert that Havana was behind the whole thing, leading to war with Cuba and the USSR "in no time".

Hunt's deathbed confession

CIA agent E. Howard Hunt was also said to be involved in this dynastical battle and, in April 2005, *Rolling Stone* magazine ran the "deathbed confession" in which he fingered LBJ for giving the go-ahead to the CIA assassination team and for guiding the Warren Commission cover-up. Hunt also blamed a raft of CIA men linked to the Bay of Pigs invasion (including Cord Meyer, whose wife slept with JFK), and operatives later associated with Watergate and the Iran–Contra affair. Other conspirators, according to Hunt, included a bevy of top Mafia men, Cuban exiles and David Sanchez Morales (also cited in the killing of Robert F. Kennedy, see p.39), for various reasons involving their mutual gain and self-preservation. George H.W. Bush's name appears in the papers of one of Oswald's CIA handlers and on one of Hoover's memos, and he was also linked to some anti-Castro Cubans, a clique of Texans, the Mob and the Republicans. In 1973, Bush went on to chair the Republican National Committee, where he endeavoured to keep President Richard Nixon out of trouble over Watergate – itself apparently a cover-up of the JFK assassination, according to journalist Larry Chin, commenting on the *Rolling Stone* piece on conspiracy website www.rense.com.

National security and pillow talk

Fortunately, some simpler sex theories also abound. One twist to the possible involvement of the CIA and/or FBI argues that John Kennedy was brought down by his own sexual promiscuity. His pillow talk may have so compromised national security that it became necessary to kill him. Supposedly, JFK's liaisons with Ellen Rometsch, who was suspected of being a Stasi agent, were on the point of being investigated by Congress before the shooting. Along the same lines, there's also another link with the Mafia, in that JFK also had trysts with Judith Campbell, the girlfriend of Chicago boss Sam Giancana.

The Nazis

Conspiracy theorist Mae Brussell outlined an almost senselessly elaborate theory that put Nazis behind Kennedy's killing, with Nazi hit men hired through the Org (see p.365). In 1971, a French paper headlined a news story – "Martin Bormann Behind the Kennedy Murders" – pointing at an international band of killers in Texas, while a 1977 *Guardian* report, "Bormann Linked With Kennedy Murder" (based on *Treason for my Daily Bread* by Mikhail Lebedev), placed Hitler's deputy, missing since 1945, behind the killing. By this account, anticipated cuts in missile programmes under Kennedy led to anger among the ex-Nazi scientists working on NASA's space programme, and they, with the FBI, military-industrial complex and the Las Vegas Mob had Kennedy shot. In *NASA, Nazis and JFK: The Torbitt Document and the Kennedy Assassination*, William Torbitt and Kenn Thomas claimed that the firms involved in the killing were also behind the failed attempt on Charles de Gaulle's life in 1962. When de Gaulle realized that the companies behind the assassination bid against him were the same ones who supplied NATO, he took France out of the pact.

JFK the movie

In 1992, Oliver Stone's movie *JFK*, which is said to be filled with subliminal imagery suggesting Masonic and homosexual links to the assassination, brought the Garrison trial back to public attention shortly before the thirtieth anniversary of Kennedy's death. The American Bar Association conducted a mock trial of Oswald, while Congress approved the JFK Assassination Records Collection Act to ensure the speedy declassification of all files. "Speedy" in this context, however, means that the records needn't be made public until 2017, and that date can be postponed if the president certifies that release could "harm the military, defense, intelligence operations", and/or "outweighs the public interest in disclosure".

The big picture? The Masons and other strange phenomena

For a truly global conspiracy, how about the idea that the assassination of JFK was a Masonic coup to get rid of the first Catholic president, who but for the pope was the most powerful Catholic in the world? Lyndon B. Johnson, Earl Warren and J. Edgar Hoover were all Masons. So too were Gerald Ford, who "edited" the Warren Report, and another leading member of the Commission, former CIA director Allen Dulles.

Other notably left-field suggestions include the following: Kennedy, who was a much sicker man than the public knew, arranged his own shooting so that he could die a martyr before his various ailments claimed him; he faked his own death to escape the burden of the presidency; Jackie Kennedy was sufficiently tired of JFK's philandering to take out a contract on her own husband; and finally, the Roswell aliens (see p.342) shot Kennedy to prevent his space programme from revealing all their interstellar secrets.

Next comes the odd "0" coincidence. Every president elected in a year ending zero has died in office: William Harrison, elected in 1840; Abraham Lincoln, 1860; James Garfield, 1880; William McKinley, 1900; Warren Harding, 1920; Franklin Roosevelt, 1940; John Kennedy, 1960. Ronald Reagan, 1980, bucked the trend, but only by a hair's breadth, when he survived an assassin's bullet in 1981. George W. Bush, 2000, has yet to dispel the curse.

Further bizarre coincidences link Kennedy to Abraham Lincoln. Kennedy's vice president was Lyndon B. Johnson, while Abraham Lincoln's was Andrew Johnson. Both Johnsons were Southerners, while Lincoln and Kennedy were Northerners. Kennedy had a secretary called Lincoln; Lincoln had a secretary called Kennedy. Both Kennedy and Lincoln were noted for their commitment to civil rights.

Back to square one

And still the debate continues. Forty years after the killing, as if to complete the circle, the BBC broadcast a documentary that came down in favour of the original story: Oswald was a lone Marxist sniper. Notes from his years in the Marine Corps prove that Oswald was a crack shot even without telescopic sights. Kennedy was clearly visible, and the limo was moving so slowly that shooting him was easy. Oswald didn't need to take three shots in the few available seconds, just two – the so-called "magic bullet" could indeed have followed the trajectory described in the Warren Report if, as a computer simulation showed, and the limo's design makes plausible, Connally was placed slightly inboard and down from Kennedy. That said, anyone can programme a computer to do anything, and it remains just one theory among hundreds.

In June 2007, Italian news agency ANSA reported that the Italian Army had tried to re-enact Oswald's three-shots-in-seven-seconds, according to the Warren Commission, using the same model of Carcarno bolt-action rifle. In the test, the best time was nineteen seconds, almost three times as long. Furthermore, a bullet fired through two large pieces of meat (in a tactful simulation of the single shot that traversed Kennedy and Connally) came out "deformed", whereas the bullet from the Commission's version of reality was intact.

The theories continue

So far, around two thousand books have been devoted to the assassination of JFK, creating a self-sustaining sub-industry that also includes TV documentaries, websites, films, essays, magazine and newspaper articles, PhDs, memorabilia and sheer conjecture. Every year, researchers and conspiracy enthusiasts meet in Dallas for the "November in Dallas" convention, sounding out new theories and evidence. Dallas even has its own Conspiracy Museum. Over thirty gunmen have been named as acting either in cahoots with or separately from Oswald, and a hundred witnesses are said to have been killed as a result of the conspiracies that surround the deaths of Kennedy, Oswald and Ruby.

While the assassination was a spectacular and deeply affecting event in itself, a more subtle dislocation in the minds of the American public began to set in with the shootings of Malcolm X, Martin Luther King Jr and Robert Kennedy later that same decade. It became increasingly hard to believe in Oswald as a "lone nut". Just how many "lone nut" killers, and successful ones at that, could there be? As the later deeds of the CIA and FBI were revealed, the atrocities in Vietnam were televised, and the Watergate scandal saw the president of the United States incontrovertibly linked to a grubby burglary and an even grubbier cover-up, the potential depth of the government's duplicity seemed limitless.

Multiple investigations, whether Congressional, judicial, intelligence agency or simply private, have pored over not only the assassination but also every previous investigation. Every item of evidence, and every conclusion drawn from it, has been examined and re-examined from every angle. Doubts have been cast on everything from the "magic bullet" to the autopsy X-rays; has even the Zapruder film been altered? (Doubts have also been cast on the death of JFK's son John Kennedy in a plane crash in 2000, but that's another story.)

So, anyway, where were *you* when Kennedy was shot?

SOURCES

Books

Stewart Galanor Cover-up (1998). A concise outline of the cover-up in government and the press over key elements of Kennedy's death.

Mikhail Lebedev Treason for my Daily Bread (1977). One of the more fringe theories, though a bit dry to read.

Jim Marrs Crossfire: The Plot that Killed Kennedy (1989). A fascinating tour of the big theories behind Kennedy's assassination, cited by Oliver Stone in *JFK*.

Sylvia Meagher Accessories After the Fact (1967/1992). One of the first big conspiracy works, imbued with the sense of wide-eyed disbelief that such a thing could be lied about.

Mark North Act of Treason (1991). J. Edgar Hoover's involvement, or lack of it, in events preceding Kennedy's death. Could he have warned the president?

Gerald Posner Case Closed (1994). A somewhat overly confident book that triumphantly proves Oswald did it alone.

Robin Ramsay Who Shot JFK? (2000). An excellently researched, tightly written tour through the thinking (or lack of it) behind Kennedy's assassination. Ramsay's *Conspiracy Theories* (2000) is of a similar calibre.

David Schiem Contract on America (1988). "It wuz da Mob."

Peter Dale Scott Crime and Cover-up: The CIA, the Mafia and the Dallas–Watergate Connection (1977). The same names seem to keep cropping up in all these political scandals, and Scott refuses to accept that this is a "coincidence".

Anthony Summers Conspiracy (1980). Another highly praised summary of the main theories surrounding Kennedy's death.

A.J. Weberman and Michael Canfield Coup D'Etat in America (1975). The focus here is on the three hoboes and the grassy knoll.

Websites

Ⓦ **www.archives.gov/research_room/jfk/warren_commission/warren_commission_report.html** The report that started it all – all 888 pages of it.

Ⓦ **www.newsmakingnews.com/mbnaziconnect.htm** Devilishly convoluted theory that puts a cabal of Nazis behind the killing.

Ⓦ **www.rense.com/general76/hunt.htm** Journalist Larry Chin's commentary on Hunt's deathbed confession revealing JFK's killers.

Ⓦ **www.rollingstone.com/politics/story/13893143/the_last_confessions_of_e_howard_hunt** Former CIA operative E. Howard Hunt tells all to Erik Hedegaard of *Rolling Stone* magazine in 2005.

Malcolm X

In the late 1950s and early 1960s, Malcolm X was the most visible spokesman of radical black America. Establishing a powerful public persona as the principal mouthpiece of the Nation of Islam (NOI), he rejected the passive civil disobedience advocated by Dr Martin Luther King Jr, and argued that it was up to blacks to resist oppression "by any means necessary". In 1964, he split with the so-called "Black

Muslims" and set up his own Organization of Afro-American Unity (OAAU). Reaching out to other domestic and international leaders, he appeared to espouse the idea that it might be possible for different races to live in equality in the US. On February 21, 1965, however, immediately after delivering a speech, Malcolm X was shot dead on stage at the Audubon Ballroom in New York City. Three men – Talmadge Hayer, Thomas "15X" Johnson and Norman "3X" Butler – were convicted of his murder in March 1966.

However, Hayer always maintained that the others were innocent, and there were doubts as to whether Johnson and Butler were even at the meeting. Whereas initial press reports said that two people had been rescued from the furious crowd, including Hayer, who had himself been shot, both press and police said later that Hayer was the only one arrested. Although there was usually a high police presence at Malcolm's speeches, there were almost none there on that fateful day. The police claimed that Malcolm had turned down their protection, but his widow, Betty Shabazz, insisted that was a lie. It also took half an hour for help to arrive from a hospital directly across from the theatre. Finally, shortly after Malcolm's death, an OAAU activist announced that he had evidence of government involvement. But he collapsed and died from "epilepsy" the following day, even though he'd never suffered from the disease before.

The FBI and the CIA

According to Roland Sheppard, who attended many of Malcolm X's lectures and had been a presence in both the OAAU and the NOI, Malcolm X had become the focus of a high-level conspiracy within the government. Malcolm's conviction that American capitalism was irredeemably rooted in racism, and that the struggle for civil rights was just part of a larger economic and social struggle, combined with his opposition to the Vietnam War to attract the attention of the FBI.

Then there was the international company that Malcolm was keeping. He met with Fidel Castro and Che Guevara in 1964, and planned to petition the International Court in the Hague with a list of abuses against blacks in both the US and South Africa. In addition, Ahmed Ben Bella of Algeria had invited Malcolm, along with other independence leaders, to the Bandung conference in March 1965, at which Malcolm intended to make a concerted effort to create a global black power base. This, in turn, was anathema to the CIA, which was desperate to hold onto its raft of friendly states in Africa, where Western and Soviet agencies were fighting a covert but deadly battle to maintain their spheres of influence.

In *The Judas Factor*, Karl Evanzz of *The Washington Post* contends that the CIA decided to "neutralize" Malcolm. Both Evanzz and Sheppard believe that the FBI and/or CIA had infiltrated agents into the Nation of Islam to disrupt its activities, and possibly precipitated the split between Malcolm and NOI leader, Elijah Muhammad. Evanzz argues that one key high-level informant, a "Judas", was largely responsible. That said, even if there was a conspiracy to stir up trouble in the Nation of Islam, there's no sign of the proverbial "smoking gun" – a documented order to kill Malcolm X.

Drugs and the Klan

There were also rumours that Malcolm X was killed by Chinese drug traffickers who stood to lose out from his campaigns against inner-city drug abuse. Another rumour suggested that Malcolm X was killed by NOI members because he was going to reveal that the group had received money from the American Nazi Party and the Ku Klux Klan (on the basis that the NOI, the Nazis and the KKK all agreed with the idea of racial segregation).

Turf war

Hayer himself never denied pulling the trigger. He was a member of the Nation of Islam, and the most popular theory continues to ascribe Malcolm X's murder to a straightforward act of vengeance. Malcolm had founded the Organization of Afro-American Unity while on suspension from the Nation of Islam, ostensibly for the controversy he aroused by saying "chickens coming home to roost never did make me sad", in reference to the assassination of JFK, but also because he publicly alleged that Elijah Muhammad had fathered numerous illegitimate children. Muhammad, livid at both that charge and Malcolm's defection, reportedly said in 1964: "It's time to close that nigger's eyes."

Equally outraged was a one-time supporter of Malcolm's, Louis Farrakhan, who called Malcolm a traitor and wrote two months before the killing that "such a man is worthy of death". Michael Friedly outlined the likelihood that the shooting was an inside job in *Malcolm X: The Assassination*, pointing out there had been four attempts on Malcolm's life in the weeks preceding the shooting. Malcolm's widow Betty Shabazz publicly accused Farrakhan of involvement in his murder, and that suspicion remained strong enough for Malcolm's daughter Qubilah to attempt to hire a hit man – who turned out to be an FBI informant – to kill Farrakhan in 1994.

Admission and contrition

In 2000, Farrakhan, who by then had been leading the NOI for some years, told CBS News and Malcolm X's daughter Atallah Shabazz: "I may have been complicit in words that I spoke leading up to February 21 [1965] … I acknowledge that and regret that any word that I have said caused the loss of life of a human being." Atallah replied "My father was not killed from a grassy knoll", and said she still believed that the FBI were involved in Malcolm's death, even if it was young black men who shot him. Nonetheless, while Farrakhan has made his peace with the Shabazz family, and has also acknowledged that "I know that members of the Nation were involved in the assassination of Malcolm X", some theorists continue to believe that he was directly involved. But that doesn't, of course, preclude the possibility that government agencies also played a part. The FBI is still refusing to release the 45,000 documents it holds on Malcolm X.

In December 2007, Thomas Johnson (having since renamed himself Khalil Islam) added fuel to the conspiracy fire when he told *The Voice* newspaper that neither Farrakhan nor Elijah Muhammad were behind the hit. He said it was Hayer leading four "known criminals" – "brothers" acting in the throes of the "jealousy and hate" that were afflicting the Brotherhood at that time. The FBI were not behind the killing, but Johnson was duly framed because of his seniority in the Brotherhood and because of the "threat" he posed as Malcolm X's likely successor. Despite witness statements placing Johnson at home ill on the day of the murder, the shotgun killer being described as dark-skinned and bearded (Johnson was neither), the fact that he passed a lie-detector test paid for by Muhammad Ali, and Hayer's affidavit naming his four collaborators – none of which were Johnson or Butler – Johnson spent 22 years in jail for the murder of Malcolm X.

SOURCES

Books

Karl Evanzz The Judas Factor (1992). While holding the Nation of Islam responsible, Karl Evanzz also charts the shadowy influence of the FBI and CIA, in a detailed write-up that covers Malcolm X's life and works too.

Michael Friedly Malcolm X: The Assassination (1992). A neat summary of the many theories that surround Malcolm X's death, this concludes that the Nation of Islam was responsible (and, as a result, it has been decried by some as an FBI cover-up).

Films

Spike Lee Malcolm X (1992). Denzel Washington captivates as the eloquent, angry Malcolm.

Websites

Ⓦ **www.cmgww.com/historic/malcolm/** The official Malcolm X website maintained by his estate.

Ⓦ **www.voice-online.co.uk** Thomas Johnson (aka Khalil Islam) breaks his silence.

Dr Martin Luther King Jr

While civil rights leader Dr Martin Luther King Jr could draw crowds of millions, and bring them to tears with his impassioned vision of black and white living in harmonious equality, his vision also drew murderous hate. On April 4, 1968, while he was visiting Memphis to mediate in a strike by local authority workers, King was shot dead on the balcony of the Lorraine motel. A single shot went through his neck, severing his spinal cord and killing him almost instantly. After a worldwide manhunt, the man blamed for the killing, petty criminal James Earl Ray, was charged and convicted of King's murder and sentenced to 99 years. Accusations and rumours of conspiracies have continued to rumble ever since.

The case against Ray

Moments after King was shot, someone was seen to leave an apartment building opposite the motel, and race away in a white Mustang. The shot was later traced to the bathroom of one apartment, a classic "sniper's nest" equipped with binoculars and a rifle with telescopic sights, and enjoying a perfect view of the motel balcony. All, police later claimed, were covered in the fingerprints of James Earl Ray, and a warrant was put out for his arrest. By now, Ray was on a complicated and expensive fugitive flight through Canada, England and Portugal. He was finally detained, after two months on the run, at London's Heathrow airport, en route to start a new life as a mercenary in southern Africa.

This inept car thief appeared to have done his best to get caught. As well as leaving his prints everywhere, he had also dropped a bundle of personal effects on the pavement as he fled the apartment building. At his trial, Ray pleaded guilty, and thereby avoided a full trial, which he was told would end in his execution.

Questions arise

Three days after his conviction, Ray began to protest his innocence, saying that he'd been framed by a gun-smuggler called "Raul" or "Raoul". Questions were, in any case, being asked. Where had this habitual petty criminal obtained the $10,000 needed to fund his globetrotting escapade, and how had he managed to pull off a major assassination, only to leave such incriminating evidence at the scene? How come his prints were neither all over the boarding-house room nor on a box of bullets? Why did Memphis police withdraw King's police protection the day before he died, despite his receiving more than fifty death threats? Hours before the shooting, two firemen and a detective posted near the motel were sent off on spurious tasks. The infamous photo of King lying on the balcony, taken moments after the shooting, shows all his aides pointing up to the motel roof opposite, not towards the apartment. In addition, Charles Stephens, the only witness who identified the mystery Mustang man as Ray, was drunk at the time and later retracted his story, while his similarly unreliable wife Grace said that Charles couldn't see the mystery man from where he was at the time, whereas she could – and it wasn't Ray. She was later put in a mental hospital. Furthermore, it was no secret that FBI boss J. Edgar Hoover had hated King for years, hounding him in the hope of destroying his reputation. It took FBI investigators more than two weeks merely to announce that they had found Ray's things in the street, shortly after the car sped off.

The House points to conspiracy

The 1977–78 House Select Committee on Assassinations found that, while Ray did shoot King, there was a "likelihood" that he did not act alone. The House considered whether the CIA was involved in framing Ray, in view of the numerous fake IDs and documents found on him when he was arrested. One alias, which he'd used before the shooting, belonged to a Canadian named Galt. Galt strongly resembled Ray, and was a crack shot into the bargain. However, Ray's initial escape to Canada, where a "fat man" gave him the money to get to England, was the first time he had ever visited the country.

Martin Luther King Jr at a civil rights march in Washington DC in 1963.

Jowers "confesses"

Another twist came in 1993, when Loyd Jowers, the owner of a grill bar opposite the motel, told ABC TV that he had been asked to help in the assassination, and had been told there would be a decoy, namely Ray. Jowers said that a cast of Memphis police and government agents met in his restaurant in the days prior to King's death; that a mobster dropped off money there; and that a man named Raul arrived the day before, and left a rifle which reappeared, smoking, after the shooting.

The story unravels

Ray's lawyer, William Pepper, accused the Green Berets of carrying out the killing. In his 1995 book *Orders to Kill: The Truth Behind the Murder of Martin Luther King*, he says that members of the 20th Special Forces Group, including several with experience of CIA missions in Vietnam, were scattered in and around Memphis in the period leading up to the shooting. Then in 1998, an FBI agent came forward and claimed that he had once had papers from Ray's car with FBI phone numbers and "Raul" written on them, which were subsequently stolen. In August that year, Attorney General Janet Reno ordered the Justice Department to reinvestigate King's death. Focusing mainly on the Jowers story, they completed their report in 1999. Their conclusion? Ray did it, and there was "no reliable evidence that Dr King was killed by conspirators who framed James Earl Ray". They continued: "nor have any of the conspiracy theories advanced in the last thirty years … survived critical examination." It was Ray, and Ray alone.

The Kings say it wasn't Ray

However, in December 1999, a Memphis jury in a wrongful death lawsuit determined that there was a conspiracy to kill Dr Martin Luther King Jr by Loyd Jowers and "other unknown conspirators" – understood to mean government agents of some kind – and awarded the King family a symbolic $100. The trial had to be a civil suit because US intelligence agencies can only be tried in criminal courts with Federal government consent, which wasn't forthcoming. King's wife, Coretta Scott King, and his son Dexter have also said that they believe he was killed in a larger conspiracy, involving the CIA, the FBI, the army and President Johnson. Dexter visited Ray in jail in 1997 to say that he and the Kings believed in his innocence, but Ray died the following year. Both the Lorraine motel and the "sniper's nest" in the apartment building are now open to visitors as memorials to Dr King, and an exhibition approved by the King family lays out the assorted conspiracy theories in copious detail.

SOURCES

Books

William Pepper Orders to Kill: The Truth Behind the Murder of Martin Luther King (1995). The fact that these charges come from a source as close to the facts, and the family, as King's lawyer renders them all the more extraordinary.

Websites

ⓦ **www.consortiumnews.com/2000/022100a.html** Plenty of Martin Luther King conspiracies.

ⓦ **www.usdoj.gov/crt/crim/mlk/part1.htm** The official verdict of the Justice Department in 1998.

Robert Kennedy

For a brief, heady moment in 1968, it looked as though Robert F. Kennedy was going to fill the presidential shoes of his slain brother John. The great white hope of liberal America, Robert had recast himself as a handsome, idealistic young knight, crusading across an America that was bitterly divided over civil rights and the worsening situation in Vietnam. It's hardly surprising that when Robert was shot dead on June 4, 1968, a mere two months after the killing of Dr Martin Luther King Jr, three quarters of Americans are said to have believed he was the victim of a conspiracy.

That day, RFK won the crucial Democratic primary election in California, which made him the frontrunner to become the Democrats' presidential nominee that autumn. As the results came in, he celebrated at Los Angeles' Ambassador hotel. At 12.15am, engulfed by a throng of supporters, press, guards and others, he was being escorted out through the hotel pantry when someone managed to get a clear shot at him. A hail of bullets left RFK bleeding to death on the floor.

A small Palestinian man, Sirhan Bashira Sirhan, gun in hand and firing wildly, was wrestled down by the security men who had so palpably failed to protect Kennedy. A "lone nut" protesting against RFK's plan to sell American bombers to Israel, Sirhan had apparently snapped on seeing the senator's pro-Israeli statements in late May and shot him just days later. Put on trial and convicted of murder in the first degree, Sirhan was sentenced to life imprisonment.

A case riddled with holes

For many observers, however, too much about the case simply didn't add up. For a start, there were too many bullets. Sirhan's pistol held eight rounds, but RFK took three wounds, one bullet went through his clothing and five others were also fired – which makes nine bullets. According to the Los Angeles Police Department, some bullets must have hit more than one person. However, the *Los Angeles Free Press* newspaper reported, with photographic proof, that more bullets were lodged in a doorframe in the pantry. Indeed, the total fired reached thirteen, and thus pointed to the presence of at least one more gunman. It was shown that the police had indeed documented the extra hits, but had failed to disclose that information at the trial, after which the doorframe and all forensic evidence had been destroyed. On that basis, Congressman Allard Lowenstein attempted, unsuccessfully, to start a reinvestigation in 1974, backed by Hollywood celebrities such as Robert Vaughn. Lowenstein was later shot dead in his law office by "a disgruntled client".

According to Court TV, Lowenstein's investigation was largely sabotaged by the intransigence of the LAPD. After much media pressure, the LAPD released its crudely censored records of the events in 1986. Further pressure led to the release of fifty thousand more documents in 1988, but these still excluded not only the doorframe evidence but also the trial testimonies of seven forensic experts.

To add fuel to the furtive fire, the Discovery Times channel broadcast a programme in June 2006 called *Conspiracy Test: The RFK Assassination*, which featured the first-ever public broadcasting of the only known audio recording of the shooting. It was captured at the scene by a newspaper reporter, but buried in the California State Archives for nearly forty years. Three audio experts said they identified betweeen ten and thirteen gunshots on the recording, scotching the theory that Sirhan, with his eight-shot pistol, could have fired them all. They also deemed that some of the shots were fired at too rapid a rate for a single gunman.

Crucially, coroner Thomas Noguchi (who also attended the corpses of Marilyn Monroe and John Belushi) reported that the fatal wound was caused by a .22-calibre bullet that went into the back of RFK's head. Powder burns indicated that the gun was fired from a distance of no more than three inches. However, every witness put Sirhan several feet in front of RFK, and no one said that Kennedy had turned away. Noguchi, who examined the bullet-ridden doorframe, later wrote: "The existence of a second gunman remains a possibility. Thus, I have never said that Sirhan Sirhan killed Robert Kennedy."

Sirhan remembers nothing

Sirhan himself said, after the trial, that he had no memory of the shooting. Bernard Diamond, a psychiatrist working for the defence, diagnosed Sirhan as a paranoid schizophrenic, but the trial judge didn't allow them to use the defence of insanity. Diamond did not rule out the possibility that Sirhan had been hypnotized, and Dr Eduard Simpson, who examined him in jail, said hypnosis was utterly credible. Hypnosis by state doctors has since failed to evoke any memory of the shooting from Sirhan.

In *RFK Must Die!*, former journalist Robert Blair Kaiser, who also worked for Sirhan's defence team, wrote that Sirhan was programmed to kill Robert Kennedy and then forget his programming. Notebooks presented by the prosecution at the trial, which supposedly belonged to Sirhan and contained the phrases "RFK must die" and "must be assassinated", were claimed to be forgeries and described as "automatic", implying hypnotically induced writing. Ex-FBI agent William Turner lent his support to the theory that Sirhan was a so-called "Manchurian candidate" or brainwashed assassin.

Half a dozen witnesses to the murder reported seeing a "girl in a polka-dot dress" fleeing the scene, screaming "We shot him!" Asked "who?", she replied "Senator Kennedy!" Sirhan's last memory prior to the shooting was of drinking coffee with a woman, who he said wore a polka-dot dress. The theory runs that the woman gave Sirhan his final preparations, using techniques mastered under the CIA hypnosis program, MK-ULTRA (see p.210). If the CIA were involved in hypnotizing Sirhan, a possible motive might be fear that if RFK reached the White House he would order a proper investigation into his brother's death, and thus discover the part played by the CIA. But that doesn't answer the riddle of the point-blank shots fired from behind him.

The security guard

Despite the fact that the would-be president was appearing in front of two thousand people – and not forgetting the fate of his president brother just five years before – Robert Kennedy's security protection was rather limited. His security retinue comprised unarmed Olympic decathlete Rafer Johnson and American football player Rosey Grier – both tough men, but not exactly a Wall of Steel for a potential president. On that fateful night, he was also guarded by Thane Cesar, who was employed by the private security company Ace. Witnesses reported that Cesar was standing right behind Kennedy, and Cesar himself admitted that he was in a perfect position to shoot Kennedy at point-blank range. However, despite being a crucial witness, he was not called to testify at Sirhan's trial. Cesar told the LAPD that he had owned a .22-calibre pistol, but that he had sold it before the shooting. Interviewed in 1994 by Dan Moldea,

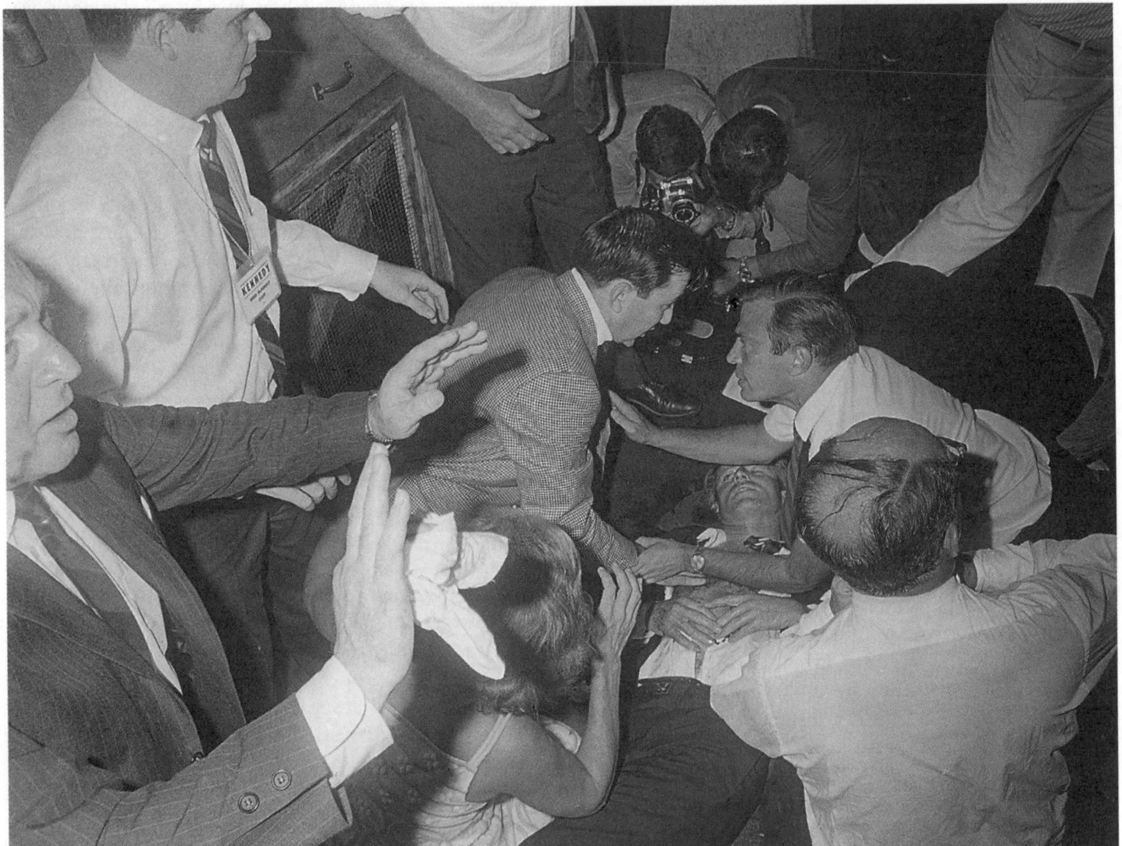

Robert Kennedy – surrounded by supporters, security and press – lies dying on the floor of the Ambassador hotel.

author of *The Killing of Robert Kennedy*, Cesar passed a polygraph test in which he denied shooting Kennedy. But had he been programmed as well?

The CIA, the Mafia and the arms industry

So who wanted Kennedy dead? It wasn't beyond the CIA to get the Mafia to do the job, but equally it wasn't beyond the Mafia to do it themselves. As Sam Giancana's brother and grandson wrote in *Double Cross*, the Mob hated Robert Kennedy for his war on organized crime. The Giancanas also charged that Marilyn Monroe's death was a bid by the Mafia to topple Robert Kennedy (see p.18). In 2004, Court TV reported that Giancana's supposed ally in bumping off Monroe, Teamsters' union leader Jimmy Hoffa, had told an informant in 1967 that he had a contract on RFK and he'd be dead if he ever won a primary.

Another much-touted suspect is the "military-industrial complex", which didn't want Kennedy to end the lucrative Vietnam War. However, it should be remembered that the president who ended the war, Richard Nixon, wasn't killed… but then he did resign in disgrace. For that matter, the neo-Nazis didn't want an advocate of civil rights in the White House, and they may have been aided by FBI boss J. Edgar Hoover. In 2005, one writer linked the CIA, FBI and Aristotle Onassis in the plot to hypnotize Sirhan, but again failed to address the bullet-from-behind conundrum.

The CIA and Cuba

Screenwriter and reseacher Shane O'Sullivan, who made the 2007 documentary *RFK Must Die: The Assassination of Bobby Kennedy*, found himself drawn into a world of "second guns" and "Manchurian candidates". His research, first broadcast on the BBC's *Newsnight* programme in November 2006, but subsequently fiercely contested, showed new video and photographic evidence that appeared to put three senior CIA operatives in the frame: David Sanchez Morales and two other men, who all worked together at JM/WAVE, the CIA's secret Miami base, in the early 1960s. The programme said that all three men were spied on old films and photos that were taken in and around the hotel ballroom before and during the shooting. Sullivan cites Morales as being of particular interest, as he was described by one former Havana Embassy official as the "last person" to protect the Kennedy brothers, because of his evidently well-known hatred of them following the failed Bay of Pigs invasion. According to another of Sullivan's sources, Morales once drunkenly bragged to CIA friends, "I was in Dallas when we got the son of a bitch and I was in Los Angeles when we got the little bastard." Intriguingly, one of the same CIA operatives later acted as CIA liaison to the HSCA investigation into JFK's death – Morales was called to appear in front of the investigation, but died just weeks beforehand.

Case unsolved

Whoever was behind Robert Kennedy's killing – and whoever was standing behind him when he was killied – Sirhan continues to protest his innocence from jail. The belief of his lawyer, Lawrence Teeter, that Sirhan was hypnotized might seem absurd, but it's no more absurd than the fact that Sirhan was convicted despite the problem of the extra bullets. In the minds of many Americans, the case is still unsolved, and the actions of the LAPD in disposing of the forensic evidence hardly allay suspicion. Nonetheless, the official story, as reiterated by a 1997 congressional hearing, remains the same: Sirhan did it, and he acted alone.

SOURCES

Books

Sam and Chuck Giancana **Double Cross: The Explosive, Inside Story of the Mobster who Controlled America** (1992). This book is a must-read, not only for the vignettes of Mafia-speak, but also because it plausibly identifies a handful of Mafiosi as the men behind many 1960s assassinations.

Robert Blair Kaiser **RFK Must Die!** (1970). A contemporary account of RFK's death.

Dan Moldea The Killing of Robert Kennedy (1994). Moldea's detailed exploration of the assassination, investigation and conspiracy theories ends by upholding the official story – Sirhan acted alone.

William W. Turner and Jonn G. Christian The Assassination of Robert F. Kennedy: The Conspiracy and Coverup (1993). This book raises a lot of questions about the LAPD and CIA, but the biggest mystery is the lack of outcry from the US public.

Films

Shake O'Sullivan RFK Must Die: The Assassination of Bobby Kennedy (2007). Investigative documentary featuring new interviews and evidence of CIA agents being in the Ambassador hotel that night.

Websites

www.crimelibrary.com/terrorists_spies/assassins/kennedy/2.html A detailed, soberly written tour through the failures and questions surrounding RFK's death.

www.ss.ca.gov/archives/level3_rfkguide.html The Californian government's opinion about the RFK killing.

Salvador Allende

It's not known who exactly pulled the trigger to kill President Salvador Allende on September 11, 1973, during a bloody military coup in Chile. It remains a mystery whether he was cut down by the troops of General Augusto Pinochet as they stormed the presidential palace, which had already been bombed by airforce jets, or whether Allende took his own life in defiance. What's no longer in dispute is that the US was behind the coup, in a plot that can no longer simply be dismissed as a "conspiracy theory".

The CIA and Nixon

The official US version, in the days following the coup, was that Allende's bad leadership had obliged the Chilean military to step in and rescue the country. As President Richard Nixon put it in his memoirs, Allende's inefficient socialist government, in power since late 1970, had caused crippling strikes that resulted in an inflation rate of 350 percent by 1973. The army could no longer stand by.

However, it was hard to believe that the US had played no part in Allende's downfall, given that it had tried so hard to stop him getting into office in the first place. Richard Nixon, who was in office at the time of both Allende's accession and his death, wrote that Kennedy and Johnson had spent almost $4 million ensuring Allende's defeat in Chile's 1962 and 1964 elections, while in 1970, when Allende won, he received $350,000 from Cuba. Nixon followed his predecessors' lead, instructing the CIA to support Allende's opponents in the Chilean Congress. "As long as the Communists supply external funds to support political parties, factions or individuals in other countries, I believe that the United States can and should do the same and do it secretly so that it can be effective … To me it would have been the height of immorality to allow the Soviets, the Cubans and other Communist nations to interfere with impunity in free elections while America stayed its hand."

The election of Allende established Cuba and Chile as a "Red sandwich", which Nixon feared might export revolution elsewhere in the continent. Even so, the US appeared to accept the will of the Chilean people, until Allende's overthrow in 1973 ushered in the seventeen-year dictatorship of Augusto Pinochet, whose regime didn't so much interfere with free elections as outlaw opposition on the pain of murder.

The problem with Allende

Salvador Allende nationalized Chile's banks and its copper industry, and received aid from both Cuba and the USSR. By contrast, the US government curtailed its trade with Chile, and cut off aid, while the CIA increased its support to the Chilean military in terms of arms and advice, and encouraged right-wing paramilitary groups. Once the pro-capitalist Pinochet was installed, US trade and aid with Chile resumed. Pinochet cut government spending and social subsidies, lowered tariffs and opened Chilean markets to massive imports, causing wages to fall and industries to close. As the working poor faced starvation, the US government propped up the Pinochet junta with financial aid.

The smoking guns

While this was all common knowledge, it amounted to little more than circumstantial evidence that the CIA was behind the coup – until the Clinton administration declassified the relevant CIA documents in 2000. US strategy was summarized in a memo dated September 27, 1970, which outlined a programme of economic, political and psychological warfare that might ultimately bring down Allende. "Surface ineluctable conclusion that military coup is the only answer. This is to be carried forward until it takes place … [but in production being] diffuse, denatured, and ineffective … Eventually we may use propaganda to persuade the military that it is their constitutional duty to prevent Allende from holding power." CIA director Richard Helms said that he intended to "make the Chilean economy scream".

In September 1973, the plan came off. The reason Nixon declined to take credit for the coup is revealed in a transcript of what national security adviser Henry Kissinger told him on September 16, 1973. Kissinger lamented the fact that US newspapers were "bleeding because a pro-Communist government had been overthrown … instead of celebrating – in the Eisenhower period we would be heroes." The documents also revealed that, in 1964, the CIA had not considered Allende to be all that dangerous, or regarded him as a genuine ally of the Soviets. "The US has no vital national interests within Chile", it reported, or at least none that could be threatened by distributing free milk or nationalizing industries, or even by expanding trade with the Soviets.

Suspicions proven

The declassification of the CIA documents confirmed beyond doubt the extent of the US government's determination to bring down Allende. Under the ensuing Pinochet dictatorship, 130,000 Chilean citizens were placed under political arrest, 3100 "disappeared", and torture was widespread. True, inflation was brought under control and some economists cited Chile as a model for other Latin American countries; it also, however, came to rank seventh in the world for inequality of income distribution.

While in the UK for medical treatment in 1998, Pinochet was placed under house arrest (despite the support of powerful friends like Margaret Thatcher) when a Spanish judge issued a warrant for his arrest for the murder of Spanish citizens in Chile. However, he was released in 2000 – on medical grounds – without facing trial and allowed to return to Chile. When his plane landed on the tarmac in Santiago, the healthier-looking general was greeted by a military fanfare and the news that Congress had just moved to grant ex-presidents immunity from prosecution.

But a happy retirement was not to be. Over the following years, allegations, revelations and criminal charges for murder, kidnap, torture, the use of bio-chemical weapons on political opponents, cocaine smuggling and tax evasion were levelled at home and abroad. His immunity from prosecution was contested, overturned, reinstated and re-contested. Finally, in December 2006 – just weeks after a second raft of charges for kidnap, torture and murder were levied and another attempt at evading trial on the grounds that he was suffering from dementia was foiled – Pinochet did the decent thing and died.

SOURCES

Books

Richard Nixon The Memoirs of Richard Nixon (1978). A good read, and an insight into what the world's most powerful man will choose to delete, forget or subliminally reappraise.

Websites

www.worldpress.org/Americas/1591.cfm A brief, political summary of events; there's more detail (although uncorroborated), at www.rrojasdatabank.org/coup1.htm.

Elvis Presley

Elvis Presley, "The King" of rock'n'roll, was found dead in the bathroom at Graceland, his home in Memphis, on August 16, 1977. Tributes poured in from around the world, from The Beatles to The Beach Boys, and President Jimmy Carter made a statement. The medical examiner in Shelby County reported the cause of death as heart failure, brought on by chronic heart disease. However, Elvis was only 42, and rumours ran rife that he'd simply faked his own death to escape his unrelenting, obsessive fans. Those rumours have snowballed into a veritable industry, as magazines like the *National Enquirer* publish a steady stream of bread-and-butter stories that Elvis has been spotted everywhere from Antarctica to the moon.

Chips and fixes

Compared to the young sex-god who had shown America's teens what hips were really for during the 1950s and 60s, Elvis had become a physical and mental wreck by the 1970s. He both dealt with and exacerbated his decline by ingesting copious quantities of food and prescription drugs. The same evergreen core of devotees who went to his shows, and thus provided him with the audiences he craved, also staked out his mansion, flooding his mailbox with letters, flowers, tributes and declarations of undying love. All of which served to fuel Elvis's paranoid fantasies that he too would fall victim to a lone nut. When he stayed in hotels on tour, Elvis often used the pseudonym John Burrows. Just days after the King was announced dead, someone with that name, who very much resembled Presley, was supposedly seen buying a ticket for South America. Had Elvis chosen to escape from his own glamorous but destructive existence for a life of anonymity?

Elvis meets Nixon

Although some have suggested that Elvis was murdered by right-wing government elements, Elvis considered himself to be very much in line with that mindset. So much so that he took himself to Washington DC in 1970, to meet first Vice President Spiro Agnew and then, a few weeks later, Richard Nixon. He told the president how America's youth was being morally degraded by rock degenerates such as The Beatles, and offered his services. Nixon responded by appointing him as "Federal Agent at Large" against drugs.

Elvis messes with the CIA

Did Elvis's desire to help the government run deep enough to allow the CIA to use Graceland as the cover for a massive secret underground installation? The very idea was so ludicrous, of course, that no one would ever suspect the truth. Then Elvis, forgetting quite who he was dealing with,

President Nixon shakes hands with the King at the White House in 1970.

is said to have threatened to expose the scheme unless the CIA moved out from beneath him – paying the price with his life. Equally ludicrously, some have blamed Elvis for assassinating JFK, suggesting he was enraged by the way the handsome president was barging into his limelight. Elvis was then killed in revenge.

Elvis on drugs

Perhaps, on the other hand, Elvis died of an overdose of prescription drugs. It's been alleged that Elvis's father, Vernon, was so afraid that the news would tarnish his son's anti-drugs image forever that he bribed medical officials to say that he'd died of a heart attack. *The Washington Post* reported the coroner's verdict that "there was no sign of drug abuse": a striking observation to make if it had simply been a heart attack. Vernon's widow Dee has told of seeing autopsy papers that blamed drugs for Elvis's death. The Shelby County Commission has filed for a second autopsy, but it has been continually resisted by the Elvis estate. While the official cause of death remains cardiac arrhythmia, many Internet sites and bloggers have decided that Elvis's heart may well have packed up – but not without the influence of a cocktail of tranquillizers and barbiturates, which Elvis imbibed in a range and quantity way beyond what any kosher doctor would individually prescribe.

There was only one Elvis – and he's gone

The reason there have been so many Elvis sightings is very simple: there's a lot of money, entertainment and just plain comfort to be derived from reporting yet another sighting, even decades after his death. On top of that, of course, countless men the world over still pay homage to the King by dressing up and singing like him – so it's hardly surprising some of them get "spotted".

Ultimately, heart failure makes the most sense, given Elvis's extraordinary appetite. This was a man who considered a dozen two-foot baguettes, stuffed with pounds of bacon, jam and peanut butter, literally worth flying to Las Vegas for. His frenetic stage performances also forced him into a horrendous seesawing cycle of weight gain and loss. In the end, it was a question of time as to which organ would shut down first, as the world's most famous star gorged himself to death.

SOURCES

Books

Paul Simpson The Rough Guide to Elvis (2002). Contains a very detailed overview of the many theories and rumours that surround the death of the King.

Websites

Ⓦ **www.deadoraliveinfo.com/dead.nsf/pnames-nf/Presley+Elvis** For those who suspect that Elvis isn't even dead.

Ⓦ **www.elvispresleynews.com** For die-hard fans.

Ⓦ **www.nationalenquirer.com** For those who know that Elvis isn't dead.

Pope John Paul I

When Albino Luciani, a humble, almost timid man without a high-profile career in the Vatican hierarchy, was elected pope on August 26, 1978, the cardinals in the papal conclave seemed as surprised as Luciani himself. But he was proudly acclaimed as "God's candidate", and soon acquired the nickname, the "Smiling Pope". Catholics all over the world responded warmly to his modesty – at his coronation, he refused the customary papal tiara and only reluctantly agreed to be carried aloft on the traditional gestatorial chair. Shortly after 5am on September 28, however, just 33 days after his election, Pope John Paul I was found dead in the papal lodgings. The Vatican initially claimed that his body was found by his papal secretaries, Magee and Lorenzi – propped up in bed with a copy of Thomas à Kempis's *The Imitation of Christ* – but afterwards revealed that he was discovered by a nun who had brought him his morning coffee. The papal doctor, Renato Buzzonetti, declared him dead of a heart attack. At 5.15pm, the Signoracci brothers, embalmers to the Vatican, were summoned. They began work within two hours. There was no autopsy.

For any pope, let alone such a popular one, to die just a month after his election was unimaginable. Conspiracy theories abounded, the most persuasive and persistent of which were eventually researched, tidied up and presented in David Yallop's 1984 bestseller, *In God's Name*. The book accused an unholy trinity of Vatican conservatives, Mafia bankers and right-wing Italian Freemasons, claiming that Luciani had been poisoned with digitalis heart medicine.

Vatican conservatives

The Second Vatican Council of 1962–65 proclaimed a new, more open Catholic Church, and finally permitted a vernacular rather than a Latin liturgy. But the Church was riven by factions. Some thought "Vatican II" had been dangerously liberal, others that it hadn't gone far enough. Although birth control was outlawed, the election of a liberal pope might change that. John Paul I, according to David Yallop, was that liberal pope, and was on the brink of authorizing contraception when he was killed.

But was Luciani really a liberal? Yes, he apparently rejected some traditions by toning down his coronation and by referring to himself as "I", not "we", but these might simply have been the actions of a modest man, rather than a reformer. Yallop alleges that Luciani had advised Paul VI – in a document never cited by any other researcher – not to outlaw contraception in his rule-making encyclical *Humanae Vitae*. Although publicly Luciani always supported the conservative line on birth control, Yallop's supporters claim that his speeches on the subject were subtly censored in the Vatican mouthpiece newspaper, *L'Osservatore Romano*, which did, it is true, change his "I"s to "we"s.

God's bankers

According to Yallop, Luciani's allegedly liberal views on contraception were only a side issue. He says the real danger was his desire to clean up the Istituto per le Opere Religiose (IOR), the Vatican Bank. The story is murky, complex and highly disputed. Sicilian tax expert and international financier Michele "the Shark" Sindona had apparently become a key middleman between the IOR, which was seeking to limit its new tax liabilities, and the Mafia, which needed its money laundered – preferably through an opaque, hard-to-touch financial institution. Sindona's key instrument was Roberto Calvi (see p.51), who handled the IOR's riskier and shadier speculations through the Milan-based Catholic bank, Banco Ambrosiano, including the transfer of billions of dollars into ephemeral and sometimes nonexistent offshore accounts, allegedly in partnership with the American archbishop and IOR director, Paul Marcinkus.

Nicknamed "the gorilla" (though he also shared the soubriquet of "God's banker" with Roberto Calvi), Marcinkus has always denied any involvement; until his death in 2006, he worked freely as a priest in Arizona – thanks in part to Pope John Paul II granting him special immunity. Equally, the Vatican never accepted responsibility for Banco Ambrosiano's collapse under Calvi, though it paid out some $250 million to creditors – allegedly with the help of Opus Dei (see p.166). Sindona's fraudulent banking deals, by contrast, were exposed when his Franklin Bank collapsed in 1974 – the largest bank failure in US history. Sindona was later forced to fake his own kidnapping by "left-wing terrorists" in order to escape criminal charges, but eventually went on trial in Italy. There, he arranged the contract killing of a prosecution witness, a classic Mafia crime for which he was convicted by an Italian court in 1986; that same year, while in prison, he was murdered with a cup of poisoned coffee.

Masons in the Vatican

Blowing the whistle on the Vatican Bank was the least of Luciani's alleged threats. Millions of people in Italy – almost a third, some polls suggest – believe he was also poised to expose the existence of a powerful Masonic cabal within the Vatican. Among the Masons, it is claimed, were Cardinal Villot (the Vatican secretary of state, and number two to the pope) and Archbishop Marcinkus. They are supposed to have belonged to the lodge Propaganda Due, better known as P2 (see p.134), which was half quasi-Masonic network and half murderous terrorist cell dedicated to the establishment of a fascist state. A police raid in 1981 turned up a list of members that included countless powerful state officials, police chiefs, businessmen and media figures. Roberto Calvi and Michele Sindona were on the list too, but curiously, no Vatican prelates were named. This doesn't bother Vatican conspiracists, however, because

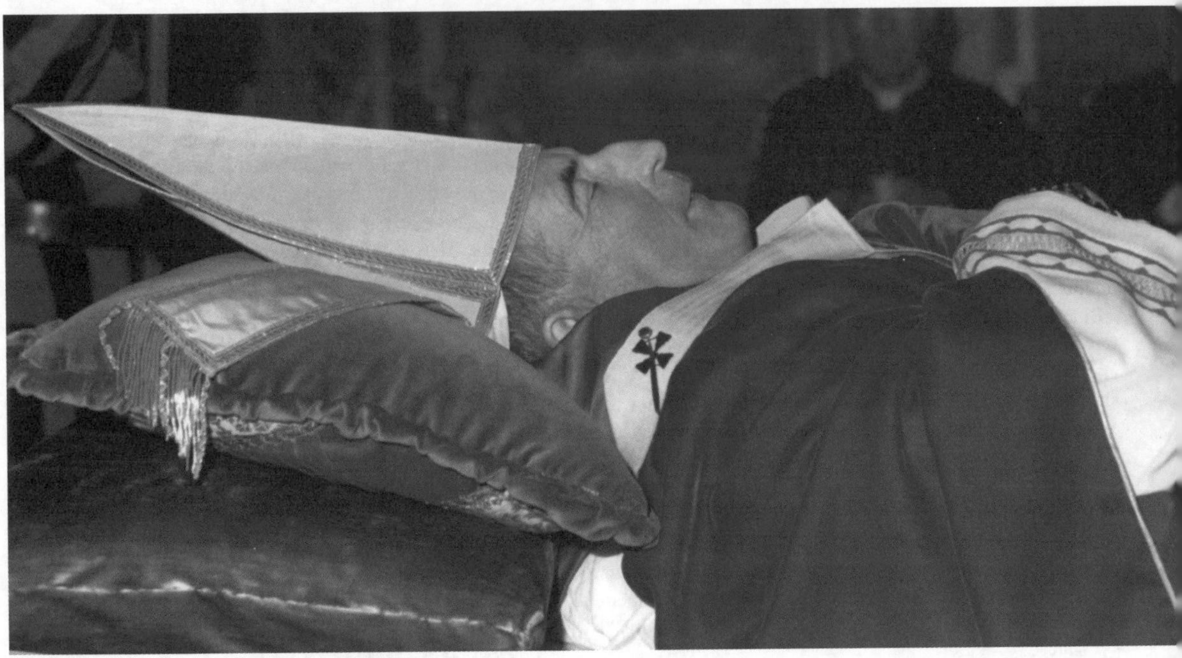

Not smiling any more: Pope John Paul I lies in state at the Vatican in 1978.

self-confessed repentant P2 member and tabloid journalist Mino Pecorelli claimed in 1978 that both Marcinkus and Villot had, in fact, been members. As the sole witness to have come forward, Pecorelli is less than reliable, though perhaps his credibility rose after he was killed in March 1979 – the first of a number of implicated figures and investigators who were murdered that summer.

A thief in the night: Cornwell's counter-claims

In the wake of the scandal that surrounded Yallop's book *In God's Name*, Vatican officials asked English journalist John Cornwell to conduct a thorough, independent investigation, and write it up in popular form. Written like a thriller, *A Thief in the Night* appeared in 1989. Pope John Paul I, it said, had died of a pulmonary embolism. Cornwall's evidence was persuasive. Luciani was known to have had severely swollen feet. He complained of feeling unwell the day before he died. He suffered a bad bout of coughing in front of his papal secretaries. And he unwisely ran to answer the telephone that evening. Sure-fire grave-fodder, then. All this, Cornwell claims, points to the development of an embolism that was dislodged and finally reached the heart at around 9.30pm. Cornwell convincingly demolishes some key points in Yallop's argument – especially his claims that Cardinal Villot called the embalmers in before he let anyone else in the Vatican know about the pope's death, and disposed of the pope's allegedly vomit-stained glasses, slippers and heart medicine. His own theory has one weak point, however: it relies on the papal secretaries having manoeuvred the pope's body into a more dignified position in bed and having lied about it forever after.

Lefebvre and the sedevacantists

The death of John Paul I continues to have political reverberations within the Catholic Church. Arch-traditionalist "sedevacantists", who believe that all popes since Vatican II have been false popes, are as ready to believe in conspiracies as left-wingers. As early as August 28, 1978, maverick French sedevacantist bishop Marcel Lefebvre claimed that the papal conclave had elected its candidate with suspicious haste, given that the necessary two-thirds majority had been achieved at only the third ballot. Some Lefebvrists even went on to claim that Pope Paul VI had been replaced by an impostor.

As for Luciani's successor, Pope John Paul II, he was at various times dubbed a communist sympathizer on the one hand, and a tool of liberal capitalism – personally responsible for the collapse of the Eastern Bloc – on the other. It's a question of political sensibility. The Left is sure that the CIA was behind Luciani's death, while the Right is convinced the KGB were involved. Catholics smell Masonic plots, while secular Italians see the machinations of the Vatican. Like so much in Italy, Italian history seems to be a matter of taste.

SOURCES

Books

John Cornwell A Thief in the Night (1989). A thriller-writer's authorized counter-blast to David Yallop.

David Yallop In God's Name (1984). The chief conduit by which the conspiracy theories raging in Italy and the Catholic world reached the Anglo-Protestant hemisphere. Not big in Catholic bookshops.

John Lennon

There has never been any mystery as to who fired four bullets into John Lennon's back, outside the Dakota apartment building in New York City, on December 8, 1980. Indeed, as the former Beatle and prominent anti-war activist lay dying in the arms of his wife Yoko Ono, the man with the revolver, Mark David Chapman, relaxed his military-style shooting stance, and instead of fleeing, began to read *The Catcher in the Rye*. A witness asked him if he knew what he'd done. "I just shot John Lennon", Chapman replied, having flown in from Hawaii, with the revolver, to do just that. A few months later, Chapman, officially deemed to be a "deranged fan" with the catch-all loser motive of "wanting attention", pleaded guilty and was sentenced to twenty years to life. Lennon appeared to have been slain by a lone nut. But was he?

It was strange of Chapman suddenly to plead guilty, after lawyers had spent six months preparing his defence. He did so, he said, on orders from a "voice" he heard in his cell. A psychiatrist for the defence, Dr Bernard Diamond, who coincidentally had also testified on behalf of Robert Kennedy's assassin Sirhan Bahira Sirhan (see p.37), called Chapman a "paranoid schizophrenic".

Nonetheless, Chapman was deemed rational enough to stand trial, and was sent not to a mental institution but to a normal jail. One detective commented that there was

PAUL MCCARTNEY IS DEAD

With John Lennon and George Harrison both dead, Ringo Starr and Paul McCartney are the only Beatles to survive. Or is Starr the only true survivor? According to a rumour that spread like wildfire during the late 1960s, McCartney was actually the first to die, killed in a fiery car crash in 1966. As that would have finished the Fab Four, a look-alike replacement named Billy Shears was found. With a little plastic surgery and the growth of some scar-covering facial hair – matched by George, Ringo and John for the sake of fashion consistency – The Beatles kept on rocking. The ongoing aversion of "McCartney" to spontaneous photography is said to be owing to his fear that the cover-up will be rumbled.

However, The Beatles couldn't keep the truth hidden, and their post-Paul songs and albums are riddled with hints at Paul's death. The photo on the cover of the *Abbey Road* album depicts The Beatles crossing the road with Lennon dressed in white, like a minister; Starr in black, like a pallbearer; and Harrison wearing the garb of a gravedigger. The barefoot McCartney is walking out of step with the others because… he's dead. The number plate of a VW car reads 28IF LMW: Paul would have been 28, *if* he'd been alive to make *Abbey Road*, as Linda McCartney Weeps. The lines "Come together / Over me" from "Come Together" refer not to a kinky sexual fantasy, but to the three remaining Beatles standing over Paul lying in state, while "Your Mother Should Know" somewhat tactlessly points to the most qualified person to distinguish Paul from the impostor.

The famous sleeve of *Sergeant Pepper* is even more explicit, showing a crowd of famous dead people, with The Beatles centre, all facing Paul, behind a BEATLES wreath. Wax figures of the band stand overlooking a grave. Splitting the words on the drum with a mirror reveals HE ^ DIE, pointing at Paul. There's also a left-handed bass guitar, as played by Paul, with three sticks to symbolize the remaining Beatles, and a doll in a red-lined dress, holding a toy car: that's a blood-soaked Jane Asher with the car Paul died in.

Inside, the sleeve shows Paul wearing an armpatch with the letters OPD: Officially Pronounced Dead. The lyrics tell it all: "Let me introduce to you the one and only Billy Shears / And Sergeant Pepper's Lonely Hearts Club Band". "She's Leaving Home" reveals the time and day of the accident to be "Wednesday morning at five o'clock". That's confirmed in the lyrics of "Good Morning, Good Morning" – "Nothing to do to save his life", "People running around / It's 5 o'clock". The song also describes how Paul's loss of concentration caused the crash, "Watching the skirts you start to flirt / Now you're in gear". The climactic "A Day in the Life" tells of a man who "blew his mind out in a car", while "A crowd of people stood and stared / They'd seen his face before". Of course they had: it was Paul McCartney.

The so-called "Paul is Dead" theory has circulated since Michigan University student and musician Fred LaBour made it up in the *Daily* newspaper in 1969. LaBour's Byzantine version also mentioned "I Am the Walrus", claiming that "walrus" means death in Greek – it doesn't – while a hand apparently visible behind Paul's head was a mystic sign of his death. LaBour told the *Nashville Tennessean* years later that people used to call him to ask if Paul was really dead. "How did I know? I was just a college kid!" he laughed.

something vacant or "programmed" about Chapman on the day of the killing, adding that Chapman "did not want to talk to the press from the very start", which cast doubt on Chapman's supposed craving for attention. Chapman has since agreed to just one press interview (with James Gaimes of *People* magazine), in which he said: "He [Lennon] walked past me and then I heard in my head, 'do it, do it, do it', over and over again … I don't remember aiming" – and that he felt "no emotion, no anger".

It's also puzzling why Chapman made no attempt to escape. With a couple of bullets left, several credit cards and $2000 in cash, he could have got a long way. In any case, where did he get the money? And where did an untrained civilian learn to shoot like that?

Lennon, Nixon, Chapman and the CIA

One theory, proposed by author Fenton Bresler in *Who Killed John Lennon?* and supported by radio journalist Mae Brussell, suggests that Chapman's madness was the result of being a brainwashed CIA assassin, who was programmed to kill Lennon by right-wing elements within the US government. They argue that Chapman, while working for World Vision as a children's counsellor in refugee camps from Laos to Beirut, fell into the clutches of just the sort of covert operatives you'd expect to find in such war zones – the CIA.

Chapman's sojourn in Beirut coincided with the presence of CIA assassination squads and, in 1976, he appeared in Hawaii, a centre for CIA and Special Forces operatives, where mental ill-health and hospitalization caused him to drift from job to job. Somewhere along the way, it's speculated that the CIA hypnotized and drugged Chapman under their MK-ULTRA programme (see p.210), and brainwashed him into killing Lennon. Although Chapman was certifiable, no paperwork prevented him from buying a gun, and there was no metal detector to stop him from taking it to the mainland. Somehow, this indolent lunatic had the funds in October 1980 to travel to Switzerland and Georgia, and from Hawaii to New York and back, on what was perhaps an abortive killer-run, in which he managed to resist the "master inside himself". In December, however, he succumbed, and killed Lennon.

So why would the government want a hippy singer like Lennon dead? Because John Lennon was much more than that. He was an outspoken activist, demonstrating against the Vietnam War, marching for the IRA and CND and supporting striking shipbuilders. During the 1970s, John and Yoko supported radicals like jailed White Panther John Sinclair, and the anti-establishment Yippies (the pro-pot "Youth International Party"), and planned a series of anti-war concerts across the US.

To President Nixon's right-wing administration, anti-war meant anti-them. And Lennon, allegedly able to "draw out one million anti-war protestors in any given city in 24 hours", seriously threatened their ability to mobilize for war. FBI boss J. Edgar Hoover wrote on Lennon's file "ALL EXTREMISTS SHOULD BE CONSIDERED DANGEROUS." Agents tapped Lennon's phone and stalked him everywhere. Right-wing senator Strom Thurmond urged that Lennon's 1968 marijuana conviction in the UK – a set-up in itself – should be used to stop his immigration to the US. Later, Senator Frank Church's committee hearings outlined the dangers of the anti-war "new Left", and cited Lennon as a prominent member.

Lennon remarked in 1972 that "if anything happens to Yoko and me, it was not an accident". As the continual threat of deportation, and harassment by the FBI, strained Lennon's career and marriage, the birth of his son Sean in 1975 pushed the Lennons into seclusion. However, John then got his green card and, after 1976, his 300-page FBI file was left to gather dust. The fact that he was keeping quiet may have kept everyone off his case, or perhaps it was simply because Nixon had left office in 1974, and the Republicans were dumped in 1976.

In 1980, Lennon's career was relaunched by the relase of the *Double Fantasy* album, and the Republicans returned to the White House, when Ronald Reagan won the presidency on the back of future CIA chief William Casey's election campaign. Their plan to square up to the USSR, flood the Pentagon's coffers and kick off numerous covert operations in Central America wouldn't have been popular with the rabble-rousing likes of Lennon. At the time, Mae Brussell said "the old assassination teams are coming back into power". The very next day, the drugged-up Chapman cut Lennon down.

Spooky lyrics

According to a spokesman for Lennon's record label Parlophone, certain of Lennon's songs contain "spooky" clues that predicted his death. Some read significance into the US release of The Beatles' *Magical Mystery Tour*, which showed a picture of Lennon next to a sign that read "The best way to go is by MD & C" – Chapman's initials. The lyrics from The Beatles' "Helter Skelter" formed part of Charles Manson's twisted logic in the brutal killing of the pregnant Sharon Tate. And Tate's husband, film director Roman Polanski, made the film *Rosemary's Baby* about the birth of the Antichrist at the Dakota B
in New York! Even more eerily, CNN reported i

"Dangerous extremists" John Lennon and Yoko Ono attend an anti-war rally in New York.

that Lennon apparently foresaw his own death in the 1980 song, "Help Me to Help Myself", with lyrics including "The angel of destruction keeps on hounding me" and "Oh help me, Lord".

Threat to the RNC

In 2005, it was reported that declassified FBI files showed that the Bureau *was* concerned about the threat Lennon posed in the early 1970s. But that threat was less to the US political establishment as a whole than to the Republicans specifically and, in particular, to the 1972 Republican National Convention (at which Richard Nixon won his second run as the party's presidential candidate). Lennon's renewal of his travel visa at that time apparently fuelled FBI fears about his planning to attend and disrupt the RNC. However, the Feds finally concluded that any threat was essentially emasculated by Lennon's copious drug intake. Agents concluded he was too out of it to do any damage – except presumably to himself.

Still believing

Brussell and Bresler's story is a fantastic concatenation of events and themes. Bresler obtained his information on Nixon and the FBI's pursuit of Lennon through the Freedom of Information Act, but as no files on Chapman have surfaced, Bresler himself acknowledges that his theories are speculative. In any case, Chapman's mental state seems parlous enough for him to have committed any kind of psychotic behaviour – including killing Lennon on his own initiative. His madness is so readily apparent that the killing has never been reinvestigated at any official level – but then, if there was a conspiracy, that's exactly what the plotters would be banking on.

Whether or not they buy Bresler's version, Yoko Ono and Sean Lennon have armed minders to this day. Sean told the *New Yorker* in April 1998: "He [Lennon] was dangerous to the government. If he had said, 'Bomb the White House tomorrow', there would have been ten thousand people who would have done it. These pacifist revolutionaries are historically killed by the government."

SOURCES

Books

Fenton Bresler Who Killed John Lennon? (1989). This well-sourced book makes a swift and fascinating read.

Jack Jones Let Me Take You Down: Inside the Mind of Mark David Chapman, the Man Who Killed John Lennon (1992). Considering Chapman claimed he never did it for the publicity, this insight into the man seems to have had a lot of assistance from the said killer.

Films

Andrew Piddington The Killing of John Lennon (2006). Gritty portrayal of Chapman's mental descent as he sought to end his anonymity by becoming a celebrity stalker and killing a real somebody.

God's banker: Roberto Calvi

In June 1982, a stock-market slide caused the secretive financial walls around Roberto Calvi, a director of the Milan-based Banco Ambrosiano, to collapse. The foundations of his self-built banking castle were exposed as nothing but $1.3 billion's worth of sheer air. Calvi was already under a suspended sentence for currency trading violations. Now, he knew he faced a worse fate, as he and his co-conspirators in the Vatican Bank had been ripping off the Mafia for years. Calvi had already earned the enmity of Michele "the Shark" Sindona – allegedly the financial middleman between the Vatican Bank and the Mafia – for failing to bail out Sindona's beleagured Franklin Bank in 1974. Now his enemies included the bosses of Italy's clandestine, right-wing Masonic lodge, Propaganda Due, or P2. It would all end fatally for Calvi before the month was out.

The road to Blackfriars

Calvi's reported attempts to negotiate a financial rescue package came to nothing. He was rumoured to have sought non-spiritual succour from the right-wing Catholic organization Opus Dei (see p.166), though the group has always vigorously denied it. The story seems to emanate from Calvi's daughter, Anna, who said her father told her as much. Calvi's son Carlo, meanwhile, claims the banker even met John Paul II – though again, the Vatican categorically denies the allegation. Calvi certainly wrote to the pope, warning – threatening, some think – that his bank's collapse would cause "a catastrophe of unimaginable proportions in which the Church will suffer the gravest damage". The letter failed to bring any financial aid.

Calvi was a desperate man – desperate enough, perhaps, to try to raise emergency funds by threatening to reveal all he knew. And Calvi knew a lot – he wasn't nicknamed "God's banker" for nothing. He knew about Banco Ambrosiano's laundering of heroin money for the Sicilian Mafia through offshore shell (or dummy) companies. He knew about the murky financial dealings of the Vatican Bank, Istituto per le Opere Religiose (IOR), under its boss, American archbishop Paul Marcinkus (who died in semi-disgrace in 2006, having remained silent about the whole Ambrosiano affair). Calvi knew about the right-wing conspiracy to control Italian politics through the secret Masonic lodge P2 (see p.134). He knew about illegal arms sales to Argentina, where P2 boss Licio Gelli maintained high-level contacts with Juan Perón's populist authoritarian regime. He knew, some claim, about secret funding supposedly channelled from the Vatican via the Mafia to anti-communist groups in Poland and South America.

Fearful of arrest – he had only recently been released from jail pending an appeal against a conviction for breaking currency laws – and probably more fearful of a violent death, Calvi fled to London on June 11, where he desperately tried to raise funds. A week later, on June 18, 1982, he was found hanging below London's Blackfriars Bridge on the end of a noose of orange rope, with $15,000 in cash – mostly dollars – stuffed into his pockets. Some observers saw Masonic significance in the choice of venue – a "black friar" is supposedly one of the symbols commonly used in Italian Freemasonry.

Judgement...

Somehow, a British coroner, who perhaps hadn't come across many Mafia or Masonic killings, recorded a verdict of suicide. It was greeted with incredulity in Italy. Calvi was in his sixties, unfit and a vertigo sufferer. He also had a sizeable collection of barbiturates back in his hotel room. (It has since been claimed that the coroner's incisive analysis was designed to conceal glaring mistakes in police procedure.) Coincidentally, Calvi's secretary committed suicide in Milan on the very same day. On the face of it, Calvi's death certainly looked like a punishment killing. He had been half-strangled and then hung from an iron ring, his feet in the water and bricks in his pockets; he would have died over an agonizing hour as the tide dropped away beneath him.

In 1992, Mafia supergrass Francesco Mannino Mannoia declared that Calvi had been throttled by another *pentito* (government witness) on the orders of Cosa Nostra boss and Mafia "ambassador to Rome", Pippo "the Cashier" Calò. Italian prosecutors further alleged that above Calò was the notorious grandmaster of P2, Licio Gelli. A former Blackshirt and Nazi informant, Gelli had been pursued by Italian magistrates for years for alleged acts of right-wing subversion during the "strategy of tension" years (see p.132), and had already been convicted of fraudulent involvement in the collapse of Banco Ambrosiano. In Italian conspiracy circles, Gelli is typically assumed to be behind practically every right-wing or Mafia conspiracy. If the plot had a mastermind, they would argue, it was surely him.

...deferred

In April 2005, Pippo Calò was charged in a Roman court with conspiring to murder Calvi. There were four alleged co-conspirators: the Sardinian businessman (and friend of Italian prime minister Silvio Berlusconi), Flavio Carboni; his girlfriend, Manuela Kleinszig; his bodyguard, Silvano Vittor; and the Roman businessman, Ernesto Diotallevi. Most commentators thought the mystery was about to be neatly sewn up – until all five of the accused were acquitted in June 2007. Kleinszig was fully cleared, while the four men – Calò, Carboni, Diotallevi, Vittor – were acquitted for lack of evidence.

Some believed that this ever-so-slightly hazed verdict would leave the door open for an appeal. Others thought the case was a smokescreen for a deeper conspiracy. Calvi's son Carlo, for one, is sure that the murder was designed to protect the powers behind the Vatican Bank – Paul Marcinkus in particular – and the institutional conspiracy that lay behind the P2 lodge, of which Calvi was a member. A dead man can't squeal, and neither can he blackmail his former co-conspirators. The peculiar style of his killing certainly seemed designed to send a message. Any other businessmen thinking of leveraging their insider knowledge to raise some emergency capital might just think twice.

As for the black hole left in the Vatican's finances by Banco Ambrosiano's collapse, persistent (and just as persistently denied) rumours claim that Opus Dei footed the bill, thus buying its way into the heart of Vatican counsels. In Italy, allegations that the membership of Opus Dei crosses over with that of P2 have dogged the group. Certainly, there's a significant correlation in terms of personality profile – high-achieving, authoritarian and conservative. The same is true for CIA agents, a disproportionate number of whom are said to be Opus Dei members. Some US conspiracy theorists (feeling left out of a good international conspiracy, perhaps) even claim that Ronald Reagan helped to plug the Vatican's finances with $300 million of CIA discretionary funds – and, in doing so, bought "the Catholic vote".

"God's banker" Roberto Calvi

SOURCES

Books

Paul Williams The Vatican Exposed: Money, Murder and the Mafia (2003). A wide sweep of anti-Catholic history, focusing on the murky past of the Istituto per le Opere di Religione (Vatican Bank).

Philip Willan The Last Supper: The Mafia, the Masons and the Killing of Roberto Calvi (2007). Published prior to the 2007 trial result, this has become out of date, but it remains a fascinating journey into the huge number of conspiracy theories circulating about the case in Italy.

Films

Francis Ford Coppola The Godfather Part III (1990). The last in the great Mafia trilogy. The character Frederick Keinszig is widely thought to be a caricature of Calvi – who is said to have carried a copy of Mario Puzo's original novel with him like a Bible.

Giuseppe Ferrara Il Banchiere di Dio (God's Banker) (2002). We don't recommend many foreign-language films, but this one has a history: the director was successfully sued by Flavio Carboni – but then won the case on appeal.

Websites

Ⓦ **www.nytimes.com/2006/02/22/business/22marcinkus.html** Obituaryof Archbishop Paul Marcinkus – a man who shared Calvi's soubriquet of "god's banker", but who was also known as "the pope's gorilla" on account of his size and his semi-official role as papal bodyguard. The Vatican protected him from prosecution to the end.

Ⓦ **www.theboot.it/calvi_affair.html** Respected historian and Italy-watcher Robert Katz provides a dated (1987), but in-depth, account of the role of Marcinkus and the Vatican Bank in the Calvi affair.

The princess and the tunnel

On the morning of August 31, 1997, the British public woke to shocking news. In the early hours, while driving through an underpass beside the River Seine in Paris, Princess Diana and her new boyfriend, Dodi Al-Fayed, had been killed in a cataclysmic car crash along with the driver, Henri Paul. Only their bodyguard, former soldier Trevor Rees-Jones, had survived. As families wept openly along the Mall and bunches of flowers lay in drifts at the gates of Kensington Palace, Diana was transformed into *the* icon of late twentieth-century Britain. The new, young and then popular prime minister, Tony Blair, cannily dubbed her the "people's princess".

In the weeks following the accident, the scale and significance of the public reaction to Diana's death seemed to dwarf the banality of a car crash. Could something so profound really have been caused by something so simple? As the years went by and the public investigations were repeatedly delayed, the conspiracy theories grew and grew. A 2006 BBC poll found that 31 percent of Britons thought Diana's death was not an accident, while a CBS survey found that 76 percent of its respondents thought they would never know the whole truth.

Mercedes and the Alma

En route between the Ritz hotel and the Al-Fayed apartment in Paris, shortly after midnight, driver Henri Paul attempted to outrun a persistent group of motorcyclist photographers in his powerful Mercedes S280. Entering an underpass beneath the Place de l'Alma, the Mercedes clipped a white Fiat Uno, then skidded alongside it for nineteen metres with two wheels in the air. As he fought to regain control, Paul turned to the right to get ahead of the Fiat, but found the path blocked by a Citroën BX. He over-corrected to the left and the car entered another skid, heading straight for the infamous thirteenth pillar, which it struck head-on with devastating impact before rebounding into the tunnel wall. The airbags inflated, saving the bodyguard in the passenger seat, but Paul was killed outright by the steering column. Without seatbelts, the celebrity passengers in the rear stood no chance: Dodi was killed and Diana terribly injured.

When the paparazzi caught up they took a gruesome sequence of photographs and called an ambulance – in which order remains disputed. The ambulance arrived at the Pitié-Salpetrière hospital 103 minutes after the crash. The journey took 26 minutes, but treatment at the scene was prolonged and the ambulance had to stop twice en route because of Diana's plummeting blood pressure. She died shortly before entering surgery.

At the close of the official French inquiry, the prosecutor, Mme Coujard, summed up: "The direct cause of the accident is the presence, at the wheel of the Mercedes S280, of a driver who had consumed a considerable amount of alcohol, combined with … medication, driving at a speed … faster than the maximum speed-limit in built-up areas."

A confusion of witnesses

At first, everyone blamed the paparazzi. Many fled the scene; some had taken snapshots of the crash. Some were even charged under France's "good Samaritan" law for failing to give proper help. But this wasn't a conspiracy so much as criminally irresponsible behaviour. The paparazzi may have hounded Diana to her death, but the last thing they wanted was to slay the goose that laid the golden eggs.According to witnesses, however, it wasn't just paparazzi at the scene. One French family saw a powerful, dark car travelling close to the Mercedes, and a taxi apparently blocking the entrance to the tunnel moments after the crash. They also claimed to have witnessed a young, athletic man running into the tunnel.

In the early months after the crash, rumours of a clamp-down on witness evidence proliferated. Why were the CCTV cameras in the underpass turned off "for repair"? (There was only a single traffic-monitoring camera, and it was never used to record.) Why did none of Paris's CCTV devices record the Mercedes' final journey? (There were only ten between the Ritz and the Alma, and most were private cameras pointed at main entrances.) Why did all of Paris's police radios go dead moments before the crash? (They didn't.) Why did the Parisian authorities clean the tunnel so thoroughly after the accident? (Why would they do it sloppily?)

Andanson and the white Uno

Intense attention focused on the mysterious white Fiat Uno, the accident's apparent catalyst. Despite a giant-scale search, the French police never managed to definitively trace the car, and it became a totem for the failure of the investigation to provide a convincing explanation.

Suspicions of a cover-up were fuelled in May 2000, when the body of paparazzo James Andanson was found in a burned-out BMW in the south of France. Suicide provoked by marital difficulties was the official cause of death, but Andanson, it turned out, had been following Diana on her yacht that August. He'd also been investigated as the owner of a white Uno at the time of the Paris crash. His wife had provided a convincing alibi for the early part of the night in question, and he had produced motorway toll-station receipts showing that he was travelling *towards* Paris in the early hours of the morning.

Forensic tests also suggested that the paint on Andanson's car was not the same kind of white as the traces found on the Mercedes: it was "Bianco 210", not "Bianco Corfu 224". The French investigators concluded that the Fiat involved in the collision probably wasn't Andanson's. "Probably." It turns out that Bianco 210 *could* have produced a match for the traces on the Mercedes (if not as close a match as Bianco Corfu 224). But investigators claimed that the rear left wing of Andanson's car

INQUESTS AND INVESTIGATIONS

The establishment took the conspiracy allegations about Diana's death seriously. Not content with the massive French investigation – which concluded her death was an accident caused by drink-driving and speeding – Michael Burgess, the coroner to the Queen's household, commissioned an investigation in 2004, codenamed Operation Paget. Its head, retired London police chief Lord John Stevens, analysed the 6000-page French report, interviewed British intelligence chiefs and even scanned the Alma tunnel with lasers.

Unfortunately, Stevens had no power to force witnesses to come forward – and many did not. Some questioned his ability to manage Paget alongside an inquiry into football corruption and a career as a non-executive director, university chancellor, charity patron, after-dinner speaker and journalist. However, the report was finally released in December 2006. It had 832 pages – more than the 9/11 Commission, but slightly fewer than the Warren Report into JFK's death. "There was no conspiracy", it concluded.

The coroner's inquest could now resume. But, after twenty years service, coroner Michael Burgess stepped down in July 2006, citing a heavy workload. His replacement, high court judge (and former chairman of the Security Commission) Baroness Elizabeth Butler-Sloss, resigned in June 2007, after losing the battle to hold her hearings in private. She didn't have the "necessary experience", she said.

The exceedingly senior appeal court judge Lord Justice Scott Baker brought matters to a conclusion in April 2008. There was not a "shred of evidence" of a conspiracy, he summed up, and the jury found by a nine-to-two majority that Diana's death was an "unlawful killing" caused by the "gross negligence" of driver Henri Paul and the paparazzi. Three million words were spoken in court, 278 witnesses were called, £7 million spent, and the inquest broke all precedents for transparency – with full transcripts posted online almost as the words were uttered.

Yet critics were still not satisfied. All but one of the French paparazzi involved in the crash refused to testify, the Queen and the Duke of Edinburgh were never called and the driver of the Fiat Uno was never found. For dedicated conspiracists, these threads were loose enough to begin knotting again.

had been touched up with another kind of white paint some time before the night of Diana's death. Witnesses reported seeing a large dog wearing a reddish-coloured bandana or muzzle in the back of the car at the time of the crash. And Andanson's wife admitted having bought her labrador a red bandana.

The subsequent British investigation into the accident, codenamed Operation Paget and led by Lord John Stevens, was very sure that Andanson wasn't involved. "If you were part of a sophisticated assassination plot of such high profile", it asked its readers, "would you use your own car, registered in your own name? Would you use an old, small-engined car? Would you subsequently part-exchange that car with a local garage and relinquish all control of the vehicle to them?" Perhaps not.

But there are some curious codas to the Andanson affair. His death is presented as a clear-cut case of suicide: he'd talked about it to friends beforehand; he'd left all his personal possessions at home; and he'd asked his photo agency to transfer all royalties into his wife's name. However, a fireman who'd attended the scene reported seeing two bullet holes in Andanson's temple. A forensic specialist countered that these holes were caused by the heat of the fire – and added that no bullets were found. (By curious coincidence, it seems Andanson may have been present in the town of Nevers on the day that politician Pierre Bérégovoy committed suicide in 1993 – having put two bullets in his own head.) And then there's the strange coincidence that Andanson's photo agency was burgled by three masked and armed men after his death. The agency firmly denied any link, saying that nothing connected with Andanson was stolen, that the intrusion was "amateurish" (a security guard was shot in the foot) and that the burglars were almost certainly looking for compromising photographs of an (unnamed) aggrieved celebrity.

Rings and things

Nine days after the crash, controversial Harrods owner Mohamed Al-Fayed announced that his son Dodi had bought a $200,000 ring for Diana when the couple were on a yachting trip the week before their deaths. Was it an engagement ring? Diana never told anyone she was getting married, though Al-Fayed butler, René Delorm, claims that Dodi told him to "have the champagne ready" as he was going to ask Diana on the night she died. He later recalled further details, such as seeing Dodi "on one knee in front of her, caressing her belly and she was looking at her hand. The only thing I heard, was her say the word 'Yes.'" When asked why he hadn't previously volunteered this information, he replied, "I didn't want to get involved".

Diana had told her friend Annabel Goldsmith that she needed marriage "like a rash on my face". Another friend, Rosa Monckton, recalled that Diana knew there was a ring but said "it's going very firmly on my right hand". Diana's butler, Paul Burrell (dubbed a "liar by his own admission" by coroner Scott Baker), agreed, claiming: "She didn't want to accept it but didn't want to offend Dodi."

Embalming the truth

Rosa Monckton (who is married to the influential conservative journalist and climate-change sceptic Dominic Lawson) was instrumental in denying another related rumour: that Diana was pregnant. Diana had apparently mentioned her period starting when the friends last met on August 20, 1997. Lord Stevens' Operation Paget report was weirdly prudish about this crucial snippet, saying only "The personal and intimate nature of that evidence suggested it to be inappropriate to include details". Diana had also visited a consultant seeking relief from pre-menstrual syndrome. However, Mohamed Al-Fayed insisted that Diana was expecting a child. He even described a phone call in which he spoke to her about it. Photographs of Diana in an animal-print swimming costume duly appeared. They revealed a noticeable bulge. Unfortunately, they turned out to have been taken in July 1997 – before her relationship with Dodi began.

No pregnancy test was done during the autopsy – but there was no reason to do one, said the authorities. The autopsy, however, isn't the most controversial part of the affair: it's the embalming of the body. Conspiracists are convinced this was done to remove evidence of a pregnancy. The British ambassador in Paris, Sir Michael Jay, is sometimes accused – without evidence – of ordering the embalming, but officials insist it went ahead for the usual reason: the body was starting to deteriorate and could not be decently presented to a grieving family.

Philip's plot

The idea that Diana was engaged to Dodi Al-Fayed, and pregnant by him, was vociferously promoted by the team representing Dodi's father, Mohamed Al-Fayed. A wealthy, Egyptian-born UK businessman, he had previously brought down a Tory MP (who had admitted receiving money from him in return for political influence) in the so-called "cash for questions" scandal. Al-Fayed had no reason to love the British Establishment, and became convinced that it was behind the deaths of Diana and his son. Surely the British Establishment would never accept a Muslim marrying the mother of the heir to the throne? Someone would have stepped in to prevent it.

That someone, surely, would be the sinister racist and arch-imperialist Prince Philip, Duke of Edinburgh (such is he characterized by conspiracy theorists, see p.114), acting through the British secret intelligence service, MI6. Sceptics protested in vain that Diana's previous relationship with Muslim heart surgeon Hasnat Khan hadn't caused the establishment – or Philip – any obvious palpatations.

Tomlinson's blinding flash

Many British theorists prefer to leave Prince Philip out of the equation. Instead, they say, a rogue cabal of ultra-conservatives was acting under its own instructions. Maverick ex-MI6 agent Richard Tomlinson bolstered these theories when he observed: "there's an arrogant faction inside MI6, part of the Eton/Oxford/Guards clique, who see themselves literally as defenders of the realm – and for them, that means the royals." Could this self-perceived role have extended to murder? Tomlinson seemed to suggest as much when he recalled that MI6 had come up with a plot to assassinate Serbian president Slobodan Milosevic using blinding flashes of strobing light to cause a crash in a road tunnel.

Blinding flashes were exactly what witness François Levistre said he saw that night in the Alma tunnel. He reported seeing a motorcycle overtaking the Mercedes, and then a blinding white flash. The bike then stopped. The pillion rider got off, peered inside the car and gestured as if to say "job done" before remounting. The bike then roared off into the Parisian night.

Unfortunately for this theory, analysis of skidmarks show the Mercedes began weaving some distance before it even got to the tunnel. And neither Levistre not Tomlinson has come off too well under closer examination. Levistre had a hard time explaining inconsistencies in the accounts he gave to French police, French magistrates and British TV crews and investigators. According to Operation Paget, Tomlinson remembered the crucial details of the MI6 plot only after Diana's death. His banned memoir, written *before* 1997, refers to a plot to kill the Serbian leader in a drive-by shooting, but there is no mention of blinding flashes. Tomlinson has since admitted that this idea of a Balkan plot came from a 1992 MI6 memorandum, which floated the idea that a certain genocidal extremist might be assassinated in an ambush.

A simpler explanation of any white flashes seen that night would be the swarm of flash-touting paparazzi following Diana's Mercedes. Conspiracists have an easy counter to this argument, of course: the paparazzi's flashes provided the perfect cover.

MI6 manoeuvres

The allegations of MI6 involvement don't rest only on some white flashes. There's also the mystery of the two senior MI6 agents operating as Foreign Office officials who were said to have arrived in Paris just before the crash. In fact, one diplomat indeed arrived on August 26, 1997, but he had been appointed to his position a year before, while the other man had been stationed there since 1994. Undeterred, the British press circulated rumours that a "stream of informants" had insisted that the pair were implicated in Diana's death.

Then there was the Lord Fellowes accusation. According to the *Daily Mail*, an unnamed wireless operator at the British embassy in Paris said he had been turfed out of his office by two posh British men just before midnight. He is later said to have named one of them as Lord Robert Fellowes. Apart from being an Old Etonian and an ex-Guardsman, Fellowes was also Diana's brother-in-law and assistant private secretary to the Queen – a trusted courtier, no less. Leaving aside the question of what a "wireless operator" was doing in an embassy at the end of the twentieth century, the official Operation Paget report noted that "all of the evidence shows" that Lord Fellowes was at home with his family on the night in question. Sadly, the report didn't trouble to present any of this evidence, which would no doubt have scotched the smears very convincingly.

Another diplomat, military attaché Brigadier Charles Ritchie, happened to be walking past the Ritz when Diana was inside. He'd been dining with his family; pure coincidence.

Agents Rees-Jones and Paul

Some conspiracy theorists accuse Diana's bodygard, Trevor Rees-Jones, of being a spy, falsely citing a service history in the secretive and elite SAS. (He was actually in the crack Parachute Regiment.) His post-accident amnesia – which continues at the time of writing – has hardly helped convince conspiracists of his innocence. For a time, there were wild rumours that he had conveniently lost his tongue in the accident. (He hadn't, though his multiply broken jaw was briefly wired shut.) Some wondered why had he been wearing a seatbelt, against the rules of his profession. (He hadn't, though he had tried to buckle it in the final seconds of the skid.) Dodi's father, Mohamed Al-Fayed, questioned whether Rees-Jones could have been "turned" after the event. Most theorists, however, generously treat Rees-Jones as collateral damage, observing that he received threatening phone calls after the crash. "If you don't keep quiet", the caller whispered, "we'll do you".

Former MI6 agent Richard Tomlinson continued to stir the waters, telling the judge in charge of the French inquest that driver Henri Paul had been passing gossip to the secret services. He recalled seeing documents relating to someone with an English surname staying at the Ritz in Paris. For some observers, this instantly cast Paul as an MI6 stooge who deliberately took the Alma tunnel route in order to bring his car within range of the secret service's assassins.

Princess Diana in Angola for the Halo Trust's anti-landmine campaign.

It later transpired that Paul had nothing to do with MI6, but he did have dealings with the Direction de la Surveillance du Territoire (DST) – the French equivalent of the FBI. According to American reporter Gerald Posner, citing sources in US intelligence, Henri Paul had met up with his DST handler earlier that evening. But as deputy head of security at the Ritz, it would be suprising if he didn't have links with French intelligence. More controversial were the five unexplained 40,000 franc deposits (amounting to tens of thousands of pounds) found in Paul's account. Were these cash bonuses from his boss, Mohamed Al-Fayed, who was known to reward loyal staff in this way? Were they generous tips from hotel guests? Were they payments, some whispered, from the DST?

The blood test

Quite why Henri Paul would have cooperated in an assassination plot that also culminated in his own death is never explained. Unless, of course, he wasn't a willing participant. The French inquiry found that he had three times the legal limit of alcohol in his blood (roughly twice the UK limit) as well as traces of the prescription drugs fluoxetine (an anti-depressant) and tiapride (used to treat alcoholism). Was that really it? Was it just an accident caused by speed and an intoxicated driver?

Conspiracists screamed foul. Henri Paul wasn't an alcoholic, they said, and didn't look drunk on the CCTV images from the Ritz. He'd even tied his own shoelaces! Press attention focused on the abnormal carbon monoxide levels discovered in Paul's blood. Proof, said the conspiracists, that his blood had been switched with a suicide's. No one could have driven with that much carbon monoxide in their bloodstream. The authorities replied with DNA evidence showing that if it wasn't Henri Paul's blood, it belonged to someone from his immediate family. Then they admitted there had indeed been a mistake with the blood test, but it was in labelling the sample "cardiac blood" instead of chest cavity blood. Blood from the chest cavity, it appears, can easily be contaminated and provide unreliable readings of carbon monoxide levels.

Diana's fears

A sensational twist came in October 2003, when Diana's much-vilified butler, Paul Burrell, published one of her letters in the *Daily Mirror* newspaper. "This particular phase in my life is the most dangerous", she wrote, "XXX [the name was blanked out in the published version] is planning 'an accident' in my car, brake failure and serious head injury to leave the path clear for [him] to marry." The deleted words were later revealed to be "my husband". (The intended spouse – surprisingly enough – was not Camilla Parker Bowles, but Tiggy Legge-Bourke, the family's former nanny. Lord Stevens' report comments, rather stiffly, that Tiggy was "a family friend".) Burrell refused to say whether he thought the note was a coincidence or something more sinister. Others charge that the more suspicious coincidence is that Burrell released it to coincide with publication of his book, *A Royal Duty*, rather than at the time of the accident.

Diana was prey to fears of assassination. Her critics call her paranoid – a conspiracy theorist, even. The trouble began in October 1995. She called a meeting with her private secretary, Patrick Jephson, and her lawyer, Lord Mishcon, claiming that "reliable sources" had informed her that there was a plot to injure or debilitate her, possibly involving an accident or pre-arranged brake failure. She was terrified that the death of her former bodyguard, Barry Mannakee, in a motorbike accident had, in fact, been murder. Jephson claimed that she was "playing into the hands of those who wished to dismiss her as mentally frail and a liability to the Royal Family".

Diana shared her fears with her intimate circle. She sent an urgent note to her therapist, Simone Simmons, which read: "as you know, the brakes of my car have been tampered with. If something does happen to me it will be MI5 or MI6 who will have done it." Simmons claims that Diana once let her listen in on a phone conversation in which a male voice threatened: "Don't meddle in things you know nothing about because you know accidents can happen". This was shortly after Diana's much-publicized campaign against landmines. Diana's longstanding friend Roberto Devorik claimed the princess was convinced that "they" were going to kill her. By "they", he thought she meant the British establishment, or possibly Buckingham Palace officials. Devorik recalled that she feared three people in particular: Conservative MP Nicholas Soames; Sir Robert Fellowes, then private secretary to the Queen; and the Duke of Edinburgh.

Windsors? Landmines? Merovingians? Bin Laden?

Perhaps the most widespread conspiracy theory is that Diana was killed to prevent a Muslim marriage and/or pregnancy. Diana's former butler, Paul Burrell, told the Scott Baker inquest that in the summer of 1997 the "establishment" had "concerns" about her relationship with the Al-Fayed family. Others believe her death was the result of public relations fallout. Diana's antics – her lovers, her shrinks, her interviews – threatened the House of Windsor. Had she finally had enough of "the Firm"? Was she going to reveal the royals' murky – or at least mucky – sercrets, triggering so much public outrage that the monarchy would fall? Would she blow the lid on the secret networks of power that made up the British establishment?

Anti-corporate conspiracists suspect that Diana, through her high-profile charitable work with the anti-landmine organization Halo Trust, became a threat to organizations with an interest in continued landmine production. Her visit to Angola in January 1997 caused a junior defence minister in John Major's Conservative government to describe her as a "loose cannon", and set off a minor (and, at the time, entirely secret) diplomatic crisis. Leaving aside the views of panicky Tories about to lose an election, the landmine theory is enticing, but it rather overstates Diana's influence. The Canadian government, chief instigator of the 1997 Ottawa Convention banning landmines, was probably more of a danger to the landmine peddlers than a celebrity figurehead. Though harder to take out in a tunnel.

In the wake of 9/11, a new theory implicated none other than Osama Bin Laden. He was apparently very worried that Muslim women were identifying with Diana, and that her marriage (how did he know?) to well-known devout Muslim Dodi Al-Fayed would "give her more of an entrée" into Muslim society. Another theory paints the whole crash as an elaborately staged escape bid. Diana was trying to fake her own death before disappearing into a new and private identity. Some think the plan went disastrously wrong. Others think it worked perfectly…

Surely the most baroque theory of all claims that the death of Diana was a ritual sacrifice. Isn't her name the same as that of the goddess worshipped by the ancient Franks? Isn't the Place de l'Alma in Paris built over an underground chamber dedicated to Diana-worship? Isn't the torch monument on the spot of an ancient sacrificial symbol? Isn't Diana associated with the goddess Hecate, whose satanic sacrifices are traditionally held on August 31, at a major crossroads such as the Place de l'Alma? Wasn't Diana's Spencer family related to the Stuart royal family, which was in turn related to the French Merovingian dynasty, direct descendants of Jesus and Mary Magdalene? Didn't Diana bleed to death, as prescribed in ritual sacrifice? Didn't the car hit the thirteenth pillar? The fact that the answer to all these questions – except the bleeding and the thirteenth pillar – is a resounding "no" hasn't stopped the speculation. Neither, unsurprisingly, has the 2008 conclusion of the coroner's inquest: that there was no conspiracy.

SOURCES

Books

Noel Botham The Murder of Princess Diana (2004). An intelligence service–royal family conspiracy unmasked/posited.

Sarah Bradford Diana (2007). The best Diana biography. Bradford doesn't buy into conspiracies, but she does remark: "If she had been surrounded by royal protection, then there wouldn't have been the speeding through tunnels and the charade of the paparazzi."

Tina Brown Diana Chronicles (2007). The Diana story, complete with seven pages of self-serving celebrity acknowledgments.

David Cohen Diana: Death of a Goddess (2004). "The story of a young Englishwoman who found herself out of her depth in the company of drugs dealers, arms dealers and secret service operators." Heady stuff, which includes a curious final chapter on the wackier conspiracy theories.

Martyn Gregory Diana: The Last Days (2004). A sceptic's response to Mohamed Al-Fayed. Get the 2004 updated edition.

Jon King and John Beveridge Princess Diana: The Hidden Evidence (2001). Four hundred-plus pages of pure Diana conspiracy.

Trevor Rees-Jones The Bodyguard's Story: Diana, the Crash and the Sole Survivor (2000). This would be interesting as a bodyguard's-eye view of Diana's strange world even if it weren't for the eyewitness crash details. Lots on Rees-Jones himself.

Films

Steven Frears The Queen (2006). A sensitive portrait of Tony Blair and the royal family in the crisis days after Diana's death. Humanizes both, with controversial degrees of accuracy.

Websites

Ⓦ **www.alfayed.com** The official site of arch-conspiracist and grieving father Mohamed Al-Fayed. Packed with Diana-related material.

Ⓦ **www.davidicke.com** Search the site for a plethora of Diana-related opinion pieces pushing Icke's inventive "reptilian Windsors" line.

Ⓦ **www.dianaconspiracy.com** "It has been 2998 days since Diana's Death." And counting. Includes a disputatious "forum" section.

Ⓦ **www.direct.gov.uk/en/Nl1/Newsroom/DG_065122** The full text of Lord Stevens' Operation Paget report.

Ⓦ **www.londonnet.co.uk/ln/talk/news/diana_conspiracy_news.html** Atravel guide to London is an odd place to host a website devoted to Diana's death and the conspiracy theories around it, but there are lots of useful pages nonetheless, with regularly updated news.

Ⓦ **www.news-alliance.com/the_oxbridge_spooks.html** Moncktons, Lawsons and nests of Oxbridge spies.

Ⓦ **www.public-interest.co.uk/diana/dianawhydie.htm** Dated but useful Diana site featuring lots of news articles related to her death.

Dr David Kelly

Dr David Kelly, British microbiologist and biological weapons expert, was found dead in woods near his Oxfordshire home on July 18, 2003. His death marked the pinnacle of a spectacular row over the British government's justification for a war on Saddam Hussein's Iraq. Officially, Kelly killed himself. However, many people think that the man who blew the whistle on the case for war just wasn't the kind to commit suicide.

In late 2002, Britain's Labour government was busy trying to convince Parliament and the public that Iraq posed a clear and immediate threat to the world through its possession of weapons of mass destruction (WMDs) – weapons that Iraq should have destroyed in 1991, after the First Gulf War, but had instead not only hidden but also continued to manufacture. According to the government, sanctions, bombing and endless weapons inspections had no effect. It published two dossiers outlining the Iraqi threat. The first, in September 2002, created headlines throughout the world by claiming that Iraq had WMDs that were deployable within 45 minutes. The second, in February 2003, described Iraq's secret network of arms programmes.

The February dossier swiftly became known as the "dodgy dossier", when it was exposed as being largely based on an article by a postgraduate student that had been published on the Internet. Even so, the Iraq War began in March, with the UK's involvement backed by both Parliament and, to a lesser extent, the public. Then the September dossier began to look suspect too. On May 29, journalist Andrew Gilligan told BBC Radio's *Today* programme that a senior source at the Ministry of Defence (MOD) had told him that the government had "sexed-up" the September dossier with its 45-minute claim. Gilligan went further in a newspaper article on June 1, saying that government spin doctor Alastair Campbell was responsible for the sexing-up. The BBC's *Newsnight* programme also cited a senior MOD source as stating that the government had inserted the 45-minute claim.

Infuriated, the government insisted that the BBC should reveal the source of this outrageous allegation. Meanwhile, Dr David Kelly told his MOD superiors that he had spoken to Gilligan. The government announced on July 8 that the source had been found; then, in a highly controversial move, Kelly was "named" by the MOD to the press on July 9. (As an indication of the kind of petty game-playing that was going on, Kelly's name was confirmed when a journalist read through a list of suspects, and Kelly's was the one to which an MOD official didn't respond by saying "no".) On July 15 and 16, Kelly was grilled by a House of Commons Foreign Affairs Select Committee and by the Intelligence and Security Committee. He said he didn't think he was the source of the "sexing-up" allegation. On July 17, Kelly left his Oxfordshire house for an evening walk. After he failed to return, a search was begun. His body was found the next day in woods two miles from his home. The BBC confirmed on July 20 that Kelly had been their source.

An autopsy led by Dr Nicholas Hunt reported that Kelly was discovered with his left wrist slashed, and that he had taken a large quantity of Coproxamol painkillers. The verdict: suicide. Senior judge Lord Hutton subsequently conducted an inquiry into the circumstances that led to Kelly's death, and into the role of the BBC and the government. In his January 2004 report, Hutton castigated the BBC and largely exonerated the government of plotting to expose Kelly. He drew attention to Hunt's conclusion: "I am satisfied that Dr Kelly took his own life", and determined that no other person was involved. Instead, the exposure of "such a private man", and the possible jeopardizing of his career, caused Kelly to withdraw into himself, with fatal consequences.

Who said it was suicide?

However, the verdict cited by Hutton was not that of an official inquest. Neither was Hutton's inquiry given the remit to investigate Kelly's death as such, only the actions of the government and the BBC that preceded it. The inquiry was not given tribunal powers to subpoena new witnesses, or to call for new evidence. Of three hundred witness statements concerning Kelly's death, only seventy were submitted to the Hutton Inquiry.

The crucial point was that the *inquest* into Kelly's death, as opposed to the autopsy, had not delivered a final verdict; the Lord Chancellor had ordered the inquest adjourned for the duration of the Hutton Inquiry. And the inquest never did deliver a verdict. Oxford coroner Nicholas Gardiner said on March 16, 2004, that the inquest into Kelly's death would not be resumed. The verdict, as Hutton said, was suicide. Those who questioned that view were, according to Gardiner, "conspiracy theorists".

"Conspiracy theorists"

Some of those supposed theorists, including doctors and barristers, formed the Kelly Inquiry Group and demonstrated outside the coroner's court. Among them was UK national security lawyer Michael Shrimpton, who, the BBC reported, asked why the forensic report could not confirm whether Kelly had taken 29 Coproxamol tablets. Somehow, Kelly had managed to perform the dextrous feat of slashing his ulnar artery but not the radial one, and still bleed to death.

Three doctors, anaesthetist Searle Sennett, trauma specialist David Halpin and radiologist Stephen Frost wrote to *The Guardian* on January 27 to express their doubts, followed on February 12 by a letter from vascular surgeon Martin Birnstingl, pathologist Dr Peter Fletcher and public health consultant Dr Andrew Rouse. All agreed that the stated primary cause of Kelly's death – bleeding to death from a severed ulnar artery – was "highly improbable". The idea was "against classical medical teaching". The toxicologist who measured Kelly's Coproxamol level said it was just a third of what was usually regarded as fatal. A concurrent debate in the *British Medical Journal* mentioned that Kelly had "ischaemic heart disease" and the possibility that he had died of heart failure, but the pathologist, Dr Nicholas Hunt, had ruled that out.

Shifting evidence

The Indymedia website reported that Louise Holmes and Paul Chapman, the two volunteers who first found Kelly, discovered his body propped against a tree. On their way to tell Abingdon police, they met three "plain-clothes detectives", who continued on to the body. Witnesses later placed the body flat on its back, away from a tree, and the postmortem reported that Kelly must have died on his back. Paramedic Vanessa Hunt reported finding very little blood at the scene, either in quantity or sprayed around, whereas a fatal hemorrhage usually amounts to five pints. Scratches and bruises suggested that Kelly had been "stumbling around" in the undergrowth, but police found no trampled vegetation. And why had a police support operation, codenamed Mason, begun nine hours *before* Kelly was reported missing?

According to the *Daily Mirror*, there was no suicide note. Channel 4 reported that the day before he died, Kelly emailed a friend: "Hopefully it will soon pass … and I can get to Baghdad and get on with the real work." The Ananova website stated that he had mentioned "many dark actors playing games" in an email to a journalist just hours before his death. Then there were Kelly's own alleged dark comments, supposedly made in February 2003, that "if Iraq is attacked, then I might be found dead in the woods".

If it was murder, who did it?

Allegations that Kelly was murdered centre on the belief that he was seen as a loose cannon who needed silencing. He was certainly an expert in biological warfare and weapons, having worked at the Institute of Virology at Oxford and the MOD's Porton Down research centre (see p.289), before becoming an adviser to both the MOD and Foreign Office. As a UN weapons inspector, he visited Iraq nearly forty times to investigate its WMD programmes. If he was prepared to tell the press that the government case for war was full of holes, what else might he spill?

Michael Shrimpton told US listeners to the Alex Jones radio show in February 2004 that although 29 Coproxamol tablets were apparently missing from the blister packs found beside his body, Kelly's stomach contained less than a fifth of one tablet. He argued that Kelly was injected with traceless succinyl choline, and that his wrist was cut to cover the injection site. The assassination, he suggests, was probably carried out by French intelligence services. Alex Jones's website (www.prisonplanet.com) states that Shrimpton believes the UK media covered up the assassination, one reason being that they didn't want to depose the pro-Europe prime minister, Tony Blair, as that could thwart plans for the UK to adopt the euro.

Senior US and UN bio-weapons inspector Richard Spetzel, who worked for years in Iraq with Kelly, said he believed it was the Iraqi intelligence service because of their "long-standing enmity … towards David". Both he and Kelly were on a Iraqi hit list.

Back to the BBC?

In February 2007, a BBC-commissioned poll indicated that over a fifth of the British people believed Dr Kelly did not commit suicide. The figure was published on the corporation's website, amid other doubts about Kelly's death and links to various conspiracy theory features, paranoia investigations and the like, as promotion for the TV series *The Conspiracy Files*. But, for all this determination that the programme shouldn't be taken too seriously, it was indeed revealing. Much of its evidence had been obtained by Liberal Democrat MP Norman Baker, who had left the shadow cabinet in 2006 to spend a year looking into "unanswered questions" about Kelly's death. He stated, "I'm satisfied it was not suicide", thereby leaving only the conclusion that Kelly's life was deliberately taken by others.

Baker cited Kelly's low dosage of pills and commented that his suicide method was neither "recognized nor effective".

He also opined that the Hutton Inquiry had "blatantly" failed to resolve the question of Kelly's death, and presented letters suggesting the coroner, Nicholas Gardiner, had expressed doubts about its ability to do just that. The coroner's inquest had been abandoned on the order of the Lord Chancellor (and Tony Blair's former flatmate), Lord Falconer, and Gardiner wrote to him requesting it be resumed because the preliminary cause of death "no longer represents" the pathologist's final view. He also commented that coroners could compel witnesses to attend, but that the public inquiry had "no such powers". Lord Falconer's office replied, in August 2003, that the inquiry would "adequately" investigate the cause of death. And although Falconer requested the inquiry be as short as possible and accepted some evidence in writing, later at the final hearing in March 2004, Gardiner expressed satisfaction that there were "no exceptional reasons" for the inquest to be resumed.

It's interesting that the BBC, also linked to Kelly's demise, encapsulated all this evidence under the banner of just another conspiracy theory. Was the BBC performing a volte-face by shrouding this new information within a veil of sneers and speculation? Or was this the only way the corporation, in its state of post-Hutton condemnation, could get the news out at all?

A theory by conspiracy theorists

Although many doubts have been mooted in the media about Kelly's death – with the *Evening Standard* once running the headline "Was Kelly Murdered?" – only Michael Shrimpton has consistently asserted that he was murdered and pointed at possible suspects. The fact that he has only been able to make his accusations on the Internet is significant, as he himself acknowledges. Use of the word "murder" seems to be restricted to "alternative" news sources, such as www.propagandamatrix.com, www.prisonplanet.com and www.rense.com. None of the newspapers to raise serious doubts over Kelly's death has taken them to any conclusion, except to report that Hutton was interrupted announcing his findings by criminal psychologist Patricia Rodrigues-Walsh, who shouted that Kelly had been murdered.

As time has gone by, the story has been buried by other events – yet no weapons of mass destruction have ever been found in Iraq. The Hutton Inquiry's biggest impact was on the BBC: journalist Andrew Gilligan, the director-general and the chairman all resigned; the government seized the opportunity to rein in the BBC's proclivity for questioning the state; and the corporation remains in a mind-set of post-Hutton fear and restraint (compounded by the government's swingeing budget and staff cuts, rows over the future of the licence fee and snipes about the BBC being innately "left-liberal" and "anti-business").

But questions remain. Could a modern government really kill someone like Kelly so audaciously, in the midst of a media maelstrom? Perhaps only a government also audacious enough to base its public case for going to war on shamelessly inadequate intelligence. It does seem strange that the press, which usually lays siege to anyone in the public eye, was not surrounding Kelly's home in sufficient strength to deter him from going out that night.

As coroner Nicholas Gardiner remarked: "This hearing will do little to put an end to the controversy relating to the death of Dr Kelly." Kelly was a scientist who lost his life after his painstaking, dangerous work for the intelligence services was meddled with and squandered by governments with their own agendas – and after exposing government spin used to justify a controversial war. His Baha'i faith prohibited him from having any political affiliation, but Baha'i also forbids suicide.

In January 2008, the British government yet again rejected calls for an inquiry into Dr Kelly's death following the publication, the previous month, of Norman Baker's investigations in a book, *The Strange Death of David Kelly*.

SOURCES

Books

Norman Baker The Strange Death of David Kelly (2007). The MP's fully-fleshed investigations, leading him to conclude that Kelly's death "was not suicide".

Films

Peter Kosminsky The Government Inspector (2005). Channel 4 docudrama about the life and death of weapons inspector Dr David Kelly, pushing the suicide explanation for his death.

Websites

- **en.wikipedia.org/wiki/David_Kelly** A succinct summary of Kelly's life, work and tragic death.
- **www.guardian.co.uk/letters/story/0,3604,1131833,00.html** Doctors cast doubt over the "suicide" verdict.
- **news.bbc.co.uk/1/hi/programmes/conspiracy_files** Official site of the BBC TV series *The Conspiracy Files* which explores the theories surrounding Kelly's death before arbitrarily rubbishing them all.
- **www.prisonplanet.com/archive_murder_of_kelly.html** US radio presenter and conspiracy theorist Alex Jones provides an archive of news reports and background information about Kelly's death.
- **www.rense.com/general49/kelll.htm** Alex Jones talks to Michael Shrimpton, who asserts that Kelly was assassinated.
- **www.the-hutton-inquiry.org.uk** The official version as to who was to blame for outing Kelly.

Death of a spy: Alexander Litvinenko

Alexander Litvinenko – a former officer of the Russian secret service, the FSB (successor to the KGB), valiant expurgator of high-level corruption, a marked man in Moscow, and a dissident, exiled in London – became the world's first ever victim of nuclear terrorism in November 2006, under the mesmerized eye of the world's media, which whipped up a storm of conspiracy theories.

Litvinenko's story, by his own account, is extraordinary. As a lieutenant-colonel in the FSB in the 1990s, Litvinenko conducted investigations into corruption and organized crime that all too often led to the doors of senior FSB and government officials. But he really incurred the wrath of the state in 1998, when he went on Russian TV with four colleagues to defy and denounce an order to assassinate billionaire Russian tycoon and dissident Boris Berezovsky. Two years later, Litvinenko began to vocalize the shocking theory suggested by many people of high repute: that the Moscow apartment bombings of September 1999 (see p.388) were carried out not by Chechen terrorists, but by FSB agents seeking – and achieving – a new war in that troubled Caucasus state in southern Russia. He went on to make similar claims that the terrorists at the Beslan school massacre (see p.391) were "100 percent" FSB.

An avalanche of trumped-up charges, arrests, trials and prison sentences soon befell Litvinenko and, in 2000, he fled to the UK, seeking political asylum. In London, Berezovsky supported him and his family, helping them find work and accommodation and assisting in the publication of Litvinenko's book, *Blowing Up Russia*, which fully fleshed out his FSB-Moscow bombings theory. Litvinenko became fairly well-known in the West as a freelance writer and anti-Putin polemicist and, as such, was profiled in *The Times* in 2005 as a "spy in hiding [who] fears he will be silenced" (a pram full of Molotov cocktails had been shoved at his London front door only the year before). This portrait of a fearful figure in hiding is curiously anomalous with the man publishing books, speaking at the Oxford Union and telling all to *The Times*. Yet, worldwide fame came only at the end…

Polonium poisoning

In October 2006, Russian journalist Anna Politkovskaya, tireless campaigner against atrocities and human rights abuses in Chechnya, was shot dead in the lift of a Moscow apartment block. Litvinenko assumed it was her work that led to her killing, and thus started his own investigation into her death. On November 1, he met businessmen – and former Russian agents – Andrei Lugovoi and Dmitry Kovtun in the Pine Bar at the Millennium Hotel in London's Mayfair. That afternoon, he met Italian academic Mario Scaramella, who was also investigating Politkovskaya's death, at a sushi bar in Piccadilly. Scaramella told police and the CBS News programme *60 Minutes* that he showed Litvinenko an FSB hit-list with both of their names on it, as well as Politkovskaya's and Berezovsky's (who Litvinenko immediately went on to warn).

Later that same day, Litvinenko was hospitalized with severe stomach pains. And so began a prolonged, tortuous decline that lasted more than three weeks. Under armed police guard in hospital, Litvinenko told the BBC's Russian Service that he was the victim of a "serious poisoning"; as his hair fell out and his weight plummeted, global media interest grew. On November 20, pictures of his ghostly pale, thin face and head, rapidly rendered hairless, were printed worldwide, not least because what was killing him remained unknown. It was only after his death on November 23, that it was sensationally discovered that Litvinenko had been poisoned with polonium-210, a radioactive isotope that comes out of the bowels of nuclear reactors – and, hence, an isotope subject to the strictest state controls.

This strongly suggested that the poison had come from high-level sources with high-level state sanctions, people who were also making, as *The Economist* put it, the most "intentionally sensational" point. The police finally traced the source of the "massive" dose of polonium-210 to that most British of things, a teapot, used to serve Litvinenko at his meeting in the Pine Bar with Lugovoi and Kovtun. (Meanwhile, London went into a polonium panic, with doctors reportedly faced not with the usual complaints about winter flu, but with people fearing they had polonium poisoning, for which several Millennium Hotel staff were, in fact, treated.)

The police investigate

All the while, the British police were working their way through a list of people in the UK connected to Litvinenko: Berezovsky, Scaramella, Kovtun and Lugovoi. Indeed, the last three were all contaminated themselves to the point of illness, as the trail of radioactive polonium contamination, spattered across London, led police to Litvinenko's home, the sushi bar, Berezovsky's office, a lap-dancing club, a football stadium and a shisha pipe restaurant. Further investigation in December 2006 led to Germany, where minute amounts of the radioactive isotope were found in aircraft, cars and a flat in Hamburg, which were all used by Kovtun before and after Litvinenko's death. The polonium trail was ultimately traced all the way to the Russian capital (including to the British embassy there), where Kovtun and Lugovoi had since returned.

Outside of the UK, there was, of course, Russian president Vladimir Putin, the man Litvinenko had pointedly accused in a statement from his deathbed: "You may succeed in silencing one man, but the howl of protest will reverberate, Mr Putin, in your ears for the rest of your life." Berezovsky, himself the victim of several attempted hits on his life, also blamed the "bandit" Putin. (He also frequently attacked the Russian government and the FSB, particularly for the re-establishment of KGB killings as a common Kremlin policy tool.) Litvinenko's wife Marina later said that Putin's government was "absolutely" responsible for the murder, which could only have happened with his knowledge, if not his direct order. She has since been involved in setting up the Litvinenko Justice Foundation, which lists Putin as a "key figure" in his death, and notes that, in July 2006, Putin signed a bill authorizing Russia's Special Forces to assassinate "Russia's enemies" anywhere in the world.

Many deaths and many enemies

Sergei M. Mironov, chairman of the upper house of the Russian parliament, noted that Litvinenko and Politkovskaya's deaths came just before Putin's tour of

Europe – not an "accidental" coincidence, he claimed, possibly suggesting Putin was giving the Europeans one hell of a reminder about how the Russians do business. There was also the Chechnya connection: Chechen leader Movladi Baisarov – the Fidel Castro-lookalike that the FSB had long blamed for the 1999 Moscow apartment bombings – was also slain around the time of Litvinenko's poisoning. Baisarov's murder in November 2006 went "almost unnoticed", in the words of *The Guardian* journalist John Flower; "Baisarov was shot dead by police in Moscow at the same time Litvinenko was dying in a hospital bed." But the Baisarov conspiracy was just one of the many theories put forward by journalists, conspiracists and investigators. For, as Flower put it, the Litvinenko affair had led the conspiracy theory to "come of age", with an entire "runaway catherine wheel" of suspects, scenarios, claims and denials.

Too slow, too sensational, too obvious: the Russian response

Was Litvinenko's murder, *The Economist* opined, merely a bid to damage Putin's reputation? Many Russian commentators thought that his slow death by radioactive poison was simply too spectacular, even for the Kremlin. Therefore, they were convinced it had to be a ruse to frame Putin and his government, not least because the manner of his death meant that Litvinenko was granted several weeks in the full glare of the world's media to make all the allegations he wished. Putin himself added to this line of conspiracy questioning, asking why Litvinenko's final statement implicating him "was not made public when he was still alive?", when Berezovsky's lawyers had supposedly taken it down two days before his death.

Russian politician Anatoly Chubais suggested that Litvinenko and Politkovskaya's deaths were part of a wider plot to smear Putin, a claim backed by former Russian prime minister Yegor Gaidar, despite his being a critic of Putin's. (Gaidar had himself fallen ill the day after Litvinenko died, leading to suspicions that he may also have been poisoned.) Chubais was quoted in *Time* magazine, saying: "The deadly triangle – Politkovskaya, Litvinenko and Gaidar – would have been quite desirable for some people who are seeking an unconstitutional and forceful change of power of Russia."

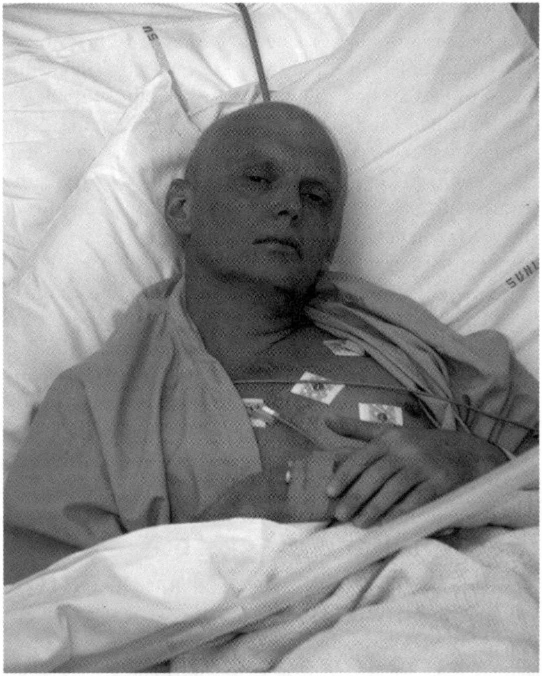

Former Russian spy Alexander Litvinenko lies in a hospital bed in London, the victim of polonium posioning.

The Berezovsky theory

Despite supporting Litvinenko when he first arrived in London in 2000, Boris Berezovsky was interviewed with a view to eliminating him from enquiries amid rumours that he had cut his funding to Litvinenko and his family. Was Berezovsky one of the prominent Russian businessmen Litvinenko was allegedly lining up to blackmail, as outlined by CBS's *60 Minutes* in January 2007? Gathering information was what Litvinenko had been trained to do, and Julia Svetlichnaya, a Russian student who sought his help to write a book, claimed that the impecunious ex-spy continually and casually talked of blackmailing "one of the Russian oligarchs which resides in UK" who had connections to both Putin and the Kremlin. However, the British police investigated Berezovsky, and cleared him of any involvement in Litvinenko's murder.

Svetlichnaya also claimed that Litvinenko behaved in an exaggeratedly furtive manner, so that he – and his claims – would be taken more seriously. This gives oblique support to Putin's comments that Litvinenko's allegation of the FSB being behind the Moscow apartment bombings was "delirious nonsense" from a man with "no access to state secrets", who had only ever really been assigned duties like troop escort. That said, Svetlichnaya's perspective has also been criticized precisely because it seems to support Putin.

Blackmail and black gold

Former KGB agent Yuri Shvets told BBC Radio 4 that Litvinenko was in possession of a dossier that may have played some role in his death. The "Yukos dossier" was said to refer to people who had controlled the Russian oil company Yukos before Putin had made the violent overthrow of its owners a cause célèbre in his war on oligarchs. Precisely who Litvinenko might have sought to blackmail with this dossier, or how he would have done so, Shvets did not make clear. However, American investigative journalist Edward Jay Epstein expanded on Shvets' notion by commenting that Litvinenko had travelled to Israel in October 2006, just weeks before his death. There he apparently gave information to the former deputy head of Yukos about the deaths of several of the company's employees and the imprisonment of former CEO, Mikhail Khodorkovsky.

Yukos, Israel and energy formed links in a bigger conspiracy chain hung by journalist Wayne Marsden on Poland. He refers to the fact that polonium was discovered by the fiercely patriotic physicist Marie Curie from Poland, or to give the country its Latin name, Polonia. In essence, Marsden's theory was that the Poles were seriously displeased about the 2005 Russo-German deal to build a gas pipeline under the Baltic Sea, rather than through Poland, which was the original plan backed by Yukos. In revenge, Poland – now an ops-base of sorts for international Russian, Polish, British, Israeli and Ukrainian crime syndicates – sought to embarrass the resurgent Russians by framing them for Litvinenko's death. The trouble with this theory is that nothing whatsoever to back it up emerged in Litvinenko's final, talkative weeks – but then again, the contents of the Yukos dossier have yet to be disclosed...

International oil may be a dirty, murky business, but was it Yukos, oil pipelines and blackmail that Litvinenko wanted to discuss with Kovtun and Lugovoi in the Millennium Hotel's Pine Bar on November 1? Was that the mysterious "business proposition" they claimed he had for them? Another unanswered question is exactly how many Russians Litvinenko actually met at the hotel bar that day. The police are apparently still seeking a third individual – a possible accomplice? – described as a "tall and muscular man with Asian features", who travelled to the UK on three fake passports and was caught on CCTV in London.

FSB factions

One theory is that the hit on Litvinenko may have been orchestrated to give the appearance of the Kremlin being wracked by murderous factionalism, possibly as part of a longer game. According to *Time*, the deaths of prominent Russians and stories of violent factionalism within the government actually matter less than the president's ability to sustain the illusion that people are plotting against all Russians, thereby reinforcing the notion that "Putin's vigilance remains indispensable" to protect the country from dangerous enemies from both home and abroad.

Putin's tenure as president is due to end in 2008 (as in the US, Russian presidents are limited to two terms in office).

And the theory goes that a faction of Putin supporters was seeking to frighten the Kremlin into wrangling him a third term in office. Possibly. Although, apparently not with Putin's sanction. Russian radio host and magazine editor Aleksei Venediktov posited that Litvinenko's killers may have been linked to Putin, but they were not acting in his name. However, guilt-by-association could compel Putin to change the constitution limiting presidential terms, so that he could stay in office and enjoy presidential immunity from any prosecution related to Litvinenko's death.

Alternatively, another theory suggests that the killer or killers could have been completely indifferent to any consideration of what the big boss may or may not have wanted. Former KGB officer Oleg Kalugin told NBC's *Dateline* that a hardline "brotherhood" of ex-KGB/FSB spooks, called "Dignity and Honour", had been mercilessly hunting down "traitors" for over a decade, something that Putin could easily appreciate, if not sanction. Was it all a plot by the Kremlin, against the Kremlin, from within the Kremlin, or just down the road from the Kremlin? *The St Petersburg Times* quoted Putin himself: "Openly speaking, I don't believe in the conspiracy theses."

More bombs

Other conspiracy theorists speculate that Litvinenko's poisoning was, in fact, self-inflicted. A Russian website called Russia Blog carried a series of posts proposing that the poisoning wasn't an assassination at all, but a "botched polonium smuggling operation", and that Litvinenko inadvertently imbibed some of the stuff from a leaky container in his hotel room. Citing the use of polonium-210 in nuclear weapon triggers and guessing that the quantity would have a street value of around $25 million, bloggers asked whether Litvinenko might have been trying to peddle the stuff on the black market to Iran or North Korea. The Russian newspaper *Izvestia* carried this idea, then added a twist – that Litvinenko and a shadowy accomplice were making a nuclear bomb to help the Chechnyan separatists. The counter-spin to this theory was that the polonium trail leading back to Moscow was the work of anti-Putin plotters attempting to implicate the Russian government in peddling bootleg bombs to rogue states. At least, that was the theory according to the pro-Putin defenders.

The Russian job: the KGB's men in the EC

Another angle focuses on the involvement of the Italians, and the influence of Russia, or rather the USSR, in the top echelons of Europe's governments. Italian investigator Mario Scaramella, who met Litvinenko in London on the day he was hospitalized, was also a consultant for the nuclear energy industry, so he conceivably had access to radioactive substances like polonium-210. But was he also really a hit man? Scaramella was known to Litvinenko through his work on another of the former Russian agent's allegations: that Romano Prodi, the former European Commission president and current Italian prime minister, was once a top KGB agent. These allegations were aired on British television by the BBC and ITV in January 2007, and UKIP MEP Gerald Batten demanded their investigation at the European parliament in early 2006. Scaramella had been investigated by the British police, and cleared of any involvement in Litvinenko's poisoning.

Extraditions, expulsions and further conspiracies

All this conspiratorial theorizing has almost obscured (perhaps deliberately?) the fact that the British police continued to doggedly pursue the case. And the detectives' suspicions mostly pointed to Moscow. In May 2007, British prosecutors announced that their chief suspect, former FSB agent Andrei Lugovoi, should be charged with Litvinenko's murder. Lugovoi insisted that the allegation was "a lie … created and spread in the West". A formal request from the British Foreign Office for his extradition followed on May 28, 2007, a move that President Putin called "foolish". In June 2007, Russia's prosecutor-general, Yuri Chaika, declared that extradition was "out of the question", and in July, his office officially refused the request.

Soon after the extradition refusal, four Russian diplomatic staff were expelled from the Russian embassy in London, followed just days later by the expulsion of a quartet of British diplomats from the British embassy in Moscow. Was Russia's refusal to give up Lugovoi simply a retaliatory protest to Britain's longstanding refusal to extradite dissident Russian businessman Berezovsky back to Russia? Or was it some kind of comment concerning wrangles with the British oil giant BP over a gas project in the far east of Russia? Or perhaps it was some kind of proxy-protest about the proposed placing of US anti-ballistic missile systems in Europe? Russian magazine editor Aleksei Venediktov commented: "As long as the public is not informed, conspiracy theories will multiply and grow." But he then cryptically added: "This does not mean there is no conspiracy."

Not only were the Russians deliberately obstructing a British murder investigation, but the FSB also declared that it was going to investigate Lugovoi's counterclaims linking Litvinenko with Britain's MI6. The FSB then began its own enquiries into British espionage efforts within Russia. Lugovoi, who remained Britain's chief suspect, suggested that Litvinenko was on the payroll of MI6, and that he was involved in selling nuclear material on the black market – and had accidentally killed himself through his own carelessness with the material he was smuggling. "How was his former boss [in MI6] supposed to explain his death?" Lugovoi exclaimed at a Moscow press conference on the first anniversary of the killing, saying that MI6 had also tried to recruit him, but had then set up a plot to elaborately frame him and Moscow for Litvinenko's death, when the polonium had actually originated in the UK. Whatever merit there may be in that theory, it poses yet more questions, particularly when you consider that Lugovoi and Litvinenko ostensibly met in the Pine Bar for "business" reasons. Also, how could Lugovoi have come to be informed about all this cloak-and-dagger behaviour going on in the British intelligence services?

The first anniversary of Litvinenko's death was marked by his widow reiterating her belief that Putin was behind the killing. Whether or not Putin was ultimately culpable, his moves to stifle the Russian press and to centralize power in a resurgent, authoritarian Kremlin would have made him a suspect regardless. As a journalist with *The New York Times* pointed out in December 2006, the Russian president remained suspicious not least because "the Kremlin's critics ... keep dying in circumstances that investigators have yet to solve". Litvinenko's killing has also revived interest, and credibility, in his thesis on the FSB's complicity in the 1999 Moscow apartment bombings. As writer Jack Langer commented in *Human Events*: "with every step that Putin's government takes to strangle Russian democracy, and with every Putin critic who turns up dead from some exotic poison, the more wild conspiracy theories like those told by the late Litvinenko seem plausible."

But despite this proliferation of conspiracy theories, Putin's position as president was, in no palpable way, jeopardized by Litvinenko's death or the accusations made against him. And while he did not change the law to allow himself to serve a third term, Putin did announce, in October 2007, his plan to become prime minister when his preferred candidate, Dmitry Medvedev, becomes president in 2008, to reportedly widespread popular appeal. Meanwhile, in the December 2007 Duma elections, Lugovoi stood for – and won – a seat!

In reference to Litvinenko's death, US-based security consultant and Russia expert Paul Joval said on *Dateline NBC*: "A message had been communicated to anyone who wants to speak out against the Kremlin: 'if you do, no matter who you are, where you are, we will find you and we will silence you – in the most horrible way possible.'" Joval himself was severely wounded in a shooting in Washington DC just days after making this comment. Former KGB agent Yuri Shvets would say that Litvinenko's "greatest agony" was the professional failing of having drunk a cup of tea that was not made in front of him. Shvets had warned *The New York Times* in 2004 that the FSB was still operating a former KGB poison lab...

SOURCES

Books

Alexander Litvinenko and Yuri Felshtinsky Blowing Up Russia (2007 update). The book that helped the dissident FSB agent to live famously – and die infamously – in exile.

Marina Litvinenko and Alex Goldfarb Death of a Dissident: The Poisoning of Alexander Litvinenko and the Return of the KGB (2007). The victim's wife tells her story, and points the finger at the Russian authorities.

Martin Sixsmith The Litvinenko File (2007). Former BBC journalist charts the Kremlin's war on its critics back to 2000 – the year Putin came to power.

Websites

www.cbsnews.com/stories/2007/01/05/60minutes/main2333207.shtml *60 MInutes* reports on the murder.

commentisfree.guardian.co.uk/john_flower/2006/12/has_the_conspiracy_theory_come.html Journalist John Flower gives his kopeck's worth.

www.economist.com/world/displaystory.cfm?story_id=8407464 Someone's going to pay for this, according to *The Economist*.

www.litvinenko.org Site of the bilingual Litvinenko Justice Foundation set up by Marina Litvinenko and other supportive friends and associates.

www.litvinenkomurder.org A much more conspiratorially contrived site about Litvinenko's death, including his final deathbed statement.

Death in a sunroof: Benazir Bhutto

On the afternoon of December 27, 2007, Pakistani opposition leader Benazir Bhutto left a political rally in Rawalpindi in her bulletproof Toyota Landcruiser. She was both exhausted and exhilerated: the last two months had been intense. She had returned from "exile" in Dubai – where she had fled more than ten years before to avoid facing corruption charges – to be instantly engulfed by the chaotic politics of Pakistan.

Her supporters gave her a rapturous welcome, but not everyone in Pakistan was pleased to see her. The very day she landed, on October 17, 2007, a suicide bomber at a rally in Karachi greeted her return with a lethal blast. Soon after, the dictator-president, Pervez Musharraf, put Bhutto under house arrest, and rebel warlords and Taliban sympathizers issued her with death threats. However, that day in Rawalpindi, the crowds were behind her. If she was going to win the promised elections, she needed the people's support. As she was driven away from the rally in her bulletproof Toyota, she decided to stand on the back seat and poke her head and shoulders out of the sunroof. She waved and smiled at the party faithful surging around the vehicle. It was a fatal mistake. Suddenly, a succession of gunshots punctuated the noise of the crowd. Before anyone could run, a bomb exploded. Bhutto, along with many others, was killed.

Extremists–terrorists–militants–Taliban–Al Qaeda

Within hours, President Pervez Musharraf was vowing that he would not rest until "we eliminate all the terrorists". Half a world away, President Bush was hitting the television networks to announce his regret for the murder of a democrat by "extremists and terrorists". Soon enough, this speedily reached conclusion was apparently backed up by jihadi websites claiming the killing as the work of "Al Qaeda".

There were plentiful reasons to suspect Islamic militants. Bhutto had once supported the Taliban, but now she cultivated a cosy relationship with the US, and she promised to attack religious extremism in Pakistan if elected. She had received counter-threats from Taliban sympathizers, including the powerful (and little-photographed) jihadi warlord Baitullah Mehsud, who was fighting a war against the Pakistan government from his homeland in the South Waziristan region of northwest Pakistan, on the Afghan border. After the suicide bombing in Karachi, Bhutto claimed to have received a letter from a "friend of Osama bin Laden" which threatened to slaughter her "like a goat".

From the outset, the Pakistani government insisted that Al Qaeda was behind Bhutto's killing. Baitullah Mehsud – who is widely suspected of having a leading role in the organization – denied any knowledge of an assassination plot. However, within 48 hours of her death, the government released a transcript of a phone conversation in which a man said to be Mehsud asks whether the killers were "our men". On being told that they were, "Mehsud" offers his congratulations. "They were really brave boys", the transcript reads, "who killed her". British and US officials pronounced the transcript "credible". The CIA went further, with Director Michael Hayden blaming the killing on "that network around Baitullah Mehsud", a network he described as being part of the "nexus between Al Qaeda and various extremists and separatist groups". Given that Al Qaeda itself is a nexus between extremist and separatist groups, this clarification wasn't altogether helpful.

President Musharraf

Many in Pakistan were not convinced of the transcript's authenticity. In fact, the shockwaves had hardly dissipated when the first conspiracy theories began to grind their way around the Pakistani rumour mill – or rather, ring their way around the phone networks. Rioting even broke out in Karachi, amid fears that the city's water supply had been poisoned.

Pakistani suspicions also broke out like a rash in the international press. "White-haired Mohamed Sharif, 61, who runs a sidewalk barber's shop", reported *Time* magazine on December 28, said that the chief rumour was that "America is involved in this with Musharraf's help". M.A. Mohamed, who "runs a car parts company," opined that "America sent Benazir and later killed her with the help of Pervez Musharraf". On December 29, renowned Middle Eastern commentator Robert Fisk published a front-page analysis in *The Independent* under the headline "They Don't Blame Al-Qa'ida. They Blame Musharraf".

Fisk put the case succinctly: "Question: Who forced Benazir Bhutto to stay in London and tried to prevent her return to Pakistan? Answer: General Musharraf. Question: Who ordered the arrest of thousands of Benazir's supporters this month? Answer: General Musharraf. Question: Who placed Benazir under temporary house arrest this month? Answer: General Musharraf. Question: Who declared martial law this month? Answer: General Musharraf. Question: Who killed Benazir Bhutto? Er. Yes. Well quite."

President Musharraf was not a popular man. He had promised to defeat the Taliban – and had been sucked instead into an unwinnable conflict. He had promised elections – and instead watched the country slide into chaos. According to Liaqat Baloch, an official in the Islamic party Jamaat-e-Islami: "This assassination was fabricated by the present government. It is part of the American strategy to scare people that Pakistan is falling apart." An excuse, then, to further postpone elections that Bhutto looked increasingly like winning?

Military insiders and the ISI

After the suicide bombing in Karachi, Bhutto had made her own suspicions public. She wrote to one journalist saying: "If it's God's will, nothing will happen. But if something should happen, then I will hold the people I have named in my letter to Musharraf of 16 October, and Musharraf himself, responsible." A similar email was sent to the British foreign secretary, David Milliband. Bhutto also told David Frost on the Al Jazeera network: "These are the people whom I suspect of wanting not only to stop me, but the whole process of democratization in Pakistan."

Bhutto's letter to Musharraf did not accuse the president himself, however, but rather urged him to watch four

– some say three – named men closely. "I'm not accusing the government", she said on one occasion, "I'm accusing certain people who abuse their powers". The identities of those "certain people" are much debated, but most of the names that circulate the rumour mill have one thing in common: they were all thought to work or to have worked for the ISI, Pakistan's Inter-Services Intelligence agency. Vast, corrupt and powerful, the ISI has been called a "state within a state". Many of its top officials, or former officials, had careers extending back to the regime of General Muhammad Zia-ul-Haq, the military dictator who deposed and executed Benazir Bhutto's father, former prime minister Zulfikar Ali Bhutto, in the late 1970s. There had long been bad blood between the ISI and the Bhutto clan, so was the assassination of Benazir Bhutto just another move in a long-running vendetta?

In fact, the ISI had concrete reasons to fear a Bhutto regime. On the day she died, Benazir Bhutto is supposed to have been on the point of handing over evidence that the ISI was siphoning off millions of the billions of dollars that the US had granted to Pakistan to fight Islamic extremists. Some of this money was even thought to have been earmarked for rigging the elections that might otherwise have allowed Bhutto to come to power.

The accused may have had one other, even more compelling motive for wanting Benazir Bhutto dead. Like so many powerful men in Pakistan – and like much of the ISI itself – they were also said to have links or sympathies with Islamicist extremists.

Political rivals

One leading figure in the ISI called the allegations "bunkum", while also admitting that "it's very convenient for the security forces to call it a suicide bomber because they can cover up the possibility someone else was behind the attack". That someone else, according to Bhutto's widower Asif Ali Zardari, may have been the governing Pakistan Muslim League (PMLQ or Quaid-e-Azam) – at least, if that's the meaning that can be construed from Zardari repeatedly calling the party, the "killer league". The other political possibility was the confusingly named PMLN, or Pakistan Muslim League (Nawaz), the rival opposition party headed by former prime minister Nawaz Sharif. Like Bhutto, Sharif had recently returned to Pakistan to contest the promised elections. Bhutto was his main rival, and relations between the two parties were troubled. Still, few thought the PMLN responsible.

The most conspiratorial suggestion of all was that Bhutto's own party, the Pakistan People's Party (PPP), were behind her death. After the first suicide bombing, in Karachi, Bhutto's husband had been accused, by an official from the government party, of staging the attack to win sympathy. Could the second bombing have been another such drama – but one that went horribly wrong?

Death by bullet, bomb – or sunroof?

Moderate conspiracists stop short of accusing Musharraf, or even elements in his government. Instead, they claim that the assassination was simply allowed to happen (much as the Bush administration supposedly allowed the 9/11 plot to proceed – see p.397). Bhutto, it is known, asked for increased security after the Karachi attack. She wanted detonator jammers, tinted glass, police escorts; she didn't get them. She wanted private security guards from Blackwater or Armorgroup; the Pakistani government refused to issue them with visas.

Of course, no form of security can save a politician who literally sticks her neck out of her vehicle's sunroof. It might, however, have prevented either the gunman or the bomber ever getting close (if they weren't the same man). If that was indeed the cause of death… The Pakistani government originally asserted that Bhutto died when she ducked inside her Toyota in response to the bomb blast. She hit her head on the sunroof's lever, they said, observing that the wound was on the right side of her head, while the gunman and/or bomber were both on her left.

The absence of complete evidence allowed speculation to flourish. The area around the bomb-scarred car was literally hosed down within hours. Eyewitnesses left the scene uninterviewed. Doctors – none of them pathologists – failed to examine Bhutto's corpse thoroughly enough to satisfy their critics. Bhutto's husband, Asif Ali Zardari, refused to give his permission for an autopsy. What was left – to feed alternative explanations – were some blurry video stills that appeared to reveal a smooth-shaven man in sunglasses with his hand raised. Another man in the photograph, who was suspiciously bearded and dressed in a shawl, was announced to have been a bystander, after the severed head of the bomber was found.

For some months, the PPP and Bhutto's family continued to insist that their former leader had been killed by two gunshots to the head and neck. But you could believe the local newspaper, *The Nation*, which quoted PPP sources as saying that her injuries were caused by a laser, and that the gunshots and bomb were decoy actions. Or you could believe the rumour-mongers who claim that, soon after the attack, a body was mysteriously picked up from the back of the hospital… and that Benazir Bhutto is actually still alive somewhere.

Wild geese

In January 2008, detectives from Scotland Yard's Counter Terrorism squad headed from London to Pakistan to help in the investigation into Benazir Bhutto's death. They quickly announced that gunman and bomber were one and the same man, and that Bhutto was killed by the bomb blast causing "a violent collision between her head and the escape hatch area of the vehicle". She banged her head on the sunroof, in other words.

The Yard may have come to its own speedy conclusions, but if Bhutto's murder is anything like those of Pakistan's first prime minister Liaquat Ali Khan (assassinated in 1951), or its most notorious dictator, General Muhammad Zia-ul-Haq (killed in a murky aircrash in 1988), it will remain unsolved – and the subject of numerous conspiracy theories – for many years to come. In a country where allegiances change more often than governments, and where the Taliban, Al Qaeda, the ISI and even the government all shade into one another, attempting to identify the mind behind the hand that pulled the trigger may turn out to be a wild goose chase.

SOURCES

Books

Benazir Bhutto Reconciliation: Islam, Democracy and the West (2008). "Benazir Bhutto", the publisher's puff piece reads "is going to be vital to that country's future". A statement of intent, now made bitter with irony.

Zahid Hussain Frontline Pakistan: The Struggle with Militant Islam (2006). An experienced international correspondent reports on President Musharraf's tussles with the militants – and the parallel Islamization of Pakistan security agencies.

Pervez Musharraf In the Line of Fire (2006). Saviour of the nation or pernicious dictator? This ghost-written memoir is in little doubt.

Mariam Abou Zahab and Olivier Roy Islamic Networks: The Pakistan-Afghan Connection (2004). Although dated, this is a clear-eyed exposé of the links between Pakistan's ISI and the supposedly "Afghan" Islamic extremists.

Websites

Ⓦ **www.benazirbhutto.org** The official website of Benazir Bhutto: "Martyred on 27-12-2007".

Ⓦ **www.counterpunch.org/fisk12312007.html** Robert Fisk's article "Who Killed Bhutto?", as first published in the UK's *The Independent*.

Ⓦ **www.time.com/time/world/article/0,8599,1698828,00.html** *Time* magazine's early take on conspiracy theories about Bhutto's death.

MEGA-CONSPIRACIES AND MASTER PLANS

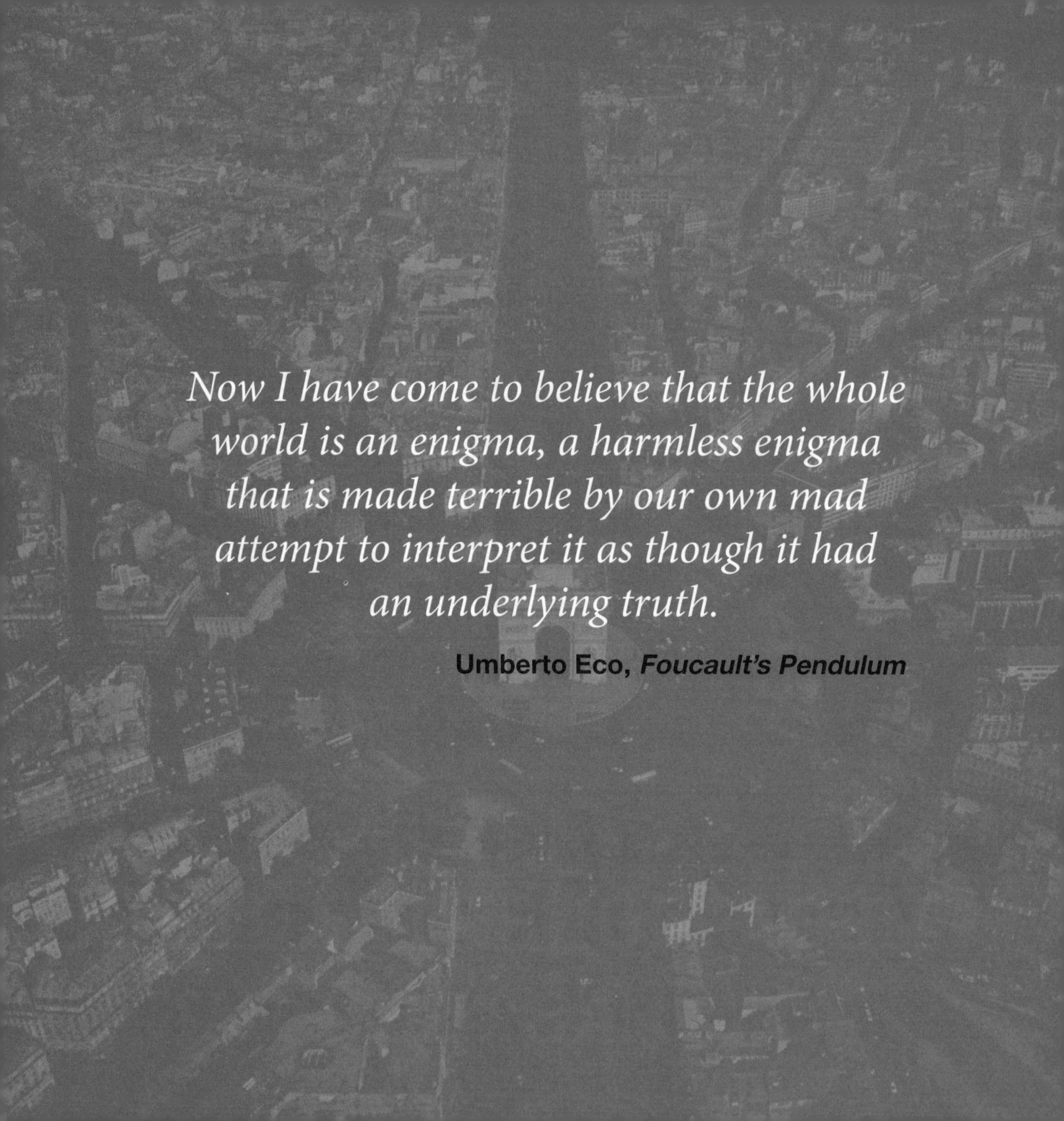

Now I have come to believe that the whole world is an enigma, a harmless enigma that is made terrible by our own mad attempt to interpret it as though it had an underlying truth.

Umberto Eco, *Foucault's Pendulum*

MEGA-CONSPIRACIES AND MASTER PLANS

Mega-conspiracies aren't so much about specific events, or even strings of conspiratorially connected events, but the groups supposedly behind them – and indeed, behind everything else going on in the world. The paranoia of mega-conspiracy theorists is reflected in the megalomania they attribute to those who hold power, especially when that power appears to be concealed from public view. The theories often concern centuries-old secret societies, so it's no surprise that the theories themselves are often centuries old too.

One group that has recently attracted the attention of a new generation of conspiracy theorists is the Knights of the Templar. Originally a corps of French mercenary knights during Europe's Christian crusades, the Templars subsequently dispersed across the continent, where their wealth made them the object of much ill feeling. They'd otherwise probably be forgotten, if not for their reappearance in Dan Brown's thriller *The Da Vinci Code*, which linked them to an elaborate cover-up in which the "real" Jesus Christ escaped crucifixion to live with Mary Magdalene and have a child. A longer-running theory is that many of the Templar orders simply reinvented themselves as the society of Freemasons.

Freemasons, also simply called Masons, are seen as mega-conspirators in their own right. For most of us, Masonry conjures up images of men wearing aprons, with rolled-up trouser legs and weird handshakes, meeting in a "lodge" bedecked with strange symbols of eyes and pyramids, and quietly running the police, the local council or golf club. However, some conspiracy theorists believe that Freemasons run the planet, dominating governments, supranational corporations, banks and even entire cities. Haven't a dozen US presidents been Masons? Aren't the movement's arcane motifs emblazoned all over the country's currency, making a dollar bill a veritable manifesto of Masonic influence? And weren't key cities like Paris, Washington and London constructed on sinister Masonic plans, with the ultimate aim of controlling and subduing their populations?

Equally obsessed with odd rites, rituals and signs are the world's various Mafia groups. The Chinese Triads are named after their triangular sign, while Japan's Yakuza can be recognized from their lack of fingers and the Russian Mafia by their little black caps, adopted in homage to their Italian-American and Sicilian counterparts. When you read about the activities of government intelligence agencies like the CIA, KGB or Mossad, though, you can't help wondering who the real bad guys are. Assuming they exist in the first place, it's a question that can also be asked of the "Men in Black": are they government agents fighting interstellar aliens, or working with them?

Talking of aliens, David Icke claims that the British royal family are from outer space. Others say the Windsors are the chief cabal of a British Commonwealth that's still seething over the loss of its American colonies and is plotting to bring the wayward United States to heel. Such narrow, nationalist theories fail to spot the powerful links between bodies like Britain's Royal Institute of International Affairs and the US's Council on Foreign Relations. This network of power is evidence of a sinister Anglo-American conspiracy – a conspiracy so powerful that it even sucks in other, non-Atlantic nations under the aegis of transnational groups like the Trilateral Commission and European Union. This mega-bloc is, of course, bent on pushing the globe steadily towards the notorious – but strangely mysterious – New World Order. Whether that Order is described as liberal-capitalist, fascist, communist or simply satanic rather depends on the theorist.

Some theorists prefer to view the world in more old-fashioned terms as a giant-scale competition between nations. While the EU is presented by many British tabloids as a "conspiracy" of Brussels bureaucrats, some Americans see it as a vast economic plot to bring down the US. In their view, the concept of global warming is an EU invention designed to hamper American economic growth. If that were so, the EU would also be taking on the US military-industrial complex, whose growing influence was the subject of a warning by the former general and US president Dwight Eisenhower – but not until he was leaving office, perhaps to escape reprisals himself.

Some secret groups only exist as fantasies. One seventeenth-century conspiracy theory that spread like wildfire across Europe concerned the Rosicrucians, a quasi-Masonic religious sect supposedly bent on spreading religious reformation across the world. The only problem was that there was no evidence of their existence – which didn't stop new groups calling themselves Rosicrucians from being set up. By then, however, there was another movement with branches scattered across Europe: a proliferation of pompous academic circles calling themselves Illuminati, or "enlightened ones". The name was also adopted by a somewhat malevolent anti-Jesuit group whose rituals and secrecy led to the Illuminati being lumped together with the Masons, a confusion that continues today.

A lethal and even older conspiracy theory is that of the "blood libel", a term used to describe the medieval belief that Jews regularly abducted, crucified and ate Christians (mainly children). Disturbingly, it's a theory that is still held to be true in certain Middle Eastern circles. In the West, meanwhile, similar practices have been ascribed to Satanists. In the 1980s, one astounding Satanism trial in the US ground on for six years, without anyone being convicted (not even those who had fabricated the evidence).

Sadly, the blood libel is just the tip of the iceberg as far as anti-Semitic conspiracy theories are concerned. In 1890, a piece of black Russian propaganda called *The Protocols of the Elders of Zion* outlined a Jewish plot to take over the world. People including Henry Ford and Adolf Hitler fell for it, and the forgery helped to fuel the hatred that led to the murder of six million Jews during World War II. But this hasn't stopped anti-Semitic Holocaust deniers like David Irving from claiming that the Holocaust never happened: works such as *Anne Frank: The Diary of a Young Girl* are themselves dismissed as part of a Zionist conspiracy.

Murder and denial, it seems, go hand in hand. The Turkish government, for example, still officially denies the genocide of some one and a half million Armenians under the Ottoman Empire during World War I, while some Serb extremists deny the Srebrenica genocide ever took place. For a country where conspiracies and conspiracy theories are part of the culture, however, you have to look to Italy, where corruption seems endemic and the long-standing political battle between Left and Right has given rise to a succession of scandals and rumours concerning assassinations, banking, Mafia connections and terrorist attacks. For some, the government of Silvio Berlusconi has made politics itself into a giant conspiracy – but in the land of Machiavelli and the Borgias, perhaps it always has been.

Knights of the shadows: the Templars

Two kinds of histories describe the Knights Templar. The first is historians' history, based on documents and contemporary descriptions. The second blends in a potent mixture of conspiracy theory, fiction and occult and esoteric "knowledge". For different reasons, the crucial date in both histories is 1312, when Pope Clement V officially dissolved the Templar Order in the Papal Bull *Vox in Excelso*. According to historians, that was that for the Knights. According to conspiracists, the Templars and their secrets survived in hiding – and continue to wield great power to this day.

Eastern origins

As the official version has it, the Poor Fellow Soldiers of Christ and the Temple of Solomon was established in 1118, when eight (or, some say, nine) French noblemen made a vow to Baldwin II, the Crusader king of Jerusalem, to defend pilgrims to the Holy Land. They took their name from the Temple quarter of Jerusalem where they had their base – just as their rivals, the Knights Hospitaller, were named after the Hospital of St John, whose inmates they cared for. Donations of property in Europe quickly made the Templars extremely rich, while donations of younger sons in search of a role in life made them more numerous. At the height of their power there were around four hundred Knights in Jerusalem, plus many more lightly mounted "Serjeants" and other hangers-on.

To assist the Templars' defence of the pilgrim passes into the Holy Land, the crusading nations entrusted the great frontier castles to their care. This wasn't philanthropy: by the latter half of the thirteenth century, the Mamelukes were threatening the Holy Land, and the Templars were gradually forced out of stronghold after stronghold. Finally abandoning their walled city of Tortosa in August 1291, they fled to the offshore island of Arwad, where they held on for another eleven years. After 1302, however, the Templars became refugees in Europe – albeit rich ones, thanks to their developing successful second careers as bankers and moneylenders. This made them no more popular than it had the Jews.

Accusations

Rumours began to spread that the Templars had been strangely corrupted by the Mohammedan ways of the East, and they were reported to have discovered "secrets" while excavating the site of the Temple of Solomon. They were accused of heresy, sodomy, worshipping cats and a mysterious head called "Baphomet", and performing strange initiation rites – denying Christ and the crucifixion, spitting on the cross, and kissing on the buttocks, mouth and penis. A mysterious "secret test" that guaranteed loyalty and silence provoked further suspicion. On October 13, 1307, Philippe IV "Le Bel" of France pounced, sending agents to arrest all the Templars in his kingdom on the same day. They were charged with heresy, but it was their money Philippe was after. Confessions were tortured out of the arrested Knights, and the rest of Europe followed the French lead. Within five years the pope had outlawed the order, and on March 11, 1314, the Templars' grand master, Jacques de Molay, was burned at the stake in Paris. He allegedly cursed Philippe IV and Pope Clement V as he died; both followed him to the grave within the year.

A twelfth-century wall painting of a Knight Templar.

In 2007, fresh light was shed on the whole murky business. Researcher Barbara Frale unearthed a long-forgotten parchment in the Vatican's secret archives entitled "Processus Contra Templarios" – the Templar Trial – which had been misfiled for centuries. It revealed that, in 1308, Clement V had decided to let the Templars off the most serious charge of heresy. Senior cardinals had interviewed the grand master and his jailed companions and concluded that the rejection of Christ was merely a type of military hazing, intended to prepare new recruits for the tortures they might face in infidel hands. Unfortunately, Clement's clemency was reversed when it was explained that Philippe IV had already spent much of their confiscated wealth.

Secret survival – the Da Vinci codswallop

The Templars' property was either seized or turned over to the Knights Hospitaller. As for the Templars themselves, those who weren't burned were forced to join other orders, or quietly disappear. They vanished from history. Unless, that is, you believe the "alternative histories" propagated by various pseudo-historians and a handful of modern neo-Templar orders. One of the most prominent, the Sovereign Military Order of the Temple of Jerusalem, for example, lays claim to a "Charter of Transmission" and a list of grand masters that traces their current chief back to de Molay. These claims are almost as dubious as those of Freemasonry, which at a certain point in the eighteenth century decided that its supposed roots among medieval masons weren't glamorous enough. Instead, it was alleged that the Templars had fled to Scotland, either joining Robert Bruce's army or establishing their own orders, which in due course became Masonic.

Even more absurd is the claim, reiterated in Dan Brown's thriller, *The Da Vinci Code*, that the Templars were a mere front organization for a "Priory of Sion" which survived the Knights' downfall unscathed. According to Brown and his sources – notably a French neofascist hoaxer called Pierre Plantard, and the books *Holy Blood, Holy Grail* by Baigent, Leigh and Lincoln and *The Templar Revelation* by Picknett and Prince – the Priory of Sion was the guardian of the Templars' true secret: that Jesus had a child with Mary Magdalene. This "holy blood" or *sang réal* is supposedly the true origin of the myth of the Holy Grail, on the grounds that the medieval French for "Holy Grail" was the similar-sounding *san graal*. (For a fuller discussion of this topic, see p.166.)

The Templars today

Templar occultists like to link the Knights to every other hermetic mystery or conspiracy theory around. The head of Baphomet is often said to have been what later turned up in church history as the Turin Shroud – which is a historical possibility. Other Templar occultists claim that the Shroud represents not Jesus, but Jacques de Molay. Others still hold that Baphomet is a mishearing for "Mahomet", or Mohammed – or even the alchemical symbol known as the Caput Mortum or "Dead Head".

Once you get this deep into unsourced speculation, you can pretty much say what you like. Which is probably why today the Templars are variously claimed to be responsible for building Europe's Gothic cathedrals and discovering America in the thirteenth century, orchestrating the French Revolution in the eighteenth century, and pulling the strings of the New World Order (see p.141) in the twenty-first. However, the Templar Order has not existed in any meaningful sense since Pope Clement V dissolved it – without papal sanction, a Templar "order" isn't anything more than a club with a fancy name, a few fragments of empty iconography and a wishful claim to historical antecedents. If the Templars are to be found anywhere today, it's only in their surviving round churches, modelled on Jerusalem's Holy Sepulchre, and in the ruined, empty castles of Palestine: Chastel Blanc, Chastel Pèlerin, Crac des Chevaliers, Safèd…

SOURCES

Books

Malcolm Barber **The Trial of the Templars** (1993). A serious study of the Templars' downfall.

Peter Partner **The Knights Templar and their Myth** (1990). Detailed and serious account not just of Templar history, but of their fantastical after-history too – hence the "myth" part of the title. Not for beginners.

Lynn Picknett and Clive Prince **The Templar Revelation: Secret Guardians of the True Identity of Christ** (1998). Even before *The Da Vinci Code* bumped this back onto the bestseller list, it was required reading for devotees of the "alternative" version of Templar history. Wildly eccentric – it calls itself "a quest through time and space" – but highly enjoyable.

Piers Paul Read **The Templars: The Dramatic History of the Knights Templar, the Most Powerful Military Order of the Crusades** (2001). Highly readable popular history, but more a general survey of the crusading era than a detailed account of the Templars.

Websites

Ⓦ **asv.vatican.va** The official homepage of the Vatican's Secret Archive (honestly). The Vatican embraces transparency? Just try getting in…

Ⓦ **www.ordotempli.org** Homepage of one of the many groups that likes to pretend it's the real heir of the Templars. Packed with popular pseudo-history.

Freemasonry: centuries of conspiracy?

Freemasonry attracts so many conspiracy theories for exactly the same reason that it attracts so many Freemasons – it has "secrets". The sheer popularity of Freemasonry just adds another dimension: the greater the number of conspirators, the greater the scale of the conspiracy. In fact, there are roughly five million Freemasons worldwide, all signed up to a creed that sounds harmless enough. As the Scottish Rite puts it: "Human progress is our cause, liberty of thought our supreme wish, freedom of conscience our mission, and the guarantee of equal rights to all people everywhere our ultimate goal."

For conspiracy theorists, however, there must be a more sinister agenda hidden away in all those "secrets". And the more influential the conspirators are, the more dangerous their conspiracy must be. Lists of powerful Freemasons – past and present – are posted all over the Internet. Most of the lists are exaggerated and highly speculative, but there *are* some remarkable facts. Well over a dozen US presidents, for instance, were definitely Freemasons, from George Washington to Gerald Ford by way of William Taft, Franklin D. Roosevelt, Harold Truman and Lyndon B. Johnson. Can any other secret society claim so much?

Stonemasons and Freemasons

Freemasonry famously claims that it's not a secret society, just a society with secrets. And the biggest secret of all is where it came from. The respected historian Frances Yates even wrote that "the origin of Freemasonry is one of the most debated, and debatable, subjects in the whole realm of historical enquiry." Plenty of writers claim to have found the answer to the mystery, however, so the legendary history of Freemasonry has easily expanded to fill the real-world vacuum.

For Freemasons, there's an obvious allure in having exotic ancestry; for opponents, long, furtive histories simply back up their darkest allegations. Some have said that Freemasonry is a descendant of the Mystery Schools of the ancient world, or Rome's Collegia, or the Knights Templar; others have said that it is the visible face of more secretive societies, such as the "Priory of Sion", the Illuminati or the Rosicrucians. According to the Orientalist Sir Richard Burton, Freemasonry was nothing less than a Western offshoot of Islamic Sufism.

The most common explanation, however, is that Freemasons were once medieval masons, the word "free" referring to their skill in the working of freestone, or fine-grained stone such as sandstone or limestone. These techniques were passed on from master to apprentice, and jealously guarded in order to differentiate skilled masons – the architects of their day – from ordinary labourers. Guilds, the medieval equivalent of unions, grew up, and gradually – so the story goes – these "lodges" of "Operative masons" began to accept non-mason members, who became known as "Speculative" or "Accepted" Masons, or just "Freemasons".

Unfortunately, there's no hard evidence of any connection between the (stone)masons of the fifteenth century – when the latest records of stonemasons' guilds date – and the (Free)masons of the mid-seventeenth century (when the earliest records of Freemasonry date). In lieu of proof, many writers cite medieval documents such as the early-fourteenth-century Holkham Bible, with its image of a Masonic-style "architect god", or the Regius Poem from the 1390s, with its Masonic-sounding phrases. It's just as likely, however, that Freemasonry adopted medieval symbolism as it is that it inherited an almost invisible medieval tradition. As for the "tradition" of secret signs, it seems unlikely that medieval stonemasons would have needed them to identify themselves to each other, as most lived on site.

Freemasonry breaks cover

The fact that there's no proof that Freemasonry existed at all before the mid-seventeenth century counts for some as further proof of its malignancy. Surely only an awesomely powerful organization could have covered its traces so well... The earliest firm evidence of Freemasonry records the admission of a Scotsman, Robert Moray, into an Edinburgh-based, military-oriented Masonic lodge in 1641, and the acceptance of an Englishman, Elias Ashmole, into another lodge in 1646. Curiously, both were key founders of the Royal Society, which established the formal study of science in England. Both were also known for their interest in Rosicrucianism, an occult pseudo-scientific fad of the era (see p.95), which is sometimes accused of having been "behind the Masons". (In this, Rosicrucianism has much in common with other groups such as the Illuminati and the Templars.)

In the later seventeenth century, Freemasonry spread rapidly among young gentlemen in England and Scotland alike. It may have owed its success partly to its alluring secrecy, partly to the enticing admixture of Enlightenment philosophy with the occult. For reasons never discovered, four London lodges "went public" in 1717, declaring themselves to be a united or Premier Grand Lodge of England, with jurisdiction over all the other lodges. Once the cat was out of the bag (and once it looked as if it wasn't about to be strangled), other lodges declared themselves too, initially in England, but soon all over Europe. Many politicians declared at the time that this was proof of a deep-rooted and wide-ranging secret network finally revealing itself. Others believed Freemasonry was just another genteel European fad, like Humanism or coffee houses.

Higher degrees

In 1725, the original two "degrees" or levels of Freemasonry were augmented by a third. Only when members had learned the mysteries of the first two degrees could they progress to the great secrets possessed by a (third-degree) Master Mason. In 1737, French Masons went one – or rather thirty – better, adding higher degrees up to the thirty-third level and calling their new system the *Rite Ecossaise*, or "Scottish Rite", after the man they believed had invented it, a Scotsman called Andrew Ramsay.

More conservative Masons, confusingly called the "Moderns", and disturbed by the thought that the "Antients" might consider themselves above their Masonic cousins, described the new levels as "side degrees". For the Antients, however, there was nothing in the past that couldn't be plundered to make Freemasonry ever more complex and exciting. The stonemason-origin story wasn't enough. Freemasonry's key foundation myth was now that it descended from the masons who built Solomon's Temple. This, then, was one of the secrets that aspiring Masons would discover once they had successfully schmoozed their way into a lodge: theirs was the most ancient club in the world.

Masonic secrets: Hiram Abiff and the Juwes

Another "secret" was the elaborate third-degree initiation ritual, which in some Masonic rites re-enacts the main event in this legendary Temple history. You won't find the story in the Bible, but according to one account, the three "Juwes" (whose names have nothing to do with Judaism, but derive from the cod-Latinate, quasi-magical-sounding Jubela, Jubelo and Jubelum) sought out Hiram Abiff, the master architect of the Temple, to discover his secrets. Hiram, of course, refused to divulge what he knew, and was murdered. Solomon sent the Juwes back to open Hiram's coffin, on the safe grounds that the first thing they found there would surely be the Secret of the Temple. The Juwes found Hiram's hand – which is one origin of the famous Masonic secret handshake.

It's an odd story (particularly as the Bible names a different Hiram – Hiram of Tyre – as the builder of the Temple) and makes little sense without a detailed explanation of the symbolism hidden in the narrative – which is exactly what initiates are given. Even odder, perhaps, is the image of adult men acting out a murder as part of their initiation (and you thought rolling up a trouser leg was weird). Of course not every Masonic lodge follows the same ritual, but the sheer creepiness of these kinds of narratives helps explain much of the resentment and suspicion that attaches itself to the Masons. It also explains a lot about the macabre rituals of later societies such as Yale's Skull and Bones (see p.237). Presumably the frat boys' dads hadn't kept their Masonic secrets too well.

Templar theories

Staking a claim to a Biblical heritage was not enough for the early Freemasons. Calling himself the "Chevalier", Andrew Ramsay delivered an "Oration" to Paris's Grand Lodge in March 1737 that set out another theory. The Masons, it seems, were the latter-day resurgence of the medieval warrior-monks, the Knights Templar – who took their name from their medieval base in Jerusalem, on the site of Solomon's Temple. Despite a complete lack of evidence of the existence of either Templars or Masons in the four centuries between 1312 (the date of the Templar suppression) and 1717 (when Masonry emerged in public), the idea caught on. Ramsay linked Masonry's early popularity in Scotland with that country's acceptance of Templar refugees in the fourteenth century – an idea later elaborated upon by conspiracy-historians Michael Baigent and Richard Leigh in *The Temple and the Lodge*.

Another modern author, John J. Robinson, outlines a different theory to explain the four-hundred-year gap in his book *Born in Blood*. He requires historians "to have one mental band tuned to the wavelength of the Masonic connection"; it's very much a conspiratorial bandwidth. Robinson sees the Masonic heritage cropping up repeatedly in various conspiratorial activities from the anti-clerical Lollard movement of the fourteenth century and the Peasants' Revolt of 1381 to the publication of Sir Francis Bacon's *New Atlantis* in 1627, which described "an unknown island guided by a learned society, told from the viewpoint of a shipwrecked gentleman". The New Atlantis, according to Robinson, was a Masonic Utopia. The shipwrecked gentleman represents a Templar fleeing persecution, washed up on the coast of Scotland, and "guiding" the society he found there towards higher learning…

A twist in the argument for a Templar origin of Freemasonry was introduced in Germany. The Scottish Rite had been introduced there by Karl Gotthelf, aka Baron von Hund, in 1755. His "Strict Observance" movement was soon joined by one Johann August Starck, who claimed to have knowledge of alchemy (much like the Rosicrucians) and to have evidence of Freemasonry's direct descent from the Templars' clergymen, who were, he said, their secret masters. (A similar idea was later revived by a French fascist called Pierre Plantard, the hoaxer behind the Priory of Sion, which later achieved worldwide fame via Dan Brown's *The Da Vinci Code*.)

For Christopher Knight and Robert Lomas, the Hiram legend is proof of the Masonic–Templar link. Their bestseller, *The Hiram Key* (another of Dan Brown's favourite sources), identifies a Pharaonic mummy with the corpse of Hiram, thanks to three "ritually placed" wounds. The Egyptians' Hebrew slaves, it seems, proudly maintained their former masters' ancient wisdom, and they employed the secret symbolism of Egyptian architecture when they built the Temple for Solomon. As a Jew and a rabbi, Jesus was also privy to these secrets, and his followers practised the resurrection ritual of Hiram. When the Knights Templar uncovered the ruins of the Temple during the Crusades, they surely discovered Hiram's secret too, which they then passed on to their Freemason descendants. It's a great story, but so flimsy that it hasn't "shaken the Christian world to its very roots", despite the promises of the book's blurb. The authors' professional backgrounds and their status as practising Masons didn't help their cause.

Revolutionary agenda: Freemasonry in France

The apotheosis of the myth of Templar origin came during the French Revolution, when the storming of the Bastille was blamed on a Templar element in the Masonic movement. Almost five hundred years after the suppression of their order by King Philippe IV of France and the immolation of their grand master, Jacques de Molay, in Paris, the Knights were still thirsty for revenge.

The Templars as a kind of Masonic Marine Corps is an alluring idea, and these kinds of accusations weren't limited to a loony fringe. An influential book published in 1797 by a conservative French clergyman, the Abbé Barruel, *Mémoires pour servir à l'histoire du Jacobinisme*, blamed Freemasons not just for the Bastille episode, but for the entire French Revolution. With the addition of a Jewish conspiracy, his book later became the basis for the infamous *Protocols of the Elders of Zion* (see p.109), in which an "Elder" states: "The Masonic Lodge throughout the world unconsciously acts as a mask for our purpose."

Many subsequent writers agreed with Barruel that Freemasons had inflamed the deliberations of the Third Estate, the parliament of landowners that set the French Revolution in motion, and believed that they had formed the backbone of the revolutionary-minded Club Breton, which became the notorious Jacobin Club. These allegations were made both by anti-Masons, eager to expose what they saw as a dangerous force in French society, and by Masons themselves, keen to lay claim to exactly this kind of power. Historians still argue the point today.

In fact, the French Revolution went too far for most bourgeois-liberal Freemasons, who tended to support the idea of a constitutional monarchy. By 1792 most French lodges had lost their members to emigration. And yet, right across Europe, Barruel's notion of a mega-conspiracy turned out to be self-fulfilling. As the idea that Freemasonry had sponsored an anti-clerical, egalitarian and progressive revolution spread, *real* revolutionaries were attracted to Freemasonry. Italy's Giuseppe Mazzini and Giuseppe Garibaldi were just two examples. Plenty more were to be found on the other side of the Atlantic.

Another revolution: early Freemasonry in America

Freemasonry had spread to North America by the 1730s, and swiftly became popular among the political classes. Benjamin Franklin jumped on the bandwagon as early as 1731, while George Washington was initiated a little later, in 1752. It seems, however, that Washington took little interest in Masonic affairs thereafter, despite his leading role in the most notorious Masonic incident of all, the laying of the foundation stone of the Capitol on September 18, 1793. (For more on the Masonic design of Washington, see p.91.)

Books and websites crawl with allegations against the Freemasons, usually exaggerated, such as the "fact" that the US Constitution was based on Freemasonry's 1723 "Ancient Charges", otherwise known as "Anderson's Constitutions", or that the design of the dollar bill is proof of a Masonic conspiracy at the heart of the US's foundation (see p.127). Participants in the Boston Tea Party are said (without any evidence) to have been Freemasons, and indeed practically anyone with any role in the War of Independence has been similarly "outed" at some point. Although lodge membership was widespread, however, it wasn't ubiquitous. Of the fifty-five signatories of the *Declaration of Independence* in 1776, it's often said that only six were not Freemasons; in fact, a mere eight (or possibly nine) were. Similarly, of the thirty-nine men who approved the Constitution in 1787, just thirteen are known to have been Freemasons.

The publication in 1797 of *Proofs of a Conspiracy Against all the Religions and Governments of Europe Carried on in the Secret Meetings of Free Masons, Illuminati and Reading Societies*, written in Edinburgh by a secretary of the Royal Society, Professor John Robison, helped to whip up rumours of a conspiracy in Europe and America alike. Curiously, many influential Freemasons in America joined up precisely because they'd heard the rumours – becoming a Mason was seen as a way of involving oneself with the cause of independence. Membership of a lodge is often hyped up by the conspiracy-minded as proof of commitment to some Masonic agenda, but in fact most American Freemasons joined primarily for social reasons. It was the ultimate fashionable gentleman's club – albeit one with a worthy political edge. Of course, membership wouldn't hurt their careers, but a little ambition doesn't turn a Founding Father into an Agent of Satan.

Masons vs Christians

It's easy to understand why conservative, eighteenth-century French monarchists would mistrust Freemasons, given that they were supposed to have been responsible for the French Revolution. What's less clear is why modern Americans would be so suspicious. If Freemasonry was a conspiracy to kick out the British and establish a democracy, it's hard to see where the problem lies.

The answer can be found in Freemasonry's rationalist roots in the Enlightenment and, perhaps, in its status as a potential rival to the church. Right from the start, the Vatican was hostile. Freemasonry's alleged complicity in the French Revolution, which dethroned a divinely appointed king and promoted a brotherly egalitarianism, was a bad start, and the bourgeois liberalism of the typical Freemason didn't mix too well with conservative Catholicism. Worse still, the Masonic conception of God as the "Architect of the Universe" smacked of rationalistic deism – anathema to a Catholicism founded on the church's apostolic authority. Some lodges were even openly atheist.

One of the earliest and most famous anti-Masonic documents was a flysheet distributed in London in 1698 that warned "all Godly people" against Freemasonry. "For this devillish sect are Meeters in secret which swere against all without their Following", it read. "They are the Anti-Christ which was to come leading them from Fear of God. For how should they meet in secret places and with secret Signs taking care that none observe them to do the Work of God; are not these the Ways of Evil-dom?"

The definitive religious tract against Freemasonry was published by the conservative pope Leo XIII in 1884. His encyclical, *Humanum Genus*, openly accused Freemasonry of being in league with the devil, and was heavily conspiracist in tone. Freemasonry's "ultimate purpose", it declared, is "the utter overthrow of that whole religious and political order of the world which the Christian teaching has produced, and the substitution of a new state of things in accordance with their ideas, of which the foundations and laws shall be drawn from mere naturalism." "By means of fraud or of audacity", Freemasonry had apparently gained "such entrance into every rank of the State as to seem to be almost its ruling power."

The relationship between the pope and the Freemasons hasn't mellowed much since then. Paul VI, pope from 1963 to 1978, declared that Freemasonry was "the smoke of Satan … penetrating and fogging the temple of God". But then, he did have the P2 lodge to contend with (see p.134). Today, Catholics are forbidden from becoming Freemasons in many countries (though the reverse is not true), and rival Catholic fraternities such as the Knights of Columbus vie with Masonic lodges for membership around the world.

Anti-Masonic feeling in America

In America, the most vehement anti-Masonic conspiracism dates back to the well-publicized disappearance in 1826 of a renegade Mason, William Morgan, who had claimed he was about to write an exposé of Masonic secrets. It is probable that he was murdered by local Freemasons, and certainly this is what most Americans believed at the time, leading to widespread anti-Masonic feeling, and even riots.

Although Protestant churches have tended to be more tolerant than the Catholic Church, in America the alignment of Freemasonry with Satanism has been enthusiastically espoused by the more rabid wing of the evangelical movement. To the evangelical ultra-Right, the esoteric symbolism employed by Freemasonry is like a red rag to a bull. According to www.thewatcherfiles.com, the "meaning" of Washington DC's street plan "is all too clear". By using such symbols as the Goathead of Mendes and the Devil's Pentagram, it seems that "occultists planned for the White House to be controlled by Lucifer in accordance with his occultic power and doctrine".

Part of the blame for this Satanic reputation can be laid at the door of Albert Pike, the great embellisher of American Freemasonry in the nineteenth century. Conspiracists love to cite his 1871 magnum opus, *Morals and Dogma of the Ancient and Accepted Scottish Rite of Freemasonry*, as evidence of Freemasonry's alleged atheism, or worse. "The God of the Christian world", Pike wrote, "is only Bel, Moloch, Zeus, or at best Osiris, Mithras or Adonai, under another name." At one point, Pike hails "Lucifer, the Light Bearer! ... Lucifer, the Son of the Morning! Is it he who bears the Light?"

Utah's Church of Latter Day Saints, or Mormon Church, has proved a longstanding opponent of Freemasonry, despite the remarkable parallels between certain rituals performed in Mormon temples and Freemasonic lodges. Some Mormons claim this is because they share a common heritage in the secrets of the Temple of Solomon, but it's more likely down to the fact that the Mormon founder, Joseph Smith, and other church leaders were Freemasons themselves. Either way, the allegation that the mob that killed Joseph Smith and his brother Hyrum (note the name) in Carthage, Illinois, in 1844 was Masonic has been repeated for generations.

UK and European conspiracy theories

In the UK, many conspiracy theories have focused on the royal family. Prince Charles, it seems, is the first male heir to the throne in two hundred years not to be a Mason. The Masonic angle is regularly blended with wild allegations about the Windsors' involvement in global power-politics (see p.113). Or with notorious murder cases... Stephen Knight's *Jack the Ripper: The Final Solution* (1976) produced an elaborate theory linking Queen Victoria's grandson, the Duke of Clarence, to the famous murders of East End prostitutes by a man known as "Jack the Ripper". The gruesome killings were supposedly ordered by the prime minister, Lord Salisbury (a Freemason), to cover up the Duke's marriage to a Catholic commoner – the prostitutes were apparently witnesses. It seems the actual killer, royal doctor Sir William Gull, left ample evidence of his guilt in the form of carefully constructed Masonic symbolism.

Most British Masonic conspiracy theories tread a more measured line. In the early 1980s, Knight went on to write one of the virtual textbooks of UK anti-Masonic theories, *The Brotherhood*, setting out the standard allegation that Freemasons have a policy of mutual preferment. They help each other into jobs and contracts, it's said, and out of jail. Freemasonry, it seems, is popular in the police force and in the judiciary.

In the early 1990s, a group of Labour MPs led by Chris Mullin tried to push through a bill that would have forced public servants to declare membership of secret societies. The MPs' legislative zeal had been stoked by the publication of Martin Short's *Inside the Brotherhood: Further Secrets of the Freemasons*, which mixed testimony from disgruntled Masonic widows and divorcées with political allegations, such as the claim that the Conservative Party was "riddled" with Freemasons. Short even implied that Freemasons had murdered Stephen Knight (in fact, Knight died of a brain tumour). England's United Grand Lodge responded to the parliamentary challenge by declaring that no democracy would ever countenance forcing individuals to declare their religious beliefs, say, or their membership of a golf club. Short retorted that Freemasonry wasn't like other clubs in that it had five disturbing features: a code of mutual aid; ritual threats directed at potential whistleblowers; rituals involving "menacing objects or disorienting devices"; secret passwords and signs; and, lastly, "widespread public concern". Short also pointed out that only seven members had been expelled from the Grand Lodge for criminal convictions in the thirty years to September 1988. It didn't help; Labour's bill failed.

Elsewhere, European Freemasonry has a more conspiracist edge – partly thanks to its profoundly more political history. In French lodges, political discussion had always been allowed, whereas it had been resolutely banned in Britain. In France, each year brings a new crop of books containing fresh allegations about the baleful influence – historical or contemporary – of *la franc-maçonnerie*. In Italy, Freemasonry has been tainted by its apparent connection with the *Propaganda Due* affair (see p.134), though it seems more likely that P2's masters were making use of Masonic networks rather than the other way round, and P2 was later expelled by the Italian Grand Lodge. Many Italians claim that Freemasonry has "infiltrated" the Vatican, to the extent that some blamed the "murder" of Pope John Paul I on Masons in the Holy See.

Racism, sexism – and persecution

The most disturbing allegations against Freemasonry aren't actually conspiracy theories: they relate to sexism and racism. On the first count, it's true that women are excluded from most lodges in the UK and the US. According to authors R.A. Gilbert and John Hamill (both enthusiastic Freemasons), women are banned because that's what the "Ancient Landmarks", or Masonic rules, prescribe. Most Masons, they say, would "echo the sentiments" of a certain John Coustos, who told the Portuguese Inquisition in 1743 that women were excluded in order "to take away all occasion of calumny and approach" – i.e. to pre-empt any accusations of orgiastic practices and general immorality – and because "women had, in general, been always considered as not very well qualified to keep a secret".

On the racism front, lodges today do not exclude people on the grounds of race. Not explicitly, at least. In the American South, many lodges do not recognize members of the (black) Prince Hall Lodge as fellow Masons. As author John J. Robinson remarks, "it is difficult to wrap one's mind around the concept of a limited universal brotherhood". Historically, there are many connections in the white South between Freemasonry and the Ku Klux Klan, with their parallel systems of symbols, signs and chivalric orders, and their odour of anti-Catholicism.

For their part, many Freemasons equate conspiracy theories about Freemasonry with similar anti-Semitic or racist arguments. Germany's defeat in World War I was widely blamed on a "Judaeo-Masonic" conspiracy. Publications such as future Nazi general Erich von Ludendorff's *The Extermination of Masonry by the Exposure of its Secrets* (1928) only fanned the flames, as did the Nazis' dissemination of *The Protocols of the Elders of Zion* – which was almost as virulent in its hatred of Freemasonry as it was of Judaism. Mussolini's Italy banned Freemasonry in 1925, while Nazi Germany sent thousands of Masons to concentration camps – where they wore blue forget-me-nots as a secret sign of recognition.

The implicit warning, of course, is that something similar could happen again, if conspiracy theorists continue attacking Freemasonry. It does, however, seem difficult to compare anti-Masonic rhetoric with the naked hatred directed against Judaism worldwide. For all the conspiracy theories, the usual stereotype of Freemasonry is of a rather dusty gentleman's club where men can enjoy genteel, boozy dinners, indulge in philanthropy and take part in rather wacky male-bonding rituals. These days, Freemasons seem more like Shriners or Rotarians than Jacobin revolutionaries.

One episode of *The Simpsons* featured a famous parody that says a lot about modern attitudes to Freemasonry. Every Wednesday, the "Ancient Society of Stonecutters" – which numbers virtually every man in Springfield – meets in a large, forbidding pyramid. Safe in their lodge, they pay homage to a Sacred Parchment before getting drunk, playing wild games of table tennis and singing their sinister song: "Who keeps the metric system down? We do!

We do! Who leaves Atlantis off the maps? We do! We do! Who keeps the Martians under wraps? We do! We do!"

SOURCES

Books

Michael Baigent and Richard Leigh The Temple and the Lodge (1991). Recounts the pseudo-history of the Masonic influence on Scotland, the main evidence being supposed Templar graves. Also throws in material on the Masons in the American Revolution. Not much on Masonic conspiracies, though – the authors say the contemporary controversies are "a storm in a teacup".

David V. Barrett Secret Societies: From the Ancient and Arcane to the Modern and Clandestine (1999). Excellent primer, with encyclopedia-style articles ranging from neo-Platonism and Hermes Trismegistus (from whom we get the word "hermetic", meaning sealed or secret knowledge), through brief histories of the Rosicrucians and Illuminati, to Nazis and modern Triads.

Dan Brown The Solomon Key (2008?). The latest novel from the author of *The Da Vinci Code* is widely rumoured to focus on Washington and its "Masonic secrets". Still unpublished at the time of writing – perhaps because Brown is trying to get his research straight.

R.A. Gilbert and John Hamill World Freemasonry: An Illustrated History (1992). From the official Masonic Aquarian Press, this holds that Freemasonry descends from medieval stonemasonry. As much a history of Masonic persecution as of Masonry itself.

Christopher Knight and Robert Lomas The Hiram Key: Pharaohs, Freemasonry, and the Discovery of the Secret Scrolls of Jesus (2001). Described in detail in the main article (see p.84).

Stephen Knight The Brotherhood (2001). Described in detail in the main article (see p.87).

Jasper Ridley The Freemasons (2000). Authoritative, balanced and well-written history; dry at times, but good on anti-Masonic conspiracy theories.

John J. Robinson Born in Blood: The Lost Secrets of Freemasonry (1990). The first half of the book is a history of the Knights Templar; the second "unlocks" the symbolic secrets of Masonry to discover their true meanings – and they have nothing to do with guilds of medieval stonemasons. Fascinating but fanciful.

Martin Short Inside the Brotherhood: Further Secrets of the Freemasons (1990). Picks over the pernicious influence of Freemasonry in UK society, especially in the police and judiciary, and in relation to the Woolard and Stalker "Affairs". Gives time to the evangelical argument suggesting Freemasonry is Satanic. Gilbert and Hamill call it a "venomous attack", full of "fables and lies".

Frances Yates The Rosicrucian Enlightenment (2001). A serious work by one of a generation's greatest and most fascinating historians. Traces the history of the esoteric philosophy behind the Rosicrucians, and puts forward some ideas about the origins of Freemasonry.

Films

Allen and Albert Hughes From Hell (2001). Horrific thriller based on the theory that Freemasons were behind the Jack the Ripper killings in nineteenth-century London. Excellent casting, including Johnny Depp as an opium-fuelled Scotland Yard detective. Based on a graphic novel by Alan Moore and Eddie Campbell.

Websites

Ⓦ **anti-masonry.info/alt.illuminati_FAQ.html** The Grand Lodge of British Columbia and Yukon has pooled lots of links to articles and sites dismissing anti-Masonic theories.

Ⓦ **www.catholicculture.org/library/view.cfm?recnum=1244** Pope Leo XIII's anti-Freemasonry broadside, *Humanum Genus*, in English.

Ⓦ **www.freemasonry.bcy.ca/fiction/cinemal** An excellent list of Freemasonry in films, including short reviews and Masonic Moments.

Ⓦ **www.freemasonry.org** Look out for the page of counter myths about Masonic influence on American Independence.

Ⓦ **www.freemasonrywatch.org** Begins by quoting JFK: "the very word 'secrecy' is repugnant in a free and open society; and we are, as a people, inherently and historically opposed to secret societies, to secret oaths and to secret proceedings." Ends in wilder conspiracies.

Ⓦ **www.masonicinfo.com** Sets out the main arguments and conspiracy theories ranged against Freemasonry, and then attempts to counter them. Unusually balanced, for the most part.

Ⓦ **www.rosicrucian.org** The homepage of AMORC, one of many organizations claiming to be the true heirs of the Rosicrucians.

Ⓦ **www.ugle.org.uk** Homepage of the original United Grand Lodge of England.

Sinister cities

Ever since the Pharoahs, powerful rulers have used architecture to express their innermost beliefs. With Egypt's masons long since in their tombs, it has been the task of historians – or, more frequently, speculative writers on the occult – to recover the secrets behind the symbolism (or the "symbology", as the occultists have it) of their great edifices. Many have tried to trace an esoteric tradition down the centuries, finding Egyptian beliefs – as transmitted to the Templars and the Masons – etched in the very fabric of the world's cities, including Paris, London and Washington DC. Exactly why Masons (or Egyptians, or Templars) would want to unmask their own secret purposes by turning them into architecture is problematic. Perhaps evil geniuses just can't help revealing their masterplans? In a few notorious cases, city planners have had less occult and more explicitly brutal purposes. Paris, famously the jewel of nineteenth-century architecture, was explicitly planned to crush dissent and allow insurrection to be more easily suppressed. Architectural theorists call it "urbicide".

Pyramids and boulevards: Paris

The most notorious case of hidden symbolism in city planning is the glass pyramid of the Louvre in Paris. In the hands of conspiracists, it has variously served as the funerary monument of former French president François Mitterrand (the Egyptophile "pharaoh" of French politics), the hidden grave of Mary Magdalene (according to Dan Brown's *The Da Vinci Code*) and the nexus of Satanic power, with its supposed 666 panes of glass (there are, in fact, 673).

The Louvre's pyramid is, however, just the latest addition to a carefully planned city-within-a-city, designed principally to trumpet the raw power of the French state. The Louvre's "grand axis" stretches all the way from the remains of France's ancient royal palace, up the Champs-Elysées, under Napoléon's Arc du Triomphe and out to the modern Grande Arche de la Défense. Some have claimed that it echoes the design of the Karnak temple complex in Egypt, but for occult rather than merely symbolic reasons. Even if you don't buy into this argument, the grand axis is as scarily absolutist a piece of power-design as you can find.

The Paris cityscape has another, still more sinister aspect: its boulevards and avenues. These arrow-straight

ROOSEVELT'S TRAILER PARKS

During the Depression and World War II, Franklin D. Roosevelt's "New Deal" helped to provide inexpensive trailer homes for America's poor. His supporters say that, in the 1930s, trailers allowed people to seek work wherever it was available, taking their homes along with them, while in the 1940s, they provided a degree of domestic security for soldiers returning from war during a housing shortage. However, Roosevelt's conspiracy-minded critics take a very different view. Trailer homes quickly ceased to be mobile, they note, running aground in ghetto-like trailer parks. These parks were particularly thick on the ground in the Midwest – which is, of course, tornado country. Roosevelt's trailers, then, were part of a nefarious scheme to rid the nation of its underclass by capitalizing on natural disasters.

Curiously, there's actually some evidence that trailers were explicitly designed to protect Americans from having their homes destroyed – albeit by nuclear holocaust, rather than by tornado. Trailer manufacturers claimed that their products would roll with the shock wave of a nuclear blast, rather than disintegrating and crushing their occupants, as would happen with a conventional home. Luckily, this theory has not – to date – been tested.

mega-roads were bulldozed right through the crumbling medieval city in the second half of the nineteenth century by Baron Georges-Eugène Haussmann, architect-in-chief to the dictator Napoléon III. The official justification for this megalomaniac project was to allow the free circulation of air (for purposes of hygiene) and traffic (for purposes of commerce) – and, of course, to create an imperial capital fit for an emperor. But, in his memoirs, Haussmann claimed that there were other, hidden reasons. The demolition of entire neighbourhoods shifted tens of thousands of workers from inner-city slums to the suburbs, where they could cause less trouble. Suspicious Parisians have long speculated that the new roads were also designed to allow troops to move speedily around the city – without having to fight their way from barricade to barricade, as had happened in the 1848 French Revolution. Marshal Bugeaud had used similar techniques of military reconstruction in colonial Algeria, after all. By some accounts, the straight lines of the avenues were explicitly created to facilitate fusillades and cavalry charges; they were, in short, instruments of government oppression.

Masons and architects I: Washington DC

George Washington was, notoriously, a Freemason, and on the occasion of the laying of the Capitol's foundation stone, in 1793, he publicly wore a Masonic apron and used a Mason's silver gavel and trowel – the symbolism could not have been more explicit. That same symbolism pervades the very geography of Washington DC. The first overall architect of the city, Pierre-Charles L'Enfant, was an associate of the Marquis de Lafayette, a French revolutionary and committed Freemason. Although there's no evidence that L'Enfant was a Freemason himself, his design for Washington was certainly informed by the kind of esoteric ideas propagated by the Masonic movement. His successor, Surveyor General Andrew Ellicott, was a Mason, however, and he worked on his plans for Washington with Benjamin Banneker, who was popularly known as the "Sable Astronomer" because of his African-American heritage and his enthusiasm for the stars.

Even ex-neoconservative historian Francis Fukuyama admits that the Masonic influence on the federal capital was "unmistakable". It's not just the prominent presence of a giant Masonic obelisk in honour of George Washington, but that the city's perfectly square layout was overlaid with diagonal avenues to create the Masonic symbols of square and compasses. Endless American websites now display maps and satellite photos of Washington DC, enhanced or marked up to reveal geometric patterns in the street layout – most notably a pentagram with its point at the (phallic) Washington Monument. These interpretations draw on everything from Mason-style pseudo-Egyptian occultism to all-out Satanism to explain the origins of the design. (Erecting a five-sided structure explicitly called "the Pentagon" during World War II was sheer Masonic chutzpah.)

One of the chief propagators of the line that Washington is a vast Masonic template is astrologist and prolific author David Ovason. He is most perturbed (or impressed) by the proliferation of zodiac signs on public buildings. Washington, he believes, is "being prepared for some future time when the stars will be seen as the living mysteries they really are". Prepared, it appears, by the Masons who first built the city and who continue to govern it. He sees the most powerful sign of all as the triangulation of the constellation Virgo created by the Federal Triangle: while federal buildings "were nominally designed to serve vast bureaucracies", he remarks in *The Secret Architecture of Our Nation's Capital*, "they were also quietly dedicated to the ancient goddess."

In their book Talisman: Sacred Cities, Secret Faith, mystical historians Graham Hancock and Robert Bauval speculate that Washington's esoteric symbolism allows it to act as a vast receiver of divine energy, thus enabling humanity to rediscover lost Egyptian wisdom. Others are more troubled by Washington's political symbolism. The stern neoclassicism of the buildings on the Federal

Parisian power-design: the "grand axis" passes through the Arc du Triomphe.

Triangle has been called Stalinist, while the very project of a geometric capital city is, to many, disturbingly authoritarian and centralist – the perfect capital for the New World Order, no less.

Masons and architects II: London

Less than one week after architect and Freemason Christopher Wren submitted plans for a new St Paul's Cathedral in 1666, a huge fire broke out, destroying not just the area around the old church but much of the rest of London besides. The authorities blamed a bakery in Pudding Lane, and London baker Thomas Farriner has carried the can pretty much ever since (though a French Catholic, Robert Hubert, temporarily confessed to being a papal agent and starting the fire, and was hanged at Tyburn in short order, despite recanting).

The Great Fire of London created a spectacular opportunity to rebuild the city in grand classical style. Ambitious plans were submitted to King Charles II. Freemasonry was deeply fashionable at the time, especially in architectural circles, and many of the new proposals drew on Masonic symbolism. This, their draughtsmen hoped, would give their work an elite, intellectual edge. Diarist John Evelyn's plan incorporated square-and-compasses street-geometry, while the designs of architect Christopher Wren – who soon after became grand master of the London Grand Lodge – incorporated a plethora of Masonic and kabbalistic symbols.

Practical difficulties prevented the grander schemes from becoming reality, but a number of impressive new churches were built nonetheless. Most notably, St Paul's Cathedral was reconstructed to Christopher Wren's grand design. Curiously, the cathedral is aligned eight degrees off the customary east-west axis. This strange kink results in it pointing directly towards Temple Church, the former spiritual home of the Knights Templar. Architect Nicholas Hawksmoor was equally bold. His church of St George's Bloomsbury is actually topped by a ziggurat-styled pyramid. For poet and "psychogeographer" Iain Sinclair, this was evidence of Hawksmoor's theistic Satanism – an idea taken up by a succession of writers. In Peter Ackroyd's disturbing novel *Hawksmoor*, the architect's London churches become the setting for a series of Satanic murders, while Eddie Campbell and Alan Moore's graphic novel *From Hell* even throws Victorian murderer Jack the Ripper into the mix. As ever, one conspiracy theory bleeds easily and smoothly into another.

SOURCES

Books

Peter Ackroyd **Hawksmoor** (1985). This colourful literary novel casts architect Nicholas Hawksmoor as a seventeenth-century Satanist bent on implanting Masonic symbolism into his work.

Robert Bauval and Graham Hancock **Talisman: Sacred Cities, Secret Faith** (2004). Traces the grand conspiracy of esoteric city design back from the Masons to the Templars and Cathars and from the Gnostic Christians to the prophet Mani of Babylon – and sees evidence of this everywhere from ancient Alexandria to London.

Scott W. Berg **Grand Avenues: The Story of the French Visionary Who Designed Washington DC** (2007). Serious, well-researched book on Pierre-Charles L'Enfant's role in the design of Washington.

David Ovason **The Secret Architecture of Our Nation's Capital: The Masons and the Building of Washington, DC** (2000). Plenty of good research on architecture and Masonic history, but overlaid by a distinctly wacky astrological angle.

Websites

Ⓦ **www.freemasons-freemasonry.com/christopher_wren_freemasonry.html** Detailed, Freemason-authored paper on Sir Christopher Wren's Masonic meddlings.

Ⓦ **www.geocities.com/area51/cavern/9748/plots7.html** A classic – surely tongue-in-cheek – exposition of the Roosevelt–trailer park theory.

Ⓦ **www.geocities.com/jussaymoe/dc_symbolism/index.htm** Well-resourced site revealing the Masonic plan of Washington – and a second plan, of the Great Pyramid – while denying any conspiracy. Masons, the author says, can simply be expected "to generate designs that feature symbols that are meaningful to them".

Ⓦ **myweb.tiscali.co.uk/zucconi/biscuit/loony/londonquest/londongeometry.htm** Fascinating application of Masonic geometry to London.

Ⓦ **thebiggestsecretpict.online.fr/nwo.htm** One of the many sites showing maps and satellite photos of the patterns in Washington's street layout, plus all kinds of other signs and symbols – all evidence of the hidden hand of the New World Order, which, for some reason, delights in showing itself to those in the know.

Ⓦ **www.theforbiddenknowledge.com/chapter3/** The Luciferic symbolism of Washington DC, luridly explained.

The Illuminati

Groups calling themselves *illuminati*, after the Latin word for "enlightened", have come and gone for centuries. The earliest had loosely Gnostic beliefs: the *alumbrados* of sixteenth-century Spain, for example, believed that the soul could communicate directly with the divine. They quickly fell foul of the Inquisition. In France, various sects have called themselves *illuminés*, including the Martinists, a Christian mystic sect that originated in the eighteenth century and still survives today.

The first group to actually call itself "the Illuminati" was closer to Freemasonry than to Gnosticism. In 1776, a Bavarian university professor, Adam Weishaupt, founded an "Order of Perfectibilists", or Illuminati. They were basically an anti-Jesuit club, with anti-monarchist and egalitarian beliefs mixed up with a Masonic-style culture of esoteric symbolism – in fact, Weishaupt and his colleague Baron von Knigge recruited mostly from Masonic lodges within Baron von Hund's popular Strict Observance rite. At first, with just five members, it seemed there weren't too many Perfectible men in Bavaria, but within ten years the group had grown to a few hundred, mostly in German-speaking Europe.

By the mid-1780s, the activities of the Illuminati and other "secret societies" – for which there was a pan-European fad – had attracted the suspicion of Bavaria's ruler, the Elector Prince Karl-Theodor. Warned by informers that these kinds of groups were stirring up political trouble, Karl-Theodor banned all secret associations in Bavaria in June 1784. In March 1785, he followed up by condemning Freemasonry and the Illuminati by name. Weishaupt fled Bavaria, and the Illuminati were disbanded.

Afterlife: growth of a conspiracy theory

Despite the order's official closure, the reputation of the Illuminati lived on, and even grew, in the burgeoning conspiracy-theory culture of late eighteenth- and early nineteenth-century Europe. The group's alleged reach was most famously exaggerated by the controversial healer, occultist and Freemason "Count" Cagliostro (who inspired the character of the Masonic enchanter Sarastro in Mozart's *The Magic Flute*). After being arrested in Rome in 1789, Cagliostro quickly confessed the "secrets" of the Templars, Masons and other groups to the Inquisition. As extravagant under duress as he was in high-society parties, Cagliostro declared that the Illuminati were plotting to overthrow the Bourbon monarchy and the papacy.

In Europe, conservatives' fears of secret societies were inflamed by the Abbé Barruel's *Mémoires* (see p.85) of 1797, which blamed the Illuminati (along with Freemasonry in general) for the French Revolution. The following year, conspiracy theories in Britain and North America were stoked by John Robison's *Proofs of a Conspiracy* (see p.85), which was as unsparing of the Illuminati as it was of the Masons. Slowly the Illuminati were mythologized as a kind of arch-Masonic group, an elite conspiracy behind a conspiracy. In 1803, a former colleague of Baron von Hund's, Johann August Starck, published his *Triumph der Philosophie im achtzehnten Jahrhundert*, an early mega-conspiracy theory tracing the growth of evil from Greek philosophy through medieval heresy to the Illuminati. (Though Starck selected the more mystically oriented Knigge as the villain of the piece, rather than Weishaupt.)

Despite a complete lack of any proof of the Illuminati's existence, the group continued to be blamed for all manner of conspiracies well into the nineteenth century. Federalists accused Thomas Jefferson of being controlled by European Illuminati (though he wasn't even a Freemason), largely on the grounds that he had expressed sympathy for Weishaupt for living "under the tyranny of despots and priests". In fact, Jefferson had written in a letter to a friend stating that if Weishaupt had lived in America he would have had no need for secrecy.

The Illuminati today

In 1924, the publication of Nesta H. Webster's *Secret Societies and Subversive Movements* catapulted the myth of the Illuminati out of the eighteenth century and right into the twenty-first. Although Webster had merely repeated the stale gossip of post-French Revolutionary Europe, *Secret Societies* became a staple reference work of the twentieth century; over eighty years after its publication, the Illuminati are once again widely tipped as the ultimate conspiracy organization.

Perhaps because of the complete lack of evidence for who the Illuminati actually are, they have simply become whatever conspiracists want them to be. Most common is the thesis that Freemasons are the unwitting dupes of the Illuminati. It's as if conspiracy theorists fire off their anti-Masonic accusations with such force that they overshoot what's actually there. It's not a problem: beyond the Masons lie the Illuminati. Alternatively, the hierarchical system of Freemasonry is offered as proof of the existence of the Illuminati: only when Masons penetrate beyond the 33rd degree, it's alleged, do they learn that the Illuminati are the master architects presiding over the grand plan. Only the most devoted Freemasons get that far, thus safely preserving the secret.

Oddly, ever since conspiracism took off on the Internet, scores of sub-Rotarian private clubs have suddenly appeared, all claiming to descend in an unbroken (but hitherto unaccountably secret) line from Weishaupt's original organization. None is any more credible than similar "Templar" groups.

THE ROSICRUCIANS

In 1614, an anonymous pamphlet was published in Germany with the ambitious title *The Universal and General Reformation of the Whole Wide World*. It announced the existence of a secret Brotherhood of the Rosy Cross – *rosae crucis* in Latin, hence the English "Rosicrucian" – which would set about that bold project. (The name was a nod and a wink to those with a knowledge of alchemical symbolism: the rose signifying female sexuality – or, alternatively, the mystical alchemical *ros* or dew of regeneration – and the cross symbolizing the male organ.) Within two years, further anonymous "manifestos" followed: the *Fama Fraternitatis Rosae Crucis*, the *Confessio Fraternitatis*, and *The Chemical Wedding of Christian Rosenkreutz*. They revealed a mysterious organization that had supposedly been founded in 1407 by a German monk, "Christian Rosenkreutz", who had learned the secrets of Arab science and medicine during his travels around the Mediterranean. On his return to Germany, he founded a secret society of eight members to preserve this knowledge and built a temple named after the Holy Spirit to which all eight would return, in secret, once a year. This "Sanctus Spiritus" was also Rosenkreutz's grave. When it was unsealed, after 120 years, a hidden seven-sided chamber was supposedly revealed, containing books, alchemical instruments and Rosenkreutz's fresh and undecomposed body.

The effect of the "manifestos" on European intellectual circles was something like the impact of Chubby Checker's "The Twist" on early 1960s America: soon everyone was dancing to the new tune. "Occult" sciences such as alchemy were deeply fashionable in the higher echelons of society, especially when polished up with an antique patina. Pamphlets were published answering the Rosicrucian call, challenges were issued and addressed, accusations levelled and denied, and open letters called on the secret society to reveal itself and its secrets – whatever they were. Some scholars actually went off in search of the "Sanctus Spiritus".

Although the clamour spread across Europe – reaching Britain in 1625 or so, if the published record is anything to go by – the Rosicrucians themselves responded with a deafening silence. Perhaps this was because they were a *secret* society, after all. Or perhaps because they were nothing more than a witty invention – a *ludibrium*, or plaything. That, at least, was the word used for the "manifestos" by the man most widely suspected of having written them, the theologian Johann Valentin Andreae, who was born in 1586. As the admirable British historian Frances Yates puts it in *Rosicrucian Enlightenment*: "The right way of looking at the question may thus be to give up the hunt for 'real' Rosicrucians and to ask instead whether the Rosicrucian movement *suggested* the formation of secret societies." (As she also noted: "when, as is often the case, the misty discussion of 'Rosicrucians' and their history becomes involved with the Masonic myth, the enquirer feels as though they are sinking helplessly into a bottomless bog.")

Even if the legend behind the secret brotherhood was a fiction, Rosicrucianism as a scientific and philosophical ideal – promoting learning and spiritual improvement, and challenging ignorance and the abuse of religious authority – was certainly real. Proto-Enlightenment Europe *was* becoming acquainted with Arab scholarship and alchemical science, and even if thinkers and specialists in Hermetic mysteries like Giordano Bruno, John Dee, Philip Sidney, Francis Bacon and Robert Fludd weren't members of a "Rosicrucian brotherhood", it was only for want of the name.

It wasn't long before Rosicrucian societies were being set up for real, the first appearing in Holland in the 1620s. It was scarcely any longer before they were denounced, with pamphlets appearing in Paris in 1623 accusing the "Invisibles" of entering into a pact with the devil. The eighteenth-century re-inventors of Freemasonry (see p.82) added a sprinkling of Rosicrucian terminology and symbolism to give their efforts a high-minded flavour, while in the late nineteenth and early twentieth centuries a number of "Rosicrucian" brotherhoods were set up. Some still exist, many claiming to be authentic inheritors of Rosenkreutz's "original" tradition. Of course, they can't all be right. You could say none of them is, but this doesn't mean they're any less "real" than the Dutch brotherhood of the 1620s. Today, you can try to join any of the Ancient Mystical Order Rosae Crucis (AMORC), the Confraternity of the Rose Cross, the Fraternitas Rosae Crucis, the Societas Rosicruciana and the Rosicrucian Fellowship, to name just a few. Ideals vary from sincere Christian philanthropy to mystifying astrological hocus pocus. Some conspiracy theorists see these organizations as mere shams. The descendants of Rosenkreutz's eight brothers are surely too busy setting about "the Universal and General Reformation of the Whole Wide World" to mess around with frat clubs…

In certain authors' hands, the power of the Illuminati has grown with impressive virulence. On the Web, the Illuminati are blamed for everything from world communism to one-world-government projects. The Illuminati are Satanists, international capitalists, Zionists. They run the CIA, the Vatican, the Freemasons, the Wide Awake Club. They murdered Lincoln, shot JFK and put the phoney "face" on the surface of Mars. For self-styled intelligence insider Milton William Cooper, author of the right-wingers' apocalyptic mega-conspiracy bible, *Behold a Pale Horse* (1991), the Illuminati are the cutting edge of a grand plan to impose an anti-libertarian one-world government. For British arch-conspiracist David Icke, they are just another name for the power-wielding elite behind the New World Order conspiracy, the Bushes, Saddams and Windsors of the world, and are thus a tool and synonym for the sinister, shape-shifting reptilians (see p.116). Curiously, both writers invert the Illuminati's historical reputation as revolutionary and anti-establishment.

The Illuminati are almost as popular in fiction as they are in the half-reality of conspiracy literature. Robert Shea and Robert Anton Wilson's cult *Illuminatus!* trilogy depicts them as a repressive, quasi-fascistic force locked in constant struggle with the chaotic, liberated "Erisians" for domination of the world. Umberto Eco weaves them into his scintillatingly cerebral *Foucault's Pendulum*, while Dan Brown's more lowbrow (and more engagingly plotted) *Angels and Demons* imagines them as a cabal of ultra-scientists pitted against Vatican philistines in a hyper-modern take on the ancient conflict between faith and reason. *Angels and Demons* also gave the world that visually pleasing, reversible calligraphy rendering of the word "Illuminati", which has so boosted the organization's ubiquity on the Web. Every secret society needs a logo, after all, and there's no story without a picture.

The most satisfyingly extravagant anti-Illuminati conspiracy theory belongs to "former MI6 agent" John Coleman. And Coleman says it is no fiction. His Illuminati, aka the "Committee of 300", have a very broad agenda. On a number of websites, Coleman breaks down their "Targets" into 21 bullet points. It begins with the destruction of "national identity and national pride", as well as "the Christian religion", and ends with the establishment of a "New World Order" (see p.141) backed by the IMF, UN and World Court. To achieve this goal, mind control will be used to help achieve drastic population reductions, with the help of "religious cults such as the Moslem Brotherhood, Moslem Fundamentalism and the Sikhs". Meanwhile, "the youth of the land will be encouraged by means of rock music and drugs to rebel against the status quo, thus undermining and eventually destroying the family unit". Devised by the Tavistock Institute, this programme is known as the "Aquarian Conspiracy". This totalitarian agenda culminates in the Illuminati "taking control of education in America with the intent and purpose of utterly and completely destroying it. By 1993, the full force effect of this policy is becoming apparent, and will be even more destructive as primary and secondary schools begin to teach 'Outcome Based Education'". A formidable threat indeed.

SOURCES

Books

Dan Brown Angels and Demons (2000). Middle-octane thriller casting the Illuminati as a bunch of high-tech anti-clericals intent on blowing up the Vatican.

John Coleman Conspirator's Hierarchy: The Committee of 300 (1992). "Can you imagine an all-powerful group, that knows no national boundaries, above the laws of all countries, one that controls every aspect of politics, religion, commerce and industry, banking, insurance, mining, the drug trade, the petroleum industry, a group answerable to no one but its members?" Coleman can.

Milton William Cooper Behold a Pale Horse (1991). Possibly the maddest mega-conspiracy book ever written. Unsummarizable, but as one online reviewer put it, "this Book has made me paranoid and explained all the visions and dreams I have had as far as the battle over Good vs. Evil". In May 2001, Cooper was shot dead by police. He was wanted for assault and had fired first – at least, that's what the police say.

Robert Shea and Robert Anton Wilson Illuminatus! Part 1: The Eye in the Pyramid (1987). *The Hitchhiker's Guide to the Galaxy* meets the world of conspiracy counterculture. A favourite among computer hackers, apparently.

Fritz Springmeier Bloodlines of the Illuminati (2002). In mocking imitation of the Twelve Tribes of Israel, Satan set up his own dozen. And a thirteenth, whose modern-day descendants are still obscenely powerful. The book is filled with all the usual suspects: Kennedy, Rothschild, Onassis, Rockefeller, McDonald, Disney etc. Written by a Christian "patriot" jailed for a bank robbery.

Lindsay Porter Who Are the Illuminati? (2005). Detailed and clear-eyed account of the Illuminati's role in conspiracist history. Scotches the usual theories without losing sight of their importance.

Websites

Ⓦ **100777.com/myron** Audio downloads of the "Myron Fagan tapes", which have long circulated in right-wing groups. Fagan delivers a deeply conspiratorial lecture on the Rothschild-backed Illuminati plot to establish a One World Government through the nefarious Council on Foreign Relations. Describes income tax as a "cancer".

Ⓦ **illuminati-order.com** One of a number of groups claiming to be the original Illuminati. "Some have tried to discredit our authenticity because we are not as secret as we are supposedly required to be. So, let us be clear here and now that we are only as secret as necessary to exist relatively unimpeded." That's solved that one, then.

Ⓦ **www.illuminati-news.com** Click on the Illuminati link and you'll be taken to a page on "Shadow Government". Also features a revolving version of Dan Brown's calligraphic rendition of the word Illuminati!

Blood Libel: the longest-running conspiracy theory of all

Forget about conspiracy theories that a bloodsucking government wants to drain your life away in the form of taxes, the "Blood Libel" or "Blood Accusation" is the real thing: the paranoid belief that Satanists, Protestants, Catholics, witches or – most frequently – Jews are actually out for your blood. Or rather your children's blood, supposedly collected in ritual sacrifices and drunk as wine or blended with other ingredients to make festival cakes.

Lost boys: William of Norwich, Little Hugh, Simon of Trent

Around 40 BC, according to the historian Josephus, the grammarian Apion accused Alexandria's Jewish community of sacrificing a Greek boy every year and eating his entrails. Apion worked the resulting uproar to his own political advantage. Before the Roman Empire adopted Christianity, similar accusations were regularly made by Roman authorities against Christians – who weren't helped by the fact that their principal ritual involved consuming the "body" and "blood" of their founder.

However, the Blood Libel was first infused into the mainstream of European history in Norwich, England, at the Easter festival of 1144, when a tanner's apprentice called William disappeared. His body was never found, but local Jews were accused of torturing, hanging – crucifying by some accounts – and perhaps eating him. Although the sheriff dismissed the claims, mob violence drove the Jews out of town. In 1255, the story reappeared a few miles away, when "Little Hugh" of Lincoln was found dead in a cesspool belonging to a Jew named Jopin. Had he fallen? Or was he, as the crowd insisted, the victim of a ritual crucifixion? After

CONSPIRACY OF FEAR: SATANIC RITUAL ABUSE

A modern twist on the Blood Libel seems to have emanated from an unholy conjunction of the psychiatrist's couch and the fundamentalist's newsletter. In the 1980s, using "recovered memory" techniques, psychotherapists "helped" hundreds of adults to "remember" that they had been sexually abused as children. In many cases, the abuse was blamed on the ritual practices of "Satanists" – whatever they were supposed to be. Some linked belief in devil-worship to paranoid fundamentalist Christians with imaginations stimulated by the old Blood Libel stories. (Others blamed hysterical feminists convinced that just as all men were rapists, so all fathers were abusers.)

Whatever the cause, the most serious consequence of the sudden growth in belief in Satanic Ritual Abuse (SRA) was a spate of so-called Multi-Victim, Multi-Offender (MVMO) cases, most famously the McMartin Pre-School scandal in Manhattan Beach, California. This kicked off in August 1983 when an alcoholic paranoid schizophrenic mother accused a part-time school worker of molesting her son. The DA dropped the case for lack of evidence, but a local police chief wrote to some two hundred parents asking them to question their children. The media quickly took up the hue and cry, as did the (Catholic) American Martyrs Church. Panic spread, and hundreds of children were interviewed using techniques now known to be highly suggestive, including leading and repeated questions. By the spring of 1984, it was declared that 360 children had been abused. Their interviews revealed a story of teachers belonging to a "Satanic Church" who ritually murdered babies and drank their blood. The children were molested on highways, buried in coffins, flushed down toilets and abused in underground networks of secret tunnels.

After six years and $15 million spent on trial costs, the McMartin jury failed to make a single conviction. Perhaps because of the publicity the affair generated, however, MVMO cases spread all over the US and beyond. Childcare professionals gave seminars on SRA and evangelical churches galvanized their members to warn others of the dangers. In the UK, these combined efforts led to almost a thousand cases of organized abuse and eighty-six cases of ritual abuse being brought between 1988 and 1991, including the Cleveland, Rochdale and Orkney scandals. In the last-named affair, children were forcibly removed from their homes in dawn raids. In an official UK government report, completed in 1994, Professor Jean La Fontaine concluded that Christians in opposition to new religious movements had been "a powerful influence encouraging the identification of Satanic abuse".

From the early 1990s, the interviewing techniques that led to MVMO cases began to be discredited. False Memory became the new buzzword in psychological circles. Yet some still saw conspiracies of Satanic abusers at large. Elizabeth Loftus, author of the 1996 book *The Myth of Repressed Memory*, was told that her work was "on the same level as those who deny the existence of the extermination camps during World War II". And as late as 2003, a group of New Agers on the predominantly Free Church (Christian fundamentalist) island of Lewis, off the west coast of Scotland, were accused of SRA – including blood-drinking, orgies with children and animal sacrifice. By July 2004, however, all the charges had been dropped.

One of the accused, a self-styled white witch or pagan, described the experience as "like a seventeenth-century witch-hunt", inevitably inviting comparisons with the late Arthur Miller's play *The Crucible*, itself a dramatic response to the madness of McCarthyism (see p.368). The message is clear: whether the finger is pointed at witches or Jews, Communists or suspected child-abusers, some conspiracy theories can all too easily tip over into collective hysteria.

confessing under torture, 81 Jews were arrested; 18 were hanged.

The Blood Libel flowed all too easily into the well of Christians' darkest fears about Jews: were they not responsible for the crucifixion of Jesus? (Never mind that it was the Romans, that Jesus was a Jew himself and that without the cross Christianity would be just another Jewish cult…) The story spread across Europe like an epidemic. In 1267, fishermen found a seven-year-old girl's body washed up near Baden. Miracles such as blood flowing fresh from the wounds "proved" the Jews were responsible. Similar cases soon surfaced all over Germany and beyond. In 1475, the Blood Libel was officially endorsed, after a boy from Trent called Simon disappeared during Holy Week. Again, the

Jews were accused of kidnapping the child, crucifying him to express their implacable enmity towards all Christians, then butchering him and collecting his blood. Again, confessions were extracted under torture. Such was the outcry that a papal enquiry was eventually set up. It concluded that Simon had been killed following "rabbinical law" to celebrate Passover with blood-leavened breads – ignoring the fact that he disappeared on the day *after* the feast. Simon was soon canonized as a martyr by Pope Sixtus V (and only de-canonized in 1965).

In late fifteenth-century Hungary, Jewish men were driven to confess, after torture, that the Blood Libel was true. And why? Because, they revealed, male Jews menstruate like women and, therefore, need to replenish their blood supply. (Oddly, Christian women seem to get by without regular infusions.) According to the sixteenth-century Jesuit writer Gottfried Henschen, Jewish men actually menstruated through their penises, and the only cure for their cramps was the consumption of Christian blood. Seventeenth-century pogroms (anti-Jewish riots) in Poland were inspired by the Blood Libel to such an extent that one Rabbi Siegel ruled that the wine used at ceremonial Passover meals – traditionally red – should be changed to white, so as not to provoke neighbours who had heard about the Blood Libel.

The Blood Libel in the Middle East

The "Damascus Affair" of 1840 saw the arrival of the Blood Libel in the Middle East, after a Capuchin monk named Father Thomas disappeared in the city. The French consul, Ratti Menton, made the old accusation, backed up by the British and American consuls. Jews were rounded up and imprisoned, but eventually released (apart from four who died) after the pasha of Egypt made an official declaration that the ritual murder claim was a nonsense.

One hundred and fifty years later, in March 1991, the accusation broke out again, when a Syrian UN Human Rights Commission delegate recommended that members should read *The Matzah of Zion*, a book published in 1983 by the Syrian statesman and onetime defence minister Field Marshal Mustafa Tlass. The cover showed a man whose throat had been cut (with a menorah, the traditional Jewish candelabrum, in the 1986 edition), and whose blood is being collected in a basin. The book describes the Damascus Affair and presents the Blood Libel as accurate – Father Thomas's blood having apparently been used in the preparation of Jewish *matzah* bread. As the introduction puts it (according to a translation published on the website of the pro-Israeli Middle East Media Research Institute), "Damascus was shocked by this loathsome crime ... now every mother warns: 'Be careful not to stray far from home unless the Jew comes, puts you in his sack, takes you, slaughters you and drains your blood in order to prepare the *matzah* of Zion.' "

In March 2002, a storm erupted after Umayma al-Jalahma, a teacher at King Faisal University in Al-Dammam, Saudi Arabia, published an article in the Saudi Arabian daily *Al-Riyadh*. Describing "The Jewish Holiday of Purim", it claimed that "Jewish people must obtain human blood so that their clerics can prepare the holiday pastries ... [The victim's] blood is taken and dried into granules. The cleric blends these granules into the pastry dough; they can also be saved for the next holiday." On return from a visit to the Lebanon, the editor commented that the article had "slipped through the cracks". The Blood Libel even crops up on television: in 2003 the TV series *Al-Shatat* on the Lebanese Al-Manar satellite channel notoriously included an episode in which a "rabbi" character cuts the throat of a Christian child and collects his blood in a basin. In the next scene the rabbi offers a Jewish man a *matzah* that is "tastier and holier because it was kneaded with pure blood".

Fighting back

That the Middle East Media Research Institute (MEMRI) translated and published on the Internet parts of Mustafa Tlass's book is typical of the efforts of a number of websites keen to expose the truth about Arab anti-Semitism (as they'd put it), or to slander their enemies (as their opponents would counter). MEMRI rightly points out that few Arab media sources are translated into English – unfortunately, this makes it hard for non-Arabic speakers to check the original sources. Sites ranging from the moderate Arab-Israeli www.mideastweb.org to the influential Anti-Defamation League and the conspiratorial www.trackingthethreat.com all spotlight anti-Semitic slanders emanating from the Middle East.

Some conspiracists have seized on an unfortunate parallel with conspiracy theory websites, in that the same allegations crop up again and again. Reports of what this or that Palestinian Authority figure may or may not have said, for instance, get cut and pasted so many times that it's sometimes alleged that these are not genuine reports of modern manifestations of the Blood Libel, but a conspiracy in themselves – a Zionist conspiracy to convince the world that Arabs are dangerous conspiracists and potential *génocidaires*. But then this kind of thinking is disturbingly close to the anti-Semitic fable of the all-powerful "Jewish lobby". There's undoubtedly a powerful moral imperative to expose these myths. The precedents of eastern European pogroms and, of course, the Holocaust (see p.101) are always close to mind, as the Blood Libel has always been an undercurrent of the most dangerous anti-Semitic rhetoric. The Nazi mouthpiece, *Der Stürmer*, for instance, was full of references to it.

While the Blood Libel itself is fairly unusual outside conspiratorial circles, its subtler manifestations are disturbingly common. Arab newspaper cartoons, for instance, may show caricatures of Israeli politicians stalking through the ruins of Palestine, their hands dripping with blood, while liberal attacks on Israel's interventions in the West Bank often focus on the deaths of Palestinian children or teenagers. You could see these as fair – if robust – attacks on Israel's policies. You could also see them as sinister takes on the old Blood Libel – Israel is, after all, a Jewish state. A libel case in 1985 became a landmark in US law, when then-General Ariel Sharon sued *Time* magazine after a cover story in February 1983 accused him of conspiracy in the massacres at the Sabra and Shatila camps, conducted by Christian Phalange militia during the Lebanese Civil War. The case was widely reported as a "blood libel". (For the record, the court found the *Time* article to be false, and the product of "negligent and reckless" reporting. It wasn't, however, malicious – and therefore wasn't libel.)

The Blood Libel today

Over two thousand years after Apion's Alexandrian accusations, the old wound is still bleeding. On January 25, 2005, twenty members of the Russian parliament from the Motherland and Communist parties signed a declaration demanding that Jewish organizations be banned throughout Russia on the grounds of their hostility to the Russian people and their practice of ritual child murder. Somehow it's not surprising that they also bemoaned the fact that "the whole democratic world is today under the financial and political control of international Jewry" – a reference to the hoary "Elders of Zion" myth (see p.109).

And the accusations have spread beyond Judaism. In 1996, evangelical Christians persuaded Senator Jesse Helms of the House Foreign Relations Committee to investigate stories that Chinese people eat aborted fetuses for their medicinal benefits. And pro-life groups frequently equate abortion with the Holocaust, characterizing feminists and other campaigners for women's rights as bloodthirsty servants of evil – terms disturbingly reminiscent of the Blood Libel.

SOURCES

Books

Alan Dundes The Blood Libel Legend: A Casebook in Anti-Semitic Folklore (1991). This collection of academic essays is one of the few serious studies of the phenomenon.

Ronald Florence Blood Libel: The Damascus Affair of 1840 (2004). Pacy and fascinating account of the Damascus Blood Libel. For a really detailed and scholarly version, go for Jonathan Frankel's 1997 doorstopper, *The Damascus Affair.*

Debbie Nathan and Michael Snedeker Satan's Silence: Ritual Abuse and the Making of a Modern American Witch Hunt (2001). Wise and considered telling of the story of Satanic Ritual Abuse scares, advocating more rights for children.

Marvin Perry and Frederick Schweitzer Anti-Semitism: Myth and Hate From Antiquity to the Present (2002). Fascinating, scholarly survey of the history and origins of anti-Semitism, ranging from the myths of the Blood Libel and *The Protocols of the Elders of Zion*, to modern-day Holocaust denial and the attitudes of the Nation of Islam.

Websites

www.adl.org/css/mix_blood_libel.asp The 1986 cover of Mustafa Tlass's *Matzah of Zion* book – just one of the blood-libelling, anti-Semitic cartoons archived at the Anti-Defamation League's site.

www.churchoftrueisrael.com/streicher/jrm/ The full text of *Jewish Ritual Murder*, an extraordinary, hate-filled book-length justification of the Blood Libel, published in London in 1938. The author, former jailbird Arnold Leese, believed he was "killing a rat with a stick". The "pro-white" (and deeply anti-Semitic) site includes lots of other "classic" racist texts.

www.memri.org "Bridging the Language Gap Between the Middle East and the West" – albeit with an agenda to show the West how anti-Semitic the Arab Middle East is. Click on "videos" to see the blood-libelling episode of *Al-Shatat*, among other clips.

www.thewatcherfiles.com/jewish_sacrifice.htm Headlines such as "Jewish Murder Plan Against White Christians Exposed" give an idea of the flavour of this long screed, written by Willie Martin with endless pseudo-historic citations of the Blood Libel. From one of Sherry "Soldier in the Army of God" Shriner's hysterical conspiracy websites.

Holocaust denial

Denying that the Holocaust ever happened is a conspiracy theory because it requires you to believe not only that all the survivors of the death camps were lying, but that they were complicit in an intricate conspiracy to agree on a story – a conspiracy that somehow embraced the scores of Nazis who admitted involvement in the death camps at the Nuremberg trials after the war. Typically, the idea that such a conspiracy exists neatly confirms Holocaust deniers' darkest and oldest fears about Jewish people – the very fears that Hitler fuelled as he marched to power.

The Holocaust: some facts

The Nazis' genocidal attempt between 1941 and 1945 to eliminate European Jewry – along with the Roma (gypsies), gay men, Jehovah's Witnesses, Communist leaders, dissenters and the physically and mentally disabled – is usually called the Holocaust. In practice, the sheer numbers of Jews killed – six million is the conventionally accepted figure – means that the term is often used solely for the Jewish Holocaust, or what the Nazis called the *Endlösung der Judenfrage*, the "final solution of the Jewish question". The phrase is known from the infamous Wannsee conference of January 20, 1942, where German leaders promised Reinhard Heydrich, deputy to SS chief Heinrich Himmler, that they would help set up – and supply – seven new *Vernichtungslager*, or extermination camps: Auschwitz-Birkenau, Belzec, Chelmno, Majdanek, Maly Trostenets, Sobibór and Treblinka II.

The origins of the "Final Solution" date back to the mid-1930s, with the increasing persecution of Jews and their incarceration in ghettos. Mass killings began even before Wannsee, as the ruthless *Einsatzgruppen* execution squads followed the German army's advance into Soviet territory from June 1941. Secret meetings between Himmler, Heydrich and Adolf Eichmann, the SS officer in charge of the Gestapo's Jewish Office, are known to have taken place in mid-October 1941. Around that time, Himmler banned all Jewish emigration, the first gas chambers were built

ANNE FRANK: TEENAGER OR FACE OF AN INTERNATIONAL CONSPIRACY?

Anne Frank: The Diary of a Young Girl was written by a Jewish girl who remained hidden in a secret annex of an Amsterdam house between 1942 and 1944. She died of typhus in Bergen-Belsen in March 1945, a month before the camp was liberated. After the war, her manuscript was published by her father, Otto Frank, the sole family member to survive the death camps.

Although some 31 million copies have now been sold, some Holocaust deniers allege that Otto Frank was selling a scam, a forgery designed to provide a convenient focus for public sympathies and to help publicize the "myth" of the Holocaust. These allegations have been tested in the courts a number of times, first in Lübeck in 1959 – where the German court ruled, after tests, that the diary was genuine and the claim was withdrawn. A flush of cases came to a head in the late 1970s: a certain Werner Kuhnt wrote in a far-right monthly that the diary was a fraud; a pamphlet by one Erwin Schönborn said it was "the product of Jewish anti-German atrocity-propaganda to support the lie of six million gassed Jews and to finance the State of Israel"; and one Ernst Römer was prosecuted for giving out the pamphlet *Best-Seller – ein Schwindel* outside a theatre showing a dramatic version of the diary. The courts allowed the first two cases to pass, on the basis of free speech, but the third went ahead. As part of the investigation, the Bundeskriminalamt (BKA), or German Criminal Court Laboratory, examined the diary manuscripts and commented in their four-page report that all the materials were of genuine wartime origin, except for some "later corrections made on loose-leaf pages written in black, green and blue ballpoint pen".

There were no ballpoint pens in Amsterdam in 1945, a fact that didn't escape an article in *Der Spiegel,* the leading German weekly. Troubled by a growing public furore, the Dutch government commissioned a detailed report from the Gerechtelijk Laboratorium (State Forensic Science Laboratory) in 1980. It ran to 250 pages and concluded that the diaries were certainly written by one person using paper and ink that dated exclusively from the early 1940s. The ballpoint pen additions were indeed later changes – added to help keep the pages in the right order.

In 1989, the *Revised Critical Edition* of *Anne Frank: The Diary of a Young Girl* was published, revealing the original unedited version along with Anne Frank's own edit, which she'd completed in 1944 as part of her efforts to write an autobiographical novel she called *Het Achterhuis* (*The Secret Annex*). The new edition also revealed that Anne's father had made some cuts, but mostly just short passages where Anne criticized her mother or made sexually suggestive or crude remarks. Of course, this hasn't stopped Holocaust deniers using this as "evidence" that the diary is a forgery.

at Belzec and Chelmno, and the first experiments with Zyklon B gas were conducted at Auschwitz-Birkenau.

Jews and Hebrew speakers today often talk about the Shoah, or "calamity". Around sixty percent of all Europe's Jews were killed, a third of the entire Jewish population of the world. In all, somewhere between 12 and 26 million people died as a result of Nazi persecution, including many millions of non-Jewish Slavs and Poles.

Conspiracy theorists in denial

A small, vocal minority dispute these facts. For them, the "history" of the Holocaust is a gigantic conspiracy to present the Jews as victims and to blacken the reputation of the Nazis. Ever since French Nazi-sympathizer Paul Rassinier began claiming in the late 1940s that the figures for the dead were grossly exaggerated, these "revisionists", as they call themselves, have presented their arguments as a contribution to the real historical debate about the exact number of Jewish deaths. Opponents, however, call them Holocaust deniers, claiming that their arguments spring not from fresh examination of the evidence, like genuine revisionist historians, but from blind, poisonous prejudice.

When "revisionist" publications are laden with anti-Semitic language, it's easy to draw that conclusion. Increasingly, however, Holocaust deniers present themselves more subtly, as champions of freedom of speech, as underdogs challenging the established, entrenched hierarchy, as seekers of truth against a conspiracy of dogma or silence, even as anti-corporate warriors against a bloated "Holocaust industry". Their enemies are legion: the Allied military men who "staged" war-film footage of "death camps"; the post-war governments intent on demonizing Germany in order to boost their own power-share in Europe; the Zionist factions bent on justifying and sustaining the creation of a Jewish homeland in the Middle East; the European Jews eager to reap spectacular profits in reparations; and the campuses filled with academics anxious to protect their profitable Holocaust-industry careers.

Most of all, Holocaust deniers blame the sheer malevolence of Jewish people. As Harold Covington, leader of America's National Socialist White People's Party, wrote to supporters in July 1996: "Take away the Holocaust and what do you have left? Without their precious Holocaust, what are the Jews? Just a grubby little bunch of international bandits and assassins and squatters who have perpetrated the most massive, cynical fraud in human history."

Zionist conspiracy?

Some on the Left point to the disparity between the amount of time and money spent on remembrance of Jewish deaths – through museums, newspaper articles, television programmes and so on – as opposed to the relatively unpublicized murders of Roma people, gays and people with disabilities. This is seen as evidence of a Jewish or Zionist conspiracy to infiltrate the media and promote their own cause at the expense of others. Such thinking is particularly common in the Middle East, fuelled perhaps by resentment or hatred of Israel. As Palestinian Authority newspaper *Al-Hayat Al-Jadeeda* put it on July 2, 1998: "The persecution of the Jews is a deceitful myth which the Jews have labelled the Holocaust and exploited to get sympathy."

Or as French philosopher Roger Garaudy has argued, Israel uses "the myth of the six million to build its state and justify attacks on Palestinians". A former Communist who converted to Islam late in life, Garaudy was lionized by the Egyptian press when he toured the country in November 1996. In January 1998, however, he was tried for breaking the French law against Holocaust denial, and specifically for "complicity in the questioning of crimes against humanity", in his book *The Founding Myths of Israeli Politics*. Despite the help of volunteer lawyers from Egypt and the Lebanon, and Garaudy's own claim that "My adversaries confuse Judaism, which is a religion that I respect, and Zionism, which is a policy that I fight", he was fined 240,000 francs – roughly $40,000 at the time.

Hot air and gas chambers

In the aftermath of World War II, Allied troops recovered letters, lists, reports, orders, photographs, films and blueprints detailing exactly how the Holocaust was arranged. All forgeries, say the deniers. The Allies also discovered trucks, chambers and mass graves packed with emaciated, sometimes tortured bodies – the result of typhus or cholera epidemics, according to the deniers.

Following the line of French literary professor and leading Holocaust denier, Robert Faurisson, it's claimed that the Nazis were technically incapable of mass murder on such a huge scale. Cleverly, this approach chimes with the sense of appalled disbelief that anyone studying the Holocaust encounters. In a book with a foreword by Noam Chomsky (defending the right to free speech), Faurisson claimed Zyklon B was used only for delousing detainees.

"Evidence" was provided, much later, by the infamous, self-published *Leuchter Report*, a 1988 tract by layman Fred A. Leuchter, who tested the Auschwitz gas chambers for cyanide and found no significant residues. (With no forensic training – unless you count his job as a builder of execution apparatus in the US – and after an interval of almost fifty years, it would be surprising if he had.) Similarly, a photograph circulates on the Internet showing a "flimsy" door on a gas chamber: in fact, this photo shows a chamber that *was* used for delousing. Most damningly, a former associate of Faurisson's, Jean-Claude Pressac, turned against his own theories after undertaking one of the most detailed studies ever published, the massive *Auschwitz: Technique and Operation of the Gas Chambers* (1989). The "shower rooms", Pressac pointed out, had gas-tight doors and lacked water connections.

Hitler's orders

One favourite tactic of Holocaust deniers is to allege that there is no proof that Hitler ordered the genocide. (Evidently, Zionist conspirators managed to forge a mountain of evidence besmirching other Nazi leaders but somehow forgot to implicate the Führer.) Like the exact figures of the dead, this claim is cleverly passed off as a contribution to a genuine historical debate: which Nazis decided what, and when? While there's no signed and dated order saying "kill all the Jews", there's no doubt that Hitler was involved in planning the genocide. As early as January 30, 1939, he was telling the Reichstag: "If international Jewish financiers inside and outside Europe again succeed in plunging the nations into a world war, the result will not be the Bolshevization of the earth and with it the victory of Jewry, but the annihilation of the Jewish race in Europe." Empty rhetoric, deniers say. Empty? Really? Coming from the man who *started* a world war by invading half of Europe later that year?

Once the war was fully underway, Hitler's intentions became increasingly clear. The head of the Gestapo's Jewish Office, Adolf Eichmann, wrote in his memoirs that, in July 1941, SS intelligence chief Reinhard Heydrich had told him that Hitler ordered the "physical destruction" of the Jews. Himmler recorded a meeting with Hitler on December 10, 1942, in which they discussed the "6–700,000" Jews in France; next to the item on the agenda is a tick, and Himmler's note "*abschaffen*" ("get rid of"). At the first Klessheim conference of April 17 and 18, 1943, Ribbentrop stated in Hitler's presence that the Polish Jews "must either be exterminated or brought to concentration camps". Hitler commented: "They should be treated like the tubercular bacillus … even innocent creatures of nature like hares and deer must be killed so that they cannot damage others."

The counter-evidence is flimsy, to say the least. Leading Holocaust denier David Irving has claimed that a note of a telephone call between Himmler and Hitler on November 30, 1941, for instance, states there will be "no liquidation" of the Jews. In fact, the note says "Jewish transport from Berlin. No liquidation." This clearly refers to a specific case, and – taken out of context – is ambiguous to say the least. (It is an order? A statement of fact? A reprimand?) As for Eichmann's "physical destruction" note, Irving comments that "you've only got to change one or two words and you get a completely different meaning". Which words? "Physical destruction", perhaps?

Whether or not Hitler was the driving force behind the genocide, and when exactly it became Nazi policy, it was certainly ordered. In October 1943, SS chief Heinrich Himmler gave a speech to senior Nazis, saying: "I regard myself as having no right to exterminate the men – in other words, to kill them or have them killed – and to let the avengers in the form of the children grow up for our sons and grandsons to deal with. The difficult decision had to be taken to make these people disappear from the earth." But then, according to David Irving, "Hitler couldn't be bothered with much that Himmler was up to. I think there was a certain lack of affinity between the two."

David Irving: anti-Semite

The front man for Holocaust denial is the bestselling British writer David Irving. In his own words: "People say to me, 'Mr Irving, do you believe in the Holocaust?' I say that I mistrust words with a capital letter. They look like a trademark, don't they?" In 1993, his work was targeted in historian Deborah Lipstadt's seminal book *Denying the Holocaust*. In response, Irving sued her and her publisher, Penguin, for accusing him of "distorting evidence and manipulating documents to serve his own purposes", and calling him "right-wing" and "an ardent admirer of the Nazi leader".

Cambridge historian Richard Evans was hired to defend Lipstadt's case, and after two years of detailed research into Irving's work he reported that Irving had indeed used documents he knew to be forgeries or inadequate material – such as the Leuchter Report – as sources. Judge Charles Gray firmly decided in favour of Lipstadt and Penguin (and Evans), declaring that comments made by Irving such as "Jews are amongst the scum of humanity" and "Jews scurry and hide furtively, unable to stand the light of day" make it "undeniable" that Irving is anti-Semitic. He concluded that "Irving has for his own ideological reasons persistently and deliberately misrepresented and manipulated historical evidence; that for the same reasons he has portrayed Hitler in an unwarrantedly favourable light, principally in relation to his attitude towards and responsibility for the treatment of the Jews; that he is an active Holocaust denier; that he is anti-Semitic and racist and that he associates with right-wing extremists who promote neo-Nazism."

Some of the thousands of gold wedding rings taken from Holocaust victims at Nazi concentration camps during World War II.

More deniers in the dock: Zündel and the IHR

In North America, legal squabbles have focused on Ernst Zündel. Until 1985, when he was sent to prison by an Ontario court for "disseminating and publishing material denying the Holocaust", Zündel ran a small Canadian publishing house producing pamphlets such as *Did Six Million Really Die?* His conviction was overturned by Canada's Supreme Court in 1992 on the grounds that the "false news" law was unconstitutional – thus allowing Zündel to parade himself as the champion of free speech against a repressive, conspiratorial government. In January 2002, Canada's Human Rights Tribunal decided that his website contravened the Human Rights Act, and ordered him to shut it down. Sympathetic websites now push his beliefs and his status as a victim of oppression, declaring that they are "fighting the New World Order" (see p.141). One such site, the Zundelsite, features a stirring cartoon of the eagle of Truth swooping down on the dragon of the "Holocaust Lie".

Online, the loudest mouthpiece of Holocaust denial is the Institute for Historical Review, founded in 1978 by Willis Carto (dubbed "America's leading anti-Semite" by detractors) and British National Party founder Dave McCalden, aka Lewis Brandon. David Irving has been a key contributor. In 1979, the IHR offered a $50,000 reward to anyone who could prove that Jews were gassed at Auschwitz. A year later, one Mel Mermelstein, Auschwitz survivor number A-4684, submitted affidavits detailing the deaths of his mother, father, brother and two sisters. When the IHR refused to pay, Mermelstein sued them. Both sides agreed to settle for a summary judgement, in which the court forced the IHR to apologize formally and pay Mermelstein the $50,000, plus a further $40,000 for causing emotional distress.

The Iranian controversy

In December 2005, a fresh Holocaust controversy burst into the world's media. In a speech published on Iranian state television's website – and swiftly republished as news headlines all over the world – President Mahmoud Ahmadinejad declared that the West had "invented a myth that Jews were massacred". This myth, he pontificated, was considered to be "more significant than God, religion and the prophets". In an interview with the German magazine *Der Spiegel*, Ahmadinejad was slightly more nuanced. "We oppose every type of crime against any people", he said. "But we want to know whether this crime actually took place or not … Why isn't research into a deed that occurred sixty years ago permitted?" He added, "I will only accept something as truth if I am actually convinced of it."

In order to debate whether or not the Holocaust had actually happened – and, not incidentally, to demonstrate to the world Iran's independence of mind and freedom of thought – a conference was convened in Tehran a year later. Unfortunately, the attendees were not leading historians of the Nazi era, but specialist Holocaust deniers such as Robert Faurisson and Fredrick Töben, alongside experts like David Duke, former oil engineer and Grand Wizard of the Knights of the Ku Klux Klan. Among the few supporting the view that the Holocaust had, in fact, taken place were representatives of the Hasidic Jewish sect Neturei Karta, a fierce opponent of Zionism.

Western pundits lined up to criticize the conspiracist strain in Middle East politics. President Ahmadinejad's comments were wielded as evidence that he was a wild-eyed paranoiac who shouldn't be trusted with a popgun let alone a powerful nation. As a spokesman for the Israeli Foreign Ministry put it, "The combination of a regime with a radical agenda, together with a distorted sense of reality that is clearly indicated by the statements we heard today, put together with nuclear weapons – I think that's a dangerous combination that no one in the international community can accept."

A counter-conspiracy arose just as swiftly. Politicians utter rabble-rousing stupidities all the time, they pointed out. Why was this particular example suddenly in the headlines? Was it anything to do with the US ratcheting up pressure on Ahmadinejad? Was the US leveraging this issue simply to muster international support for its campaign to deprive Iran of nuclear power? Was this the first step on the long road to another Middle Eastern invasion? Ahmadinejad – a far more sophisticated political operator than is usually portrayed – had his own conspiracist view of the situation. He asked *Der Spiegel*, "How long do you think the world can be governed by the rhetoric of a handful of Western powers? Whenever they hold something against someone, they start spreading propaganda and lies, defamation and blackmail. How much longer can that go on?"

Perhaps the last word should go to Javad Zarif, Iran's representative at the UN. In February 2007, he commented drily that "the Genocide of the Jews did happen. And it should not happen again."

The upshot

Historians will continue to debate the precise scale of the killings, the exact workings of the death camps and the division of responsibility among the Nazi leadership, the German population in general and European churches and governments. But Holocaust denial itself is entirely discredited. In Israel, Switzerland and seven European Union countries, including France and Germany, claiming that the Holocaust never happened is actually illegal.

Holocaust denial uses techniques familiar to anyone interested in conspiracy theories, in which evidence is used piecemeal to buttress a case whose merits were decided far in advance. The effect is similar too: whether or not there's any substance to the theories, the fact that they're "out there" in the media leaves non-experts wondering if there's some truth to them. It allows cynical politicians like the French nationalist leader Jean-Marie Le Pen to claim that the Holocaust is "a detail in the history of the Second World War" (though he was fined 1.2 million francs for doing so), and creates statistics such as the one that surfaced in Italy's *Corriere della Sera* in January 2005 – that twelve percent of Italians believe the Holocaust never happened. This leaves commentators with an ethical problem: does refuting Holocaust deniers only give them airtime they don't deserve? In this guide, for instance, should we even have mentioned the "Anne Frank fraud" theory, even if only to say it's not true? Once established, it's hard to make these kinds of myths go away.

OTHER GENOCIDES, OTHER DENIALS

The Jewish Holocaust is not the only denied genocide. Far from it. In the Srebrenica genocide, some 40,000 Bosniaks (Bosnian Muslims) living in the UN-declared "safe area" of Srebrenica were targeted for elimination by Bosnian Serb forces. Over 8000 were murdered. Many Serb extremists deny such a "genocide" even happened – which would seem to be a fairly straightforward case of perpetrators trying to downplay their culpability. In practice, the pattern of denial takes many forms. Some Serb nationalists simply downgrade the numbers of Bosniak dead, others deny that any women or children were harmed, or claim that those killed were all arms-bearing soldiers or paramilitaries. (While most of the dead were men of military age, by no means all were.) It's often alleged that the Bosniaks provoked the assault by carrying out attacks outside of Srebrenica, and some nationalists counterclaim that the Croats and Bosnians had previously perpetrated their own atrocities against Serbs – as if to suggest that the atrocities at Srebrenica were somehow deserved. Others blame the massacre on fringe groups, unwilling to accept evidence that leaders of the Bosnian Serb Republic were intimately involved in the planning. In almost all cases, the international community is cast as the sinister power behind a conspiracy to blacken the Serb name and to impose punitive retribution on the long-suffering Serb people.

In 2004, under heavy international pressure, the Bosnian Serb government finally admitted responsibility for the Srebrenica massacre and issued an official apology. The process of acceptance is taking far longer in the case of the Armenian genocide. Indeed, denial of the Armenian genocide still comes with official backing. Between 1915 and 1923, the Ottoman Empire under the government of the "Young Turks" conducted a systematic policy of deportation, expropriation and execution directed at its Armenian population. Mass starvation was combined with wholesale killings, a programme now thought to have caused the deaths of some 1.5 million people. Today, the modern Turkish government denies the Armenian genocide ever took place. In October 2007, the US Congress put pressure on Turkey by passing a resolution condemning the Armenian genocide. For Congress to make such a controversial move at a time when relations with Turkey were already strained by the Kurdish issue certainly raised eyebrows. A strangely powerful "Armenian lobby" was blamed for leveraging politicians' instinctive alignment with Christian Armenians and against Muslim Turks. As ever, the existence – or power – of any such lobby was hotly denied. For more, see www.armenian-genocide.org.

Many historians believe that they should maintain a noble silence, just as many evolutionary biologists refuse to share platforms with Creationists on the grounds that it would give their opponents a legitimacy they don't deserve. Deborah Lipstadt, however, believes the "lunatic fringe" must be vigorously challenged: "We must function as canaries in the mine once did, to guard against the spread of noxious fumes. We must vigilantly stand watch against an increasingly nimble enemy. But unlike the canary, we must not sit silently by waiting to expire so that others will be warned of the danger." In *Warrant for Genocide*, Norman Cohn warns of the dangers of some conspiracy theories. "There exists a subterranean world where pathological fantasies disguised as ideas are churned out by crooks and half-educated fanatics for the benefit of the ignorant and superstitious", he observes, adding "it occasionally happens that the underworld becomes a political power and changes the course of history."

SOURCES

Books

Christopher R. Browning The Origins of the Final Solution (2004). Still in any doubt that the Nazis planned it? These 615 pages trace the decision in painstaking detail from initial idea to implementation.

Arthur R. Butz The Hoax of the Twentieth Century: The Case Against the Presumed Extermination of European Jewry (1992). Quasi-textbook for Holocaust revisionists, which caused a huge uproar in 1977. Its author, a professor – of electrical engineering – at Northwestern University, is now associated with the IHR.

Richard J. Evans Lying About Hitler: History, Holocaust, and the David Irving Trial (2002). Evans is an excellent English writer on Holocaust denial, and was a key witness in the David Irving trial.

Norman G. Finkelstein The Holocaust Industry: Reflections on the Exploitation of Jewish Suffering (2003). Widely vilified as a Holocaust denier, (Jewish) academic Finkelstein is no such thing. He is, however, a vocal campaigner against what he calls the exploitation of the Holocaust for financial gain, through compensation cases etc.

Daniel Jonah Goldhagen Hitler's Willing Executioners: Ordinary Germans and the Holocaust (1997). Deeply controversial naming of names, a nightmarish account of the Holocaust from the side of the perpetrators.

Raul Hilberg The Destruction of the European Jews (1985). The first and most influential historical account of the Holocaust, with detailed sources.

David Irving Hitler's War (1990). Hard to find these days, except in second-hand shops, though even the judge in the Lipstadt trial agreed Irving was a fine military historian. Details the war from Hitler's point of view – from which he apparently couldn't see the plan for genocide.

Deborah Lipstadt Denying the Holocaust: The Growing Assault on Truth and Memory (1994). Written by a professor at Emory University, *Denying the Holocaust* sparked the David Irving trial. Offers a passionate overview of the recent debates, and anatomizes who supports Holocaust denial, and why.

Peter Novick The Holocaust and Collective Memory (2001). A fascinating angle on the context and the afterlife of the Holocaust, protesting against the way the scale of the Jewish genocide has masked the killings of other groups, such as gays and the mentally ill.

Michael Shermer, Alex Grobman and Arthur Hertzberg Denying History: Who Says the Holocaust Never Happened and Why Do They Say It? (2002). Historians' examination not only of the evidence for the Holocaust, but also of how "counter-evidence" has been manipulated by Holocaust deniers.

Films

Jon Blair Anne Frank Remembered (1995) From the director behind the original documentary that inspired Schindler's List. Narrated by Kenneth Branagh and Glenn Close, with powerful interviews – one with Anne's father – and even some film footage of Anne herself.

Channel 4 The Holocaust on Trial (2000). Stirring courtroom drama-documentary re-enacting British historian David Irving's libel trial against American academic Deborah Lipstadt. Includes interviews with Holocaust experts.

Claude Lanzmann Shoah (1985). "The most comprehensive account of the Holocaust available on film." Haunting, painstaking, shattering nine-hour documentary using interviews with survivors, perpetrators, bystanders and historians, plus film of extermination sites today rather than archive footage.

Frank Pierson Conspiracy (2001). Chilling and paralysingly gripping reconstruction of the Wannsee Conference, at which the Final Solution was planned. Kenneth Branagh gives the performance of a lifetime as Reinhard Heydrich.

Joseph Sargent Never Forget (1991). Straight-to-video dramatization of the Mel Mermelstein / IHR case, starring Leonard Nimoy.

Websites

Ⓦ **alt.revisionism** The main Usenet newsgroup devoted to debate – often impassioned – on Holocaust denial.

Ⓦ **www.annefrank.org** Homepage of Anne Frank's house in Amsterdam.

Ⓦ **www.holocaustdenialontrial.org** The full transcripts of the Irving–Lipstadt trial. If you're in any doubt about David Irving's motives, click the tab "the Judgment" and read part IX, "Justification: The Allegation that Irving is an Anti-Semite and a Racist".

- **www.holocaust-history.org** Compelling, authoritative site presenting essays on the Holocaust and on Holocaust denial, along with scanned versions of key Nazi documents and death-camp photographs.
- **www.ihr.org** Site of the deeply controversial Institute for Historical Review devoted to "challenging" the accepted view of the Holocaust.
- **www.iranholocaustdenial.com** Charts international responses to Iranian Holocaust denial. Oh, and also happens to chart Iran's "nuclear threats to world peace".
- **www.nizkor.org** Anti-Holocaust-denial website maintained by American anti-revisionist Ken McVay, a non-Jewish ex-gas-station manager with a cause.
- **remember.org/image/** A large collection of images of the Holocaust.
- **www.spiegel.de/international/0,1518,druck-418660,00.html** The full text of "We Are Determined", *Der Spiegel*'s in-depth interview with President Ahmadinejad, as published on May 30, 2006.
- **www.yadvashem.org.il** Jerusalem's Holocaust Martyrs' and Heroes' Remembrance Authority. A serious archive.
- **www.zundelsite.org/101.html** "Revisionist Articles Offered as a Detoxification Program to Cure the Politically Correct of the Hollywood Version of the Holocaust". You can find the "66 Q&A" elsewhere on the site – described as an "early" IHR document, though it's apparently an abridged form of the 1983 *120 Questions and Answers About the Holocaust*. (One wonders what the 54 questions and answers *not* good enough for the final cut were like.)

The Protocols of the Elders of Zion

The Protocols of the Learned Elders of Zion, to give the text its full title, first appeared in Russia in the late 1890s. It purported to be a series of lectures by the leaders of a Jewish world-domination conspiracy, in which they revealed a Machiavellian plot to prepare the ground for a world socialistic revolution, a revolution they would ultimately control for their own purposes. The text incorporated age-old anti-Semitic ideas like the Blood Libel (see p.97). The Protocols have since been published and republished, and are accepted as genuine in large areas of the world. Even where the work isn't known, the idea that a Zionist, Jewish or Semitic bankers' scheme exists to control the world is now a commonplace.

Genesis of the Protocols

Frustrated at the global success of a shabby forgery, scholars have traced the genesis of the *Protocols* with exacting care. In fact, the so-called "lectures" were probably cobbled together by the Okhrana, the tsarist secret police, in Paris in the wake of the Dreyfus case in France. The actual author was almost certainly the writer and anti-Semitic activist Matvei Golovinski. Printed privately in Russia in 1897, the first public edition was produced by a minor tsarist official called Sergei Nilus in 1905. (It's thought that he privately knew them to be a forgery while believing that the basic idea behind them was sound.) It's almost certain that the *Protocols* were created with the specific political aim of discrediting Marxism and its offshoots, and consolidating the position of Tsar Nicholas II by whipping up hysteria about an implacable and alien external threat. (Anyone with half an eye on contemporary politics will recognize a familiar manoeuvre.) In Russia, the end result was the pogroms (anti-Jewish riots). If there was an international conspiracy, therefore, it was a tsarist not a Zionist one.

The *Protocols*' Russian authors used a bizarre miscellany of sources, mostly French. Some of the basic ideas and phrasing were drawn from *Mémoires pour servir à l'histoire du Jacobinisme*, a four-volume work written in 1797–98 by a clergyman called Augustin de Barruel.

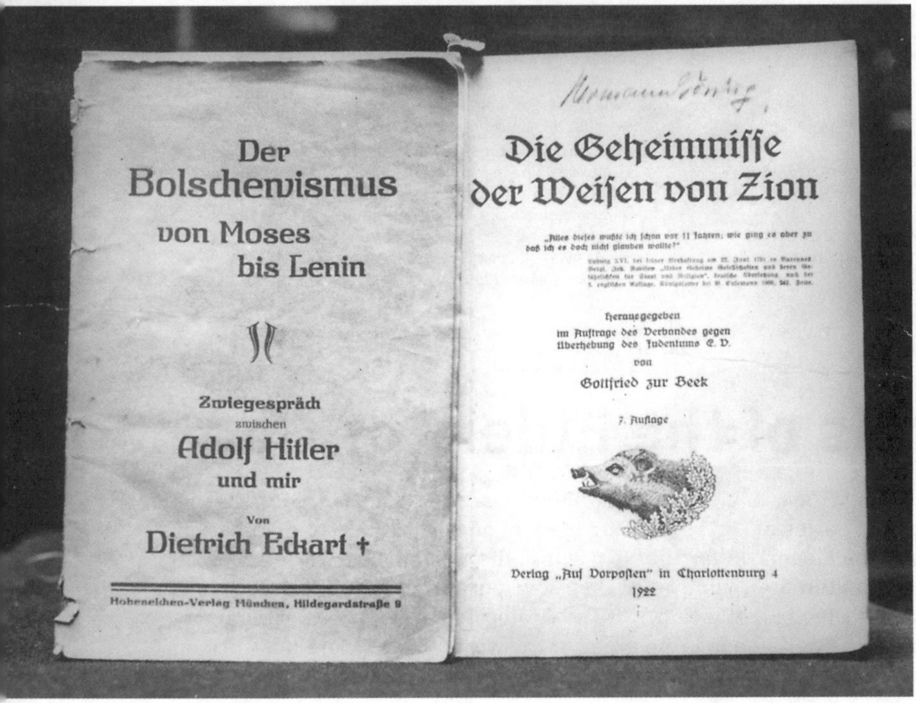

Nazi propoganda: the anti-Semitic forgery, *The Protocols of the Elders of Zion*.

This argued that the French Revolution had been secretly sponsored by Freemasons, and was highly influential in publicizing the idea that dangerous secret societies were pulling the strings behind world affairs. The idea that the Freemasons, in their turn, were the puppets of a sect of power-hungry Jews was a later twist, drawn from the so-called "Simonini Letter" sent to Barruel in response to his book's success.

The Okhrana's key source, however, was a satire written in France in 1865 by a lawyer called Maurice Joly, the *Dialogue aux Enfers entre Montesquieu et Machiavel* (*Dialogue in Hell between Montesquieu and Machiavelli*). A good fifteen to twenty percent of the *Protocols* is closely paralleled by Joly's text, its wry representations of the political machinations of the Emperor Napoléon baldly translated into the actions of the "Elders of Zion". Joly's son, Charles, is known to have worked with Golovinski.

Other sources of the *Protocols* are still more bizarre: many sections can be traced to an 1868 novel written in Prussia by a certain Hermann Goedsche under the pen name of "Sir John Retcliffe". One chapter described how the elders of the twelve tribes of Israel would meet every hundred years to plot world domination; this section was widely reprinted in Russia as a factual tract. Another key influence was French historian Gougenot des Mousseaux's 1869 *Le Juif: le Judaïsme et la Judaïsation des peuples Chrétiens* (*The Jew: Judaism and the Judaeofication of Christian Peoples*). This, by contrast, was at least a work of history – albeit a deeply flawed one – rather than outright fiction.

Hitler and Henry: the Protocols between the wars

Most likely, the *Protocols* would never have amounted to more than an obscure relic of Russian anti-Semitism had it not been for two men: Adolf Hitler and Henry Ford. Ford was apparently persuaded of the document's authenticity by a Russian émigré, and had parts of it republished in the *Dearborn Independent* throughout much of the 1920s. "They fit in with what is going on", he commented. "They are sixteen years old, and they have fitted the world situation up to this time. They fit it now." It's a pity he never read Lucien Wolf's 1920 debunking, *The Jewish Bogey and the Forged Protocols of the Learned Elders of Zion*, which first set out the evidence of Russian forgery.

The Nazis simply wove the *Protocols* into their hate literature, presenting them as authentic. No fewer than 120,000 copies of a German edition were sold in a single year. In 1935, the text was utterly discredited in the Swiss trial of two Nazis accused of peddling it. The presiding judge declared the *Protocols* "nothing but ridiculous nonsense". Ironically, he added: "I hope that one day there will come a time when no one will any longer comprehend how in the year 1935 almost a dozen fully sensible and reasonable men could for fourteen days torment their brains before a court of Berne over the authenticity or lack of authenticity of these so-called Protocols."

The judgement did nothing to slow their success. Hitler himself cited the *Protocols* as evidence that "the whole existence of this people is based on a continuous lie". In *Mein Kampf*, he makes the conspiracists' classic connection to Zionism, portraying the goal of a Jewish state in Palestine not as a place to live, but as "a central organization for their international world cheating, withdrawn from others' reach – a refuge for convicted dregs and a college for aspiring swindlers". It's not, in fact, certain whether Hitler actually believed the *Protocols* to be authentic. One leading anti-Jewish propagandist, Count Ernst zu Reventlow, privately admitted they were "a clumsy hoax" – while continuing to make use of them in public.

Nazi publications drew directly on the Tsarist example of the propaganda of fear, using the text to attack not just Jews but a supposed cabal of Jews, international financiers and Communists. It's hard to imagine representatives of the three groups sitting around a boardroom table, cigars in hand. Soviet-era propaganda, by contrast, tended to portray Jews as lackeys of the capitalist counter-revolution.

The Protocols in the Far East

Nazi anti-Semitism is a given. More surprising is the use of similar propaganda in imperial Japan. During the war, the same tsarist material was publicized there for the same purposes – with utterly bizarre success, given the almost complete absence of Jews from Japanese territory. Equally strange is the success of the *Protocols* in contemporary Southeast Asia. In Malaysia, for example, the document was first published – as fact – in 1983. Within a few years, conspiratorial and anti-Zionist rhetoric crept into public discourse, notably in the mouth of the brash, confrontational prime minister Mahathir Mohamad, who led the country for 22 years.

In October 2003, just days before he resigned, Mohamad addressed the tenth summit of the Organization of the Islamic Conference (IOC). As part of a typically undiplomatic speech aimed at giving Muslim leadership a kick in the pants, he declared "We are up against a people who think … They invented and successfully promoted Socialism, Communism, human rights and democracy so that persecuting them would appear to be wrong … With these they have now gained control of the most powerful countries and they, this tiny community, have become a world power." The words could have been drawn straight from the *Protocols* – and, indeed, they probably were. Non-Jews haven't escaped Mohamad's wrath and suspicion either: in the same years, he labelled "Anglo-Saxon Europeans" as proponents of "war, sodomy and genocide".

The Protocols in the Middle East

The Protocols of the Elders of Zion have found an unintended, but enthusiastic audience in the modern Middle East. Legend has it that the text had arrived in the region before World War I was over – the Jerusalem leader Musa Kazim al-Husayni supposedly asked Chaim Weizmann whether he and the other Zionist leaders were the same thing as the "Elders". The story is almost certainly apocryphal, as Arabic translations only emerged in the 1920s. Persian editions appeared after World War II.

DANIEL PIPES AND THE HIDDEN HAND

Anyone investigating Middle Eastern conspiracies will soon stumble across the name of Daniel Pipes. Some view him as a ruthless opponent of anti-Semitism who uses his website (www.danielpipes.org), lectures and ever-growing bibliography to expose the worst excesses of Middle Eastern rhetoric. Pipes is an undoubted authority on Middle Eastern politics, and on conspiracism in general – his books *The Hidden Hand: Middle East Fears of Conspiracy* and *Conspiracy: How the Paranoid Style Flourishes, and Where It Comes From* are towards the top of the reading list. He says that his "mantra" is "militant Islam is the problem, moderate Islam is the solution", and he is absolutely right to point out that "the twentieth century's terrible history should expunge the impression that conspiracy theories are trivial".

And yet his strong links with conservative groups that promote an aggressively pro-Israeli US foreign policy have troubled some commentators, as have his McCarthyesque "name and shame" campus campaigns against academics guilty of what he sees as anti-Semitism, and his stance on the supposed incompatibility of Islam and American-style democracy. The Orientalist scholar Edward Said described Pipes in 1996 as a pundit who sought to "make sure the (Islamic) threat is kept before our eyes, the better to excoriate Islam for terror, despotism and violence". Other critics have seized on statements such as the one Pipes made in *USA Today* after the Oklahoma City bombing: "People need to understand this is just the beginning. The fundamentalists are on the upsurge and they make it very clear they are targeting us. They are absolutely obsessed with us." There's undoubtedly something ironic about Pipes, the prolific analyst of the "paranoid style" in politics, accusing "fundamentalists" of being obsessed with "us". In response to George W. Bush appointing him to the United States Institute of Peace, a spokesman for the Arab American Institute criticized Pipes' own "bizarre obsessions" with all things Arab and Muslim. The harsher irony, of course, is that the Oklahoma bombers turned out to be right-wing American fundamentalists, not Islamic ones.

Modern editions in Arabic and other languages are now regularly republished – and even distributed free by the Saudi government in one notorious 1980s incident. More recently, the old hoax has even evolved into new media. In 2002, the *Protocols* were serialized on a number of Arab television channels as a drama-documentary, entitled *Knight Without a Horse*.

The general idea of a world conspiracy to promote Zionism is extremely widespread. It even appears in the founding charter of Hamas, the leading Islamist movement in Palestine whose political wing makes up the elected government of the Palestinian Authority. Article 32 of the charter, sometimes known as the "Hamas Covenant", states: "Today it is Palestine, tomorrow some other country or countries, for the Zionist plan has no limits, and after Palestine they want to expand from the Nile to the Euphrates… Their plan is expounded in *The Protocols of the Elders of Zion*, and their present [behaviour] is the best proof of what we are saying."

It's curious that what was once a specifically European idea, an answer to suspicions about the forces behind European revolutions, was able to morph into a general cultural prejudice, and then be retranslated into another, entirely different political situation – the issue of Israel's position in the Middle East. European liberals rightly protest against the conflation of anti-Israeli policies and cultural anti-Semitism, but it's far harder to unpick the two strands of thought on the ground in Palestine or Tehran. Ironically, suspicions of a Zionist design for a "greater Israel" have obvious parallels with the pan-Arabist movement espoused by Nasser of Egypt, and by Iraq's and Syria's Ba'ath parties.

The controversial US academic Daniel Pipes (see box above) claims that the *Protocols* are "the most important single vehicle for transmitting Christian anti-Semitism to the Muslim world" – and for passing on conspiracist thinking to boot. Pipes has collected numerous examples of *Protocols*-influenced Middle Eastern conspiracism. He describes how a 1985 Tehran edition of the *Protocols* included a commendatory introduction, as well as a map called the "Dream of Zionism" showing the supposed boundaries of "Greater Israel". He reports on how Shimon Peres's book promoting regional cooperation, *The New Middle East*, was given a new introduction in an Egyptian edition, declaring "when the *Protocols of the Elders of Zion* were discovered about 200 years ago … the international Zionist establishment tried its best to deny the plot … And now, it is precisely Shimon Peres who brings the cutting proof of their validity." He quotes an academic at Cairo's prestigious Al-Azhar University, Salih Hasan al-Maslut, as writing in 1995 that Freemasonry is "a Jewish international organization seeking to destroy non-Jewish nations and governments … as defined by the Zionists' *Protocols*". Pipes reports the professor as going on to say that the Masons weren't an effective enough tool, so the Jews went on to establish the Rotary Clubs.

SOURCES

Books

Norman Cohn **Warrant for Genocide: The Myth of the Jewish World Conspiracy and the Protocols of the Elders of Zion** (1996). The definitive story, proving that the *Protocols* were a forgery once and for all.

Will Eisner **The Plot: The Secret Story of the Protocols of the Elders of Zion** (2005). Published just before Eisner's death, this sombre, thoughtful graphic novel tells the full tale of the *Protocols* hoax.

Marvin Perry and Frederick Schweitzer **Anti-Semitism: Myth and Hate From Antiquity to the Present** (2002). See review on p.101.

Daniel Pipes **The Hidden Hand: Middle East Fears of Conspiracy** (1998). See box opposite.

Websites

Ⓦ **www.danielpipes.org** See box opposite.

Ⓦ **www.jewwatch.com/jew-references-protocols-folder.html** Full text of the *Protocols*, with arguments for its authenticity and answers to such burning questions as "Is Rupert Murdoch Jewish?" The name of the page rather gives away its disturbing political slant.

Ⓦ **www.memri.org** The Middle East Media Research Institute: a source of Arab-language articles otherwise unavailable in English, though readers may note that the bulk of its translations somehow show only a disturbing side of Arab culture.

Ⓦ **users.cyberone.com.au/myers/toolkit.html** Pro-*Protocols* attempt to discredit the "forgery" line. This highly conspiracist and racially charged site loses sight of the bigger picture as it triumphantly discovers minor errors in the main argument, but provides surprisingly handy source material on the way.

The British royal family

When the British Empire was at its height, to accuse the royal family of being behind a mega-conspiracy to rule the world would not have been entirely unreasonable. Over a hundred years later, however, most people would say that the map of world power has changed more than a little. To be sure, the Windsors have been fingered as the conspirators behind scandals as disparate as the Jack the Ripper murders of the 1880s and the death of Princess Diana in 1997 (see p.54), but two arch-conspiracy theorists paint an altogether more sinister picture. American political activist and conspiracy king Lyndon LaRouche has accused the royal family of being the puppet masters behind a host of international agencies and corporations, while prolific conspiracy author, ex-footballer and self-proclaimed Messiah David Icke has claimed that the real issue is that the Windsors are reptilian shape-shifters.

Prince Philip, the WWF and the ODA

In Lyndon LaRouche's own words, "the Queen runs from the top down, through a Privy Council. Number One on the Privy Council, after the Queen, is the Church of England, the head of the Church of England, and then a whole lot of other people, about 500. These 500 people run the British Empire, including the apparatus of its old Colonial Office. The Colonial Office was never disbanded. They call it the Overseas Development Office now."

As an offshoot of the Foreign Office, with a relatively tiny budget spent largely on aid and development projects, the ODA (now the Department for International Development) is an odd choice of villain. But then it turns out that the DFID is a pawn in a much larger global game. According to LaRouche and his co-theorists, the Windsors wield power through an assortment of agencies. As president emeritus of the World Wildlife Fund, Prince Philip – apparently "the Doge of London" – "leads the world in orchestration of ethnic conflict and terrorism". To date, successes of the WWF have included the Rwandan genocide (see p.381), which was not, as you may blindly believe, the work of marauding, machete-wielding bands of Hutu extremists, but was, in fact, executed by trained soldiers from Ugandan president Yoweri Museveni's army. (Don't be fooled by Uganda's apparent support for the opposing Tutsi rebels.) These soldiers were all trained in camps set up under the guise of the WWF's gorilla-protection programmes. Given that the Overseas Development Agency "controls" Museveni, the troops were, in fact, little more than proxies for the British.

By this account, Rwanda is far from being the only WWF operation. Anything from African coups and rebellions to ecological protests (such as those against French nuclear testing in the South Pacific) are actually the work of the SAS, the British army's elite special operations commandos. The SAS is behind what LaRouche calls the "Afghansi terrorist network" (better known today as that all-powerful and ultra-evil demon "Al Qaeda", which, according to most Western pundits and politicians, magically controls and coordinates world terrorism). According to LaRoucheites, the regiment "operates outside the British government command structure, and is directly beholden to the Sovereign". If that got out, it would be a big shock to the Ministry of Defence.

Prince Philip and the Club of the Isles

You may wonder why Prince Philip, in cahoots with the WWF, ODA and SAS, would have wanted the Rwandan genocide to happen. He has been accused of a more general appetite for population control – perhaps along the lines of the culling of game animals. In 1988, the German news agency DPA quoted Philip as muttering, "In the event that I am reincarnated, I would like to return as a deadly virus, in order to contribute something to solve overpopulation." The remark was largely received with forced or incredulous smiles – another classic foot-in-mouth joke from the Duke of the Gaffe. Conspiracists, however, saw something more sinister behind the apparently throwaway remark.

According to LaRoucheites, Philip's leadership stems from his historical role as the unofficial leader of the "Club of the Isles", an informal and highly secretive association of corporate and European aristocratic interests. According to one website, the Club of the Isles lords it over "an estimated $10 trillion in assets". Associated businesses include Shell, ICI, Lloyds of London, Unilever, Lonrho, Rio Tinto Zinc and DeBeers; as a result, the Club controls most of the world's raw materials. This oligarchy is so nefarious, according to one writer on LaRouche's website, that it even manipulates the world's food supplies, a policy that results in the deaths of tens of millions every year from "the most elementary lack of their daily bread".

The Club of the Isles, it seems, inherits its power from "Mesopotamian-Roman-Venetian" trade networks. More specifically, it represents "a new, more virulent, Anglo-Dutch-Swiss strain of the oligarchic system of imperial Babylon, Persia, Rome, and Byzantium". (US corporations may sometimes seem aggressive, but they are philanthropic by comparison.) But this doesn't explain the Rwandan genocide. It was, it seems, just one element in a super-plan drawn up by the Royal Institute for International Affairs, aka Chatham House (see p.141), as part of a "blueprint for the consolidation of one-world empire". To rule this empire according to the feudal model – and nothing else would be acceptable to Prince Philip and his blue-blooded friends in the City of London – would apparently require that the world's population be reduced fivefold to one billion people… starting with Lyndon LaRouche. According to a 1999 article in the LaRouche magazine *Executive Intelligence Review*, the publication of a distinctly negative article in the budget UK women's magazine *Take a Break* was apparently the first step in an MI6 campaign to assassinate him. One wonders why Prince Philip didn't just use the SAS.

The Windsors, the Commonwealth and the UN

As a challenge to American corporate hegemony, the Club of the Isles conspiracy theory could be compared to the highly conspiracist conception of the EU that emanates from ultra-right America (see p.138). It's also distinctly reminiscent of conspiracists' accusations about the UN. And indeed the Commonwealth. After all, as one conspiracy site's blogger puts it, "there really is no real reason for the UK to have the Commonwealth except to control the UN through the Commonwealth. Its goals are exactly those of the UN."

Joan Veon, author of *Prince Charles: The Sustainable Prince*, has noted that "every time a country was granted independence from Britain, they were given a vote at the UN". Strange that. Equally, according to Veon, the Senate's

The British royal family: reptilian shape-shifters?

ratification of the UN Charter meant that it simply reverted to British overlordship. Like LaRouche's co-conspiracists, Veon sees Prince Philip as the *éminence grise* behind the throne – and behind the UN too, "a key, behind-the-scenes mover and shaker" who follows the goals of arch-colonial capitalist and diamond baron Cecil Rhodes. (Not incidentally, Philip is also "responsible for the radical environmental agenda that perverts Genesis 1, 2, and 3 and puts the earth above man and not man above the earth as God intended.")

Drugs, The Beatles and Diana

The decimation of the world population envisaged by the Club of the Isles will obviously have seriously negative social consequences. But according to LaRoucheites, the conspirators have an ingenious plan to deal with this. By fostering a "drug-rock-sex counterculture", potential protestors will be effectively silenced. According to LaRouche devotee and self-confessed former British spy David Coleman, The Beatles were just one thrust of this campaign, designed by the Club of Rome and the Tavistock Institute for Human Relations, to create a drugged-out and conspiracy-minded population with no inclination towards effective activism.

Meanwhile, Queen Elizabeth has been busy writing science fiction, under various pseudonyms, aimed at distracting and disorienting the young and impressionable. If that isn't enough, environmental youth groups (fostered, of course, by Prince Philip's WWF) will act as a kind of Hitler Youth. The WWF's vicious "Pandas", in their distinctive Black-and-White-Shirts, will face a debilitated enemy, racked by drug use. The Windsors, it appears, control the global drug trade – a continuation, it seems, of Britain's role in China's Opium Wars. Triads and Colombian drug cartels are mere lackeys in their thrall.

David Icke and the reptilians

There's no way that a mere summary of his arguments can do justice to the fantastical conspiracy cocktail that has become the world view (and chief source of income) for former footballer David Icke since he first reported seeing visions in 1990. Icke incorporates any and all conspiracy theories in his mega-system, but the conspiracists' usual explanations, he claims, never go far enough. Icke puts it in quasi-Buddhist terms, saying that we are too habituated to "false reality". Icke, of course, can always see a deeper conspiracy lurking behind the one that other theorists claim to have exposed. The result, of course, is that his "ultimate" conspiracy is far more dramatic than anything anyone else could possibly believe in.

Humanity, Icke says, is being controlled, manipulated and, in some cases, actually drained of blood by alien reptiles. These "reptilians" are something like dinosaurs and something like dragons, only vastly more intelligent. Thanks to their origins as a consciousness from the Fourth Dimension, they are also able to change shape at will. While Icke's evidence ranges across human and mythological history, from ancient snake worship to modern "eyewitnesses", his proof rests finally on the visions experienced by him and his supporters.

Using their ability to shape-shift (as well as the relatively conventional practice of intermarriage), the reptilians have worked their bloodline (or, more specifically, their "reptilian-mammalian DNA combination") into everything from the all-powerful Illuminati (see p.93) to influential families such as the Bushes, the Rockefellers, the Rothschilds – and the Windsors. (Some suspect that beneath Icke's idea of a racial – albeit lizard-race – conspiracy involving powerful banking and political families lies a deeply anti-Semitic subtext. Others think his idea is so mad that he must be the front man for a conspiracy to give conspiracy theories a bad name.)

According to Icke, the Windsors "are not the top of the pyramid by any means", but "they are very much involved in the global agenda and in the sacrificial ritual that always goes with it". These sacrificial rituals apparently included the death of Princess Diana at the thirteenth pillar of the Alma tunnel (see p.60). One writer on the Icke-ite website www.reptilianagenda.com claims that Balmoral, the royal family's Scottish summer residence, is a "very, very nasty place. That's somewhere they want to dig underground.

They will find reptile fossils, it goes back that far." Scotland's other conspiracy landmark, the "Templar" Rosslyn Chapel, pales into insignificance.

As Icke admits, the "Windsors Are Lizards" theory is "quite something to absorb from our conditioned version of reality". But how can you gainsay an eyewitness who claims to have seen an extra membrane momentarily flicking across Queen Elizabeth's eyes? Or one who observed the Queen Mother actually transforming into a lizard? The secret of the Windsors' abilities, according to www.reptilianagenda.com, is not gin and tonic, horseracing and unimaginable wealth, but "microcurrents". Apparently, "it's much easier for them to do Frankenstein shit than it is for us. The different bodies are just different electrical vibrations and they have got that secret, they've got the secret of the microcurrents, it's so micro, so specific, these radio waves that actually create the bodies." Fortunately, these microcurrents aren't entirely negative. As the website's contributor goes on to add: "These are the energies I work with when I'm healing."

SOURCES

Books

Phil Dampier and Ashley Walton Duke of Hazard: The Wit and Wisdom of Prince Philip (2006). OK, this gets a listing mainly for its title, but its also a useful antidote to the more apocalyptic fears.

David Icke The Biggest Secret: The Book That Will Change the World (1999). It may not have changed the world, but it has done wonders for Icke's bank balance. Alternately mad, funny and shoddily written. A few of the main arguments are summarized above.

Joan Veon Prince Charles: The Sustainable Prince (1997). This former businesswoman and now devoted conspiracy theorist campaigns against the UN by means of the newsletter *UN Watch!* Her book traces the conspiratorial links between the one-world global agenda of the UN and the environmental activism of Prince Charles.

Websites

Ⓦ **www.davidicke.com** Hilarious Icke tackles the news of the moment, alongside lots of advertising for his many books.

Ⓦ **www.larouchepub.com** Lyndon LaRouche's website, featuring the online publication *Executive Intelligence Review*. As with the absence of WMD in Iraq, this gives a whole new meaning to "intelligence".

Ⓦ **www.reptilianagenda.com** Staggeringly detailed elaboration of Icke's "reptilian agenda" theory from fans around the world with an equally tenuous hold on what most of us think of as reality.

The Central Interference Agency

The Central Intelligence Agency, or CIA, has been accused of just about every conspiracy going, from trafficking drugs, covering up the existence of UFOs and leaking Watergate to assassinating JFK, RFK, Martin Luther King and Malcolm X – to name just the most famous alleged hits. It's surely the world's largest intelligence agency, though its budget, structure and even the number of staff it employs are known only to the president, to whom it reports, the National Security Council, and the congressional and Senate committees that oversee its activities. At least its objectives are known – to track and disrupt terrorism, drugs trafficking and organized crime, all of which are aspects of its brief to evaluate and challenge foreign threats to national security. It is forbidden to carry out investigations on the "homeland".

Cold warriors

For its first fifty years, however, the CIA seemed to see only one threat to national security: Communism. Its roots might have something to do with this monomaniacal focus. The CIA grew out of Roosevelt's wartime, dirty-dealing Office of Strategic Services (OSS), and was formally established in 1947 (much to the annoyance of the FBI).

VENEZUELA: THE TWO-DAY COUP

The CIA's penchant for plotting the overthrow of hostile regimes, even elected ones, has supposedly continued unabated. In Venezuela, the populist, socialist government of President Hugo Chavéz claimed that the failed 2002 "two-day coup" against them had US backing. Chavéz is an outspoken critic of the US, a determined nationalizer of his country's oil industry and a faithful disciple of Fidel Castro. Many instantly suspected the hand of the CIA, but then it was discovered that President Bush's Cuban-American policymaker for Latin America, Otto Reich, had held meetings with coup leaders in the months beforehand. An investigation by the Department of Justice's Office of the Inspector General found no evidence of wrongdoing, but few Venezuelans were convinced. If the coup hadn't had actual military or financial support from the US, they raged, then the White House had surely given the plotters the nod. Curiously, the CIA wasn't at the front of the firing line, for once. It was later proven that the Agency had known about the plot in advance, but those warnings had actually been passed on to Chavéz.

Its first real chance to prove itself came in 1950, with the Korean War. The new agency helped Chinese Nationalists to operate out of Burma, turning a blind eye to the mercenaries' preferred source of funding – opium. Thereafter, the CIA swiftly expanded its fight against Communism into what was then called the "Third World".

In 1953, the CIA pulled off one of its first coups with the installation of the shah of Iran. A year later, it actively promoted a fascist coup in Guatemala – with the help of a kill list, training for assassins and $15 million – which ushered in a procession of murderous dictators and 36 years of civil war. In 1958, the CIA tried to topple Cuba's Batista regime, in order to forestall the burgeoning revolution. This time, however, the plot failed. The CIA's Science and Technology Directorate, meanwhile, was experimenting with mind-control drugs – including LSD – under Sidney Gottlieb's MK-ULTRA programme (see p.210). In the 1960s, "The Company", as the CIA became known, plotted the assassinations of foreign leaders. Patrice Lumumba of the Congo was executed against a tree on January 17, 1961, while Rafael L. Trujillo of the Dominican Republic was shot by two carloads of gunmen on May 30, 1961. Cuba's revolutionary leader Fidel Castro survived the endlessly creative attempts to murder him concocted under Operation Mongoose (see p.19), but in 1967, with the help of CIA funding, anti-Castro agents in Bolivia successfully tracked down and killed his iconic comrade, Che Guevara.

The Vietnam War offered plentiful opportunities for clandestine action. Throughout the 1960s and into the early 1970s, the CIA was in the thick of the "Secret War" in Laos, supplying the so-called Secret Army with a private fleet of aircraft flying under the patriotic banner of "Air America". Meanwhile, the Agency was supporting a coup in the Middle East led by a certain Saddam Hussein, funding a bloody guerrilla war in Angola, helping overthrow Chile's Salvador Allende in favour of a military dictatorship (see p.40), and funding and arming Nicaragua's drug-running, torturing Contra guerrillas. In the 1980s, the Mujahedeen resistance to the Soviet occupation of Afghanistan attracted huge CIA support. Estimates of the total value of armaments, training and plain cash provided by the CIA to the Afghan insurrectionists – including a certain Osama bin Laden – are put at some $600 million.

At home, the CIA indulged in some creative Cold War campaigning. In 1969, Director Richard Helms did a little dossier doctoring, erasing a passage in a CIA report to President Nixon that expressed doubts about the ability of the Soviet military to launch a successful nuclear strike, and upping the estimates of the Russian nuclear arsenals.

Failure and humiliation

The CIA's reputation for evil genius is somewhat surprising, given how many of its plots have failed and how often its intelligence has been proved wrong. Among the hugely significant events it has failed to foresee have been the Soviet Union's development of nuclear weapons and, later, its deployment of them in Cuba. The Agency didn't predict the Korean War, the Arab–Israeli War, the Soviet invasion of Afghanistan or the Iraqi invasion of Kuwait. It didn't see the collapse of the Soviet Union coming, either. But Cuba has long been the greatest thorn in the CIA's flesh. The invasion of Cuba in 1961, at the Bay of Pigs, was an embarrassing failure, and the plots aimed at Fidel Castro, as part of Operation Mongoose, verged on the absurd.

The CIA has not been immune from domestic criticism. The first major attack was the 1975 Church Committee (see p.20), which uncovered scores of assassination plots, including some of the "successes" of the 1960s. The Church Committee's report resulted in the signing of Executive Order 11905 by President Ford, which ruled that "no employee of the US government shall engage in, or conspire to engage in, political assassination". Next came the 1983 Boland Amendment, which indirectly caused the most scandalous project to date – the Iran–Contra affair (see p.201). By throwing Lieutenant Colonel Oliver North to the wolves, the agency itself dodged the fallout, though it's widely assumed that then-Director Bill Casey had backed the scheme himself. Watergate reporter Bob Woodward even claimed that Casey had confessed as much on his deathbed, in 1987, with the words "I believed" (though no one believed Woodward). Associated rumours that the CIA was involved in the Contras' drug-trafficking have proved resilient.

9/11 and the CIA

On September 15, 2001, George Tenet presented a memorandum to George W. Bush asking for permission to engage in "lethal covert action". Bob Woodward even claimed that Tenet presented a "Worldwide Attack Matrix" which would, if activated, set in motion the assassination of some eighty targets around the world. A number of suspicious deaths followed, most obviously the killing of "Al Qaeda" operatives in Yemen on November 5, 2002, whose car was destroyed by a "Predator drone", a missile from a high-altitude, remote-controlled CIA aircraft. These kinds of operations went directly against President Ford's Executive Order (and President Reagan's clarification of it, Executive Order 12333, that "no person employed by *or acting on behalf of* the United States Government shall engage in, or conspire to engage in, assassination"), but were justified on the grounds that both excluded wartime activities. And, as President George W. Bush repeatedly reminded his electorate, he was fighting a "war on terror" and he was a "war president".

The CIA might have tried to chase down terrorists after the event, but it couldn't hide from its failure to predict the 9/11 attacks. The agency's role in the Iraqi weapons of mass destruction debacle (see p.413) didn't help – George Tenet would come to regret saying that Iraq's possession of WMD was a "slam dunk" case. In July 2004, the US Senate Intelligence Committee reported that the CIA had described the WMD danger in "an unreasonable way, largely unsupported by the available intelligence". But wasn't intelligence the CIA's job, rather than decision-making? In the ensuing political fallout, it wasn't just left-wingers and conspiracy theorists who were wondering what the CIA had been up to, but congressional leaders and senators as well. The CIA's support for Afghanistan's Mujahedeen fighters – whose resistance to the Soviet invasion had previously been trumpeted as one of the agency's greatest successes – suddenly seemed deeply ill-considered: the CIA had trained the very same Islamic militants who planned the attacks on the World Trade Center.

The Family Jewels

Rumours had long circulated about an explosive document known as the "Family Jewels" that was thought to detail all of the CIA's illegal activities in the 1950s and 60s. It was supposed to have been drawn up in-house on the orders of Director James R. Schlesinger. If they could only get it published, this document would expose a legacy of conspiracy – and prove the theorists right. Enough excerpts were leaked over the years to prove that the document did indeed exist. For instance, it revealed the CIA's illegal domestic espionage during Watergate in 1974.

Only in June 2007 was the full text finally made public. It did indeed reveal that the CIA had been knee-deep in illegal activities throughout the 1950s and 60s, but it didn't provide the explosive revelations that some had hoped for. Yes, the CIA had been bugging and trailing reporters, dissidents, anti-war protestors and Black Power campaigners – as well as former agents. Yes, it had opened mail sent to and from the Soviet Union and China. Yes, it had experimented on human subjects as part of MK-ULTRA. Yes, it had routinely subverted democracies around the world for its own ends, and trained foreign secret police in sabotage. Yes, it had tried to work out ways to kill Cuban leader Fidel Castro, Congolese president Patrice Lumumba, Dominican Republic president Rafael Trujillo and Chilean military chief René Schneider. But it hadn't succeeded in any of these assassination attempts, the report insisted, and the fact that the last three had all been assassinated anyway was merely a coincidence. Most disappointingly for conspiracy theorists, there was no startling revelation concerning the deaths of John or Robert Kennedy – although some, ever hopeful, noted that some passages had been blanked out, and some pages removed entirely. The whole truth would have to remain just one step away.

The CIA today

Since 9/11, the CIA has been progressively sidelined. Directors have come and gone with unstately frequency, and the organization has been repeatedly restructured. It is still charged with overseeing human intelligence but has been forced to give up many of its former roles – especially its paramilitary roles – to an ever-mightier Pentagon. Even the FBI now runs foreign agents. The CIA's director no longer meets the president to issue a daily briefing, the role having passed to a new director of national intelligence. Many CIA agents, meanwhile, have relinquished their jobs to join the burgeoning private intelligence sector. In 2006, half of the intelligence officers in Baghdad and at the new National Counterterrorism Center were contract staff.

The CIA's current budget is a secret, but it can be assumed that it's not less than the budget of 1997, which was made public after a lawsuit sponsored by the Federation of American Scientists. The figure then was $26.7 billion – a figure neatly matched by Chile's foreign debt, US arms exports and the global expenditure on pesticides in the same year. Curiously enough, it also matched the budget set for the new Department of Homeland Security. Critics claim that this secret budget goes against the constitutional requirement for federal spending to be published openly.

It's thought that the CIA currently has some sixteen thousand employees, most of whom work at its base at Langley, Virginia. At the time of writing, the director, or DCI, is Air Force General Michael V. Hayden. Previously an expert in the surveillance of American citizens at home, he was nominated by President George W. Bush in 2006. He oversees four directorates: Intelligence, Science and Technology, Support and the newly named National Clandestine Service. While intelligence is the most important function, it's the last directorate – formerly known as "Operations" – that has most attracted the world's attention. Covert operations are officially defined as those "conducted or sponsored by this Government against hostile foreign states or groups or in support of friendly foreign states or groups but which are so planned and executed that any United States government responsibility for them is not evident to unauthorized persons and that if uncovered the United States government can plausibly disclaim any responsibility for them."

Former CIA director Robert Gates observed that "the clandestine service is the heart and soul of the agency. It is also the part that can land you in jail." Few CIA agents ever actually seem to end up there, however. Even if the CIA could wash its hands clean of its history, its fatal combination of secrecy, power and ideology – what its mission statement calls "quiet patriotism" – will ensure that it remains the subject of endless conspiracy theories. And if history is anything to go by, a lot of them will be right.

SOURCES

Books

William Blum Killing Hope: US Military and CIA Interventions Since World War II (2003). The first part of the title leaves you in no doubt which side of the fence Blum is on.

Ronald Kessler Inside the CIA (2003). Surprisingly dull, given the subject matter. Full of facts – the journalist had unprecedented cooperation – but short on the Agency's darker past. Kessler's more recent book, *The CIA at War*, suffered from the post-publication revelation that Iraq did not, in fact, have any WMD.

Norman Mailer Harlot's Ghost (1991). Enormous, but rambling novel set in the conspiratorial world of the CIA in the 1950s and 60s.

Tim Weiner Legacy of Ashes: The History of the CIA (2007). Gritty excoriation of sixty years of failure, focusing on covert operations rather than espionage. Weiner has little time for conspiracy theories, but doesn't shut his eyes to abuse and incompetence. The style is journalistic, but it's unusually well-researched.

H. Bradford Westerfield Inside the CIA's Private World: Declassified Articles from the Agency's Internal Journal, 1955–1992 (1995). The real thing: formerly classified CIA reports, in your own hands, and all the more fascinating for it.

Websites

Ⓦ **www.cia.gov** You can click on "Frequently Asked Questions", but don't expect to get many answers. There is, however, a "CIA homepage for kids".

Ⓦ **www.gwu.edu/~nsarchiv/index.html** Homepage of the National Security Archive of the George Washington University: lots of declassified CIA material, including the full text of the "Family Jewels".

Ⓦ **www.thirdworldtraveler.com/South_America/US_Coup_Venezuela.html** Collection of newspaper articles arguing that the US backed the Venezuelan coup of 2002.

The military-industrial complex

In January 1961, departing president Dwight D. Eisenhower gave his farewell speech to the nation. Astonishingly, with the Cold War at its height, Eisenhower – a former Allied Supreme Commander, a man with years of experience of exercising power at the very highest level and a Republican to boot – took this opportunity to warn that the US arms industry had grown to an unprecedented size: "This conjunction of an immense military establishment and a large arms industry is new in the American experience. The total influence – economic, political, even spiritual – is felt in every city, every State house, every office of the Federal government ... We must guard against the acquisition of unwarranted influence, whether sought or unsought, by the military-industrial complex. The potential for the disastrous rise of misplaced power exists and will persist."

As Eisenhower's speech shows, the "military-industrial complex", a concept that permeates conspiracy-theory talk, was born at the highest levels of civilian and military governance. The following year, President Kennedy and Secretary of State Robert McNamara blamed the complex for promoting myths about a "missile gap" and a "bomber gap" between the US and USSR, pushing military spending to unprecedented levels. (While there were indeed gaps, they were in the US's favour – see p.369.) Some conspiracy theorists link Kennedy's subsequent assassination (see p.22) to his calls for cuts in military expenditure and for the token US presence in Vietnam to be withdrawn, citing as evidence his successor Lyndon Johnson's immediate increase of US

US vice president Dick Cheney, one of the founders of the Project for a New American Century, puts his hand on his heart during a press conference at the White House.

involvement in the region, especially after the fabricated Gulf of Tonkin incident (see p.373).

More recently, film director Eugene Jarecki placed the military-industrial complex at the heart of his Sundance award-winning documentary *Why We Fight*, which suggests that the complex is behind many of the US's forays abroad in the past fifty years. It's thought that the complex may actually foment wars – and fabricate threats to justify wars – in order to secure profitable contracts and more taxpayer funding. "Threats" from Iraq, Iran and North Korea have been exaggerated – demonstrably so in the case of Iraq's WMD – or provoked, like intimidating the North Koreans so that they resume atom-bomb production, thus helping to justify the otherwise redundant (and unworkable) National Missile Defense system, SDI.

In 2005, fifteen years after the end of the Cold War, the taxpayer-funded US discretionary military budget reached $420 billion – 51 percent of the total budget; seven times bigger than that for the next biggest sector, education; only fractionally less than the rest of the world's military spending put together; four times the joint total of America's fabled foes Russia, China, Syria, Iran, Libya, Cuba and North Korea; and 42 times the annual spending of all the agencies of the United Nations. This budgetary expansion, a 45 percent increase on 2000, has mostly come in the wake of the 9/11 attacks, but the policy think-tank Project for a New American Century (see p.418) – whose founders included Dick Cheney, Donald Rumsfeld, Paul Wolfowitz and George W. Bush's brother Jeb – had advocated big increases in military spending since the late 1990s.

In 2000, the alarming PNAC policy document "Rebuilding America's Defenses" (www.newamericancentury.org/RebuildingAmericasDefenses.pdf) said that a "catalyzing event – like a new Pearl Harbor" might be needed to galvanize increased spending on hi-tech weaponry, ensuring that the US can fight wars better than anyone and everyone. Despite the fact that the attacks involved just nineteen men aboard four airliners, 9/11 provided just such a catalyst. Spending on new jet fighters, tanks, satellites and National Missile Defense (NMD), meanwhile, benefits defence giants such as Lockheed Martin, Northrop Grumman, Boeing &

Rockwell, Raytheon and Litton – all big contributors to the Democratic and Republican parties, but favouring the latter by two to one.

Such political lobbying is evidence – as *Why We Fight* reminds us – of what the first draft of Eisenhower's speech referred to as a "military-industrial-congressional complex". Jarecki's film suggests that "defence" industries and their suppliers are deliberately dispersed throughout the US to spread their wealth-creating and political lobbying power (Lockheed Martin claims it has facilities in all fifty states). Local economies, the funding of political parties and local politicians' careers are all dependent on their success.

It used to be said that what's good for General Motors is good for America (economically speaking). However, as Michael Moore's 1989 film debut *Roger and Me* dramatically demonstrated, General Motors and other civilian manufacturers have shut down plants, leaving derelict, "rust-belt" towns. In *Fahrenheit 9/11*, Moore argued that for many of the young urban poor left behind, their best chance of paid employment, let alone college education or health care, is to join the army. The alternative is welfare-to-work programmes, run by companies like US defence giant Lockheed Martin. In this scenario, Americans simply become the tax-paying subsidizers and slave-wage workers of a system that's immune from the checks and balances of the peace-seeking electorate – because it owns them and their representatives.

According to the *Christian Science Monitor* of February 13, 2002, the "Iron Triangle" of the Pentagon, defence firms and Congress extends directly into the White House through the Carlyle Group, an investment firm with billions of dollars in military and aerospace. The Group is chaired by Ronald Reagan's former defense secretary Frank Carlucci, a confidant of Donald Rumsfeld, and it employs former president George H.W. Bush, his advisor and former secretary of state James Baker, and former British prime minister and Bush senior's partner in the First Gulf War, John Major.

Other Web sources reveal that between 1994 and 2001 Vice President Dick Cheney's wife Lynne earned six-figure fees as a board director of Lockheed Martin – the world's largest weapons manufacturer. According to Bill Hackwell of the International Action Center, Lockheed "has received prime Pentagon contracts totalling $30 billion" in the two years prior to 2003. Perhaps the man who best embodies the new military-industrial complex, however, is the less well-known Bruce P. Jackson, Lockheed's vice president for strategy and planning from 1999 to 2002 (and finance chairman for the 2000 Bush election campaign).

During his time as Lockheed's VP, Jackson – a board director of the Project for the New American Century – not only founded the US Committee for NATO and the Project for Transitional Democracies, but also… (wait for it) chaired the Republican Party's subcommittee on foreign policy. All of these bodies, Stephen Gowans noted in a November 2002 article in the e-zine *What's Left*, advocated more defence spending – from which Jackson's employer, Lockheed, stood to gain more than any other company. To cap it all, between 2002 and 2003, Jackson was the chairman of the Committee for the Liberation of (you guessed it) Iraq.

From another viewpoint, it's been argued that the military-industrial complex goes hand in hand with a foreign policy dedicated to preserving US supremacy and the American way of life in an increasingly competitive world. In his 1998 book, *Hidden Agendas*, award-winning UK journalist John Pilger quotes a secret (but now declassified) memo written in 1948 by George Kennan, head of the US State Department Policy Planning Staff. Noting that the US had half the world's wealth but only six percent of its population, Kennan said that the real task ahead was to devise "a pattern of relationships which will permit us to maintain this position of disparity without positive detriment to our national security". Referring to the Far East – though clearly the same principle could be said to apply elsewhere – Kennan argued that this would mean dumping "unreal objectives" like "human rights, the raising of living standards, and democratization" and instead dealing in "straight power concepts".

THE MILITARY-ENTERTAINMENT COMPLEX

Some would say that the reach of the military-industrial complex is such that there is no escape from it, even in mindless escapism, thanks to the military-entertainment complex. The World Socialist Website reported that the Pentagon, CIA and US Air Force all have "film approval" offices or liaison officers to assist films that show them in a favourable light (hence credits thanking the Department of the Navy/Army/Air Force). The lavishly assisted *Top Gun* helped increase naval aviation recruitment fivefold, aided by recruitment booths in cinemas, while Paramount offered the Pentagon recruitment advertising space on the videos of *Flight of the Intruder* and *The Hunt for Red October*.

Computer games have also been given a military tie-in, with some deliberately designed as recruiting tools. The Common Dreams website notes that *Full Spectrum Dominance*, a Microsoft Xbox game about attacking the fictional central Asian "haven for terrorists" of "Tazikhstan", had been developed in conjunction with the US Army and took its name from the Pentagon's 2000 "Joint 20/20" plan for fighting future wars. The Department of Defense, US Army and Marines have worked with the University of Southern California, the Institute for Creative Technologies and companies like Paramount Pictures to produce simulators such as *Advanced Leadership*, tank simulator *Spearhead* and *Tom Clancy's Rainbow Six: Rogue Spear*. And the online game *America's Army*, which has attracted some two million registered users since its launch in 2002, was a US Army co-production with Epic Games and *Star Wars* creator George Lucas's company Lucasfilm Ltd. But then it was *Star Wars* that supplied the nickname – and who knows, perhaps the idea – for Ronald Reagan's Strategic Defense Initiative (SDI).

In 2007, the British intelligence organization GCHQ began advertising in online games like Electronic Arts' *Need for Speed: Carbon*, Ubisoft's *Tom Clancy's Rainbow Six* and *Splinter Cell Double Agent*, and Activision's *Enemy Territory: Quake Wars*, to lure Internet-savvy graduates into "Careers in British Intelligence" (following the first open recruiting campaigns by MI5 and MI6). However, by doing so, they also risk recruiting real terrorists; as the Australian High Tech Crime Centre reported, terrorists use online games like *World of Warcraft* for realistic arms training (rendering real-world training camps redundant), risk-free reconnaissance, attack rehearsals, money-laundering and ID theft. Such is the fear that games like *Second Life* may become terror classrooms, Western agents have set up their own virtual worlds to replicate the terrorist experience, while also seeking to develop software to detect which of these gamers may be predisposed to terrorism.

Writing in 1999, American author William Blum noted that since World War II the US had carried out "extremely serious interventions" – from supplying arms for military coups to actual invasions – in more than seventy countries. These included Cambodia, China, East Timor, Korea, the Philippines, Vietnam, Chile, Cuba, the Dominican Republic, El Salvador, Grenada, Guatemala, Nicaragua, Panama, Afghanistan, Iran and Iraq – to name only "Third World" countries. Today, a US military presence "defends American interests" in over 140 states worldwide.

On the business side, US arms make up around fifty percent of global arms sales, and war zones provide a perfect showcase for the latest weapons. US firms, along with several from Western Europe, armed both sides of the Iran-Iraq War in the 1980s. The US media have been accused of promoting the brilliance of US-made smart bombs and Patriot missiles during the First Gulf War – which gave a massive boost to Israeli and Saudi Arabian demand for US arms. The publication *Foreign Policy in Focus* reported that Boeing, Lockheed Martin and Textron all lobbied for the expansion of NATO in the late 1990s as a "golden opportunity" for increased arms sales, although the move also antagonized Russia and undermined arms control talks (which the George W. Bush administration put the boot in on anyway). In early 2005, Condoleezza Rice was in India discussing closer ties with the US on practically the same day that 22 F-16 fighter jets were sold to India's neighbour Pakistan – a move hardly calculated to ease the longstanding tension between the two countries.

The reach of private companies into the US Army has increased markedly in recent years, with private firms now outsourced to provide transportation, drivers, supplies, caterers, interrogators (at Abu Ghraib) and even foot soldiers (with the steady rise of security firms, such as Blackwater USA). While private mercenaries are paid several times the salary of regular soldiers, it was not until late 2007 that it was even suggested that mercenaries be put on an equal footing in terms of rules of engagement, the same tight restrictions on the use of force, legal culpability for their actions, and even cultural awareness training – and that was only due to a controversy implicating Blackwater guards in the deaths of seventeen Iraqi civilians.

For the military-industrial complex, it would seem, business is business, regardless of the human consequences – and not just the consequences abroad. According to a 2005 UNICEF report, the US has the highest proportion of children growing up in poor households of any OECD

MEN IN BLACK

If you've recently been abducted by aliens and maybe had a mind-control chip implanted in your brain, you should expect a visit from the "Men in Black" sometime soon. The "MIB" are the *X-Files* version of the CIA, the stormtroopers of a ubiquitous, sinister agency dedicated to covering up the existence of alien life forms. Some think the Men in Black actually are government agents, perhaps thanks to their rather formal dress code of black, badly made suits, stiff white shirts and plain black ties – the uniform, coincidentally, of any self-respecting secret agent from the 1950s.

Some witnesses have reported seeing MIB travelling in 1950s Cadillacs (which, apparently, "smell new" rather than "vintage"), while others have spotted MIB using blacked-out limos or even the more up-to-date black helicopters – also the transport of choice for high-tech agents of conspiracy ranging from the CIA to the UN, according to popular ultra-right-wing legend. Some alleged MIB victims have reported more obviously extra-terrestrial features, such as "shiny skin", "pointy chins", "hands without fingernails" and metallic, inhuman voices.

As it turns out, Men in Black do come from the 1950s, or at least from a 1956 book melodramatically entitled *They Knew Too Much About Flying Saucers*. The author, a West Virginian theatrical film booker and notorious hoaxer called Gray Barker, claimed that he had been visited by a trio of terrifying dark-dressed men who had warned him off relaying details of his UFO experiences. The story drew heavily from early 1950s UFOlogy, which typically incorporated sinister government agents on a mission to suppress "The Truth". (CIA files later released showed that, in the 1950s, the Agency had indeed mounted disinformation campaigns related to UFO sightings, partly to conceal the existence of early spy planes such as the U2.)

West Virginia was again the setting for the big entrance of MIB into popular culture, via the "Mothman" hysteria of 1966–67 Point Pleasant, as documented by John Keel's book, *The Mothman Prophecies*. As well as the "Mothman" himself, townsfolk were soon reporting visits from endless dark-suited men – at least some of whom were undoubtedly Barker himself, or his friends, playing pranks.

If Men in Black are what their eyewitnesses clearly think they are – aliens conspiring to cover up evidence of UFOs – then it seems odd that they'd adopt such a time- and culture-specific costume. As a piece of fiction, however, it's a good hook, pulling on all sorts of subconscious strings related to powerful, faceless authority figures. To put it bluntly, the MIB are right out of a comic book. And, in fact, they were later turned into cartoon characters by Lowell Cunningham, whose books were, in turn, adapted into the comedy sci-fi films *Men in Black* and *Men in Black II* in 1997 and 2002, starring Tommy Lee Jones and Will Smith.

The movie version had the distinctly neofascist twist that the Men in Black are actually good cops protecting the world from an invasion of aliens – like a paranormal Department of Immigration, perhaps. By contrast, the "sentient agents" of *The Matrix* movies are more faithfully drawn from MIB mythology, right down to their sinister service of their inhuman masters – the "Machines". If the Matrix itself stands for faceless bureaucracy, the Men in Black are its federal agents. They are the men from nowhere, the waking nightmare of the disenfranchised and the fearful, whose lonely lives only mean something when these insidious government agents invade them.

country – 21.9 percent, nine times the rate in Denmark. As if to prove this point, in October 2007 – with the Iraq War alone estimated to have cost $462 billion – the Bush administration asked Congress for an extra $46 billion for war-spending in 2008, mostly for Iraq and Afghanistan. This was on top of the $147 billion already bid for by the Pentagon. And there is no end in sight for either conflict – the Iraq and Afghanistan wars are projected, by the Congressional Budget Office, to cost an additional $2.4 trillion over the next decade. The very same month that he requested the additional military spending, President Bush vetoed a $60 billion act that would have ensured all American children had health cover – on the grounds of expense. As Eisenhower pointed out in 1953, at the beginning of his presidency: "Every gun that is made, every warship launched, every rocket fired signifies, in the final sense, a theft from those who hunger and are not fed, those who are cold and are not clothed."

SOURCES

Books

Helen Caldicott The New Nuclear Danger: George W. Bush's Military-Industrial Complex (2002). Giving the military-industrial theory a modern context, Caldicott argues that the complex has used its connections to Congress and the White House to hurdle the post-Cold War downturn, and turned 9/11 into a once-in-a-lifetime business opportunity. The result is the complex tightening its grip on America's government and society more than at any time since World War II (and spending more, of course).

Aaron L. Friedberg In the Shadow of the Garrison State (2000). Friedberg doesn't actively support a complex as a good thing per se, but contends its size and growth during the Cold War has not led to a garrison state (phew!). Indeed, the process of investment in arms, technology and supportive political institutions and individuals has apparently created a stable, economically unbeatable political-economic setup. But whether that means it is a model for economic growth the world should follow, he doesn't say.

Films

Eugene Jarecki, Why We Fight (2005). Taking Eisenhower's "military-industrial complex" speech as its starting point, Eugene Jarecki's film adopts an altogether more sober approach to its subject than Michael Moore's *Fahrenheit 9/11*, and it is all the better for it. Essential viewing.

Websites

Ⓦ **www.eisenhower.archives.gov/farewell.htm** The text of Eisenhower's seminal speech.

Ⓦ **schema-root.org/commerce/corporations/military/** Covers 38 military industry topics, each with a current newsfeed.

Ⓦ **www.sourcewatch.org/index.php?title=Military-industrial_complex** SourceWatch describes itself as a collaboratively written "encyclopedia of people, issues, and groups shaping the public agenda". The article includes dozens of links to follow up.

Ⓦ **www.thirdworldtraveler.com/Blum/US_Interventions_WBlumZ.html** "A Brief History of US Interventions: 1945 to the Present" (*Z Magazine*, June 1999), by William Blum, author of *Killing Hope: US Military and CIA Interventions Since World War II*.

Currency codes: from Masonic dollars to ten-agora coins

Coins and banknotes are so familiar that people scarcely notice what's on them. Most people, that is. The conspiracy-minded, by contrast, are able to tease out a wealth of arcane imagery and symbolism

that reveals some disturbing truths: that Masons run the US government, that 9/11 is written all over a twenty-dollar bill issued in 1998, that Israel plans to colonize three quarters of the Middle East, and that John McEnroe is the front man for some pretty dark forces...

The almighty dollar: Masonic myths

Ever since 1935, the reverse side of the one-dollar bill has carried a pair of strange images framed by circles on either side of the word "ONE". To quote the State Department's official heraldic description, the image on the left shows: "A pyramid unfinished. In the zenith, an eye in a triangle, surrounded with a glory proper." The Roman numerals for the date of independence, 1776, are carved into the base of the pyramid, which has thirteen steps. Above the eye is the Latin motto *Annuit Cœptis*, while below the base of the pyramid a banner reads *Novus Ordo Seclorum*. The image on the right shows a bald eagle holding a banner reading *E Pluribus Unum*, and clutching an olive branch and arrows in its talons.

Together, these odd drawings make up the Great Seal, the official symbol of the United States of America. However, conspiracy theorists – especially those on the religious Right – see them as powerful proof that Masonry captured the heart of the republic right from the start. Never mind the slogan "IN GOD WE TRUST" written in capitals across the centre of the note, the Masons were – and still are – conspiring to build an atheistic, self-interested state on the ruins of what was once the new promised land. *Novus Ordo Seclorum*, it's said, stands for "New World Order", the much-feared Grand Plan to establish an authoritarian, probably left-wing and certainly ungodly world regime (see p.141). Latin scholars can bleat in vain that the phrase really means "a new order of the centuries", *seclorum* being a short form of *saeculorum*, and it is adapted from Virgil's fourth *Eclogue*, where the line "*Magnus ab integro seclorum nascitur ordo*" trumpets the hope that "a mighty order of ages is born anew" for the Roman Empire. Which is, not coincidentally, just what the founding fathers hoped for the American republic back in MDCCLXXVI – that it would begin a new era in which monarchies would become a thing of the past. (Now that's a real conspiracy.)

Above the pyramid, the phrase *Annuit Cœptis* translates as "He favours our undertaking" – "He" being God, who apparently looked on people born in a certain part of North America with the same indulgence he once granted the Israelites. This divine favour, the official version has it, also explains the eye in the top of the pyramid, described as the "Eye of Providence". Mason-watchers, however, see a very different interpretation. They claim that the blazing eye is, in fact, a secret symbol for the Great Architect of the Universe, the "light-filled" deistic divinity or "Supreme Being" in which deistic Freemasons are traditionally supposed to believe. The light emanating from it is nothing less than the light of Masonic knowledge – the original light of "the Enlightenment".

For once, symbol-readers aren't entirely barking up the wrong pyramid. The eye also appeared on the Masonic apron worn by George Washington when he laid the foundation stone of the Capitol in 1793. But when it comes to proof, symbols are as elusive as eels – it's counter-claimed that, in the late eighteenth century, the eye symbol was used outside Masonic circles as much as within them, so the designers of the Seal and the Freemasons were just drawing on a common stock of quasi-spiritual symbols. Turn over the dollar bill, however, and there are more clues. The US Treasury Seal shows scales, a chevron representing a carpenter's square and a key. Do these represent a balanced budget, judicious accounting and monetary security, as conventional accounts would have it? Or do they represent Masons, Masons and Masons?

George Washington was not the only high-placed Mason in the early years of the Republic. Benjamin Franklin is known to have rolled up a trouser leg as well, and it turns out that he was actually on the committee that designed the Great Seal. But then so too were Thomas Jefferson and John Adams – and there are no records of either being a Freemason, despite what conspiracy theorists believe. With the help of an artist named Pierre Eugene du Simitière, Franklin, Jefferson and Adams created some of the main elements of the Seal, including the Eye of Providence and the date of independence, along with the thirteen-striped shield and the motto *E Pluribus Unum*. By 1782, the design of the Seal had gone to a Third Committee, which devolved the hard work to William Barton, a Philadelphia lawyer and heraldic enthusiast who added the eagle – not yet bald – and the pyramid.

Barton was almost certainly not a Mason, though a contemporary with the name William Barton apparently was – a fact that has led to rich confusion. Mason or not, numerologists and symbol buffs have had plenty of fun with his designs. One of the wings of the eagle has 32 feathers – that's the number of degrees in Scottish Rite Freemasonry! Its tail has nine feathers – that's the number of degrees in the York Rite! Best of all, as www.freemasonrywatch.org has it: "the total number of feathers in the two wings is 65, which, by gematria – the assigning of numerical values to the letters of the Hebrew alphabet – is also the value of the Hebrew phrase YAM YAWCHOD ('together in unity'). This phrase appears in Psalm 133 as follows: 'Behold, how good and how pleasant it is for brethren to dwell together in unity,' and is used in the ritual of the first degree of Freemasonry." But then you can prove almost anything with numbers.

As for the pyramid, those versed in Masonic lore believe it represents the unfinished Jerusalem Temple, begun by the legendary ancestors of the Masons. Or as Henry Agard Wallace, vice president to Franklin D. Roosevelt during World War II and 32nd-degree Mason, wrote in his 1934 work *Statesmanship and Religion*: "It will take a more definite recognition of the Grand Architect of the Universe before the apex stone is finally fitted into place and this nation in the full strength of its power is in position to assume leadership among the nations in inaugurating 'the New Order of the Ages'." It was Wallace who took the decision to put the Seal on the dollar bill – by his own account at the prompting of Roosevelt himself, a fellow Mason.

A truly sinister reading of the pyramid image sees a hidden code within it implicating Jews in the conspiracy (whatever that conspiracy is). The image can be made to reveal a Star of David, as follows: one equilateral triangle is drawn using the lines of the pyramid, with its base on the letters N and M of "*Novus Ordo Seclorum*"; the second, inverted triangle has its base on the A and S of "*Annuit Coeptis*", and its point on the final O of *ordo*. And the anagram thus created reads "A MASON"... And the official view? It comes from Charles Thomson's report to Congress on the work of the three committees, from June 20, 1782. His "Remarks and Explanation", as quoted by the State Department, declares: "Reverse. The pyramid signifies Strength and Duration: The Eye over it & the Motto allude to the many signal interpositions of providence in favour of the American cause. The date underneath is that of the Declaration of Independence and the words under it signify the beginning of the New American Era, which commences from that date" (although the right-wing think-tank Project for the New American Century might argue such an era really starts with them).

The twenty-dollar prophecy

This one's a little complicated, and you'll need to have an old twenty-dollar bill in front of you (or go to www.snopes.com/rumors/20bill.htm to see how it's done). If you fold the note in half to show the top half of the White House, then fold both the left and right halves of what you're left with up underneath themselves so they point upwards at ninety degrees, you're left with a composite image apparently showing the Pentagon ablaze – just like the famous image from 9/11. Spookily, if you turn the folded note over, a tower with black smoke pouring out of it is revealed. (In both cases the smoke is dark green shrubbery from the original image.)

If you were in any doubt that something very iffy is going on, try this: a concertina-style fold allows you to spell out "Osama" from "*20 United States of America*". And here's the clincher: the note was a redesign introduced in September 1998, but it was replaced *again* as soon as October 9, 2003. But what's the conspiracy here? Did the Treasury know at least three years in advance what was going to happen on September 11, 2001? If so, it's a shame officials didn't tell the president – or did they (see p.395)?

From the unfinished pyramid and the blazing eye to the mysterious phrase, *Novus Ordo Seclorum*, Masonic symbolism can be found all over the US one-dollar bill.

The ten-agora coin: map of Greater Israel

During the early 1990s, Yasser Arafat is said to have carried around Israel's ten-agora coin in his jacket pocket. Not in case of parking emergencies but to offer "proof", as he would put it, of an Israeli conspiracy to colonize the entire Middle East. On May 25, 1990, he even spoke to the UN Security Council on the issue, showing the coin to representatives especially assembled in Geneva. The coin is engraved with the image of an ancient coin dating back to the Roman siege of Jerusalem, in the reign of the last Hasmonaean king, Mattathias Antigonus II. It is stamped with the image of a seven-branched candlestick, the Jewish menorah, and its shape is distinctive, with a broken left-hand edge curving out to a point on the lower left side.

Suspicious-minded Palestinians saw a familiar outline in that edge – it was the profile of the eastern Mediterranean shore! If the rest of the coin was superimposed on a map of the Middle East, then the right-hand side of the coin would cover half of the Middle East, stretching from the Red Sea three quarters of the way across Iraq and Saudi Arabia – almost to the Gulf. This coin, then, was nothing less than a coded reference to "Greater Israel". According to Arafat, it was "a glaring demonstration of Zionist aspirations".

This "Greater Israel" notion didn't spring from nowhere. Early Zionists had indeed planned a much larger Jewish state. Theodor Herzl, for instance, believed the Jews should settle in Palestine and Syria, and even considered settlements in Mesopotamia – modern-day Iraq. This was on the basis of two Biblical passages: in Genesis 15:18, Abraham is told "Unto thy seed have I given this land, from the river of Egypt unto the great river, the river Euphrates", while in Deuteronomy 11:24, Moses declares "Every place whereon the soles of your feet shall tread shall be yours:

George Washington lays the foundation stone for the US capital in 1793 while wearing his Masonic apron.

from the wilderness and Lebanon, from the river, the river Euphrates, even unto the uttermost sea shall your coast be". From the Euphrates to the sea? Or to the "river of Egypt" – the Nile? Jewish scholars may explain that these vague territorial claims are superseded by later, more precise Biblical delimitations of the land of Israel (and that in any case the river called "Euphrates" may in fact be a small river in Syria, while the so-called "river of Egypt" is probably another minor watercourse in the north of Sinai), but Palestinians aren't much comforted. Israel's sudden seizure of the West Bank, Gaza and, for a time, Sinai, in the wake of the Six-Day War, and the actions of Jewish settlers, seem to tell a different story – of expansion, not defence.

And then there's the issue of the Israeli flag, which shows the state of Israel, represented by a blue Star of David, standing between two blue stripes. Officially, these stripes are taken from the traditional pattern of Jewish prayer shawls. According to conspiracy lore, however, they show how Israel has designs on all the land "from the river to the river" – from the Euphrates to the Nile. Exactly as depicted on the ten-agora coin.

The ten-quid secret

When Charles Darwin elbowed Charles Dickens off the rear of Britain's ten-pound note, it was officially on the grounds that the great scientist's beard was bushier and therefore harder for forgers to copy than the less hirsute – though still impressively endowed – novelist's. If it had been the ten-

dollar bill that had swapped Dickens for Darwin, it's not hard to imagine the conspiracy theories that would have quickly flooded the Internet. Was the reserve bank run by a cabal of Masonic atheists parading their evolutionist hero in the faces (or at least the wallets) of the righteous? This being tolerant, atheist-minded Britain, however, there was no such outcry – but a secret code was soon found nonetheless. With a bit of care, the lower half of the Queen's face, from the front of the note, can be folded so that it aligns with the upper part of Darwin's. The result is striking. It's John McEnroe! Complete with earring. The attendant conspiracy theory hardly needs to be explained – first Wimbledon, tomorrow the world? As McEnroe himself would say: you can *not* be serious!

SOURCES

Books

David Ovason The Secret Symbols of the Dollar Bill (2004). A trove of arcane information, from numerology to etymology, by way of early American history.

Richard S. Patterson and Richardson Dougall A History of the Great Seal (1976). Released by the Department of State, this weighty official history tells you everything you might want to know (and probably a good deal more) about the origins of the Seal.

Daniel Pipes The Hidden Hand: Middle East Fears of Conspiracy (1998). The last word on the subject, though admittedly from a distinctly pro-Israeli perspective. Includes a map of "Greater Israel" as depicted on the ten-agora coin.

Websites

Ⓦ **www.danielpipes.org/article/247** Article-type treatment of the ten-agora affair by Daniel Pipes, the authority on Middle Eastern conspiracy theories.

Ⓦ **www.freemasonrywatch.org/onedollarbill.html** Virtuoso freestyling on the Masonic symbolism of the dollar bill.

Ⓦ **www.legendinc.com/Pages/MiscellaneousPages/USDollar.html** A good online image of the dollar, with a short key to what's on it.

Ⓦ **www.moneyfactory.com** Official website of the Treasury's Bureau of Engraving and Printing, with lots on the development of banknotes.

Ⓦ **myweb.tiscali.co.uk/zucconi/biscuit/loony/logos/logos.htm** Tongue-in-cheek page on mystical symbols in corporate logos.

Ⓦ **www.snopes.com/rumors/20bill.htm** Perfect illustration of how to fold a $20 bill to reveal the 9/11 atrocities.

Ⓦ **www.srmason-sj.org/council/journal/uzzel.html** Full Masonic biography of Henry A. Wallace, vice president and Freemason.

Ⓦ **www.state.gov/www/publications/great_seal.pdf** Download the official history of the Great Seal.

Ⓦ **thebiggestsecretpict.online.fr/nwo.htm** Analysis of everything from dollar bills to the US flag, the UN emblem, Portuguese newspaper logos and, of course, George Washington as Baphomet.

Italy: land of conspiracy

Everything is political in Italy, and everything is a conspiracy – history included. The country is divided between Left and Right in a way that makes the American divide between pro- and anti-Bush camps look shallow and inconsequential, and for decades Right and Left alike have issued frantic warnings of the dangers of Communist or Fascist coups or covert action. A politician convicted of corruption or outright criminality can easily survive until the next trial by claiming that "Communist justice" has conspired to slander him. Or, like three-times prime minister Silvio Berlusconi, by rewriting Italian law to create immunity from prosecution and to halve the statute of limitations.

As an integral part of Italian politics and culture, conspiracies are a topic of discussion as hot as football. There's even a word in Italian for conspiracy theorizing: *dietrologia* – "the study of what lies behind". According to Adriano Sofri, one of the best-known names from the ultra-conspiracist years of the 1970s, "*Dietrologia* is an air that you breathe in Italy". As he told author and conspiracy expert Tobias Jones, "It's the result of paranoia and jealousy, and it simply exalts an intricate intelligence. It's like Othello with Desdemona's handkerchief: one innocent object can spark off endless suspicions." Summing up, Sofri mused that, in Italy, "It's a game which people play, almost to show off".

Communists vs Fascists

Italy's Communists and Fascists were fighting it out long before the end of World War II, as left-wing partisans harried the retreating Nazis and the remnants of Mussolini's collapsing armies. As elsewhere in Europe, the Allies quickened the pace of their invasion, alarmed by the possibility of a Communist takeover. In Italy, the proto-CIA did its bit for peace and security by setting up a "stay-behind" network of trained anti-Communists under Operation Gladio – its name taken from a Roman stabbing sword – with caches of weapons ready for use in the event of a left-wing government coming to power. Until 1990, when scandal-dogged prime minister Giulio Andreotti admitted to the Italian parliament that the programme had indeed existed, "Gladio" had been regularly dismissed as the most absurd of conspiracy theories. Unlike in France, where the *épuration* helped to purge the country of its political tensions, Italy remained split into two semi-warring camps, with Fascist-era officials still largely in power.

By the late 1960s, the pressure had only intensified. Italy's neighbours in the Mediterranean – Spain, Portugal and Greece – were all run by Fascist, military dictatorships, and the Italian Left was in a constant state of paranoid alarm about an imminent right-wing coup. Conspiracy theories were rampant – and largely justified. The Right and the conservative establishment seem to have collaborated on what has become known as a "strategy of tension", to work on public fears of left-wing or anarchist terrorism. With Greek – and possibly US – support, the far right attempted to create the conditions for a coup, preparing the ground by claiming that Italy just wasn't ready for democracy – a claim reminiscent of apartheid-era statements about Africans.

Piazza Fontana and the Anni di Piombo

The *autunno caldo* or "hot autumn" of 1969 saw some 145 explosions. It was just a prelude. On December 12, 1969, a huge bomb exploded in Milan's Piazza Fontana, killing 16 and injuring 88. The ensuing decade of terrorism and political semi-chaos was dubbed the *anni di piombo*, or "leaden years", and Piazza Fontana became the centre of a conspiracy vortex, sucking in endless court cases and political careers, and leaving an ever-mounting death toll of murdered witnesses and judicial officials. Whether Piazza Fontana was the work of anarchists or Fascists became the ultimate test of Italian political loyalties, but the more the bombing was investigated, the harder it seemed to become to establish the truth. As Tobias Jones puts it: "There are so many words. Words everywhere, and not a shred of common sense. Documents multiply amongst themselves, which sire new pieces of paper, loosed from all logic. The longer I spent following the trial, the more it seemed like something out of Kafka."

The most notorious eddy of the Piazza Fontana tornado was the furore surrounding the death of a young anarchist and pacifist, Giuseppe "Pino" Pinelli, an event made famous by Dario Fo's brilliant farce *Accidental Death of an Anarchist*. Pinelli was arrested shortly after the bombing, and held for 72 hours in custody in Milan, before he apparently threw himself from a window and died in the courtyard below. The *questore* in charge of the investigation called his leap "a sort of self-accusation". All suicides are open to conspiracization, of course, and yet this one looked particularly iffy. No one heard Pinelli scream, there was evidence of a blow to the back of his neck, and he had no injuries to his arms – although even suicides usually instinctively protect their heads. And besides, why was a window wide open in winter?

The police commissioner in charge of Pinelli's case, Luigi Calabresi, was murdered in "revenge" in May 1972, and bombing campaigns followed throughout the 1970s. An army colonel announced that his troops were "the only bulwark against disorder and anarchy" – in reality, the far right, including more than a few military elements, was behind the destabilizing events. The *anni di piombo* culminated in the bombing of Bologna railway station in August 1980, in which 85 bystanders were murdered. Like the less murderous bombs that had preceded it, the Bologna bomb was at first pinned on radical left-wing terrorists, but many Italians were never convinced, and theories that the bombings had, in fact, been the results of a right-wing conspiracy – to discredit the Left and set a right-wing coup in motion – were widespread.

The Slaughters Commission and the Ordine Nuovo

In the late 1980s, the parliamentary *Commisione Stragi* or "Slaughters Commission" investigated Piazza Fontana. A far-reaching right-wing conspiracy with the alleged collusion of the Ministry of the Interior and the Italian (and possibly US) secret services was reluctantly dragged out of the underworld and into Italy's sunshine. Without actual convictions, however, the shadows of the past seemed just to dissipate, the evidence buried rather than revealed by the million-odd court documents.

In 2001, Delfo Zorzi, Carlo Maria Maggi and Giancarlo Rognoni were convicted of the Piazza Fontana bombing – but only temporarily, as the verdict was then overturned on appeal in 2004. Zorzi and Maggi had been members of *Ordine Nuovo*, a far-right group then led by a robust operator called Pino Rauti, and they were rumoured to be secret agents with connections to the CIA – in 2000, Italian newspapers reported that Rauti had received cheques from the US embassy in the early 1970s, though this issue, typically, remains unresolved. Rauti went on to lead another entirely legal neofascist party, the Tricolour Flame.

Murder of a president: Aldo Moro

Iconic Piazza Fontana may be, but it was overshadowed by the most shocking event of the *anni di piombo*, an incident that has been compared in its impact on the national psyche – and on conspiracy theorizing – to the assassination of JFK. On March 16, 1978, Italy's centrist, Catholic president, Aldo Moro, was kidnapped at gunpoint by members of one of the "Red Brigades" devoted to the violent overthrow of the state. He had been on his way to a meeting sanctioning a new government that, for the first time, would include Communist representation in a broad coalition. Moro was held for two months, during which time he sent letters begging Prime Minister Giulio Andreotti to negotiate. Andreotti refused. Moro's bullet-ridden body eventually turned up on the Via Caetani in central Rome.

One effect was more like that of 9/11 than JFK: a war on terrorism was unleashed (this time, with the full backing of the Communists). A flood of speculation was also unleashed. The Italian public had been horrified by its government's uncharacteristic refusal to negotiate with the kidnappers, and its rather less surprising failure to locate and free their hostage. Right-wing elements in government, including Andreotti himself, were accused of wanting Moro dead in a deliberate attempt to keep the Communists out of government. Investigators revealed that the Red Brigades had been heavily infiltrated by the secret services, while the security forces themselves were in the grip of sinister elements (later identified as the P2 group – see below). Some newspapers claimed that the CIA effectively ran certain Brigade cells. (For many, their suspicions were confirmed when Brigade members Mario

Moretti and Giovanni Senzani – both probably secret service plants – were allowed to travel to the US at a time when all Italian Communists were routinely denied visas.) A parliamentary commission even suggested that the Interior Ministry might have actually located the apartment where Moro was held, and diverted police searches to protect it.

The Vatican Bank scandal: Licio Gelli revealed

Exactly which elements in government might have wanted Moro dead only emerged in the wake of the death of Italian banker Roberto Calvi, who was found hanging below London's Blackfriars Bridge on June 18, 1982 (see p.51). As chairman of the traditionally Catholic Italian bank Banco Ambrosiano, Calvi had presided over an elaborate drug-money laundering scam on behalf of Sicilian Mafia figures, using the Vatican Bank as a conduit. Foolishly, he'd also been swindling the Mafia on the side, and had threatened to reveal the involvement of powerful political figures; his death, then, was not exactly surprising.

One of the first magistrates sent to investigate Banco Ambrosiano ended up dead, killed by "terrorists". Another magistrate sniffing around the finances of Calvi's co-conspirator, Sicilian tax expert and banker Michele Sindona, was also murdered. But slowly, the links between the various cases were pieced together, despite the outright obstruction of powerful figures in government. (Calvi, it seemed, had been paying off all of Italy's political parties for years, including making two payments totalling $7 million to Bettino Craxi, who became Italy's first Socialist prime minister in 1983.) As the magistrates approached the centre of the web, a certain Licio Gelli emerged as the key political fixer behind the whole Calvi–Sindona–Vatican affair, bribing and blackmailing politicians and Mafia grandees alike to protect the operation.

The Italian press promptly nicknamed Gelli *Il Burattinaio*, "The Puppet Master". A committed Fascist and an SS officer during the war, he had escaped to Argentina where he formed a close political association with dictator Juan Perón and dealt in arms. Conspiracists have fingered him for involvement in everything from the flight of Nazi criminals, including Klaus Barbie, to South America and the death of Pope John Paul I (see p.44) to the assassination of Swedish prime minister Olaf Palme and Reagan's October Surprise (see p.199). Certainly, Gelli's range of contacts was impressive, extending to Pope Paul VI and George H.W. Bush, never mind Juan Perón. Italian prime minister Giulio Andreotti even claimed that at Perón's inauguration in 1973, he saw the new Argentinian president kneel and kiss Gelli's ring.

P2 unmasked

Gelli, it seems, was the dark side of Italy's right wing, the point at which it shaded off into the Mafia – he was widely quoted as saying "the doors to all bank vaults open to the right". When his homes and business addresses were raided in March 1981, an extraordinary document was found in a safe. It listed 953 powerful names in politics, business, the military and the judiciary – including 38 MPs, 14 judges, 2 cabinet members, all the heads of the Italian armed services and a businessman called Silvio Berlusconi. All were supposedly members of a secret, quasi-Masonic lodge called Propaganda Due, or P2. Freemasonry buffs have tried to concoct lurid histories for P2, involving connections with a nineteenth-century "Egyptian rite" and tales of oaths made to hooded officials in Tuscan villas with Nazi decor, but the organization is thought by most to have been founded in the 1970s, allegedly with CIA support, and to be less a Masonic lodge than a political network. P2's aims lay somewhere between the promotion of Gelli's own Mafia-style mini-empire, by means of bribery, blackmail, murder and ferocious networking, and the overthrow of the Italian state and its replacement with a Fascist regime.

Shortly after the discovery of the list, a manifesto was discovered underneath a false bottom in Gelli's daughter's

The body of kidnapped former Italian prime minister Aldo Moro is discovered in Rome on May 9, 1978.

briefcase, setting out "A Plan for the Rebirth of Democracy". It involved suspending unions, controlling the media and generally putting Italy back on its Fascist feet. (Post-Berlusconi, the scheme doesn't look all that unlikely.) Never mind Piazza Fontana – for conspiracists, this was the Holy Grail, proof that a powerful, well-connected and well-hidden hand had long been directing the course of Italian affairs for its own advantage, under the cover of democracy. If P2 existed, what else might be true? P2 was quickly linked to Sindona's faked kidnapping, the failure of Andreotti's government to negotiate for Aldo Moro, the infamous Bologna railway bombing of August 1980, and indeed with most of the unsolved and unresolved outrages of the *anni di piombo* that had previously unconvincingly been laid at the door of ineffectual anarchists.

P2 obscured; Licio Gelli on the run

This being Italy, the euphoria of a conspiracy unmasked didn't last long. Slowly, the list has been chipped away, many of the names denying ever having "joined", others turning out to have had only distant connections. Or so they claimed. Like the so-called "Mafia", P2 has proved to be less an organization than a coincidence of interests; less a Masonic club, with rules, code words and curious costumes, and more a networking opportunity. Some commentators have even said that P2 was nothing more than a chimera, a sop thrown to the Left to distract its attention from the real locations of power. And yet... Gelli and his associates did repeatedly engage in the planning and execution of very real terrorist murders.

Gelli himself went on the run. He was arrested in Switzerland in 1987, probably while scrabbling together some of the missing millions for his drug-running Mafia cronies, but he escaped from prison – with astonishing ease – and made for South America. Eventually extradited to Italy, he fled house arrest, only to be arrested again in Cannes in 1998, and sent back home to face a twelve-year prison sentence.

The Mafia on trial

Less the family-run crime gang of popular legend, and more an unholy alliance of "black shirts" and "white collars", the Italian Mafia has cast an obscuring smog of disinformation across the face of Italian history. So many Mafia-inspired lies have been told in Italian courts, so many perjured confessions made by so-called *pentiti* (supergrasses), so many investigations obfuscated, and so many judges and witnesses murdered that it is almost impossible to verify anything. The so-called "maxi-trials" of the late 1980s only led deeper into confusion, as government figures were half unmasked by *pentiti*, and new lines of judicial assault opened. Seven-times prime minister Giulio Andreotti was accused of exchanging an infamous kiss of association with "boss of bosses" Salvatore "Toto" Riina – who was allegedly behind the deaths of elite anti-Mafia judges Giovanni Falcone and Paolo Borsellino, murdered by huge bombs in May 1992. The judges' landmark assassinations finally revealed the extent of government collusion with the Mafia: only someone with high-level inside information could have got through the judges' security. As with the scandals of the 1970s, the most outrageous allegations of so-called conspiracy theorists were revealed to be true.

Clean Hands and Silvio Berlusconi

The Mafia trials soon morphed into the *Mani Pulite* or "Clean Hands" investigation led by Milanese judge Antonio di Pietro. The ensuing *tangentopoli* or "bribesville" scandal revealed the breathtaking extent of corruption in the established political parties: the Christian Democrats and the Socialists. Again, conspiracy theorists were vindicated.

Into the power vacuum swooped the charismatic multi-billionaire media magnate Silvio Berlusconi who, in 1993, set up his own political party, Forza Italia, or "Come on Italy" – and became prime minister. (He won the top job again in 2001, lost the 2006 election, then won a third time in 2008.) Berlusconi was not the refreshingly unpolitical outsider he claimed to be when he first emerged on the political scene. Aside from his inclusion on the notorious P2 list (see p.134), he was a former crony of Bettino Craxi, one of the politicians most deeply tainted by *tangentopoli*, and he later played a leading role in discrediting Antonio di Pietro.

At times, Berlusconi's career seemed designed to provoke the conspiracy machine. There were the conflicts of interest between his roles as the ultimate boss of the state media network, RAI, and as the owner of the main rival private channel, Mediaset – a combination which for a time gave him an interest in an unsettling ninety percent of Italy's television news. There were the links between his financial holding company, Finninvest, and a plethora of individuals with Mafia ties (although it's true that any big fish in Italy swims in a murky pond).

Then there were the charges of sharp business practice. Accusations are one thing, convictions are another. Berlusconi has been put on trial for corruption – by "Communist magistrates", he would say – no less than seven times. Four of those trials initially resulted in guilty verdicts, but all four were later overturned on appeal. In a number of cases, Berlusconi was acquitted because time ran out, meaning that the case was thrown out under the statute of limitations. Time limits are crucial to prevent the hounding of politicians by a politicized judiciary. That was, no doubt, why Berlusconi's Forza Italia government voted to halve the statute of limitations on false accounting to seven and a half years (thus ensuring Berlusconi's own pre-office record was legally untouchable).

Immunity from prosecution for serving politicians is also very practical, which was surely why the government also declared Berlusconi to be officially immune from prosecution – while he was actually in the middle of being tried for bribing a judge during a takeover deal. The immunity law didn't last long, being overturned by a constitutional court in January 2004. But then, as Berlusconi's Forza Italia colleague Carlo Taormina commented, "only a Communist could conceive such a ruling". Blaming the so-called "red togas" – judges named after the colour of their politics, not their judicial robes – is a typical move. Any setback in Italy, it seems, must be the result of a conspiracy.

Apart from being a dangerous game in itself, any discussion of Berlusconi's legal position is jeopardized by the constantly shifting state of affairs. For the record, in October 2007, he was definitively cleared on one of the key cases made against him by his opponents – that of bribing judges to prevent the sale of food group SME to a rival company. In a Dickensian manner, the case dated right back to the 1980s. At the time of writing, inevitably, other cases were pending, although Berlusconi's third electoral victory, won in April 2008, looked set to alter the political – and perhaps judicial – landscape all over again.

SOURCES

Books

Giuseppe Genna In the Name of Ishmael (2004). Complex literary thriller featuring two Italian detectives' investigations steadily converging on a mysterious arch-villain, Ishmael, who seems to be at the centre of forty years of European conspiracies and ritual murders.

Paul Ginsborg A History of Contemporary Italy: Society and Politics, 1943–1988 (2003) and **Italy and its Discontents** (2003). Ginsborg is the pre-eminent historian of post-war Italy and the best guide to the background of its conspiracy theories. More recently, he published a compelling, insightful and hostile study of the Berlusconi era, *Silvio Berlusconi: Television, Power and Patrimony*.

Tobias Jones The Dark Heart of Italy (2005). Not just a portrait of post-war Italy, or a book about conspiracy theories, or just another "my year in the sun" publication – but all three. This describes the author's fascinating journey into the world of conspiracy theorizing.

Leonardo Sciascia The Moro Affair and the Mystery of Majorana (2004). An enthralling indictment of the Italian state – and of the Christian Democrats, in particular – by a Sicilian novelist and member of the parliamentary commission investigating the Moro murder.

Websites

Ⓦ **www.americanatheist.org/pope99/calvi.html** Full exposition of the Calvi–Gelli–Marcinkus–Sindona–John Paul I affair, with black-and-white photos of the protagonists.

The EU

This book's most surprising agent of conspiracy has to be the European Union. Al Qaeda – fine; the CIA – naturally; the Knights Templar – frankly, no, but we take your point. But the giant bureaucracy that is the European Union? Really? From one viewpoint, of course, the EU is a kind of conspiracy, inasmuch as it's an agreement between powerful nations to order affairs to their own advantage. As a legal entity ratified by parliaments, however, it's not exactly secretive or malevolent – the usual conditions for a "conspiracy" to be labelled as such. Eurosceptics – particularly of the "Little Englander" variety – might disagree, claiming that the EU, like a kind of political vampire, feeds on national sovereignty in order to grow. Unlike European national parliaments, such Eurosceptics say, the EU is neither properly democratic nor practicably accountable. Hence it may behave like a power-hungry, conspiratorial cabal.

But all this is politics, not conspiracy theorizing. Maybe the EU is democratic, maybe it isn't. Maybe its advocates do want to create a European superstate, maybe they don't. True conspiracists see more esoteric dangers. In Northern Ireland, for example, Ian Paisley's pro-British, ultra-Protestant Democratic Unionist Party liked to put about the idea that the EU is… a Catholic plot. Professor Arthur Noble, a DUP-backed speaker, is quoted on Paisley's website as saying: "The European Union was intended from the outset as a gigantic confidence-trick which would eventually hurtle the nations of Europe into economic, social, political and religious union." Thus far, most British Conservatives might agree. But Noble goes on to state that the "prime mover behind the EU conspiracy" is none other than "the Vatican". Surely not even the most Europhobic Tory could get behind that argument. In August 2003, however, Adrian Hilton – later the Conservative candidate for Slough – wrote in the *Spectator* magazine that "a Catholic EU will inevitably result in the subjugation of Britain's Protestant ethos to Roman Catholic social, political and religious teaching". (And this in the EU that so vehemently opposed inscribing any mention of religion into its new constitution.) Hilton was quickly deselected.

But neo-Paisleyan anti-Catholicism is nothing compared to some of the rhetoric coming out of evangelo-hysterical America. One conspiracy blog site recalls the Book of Revelation: "Then I saw another beast, coming out of the earth. He had two horns like a lamb, but he spoke like a dragon." The beast, it seems, has been "pretty well pegged as the second-coming of the Holy Roman Empire based out of Europe". Someone, the writer suggests, "has to run this new Holy Roman Empire from the political side" (apparently not realizing that, as Voltaire put it, the Early Modern political conglomeration that was the Holy Roman Empire was "neither holy, nor Roman, nor an empire"). The beast's master, of course, is "aspiring Marxist dictator" – to quote another US-based website – Javier Solana, the EU's high representative for foreign and security policy. Elsewhere, Solana's "meteoric rise to power" is compared to that of the Antichrist, and his office is blamed for a massive hacking attack on a good, Christian (and anti-EU) blogger. Luckily "her firewalls held", and Solana was thwarted.

Behind this kind of frothy-mouthed rhetoric seems to lie a recognition that the EU is becoming a serious challenge to US unilateralism and power. EU support for absurd, unscientific notions like climate change (see p.305) or international law is interpreted as a cynical move to limit the US's freedom of action. And not just by the wacko fringe. An adviser to George W. Bush, Myron Ebell of the Competitive Enterprise Institute (funded by Esso to the tune of $1.5 million a year), claimed on BBC Radio 4's flagship *Today* programme that the concept of global warming was EU propaganda aimed at disrupting the US economy.

The European Parliament in Strasbourg: mega-conspiracy or mega-bureaucracy?

Confusingly, left-wing Eurosceptics, especially in France, protest that the EU is behind a *right*-wing conspiracy to impose free-market neoliberalism on Europe. Meanwhile, the former British secretary of state for international development, Clare Short, has accused the EU of being behind a massive conspiracy that keeps Africa impoverished, thanks to the generous agricultural subsidies that effectively close European markets to African farmers. Which seems pretty much spot on – though the Common Agricultural Policy isn't exactly a secret.

SOURCES

Books

T.R. Reid **The United States of Europe: The New Superpower and the End of American Supremacy** (2004). The former *Washington Post* Europe chief calls the EU a "waking giant" with more people, wealth, trade and leverage in international organizations than the US (the EU is apparently also better-loved). As the euro may yet undermine all America's military supremacy and end its global dominance, Reid rings the warning bell of the threat the EU poses to the US, that Americans have been oblivious to for too long.

Websites

ⓦ**europa.eu** The official website for the European Union (the latest EU news and developments can be found at ⓦ**www.euobserver.com**).

ⓦ**www.freemasonrywatch.org/eu.html** An unofficial, unsanitized investigation into the more sinister workings of the EU.

The Council on Foreign Relations

The Council on Foreign Relations describes itself on its website www.cfr.org as "an independent, national membership organization", where policy makers, government figures, leading thinkers, journalists and others can "better understand the world and the foreign policy choices facing the United States". From its offices in New York and Washington DC, the CFR disseminates books, articles and its journal, *Foreign Affairs*, and also runs programmes to develop "the next generation of foreign policy leaders".

While the calibre and breadth of the CFR's 3605-strong membership is comparable with the World Economic Forum (see p.249) or the Bilderberg Group (see p.250) – and there's considerable crossover between the three – the CFR is exclusively American. *The Washington Post* has called it "the nearest thing we have to a ruling establishment in the United States", which has "for fifty years managed our international affairs and our military-industrial complex". Around five hundred of the members are current or former US government officials, including all the CIA directors, former secretary of state Colin Powell, his successor Condoleezza Rice, Vice President Dick Cheney, former secretary of defense Richard Perle, former assistant secretary of defense and new World Bank president Paul Wolfowitz, and Bill Clinton and practically everyone in his administration. Indeed, all of the two main parties' US presidential candidates between 1948 and 1972 (with the exception of Barry Goldwater) were members, as were all the American members of the Bilderberg Group steering committee from 1955 to 1971.

The rest of the CFR membership is composed of bank chiefs, university deans, diplomats, newspaper and news network executives and operatives, captains and executives of civilian and military industries, and the like. Professor Carroll Quigley of Georgetown University, who Bill Clinton praised as his mentor in 1992, called the CFR a bastion of policy continuums in US government, irrespective of which party was in office. Its purpose, he wrote in *Tragedy and Hope* in 1966, was that "the two parties should be almost identical, so that the American people can 'throw the rascals out' at any election without leading to any profound or extensive shifts in policy".

Officially, the Council on Foreign Relations was founded in 1921 in Paris by several Americans who had taken part in the negotiations that produced the post-World War I Treaty of Versailles. However, the CFR was not a completely spontaneous concoction. Quigley called it an "international Anglophile network" set up as the US counterpart to the Royal Institute of International Affairs (the RIIA has around 1800 members and reports in *The*

World Today and *International Affairs*), aka Chatham House. The RIIA was the source of the "Chatham House Rule", which states that participants can freely use the information received, but that they cannot reveal the identity nor affiliation of who said it or who was present at the time it was said.

THE NEW WORLD ORDER

The New World Order (NWO) crops up in countless conspiracy theories. While the detail varies as to exactly which institutions or individuals are involved, and to what ends, the basic premise remains the same: that a group or groups are seeking to establish a single, all-powerful global government (hence the theory's other moniker, the "One World Government"). According to Dr John Coleman in his 1992 book *Conspirators' Hierarchy: The Story of the Committee of 300*, the NWO is a group of "permanent non-elected hereditary oligarchists", chosen by some "feudal system" to enforce globally uniform laws, through the courts and military force.

Being an unelected institute of global governance, the United Nations is in the frame for many US conspiracy theorists as the ultimate expression of the New World Order. As such, the UN pushes its economic diktats through the International Monetary Fund, the World Bank and the World Economic Forum, and its laws through the World Court and International Criminal Court, and it enforces its rule through NATO bombers and UN peacekeepers. Other institutions supposedly in on the plot are the Bilderberg Group (see p.250), the Trilateral Commission (see p.143) and the Council on Foreign Relations (see p.140).

The NWO's agents are said to be responsible for nearly all of the major wars, economic successes and maelstroms of the last century, and are believed to have profited greatly from each. The Great Depression of the early 1930s, World Wars I and II, the Bolshevik Revolution, the Cold War, the Soviet Union's collapse – all were, apparently, NWO projects, with Communists and far-right US Republicans part and parcel of the same conspiracy. Famine, disease and AIDS (see p.290) are all supposedly NWO weapons to control and cull the world's population and reduce pressures on finite resources.

In the US, other calamities – like the chaos the "Millennium Bug" was supposed to bring (but didn't, see p.265), or terrorist events like the Oklahoma City bombing (see p.228) and 9/11 (see p.395) – have been engineered to justify the imposition of martial law under the Federal Emergency Management Agency (FEMA). This would quell the few who can't be brainwashed through mind-control methods such as MK-ULTRA (see p.210).

The idea of a One World Government is often associated with Professor Carroll Quigley, a specialist in twentieth-century US history cited approvingly by President Bill Clinton in one of his speeches. Part exposé, part apologia for rule by the elite, Quigley's 1300-page tome *Tragedy and Hope* – which, ironically, favours the cock-up rather than the conspiracy theory of history – advocates a single body of global governance.

The current manifestation of such a body is, of course, the UN, but for other conspiracists the NWO's origins reach back to mystical groups like the Illuminati (see p.82) and the Freemasons (see p.93), which are both now said to control the NWO. One Christian conspiracy theorist, Pat Robertson, traces the NWO's origins back to before the Tower of Babel, when one government and one language unified the world (or so the Old Testament has it). A single global government is also apparently foretold in the Bible's Book of Revelations, so Robertson argues that today's NWO is the work of Satan, an interpretation supported by the prevalence of war, famine, pestilence and death, the Four Horsemen of the Apocalypse.

Other conspiracy theorists claim that the expression "New World Order" is part of the currency – literally so, as it is inscribed in Latin on the US dollar bill amid all the supposedly Masonic imagery (see p.127) as *Novus Ordo Seculorum* (although the expression actually means "New Order of the Ages"). It also became a catchphrase of President George H.W. Bush, who told Congress in January 1991 that what was at stake in the impending Gulf War was "a big idea – a new world order, where diverse nations are drawn together in common cause to achieve the universal aspirations of mankind: peace and security, freedom and the rule of law".

The Gulf War (see p.412), authorized by the UN Security Council and waged by its main members, is thus seen by some as the first overt NWO war, with the White House – and the Bush family – at its helm. From this perspective, the New World Order is less about the UN subverting the power and sovereignty of the US, than about the US exploiting the UN to enforce the Order of the New World – a conspiracy theory that, for political realists, might seem to come uncomfortably close to the truth.

Indeed, the RIIA says on its website www.riia.org that it was at Versailles that "the idea of an Anglo-American institute of foreign affairs to study international problems with a view to preventing future wars" was conceived, with the RIIA set up in 1920 prior to its "sister institute". One theory is that some English Round Tablers, who were mostly of aristocratic stock, formed the Cliveden Set, who, led by Edward VIII, disgraced themselves by consorting with Hitler and advocating appeasement in the 1930s. Likewise, the CFR is said to have had senior government figures working with Nazis not only pre-1941 (as Ambassador Joseph Kennedy and Senator Prescott Bush advocated), but also immediately after the war, against the Communists (except, of course, for those members of the US government suspected of being Communist agents). After a while it seems that the CFR is guilty of something simply because it exists.

According to Robert Gaylon Ross's conspiracy manual *The Who's Who of the Elite* – which identifies the Bilderberg Group, the Trilateral Commission and the CFR as the "three major secret organizations" in the global Elite – the RIIA and the CFR weren't spontaneous setups so much as modernized versions of nineteenth-century Round Table groups. These were under the umbrella of the International Secret Society, and they were all established by Imperial Britain's most successful venturer and diamond magnate, Cecil Rhodes. There were Round Tables in India, Canada, Australia and elsewhere in the English-speaking empire to keep the imperially minded up to speed on how England sought to run the world, and on their roles within it. The Round Tables then morphed into those individual countries' Councils on Foreign Relations or Institutes of International Affairs.

Former US Navy admiral and former CFR member Chester Ward has lambasted the CFR as a gang of bankers in the pocket of those other bankers at the Bilderberg Group, all bent on global domination. Ignoring both the banking and the Anglophile angles, the right-wing US magazine *New American* has, by contrast, called it "a coterie of internationalists" – read communists – and the "architects of the New World Order", who have been "working furtively for decades to undermine America's nationhood and constitutional order" under an endless procession of UN treaties and laws. *New American* also charges that every successive "loss" to communism, from China, Korea, Cuba and Vietnam to the failure of the 1956 uprising in Hungary and the sending of aid to Communist Poland and Romania, was engineered by CFR members in the US government. The list of alleged conspirators includes the Dulles brothers, John J. McCloy, Dean Rusk, Robert McNamara, Richard Nixon, Henry Kissinger, Zbigniew Brzezinski, Cyrus Vance, Warren Christopher, George Shultz and William J. Casey. By this reckoning, the CFR is the US sector of the "Internationalist Power Elite" responsible for tens of millions of deaths in World War II, Korea, Vietnam, the Gulf, Iraq and so on, and also for the "Global Order" of the League of Nations, the Atlantic Charter, NATO, the UN, the IMF and the World Bank.

SOURCES

Books

Carroll Quigly Tragedy and Hope (1996). This is positively the bible of proof for conspiracists of the thinking and plotting behind everything from the New World Order to the International Banking Conspiracy. Quite simply, Quigley's thesis is that the planet is governed by international laws and financial flows that are ruled over by a select, unelected, unaccountable few, but whether he is advocating this system or merely reflecting it is a matter of debate.

Robert Gaylon Ross, Sr Who's Who of the Elite (2002). Ross bookends a massive list of Bilderberg, Trilateral Commission and Council on Foreign Relations members (the "three major secret organizations") with discourses on their origins, ulterior purposes and position in the global Elite, which he contends has David Rockefeller as its tsar.

Websites

Ⓦ **www.cfr.org** The council's own website, which has a list of sources on its views on the globe's hot spots and issues.

Ⓦ **www.newamerican.com** An oasis of conspiracy theories about the CFR. The magazine evidently has little time or respect for the institution, but some interesting kernels of information float up in its foaming copy.

The Trilateral Commission

Another major cabal of colluding conspirators, according to conspiracy theorists, is the Trilateral Commission. The Commission was established in 1973, when international economic pressures such as the oil crisis were piling pressures on the US as the world's major capitalist superpower. As the Commission itself puts it on its own official website: "There was a sense that the United States was no longer in such a singular leadership position as it had been in earlier post-WWII years, and that a more shared form of leadership – including Europe, and Japan in particular – would be needed for the international system to navigate successfully the major challenges of the coming years."

The Commission consists of the EU, North America and Japan (originally alone but now head of the Asian sector, which currently includes China, New Zealand, Indonesia and Malaysia) – the three main centres of industrialized, democratic power – and meets annually in the capital of a member nation. The European sector has expanded to include Eastern European states such as Estonia, Poland and Slovenia.

The Trilateral Commission was conceived by David Rockefeller, the former chairman of the Council on Foreign Relations (CFR), who funded Polish geopolitical analyst Zbigniew Brzezinksi to establish and direct it from 1973 to 1976. The then-governor of Georgia, Jimmy Carter, was also in on the group's foundation: when he became president in 1976, he appointed Brzezinski as his national security affairs adviser, defence adviser and National Security Council chief. These events are repeatedly cited in conspiracy books such as Pat Robertson's *The New World Order* and James Perloff's *The Shadows of Power* as proof of the power of the Trilateral Commission, as well as that of the "Elite" in building a New World Order – not that the Elite was able to stop Carter losing office in 1980 to non-Trilateralist and non-CFR member Ronald Reagan. It's also suggested that the Trilateral Commission is involved in some rivalry with the Council for Foreign Relations, so there can be dissenting, competing views in the quest for world dominance.

Senator Barry Goldwater, the defeated Republican presidential candidate of 1964, later dismissed the Trilateral Commission as "Rockefeller's newest international cabal". He charged that it helped Carter to win both the presidential nomination and the presidency by mobilizing "the money power of the Wall Street bankers, the intellectual influence of the academic community – which is subservient to the wealth of the great tax-free foundations – and the media controllers represented in the membership of the CFR and the Trilateral". The Commission has been further attacked by right-wingers as a coterie of bankers, stemming from the loans totalling $52 billion that were made to the developing world at the time of the oil crisis, which were allegedly spearheaded by David Rockefeller's Chase Manhattan Bank.

The Trilateral Commission certainly has a very strong economic orientation, and while its actual policy direction or constituted powers (if any) are not known, it does serve as an extraordinary networking institute. Its European chairman is Peter Sutherland, the chairman of BP plc and Goldman Sachs International, a director of the World Economic Forum and a former director general of GATT/WTO. His impressive portfolio is paralleled by many other Trilateral Commission members, who include the great and the good (or not-so-good) from past and present US governments – George H.W. Bush, Dick Cheney, Bill Clinton, Paul Wolfowitz, Henry Kissinger, Alan Greenspan – plus (at some time) Ken Lay of Enron, and to maintain the presence of the original founder's family, Senator John D. Rockefeller IV.

Other members of the Commission include directors, CEOs and presidents past and present of US, European and

East Asian companies such as Mobil Corp, Exxon, CNN, Time Warner, Chase Manhattan Bank, Citibank, Citigroup, Citicorp, N.M. Rothschild & Sons, J.P. Morgan Chase, the Carlyle Group, RAND Corp, Bechtel, Halliburton Co, Banca Sella, First National Bank of Chicago, German Council on Foreign Relations, Carnegie Endowment for International Peace, French Institute for International Relations, World Trade Organization, *The New York Times*, Fuji Xerox, and Banco Itau SA of Brazil. The list grows longer all the time, and with it, inevitably, suspicions about its intentions, influence and power.

SOURCES

Books

James Perloff The Shadows of Power (1988) and **Pat Robertson The New World Order** (1991). Both tomes are of a similar ilk, lambasting the secret world of decisions taken behind closed doors in smoke-filled rooms.

Websites

Ⓦ **www.trilateral.org** The Commission's official (and not particularly detailed or revealing) homepage, which has purpose, publications and upcoming meetings, plus membership details if you're interested in joining.

Organized crime

The very notion of organized crime implies conspiracy and corruption. Drug trafficking, gambling, loan sharking, protection rackets, prostitution... These unsavoury practices feature in countless conspiracy theories, in large part due to the shadowy profiles of the men behind them (understandable as most of the activities they're engaged in are illegal).

The Mafia

"Mafia" – meaning "hostility to the law" or "boldness" in the Sicilian dialect, while "Mafioso" means "man of honour" – is now used as a general term for secret criminal organizations, but the word originally referred to the Italian, and especially Sicilian, family gangs that formed in both Italy and the US. (The term Cosa Nostra, or "this thing of ours", is also used.) It's been claimed that the first Mafia families came to prominence in medieval times as part of the resistance to Turkish, French and Spanish rule, but by the late nineteenth century there were powerful Mafia groups all across Italy. They then developed organically in the US through Italian emigration, principally to New York and Chicago.

The Mafia became made men in the land of opportunity during Prohibition, profiting enormously from the illicit production, smuggling and distribution of booze, while having more than a few shootouts with each other and the civic authorities (which ultimately led to the formation of the FBI). Post-Prohibition, many families moved into new ventures like gambling, loan sharking and eventually drug dealing, and extended their purchasing power from bent policemen to politicians.

During World War II, the Allied invasion of Sicily and Italy in 1943 supposedly depended on the US Army working with big US-based Mafia groups still tied to their homeland. This was a good quid pro quo, as Fascist dictator Benito Mussolini had caused many Mafia men to flee to the US in the first place, so they returned – backed by US Army firepower – for the ultimate vendetta. Gangsters like Joseph "Joe Bananas" Bonanno and "Lucky" Luciano profited handsomely from the new power and honour this gave them, which carried over into the post-war battle against Communism.

The Mafia is also widely believed to have muscled in on American labour unions, particularly the Teamsters Union, which was led by Jimmy Hoffa who mysteriously disappeared without trace in 1975. (He was officially declared dead in 1983, one theory being that his body was run through a Mob-controlled fat-rendering plant.) After the war, the FBI and CIA may have fought the Mafia, but they also employed a few of them as heavies in the war against Cuba (see p.20). The Mafia have also been linked to the deaths of Marilyn Monroe, Martin Luther King and both John F. and Robert Kennedy. In Italy, the Mafia has been blamed for the murders of many Italian judges and politicians, with investigations reaching into the upper echelons of Italy's government.

In November 2007, while arresting a Sicilian Mafia boss in Palermo, Italian police reported finding a Mafia loyalty oath and a "Ten Commandments"-style list governing Mafioso behaviour. The ten dos and don'ts proclaim, among others things, that a "good mobster" cannot be related to a police officer, let alone be seen with one, and that while one's wife must be treated with respect – and other Mafiosi's wives not even looked at – not even childbirth can override being ever-available for Cosa Nostra duty (as another commandment says, "appointments must absolutely be respected"). The list doesn't say anything about "thou shalt not kill", though.

The Triads

With a similar worldwide reach are the Chinese Triads, secret criminal groups that have dominated the Chinese underworld for centuries. Based on sworn brotherhood and built on kinship, the Triads derive their name from the triangular shape – symbolizing man, heaven and earth – of the Chinese character for "secret society" that they use as an emblem. However, the name was first applied to them by the British colonial government in the Triad stronghold of Hong Kong. Triads first emerged in the seventeenth century as underground political organizations fighting the Qing dynasty to restore their Ming predecessors. After the Qing fell, the Triads lost public support and financing along with their original reason for existing, but being men of violent means, they turned to earning their daily rice through extortion and other rackets.

The Communist victory in China's Civil War in 1949 made the Triads head for Hong Kong, Macau and various Chinatowns beyond. These days it's reckoned that there are up to 60 Triad groups and a total of around 100,000 members (with major groups like the 14K Triad or Sun Yee On having several tens of thousands of members globally). Initiation ceremonies can involve drinking the blood of a beheaded cockerel before an incense-burning altar, and numbers are used to denote role and rank. Smaller groups use tricks like wearing right-handed white gloves for recognition (the imaginatively titled White-Glove Gang).

In recent years, the Triads have been moving back to the Chinese mainland and profiting (in various legal and not-so-legal ways) from China's rapid economic growth, with key figures in place in financial institutions and government. As a result, sources of Triad income are changing from smuggling to legitimate business investments in southern China (although tactics like leaking key information are causing consternation for foreign multinationals based there). Indeed, the Communists seem to tolerate this: in 1997, one Chinese law officer acknowledged the Triads as true patriots. One big issue is China's unwillingness to address issues of intellectual property, and much Triad income derives from trading fake CDs and DVDs. However, they also make money from drug smuggling, racketeering bus and taxi companies, and karaoke bars. They are also involved in the traffic of illegal immigrants to North America and Europe, through affiliated gangs referred to as "snakeheads".

Gangsters they may be, but the Triads have a strict code of conduct, worshipping the Confucian qualities of humanity, wisdom, loyalty, righteousness and obedience, as embodied by the ancient Chinese hero Lord Guan (also a deity to the Hong Kong police). Apparently it's this code and the fact that disorderly society makes for bad business that has made the streets of Vladivostock so much safer in the twenty-first century, as Triads have moved in to take over the city's illicit businesses from the brashly violent Russian Mafia. Indeed, it's reported that hundreds of millions of dollars are passing through underground banks into the Russian Far East, not just into casinos, hotels and hostess bars, but also into logging and fishing enterprises. However, neither the Chinese nor the Russians stray much into drugs, dominated as it is by Tajiks, Kazakhs, Chechens smuggling heroin from Afghanistan, and some North Korean government officials.

The Russian Mafia

The ethnic mix of groups operating across Russia belies the generalization "Russian Mafia", which covers all the gangs and groups that sprang up in the vacuum that followed the USSR's collapse. With many ex-Soviet officers, soldiers and KGB officials finding themselves unemployed in the early 1990s, crime was the surest route to riches for some and a matter of basic survival for others (such as the sportsmen and martial arts experts who became their henchmen). In Moscow, at least, you can tell a Mafioso by the fact they tend to dress darkly and wear black flat caps, with minders in bomber jackets and "officers" in long, plush coats. Some seek to show off their status by, for example, having car horns that play the theme tune to *The Godfather*. For ordinary Russians, though, it's no joke.

Across Russia and its ex-Soviet satellites in Central Asia and Eastern Europe, numerous networks of trafficking in drugs, prostitution and illegal workers have sprung up, reaching into the EU and North America. Even the ethnic identity of many Russian Mafiosi has been obscured by numerous bogus (but successful) applications for Israeli passports, and billions of dollars have gone to Israel by that route. Arms also sell well, with military stockpiles and ex-Soviet factories still producing dirt-cheap, but efficient, weaponry. It's been feared that the profusion of Soviet missile and nuclear warheads could end up being pawned off by dodgy army units and their Mafia friends.

The Yakuza

A similar level of power infiltration was once enjoyed by Japan's Mafia, the Yakuza, the backbone of a weird nexus of ultra-right-wing military officers, gangsters and government officials that used espionage, terrorism and assassination to control Japan's colonial dominions in East Asia, while profiting from the opium trade, gambling and prostitution. After World War II, the Yakuza moved into the black market to such an extent that they came to control the major seaports and fought off efforts by the occupying Americans to close them down.

It was all a far cry from the loose community of pedlars and gamblers from whom the term Yakuza originated (Ya-Ku-Sa, or eight-nine-three, was the value of the worst possible hand in a Japanese card game called Oicho-Kabu – which suggests the value of the original Yakuza to society and the seediness of their past). Roaming samurai and ronin warriors, employed as vigilante groups to protect villages, sometimes ganged up, but most were drifters who were pushed into cities by Japan's industrialization. There they engaged in commercial ventures and moved into red-light districts – if not directly investing, then "protecting" them.

These days the larger Yakuza groups also dabble in property speculation, banking and extorting stock from shareholders, and such is their quasi-legitimate presence that their offices have signs outside denoting their purpose. (The major Yakuza chapter in Kobe was instrumental – and far more effective than the civic authorities – in providing relief after the earthquake there in 1995.) In person, however, the easiest way to identify Yakuza is through their lack of fingers, as it's a Yakuza penance to cut off your digits. Ironically, this has led to problems with imported cartoons such as *Postman Pat* and *The Simpsons*, whose three-fingered characters apparently convey gangster connotations to their infant audiences.

SOURCES

Books

John Dickie Cosa Nostra: A History of the Sicilian Mafia (2004). Dickie maps the rise of the Sicilian Mafia from gangs on Palermo's streets to their "tolerated" status under Italy's post-war governments and their unnerving role in the US as an economic and political enemy–ally to the government.

Websites

Ⓦ **www.fbi.gov** and **wwww.interpol.int** The official sites of the FBI and Interpol – much of the information we have about the various mob groups comes from the law enforcement agencies that are (supposedly) battling them. Sadly, the major Mafia families seem reluctant to have their own official websites promoting their activities.

Ⓦ **www.mobmagazine.com** General interest site concerning all matters mob- and Mafia-related, both historical and more recent updates of news stories both big and small fry. The stories don't display their sources (as in the original publications, not the name of the snitch).

Secret services

It's almost a surprise to read a conspiracy theory that doesn't involve the CIA somewhere, such is the tentacular reach on the imagination of that secretive organization. But it's not the only agency to register on the conspiracy theorists' radar; when theorists twitch the curtains, they're also looking for the agents of Russia, Britain and Israel.

The KGB

The KGB, or Komitet Gosudarstvennoy Bezopasnosti (Committee for State Security), was the USSR's secret service agency. The agency had been around since 1917 (when it was known as the Cheka), a secret police charged with liquidating so much as a dissenting thought against the Communist rulers, and carrying out missions against enemies abroad. The KGB, based in the imposing Lubyanka office-cum-prison and torture chamber in Moscow, was divided into various directorates (foreign operations, internal political control, military counterintelligence and so on) which also provided bodyguards and patrolled the USSR's borders.

The KGB successfully bloodied its American and British counterparts' noses many times. Two apparent KGB spies were Americans Ethel and Julius Rosenberg, who were executed for giving the Soviets atom bomb secrets that enabled them to build their own nukes. Then there was the KGB "Cambridge spy ring" in the British Secret Intelligence Service in the 1960s, which included Kim Philby, the head of MI6's counterespionage unit. Philby saved more than a few Soviet agents while working undercover in MI6, and allowed scores of British agents to be caught and killed. Another KGB spy was George Blake; employed by MI6 in the 1950s, he was captured by the Chinese during the Korean War and became a "Manchurian Candidate" on his return to the UK, informing the KGB about British intelligence operations such as tunnels for defectors in Vienna and Berlin. Although he was eventually caught and imprisoned by the British, Blake was busted from jail in the mid-1960s and escaped to Moscow.

In the end, however, the KGB got too big for its boots. In August 1991, KGB chief Colonel Vladimir Kryuchkov helped orchestrate the hardline Communist coup attempt against President Mikhail Gorbachev. The coup failed, Kryuchkov was arrested and the KGB disbanded. The KGB was replaced by the Federalnaya Sluzhba Bezopasnosti (FSB) in late 1991, though there is precious little difference in practice between the two organizations, and the ignominy of the betrayal didn't stop former KGB chief Vladimir Putin from becoming president of Russia in 2000. Only in Belarus, under the leadership of Stalinist dictator Lukashenko, is the secret service still called the KGB, but to the locals it's the "association of crude bandits".

The Turkish man that shot Pope John Paul II in 1981 was supposedly on the KGB payroll, and it's also been suspected – but officially discounted – that JFK's assassin, Lee Harvey Oswald, was one of their agents. However, the KGB was also capable of creating its own conspiracy theories. The notion that AIDS was a concoction of the US military was a theory put about, in part, by the KGB. *The Sword and the Shield: The Mitrokhin Archive and the Secret History of the KGB,* by Christopher Andrew and Vasili Mitrokhin, describes how Soviet leaders and KGB chiefs, having never lived in the West, could never really understand it, or how America's levels of economic production and innovation were achieved with so little apparent regulation. Defector Arkadi Shevchenko noted: "Many are inclined to the fantastic notion that there must be a secret control center somewhere in the United States. They themselves, after all, are used to a system ruled by a small group working in secrecy in one place."

SIS-MI6

The Secret Intelligence Service (SIS) – aka MI6 or Military Intelligence Section 6 since World War II, or Her Majesty's Secret Service – is the UK's external secret service agency, founded in 1909. The SIS coat of arms, with the motto *semper occultus* ("always secret"), shows a grey brain contained within a green "C", a letter that stands for the SIS's founder Sir Mansfield Cumming. Every SIS director since has been referred to by the first letter of his or her surname (like "M" in the James Bond novels – Bond himself is an MI6 man). The SIS's real-life headquarters is based in Vauxhall, London; a yellow and green pile of blocks known as "Legoland" to those who work there, it also featured in the Bond film *The World Is Not Enough* (1999).

KGB spies Ethel and Julius Rosenberg under arrest in 1950 for passing US atom bomb secrets to the USSR.

In the 1920s, SIS agents were billeted to embassies around the world as "Passport Control Officers" – not the most convincing of covers – and it wasn't too long before they were rumbled. A notable early SIS venture was backing the Russian-born "ace of spies" Sidney Reilly and ex-terrorist Boris Savinkov in their bid to bring down the Soviet government, but both Reilly and Savinkov were caught and executed in 1925. Later "successes" attributed to covert SIS action (in joint ventures with the CIA) include the overthrows of the elected Iranian leader Mohammed Mossadeq in 1953 and of Patrice Lumumba, the first elected prime minister of Congo, in 1961. The SIS was also reportedly involved in triggering paramilitary conflict in the Lebanon in the 1980s and providing duff intelligence to justify the Iraq War in 2002. In the main, the SIS doesn't figure much in conspiracy theories these days, bar an attributed role in a plot to kill Princess Diana.

Mossad

A secret service with a far more fearsome reputation than the SIS is Israel's spy unit, the Institute for Intelligence and Special Operations – or Mossad (Hebrew for "institute") to most people. "Where no counsel is, the people fall, but in the multitude of counsellors there is safety" (Proverbs 11:14) is the organization's motto, and Mossad's "counsellors" engage in everything from diplomacy and intelligence analysis to covert action and counterterrorism. The Institute also works to bring Jews to Israel from countries where official agencies to facilitate Jewish migration aren't allowed, notably Syria, Iran and Ethiopia. It was created amid the chaos of the Palestine Mandate as the *Shai* or information service, and given official sanction in 1949 by Prime Minister Ben Gurion. With its base in Tel Aviv and some 2000 staff, Mossad is part of the prime minister's office and it reports directly to him.

The list of Mossad's operations and "achievements" is long and distinguished. Mossad successfully located and kidnapped top Nazi Adolf Eichmann in South America in 1960, bringing him back for trial. The Institute also found and killed all those responsible for the Munich massacre of Israeli athletes at the 1972 Olympic Games. Mossad kidnapped the Israeli nuclear scientist Mordechai Vanunu from Italy (Vanunu had let on that Israel had nuclear bombs) and set up Iraq's Osiraq nuclear reactor for air strikes in 1981. Mossad agents with fake Canadian passports were caught in Jordan in 1997 trying to poison a Hamas leader, and a number of assassinations of Palestinian nationalists can also, no doubt, be laid at their door.

Conspiracy theorists have also put Mossad behind the assassination of John F. Kennedy, apparently over his opposition to Israel developing nuclear weapons. Mossad has even been blamed for the 9/11 attacks by anti-Semitic conspiracy theorists, who claim that many thousands of Jewish workers at the World Trade Center were absent on that fateful day (see p.402). Czech-born British newspaper tycoon Robert Maxwell was supposed to be a KGB agent, rescued by Communists from the Nazis, but was also apparently a Mossad agent; when Mossad found out about his KGB connection, Israeli frogmen are said to have assassinated Maxwell on his yacht. Apparently, it was also Mossad that brought down British cabinet minister David Mellor after he made a pro-Palestinian statement in 1988. Mossad tapped Mellor's phone and rumbled his extra-marital affair; when the press learnt of Mellor's philandering antics, he resigned from office.

SOURCES

Books

Christopher Andrew and Oleg Gordievsky KGB: The Inside Story of its Foreign Operations from Lenin to Gorbachev (1992). Coming out just as the Cold War ended, this tome, co-written by an ex-KGB colonel, uncovers quite how successful the Soviet's shadowy spies were at recruiting foreign traitors, setting up coups and "liquidating" opponents. Somewhat academic in tone, but worth a read.

Christopher Andrew and Vasili Mitrokhin The Sword and the Shield: The Mitrokhin Archive and the Secret History of the KGB (2000). Andrew returns to his subject with KGB defector Mitrokhin and unveils more covert ops to discredit every American in the public eye, from Martin Luther King to Ronald Reagan, while leaving deep-cover sleeper agents strewn across the West, along with booby-trapped caches of arms and little sideshows such as trying to link Lee Harvey Oswald to the CIA.

Stephen Dorril MI6: Inside the World of Her Majesty's Secret Intelligence Service (2002). In this book the UK government apparently tried to suppress, Dorril portrays a blundering British spy organization that can't quite put together plots to kill or bring down Libya's Colonel Qaddafi, Albania's Enver Hoxha or Serbia's Slobodan Milosevic, but did manage to employ Nelson Mandela to tell all on Libya's funding for the IRA.

Films

Steven Spielberg Munich (2005). One of Mossad's most infamous capers – executing those responsible for the 1972 massacre of Israeli Olympians – is put on celluloid by the influential Hollywood filmmaker.

Websites

Ⓦ **www.bbc.co.uk/crime/fighters/mi6.shtml** A good brief on the British secret service, from the UK's state broadcaster.

Ⓦ **www.fas.org** Interesting write-ups about the past and present espionage capers of all the intelligence services can be found at the Federation of American Scientists' Intelligence Resource Program.

Ⓦ **www.fsb.ru** The official FSB site is only useful for Cyrillic-script readers.

Ⓦ **www.mossad.gov.il** Official homepage of Israel's spy unit.

Ⓦ **www.mi6.gov.uk** The official homepage of the British secret service.

SECRETS, MYTHS AND HOLY LIES

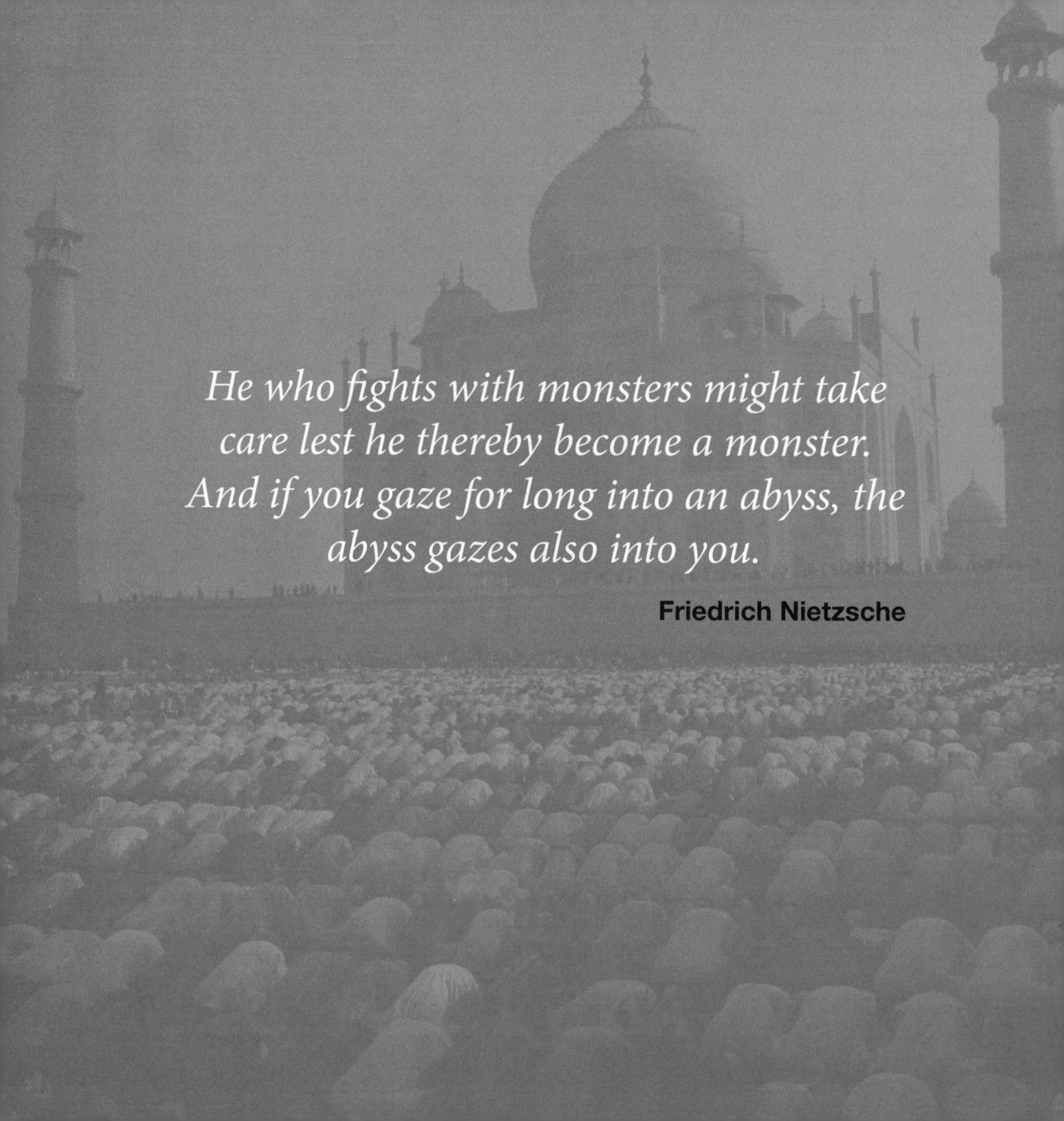

He who fights with monsters might take care lest he thereby become a monster. And if you gaze for long into an abyss, the abyss gazes also into you.

Friedrich Nietzsche

SECRETS, MYTHS AND HOLY LIES

Easily the oldest conspiracy in this book, predating the assassination of Tutankhamun (see p.4) by thousands of years, is the suppression of matriarchal religion. Not until the last fifty years have women, in the shape of female archaeologists, finally started to fight back, but things still haven't changed much. Men – or at least male academics – appear to have closed ranks to deny that the so-called "Great Goddess" ever existed. Archaeological infighting was also the key feature of the bizarre Taj Mahal conspiracy, in which some firebrand Hindu nationalists claimed that the world-famous Muslim tomb was, in fact, a Hindu temple.

The Dead Sea Scrolls controversy also transformed digging around in ancient dirt into high-octane religious politics. Some claimed that these ancient Jewish texts, discovered in the desert near Jerusalem in the 1940s, could seriously undermine Christianity. Unfortunately, the Vatican was busy burying the evidence as fast as it could be dug up.

And that wouldn't be the first time: the early Church supposedly conspired to suppress the alternative, "gnostic" accounts of Jesus' Crucifixion, some of which maintained that Jesus had never died at all, or that he was only a man, and not a god. Gnostic theories were revived by the medieval Cathars, who were exterminated by the established Church, and have been woven into religious conspiracy theories ever since, as guardians of unmentionable secrets. Modern theologians, meanwhile, attempted to prove that "Jesus" was nothing more than a water-walking collection of myths.

Parallel to the Jesus story is the conspiracy theory that early Christians covered up the truth about Mary Magdalene, who's said to have been Jesus' true apostle, or his wife, or even his divine consort in a male–female holy union. That at least was the tale trumpeted by Dan Brown's super-selling thriller *The Da Vinci Code*, which resurrected some ancient conspiracy theories, while finding time to publicize some new ones too. The book did little for the reputation of Opus Dei, a severe and some would say secretive Catholic group, but at least it took the heat off the Jesuits, the long-term historical also-rans to the Masons in the conspiracy stakes.

Not all religious conspiracy theories are ancient history. The current pope, Benedict XVI, has been the focus of plentiful speculation thanks to two previous jobs – as the Vatican's chief inquisitor in child-abuse cases and a teenage member of the Hitler Youth. And in 2007, some longstanding conspiracy theories about Mormons crept back into the news, thanks to Mitt Romney, a member of the Church of Jesus Christ of Latter-Day Saints, campaigning to be the Republican presidential nominee. Never mind a black man or a woman; could a Mormon ever really be US president?

The great conspiracy: patriarchy and the Great Goddess

The idea that patriarchy has suppressed the fact that women once ruled the world while goddesses ruled the roost in the heavens is the original mega-conspiracy. The main argument, put forward by some controversial archaeologists, is that European Palaeolithic and Neolithic culture, dating from around 25,000 BC until 2500 BC, was at root matriarchal, and the chief objects of worship were fertility goddesses, or even some original Great Goddess. This theory, of course, runs directly counter to Judaeo-Christian mythology, and the debate is hot: the "Goddess" thesis encompasses not just a millennia-long conspiracy to oppress women and suppress the worship of the feminine, but also a live, ongoing academic conspiracy to conceal the alleged discovery of that original, patriarchal conspiracy.

Early Amazons

From around the seventeenth century, evidence began to filter back from travellers that Europe's patriarchal social structure might not be the only possible form human society can take. The first to put forward a theory of an early, female-dominated culture was a Swiss philologist, Johann Jakob Bachofen, who in 1861 published the catchily titled *Mutterrecht*, or *Mother Right: An Investigation of the Religious and Juridical Character of Matriarchy in the Ancient World*. Bachofen speculated that, at some point in the distant past, women revolted against an earlier epoch of sexual subjugation and established matriarchy through the institution of marriage, and that this "Amazonian" world had, in turn, evolved into the patriarchal society of his day.

The earliest apparent evidence of matriarchal societies emerged during the first half of the twentieth century, when archaeologists dug up endless apparently ritual figurines of women at megalithic sites across Europe, and indeed all over the world. Palaeolithic and Neolithic statuettes were found with emphasized feminine characteristics such as breasts, buttocks and vulvas, or pregnant bellies. Some were apparently sitting on altars or thrones, or had animal heads – often seen as indicating the portrayal of a deity. Others were surrounded by eggs and animals, which are fertility symbols, or were depicted actually giving birth.

Gods and goddesses

From the 1950s onwards, religious historians and anthropologists began to provide corroboration in the form of myths about men overthrowing female power, which are particularly common among so-called "primitive" peoples

THE NEW WORLD RELIGION CONSPIRACY

For the alternative view, look no further than those arch-conspiracists, the Christian ultra-right. As they see it, New Age blasphemers have taken up the Goddess theory with enthusiasm, recreating Goddess-oriented rituals and rediscovering the joys of Goddess worship. This worship of the feminine is clearly nothing less than worship of the devil, and proof is found in other, older religious crimes, too: Catholic Marian cults and black Madonnas, Hindu Devi worship, Buddhist veneration of Tara. Yes, this is the work of Satan, the original and greatest conspirator, drawing his followers together into One World Religion – probably in league with the UN. Just wake up and smell the sulphur.

in Australia, Melanesia, Africa and the Amazon basin. There are also parallels within Indo-European culture: the Minoans, Etruscans and early Greeks, for example, all seem to have had elements of goddess or nature worship in their ideology, while legends of male priests taking control of the female Oracle were attached to the great shrine of Apollo. Some have tried to demonstrate, through the analysis of parallel symbolism, that the powerful goddess figures worshipped across the Mediterranean – Isis, Artemis, Astarte – all refer back to one Great Goddess or god-mother.

Similarly, in Hinduism, the many goddesses are supposed to refer back to one original Devi, sometimes called Ekakini, "the Only". The cultures of many of India's "tribal" peoples also contain elements of matriarchal society and goddess worship, albeit variously intermixed and overlaid with patriarchal beliefs, allegedly of later, "Aryan" origin. Some historians of Judaism claim that, in the distant past, the early Israelites worshipped a goddess called Asherah. The Jewish scholar Raphael Patai even maintained that Asherah's statue stood in the Temple for hundreds of years, before being driven out by the god who was once her consort and who later became the monotheistic, jealous god of the Hebrews. In Arabia, the triumph of Islam is sometimes described as a victory over a triad of goddesses: as Mohammed said in one of the *hadith* sayings, before the revelation of the Koran the Arabs worshipped only women. And Christianity may have its own alternative tradition (see p.162).

Even more controversial is "evidence" drawn from modern anthropology. Many contemporary hunter-gatherer societies, it has been found, have relatively emancipated gender relations – a fact that runs counter to the popular intuition of man the hunter as man the master. Perhaps, then, it was when people settled down into an agrarian society that men started lording it over women. Unfortunately, this notion is bound up with a suspect, and maybe racist, assumption that modern hunter-gatherer societies are somehow more "primitive" and closer in culture to earlier humans.

Pornographic statuettes

Opponents of the Goddess theory have come up with endless alternative explanations for all those Neolithic and Palaeolithic statuettes. They could be pornography, toys, sex-education aids, dolls or even, as art historian LeRoy McDermott maintains, self-portraits (McDermott claims that the anatomical distortions aren't so much about ritual fertility as familiar female fears about fat bums and heavy thighs). The more theories emerge, the more confident mainstream archaeologists become that it's all just speculative interpretation and that no one can ever really know what these figurines were used for.

Some archaeologists think that there are just as many male, gender-neutral or animal figurines anyway. Why postulate a Great Goddess, they ask, when there could be any number of other kinds of deities? Others point out that even if the figurines are overwhelmingly buxomly female, this could point to the existence of a widespread fertility ritual, and that the leap to Europe-wide goddess-worship is a leap of faith, not reason. A kind of reverse sexism, perhaps. As for drawing on later Indo-European myths to

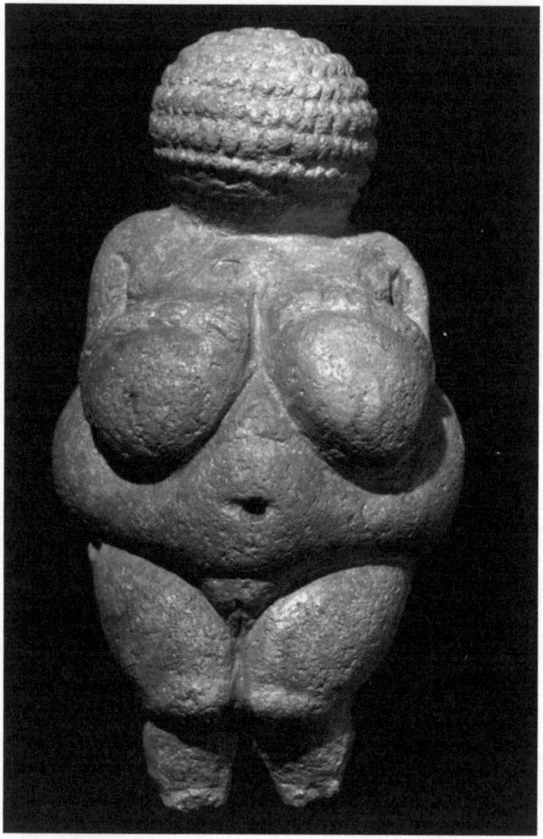

Venus of Willendorf (c.28,000 BC): mother-goddess figurine or prehistoric pornography?

find out about the myths that went before, they say that's just sloppy methodology – pursuing a feminist agenda by comparing like with unlike.

Feminists and archaeologists

The eminent archaeologist Jacquetta Hawkes described how, before World War II, she was advised to keep quiet about her discoveries of material that seemed to suggest female-led societies. No one, she was told, would take her seriously. She eventually published *Early Britain* in 1945, which speculated about generalized worship of a European "Great Goddess" in the megalithic era.

But the totemic figure who really developed the Goddess theory was Marija Gimbutas, professor of archaeology at UCLA for a quarter of a century. She developed the leading hypothesis about the origins of Indo-European people and practically invented a new discipline (never a good idea in academic circles), which she called archaeomythology. In 1974, her book *Goddesses and Gods of Old Europe* (her publisher changed the title of the first edition to *Gods and Goddesses of Old Europe*) set out her stall for a wider public. According to Gimbutas, peaceful, "matristic" Palaeolithic and Neolithic Europe was suddenly invaded by the warlike, patriarchal Indo-Europeans. Europe inherited most of its religious ideas from the invaders, but key elements of Goddess worship survived underground and in folk tales, leaving only hundreds of thousands of feminine figurines as evidence of Old Europe's once-dominant belief system.

Curiously, Gimbutas's theories only became truly controversial after the feminist movement got going. "Some people", she claimed, are now "automatically not accepting" her ideas. In fact, the debate over her work is so politicized and heated that some archaeologists claim they can't even discuss it without being sidelined, as if there were a conspiracy to undermine her work. But while it is true that some male archaeologists advancing similarly bold, speculative theories have been treated rather differently – with admiration or at least indulgence – many archaeologists frown on all interpretations or speculations about religious and social beliefs, whether they concern goddesses or not.

Feminists have also been known to gang up on the Goddess theory. Religious scholar Cynthia Eller thinks it is an "ennobling lie" that ultimately shoots feminism in the foot because it buys into the oppressive idea of societies naturally evolving towards an "advanced" patriarchal society. Or as feminist historian Gerda Lerner put it: "The creation of compensatory myths of the distant past of women will not emancipate women in the present and the future."

SOURCES

Books

Cynthia Eller **The Myth of Matriarchal Prehistory: Why an Invented Past Won't Give Women a Future** (2000). A feminist attempts to demolish the Goddess theory, with some success and a lot of publicity.

Marija Gimbutas **The Goddesses and Gods of Old Europe, 6500–3500 BC** (1974). Gimbutas's original Goddess theory – overreaching, but fascinating nevertheless. *The Language of the Goddess* (1989) focuses on the actual figurines, with beautiful photographs.

Merlin Stone **When God Was a Woman** (1976). The improbably named Merlin Stone argues that a patriarchal conspiracy has perverted Goddess worship from its real origins in the devotion to wisdom and fertility.

Websites

Ⓦ **www.belili.org/index.html** A good site dedicated to Marija Gimbutas, with a streaming documentary. Set up by Starhawk, an eco-activist and the reviver of Wicca, or Goddess worship.

Ⓦ **www.levity.com/mavericks/gim-int.htm** Another site devoted to Marija Gimbutas, with a fascinating interview transcript.

Ⓦ **www.suppressedhistories.net/articles/eller.html** A sustained and well-argued defence of the Goddess theory against Cynthia Eller's well-known published attack.

Jesus the myth

At the core of Christianity lies the belief in a miracle: Jesus was crucified and, three days later, rose from the dead. Christians see this miracle as proof that Jesus was the Son of God. Sceptics, of course, think it proves the opposite: people just don't come back to life, and thus there was no Resurrection. If such sceptics can undermine the bedrock of the Resurrection, they could be on their way towards bringing the whole Church crashing down. As a result, the story of the Passion has attracted as many conspiracy theories as any event – or nonevent – in history. It's the original JFK, the dark wood where anyone with an axe to grind soon finds themselves thrashing about wildly among the trees.

The hero of a thousand faces

The simplest theory states that Jesus never existed – or at least existed only as a man, and not as the Son of God – and that the early Church concocted the whole story out of earlier myths. Variations hold that, divine or not, Jesus was never actually crucified, or that he never came back from the dead. Most shocking of all is the theory that the Resurrection was an elaborate fake by a group of cunning conspirators.

Many scholars and researchers have pointed out that much of Jesus' story is surprisingly reminiscent of earlier "pagan" myths. (For Christian apologists, of course, this just shows how Christ fulfils the divine plan and, not incidentally, supersedes all other figures of wisdom.) In his quixotic search for what he called the "Monomyth", mythologist Joseph Campbell came up with the idea that behind the major myth systems of the wider Mediterranean region was a figure he dubbed "The Hero of a Thousand Faces". Ever since, sceptical researchers have trawled through everything we know about early, non-Christian religions, cults and myth groups in search of material that might undermine Christianity's claims to uniqueness. Prime candidates for proto-Jesus status are Mithras, the

THE JESUITS

The Jesuits were not originally supposed to be "the shock troops of the Counter-Reformation". When St Ignatius Loyola began to gather followers in Paris in the 1530s, it was with the idea of imitating the life of Jesus. Then came Pope Paul III, who helped transform Loyola's idealists into the missionary, militant "Societas Jesu", or Society of Jesus. At first, the Jesuits were sent out to win converts across the world, but they were soon operating secretly in Protestant countries.

The earliest conspiracy theories about Jesuits stem from their zealous efforts at conversion and the fact that, uniquely, they came under the direct control of the pope. They were accused of hair-splitting, morally evasive logic and Machiavellian plotting. It was said that they followed the motto "the end justifies the means" and had a finger in every political pie – they even acquired the role of private confessors to Europe's kings. It quickly became as common to "blame the Jesuits" as it was to blame the Jews. (Of course, in England the Jesuits really were conspiring against the Protestant monarchy.) The Society's reputation in France was damaged in the early seventeenth century by their vicious theological spat with the Jansenists, which was fuelled by wild allegations. At one point, the Jesuits accused the Jansenists of meeting secretly in a monastery at Bourg-Fontaine to discuss a conspiracy to overthrow Christianity itself, and to establish deism in its place.

Over in the New World, the Jesuits were more the victims of a conspiracy than the instigators. They had set up missions among Native Americans in the colonial possessions of Spain, Portugal, France and England, and for 150 years, from 1609, they administered the huge Republic of Paraguay, where Guarani Indians lived free of slavery. Their work threatened Spanish and Portuguese commercial interests, and from the mid-eighteenth century they were gradually expelled from countries across the New and Old Worlds – from Portugal in 1759, Louisiana in 1763, France in 1766 and Spain in 1767. In 1773, the Society was officially suppressed by Pope Clement XIV, under heavy pressure from half the monarchs of Europe. As the French Revolution ignited, the Jesuits were suspected of fanning the flames in revenge – and they remain prime candidates for conspiracy theorists' accusations. Either them or the Jews. Or the Masons.

When the Society was finally restored in 1814, under Pope Pius V, the European nations hadn't lost any of their suspicions. French novelist Eugène Sue's *The Wandering Jew*, published in 1844, recycled old anti-Masonic and anti-Semitic myths, but substituted a mysterious, conspiratorial Jesuit under the command of a "Black Pope" as the villain. In the US, the anti-Masonic hysteria of the 1820s and 30s swept the Jesuits along with it, with Protestant preachers seemingly convinced that

hero-god of Roman soldiery; the Egyptian gods Osiris and Horus; the Greeks' Dionysus and Adonis; the Babylonian Tammuz; and even Hinduism's Krishna.

Dionysus

Bearing in mind that if you pick and choose your versions of a story from a wide enough area, you can pretty much come up with anything, there are still some striking similarities between stories of Jesus' life and those told about other god-heroes. It looks pretty striking that, for example, Dionysus was allegedly born to a virgin in a cave in mid-winter; he miraculously turned water into wine; he rode an ass through a crowd waving branches; and he died as a sacrificial victim at around the spring solstice, before descending to hell and rising to heaven after three days. On closer examination, however, the parallels aren't as straightforward as claimed.

The December 25 or January 6 datings of Christmas are widely known to be later pagan borrowings anyway. Dionysus, according to most versions, wasn't exactly born to a virgin but from his father's thigh – more like Buddha than Jesus. Dionysus was the god of wine, so many of his miracles obviously involve making wine magically appear. And, in any case, the earliest known story of the Dionysus wedding miracle dates from well after Jesus' time, so the argument could just as well be reversed. As for the entry into Jerusalem on a donkey, Jesus could have been making a deliberate symbolic statement about his kingship, relying on his audience's knowledge of older myth patterns. The

American doors were big enough for Jesuit, as well as Masonic, bogeymen to hide behind. Later in the century, Jesuit machinations were once again seen everywhere in France, and the order was variously accused of being behind the Franco-Prussian War of 1870–71, the Dreyfus affair and a number of assassinations.

The most famous element of anti-Jesuit conspiracy theories is alive and well in the twenty-first century: the so-called "Jesuit Oath" or "Oath of the Knights of Columbus" can be found reprinted all over the Internet, often with portentous references to its appearance in the Congressional Record. It's red-hot stuff: "I do … promise and declare that I will, when opportunity presents, make and wage relentless war, secretly and openly, against all heretics, Protestants and Masons … that I will spare neither age, sex nor condition, and that I will hang, burn, waste, boil, flay, strangle, and bury alive these infamous heretics; rip up the stomachs and wombs of their women, and crush their infants' heads against the walls in order to annihilate their execrable race. That when the same cannot be done openly I will secretly use the poisonous cup, the strangulation cord, the steel of the poniard, or the leaden bullet."

Like any good regional news item, the website of the gravel-voiced, ultra-Protestant Northern Irish politician Ian Paisley (www.ianpaisley.org) once added some locally specific information to the end of the oath: "That if two Catholics are on the ticket I will satisfy myself which is the better supporter of Mother Church and vote accordingly. That I will not deal with or employ a Protestant if in my power to deal with or employ a Catholic … That I will provide myself with arms and ammunition that I may be in readiness when the word is passed." Luckily for Paisley – and all the other Protestants (and Masons) at risk of being hanged, burned, wasted and boiled – the Jesuit Oath was, in fact, a seventeenth-century forgery aimed at thwarting the accession of the Catholic monarch James II. The author was one Robert Ware, a "literary skunk", as the nineteenth-century writer and Catholic convert Father Thomas Edward Bridgett dubbed him in *Blunders and Forgeries*.

As for the oath's appearance in the Congressional Record, it turns out to be a document submitted as evidence in a quarrel between two congressional candidates in Pennsylvania in 1912, Democrat Eugene C. Bonniwell and Republican Thomas S. Butler. Bonniwell lost the election, then protested that Butler should be disqualified as he'd (illegally) campaigned against Bonniwell's Catholicism, using the oath as a supporting document. Both men accepted that the oath wasn't authentic, but there it remains, forever in the Congressional Record. These days, allegations that politicians belong to conspiratorial Catholic organizations seem to have shifted their focus away from the Jesuits and towards a relative newcomer, Opus Dei (see p.166).

Dionysian "Easter" is based only on a loose link with spring in a few reported early festivals, and Dionysus was hardly a redeeming figure, even if he did rise up to heaven thanks to his father, Zeus. And again, the Jesus of the Gospels deliberately chose the Jewish (spring) Passover festival to enact his Passion – he wasn't the first to note that it seems the most spiritually appropriate time.

Throw enough copycat incidents together from obscure references in James George Frazer's myth-soup book, *The Golden Bough*, however, and you get what Timothy Freke and Peter Gandy (the authors of *The Jesus Mysteries*) call "nothing less than the greatest cover-up of all time". According to Freke and Gandy, "Christianity's original Gnostic doctrines and its true origins in the Pagan Mysteries had been ruthlessly suppressed by the mass destruction of the evidence and the creation of a false history to suit the political purposes of the Roman Church." Their argument is oddly reminiscent of the second-century writer Tertullian's view that "the devil, whose business is to pervert the truth, mimics the exact circumstances of the Divine Sacraments … Let us therefore acknowledge the craftiness of the devil, who copies certain things of those that be Divine."

Jesus the man

Throughout the 2000-year life of Christianity, more than a few radicals and religious sects have argued that Jesus was no Son of God, but simply a revered prophet – much as Muslims view Mohammed. Today, some scholars even argue that this was actually the original "Christian" message and that all of the "redeeming Saviour" stuff came later. In the earliest version of the Gospels, it seems there may have been no talk of virgin mothers, angels, mangers and wise men at all, and no mention of Last Suppers, trials, crucifixions and empty tombs. History, they theorize, was literally rewritten, and compelling new material presenting Jesus as the Son of God was woven into the Gospels. Paul, it's pointed out, says surprisingly little about crucifixions.

The alternative version of Jesus' story seems to have survived at least until the third or fourth century, when the Church successfully drove it into the darkest corners of human memory. However, it came to light once again in 1945 when a dozen ancient codices were found by chance near Nag Hammadi in Egypt (see p.162). One of the texts discovered, the Gospel of Thomas, seemed much simpler and more basic than the Gospels of the New Testament. In Thomas, Jesus is no Messiah, no Son of God, just a prophet announcing the arrival of God's kingdom. Was this a version of the lost "Q", a text scholars think may have been used as a source by the Gospellers? Or was it a later, boiled-down version of the Gospels?

Crucifixion cover-up

One of the Gnostic texts, The Second Treatise of the Great Seth, even makes the astounding claim that the man on the cross between the two thieves was not Jesus, but Simon of Cyrene, acting as a remarkably generous stand-in. So instead of there being a conspiracy between the Pharisees and Romans to get rid of Jesus, the conspirators were, in fact, Jesus and his followers, staging a dramatic endgame scene to fool the onlookers. The text has Jesus saying: "It was another, Simon, who bore the cross on his shoulder. It was another upon whom they placed the crown of thorns. But I was rejoicing in the height over … their error … And I was laughing at their ignorance."

The Gnostic Apocalypse of Peter takes a slightly different line, claiming that while the Crucifixion took place, it was only of a "Living Jesus", a kind of physical projection of the real, divine Jesus projected onto Earth for the benefit of humanity, thus keeping the wicked flesh and pure spirit nicely separate, in the Docetic tradition. "He whom you see above the tree, glad and laughing, is the living Jesus", the Apocalypse of Peter adds. "But he into whose hands and feet they are driving the nails is his fleshy part, which is the substitute." This story seems to be the origin of a theory common in Muslim countries, and found in the tenth-century Koran commentary of Tabari, that a switch was made, and someone else was crucified in Jesus' place. According to some Muslim traditions, the substitute was a disciple-volunteer; according to another, it was a divine punishment for a would-be assassin; elsewhere it's said that God made all the disciples look the same as Jesus and the Romans crucified only one of them – which wasn't altogether cunning.

The Acts of John – a Gnostic text which the fifth-century pope, Leo the Great, wanted "not only forbidden, but entirely destroyed and burned with fire" – finds the bodily Crucifixion and Resurrection similarly distasteful. It argues that Jesus was a purely spiritual rather than physical figure, and that his appearance changed depending on who was looking at him. He was a man who left no footprints and who never blinked.

Passover plots and shrouds of conspiracy

Perhaps Jesus only seemed to be crucified? Perhaps it only appeared as if he came back to life? Hugh Schonfield's *Passover Plot* imagines Jesus at the centre of his own conspiracy. Knowing the Messianic prophecies backwards, as a good rabbi would, he apparently deliberately shaped his own life in order to fulfil the scriptural predictions. Unfortunately, the grand finale of Crucifixion and Resurrection went wrong, as he didn't expect to be speared in the side. The disciples were then forced to cover up the debacle by staging the Resurrection themselves. Even further out on the left field is Barbara Thiering, who creatively uses an archaic Jewish method of interpretation known as *pesher*. Not only does she believe that Jesus was, in fact, crucified – at Qumran, the home of the Dead Sea Scrolls (see p.170), rather than in Jerusalem – but she also says he didn't die, but went on to have children with Mary Magdalene (see p.162).

Jesus having an extended post-Crucifixion afterlife is a common theme, with many writers weaving theories about the Turin Shroud and legends of Jesus going to southern India or Kashmir into a lurid tapestry. Best of the lot is Holger Kersten and Elmar R. Gruber's *The Jesus Conspiracy*, which uses "scientific" analysis of the Turin Shroud to reveal a shocking truth: Jesus was still bleeding when he was stitched up in it and was, therefore, still alive. According to the authors, the shroud isn't a medieval fake (as the official carbon-dating tests showed), but the real thing – thus bringing the Vatican into an apparently perverse conspiracy to prove that its own relic is a fake.

Kersten and Gruber point the finger at gravemen Joseph and Nicodemus as the prime conspirators, while the centurion of the Gospels was apparently in on the fraud too, giving Jesus an unusually quick three-hour Crucifixion and helping him to stage his "death" with a heavy dose of opium, delivered in the famous vinegar-soaked sponge. Upon burial in the tomb – or, rather, upon being evacuated to a hospital cunningly disguised as a tomb – Jesus, still bleeding, was wrapped in a cloth soaked in healing myrrh and aloe according to a secret Essene recipe. (How do the authors know this? Because they recreated the shroud's image using a similar concoction.) The grand finale – Jesus' reappearance three days later – was, therefore, a case of recuperation, rather than Resurrection.

Did he or didn't he?

However indigestible sceptics have found the idea of Crucifixion and Resurrection, they've had a surprisingly hard time arguing against it. The most detailed, apparently authentic evidence there is comes from the Gospel writers, who of course believed it. Even the non-Christian Roman writers Tacitus and Josephus mention the Crucifixion of Christianity's founder as fact. The controversial Gnostic texts have been brandished as crucial counter-evidence, but it's hard to get around the fact that they postdate Matthew, Mark, et al.

The upshot, then, is pretty much the same as it has been for 2000 years: if, like the earliest Christians, you believe that Peter and the other apostles saw the bodily resurrected Jesus, you'd better get yourself to a church. If you believe they didn't see what they said they saw, or what they saw wasn't what they believed it to be, you don't need to bother. Incidentally, it wasn't actually Peter who saw the raised Jesus first, it was Mary Magdalene. But according to the early Church only certain sightings – all by male apostles – count. Which is another conspiracy theory in itself.

SOURCES

Books

Acharya S. The Christ Conspiracy: The Greatest Story Ever Sold (1999). Fanciful and poorly written book by (according to her own website, www.truthbeknown.com) "scholar, visionary" Acharya S. Jesus was apparently the product of a conspiracy of secret societies and mystery schools to create a single Roman state religion. The heavy reliance on astrology will hardly convince sceptics.

Earl Doherty The Jesus Puzzle (1999). Doherty pushes the view that Western society has been "the victim of the greatest misconception in history". Namely, that Jesus was conjured into existence by Paul and his co-conspirators as proof for their Christ myth.

Timothy Freke and Peter Gandy The Jesus Mysteries: Was the "Original Jesus" a Pagan God? (1999). It's difficult to think about the New Testament in the same way after reading this, though many of the "facts" about pagan religions have been used creatively.

Holger Kersten and Elmar R. Gruber The Jesus Conspiracy: The Turin Shroud and the Truth about the Resurrection (1992). Described in detail in the main text above.

Hugh Schonfield The Passover Plot (1963). This conspiracy theory is described in detail in the main text opposite. It was also turned into a film in 1976, with Zalman King as Jesus and Donald Pleasence as Pontius Pilate, washing sticky dates off his hands.

A.N. Wilson Jesus (1993). Sober but superbly readable biography, which covers speculation that Jesus may have been married.

Films

Mel Gibson The Passion of the Christ (2004). Gibson's pet project focuses – relentlessly – on the physical suffering of Jesus (Jim Caviezel). Nothing particularly conspiratorial about that, but the film has been interpreted in some pretty conspiracist ways, thanks largely to Gibson's father's controversial Sedevacantist beliefs.

Martin Scorsese The Last Temptation of Christ (1998). See p.169.

Websites

www.bede.org.uk/jesusindex.htm Run by a "Christian intellectual", this website boils down lots of arguments for the authenticity of mainstream Christianity based on "faith and reason".

www.tektonics.org Another Christian apologetic's site, managed with a high regard for accuracy and rigour by the burgeoning Internet celebrity, J.P. Holding. Lots on the Jesus myth.

The suppressed apostle: Mary Magdalene as feminine divine

In Dan Brown's multi-million-selling novel *The Da Vinci Code*, historian Leigh Teabing reveals to the book's hero, "symbologist" Robert Langdon, the existence of a set of ancient, leather-bound manuscripts found in Egypt in 1945 that reveal the truth about Mary Magdalene. She was, he explains, the bride of Christ, and the manuscripts are the sole remnant of "thousands of pages of unaltered, pre-Constantine documents" that perished in a presumed firestorm unleashed by the early Church.

Teabing seems to have got his plot largely from a dubious book by Lincoln, Baigent and Leigh (notice anything about those last two names?) called *Holy Blood, Holy Grail*, whose high-octane ingredients include Mary Magdalene, Leonardo da Vinci, the Holy Grail and a mysterious/spurious quasi-Templar society called the Priory of Sion. But how much of this mega-theory is true? Was Mary Magdalene married to Jesus? Was she ever revered as the feminine divine? And did the Church really conspire to suppress knowledge of her true status – whatever that was?

The finds at Nag Hammadi

In December 1945, an Egyptian peasant called Muhammad 'Ali al-Samman was out in the Jabal al-Tarif, a rugged upland near the town of Nag Hammadi, digging for a special kind of soft soil for fertilizer. He hit upon a three-foot earthenware jar buried in the earth, inside which were more than a dozen leather-bound papyrus books. The story is strangely parallel to that of the Dead Sea Scrolls (see p.170). He took the codices home, where his mother used some as kindling for the fire (holy smoke indeed!). What was left found its way to the antiques dealers of Cairo, and thence to the Coptic Museum, where they were discovered to be fourth-century copies of the long-lost gospels from the second-century Gnostic tradition of early Christianity.

Just as the Dead Sea Scrolls were to present a new picture of Judaism, the Gnostic texts of Nag Hammadi showed that early Christianity was far more heterodox than previously believed. The collection of theological tracts and alternative "gospels", probably dating from around 150 to 250 years after Jesus' death, share an influence from Greek philosophy and an emphasis on personal spiritual insight or understanding – in Greek, *gnosis* means "knowing". They contain some provocative ideas. At times, God is described as Father and Mother; elsewhere Jesus' Crucifixion is interpreted as symbolism rather than literal fact.

THE CATHARS

Whether or not you believe the Church conspired to stamp out Gnostic heresies in the early years of Christianity, there's no doubt that it brutally suppressed a medieval outbreak of Gnosticism, the Albigensian heresy of the early thirteenth century. Like their Gnostic forebears, the Albigensians lauded the feminine principle in religion, condemned luxury and pleasure, held that Jesus was only a kind of Holy Ghost unsullied by human flesh and, most dangerously of all, rejected the need for priests to intercede between man and God. Though known to their contemporaries as Albigensians, on account of their stronghold town of Albi in southern France, they called themselves Cathars, from the Greek *katharos*, or "pure ones".

If the Cathars stood for "purity", Pope Innocent III was firmly on the side of the impure. The Cathars were decried in much the same terms that the Templars would be in the following century: accused of heresy (true enough), devil worship (well, they did hold that the creator of the world, the God of the New Testament, was the Demiurge or devil) and buggery (perhaps because of their alternative name Bougres, or Bulgarians, a name acquired through the theology they shared with the Bogomils of Thrace). These attacks quickly developed into a kind of civil war between those northern French nobles aligned with the papal cause and the local opposition, and culminated in entire Cathar towns being sacked and burned. The most infamous massacre was at Béziers, where the papal legate instructed Simon de Montfort's besieging forces to spare none of the townspeople, neither Cathar nor Catholic. "Kill them all", he said, "God will know His own."

Modern Cathar conspiracy theories have less to do with the conspiracy to wipe out the Cathars and more to do with the belief that they were guardians of a secret that gave them great power. In 1885, Berenger Saunière, the village priest at Rennes-le-Château, deep in Cathar country, claimed to have discovered a group of parchments in a hollow column underneath the altar. Saunière took his find to Paris, where he moved in wealthy circles – occult mysteries have always been fashionable in Paris – before returning to Rennes-le-Château as an occult expert, and a very wealthy man. Local legend, bolstered by pseudo-historical books like *Holy Blood, Holy Grail*, has it that Saunière discovered the legendary Cathar treasure hoard. Was this the very same treasure that the Templars had discovered in Jerusalem? Was it the Holy Grail itself (whatever that was)? Or was it, as the author of *The Jesus Conspiracy* believes, evidence that the Cathars had been the guardians of the Turin Shroud and its mysteries?

In extreme conspiracy circles, the Cathars are spoken about in much the same way as the Templars, the Masons or the Bavarian Illuminati. All survived faked or unsuccessful conspiracies to exterminate them. All possessed powerful secrets. All are now players in the battle for world domination. Ironically, if the Cathars hadn't been such implacable opponents of worldly power, the idea of playing a part in a grand battle between good and evil would have fitted right in with their world view.

Most controversial of all, in the cultural context of the post-war West, is the emphasis some of the Nag Hammadi gospels place on the role of Mary Magdalene. In the Gospel of Philip, a theological-spiritual tract probably dating from around the middle of the third century (though some say it's a hundred years older), Mary appears as a deeply spiritually significant figure. Symbolically, she represents the psyche, the wisdom goddess Sophia, the spiritual consort of Jesus and the unique recipient of a tradition of alternative wisdom. The most controversial passage of Philip goes further still, declaring that Jesus, as "the partner of Mary Magdalene, loved her more than all the disciples and often kissed her on the mouth" (63.34–35). This, her supporters say, is proof that Mary Magdalene was not just spiritually, but literally, the bride of Christ.

Looked at more closely, however, problems become apparent in this interpretation. In the New Testament, the same Greek word for "partner" refers to a companion rather than a sexual partner, and in Gnostic terms it means something more like "spiritual consort". Kissing on the mouth was probably more like giving a kiss of peace or of spiritual initiation rather than a sexual kiss. And the damaged papyrus actually reads as follows: "the companion of the … Mary Magdalene … her more than

… the disciples … kiss her on her m…".

Yet, the same text goes on to describe the disciples asking Jesus why he loves Mary more than them. His answer, while extremely cryptic in typical Gnostic style, segues into a discussion of marriage. There's even a Gospel of Mary, which may date from the early second century. According to this text, Mary Magdalene tells how she had a private vision of Jesus in which he passed on hidden knowledge to her (frustratingly, four pages are missing at this point, so we never find out what it was). An angry Peter questions why Jesus would have given secrets to a woman, but Levi defends Mary, saying: "Surely the Savior knows her very well. That is why he loved her more than us."

Patriarchs, heretics and conspirators

Peter's jealousy, conspiracists allege, was just the start of 2000 years of suppression of the alternative, Mary Magdalene-focused version of Christianity. In the Pistis Sophia, one of the few Gnostic texts still in circulation before the finds at Nag Hammadi, Mary Magdalene tells Jesus that she is afraid of Peter "because he is wont to threaten me and hateth our sex". Elaine Pagels, scholar and author of the bestselling *Gnostic Gospels*, sees this rivalry as a metaphor for the power struggle being fought out between the authoritarian Church hierarchy, headed by Peter, and the Greek-influenced, spiritual tradition represented by Mary Magdalene, Jesus' mystical consort. Peter "the Rock" in the red corner; Mary "the Spirit" in the blue. Karen King, of the feminist Harvard Divinity School, claims that it's no coincidence that the Gospel of Mary and Paul's woman-subjugating Letter to Timothy were (possibly) written at the same time.

Things only got worse for the Gnostics. Powerful figures in the early Church declared their ideas heretical and their "gospels" invalid. As the Second Treatise of the Great Seth, a Gnostic text found at Nag Hammadi, puts it: "We were hated and persecuted, not only by those who are ignorant, but also by those who think they are advancing the name of Christ." In his *Against Heresies* of AD 187, Irenaeus raged against Gnostic beliefs in such fuming detail that, ironically, his writings were the chief source of modern knowledge about Gnosticism until the Nag Hammadi codices came to light. Tertullian's *Prescription Against Heretics*, from around AD 200, takes up the cudgel with enthusiasm, taking some hefty sideswipes at women for good measure, protesting that heretical women are "wanton … bold enough to teach, dispute, exorcize, heal, even baptize". Perhaps even bold enough to tell a different story about Mary Magdalene.

In AD 325, Bishop Eusebius furthered the cause of orthodoxy by promoting the idea of a single Church doctrine at the Council of Nicea. He also drew up a list of which gospels were divine and which, he thought, would be better on a bonfire. Following his lead in AD 367, Bishop Athanasius of Alexandria commanded the monks of his diocese to destroy all the unorthodox writings found in their libraries. It's presumed that similar orders went out all over the Christian world. Was this a conspiracy to suppress the truth? Or the cleaning up of a later, decadent tradition that risked perverting the truth about Jesus as reported by those who knew him best? Were the Gnostic gospels a hidden, elite tradition? Or, as Catholic historian Raymond Brown put it, "the rubbish of the second century"? (He added, sniffily, that they were "still rubbish".) Whatever their reasons, somebody disobeyed Athanasius and buried the forbidden texts in a cave at Nag Hammadi, where they remained hidden for almost 1600 years.

Pope Gregory "the conspirator"?

Even if the Gnostic gospels aren't saying that Mary Magdalene was Jesus' consort – or even if they are and they're wrong – she is still a crucial figure in the story of Jesus. In the four orthodox Gospels, it is the women in Jesus' group – not the male disciples – who do not flee the Roman soldiers at Jesus' arrest, who witness the Crucifixion and burial, who discover the tomb and who are first with the news of the Resurrection. And yet by the sixth century, women in general were shunned by the Church, and Pope Gregory "the Great" had declared that Mary Magdalene was an ex-prostitute. For anyone trying to discern an undercurrent of Magdalene-hating in the confused waters of early Church history, that is the equivalent of coming across some serious rapids.

Pope Gregory announced that three women in the Bible – Mary Magdalene, Mary of Bethany and an unnamed "sinner" forgiven by Jesus immediately before the Bible's first mention of Mary Magdalene – were, in fact, one woman. Magdalene was the sinner and the sinner was a whore. For Mary – once herald of the Resurrection and guardian of Jesus' secret tradition, but now, as author Susan Haskins put it, "an effective weapon and instrument of propaganda against her own sex" – this was some fall from grace.

But was Gregory really conspiring to bury the feminist, Gnostic truths believed by early Christians? Religious historian Jane Schaberg sees the sexual denigration of powerful women as such a common historical pattern that she has created a word specially for it – harlotization. Or was Gregory just trying to simplify the Bible? Was his conspiracy nothing more than an attempt to paper over confusing cracks in its narrative? One problem with the patriarchal conspiracy theory is that Mary continued to be a significant and hugely popular devotional figure even after Gregory's declaration, albeit as a penitent sinner.

Fresco of St Mary Magdalene and a kneeling Franciscan friar, c.1309.

Holy smoke, holy fire

According to Michael Baigent, Richard Leigh and Henry Lincoln, the authors of *Holy Blood, Holy Grail*, after pulling off the mock Crucifixion (see p.161), Jesus and his family fled from Palestine and the clutches of the quasi-fascist St Peter. Jesus' wife, Mary Magdalene, apparently ended up in France, where she founded the Merovingian dynasty, a family line that still preserves the *Sang Réal*, aka Holy Blood, aka the Holy Grail. This is the alternative version of history long hidden (but recently revealed) by a secret (yet self-publicizing) society called the Priory of Sion.

The skeleton of this story had long circulated in France, but it was given a fillip by a bunch of 1950s typescripts supposedly "deposited" in Paris's Bibliothèque Nationale and dubbed the *Dossiers secrets*. Of course, the dossiers can't have been all that secret in a public library, and (unfortunately for the authors of *Holy Blood, Holy Grail*) the man who'd put them there later turned out to be an odd crypto-fascist and acknowledged hoaxer called Pierre Plantard.

The admirably erudite historian Marina Warner famously called *Holy Blood, Holy Grail* "a heap of hooey". Its tactics are certainly dubious, and the authors have a peculiar logical tic. When they can find no substantiating evidence for their claims, they say this only shows how powerful the conspirators were, and how successful in covering their traces. Genealogical links become evidence of a conspiracy; people who "must have met" other people are transformed into co-conspirators; anagrams are wielded as coherent proofs; and no smoke is left to drift away without throwing its imagined fuel onto the conspiratorial bonfire.

The Holy Grail

The idea of a Holy Grail was dreamt up by the twelfth-century French poet Chrétien de Troyes, in his *Conte du Graal*. As Umberto Eco snorted in a television interview:

OPUS DEI: THE HOLY MAFIA

Latin countries have been hearing dark whisperings about Opus Dei, "the work of God", for decades. In Spain, where the Catholic group was founded in 1928, it was dubbed the "Holy Mafia". Members virtually controlled the economic policies of Franco's fascist government during the 1960s, and resurfaced in the late 1990s under the conservative leadership of José María Aznar, whose wife was close to the organization. In Italy, despite a complete lack of evidence, Opus Dei was rumoured to have had connections with the P2 Masonic conspiracy and with the rescue of the Vatican Bank (see p.53).

In Peru, the group was a motivating force in the coalition that bankrolled (corrupt) President Alberto Fujimori, while a hardline conservative Peruvian archbishop, Juan Luis Cipriani, became Opus Dei's first cardinal in 2001. Peruvian conspiracy theorists have unsuccessfully attempted to link Cipriani (a known sceptic of liberal human rights policies) with the murder of his predecessor, liberal Jesuit Augusto Vargas Zamora – a "killing" allegedly orchestrated by Fujimori's jailed spy chief, Vladimiro Montesinos. In the Vatican, the speedy canonization of Opus Dei's founder, Josemaría Escrivá de Balaguer y Albás, in 2002 – just 27 years after his death – was seen as evidence of the extent of the organization's power, as was the fact that, in 1994, Pope John Paul II kneeled in front of the coffin of Escrivá's successor, Alvaro del Portillo, who is now in the process of being canonized.

In the Anglophone world, by contrast, the group only made headlines after it was caricatured in Dan Brown's conspiracy thriller *The Da Vinci Code* in 2003. Seemingly, no one had noticed the seventeen-storey US headquarters Opus Dei had built on New York's Lexington Avenue, at an estimated cost of $42–54 million (viewable at www.maypinska.com/pages/projects/buildbodylex.htm). But suddenly, the group was everywhere. In the UK, Labour education secretary Ruth Kelly was forced to admit that she was a "Supernumerary" (see below), while rumours circulated that the high-powered and well-connected barrister Cherie Booth was involved at some level, perhaps along with her husband, Tony Blair. These last rumours arose chiefly on the grounds that Blair was thought to be on the point of converting to Catholicism in his last years as prime minister; he finally went over to Rome in December 2007 – safely after leaving office.

In the US, a number of conservative politicians have close links with Father C. John McCloskey III, an Opus Dei priest with a big media presence. Supreme Court Justice Antonin Scalia is widely rumoured to be an Opus Dei member (which he denies), as is former FBI director Louis Freeh (also denied) – though largely on the grounds that his son went to an Opus Dei school, and that his professional career was paralleled by FBI agent, Opus Dei member, sexual exhibitionist and Russian spy Robert Hanssen. (The Hanssen scandal is dramatized in the 2007 film, *Breach*.)

Just what is it that critics find so sinister about Opus Dei? Why do they persist in calling it a cult, in spite of Opus Dei's

"The historical reality of the Holy Grail is the same as the reality of Pinocchio and Little Red Riding Hood." Some of Chrétien's themes and symbols may be drawn from earlier traditions – the setting in the kingdom of the Britons is taken from Geoffrey of Monmouth's reinvention of stories about a legendary King Arthur, written some fifty years previously – but otherwise there's no evidence anywhere that the idea of a Holy Grail existed before Chrétien wrote about it. Unless you're willing to believe that the poet was the inheritor and maverick first publicist of a secret tradition, that is, or that some medieval entity with a secret agenda managed to systematically destroy all earlier texts that mentioned the Grail.

As for the idea that the Holy Grail was not, as all medieval authors stated, the chalice used by Jesus at the Last Supper (which was later reused to catch his blood at the Crucifixion), but in fact a code word referring to the bloodline of Mary Magdalene, this was popularized by the authors of *Holy Blood, Holy Grail* in the 1980s. The main ingredient of their story seems to be an ancient, nationalistic French legend that a pregnant Mary Magdalene had fled from Palestine to France (a legend paralleled by many other countries' "founding myths" which, when put together, would have half the figures in the Gospels magically transported all over the Mediterranean in boats in various states of ruin and decay – rudderless, sail-less,

aggrieved denials? Is it the air of secretiveness that surrounds membership? The way recruits are welcomed into a new family within the organization? The way the group's activities are exposed to the media in a tightly controlled way? Or is it Opus Dei's notorious advocacy of mortification which, in its most extreme form, includes the use of the cilice (a spiked belt worn around the thigh) and the discipline (literally, a whip for your own back)? However repellent, these aspects don't amount to a conspiracy theory.

The problem, as always, is power. Opus Dei's stated aim is to "sanctify work", creating a new model for an active religious life in the professional community. Opus Dei's critics, however, claim its real project is to recruit high-flyers – government ministers and congressmen, for instance. The resulting mixture of religion, tightly controlled organization and political influence would be potent – like the Masons, only with the fires of hell added for encouragement. On its official website (www.opusdei.org), the group declares that members separate their professional decisions from their private religious life anyway. Websites such as the Opus Dei Awareness Network (www.odan.org), however, counter with a quotation from the Spanish founder of Opus Dei, St Josemaría: "Have you ever bothered to think how absurd it is to leave one's Catholicism aside on entering a university or a professional association or a scholarly meeting or Congress, as if you were checking your hat at the door?"

Politically, Opus Dei has been linked with fascism. Its emphasis on work is certainly reminiscent of fascist ideology, as is the commitment to a charismatic leadership, the emphasis on purity and the deeply hierarchical internal structure. Escrivá's own writings make clear he is no friend of socialism or modernism, and he is alleged to have said "Hitler against the Jews, Hitler against the Slavs – this means Hitler against Communism". As Spanish theologian Juan Martin Velasco commented bitterly: "We cannot portray as a model of Christian living someone who has served the power of the state and who used that power to launch his Opus, which he ran with obscure criteria, like a Mafia shrouded in white."

Opus Dei is certainly building a powerful network of conservative Catholics. Its members include not only celibate "Numeraries", who have ordinary jobs but live in single-sex, monastic-style houses and give over all their income to Opus Dei, but also "Supernumeraries", who can be married and merely hand over large portions of their salaries. In all, there are some 85,000 lay members, three thousand of them in the US. Even if you don't buy the hostile assertions of critic Robert Hutchison – namely that Opus Dei has a media network "as large as Rupert Murdoch's", that it runs "an immense intelligence network" and that it is "preparing for what the organization regards as Christendom's inevitable showdown with radical Islam" – that's quite an army.

leaky, made of stone and so on). To this, they added a whimsical bit of false etymology by translating Chrétien's *saint Graal* not as "Holy Grail", but as "holy blood" (*sang royal*), via a corruption of the Old French *sang réal*.

This translation trickery apparently descends from a turn-of-the-century wave of popular pseudo-history. The writer Saki, for one, picked up on it when he called one of his long-running characters "Clovis Sangrail" – Clovis being the name of one of France's Merovingian kings. Ironically, Mr Sangrail appears in a number of short stories satirizing the gullibility of Edwardian society. In the story "The Unrest-Cure", the character even foments a conspiracy theory that his bishop is plotting to massacre local Jews.

Picknett, Prince and the Leonardo da Vinci connection

The notion of Leonardo da Vinci as the guardian of the secret Magdalene tradition was another idea concocted by Baigent, Leigh and Lincoln in *Holy Blood, Holy Grail*, on the basis of the dodgy *dossiers* of the "Priory of Sion", which list the artist as one of the Nautonniers, or Grand Masters. This theory was further investigated by Lynn Picknett and Clive Prince's *The Templar Revelation*, which also draws on the Gnostic gospels to promote Mary as the object of quasi-goddess worship. Ignorant, perhaps, of the artistic tradition that John the Evangelist is typically portrayed as a youthful, beautiful, beardless figure, Picknett and Prince seize on John's feminine features as painted in Leonardo's *The Last Supper* as proof that "he" is, in fact, "she", and that she is actually... Mary Magdalene.

Skirting gingerly around the whole Priory of Sion chimera, it's not hard to lance this rather swollen theory. Even on a casual visual impression, John/Mary could just as easily be a young man as a woman. And the extremely fragile *Last Supper* fresco has been restored so many times – eight, to be exact – that it's doubtful whether much of Leonardo's original paintwork actually survives. And if the contentious figure isn't John, where is he? And even if Leonardo did paint a figure of a woman beside Jesus in his *Last Supper*, that doesn't mean she was actually there at the Last Supper. As for all the pseudo-art theory that bolsters the idea, such as the "V" composition between Jesus and John/Mary (recalling the vagina), and the red and blue colours of their robes (supposedly suggesting royal blood), it's an enticing taste of flamboyantly ingenious art criticism, but nothing more.

Unless, that is, you buy the more recent theory from Italian "amateur scholar" Slavisa Pesci. The media breathlessly reported in July 2007 that *The Last Supper* contained a "hidden image" of a Templar knight and a woman holding a child. The image is certainly well-hidden: to see it, the painting has to be "superimposed with its mirror image", both have to be made "partially transparent", and then one has to be nudged sideways until the Christ figures are aligned...

Admissions and restorations

Whatever its past misdemeanours, the Catholic Church now recognizes that Mary Magdalene and the "unnamed sinner" were two different women. Of course, it hasn't gone as far as accepting the authenticity of the Gnostic gospels, and continues to stick with Bishop Eusebius' notion that only the gospels written by apostles count. That said, the Vatican also admits that the four principal Gospels weren't actually written by Matthew, Mark, Luke and John, only written "according to" their version of events. Even supporters of the authenticity and importance of the Gnostic gospels don't buy the *Holy Blood* idea that Jesus was married. As Elaine Pagels, of Princeton University, stated in a television interview on *ABC News*: "If I were guessing, and we are guessing, I would guess that there was a special relationship between Mary Magdalene and Jesus. I would also guess that it did not take a sexual form."

The various theories haven't done Leonardo da Vinci's reputation much harm, mostly just reinforcing his celebrity status as the artist-genius *par excellence*, according to the familiar romantic myth. Unfortunately for Leonardo conspiracists, the *Last Supper* fresco was revealed in 1999, after a twenty-year restoration, with many of the previously usefully murky details clarified. The old smudges on John/Mary that could have been said to look like the swelling of a breast were gone. End of story? No; Lynn Picknett apparently believes that someone took advantage of the restoration to literally clean away the evidence. As for the Priory of Sion, in the hands of conspiracy theorists it has mushroomed into a vast secret society accused of being on the verge of establishing a United Theocratic States of Europe. Pierre Plantard would have been delighted.

SOURCES

Books

Michael Baigent, Richard Leigh and Henry Lincoln Holy Blood, Holy Grail (1982). The fertile source behind Dan Brown's *The Da Vinci Code*.

Richard Barber The Holy Grail: Imagination and Belief (2004). The true biography of a medieval myth. Serious and reliable.

Dan Brown The Da Vinci Code (2003). Described in detail in the main text above.

Bart D. Ehrman Lost Christianities: The Battles for Scripture and the Faiths We Never Knew (2003). Reliable, earnest and fascinating account of the withering of early Christian beliefs in the face of orthodoxy and the authorized New Testament.

Timothy Freke and Peter Gandy Jesus and the Lost Goddess: The Secret Teachings of the Original Christians (1999). Freke and Gandy analyse the Gnostic gospels as the springboard for their own theories about the "original" Christianity as another manifestation of the god-man/god-woman dualism inherent in all religion.

Michael Haag and Veronica Haag The Rough Guide to The Da Vinci Code (2004). This pocket-sized guide to the not-so-wonderful world of Dan Brown has a wide brief, encompassing everything from the truth about heresies to the real locations in Paris and London.

Susan Haskins Mary Magdalene: Myth and Metaphor (1993). Scholarly, readable history of Mary Magdalene and her place in art, history and literature.

Elaine Pagels The Gnostic Gospels (1980). The original and best book on the subject. Pagels is the leading authority on the Nag Hammadi texts, and remains open to their potential significance while resisting the lure of sensationalizing them.

Lynn Picknett and Clive Prince The Templar Revelation: Secret Guardians of the True Identity of Christ (1997). Key source for Dan Brown – the book even appears on Teabing's bookshelves – and rather less wildly credulous than *Holy Blood, Holy Grail*. Picknett went on to write *Mary Magdalene: Christianity's Hidden Goddess*, which reaches far-out conclusions, for instance that Mary "was probably a black woman from Ethiopia, who bore Jesus' mixed race child".

Margaret Starbird The Woman With the Alabaster Jar: Mary Magdalene and the Holy Grail (1993). Starbird sees beyond the squabbles about Mary's role and into a sacred world where the feminine divine is celebrated and worshipped.

Barbara Thiering Jesus the Man (1992). Based on an idiosyncratic reading of the Dead Sea Scrolls, this has Jesus married to Mary with two sons and a daughter – before she leaves him and he remarries. Some ambitious leaps of argument, such as claiming that "the Word of God increased" (Acts 6:7) refers to Jesus having more children.

Films

Martin Scorsese The Last Temptation of Christ (1988). Based on Nikos Kazantzakis's novel of the same name, this finely crafted biopic caused huge waves of controversy for its dream-sequence on the cross, in which Jesus (Willem Dafoe) imagines how his life would have been as an ordinary man – including the love affair he could have had with Mary Magdalene.

Websites

Ⓦ **www.beliefnet.com** This US-based open religious discussion site has lots of Magdalene-related chatter – try searching for articles by Sandra Miesel or Margaret Starbird.

Ⓦ **www.gnosis.org** Website of the LA-based Gnostic Society, with endless information on Gnosticism including translations and photographs of the Nag Hammadi codices.

Ⓦ **www.lionardofromvinci.com** More mirror-image Leonardo fun.

Ⓦ **www.milano.arounder.com** Milan's official tourist site contains a link to a high-resolution image of *The Last Supper* (simply "zoomify").

Ⓦ **www.newadvent.org/cathen/09761a.htm** Mary Magdalene, the authorized version, according to the authoritative *Catholic Encyclopedia*.

Ⓦ **www.ordotempli.org/priory_of_sion.htm** Reams of unfiltered pseudo-fact on the Priory of Sion from one of the many groups that like to make out they are the modern-day Knights Templar.

Ⓦ **www.religioustolerance.org/cfe_bibl.htm** Handy overview of Jesus' teachings regarding women, from a liberal website aiming to break down fundamentalism based on the lack of information.

Ⓦ **www.thelastsuppertheory.com/** Pesci's mirror-image theory: judge for yourself.

The Dead Sea cover-up

The story of the discovery of the Dead Sea Scrolls reads like a Hollywood yarn, featuring an elusive Jewish sect, lost treasure and the Arab-Israeli War. A vicious academic spat, complete with accusations of texts going missing and evidence being suppressed, ensured that the affair was widely publicized, but what really seized the public's imagination was the idea that locked away in the scrolls was a lost truth about Jesus.

Bedouins, Dominicans and lost scrolls

In early 1947 – or possibly late 1946, no one is quite sure – a Bedouin shepherd of the Tacâmireh tribe, Mohammed "the Wolf", was searching for a lost goat in crags near the shore of the Dead Sea, in what is now the occupied West Bank. Throwing a stone into one of the many small caves in the area, he was surprised to hear the sound of breaking pottery. By chance, he'd hit a jar containing an ancient scroll. It was the first of many. Through various intermediaries in nearby Jerusalem – including an antiquities dealer known only as Kando, and the more extravagantly named Mar Athanasius Yeshua Samuel, the archimandrite of the Syrian Orthodox Monastery of St Mark – Mohammed and his friends managed to sell a handful of scrolls and scroll fragments.

News of the discoveries in the desert slowly leaked out over the course of the following year, and by the spring of 1948 academics had seen enough scroll fragments to date them tentatively to around the first century BC. Unfortunately, the eruption of the Arab-Israeli War in May of that year ruled out the possibility of a proper archaeological survey of the Qumran cave site. Meanwhile the Bedouin kept searching. By the early 1950s, the situation was calmer, and a series of expeditions and digs led by Roland de Vaux, a Dominican Biblical scholar based in Jerusalem, uncovered a total of eleven caves containing every known book of the Hebrew Bible, as well as the related works sometimes called the Apocrypha and Pseudepigrapha. At last scholars had a chance to compare the text of the Bible, as it has survived to this day, with much earlier – and perhaps less corrupt – versions.

The Qumran caves also contained a number of hitherto unknown texts, suggesting that the site belonged to a sect with ideas and scriptures of its own. A document containing laws regulating the life of the Qumran community was named the "Community Rule". An apocalyptic text was dubbed the "War Scroll", while a text describing an ideal temple city became known as the "Temple Scroll". Most famous of all was the "Copper Scroll", whose metal construction long resisted attempts to open and read it. (Once opened, it turned out to be a treasure map – though no one has yet successfully deciphered it, and many think it describes a fictional treasure.)

Academic rivalry or Vatican censorship?

While all the finds from Mohammed the Wolf's "Cave 1" had been released by 1956, material found in other caves took a surprisingly long time to see the light of day. Roland de Vaux had set up a team of eight scholars to study, edit and publish the forty thousand scroll fragments from the richest trove, Cave 4. Outsiders were jealously kept in the dark by virtue of a so-called "secrecy rule". Some claimed that this was for political reasons – de Vaux and some other members of the team had refused to cooperate with Israeli scholars in the highly charged atmosphere of the time. Others argued that it was all about academic rivalry, with every team member anxious to announce their own career-gilding discovery.

Others smelled a more troubling conspiracy. French academic André Dupont-Sommer had pointed out a number of parallels between Jesus and a figure called the "Teacher of Righteousness" in the texts, and in a BBC broadcast of 1956 maverick team-member John Allegro went further still, claiming that the Qumran sect worshipped a crucified Messiah. He went on to accuse de Vaux, among others, of suppressing texts that contained evidence of similarities between the Qumran sect and Christianity. (In later life, Allegro really went for the jugular, claiming that Christianity had originated as a hallucinogenic mushroom cult.)

Pauline propaganda?

For Professor Robert Eisenman – one of the key figures in freeing the scrolls from the clutches of the original team and releasing them into the public sphere – the community that produced the scrolls didn't just pre-echo Christianity, it was a Christian group. Eisenman identified the Teacher of Righteousness as James the Just, the brother of Jesus and the original founder of the Christian tradition. He also saw the figure described in the scrolls as the "Man of the Lie" as Paul the Apostle, who in the eyes of the Qumran community was a Roman agent conspiring to obscure and discredit the claims of James and his co-religionists. Given Paul's crucial role in spreading the word, this opened up the possibility that Jesus' "original message" had been lost, concealed – or even perverted.

In a grand-scale conspiracy finale, the writers of what might be called "alternative history" Michael Baigent and Richard Leigh worked up Allegro's complaints and Eisenman's theories into their bestselling book *The Dead Sea Scrolls Deception: Why a Handful of Religious Scholars*

Fragment of one of the Dead Sea Scrolls.

MISCELLANEOUS FOR SALE

By 1954, the Archimandrite Mar Athanasius Yeshua Samuel clearly hadn't managed to shift all the scrolls he'd bought from his Bedouin contacts, because on June 1 he placed an advertisement in *The Wall Street Journal*, under the category Miscellaneous For Sale. "THE FOUR DEAD SEA SCROLLS", it read. "Biblical Manuscripts dating back to at least 200 BC are for sale. This would be an ideal gift to an educational or religious institution by an individual or group. Box F206."

Conspired to Suppress the Revolutionary Contents of the Dead Sea Scrolls. According to them, de Vaux was a tool of the Vatican, bent on destroying texts that revealed the truth about Paul, and therefore the truth about Jesus.

Anti-Semitism at work?

While the presence of Protestants among the scholars originally chosen by de Vaux makes the Baigent and Leigh theory of a Vatican conspiracy look more than a little shaky, it is odd that the team chosen to analyse the most important collection of Hebrew Biblical texts ever discovered did not contain a single Jewish member. It's hard to imagine the outcry that would have ensued if the Gnostic gospels discovered in Egypt in 1945 (see p.162) had only been examined by Muslim scholars. Let alone if one of such a team had described Christianity as a "horrible religion", which is what Dead Sea Scroll scholar John Strugnell called Judaism in a 1990 interview for the Israeli newspaper *HaAretz*...

Digging – and covering up

The furore wasn't limited to the scrolls alone. Archaeologists debated the nature of the "monastic" ruins adjacent to the cave sites with equal fervour. At first, just a few mavericks challenged the majority view that they were the home of the Qumran community that had written the scrolls. Some Israeli scholars accused de Vaux of suppressing finds such as jewels and cosmetics, which if they existed would have undermined the consensus theory that Qumran was the home of the Essenes – the so-called "Essene hypothesis". It seems that this strict, ascetic Jewish group, which may have been related to the followers of John the Baptist, wouldn't have had much truck with self-beautification.

In 1995, Professor Norman Golb of the University of Chicago even alleged that de Vaux and other scholars had "buried" archaeological evidence confirming Golb's own theory that the Dead Sea Scrolls were not a treasured, coherent collection of sacred texts, but a miscellaneous collection drawn from various libraries in Jerusalem – including the Temple library. If Golb's "Jerusalem theory" was correct, the dramatic conclusions some scholars and commentators had drawn about the "nature of Judaism/early Christianity" wouldn't amount to a hill of beans. When the San Diego Natural History Museum exhibited the scrolls in 2007, its failure to give due weight to the "Jerusalem theory" – which was, by then, attracting significant support – dragged the exhibition into controversy. A few critics even accused the museum of having a Christian evangelical agenda.

Publish and be damned

The Dead Sea Scrolls were finally published in 1991. Admittedly, when the Huntington Library in California released a complete set of photographs, they did so against the wishes of the official team, but an official microfiche edition followed in 1993 nevertheless, and the printed versions have been rolling out ever since. Unless you believe the unsubstantiated – and unverifiable – theories that key scrolls have been destroyed or buried in the Vatican library or, like a very few bloody-minded scholars, you can conjure entire Gospel texts out of a few fragmentary Greek letters on scraps of untested scroll, the fact of official publication pretty much lays the old conspiracy theories to rest. There is, however, one last chance for new controversy. In 2007, a British team announced they would use ultra-powerful x-rays to "read" scrolls previously considered too fragile to open. "Until we start looking", the lead researcher announced, sagely, "we don't know what's there".

The most tenacious anti-Vatican theorists like to try one last argument in favour of the suppression theory. Even if the scrolls predate Christ, they say, they still reveal some worryingly familiar facts about the Qumran community. They believed that the end of the world was approaching, that private property was iniquitous, that ritual meals should involve the blessing of food and wine and that enemies should be loved. This, the theorists claim, was the uncomfortable truth that de Vaux and his Vatican backers wanted to suppress – that Christianity wasn't all that original. Except that Christian scholars knew that already. And, for Christians, similarities with earlier Jewish practices are positive proof of Christianity's fulfilment of history in the New Covenant. Divine history, they say, works that way.

Carbon-14 controversy

As for those who believe that the Qumranites were actually Christians, Carbon-14 dating on the linen coverings of fourteen of the scrolls has now shown that they were all made in the last two centuries BC, a dating that agrees with the earlier palaeographic and archaeological evidence. Of course, some people maintain that the tests were faked, or that the scrolls must have been supernaturally buried at Qumran outside normal timeframes – presumably by the same whimsical power that hid fossils in rocks at the Creation.

Media attention built on conspiracy theories has all but died away, allowing the real importance of the scrolls to be publicized. They are still, by about a thousand years, the oldest Hebrew writings to have been discovered. They reveal the diversity of Jewish thought around the time of Jesus. They prove that many Biblical texts originally came in different versions, and that variations in the earliest Bible translations may reflect differing originals rather than mistranslations. They show that Greek thought had influenced Jewish religion long before anyone realized. And they demonstrate that texts are wide open to interpretation, and that it's almost impossible to impose an official view.

SOURCES

Books

John Marco Allegro The Dead Sea Scrolls and the Christian Myth (1979). Allegro plays up the Essene hypothesis and pagan myth, and plays down the originality of the Jesus story and the historicity of Jesus' life. He also includes the chapter title "Will the real Jesus Christ please stand up?"

Michael Baigent and Richard Leigh The Dead Sea Scrolls Deception (1991). The original conspiracist version of the history of the Dead Sea Scrolls.

Robert Eisenman James the Brother of Jesus: The Key to Unlocking the Secrets of Early Christianity and the Dead Sea Scrolls (1992). Almost a thousand pages of serious early Christian history, but essential conspiracist reading. Up James; down Paul.

Robert Eisenman and Michael Wise The Dead Sea Scrolls Uncovered: The First Complete Translation and Interpretation of 50 Key Documents Withheld for Over 35 Years (1992). The bestselling translation, plus controversial editorial commentary.

Barbara Thiering Jesus and the Riddle of the Dead Sea Scrolls: Unlocking the Secrets of His Life Story (1992). A contentious version of events, which makes the Qumranites Christian, dates the scrolls in New Testament times and employs an esoteric "pesher" method of reading to uncover a radically different version of Christianity.

Geza Vermes The Dead Sea Scrolls in English (1987). Exactly what it says it is.

Websites

Ⓦ **www.historian.net/4Q285.html** Photograph of the controversial "Slain Messiah" fragment, with a suggested translation.

Ⓦ **www.ibiblio.org/expo/deadsea.scrolls.exhibit/intro.html** The website of the Library of Congress exhibition, showing photographs of a few key scrolls along with accompanying translations.

Ⓦ **oi.uchicago.edu/research/projects/scr/** Detailed academic site linked to Norman Golb that attacks the Essene hypothesis.

Taj Mahal: Muslim tomb or Hindu temple?

India's Taj Mahal is one of the world's most iconic and beloved structures. The love story on which it is founded is scarcely less celebrated – it was built by the Indian emperor Shah Jahan as a mausoleum for his beloved consort, Mumtaz Mahal, who died in childbirth in 1631. The Taj is universally recognized as the sweetest architectural flower of the Mughal era, when India was ruled by Muslim emperors. That is, it's almost universally recognized as such. A few Indian zealots maintain that the Taj Mahal is, in fact, a Hindu temple. These revisionist claims are, on the face of it, outrageous. If they're true, the entire history of Indian architecture would have to be rewritten (which is exactly what their supporters want). Scholars regard such breathtaking unorthodoxy with derision, but it's not something to be laughed at. The idea has won international fame and the support of perhaps millions of nationalists. A similar dispute in Ayodhya, meanwhile, led to the destruction of a beautiful mosque and the deaths of over 2000 people.

The elusive "Tejo Mahalaya"

To say that the Taj Mahal is not a Muslim mausoleum but a Hindu temple is rather like claiming that St Paul's Cathedral has links to the Templars or that the Capitol was built by renegade Freemasons. (In fact, both of these unlikely sounding ideas have their supporters, see p.91.) This is, however, exactly what Professor Purushottam Nagesh Oak, founder and president of the Institute for Rewriting Indian History, has argued. (Well, he used to think the Taj was a palace, but later changed his mind, concluding that it was a temple dedicated to the Hindu god Shiva.)

Oak found his key piece of evidence in Emperor Shah Jahan's own chronicle, which declares that the necessary land was bought from the Hindu king Jaisingh, and was a site "on which before there was this mansion". To work back from palace grounds to an ancient temple would have presented Oak with a problem, if it wasn't for the riddle of the building's name. Taj Mahal is not, as the historians say, an abbreviation of Mumtaz Mahal (which means "glory of the palace", and was an honorific title for Shah Jahan's favourite wife). It is, according to Oak, short for "Tejo Mahalaya", Tej being one of the god Shiva's many pseudonyms and *mahalaya* meaning "great dwelling place".

The proof of the matter is concealed in the minutiae of the building's decoration. There are stone carvings which, if cleverly reversed or looked at from a certain angle, look like images of the Hindu god Ganesh or the sacred syllable "Om". Similarly, the golden pinnacle at the top of the Taj Mahal is not an Islamic star and crescent, but a Hindu lotus topped with a Shaivite trident. Oak also cherry-picks inconsistencies and gaps in the records of the chroniclers to bolster his case, sprinkling the fruits liberally over a base of puffed-up speculation. A 1652 letter from Shah Jahan's successor, Aurangzeb, in which he complains of having to plug leaks in the Taj Mahal, becomes incontrovertible proof that the building was, by then, already ancient.

Psychology provides Oak with his final proof. The idea that a disconsolate, mourning Shah Jahan could suddenly resolve to build the Taj is, according to Oak, "a psychological incongruity. Grief is a disabling, incapacitating emotion." Equally, Shah Jahan's love for Mumtaz was "carnal, physical, sexual" and "a womaniser is ipso facto incapable of any constructive activity. When carnal love becomes uncontrollable the person either murders somebody or commits suicide. He cannot raise a Tajmahal."

What lies beneath

Like all the best conspiracy theorists, Oak and his supporters regard the refusal of the authorities and the academic world to answer their claims not as proof of their inherent implausibility, but as evidence of a cover-up. Oak's 1965 book, *Taj Mahal was a Rajput Palace*, went through two editions before the publisher dropped it "like a hot brick". Unsatisfactory sales or inadequate ideas could not explain this. "Perhaps the Congress Party in power in India dropped dark hints through its secret service of dire consequences to the publishers", Oak speculated. The Congress Party apparently had many reasons to ensure his silence: they could not afford to alienate the Muslim vote, undermine relations with "international Muslim business interests" or jeopardize Agra's tourist industry.

If Oak is right, the government's archaeologists have something – quite literally – to hide. He claims that there are seven levels of secret corridors and chambers underneath the Taj Mahal. Stephen Knapp, a US-based author and ardent convert to Hinduism, got hold of an album of photos of the Taj taken by the Archeological Survey of India (ASI) in the 1930s. He claims that they prove the ASI were investigating the Taj's non-Muslim origin. The photos show a few rooms not usually shown to the public, as well as some bricked-up arches on the river side of the building – all evidence that the Taj just had to be something more than a mere mausoleum. If a duplicitous government would ever consent to have these rooms unsealed, they would surely reveal the truth.

Oak records the story of a man who peeked into one of these hidden chambers in 1934: "To his dismay he saw a huge hall inside. It contained many statues huddled around a central beheaded image of Lord Shiva." This decapitation was a symbol of something far larger – an attempt to destroy the very foundations of Hinduism. Destroying a temple and building a mosque over it was, according to many Hindu nationalists, simply the Mughal way. The case of the Taj Mahal was more damaging still: in giving the Taj a cosmetic refit and claiming it was an original Muslim structure, the Mughals were stealing Hindu history itself.

Some conspiracists would be quite happy to reverse the process, and rewrite Muslim history for their own ends. According to a thread posted in 2006 on an anti-"Islamofascist" website, www.jihadwatch.org, "if impartial evaluation were to show that most of the above ground portion of the Taj Mahal predates Shah Jahan then this would turn the Taj Mahal from an icon of undying love and Muslim creativity into an icon of Muslim aggression and theft."

Godbole's "Great British Conspiracy"

Oak's critics have observed, drily, that if he is right, the entire history of Indian architecture would have to be revised, as many other Mughal-era buildings share the same Indo-Islamic designs and motifs as the Taj Mahal. Oak has the simplest of all answers to this criticism: yes, the history of India should be rewritten; all Mughal-era buildings are Hindu in origin. One of Oak's principal followers, V.S. Godbole, developed this line into a sub-theory in his book, *Taj Mahal: The Great British Conspiracy*. He asked himself, "Were the British scholars just a third neutral party who were misled by the prolonged misuse of Hindu buildings as Mosques and Tombs and were not cunning enough to see through chauvinistic Muslim claims? Or did they know the truth about Taj Mahal and other monuments all along but had, for political reasons, vowed to hide the truth?" He concluded, on reviewing the evidence, that a British conspiracy had suppressed the truth for the last 200 years. This was, he said, part of a systematic attempt by the British to demoralize Hindus – the better to exert imperial control.

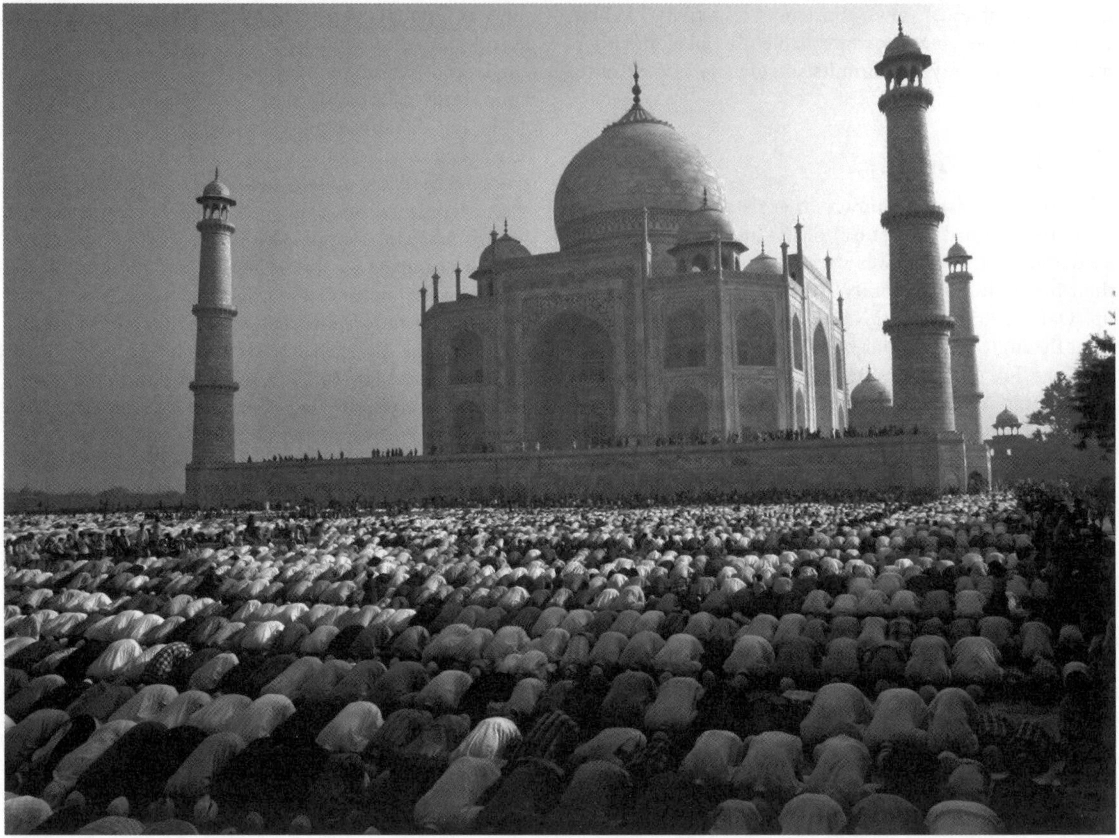

Indian Muslims taking part in Eid al-Fitr prayers outside the Taj Mahal in 2004.

Nationalism and the destruction of Babur's mosque

These types of theories can generate more support in India and among Indian expats than many may think they deserve. The reason for this is simple: the claims chime perfectly with the aspirations of the Hindutva, or Hindu nationalist movement. Hindutva is to India something like Zionism is to Israel (although some have accused it of being more akin to fascism, with its rhetoric of religion, work, family and fatherland, its sexual conservatism, and its theories of ethnic supremacy – which are, coincidentally, built on a concept of "Aryan" idealism similar to that adopted by the Nazis). Some Hindu nationalists want to turn back the clock on India's long history of foreign immigration and invasion. Their methods involve anything from attacking the idea that Indian culture is founded on an Aryan invasion to asserting that the Taj Mahal was once a Hindu temple. Their actions range from attempting to dismantle India's more overtly secularist laws to knocking down actual Muslim mosques.

In 1992, the Babri mosque in Ayodhya, in northern India, was attacked by a hundred-thousand-strong mob of Hindu extremists, and utterly destroyed. The crowd's anger had been stirred up by repeated assertions that the sixteenth-century mosque had been built – by the first Mughal emperor, Babur – on the foundations of an exceedingly holy temple to Rama, one of the most revered Hindu deities. The site, it was claimed, was the Hindu god's birthplace. This kind of claim is relatively common in India. (In fact, Oak and his followers are particularly unusual in saying that the Taj Mahal is a Hindu temple, rather than that it was built on the ruins of one.)

Similar claims about Islam's supposedly innately aggressive architectural tendencies also crop up outside of India. In 2001, Israeli apologist Daniel Pipes wrote in *The Jerusalem Post* that the Ayodhya controversy reminded him of the dispute over Jerusalem's Temple Mount. "Moslems have habitually asserted the supremacy of Islam through architecture", he observed, "building on top of the monuments of other faiths (as in Jerusalem and Ayodhya) or appropriating them (e.g. the Ka'ba in Mecca and the Hagia Sophia in Constantinople)." Pipes warned of the danger that "religious hotheads can trump governments". That said, if a Hindu temple was rebuilt in Ayodhya over the ruins of Babur's mosque, Pipes thought it might nicely "deflect the Islamic attention that for months has been heavily focused on Jerusalem".

Bees in their bonnets

If Hindu extremists aren't generally to be found knocking down mosques, they're certainly trying to undermine their historical foundations. It is possible to find alternative ideas that make the "Tejo Mahalya" theory look positively orthodox. Hindu culture, it is claimed, underpins the entire world: Baghdad was originally the ancient Hindu city of Bhagwat Nagar ("City of God"), Rome was once Ramanager ("City of Ram"), and the Vatican gets its name from the Sanskrit word *vatica*, meaning a woodland hermitage. In the real world, however, the secular arms of the Indian state remain resistant to the wilder Hindutva claims. The surveys and legal cases surrounding Ayodhya continue to drag through the courts, but the Taj Mahal has seen swifter justice. When Oak brought a Public Interest Litigation suit to the Indian Supreme Court in 2000, demanding that the Taj be surveyed, Justices S.P. Bharucha and Ruma Pal dismissed it outright, saying that the suit must have been filed by someone who had a "bee in their bonnet".

SOURCES

Books

Francois Gautier Rewriting Indian History (1996). The long-time Indian correspondent of *Le Figaro*, one of France's leading newspapers, is the most vocal foreign apologist for Hindu nationalism. This book is provocative, decrying colonialism and Islam, as much as it lauds the achievements of Hindu culture.

Stephen Knapp Proof of Vedic Culture's Global Existence (2000). A self-published screed whose title is self-explanatory (Vedic culture being ancient Hindu culture). Covers the Taj among "many mosques and Muslim buildings" that "were once opulent Vedic temples".

Ebba Koch The Complete Taj Mahal and the Riverfront Gardens of Agra (2006). Scholarly and lavishly illustrated book by the professor of art history at the University of Vienna – who is, no doubt, part of the conspiracy.

P.N. Oak Taj Mahal: The True Story (1989). This book was once called *The Taj Mahal was a Rajput Palace* (1968), but the title had to be changed – along with the author's mind – after he decided the Taj was actually a Hindu temple.

Salman Rushdie The Moor's Last Sigh (1996). This rich, satirical magical-realist novel contains a Hindu fundamentalist character, and features the storming of Ayodhya by nationalist crowds.

Websites

Ⓦ **www.geocities.com/Athens/Ithaca/3440/tajm.html** "An Architect Looks at the Taj Mahal Legend" by Marvin H. Mills of New York – who supposedly had a piece of a Taj doorway carbon dated and found it to be fourteenth century. (Unfortunately, the results cannot be found in the journal they're claimed to be in.) Mills' book, *The Origins of the Mosque of Cordoba*, declares the famous mosque "goes back to Atlantis".

- **www.hindunet.org/hindu_history/modern/moghal_link.html** Includes links to Godbole and Oak's arguments in full, plus material on the origins of the Kutubminar tower, the "real" Mughal emperor Akbar and the "Hindu genocide".
- **hindusarise.com/tajmahal.html** Online text of Oak's *Taj Mahal was a Rajput Palace*, revised and extended.
- **home.freeuk.com/tajmahal/index.htm** Oak's own website, with photos of a secret chamber – which is, disappointingly, sealed shut.
- **www.stephen-knapp.com/question_of_the_taj_mahal.htm** "Stephen has dedicated himself to spreading the deepest and most practical levels of spiritual knowledge about the soul – our real identity." He is "brahminically initiated" and "worked in the health field".

The Mormon conspiracy

Unlike other religions and organizations, the Mormons are quite open about the fact that they'd rather like to take over the world. For them, it's called guiding others to salvation. Your average Mormon, however, would be horrified to be called a conspirator as a result. As with Freemasonry, its members are generally thought to be decent and well-meaning – though possibly duped. It's what the elite are up to that conspiracists consider sinister. Critics see this as ranging from acting like a manipulative cult to creating what one Web-based commentator called "the infant state of an Orwellian New World Order".

Mormonism: the facts

Much like Islam, the Church of Jesus Christ of Latter-Day Saints – aka the LDS, aka the Mormon Church – was founded by a charismatic prophet granted the revelation of new holy books that built upon the foundations of previous revelations. But while the angel dictated the Koran verbatim to Mohammed, Joseph Smith's route to prophethood was more roundabout, though he too received his instructions from an angelic messenger. Smith's angel was called Moroni. (An unfortunate name, and not just because it sounds like an Italian lager.) According to Smith, in 1827 he found a set of ancient golden plates buried in a hillside near his home in upstate New York. The treasure was supposedly interred in around AD 400 by a white race descended from the Israelites who turned away from God, were cursed with dark skin – cue allegations that Mormons are racists – and waited around for Columbus to discover them a thousand years later, during which time they had entirely forgotten their own history. The plates were apparently engraved with new and improved books of the Bible that Smith alone could translate using an esoteric technique that involved putting his magical "seer stone" into a hat, burying his face in the same hat and then reading out, one by one, the strange characters – and their accompanying translations – that he saw mystically appear inside it.

The *Book of Mormon* was published in 1830, the same year that Smith founded the Church of Latter-Day Saints, with himself as president. In the 1840s, Smith's successor, Brigham Young, led the fledgling Church west to Utah, where they founded Salt Lake City. The Mormons are seriously evangelical, and they work hard to convert all those who persist in the error of not recognizing the *Book of Mormon*. At the time of writing, the Mormon Church had some ten million adherents, backed by billions of dollars in assets (exactly how many billions is disputed).

Conspiracy to convert

The Mormons' official evangelical policy means that there's not much "theory" in the conversion conspiracy. Yes, a powerful organization wants you to give up your former life, live by its rules, obey its authorities and donate ten percent of your income towards its costs. And yes, ideally it would like the whole world to do the same. The question is: how sinister are those aims, and the methods used to achieve them?

All over the world, but especially in Catholic countries, you'll come across young American men and women, dressed soberly, with well-brushed hair, well-shined shoes and natty name-tags. (Some conspiracists see this costume as suspicious, and as evidence of links with the CIA or FBI, who are known to adopt similarly effective disguises.) They are Mormons, busy doing a spot of overseas missionary work. According to navy veteran Charles L. Wood, on mormonconspiracy.com, there are 60,000 of these "fully trained" missionaries, and because they have "served in and studied the languages of foreign countries throughout the world", large numbers of them have been hired by the CIA – and are, therefore, "in control of a significant amount of CIA activities". Other young Mormons, he warns, have made it into the FBI…

Wood's website makes a better point when it notes that people who order the *Book of Mormon* online also get a free additional gift – a couple of Mormon missionaries leaning on their doorbell. This is where the hard questions about Mormonism really begin. One missionary tactic is to ask the curious just to read the *Book of Mormon* and decide for themselves. Seems reasonable, but beware the sting: the book states that those who read it and subsequently reject it are condemned to eternal damnation. Another questionable technique is the classic bait-and-switch: people expressing an interest in Mormonism are first given Bible quotations to ponder; quotations from the *Book of Mormon* are only gradually introduced thereafter.

Certainly, the section of the Mormon Church's official website on "basic beliefs" says a good deal about God and Jesus Christ, while keeping Joseph Smith and his golden plates relatively under wraps. Mormon apologists say this is because their primary mission is to spread the gospel. However, the uncertain area between the Church of Jesus Christ of Latter-Day Saints and more orthodox Christian denominations has led many evangelicals to accuse the Mormons of masquerading as Christians for their own sinister purposes. And what purpose could be more sinister than turning the US into a religious theocracy?

Mitt Romney and the religious theocracy

Anti-Mormon conspiracists believe that the LDS authorities want more than just America's souls, they want their political minds as well. Mitt Romney's campaign for the Republican candidacy in the 2008 presidential election was occasionally ruffled by questions about his Mormonism. Was his great-grandfather really a polygamist? Does he wear embroidered Temple undergarments? Did he intend to work secretly to establish the kingdom of Mormon in the US? One of those questions got the answer: "I'll just say those sorts of things I'll keep private".

A more intriguing line of attack was taken by *The Boston Globe*, which revealed in 2006 that one of the LDS's twelve "apostles", or elders, had discussed promoting Romney's campaign through the alumni association. The newspaper also reported that office computers at Brigham Young University had been used to send out campaigning emails backing Mitt Romney. This might sound like fairly innocuous stuff to non-American observers, but at stake, according to critics, is the Mormon Church's tax-exempt status as a politically non-partisan religious organization and, beyond that, the very existence of the much-cherished separation of Church and state in the US. Responding to conspiracist murmurings, mother-of-three Heather Johnson, founder of the "Moms4Mitt" campaign, told *The Washington Post* in April 2007, "some people make out like it's a conspiracy, but it's a natural networking system. It's just the way our Church is set up."

Conformity or mind control?

Individual political actions aside, conspiracists claim that the Mormon mission subverts the core American values of individualism and freedom of thought. Certainly, once you're inside the Church, the pressure to stay in and stay down is powerful. As a much-quoted 1945 Mormon newspaper put it: "when our leaders speak, the thinking has been done. When they propose a plan, it is God's plan … To think otherwise, without immediate repentance, may cost one his faith, may destroy his testimony, and leave him a stranger to the kingdom of God".

Charles L. Wood comments that the Church authorities use "brainwashing" techniques to stop people asking questions – doubters are told to pray harder and not to give in to sinful thoughts. Worse still, "doubters of the truth of Mormonism are told that they are risking apostasy and separation from their families for eternity. This line is a powerful mind control tactic." The Church has been accused of putting pressure on devout members to divorce sceptical spouses, even while loudly preaching "family values".

Higher education is also angled towards the promotion of Mormon values. According to a survey conducted at Brigham Young University, 98 percent of the students believe that the Mormon Church is "the only true Church on the face of the whole earth". Impressive holiness, or disturbing conformity? Mormons who have fallen foul of the authorities – perhaps by failing to pay their ten percent tithe tax – can be barred from Temple events, including, if necessary, the weddings of their own families. And many ex-Mormons have found leaving the Church very traumatic, as family and friends may shun the unfortunate recusant, and the Church's elaborate support networks (control networks, some would say) are withdrawn.

The Mormon Church casts its net wide. Anyone researching their family tree will find the genealogical tables created by distant Mormon relatives extremely helpful. But why this obsessive interest in bloodlines? It seems that the Mormons don't just want to convert the entire world, they want to convert (well, baptize, technically) the dead too – and they need their names to do so. They don't just want you; they want your ancestors.

Chloroform in print

As the foundation stone of the Mormon Church, the *Book of Mormon* has been the focus of some fairly aggressive chisel-work. Many sceptics have wondered why, if it was a divinely inspired version of the original rather than a mere human translation, the book would have adopted the seventeenth-century style of the King James Bible. As Mark Twain put it in his travel book, *Roughing It*: "The author labored to give his words and phrases the quaint, old-fashioned sound and structure of our King James's translation of the Scriptures … Whenever [Smith] found his speech growing too modern – which was about every sentence or two – he ladled in a few such Scriptural phrases as 'exceeding sore', 'and it came to pass' etc, and made things satisfactory again. 'And it came to pass' was his pet. If he had left that out, his Bible would have been only a pamphlet." Twain added that the *Book of Mormon* was "chloroform in print".

Numerous parallels have been found between the *Book of Mormon* and various texts published shortly before Joseph Smith's time, including works by Solomon Spaulding (though these, rather conveniently, seem to have been lost). Ethan Smith's *View of the Hebrews* (1823) and Josiah Priest's *Wonders of Nature and Providence Displayed* (1825, and published just twenty miles from Smith's home) even present the "uniquely Mormon" revelation that Native Americans are descended from the Israelites.

Most uncomfortably anachronistic is an echo of *Hamlet*. For Shakespeare's melancholy prince, the afterlife is "the undiscovered country from whose bourn/No traveller returns". Compare this with a line by the supposedly seventh-century BC figure of Lehi (speaking via the angel Moroni and Joseph Smith in 2 Nephi 1:14 of the *Book of Mormon*), who describes "the cold and silent grave from whence no traveler can return". Hard-core dirt-diggers have even found a similarly garbled version of *Hamlet* in Josiah Priest's work, where death is the country "from whence no traveler returns". As for the scene in the *Book of Mormon* where Nephi is ordered by a spirit to kill his own uncle, this may just be coincidentally similar to *Hamlet*'s plot. But in plagiarism trials, parallel misquotations are the equivalent of bloodstained fingerprints.

Cherchez le maçon

If Hercule Poirot (quoting Alexandre Dumas) had "cherchez la femme" as his investigative motto, conspiracists would say "cherchez le maçon" – look for the Mason – instead. And they have a prime target in Joseph Smith, who entered the Freemasons' Nauvoo lodge, by his own admission, in March 1842. Two months later, he created the Temple Endowment Ceremony for his own Church, a ceremony that has caused many conspiracists to fear a Masonic agenda lurking behind the Mormon Church.

In 1990, the offending ceremony was adapted to remove the striking Masonic symbolism – which included clothing turned about the waist and the use of the square and compasses symbol. Was this latter-day modification a change of policy? Or perhaps a cover-up? With admirable ingenuity, Mormon apologists can claim that any similarities between their own traditions and Masonic rites can only prove the truth and antiquity of Mormon ceremonies, as they preserve the lost rituals of Solomon's temple. Yet few Masons believe that their society's supposed link with Solomon's era is anything more than a legend.

The most ingenious Masonic theorists tie the Mormon interest in genealogy and their acceptance of "plural marriage" – polygamy – with a desire to protect and strengthen the bloodline of the families of Joseph Smith and Brigham Young. The Mormon founders, it seems, learned of their Merovingian lineage after their initiation into the secrets of Scottish Rite Freemasonry (see p.83). And if this strain of Masonry didn't appear to exist in early nineteenth-century America, it's only because it was shady enough to need to be well hidden.

Nukes, aliens and David Icke

Beyond Freemasonry, things start to get seriously left field. The doyenne of theorists, California's Mae Brussell, claimed that she had documentary evidence that, by leveraging their infiltration of the FBI and CIA, the Mormons had got their hands on "tons" of uranium. Apparently, they then exported it to Australia, where it was "beyond the control of the federal government" (though, presumably, the federal government of Australia was quite happy about it all), ready to use it as part of the Church's campaign for a new, unified, Mormon (this time) world government. The credibility of Brussell's document is undermined by its apparent claim that President Johnson shipped ten million tons of ore in the same direction. Presumably, in a giant flotilla of stealth mega-tankers.

Internet rumour-mongers have also spread unsourced eyewitness tales about construction workers finding super-scale catacombs under the Mormon-founded Salt Lake City. Some, the workers must have confidently assessed, predated the colonization of Utah. Others run through to the Western Rockies where, in the Cottonwood Canyons, giant storage chambers and a secret Masonic temple can be found. And three-toed footprints have allegedly been seen in the caverns... Enter British conspiracy theorist David Icke, who draws all the evidence together magnificently. The footprints were left by his "reptilians" (see p.113), who control the higher echelons of Mormonism. This über-lizard bloodline – which matches that of the elite Illuminati and the heirs of the Merovingians – is the real secret sought by the conspiratorial programme to compile the entire world's family tree. Oh, and the Mormons are really Satanists, too.

SOURCES

Books

Fawn M. Brodie No Man Knows My History: The Life of Joseph Smith (1945). Controversial biography – because it diverges some way from the official line – by an eminently readable biographer.

Charles L. Wood The Mormon Conspiracy (2006). An angry ex-teacher is keen to convert you to believing in the existence of a dangerous Mormon conspiracy to take over the world.

Films

Gary Rogers The Book of Mormon Movie (2003). Begins with Joseph Smith finding his golden plates and then runs through the Book of 1 Nephi and the first part of 2 Nephi. As one Web reviewer put it: "think high school kids in bathrobes with sheets on their heads". Even the official Mormon website tactfully admits that "as the Book of Mormon is one of the most perfect books ever written, I'm not sure any movie made by anybody would be able to fulfill such high expectations."

Websites

Ⓦ **www.exmormon.org** In the site's own words: "for those who are questioning their faith in the Mormon Church and for those who need support as they transition their lives to a normal life".

Ⓦ **www.irr.org/mit** Capacious (anti-)Mormon area of a Christian website dedicated to "investigating" (read: attacking) the claims of Christian fringe groups and non-Christian religions.

Ⓦ **www.lds-mormon.com** Devoted to challenging Mormonism on the basis of "scientific fact", with an extensive archive of articles and quotes.

Ⓦ **www.lds.org** Official web presence of the Church of Jesus Christ of Latter-Day Saints. If the number of hyperlinks are anything to go by, "How do I give gifts and donations?" is a very frequently asked question.

Ⓦ **mormonconspiracy.com** The website of Charles L. Wood, including significant excerpts from his book, *The Mormon Conspiracy*.

The Panzer Pope

In the aftermath of Cardinal Joseph Ratzinger's election as Pope Benedict XVI in 2005, *The Times* collected some choice quotations. At various points in his long career, the new pope has called homosexuality an "intrinsic moral evil", declared rock music to be a "vehicle of anti-religion" and announced that Anglicanism and Protestantism are "not proper Churches". Oh, and he thinks that Turkey joining the EU is "an enormous mistake". But liberal sneers at conservative Catholic views don't amount to conspiracy theories.

What is unashamedly conspiracist is the "Panzer Pope" theory, which imagines Ratzinger as having a Nazi agenda on the basis that the Bavarian-born cardinal was a "former Nazi". He was, in fact, a member of the Hitler Youth. At age fourteen. At a time when it was illegal for young Germans not to join. In reality, his father was an active opponent of Nazism. Similarly, Ratzinger's service in the German flak (anti-aircraft) corps was more a matter of conscription than conviction, and he deserted shortly before the German surrender. Some conspiracists also like to make out that Ratzinger was complicit in the "murder" of Pope John Paul I (see p.44) – not that there's any evidence. At best, the man they call the "Killer Cardinal" was one of the conservatives who weren't supposed to be too pleased about having a liberal pope poking his nose around the Vatican Bank's accounts, or its lists of Masonic members.

Chief inquisitor

There's rather better evidence for Ratzinger's involvement in a cover-up of the Catholic Church's sex-abusing priests scandal. As prefect of the Congregation for the Doctrine of the Faith (CDF) – or chief inquisitor, to give the job its old-fashioned name – it was Ratzinger's job to handle all sex abuse cases. On May 18, 2001, the cardinal sent a letter – written in Latin – to all the Church's bishops pointing out that sex abuse investigations were a matter for the CDF alone, and that all details were to remain strictly confidential.

Also in 2001, Jason Berry and Gerald Renner, writing in the *National Catholic Reporter*, reported that the Congregation had declined to pursue nine separate allegations of sex abuse made against Father Marcial Maciel, the founder of the Legion of Christ. This decision was laid at the door of Ratzinger, as prefect. Some speculated – without any documentary proof from the famously secretive Vatican – that he was anxious to protect from any embarrassment Pope John Paul II, who had been a warm supporter of Maciel. John Paul II himself apparently considered the allegations to be part of an anti-conservative and anti-papal conspiracy. Ratzinger finally reopened the investigation in 2004, as John Paul II was nearing the end of his life. In 2006, a year after John Paul II's death, the Vatican "invited" Father Maciel to retire into a life of prayer and penitence, which wouldn't involve either celebrating Mass or giving interviews. A trial was apparently ruled out on the grounds of Maciel's age and ill health. The Legion of Christ responded by reasserting Maciel's innocence, and noting that Maciel, "following the example of Jesus Christ", would not defend himself.

The facilitation of evil

As prefect of the CDF, Ratzinger was also instrumental in promulgating the Vatican's policy on birth control and condom use. Following the publication of "The Many Faces of AIDS" by the National Conference of Catholic Bishops' Administrative Board, Ratzinger wrote a widely publicized explanatory letter to Archbishop Pio Laghi on May 29, 1988. Discussing the Church's position on educational programmes about condoms in government schools, he wrote: "one would not be dealing simply with a form of passive toleration"; this was "a kind of behaviour which would result in at least the facilitation of evil". (Whereas telling a woman whose philandering husband is HIV-positive that if they use a condom she will go to hell is pure goodness.)

It must also have been Ratzinger's conservatism that made him write to US bishops in June 2004, declaring that priests must refuse the sacrament to "pro-choice [illegible]cians. Supporting abortion laws was "a grave sin". Ratz[illegible] specifically mentioned "a Catholic politician consisten[illegible], campaigning and voting for permissive abortion and euthanasia laws". No names, of course – that might unfairly influence Catholic voters in the upcoming presidential election. An American who voted for a pro-choice candidate would be "guilty of formal cooperation in evil and so unworthy to present himself for Holy Communion." (Himself? Presumably the cardinal temporarily forgot that women also vote.)

International links

Chris Floyd of the *Moscow Times* thought Ratzinger had other reasons to support George W. Bush. He seized on a www.newsday.com article of April 21, 2005, which revealed that the cardinal sat on the board of the Swiss Foundation for Interreligious and Intercultural Research. Also on the board was none other than Neil Bush, the president's younger brother, a man best known not for his contributions to religious debate, but rather for his business failures, notably as a director of the failed Silverado Savings and Loan bank, whose collapse cost the federal government $1 billion.

Floyd thought it fishy that the foundation was registered as a "management trust" rather than as a religious foundation. "A cynic", he wrote, "i.e. anyone with the slightest acquaintance of Bush business practices – might think that a 'management trust' masquerading as a religious charity would be an excellent place to launder money or park assets away from the taxman's prying eyes." Was Ratzinger obscurely paying a debt to the US when, in May 2005, he appointed the conservative archbishop of San Francisco, William Levada, to the recently vacated post of prefect of the CDF?

At the crazier end of the conspiracy scale was the story, reported in the obscure *Hertfordshire Mercury* on April 29, 2005, that a "German former cardinal" had called a historian at Hertfordshire's County Hall for details of the "Hertfordshire branch" of the Knights Templar. A certain Tim Acheson, one of the Hertfordshire Knights, commented that "perhaps it is the revenge of the Templars that the Church fears, since the origin of Freemasonry is rooted in the persecution of the Templars by the Church." Or perhaps Ratzinger was recruiting? Acheson also pointed out that the pope's birthplace, Bavaria, was also the home of the mysterious Illuminati (see p.93)…

SOURCES

Books

Jason Berry **Vows of Silence: The Abuse of Power and Sexual Crisis in the Papacy of John Paul II** (2004). The reporter who broke the Marcial Maciel story deals with it in this book-length attack on the papacy's handling of sexual abuse scandals.

Websites

Ⓦ **context.themoscowtimes.com/stories/2005/04/29/120.html** Chris Floyd's April 29, 2005 broadside against the pope and Neil Bush. Originally from the *Moscow Times*, but picked up by conspiracy sites everywhere.

Ⓦ **www.legionaryfacts.org/comunicados.php** The Legion of Christ maintains an entire website dedicated to replying to its critics. Responses to criticisms of Maciel take up only a few of its pages.

Ⓦ **nationalcatholicreporter.org/update/bn051806.htm** The first and most detailed report on Maciel's 2006 punishment, with links to the Vatican's communiqué on the subject, and the Legion of Christ's reply.

THE LAND OF THE FREE

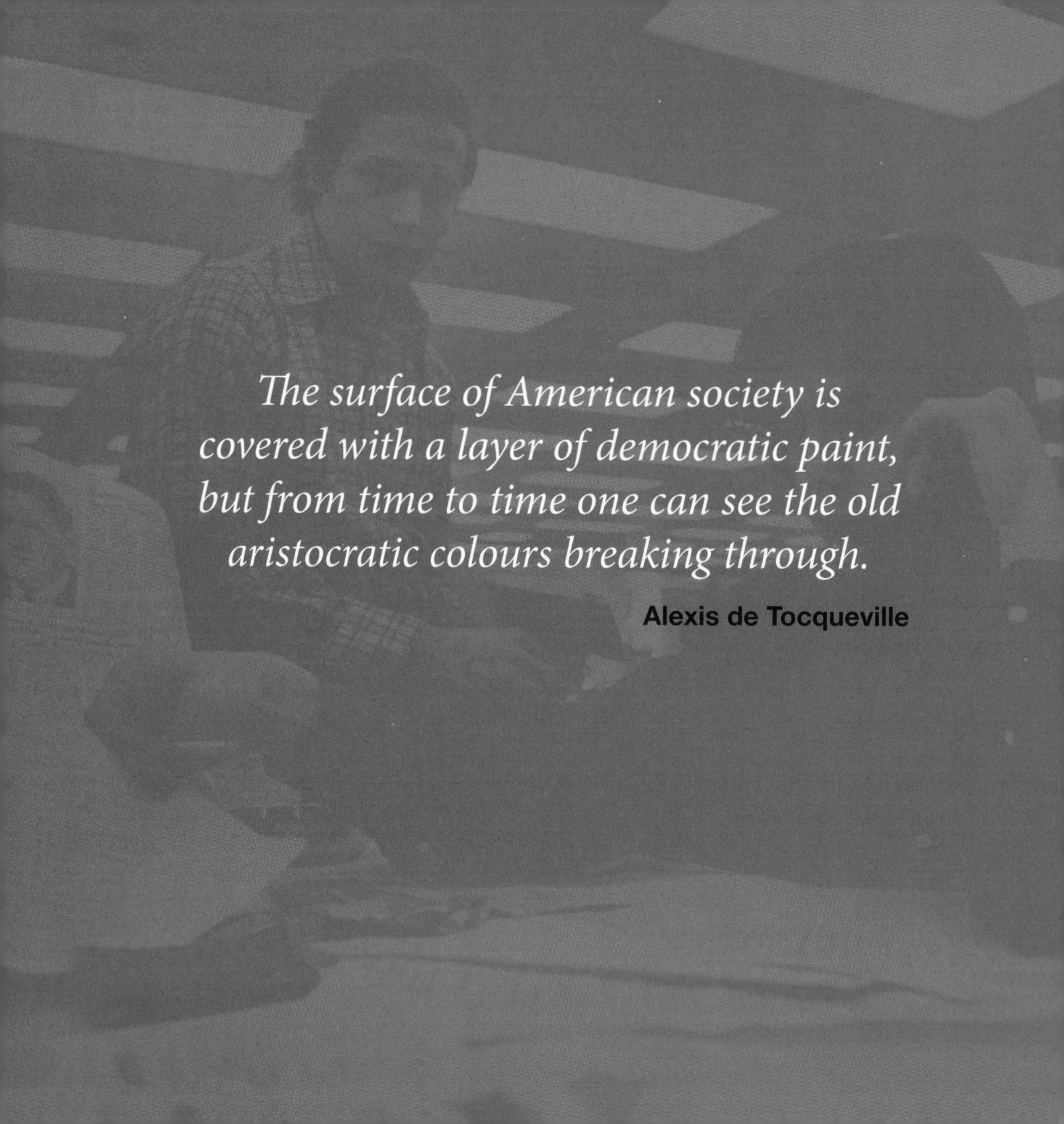

The surface of American society is covered with a layer of democratic paint, but from time to time one can see the old aristocratic colours breaking through.

Alexis de Tocqueville

THE LAND OF THE FREE

For sheer presence, the United States is far and away the leader in conspiracism. American domestic politics, the focus of this chapter, is rife with conspiracy theories. They have even been blamed for a generalized breakdown in trust in the political system. Conspiracists counter that it's not the theorists that are to blame so much as the actual conspirators...

The US even gave the world a word for a conspiracy theory whose proof leads to a politician's downfall: a Watergate. Nixon's original Watergate affair didn't just create a new word; it also set the pattern for three decades of American presidential conspiracy theories based on dirt-digging and the obvious corollary, mud-slinging. Most damaging perhaps were the various "gates" that dogged Bill Clinton's presidency. The heat that emanated from Republican-funded researchers was intense enough for Hillary Clinton to declare that there was a "vast right-wing conspiracy" to bring her husband's administration down. Politicized conspiracy theorists were no less hard at work during George W. Bush's presidency. In 2000, his very election was enmired in conspiracy theories about the electoral and legal processes that had brought him to power, not to mention the secret societies, such as the Skull and Bones, that supposedly backed – or controlled – him. Eight years on, the same issues haunted the US presidential election once again.

It wasn't the first time that conspiracy theories had swarmed around a presidential election. Ronald Reagan's inauguration speech in 1980 was magically blessed by the simultaneous release of American hostages in Iran, but in future years this October Surprise became more of a curse on Reagan's reputation, as theories about the timing of the incident refused to die down. The rumours were underpinned by the very real conspiracy behind the Iran–Contra affair, which in turn buttressed the long-running theory that the CIA were behind an elaborate scam to bring crack cocaine into the US and support the Nicaraguan Contras at the same time.

The most radical right-wing American conspiracy theorists dismiss talk of Bush, or Reagan, or Clinton, as the mere rumblings of partisan politics' grubby underbelly. Left-wing theorists may concoct conspiracies with Reagan or Bush at their centre, they say, and right-wingers can do the same for Clinton, but their targets are no more than front men for the sinister federal machine. Indeed, the ultra-conservative John Birch Society has made political hay, for more than half a century, out of the notion that even the most right-wing Republican presidents have been complicit in a vast communist plot.

In the eyes of ultra-right "Patriot" or "Christian Identity" groups, the all-powerful and all-evil federal machine's workings have been exposed by such atrocities as the Jonestown massacre of 1978, or the Waco killings of 1993. Conspiracy theories about the latter actually inspired Timothy McVeigh to carry out the Oklahoma City bombing of 1995 – about which the ultra-right have plenty more conspiracy theories. But when it comes to the secretive conclave of Bohemian Grove, issues of Right versus Left or federal versus corporate don't even come into play. Conspiracists of all colours unite in their distrust of this weird Californian shindig and its spooky annual ceremony, the so-called "Cremation of Care".

Note that America's role in foreign conflicts – from the attack on Pearl Harbor during World War II to the Second Gulf War – is covered separately in the "Warplay" chapter (see p.353), while US weapons technology is discussed under "Real weapons of mass destruction" (see p.277). For conspiracy theories centred on the alleged assassinations of famous Americans, including Robert Kennedy, Malcolm X and, of course, John F. Kennedy, see the dedicated chapter (see p.1). Alleged CIA plots to kill Salvador Allende and Fidel Castro are also covered in "Assassinations", while the CIA gets a whole well-deserved section to itself under "Mega-conspiracies and master plans" (see p.75).

The John Birch Society

The John Birch Society, or JBS, is an ultra-conservative, anti-Communist political group set up in the US at the height of the Cold War, with its self-professed aim being "To bring about less government, more responsibility, and – with God's help – a better world..." By the mid-1960s, the JBS had up to 100,000 members, many of whom were also members of parent-teacher groups, or school and library boards, or held other local offices. They were organized into hundreds of local chapters and front groups across each of the fifty states (and now online), all of which were doing the good work of spreading the message of defending the God-given US Constitution against the forces of Communism, whose agents were everywhere – everywhere! Abortion, VD, drugs, you name it, the Commies apparently peddled it – the literature of the Society is riddled with the language of conspiracy, raging against the "Insiders" and the "Communists" who staff the "global power elite", and the "Establishment" who are attempting to implement the "New World Order" (see p.141).

The JBS was itself founded on conspiracy. A young American man named John Morrison Birch worked as both a Southern Baptist missionary and a US Army intelligence officer in China during the 1940s – two dangerous careers in a troubled land and time. Shortly after the end of World War II, he was shot dead by Chinese Communists. However, according to the Society, news of his "unprovoked murder" was suppressed by the US government, "in its desire to depict the Red Chinese as innocuous 'agrarian reformers'," and because Communist China and Capitalist America were really Communist allies in it together. Seeking to raise the memory of this "selfless Christian patriot" from shameful oblivion, industrialist Robert Welch created a new organization in 1958 that he named the John Birch Society.

Exposing the Communist plot

Since its inception, the Sociey's bread-and-butter endeavour has been to regularly check – and expose – congressmen's voting records, particularly in relation to federal spending programmes and any US aid going to countries with Communist governments. (The JBS claims that its "carefully prepared exposés" have thwarted numerous "would-be domestic terrorists" and "liberal incumbents".) Any offensive act – and there are many – by a poor civic official will warrant a carpet bombing from the Society's legions of letter-writers, and the JBS also has profligate use of local radio and TV stations to blitz the airwaves with its political messages. Ironically such tactics, although not exclusive to the Society, have been likened to those of the Communists. Indeed, the book of the Society's founding meeting was published as *The Blue Book* (or *The Blue Book of the John Birch Society*), reminiscent of the *Little Red Book* of Chinese Communist Party leader, Chairman Mao Zedong.

Some pretty outrageous charges have arisen from the Society's exposés over the years, but particularly during the Cold War. Not only presidents Harry S. Truman and Franklin D. Roosevelt, but even Dwight D. Eisenhower was accused of being an agent of the "Communist Conspiracy", pretty stiff allegations considering how many of the JBS's members were Republicans (unless the Society had rumbled some greater, unadmitted plot within the party's ranks). The JBS was influential enough in the 1960s for Republican senator Barry Goldwater to accept its support during the 1964 presidential election. The senator also adopted "A Choice, Not an Echo" as his campaign slogan, taking the phrase from the title of a conspiracy theory book written by JBS member and activist Phyllis Schlafly, who alleged that the Republicans were being controlled by the "Communist" Bilderberg Group (see p.250). When Goldwater lost the election to Lyndon B. Johnson, the Society took it as proof of darker forces at work.

Vassals of the New World Order

The Bilderberg Group isn't the only secretive, elite organization to experience the wrath of the John Birch Society. The JBS has also long damned the Council on Foreign Relations (see p.140) as a cabal controlled by the Rockefeller family, and it holds the Trilateral Commission (see p.143) in the same contempt, believing that all such groups are simply vassals for the great Communist plot – the embodiment of the Freemasons' (see p.82) grand plan to run the world. But such plots aren't just the preserve of conspiratorial cabals. The JBS also believes the US government is in on the act. For instance, "gun control" is really just a ruse to disarm Americans before the New World Order "democide (the murder of civilians by the governments that rule them)" ensues, because gun control is allegedly about enabling governments to murder civilians, not preventing civilians from murdering each other.

However, it is the United Nations that seems to have stoked the Society's ire hottest over the past fifty years. The JBS launched its "Get US out! of the United Nations" campaign in 1959 – arguing that "world government through the United Nations is a serious threat to the freedom of all Americans". The Society claims that the UN does not recognize the divine origins of the US Constitution or its protection of individuals' rights, and that those rights are being sacrificed by US government traitors on the UN's "anti-American" altar in the pursuit of the New World Order. (Evidence for this supposedly includes President George H.W. Bush calling for a "new world order" during the First Gulf War and referring to the involvement of the UN in both the war and in establishing that new world order.) But the US–UN relationship is not all one way, according to the Society's literature: "From Korea and Vietnam to the Persian Gulf, Somalia, and Kosovo, the UN is hardly a 'peace' organization but a cover for American presidents to conduct undeclared wars."

NAU paranoia

The Society's lowest ebb came in the 1980s, when its chairman, Congressman Lawrence McDonald, was on board flight KAL 007 when it was shot down by Soviet fighters (see p.327) – an "assassination" in the eyes of the John Birch Society. His death coincided with a fall in both numbers and power. Since then, however, membership has been rebuilt to approximately 60,000, as US sovereignty is further threatened by the North America Free Trade Agreement, the Free Trade Area of the Americas (an initiative the Society claims is "shrouded in deception and misrepresentation") and other plans that will rob Americans of control over their own destinies, properties and rights. Even worse is the North American Union (NAU) conspiracy, under which Canada, the US and Mexico would all be bound by a common currency, a central bank, parallel systems of regulation, justice and security, and ultimately, a single constitution and government – much like the dreaded EU. (The Society lauds itself for having predicted the threat posed by that "socialist regional superstate" decades ago.)

The Society has been ridiculed from several quarters, including the Southern Poverty Law Center, as "paranoid" for its warnings about the NAU and its other "Nativist Conspiracy Theories", and these ideas have been cast in the same mould as conspiracies about JFK's assassination (see p.22) and the Apollo moon landings (see p.347). However, the JBS accepts such challenges and forcefully rebuts them on its website – where you can also read about all its current campaigns and find out how to send your kids to one of its "Youth Meets Truth" summer camps.

SOURCES

Books

Emanuel Mann Josephson Rockefeller, "Internationalist": The Man Who Misrules the World (1952). One of the Society's first members blames the Rockefellers for everything evil in the US.

Phylis Schlafly A Choice Not an Echo: The Inside Story of How American Presidents are Chosen (1964). For Phylis Schlafly US presidents are chosen in smoke-filled rooms, not by ballot box.

Dan Smoot The Invisible Government (1962). Tackles the Council on Foreign Relations and the sinister government figures who "want America to become part of a worldwide socialist dictatorship, under the control of the Kremlin".

Robert Welch The Blue Book (1958). The whole of Welch's two-day presentation on the founding of the JBS in print form (also available online at www.jbs.org/node/22).

Websites

Ⓦ **www.jbs.org** The Society's official website includes details on all its campaigns, its youth summer camps, blogs, bulletins, podcasts and the full text of *The Blue Book* – plus membership details, of course.

Ⓦ **www.publiceye.org/tooclose/jbs.html** A scathing dissection of the Society by the "progressive think-tank" Public Research Associates.

Ⓦ **www.splcenter.org/intel/intelreport/article.jsp?aid=797** The Southern Poverty Law Center's report on the North American Union conspiracy theory pushed by "paranoid far-right groups" like the JBS.

Ⓦ **www.thenewamerican.com** This online and print magazine, with its motto "That Freedom shall not perish", is the JBS's main publication.

Watergate: a third-rate burglary

These days, a botched break-in at a fancy Washington hotel doesn't sound like a big deal. But we're not talking about just any burglary. This was a genuine conspiracy whose uncovering brought down a president, the *original* "-gate" scandal, the one that lent its name to every sleazy affair in American politics that followed and inspired a generation of investigative journalists – as well as conspiracy theorists who like to imagine they're investigative journalists. Remember Travelgate, Filegate, Contragate, Zippergate and Fajitagate? Or Britain's Squidgygate and Camillagate? Not forgetting the Clintons' Whitewatergate, of course, and San Francisco's less well-known Watermelongate.

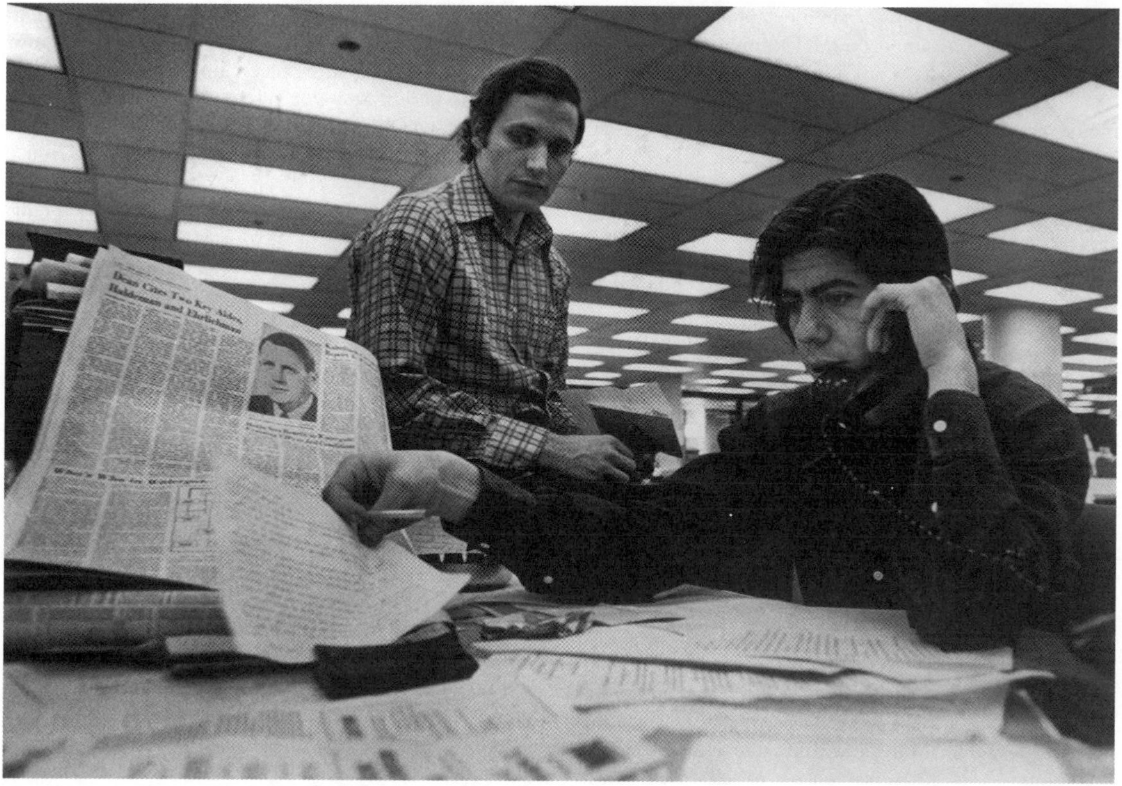

Journalists Bob Woodward and Carl Bernstein investigating Watergate at *The Washington Post* in 1973.

It all began in the early hours of June 17, 1972, when a security guard spotted a piece of tape holding a door unlocked in the basement stairwell of the Watergate complex, a Washington DC hotel and apartment building heavily patronized by the political establishment. Suspicious, he called the police, who in short order discovered five burglars in the offices of the Democratic National Committee. Two were CIA-trained Cuban exiles, another, James McCord, claimed to be an ex-CIA agent (as if they're ever "ex"…). The "black bag" team were apparently adjusting or replacing bugging equipment. The story made headlines in *The Washington Post*, but President Nixon's press secretary dismissed it as a "third-rate burglary", and it probably wouldn't have run much further had two staff writers not done a bit of checking.

All the Post's men

On June 19, Bob Woodward and Carl Bernstein of *The Washington Post* published an article pointing out that McCord was not just a former spook, but the actual, current, right-now security chief for Republican president Nixon's re-election campaign, the Committee to Re-Elect the President, aka CRP – or CREEP, as the press put it.

The dynamic duo kept on digging, helped by an anonymous inside source who was dubbed "Deep Throat" by *Washington Post* insiders, after a porn film making headlines at the time. He advised them to follow the money trail, and repeatedly confirmed what other, single sources were saying – which, as sceptics point out, was all rather convenient for the two journalists. Woodward and Bernstein linked a White House consultant, E. Howard Hunt, to at least two of the burglars, and discovered that a CRP consultant and former FBI agent, G. Gordon Liddy, had been fired shortly after the incident. On August 1, they reported another puzzling fact. A $25,000 cheque earmarked for the Nixon campaign had somehow found its way into the account of one of the Watergate burglars, through funds managed by former attorney general John Mitchell. Bernstein called Mitchell for comment, only to have his ear blistered with the response: "Katie Graham's gonna get her tit caught in a big fat wringer if that's ever published."

Katie Graham was the *Post*'s publisher, but she did, indeed, put her tits on the line. On October 10, her rising-star reporters' article opened with a thunderous (if awkwardly phrased) salvo: "The Watergate bugging incident stemmed from a massive campaign of political spying and sabotage conducted on behalf of President Nixon's re-election and directed by officials of the White House and the Committee for the Re-election of the President." But outside Washington, the American people didn't seem to have noticed. On November 7, 1972, "Tricky Dicky" was re-elected in a landslide.

Lies and audiotape

The Watergate burglars, along with Hunt and Liddy, went on trial in January 1973, and were duly convicted of conspiracy, burglary and wiretapping. Facing thirty years in prison, McCord confessed that CREEP had conspired not only to plan the burglary, but also to pay off the burglars to plead guilty and keep schtum in court. McCord started to finger more and more of the "President's Men" for involvement. The fire was spreading upwards, fast. On April 30, desperate to clear a firebreak beneath him, Nixon fired several senior White House officials and campaign staff.

But White House Counsel John Dean turned on his former boss, testifying to Nixon's involvement before a televised Senate committee of inquiry. Then, on July 13, a presidential aide casually mentioned that the White House had made tape recordings of every single presidential conversation. The Senate and newly appointed special prosecutor Archibald Cox pounced, subpoenaing Nixon for the tapes. Nixon refused, ordering Cox to drop the subpoena. On October 20, 1973, after Cox refused to back down, Nixon went on the rampage, sacking first Cox and then official after official in an attempt to find someone who'd do what he was told. The president declared: "I am not a crook."

In March 1974, a grand jury named Nixon – off the record – as a "co-conspirator", and in April, he was forced to give up 1200 (expurgated) pages of transcripts of the White House tapes. A wide-eyed public could now hear its president plotting how to pay off blackmailers and get conspirators off the hook, swearing profusely (or at least apparently saying "expletive deleted") and fulminating against blacks and Jews.

And what on earth was missing from one particularly glaring eighteen-and-a-half minute gap? The White House claimed that Nixon's secretary, Rose Mary Woods, had accidentally erased the tape by pushing a foot pedal while answering the phone. Photo reconstructions in the newspapers, however, showed this to have been ergonomically impossible, while scientific analysis of the original tape revealed that the "gap" had been erased not once, but over and over again.

Finally, the famous "smoking gun" tape was released, showing Nixon had known about the cover-up within one week of the original break-in. The House Judiciary

Committee voted 27–11 to impeach the president on three articles: obstruction of justice, abuse of power and contempt of Congress. Before the Senate could try him, however, the famously grudge-bearing, paranoid president resigned on August 8, 1974, saying: "I have never been a quitter. To leave office before my term is completed is abhorrent to every instinct in my body. But as president, I must put the interest of America first ... let me say I leave with no bitterness toward those who have opposed me."

Entrapment theory

As a conspiracy unmasked, Watergate has plenty of sleazy allure, but one fact has struck generations of commentators: the game wasn't worth the candle. Why would the president risk everything just to find out a few details about his rival's campaign? Or was there more to it? For a start, Liddy claims they were bugging Larry O'Brien, the chairman of the Democratic campaign. Hunt and the Cubans, however, say that another area of the office was being targeted. Nixon summed up the most common conspiracy theory himself. "The whole thing was so senseless and bungled", he wrote in his memoirs, "that it almost looked like some kind of a set-up." He guessed that the Democrats had known about the break-in, and had set Nixon up for a fall. The Senate investigation, he pointed out, had found some evidence that Larry O'Brien's deputy had been tipped off about a spying job.

The focus of the "Democratic Entrapment" theory is Carl Shoffler, the policeman who answered the Watergate security guard's call. It was Shoffler's birthday – and yet he'd signed up for an eight-hour night shift. Who would do such a thing unless they'd been paid off? Shoffler himself had a simpler explanation: "I just felt like it", he said. More murkily, a friend of Shoffler's called Edmund Chung claimed that Shoffler had suggested to him over dinner that he'd known about the burglary in advance. Shoffler counterclaimed that Chung had offered him $50,000 if he confessed to foreknowledge. But where would that kind of money have come from? Perhaps Nelson Rockefeller, soon to rise to new heights of wealth and influence as Gerald Ford's (unelected) vice president. Or perhaps – as Nixon himself suspected – Howard Hughes. Others turn the last theory on its head, claiming that the real aim of the break-in was for Nixon to find evidence of Hughes's undoubted financial connections to the Democrats...

Secret agenda, silent coup

Jim Hougan, author of *Secret Agenda*, thinks that the visible evidence we've seen is just the tip of a murky iceberg. McCord, he believes, was trying to sabotage the original break-in, possibly to cover up a separate CIA bugging operation aimed at collecting details of Democratic sexual indiscretions. Hougan's line was spun into a giant web by Len Colodny and Robert Gettlin, whose book *Silent Coup: The Removal of a President* was the last, Nixon-defending word in Watergate conspiracy theory literature – a theory so far out that *The Washington Post* didn't even see fit to report it. A White House insider, the book alleged, had arranged the Watergate break-in to find and presumably destroy evidence of a prostitution ring that compromised a close acquaintance. Only afterwards did Nixon jump in to protect his aides.

The *Silent Coup* theory led to a welter of lawsuits. Most have been settled out of court, with the result that *Silent Coup* has been withdrawn from publication. There is one major problem with Colodny and Gettlin's theory. Integral to their allegations was the notion that the influential four-star general (and, later, Nixon's chief of staff) Alexander Haig was the legendary "Deep Throat" who acted as Woodward and Bernstein's main source, and that Watergate was the conclusion of a campaign led by Haig and his CIA/Pentagon backers to bring down a president who wanted out of the Vietnam War. Oops. On May 31, 2005, "Deep Throat" finally revealed himself to be FBI number two, Mark Felt, which Woodward and Bernstein later confirmed. Many conspiracy theorists felt oddly disappointed; others refused to believe it.

From Watergate to Dealey Plaza, via the Bay of Pigs

Much has been made of the backgrounds of the Watergate burglars. Three of them, Frank Sturgis and two Cuban exiles, had been heavily involved in anti-Castro plots – as had their handler, ex-CIA asset E. Howard Hunt. Sturgis had surfaced in the conspiracy world once before, when he ran a media campaign to blame JFK's assassination (see p.22) on Cuban Communists. And there were other, more puzzling links with Cuba. The White House tapes revealed that Nixon had sent his first chief of staff, H.R. Haldeman, to persuade Richard Helms at the CIA to pressure the FBI into dropping the Watergate investigation. Nixon threatened, mysteriously, that if the FBI proceeded, it would "open up the whole Bay of Pigs thing again".

What about the Bay of Pigs? Were the Watergate gang connected to the CIA plots to kill Fidel Castro (see p.19)? Or were they connected to an even more sinister assassination plot? H.R. Haldeman claimed in *The Ends of Power* that "the whole Bay of Pigs thing" was actually coded talk for "the whole JFK thing". Howard Hunt and Frank Sturgis, it's pointed out, look rather like two of the famously overdressed "three hoboes" who were arrested in Dealey Plaza on the day JFK was assassinated – and promptly released. Strangely, Nixon himself was in Dallas that day, working as a lawyer for the Pepsi Corporation…

The system prevails

On September 8, 1974, Nixon's successor Gerald Ford granted him an official pardon, thus making the former president the only major player in the Watergate affair to avoid prosecution. The fact that forty government officials involved in the scandal were indicted or jailed is evidence, according to the establishment, that integrity prevailed in the system. The press and the law courts did their jobs. Sceptics wondered about the handy timing – Nixon's fall provided symbolic closure for the Vietnam War, sparing the US any real soul-searching about what had gone wrong. It has also been suggested that Nixon's pardon had been a precondition of his offer to make Ford his vice president in December 1973, following the resignation of his disgraced vice president Spiro Agnew.

After Watergate, major changes were made in campaign finance law, and senior government figures were required to make their private finances significantly less private. Government, as a result, is supposed to be cleaner. Certainly, bugging is no longer routine (or, if it is, it's well hidden) and no one tapes the White House. Which is lucky for Bill Clinton and Monica Lewinsky (see p.221). It's fascinating to compare Clinton and Nixon. Both have been called the greatest – and most flawed – presidents of their generations. Both tried to bury a relatively minor incident, only for the cover-up itself to become the issue. There was, however, one key difference: Tricky Dicky fell on his sword, while Slick Willy lived out his full term.

SOURCES

Books

Carl Bernstein and Bob Woodward All the President's Men (1974). A gripping, novella-like exposition of Woodward and Bernstein's investigation.

Len Colodny and Robert Gettlin Silent Coup: The Removal of a President (1991). "One of the most boring conspiracy books ever written", according to *The Washington Post*, but high-octane enough to storm the bestseller lists, and then be withdrawn following successful libel suits.

Fred Emery Watergate (1994). Uses memoirs and newly released White House tapes to tell the whole story afresh. Pulls no punches when it comes to describing the details of Nixon's fall, but is equally focused on the political context of the scandal.

H.R. Haldeman and Joseph Dimona The Ends of Power (1978). Since disavowed by former White House chief of staff "Bob" Haldeman as ghost-written and sensationalizing, it has also been called a rare moment of clarity from an insider who defends Nixon without whitewashing him. "Most of us would have been willing to sacrifice ourselves", says Haldeman, "to save the Presidency that we believed in."

Stanley I. Kutler Abuse of Power (1998). In 1996, Kutler and the advocacy group Public Citizen won a landmark decision to release the White House tapes. Using this new source, Kutler shines a new light into the dark workings of Nixon's White House.

Films

Alan J. Pakula All the President's Men (1976). All the gritty glamour of Bernstein (Dustin Hoffman) and Woodward's (Robert Redford) relentless investigation. A hugely watchable advert for journalism, though it doesn't much clear up what actually went on at Watergate.

CBS News Watergate: The Secret Story (1992). The documentary (made with *The Washington Post*) naming FBI director L. Patrick Gray as Deep Throat.

Websites

Ⓦ **www.asianweek.com/2002_08_30/opinion_emil.html** Watermelongate. You read it here first. (You won't find it anywhere else.)

Ⓦ **www.millercenter.virginia.edu/academic/presidentialrecordings/** Downloadable audio files of tapes secretly recorded by Nixon, LBJ, JFK and others.

Ⓦ **www.nixon.archives.gov** The original transcripts of the White House tapes, courtesy of the US government.

Ⓦ **www.washingtonpost.com/wp-srv/national/longterm/watergate/chronology.htm** Handy timeline containing links to the original *Washington Post* stories. All the mucky details, straight from the horse's mouth.

Jonestown

At the end of the 1960s, California was the epicentre of the worldwide "hippy scene". Many adherents had gathered together to live in large communes, run according to belief systems far removed from the accepted norms of Main Street America. Prominent among those infused by strong religious or mystical elements was the People's Temple, a utopian, agrarian community in Ukiah, near San Francisco. Its founder, lay preacher Jim Jones, was originally from Indiana, where his father had been a Klansman. A flourishing, well-funded development, the Temple propounded a peaceful, multiracial mission of harmonious, godly existence, and became a haven for the poor. Hundreds of followers lived and worked in the camp, while thousands more spread the Temple's message throughout California.

However, lurid tales in the press spoke of beatings at the camp, and alleged that followers were subjected to brainwashing and ritual abuse. There were even rumours that escapees were being murdered. Jim Jones had already used the Temple's not inconsiderable funds to buy a large plot of land in Guyana, and when the state began to investigate his tax affairs in 1977, he decided to move his whole flock to South America. The heart of the Guyanese jungle was just the place for the spiritual fiefdom of "Jonestown" to prosper.

Horror stories continued to filter back from Guyana, via the press and the concerned relatives of followers, telling of abuse, torture and murder. A worried California congressman, Leo Ryan, decided to investigate. He arrived in Guyana with a group of journalists on November 14, 1978, and toured Jonestown with the deputy from the local US embassy, Richard Dwyer. The visit was fraught; they were escorted around the camp by Jonestown minders, who refused them access to some parts of the camp and repelled followers who approached the visitors begging to leave with them. Jones himself became enraged at the delegates' failure to be taken in by the staged tour.

A few Jonestown families chose to defect and went to the airport with Ryan's party the next day. However, as the delegation and the defectors attempted to board two aircraft late that afternoon, they were ambushed by Temple followers. Ryan and four other passengers were shot dead, and several more were injured. Meanwhile, back at the camp, Jones was apparently recorded talking about how he knew of the ambush, but had not authorized it, saying it's "too late" and "Ryan's already dead". According to an audio recording known as the "Jonestown Death Tape", he spoke of his fear of a violent military reprisal, before declaring "We better not have any of our children left with us". Then the massacre began.

At the camp, Jones reportedly told his followers to drink cups of a soft drink laced with cyanide, or face execution from his armed guard. Jones was himself killed by a gunshot wound to the head, although it's unclear if he shot himself, or was shot by one of his followers. Photos of the camp depict hundreds of dead bodies, dressed in apparently clean, casual clothes, laying in an eerie orderly array, as though sleeping among the huts and trees. Most were women. Most were black. There were 913 victims in all, including 276 children.

The tragic victims of the Jonestown massacre in Guyana, November 1978.

The official verdict

In 1979, back in the US, the House Foreign Affairs Committee (HFAC) concluded that the massacre was the result of Jones's "extreme paranoia". Its 782-page report detailed what it called a mass suicide at Jonestown, a verdict already reached by two books written with astonishing speed in 1978, *The Suicide Cult* and *Guyana Massacre*, and by similarly themed 1979 articles in *Time*, *Newsweek* and *Rolling Stone* that described a crazy cult of death.

Too many dead people

But not everyone agreed. *The New York Times* and *The Baltimore Sun* originally reported that four hundred bodies had been found at Jonestown, while around seven hundred people had fled into the jungle. Yet a week later, the death toll was over nine hundred, suggesting that hundreds of the people that reportedly fled into the jungle were also killed. Local papers, such as the *Guyanese Daily Mirror*, reported that over a hundred Guyanese troops, as well as several score US Green Berets and members of the UK's Black Watch, were on exercise in the jungles around Jonestown at the time. Doing what, exactly? What happened, the *Mirror* asked, to the Jonestown followers who ran into the jungle in the hope of escape, but came out dead?

The gun that killed Jones was found two hundred feet from his body, while the rest of the bodies, laying face down in neat rows, showed no signs of the contorted rigidity induced by cyanide. As reported in *The New York Times* and *The Miami Herald*, Guyanese pathologist Dr Leslie Mootoo told the coroner's court that he found gunshot wounds on some victims, but strange, needle-like puncture wounds on many, many more. Nonetheless, the US Army said that as the cause of death was not in dispute – suicide by drinking cyanide – no autopsies were required. Under pressure from the families of the deceased, there were eventually a handful of autopsies – seven out of more than nine hundred deaths. The bodies were left to rot in the sun, stripped of identification and then flown to a remote US base, with several corpses lumped into each casket. Many were embalmed or cremated posthaste. According to the National Association of Medical Examiners, the military "badly botched" procedures.

The CIA

Several theories about Jonestown involve the CIA, with the most prevalent seeing the entire incident as a CIA-backed exercise in mind control and brainwashing. According to John Judge, writer and conspiracy theorist, in his article "The Black Hole of Guyana", Guyana was a CIA hotbed: its government was installed by a CIA-backed coup, the US embassy in Georgetown was a CIA headquarters and Dwyer, who escaped the killing at the airport, was a CIA agent. Judge relates that Jonestown survivor Teresa Buford – who was Jones's mistress and financial manager of the People's Temple in California, as well as the daughter of a former naval commander and spy – described brainwashing and mind-control methods being used in the Temple. Another senior Jonestown member was Larry Layton, whose father ran the US Army's Chemical-Biological Weapons Research unit. The stashes of drugs found at Jonestown were said to include many used in the CIA's MK-ULTRA programme (see p.210), which involved experimenting with the use of drugs for brainwashing and mind control; a programme that the agency claimed to have stopped in 1973.

Judge's story runs that Jones was employed by the CIA in Brazil, under the auspices of the CIA-linked charity World Vision. He then moved to California, where he founded a children's home before establishing the Temple at the behest of the CIA. After being forced to relocate to South America when the Temple's activities attracted too much public opprobrium, Jones developed acute megalomania. The leader's loss of control meant that the CIA risked having its programme exposed, so the agency terminated the Temple in the most effective way imaginable: everyone was killed. Former Jonestown director Joyce Shaw called it a mass experiment in brainwashing and exterminating blacks.

A variation, supported by Robert Sterling in *The Jonestown Genocide* and Michael Meiers in *Was Jonestown a CIA Medical Experiment?*, argues that the Jonestown experiment was not only instigated by the CIA, but that the camp was still under the agency's control at the time of the massacre. Congressman Ryan was apparently on the verge of exposing the CIA's involvement, which is claimed as the reason why he was killed at the airstrip. It's also worth noting that, despite the evident dangers of Jonestown, Ryan wasn't provided with a US military escort. It is a fact that, just a few years prior, Ryan had been behind the Hughes-Ryan Amendment, a bill that was supposed to force the CIA to disclose covert operations before carrying them out. The link between this bill, Ryan's apparent antipathy to the CIA and his death has also been made in the Church of Scientology magazine *Freedom*.

The threat that Ryan posed in relation to the CIA and Jonestown has been given another twist by conspiracy theorists on the Internet. It's alleged that fugitive Nazis Dr Josef Mengele and Martin Bormann were overseeing medical experiments at Jonestown, which would have proved more than embarrassing to the CIA if anyone had found out. Some say, on the other hand, that the CIA destroyed Jonestown when they cottoned on to the Nazi connection, believing the camp was a threat to the US.

If Larry Layton was a CIA operative, his high connections didn't save him from receiving a life sentence in 1986, although he was later released in 2002. After two trials, in which he pleaded not guilty, Layton was jailed for his part in the killings at the airstrip – having got to the airport by pretending to Ryan that he wanted to defect, he produced a gun and shot and injured two people. Larry's sister Deborah, the Temple's financial director, had indeed defected in May 1978, and told the US government and the CIA in a 37-page affidavit that Jones was drilling his followers for a mass suicide. However, the House Select Committee on Intelligence concluded in 1980 that Jones had never had anything to do with the CIA, and that the agency had no prior knowledge of the impending massacre.

The Soviets

It has also been reported that the Soviets were somehow linked to Jonestown. Around $500,000 was allegedly taken from Temple funds and given to the Soviet embassy in Guyana shortly before the massacre, while Jones is said to have met frequently with officials from the Soviet and Cuban embassies. Was that what spurred so much interest from the CIA, or was the camp just a front to lure in communist interests? Conspiracist Dr Peter Beter told the listeners to his "audio letters" just weeks after the Jonestown massacre that the mass deaths were a cover for a large military operation against a Soviet missile base in Guyana. He said that Jones was actually a Jew, who had organized Jonestown like a kibbutz, and he had been spirited back to Israel by Israeli troops working with the US on the strike against the Russians.

The Californian conspiracy

Jones also had strange links in Californian politics. A week after the massacre, *The Washington Post* described Jones as a "West Coast power", referring to the presence and utilization of Temple followers in Californian politics. *The Washington Times* reported that President Jimmy Carter's wife Rosalynn had invited Jones to dinner. Jones's twenty thousand followers in California were pivotal political foot soldiers, albeit crooked ones. *The New York Times* and *San Francisco Examiner* detailed how multiple ballots were cast to rig the 1975 San Francisco mayoral election for Jones's ally, Democrat George Moscone.

Further rigged votes, threats and blackmail allegedly got more Temple men into public office in San Francisco, enabling the funnelling of $26 million from welfare and housing budgets into offshore bank accounts. Just days after Jonestown, Moscone and prominent gay activist Harvey Milk (who was, at one time, a Temple follower) were shot dead by disaffected civic councillor Dan White, who later "killed himself". *USA Today* economics editor Jeff Schnepper has said that White was not the kind to commit suicide, and that his death was "never investigated fully". *The New York Times* carried a charge from then-governor

Ronald Reagan that Jones "was close to Democrats". Was Jones so close to the Democrats that his Californian corruption ultimately got him killed?

John Judge makes another odd connection, arguing that Jones became Temple leader around the time that Richard Nixon moved into the White House and set in place a massive increase in covert FBI surveillance and infiltration of political groups. Jones installed uniformed, armed guards in the Temple in both California and Jonestown, and used various techniques of coercion and blackmail against his followers – sinister methods that Judge insinuates may have had federal origins. Another theory on the Web suggests that Jones fell between the stools of a Republican sting and Democrat politicking. But if Jones, Moscone and Milk were all murdered for their supposed corruption, surely Jones could also have been silenced without having to kill a thousand innocents as well?

Still unresolved

Little new evidence concerning Jonestown has emerged in recent years, though theorists are tantalized by the fact that five thousand documents from the HFAC hearings in 1979 have remained classified ever since. The committee's chief consultant, George Berdes, told CNN in 1998 that the documents would be declassified soon, but there's still no sign of them. At that time, CNN described the relatives of the dead as still asking questions and demanding answers, despite the prevailing media consensus of mass suicide. In 2004, the BBC reported the poignant fact that 412 of the bodies discovered at Jonestown have never been claimed. They remain buried in a mass grave in Oakland, California.

SOURCES

Books

Jim Keith (ed) Secret and Suppressed (1993). Worth seeking out for John Judge's long, very detailed article, "The Black Hole of Guyana", cited by virtually all subsequent works on Jonestown.

Michael Meiers Was Jonestown a CIA Medical Experiment?: A Review of the Evidence (1989). Although Meiers' claim that Jonestown was a CIA medical experiment remains unsubstantiated, he shows that there was much more to Jones, the Temple and Jonestown than is usually covered.

Films

Stanley Nelson Jonestown: The Life and Death of People's Temple (2006). The wilder theories don't get an airing, but this includes some fascinating background on Jones and interviews with ex-Temple members, which makes for an absorbing, disquieting film.

Websites

Ⓦ **www.deborahlayton.com** Deborah Layton's own account of life in the People's Temple, also published in 1999 as *Seductive Poison: A Survivor of Jonestown Shares her Story*.

Ⓦ **jonestown.sdsu.edu/AboutJonestown/Articles/conspiracy.htm** This site by Rebecca Moore covers many of the major conspiracies about Jonestown.

Ⓦ **www.parascope.com/articles/0997/jonestown.htm** Robert Sterling's *The Jonestown Genocide* is now available on the Web.

Ronald Reagan and the "October Surprise"

On January 16, 1979, following mass street protests, Shah Reza Pahlavi fled Iran. Islamic opposition leader Ayatollah Khomeini returned from exile to fill the power vacuum, imperilling the country's long-cosy relations with the US. On November 4, 1979, pro-Khomeini student revolutionaries seized the US

embassy in the capital Tehran, denouncing US support for counter-revolutionaries. They took more than sixty hostages and promised not to release them until the shah was returned to Iran for trial and President Carter's administration unfroze $12 billion of Iranian assets being held in US banks. The plight of the hostages – 52 of them, once a number of the women had been released – consumed the attention of the American public.

A year later, with the November 1980 US presidential election approaching, the hostage crisis was the key issue of the campaign. Seeking a second term, President Jimmy Carter was facing strong opposition from the Republican ticket of Ronald Reagan and his prospective vice president, CIA chief George H.W. Bush. Polls showed the two parties racing neck and neck. Bush commented that he feared an "October Surprise" by the Democrats, whereby they would somehow pull off the hostages' release by the end of the month. (So the "October Surprise" label actually refers to a conspiracy theory that didn't happen, rather than one that allegedly did.) Meanwhile, Carter had declared an oil and weapons embargo and was negotiating hard with Khomeini's government. Iran was just as eager as the US to find a solution – it urgently needed weapons to resist an invasion by Iraq that had begun in late September.

Carter's negotiations somehow broke down in October, and on November 4, 1980, Reagan won the election. The Republicans entered new talks with Iran through Algerian intermediaries. Reagan's inauguration speech of January 20, 1981, trumpeted new beginnings: "Let us begin an era of national renewal", he said. "Can we solve the problems confronting us? Well, the answer is an unequivocal and emphatic 'yes'." Within minutes, it was announced that the hostages had been freed. That day, the Republicans had unfrozen $8 billion of Iranian assets. In the weeks that followed, the US government secretly began selling billions of dollars worth of weapons to Iran, mostly through the good offices of Israel.

The theory

So, had regime change in the US simply resolved the impasse? Or, as conspiracy theorists charged, was there more to it than that? Was the 1980 election, as one commentator alleged, a "covert political coup"? The theory runs that Reagan's team secretly negotiated with the Iranian revolutionary government behind Carter's back – aiming not only to release the hostages, but also to deliberately undermine Carter's own efforts. The Republicans supposedly made a deal: if the Iranians would delay the good news until inauguration day, the new Reagan administration would make sure they were handsomely rewarded.

At the heart of the story are the Hashemi brothers, Jamshid and Cyrus, Iranian arms dealers and businessmen who claim they brokered secret meetings between Khomeini's representatives and Reagan's campaign director, William J. Casey. (An American spy chief during World War II, Bill Casey went on to become Reagan's CIA chief.) Contact was first made in July 1980 in Madrid, and the deal firmed up at a Paris hotel (which one depends on whose version of events you believe) on either October 18, 19 or 20 (again, depending on whose account you follow) – which was exactly when Carter's negotiations stalled. It's claimed that George H.W. Bush was present at one or all of the meetings, possibly along with CIA agents Donald Gregg and/or Robert Gates (the latter went on to become Bush's CIA director).

A conspiracy of journalists: the prosecution on trial

From its inception, the October Surprise conspiracy theory was pieced together – or, if you prefer, concocted – by journalists. By the 1980s, everyone wanted to be a Woodward or a Bernstein (see p.191). *Executive Intelligence Review*, the mouthpiece of Lyndon LaRouche's leftist/crypto-fascist/conspiracy theorist political group, was

IRAN–CONTRA: NO THEORY

In 1979, the Frente Sandinista de Liberación Nacional, aka the Sandinistas, concluded their war against Nicaragua's brutal and corrupt Somoza government by taking power. They established a paternalistic, left-wing regime and, in 1985, held and won internationally recognized democratic elections. Against them, right-wing loyalists branded "contras" (from "contra-revolutionary") were fighting a brutal campaign – in 1982 a congressional intelligence committee reported that the Contras "raped, tortured and killed unarmed civilians, including children". They had been trained and funded by the CIA. Under the 1983 Boland Amendment, however, Congress banned the spending of federal money on the Contras.

Faced with the ongoing hostage-taking of Americans in Beirut, the Reagan administration stepped up its programme of selling arms to Iran in return for Iranian help in freeing American hostages held by pro-Iranian militias. By November 1985, General Colin Powell was attempting to sell Iran five hundred HAWK anti-aircraft missiles through the Israeli government. As the value of the deal topped $14 million, however, officials realized it would have to be declared to Congress. Spotting a way to kill two birds with one stone, Reagan's campaign chief, William J. Casey, devised the so-called "Iran–Contra scheme", originally known only to a few top officials under the code name "the Enterprise". The money from the missile sales would be diverted directly to the Contras to avoid awkward questions, troublesome domestic laws and UN agreements. The hostages would be freed and Nicaragua liberated from left-wing oppression. Everyone was a winner. Especially Bill Casey, who Reagan rewarded with the post of director of the CIA.

On November 3, 1986, the Beirut weekly *Ash-Shiraa* scooped the world with news of the scheme. On November 21, Oliver North, the National Security Council member responsible for actually running Iran–Contra, began to shred documentary evidence. Four days later, US attorney general Edwin Meese confessed to the Contra side of the scheme, and on November 26 Reagan announced the opening of the Tower Commission to examine the affair. As with the Watergate controversy (see p.190), the key issue was how much the president knew, and how early he knew it. The handsome Colonel Oliver North, aide to National Security Advisor John Poindexter, became the public whipping boy – and media darling – of the affair, but Congress's final report, released on November 18, 1987, failed to clarify the extent of Reagan's knowledge. This was despite Reagan's diary entry of January 1986, which clearly stated "I agreed to sell TOWs to Iran", and despite North's testimony that he'd written five memos for the president describing the Contra angle. Reagan even delivered a bizarre apology on March 4, 1987: "A few months ago I told the American people I did not trade arms for hostages. My heart and my best intentions still tell me that's true, but the facts and the evidence tell me it is not."

North and Poindexter were convicted on numerous counts of lying, conspiracy and obstruction of justice, but their convictions were overturned on appeal on the grounds that their testimonies to Congress had been used against them, despite their being granted immunity. The CIA emerged without a stain on its reputation, though it's widely assumed that the agency played a key role in the affair, possibly to the extent of providing extra covert funds for the Contras by assisting their drug-trafficking business (see p.213). Also escaping lily white was Robert Gates, the CIA's number two at the time. (He subsequently became CIA director and, in 2006, was appointed secretary of defense by George W. Bush.) No one thinks Gates was involved in Iran–Contra, but some suspect he knew more about it than he has admitted. Certainly, Gates's 1991 claim to have "forgotten" being warned by a senior official of his suspicions about the operation was, to quote the prosecutor of the Iran–Contra affair, "disquieting".

Much about the Iran–Contra scandal makes the October Surprise theory look worryingly plausible: Casey's involvement, the use of CIA contacts, the conduct of secret negotiations with Iran, and the evident willingness of the Reagan administration to work secretly and in contravention of both US and international law.

the first to publish the theory, as early as December 1980. However, in those pre-Internet years, the rumours largely remained word-of-mouth whisperings until an article by Gary Sick, former navy captain and Carter's White House aide for Iran during the hostage crisis, appeared in *The New York Times*, on April 15, 1991.

Sick attracted support from former president Carter himself, but his investigation was questioned by a leading sceptic of the October Surprise theory. In 1992, former CIA man and journalist Frank Snepp claimed in the *Village Voice* that much of Sick's information seemed to have come from correspondence with another journalist, Martin Kilian, the Washington correspondent for Germany's leading political review, *Der Spiegel*. Snepp alleged that Sick took these snippets of second-hand information and "built them into the scaffolding of his conspiracy theory, thus erecting an edifice of compounded error".

Snepp came up with a sophisticated counter-theory that penetrates right to the heart of the problem with conspiracy theories in general. He claimed that researchers and journalists cross-fed each other information and, worse still, that they allowed their sources to cross-reference each other in turn. "The truth", Snepp wrote, "may be lost to the confusion they generated." It was an unwitting conspiracy of journalists and sources. Sick responded that "there was no conspiracy … this was a voluntary group of people working on the story which I regard as almost the best of investigative journalism."

The evidence: American alibis

The revelation of the Iran–Contra scandal (see p.201) made the October Surprise theory "feel" very substantial. But it wouldn't be enough in court – it's all circumstantial. Investigative journalists have spent thousands of person-hours trying to place George H.W. Bush, Donald Gregg, William Casey and Robert Gates in the right place at the right time. Bush's alibi seems fairly sound: he is known to have campaigned in Pennsylvania and New Jersey on October 17, and to have visited his Washington country club, Chevy Chase, on October 19 – between 10.29am and 11.56am, according to Secret Service logs. But, it's alleged, he *could* have made it to Paris and back between times, if he'd had use of a military jet. Gregg's alibi seems even more solid. He was on vacation in Delaware, spending most of his time down on the beach. But as German journalist Martin Kilian pointed out, weather reports for the days in question describe overcast, cool conditions – as low as 55 degrees.

None of this would stand up in court, but some find it curious that no one has yet produced a convincing alibi for Casey. (Even the alibi that was produced for him showed a strange ability to change: he supposedly couldn't have made the Madrid meeting in July because he was at a historical conference in London, or rather he was at the Bohemian Grove gathering in california – or was that the following weekend?) And there is some troubling circumstantial evidence. In 1983, a congressional subcommittee headed by Democrat Don Albosta was set up to examine "Briefing-gate", a scandal that centred on the theft of President Carter's briefing book during the 1980 campaign. It uncovered a network of Reaganite "foreign policy consultants" who appeared to have deliberately leaked disinformation about the progress of negotiations in an attempt to unnerve the Iranians and perhaps prevent an October Surprise – the campaign was headed by William Casey.

The evidence: witnesses

On the one hand, the alleged conspirators are CIA-linked Republicans who all vociferously deny involvement. On the other is a bizarre line-up of businessmen, arms dealers and self-described ex-intelligence operatives who all claim – just as loudly – to have been key players. The arms dealers, Jamshid Hashemi and his brother Cyrus, are often cited as key witnesses. Cyrus, unfortunately, can't talk – he was murdered in London in July 1986. That hasn't stopped Jamshid, however, who confirmed details of the October Surprise meetings to journalist Craig Unger. It also hasn't silenced another arms dealer and witness, Hushang Lavi, who was reported as having helped to open negotiations with the Iranian government.

Meanwhile, voluble Oregon businessman Richard Brenneke places himself in Paris and Madrid as a kind of fixer. Brenneke's story is backed up by one Heinrich Rupp, who said that he was a CIA pilot and had flown Casey to Paris on October 18, where he'd caught sight of Bush waiting at the airport. Brenneke cross-confirms his story. Bush himself, along with Gregg, is supposed to have been flown home by one Gunther Russbacher, also said to be a former CIA flier, who claims Bush attended one meeting at the Hôtel Crillon and another at the George V, negotiating with Hashemi Rafsanjani (Khomeini's number two) and Saudi Arabian businessman Adnan Khashoggi. Russbacher named $40 million as the price for the delayed release of the hostages.

The US arms sales to Iran were to be channelled through the Israeli government, an angle of the deal covered by the self-confessed presence in Paris of Ari Ben-Menashe – by his own account a former Mossad agent working as a fixer for the Israelis. He claims to have met Casey, Bush, Gates and Gregg at the Paris Hilton on October 19 or 20. Supposed Mossad man Ahran Moshell makes similar claims.

An authoritative-sounding source for the October Surprise theory was Abol-Hassan Bani-Sadr, the first president of Iran under Khomeini. (So, no axe to grind there.) Speaking to researcher Barbara Honegger in 1988, he said that his knowledge of the affair came from a message he'd been sent by the Iranian foreign minister in September 1980. Bani-Sadr also believes that Carter's national security advisor, Zbigniew Brzezinski, helped Saddam Hussein plan the invasion of Iran. (Which isn't all that unlikely – after all, in 1998, Brzezinski publicly admitted that the CIA started arming the Afghanistani Mujahedeen in July 1979, six months before the Soviet invasion.)

In the witness box: the sources on trial

Self-described intelligence freelancer, Oswald "Razine" LeWinter, is central to the theory's claims. He originally told researchers Martin Kilian and Barbara Honegger that he'd read a secret memo about the affair in a CIA report. Later, he said that he'd been employed to get rid of evidence that the Paris meeting(s) had ever taken place. Later still, he placed himself in Paris at the time. Why did his story keep changing? Perhaps it was because he was a chronic myth-spreader – he once claimed he'd been paid $40,000 in 1988 to propagate the October Surprise theory. Later in his career, he materialized as a witness to the conspiracy theory surrounding Pan Am Flight 103 (see p.331), and was jailed for trying to con $10 million out of Mohamed al-Fayed for "proof" that Dodi al-Fayed and his girlfriend, Princess Diana, were assassinated by MI6 (see p.54).

LeWinter is not the only witness whose role seems to have grown over the years. Talking to a researcher in 1980, Jamshid Hashemi discussed the October Surprise theory without mentioning his own presence in Paris, and later changed his story regarding Casey's presence at negotiations. It's also strange that LeWinter was accused of involvement in the smuggling of small quantities of petty arms to Iran in 1980. Would he have been involved in such a job, it's asked, if he was simultaneously at work on a multimillion arms-to-Iran deal? As for Ari Ben-Menashe, he has never been able to prove his presence at the Paris hotel, and his credibility may be somewhat undermined by his boast of having planted a homing device at Iraq's Osirak reactor to enable Israeli planes to locate and destroy it – an unsubstantiated story that's too James Bond for some stomachs.

The other pilot regularly named as a witness, Gunther Russbacher, turns out to have been found guilty of the misuse and misappropriation of government properties and the misuse of government jets. Is his claim of involvement in the October Surprise the desperate squirming of a guilty man trying to get out of trouble? Or is he the victim of trumped-up charges designed to discredit him?

Conspiracy to create a conspiracy theory?

Quite apart from the main sources' individual credibility gaps, some people detect a problem in the fact that many of them already knew each other and had dealings in the past. A US Customs sting in April 1986, for instance, nabbed Brenneke and LeWinter, among others, for illegally exporting arms to Iran. The insider informant was one Cyrus Hashemi… Did LeWinter and Brenneke want to pay the Americans back? Or did they want to clean up

OCTOBER SURPRISES

The phrase "October Surprise" has since lent itself to a number of post-1980 US presidential elections. George H.W. Bush's 1992 campaign was supposedly hijacked by the Democrats' timing of the indictment of Defense Secretary Caspar Weinberger on Iran–Contra conspiracy charges – four days before the election. In 2000, it was George W. Bush's turn, with the "discovery" of his old arrest for drink-driving. During the 2004 George W. Bush vs John Kerry race, accusations were hurled by both sides. There was the well-timed release of the story that US troops had allowed huge quantities of explosives to disappear from an Iraqi warehouse, and the equally well-timed delay in the release of the results of the Iraq Survey Group, which failed to find any WMDs. Widespread suspicions also held that Bush would suddenly announce the capture of Osama bin Laden. In fact, only a video appeared, in which bin Laden directly addressed the American people – "I tell you in truth, that your security is not in the hands of Kerry, nor Bush, nor Al Qaeda. No. Your security is in your own hands." It wasn't much of an October Surprise, however, as commentators failed to agree which side bin Laden's intervention had favoured.

their reputations by associating themselves with something bigger than minor fraud and petty arms dealing? Or did Brenneke just want to make some money from the book he was planning?

Perhaps there were other more pressing reasons for inventing such a scam? In 1988, Brenneke had to testify at a case in which two Customs informants had supposedly claimed fraudulent expenses for a separate sting that had gone wrong. Brenneke supported his friend Heinrich Rupp's claim that he thought he had been acting under CIA instructions, citing his own involvement as a CIA agent flying arms into Iran from 1980 to 1982. Both men testified to each other's involvement in the October Surprise negotiations. Unimpressed, the government charged Brenneke with perjury – only for Brenneke to repeat his claims, bringing George H.W. Bush into the picture too.

Brenneke was eventually cleared on five counts of lying – though journalists later contended that the prosecution could have proved, from his credit-card receipts, that he was nowhere near Paris in mid-October 1980 (a claim that Brenneke denies). As Steve Emerson and Jesse Furman put it in "The Conspiracy that Wasn't" (*New Republic*, November 18, 1991), these super-sources had "discovered that it was possible to get away with any allegation in the national security area … if an intelligence agency, already suspect in the public's mind, denied something, that merely reinforced the authenticity of the charges." That observation has since become an axiom of conspiracy theorizing.

Counter-theories: Carter's surprise

One Iranian theory brilliantly turns the tables on President Carter. Far from being the victim of an evil electoral fraud, it's claimed that he was partly responsible for the hostage crisis in the first place – not to mention the Iranian revolution. The evidence? The quick-slow, stop-start speed of the Iranian students marching on the US embassy. It seems their procession was being controlled by a mullah – who was receiving commands by radio from the Iranian government. These delays were aimed at giving the Americans time to destroy crucial documents, and for senior diplomats to take refuge in the Iranian foreign ministry. But why would the revolutionary government have done this favour for the US? Because, it seems, they owed Carter one after he had secretly withdrawn support for the shah, who had refused the Americans' demands for oil kickbacks. This may be an outlandish theory, but there's some evidence that Carter's team may have undermined their own negotiation efforts by simultaneously pursuing arms deals – perhaps through none other than Cyrus Hashemi.

Lingering suspicions

In 1992, after pressure from former hostages and former president Carter himself, the House of Representatives investigated the October Surprise charges, concluding that "there was no October Surprise agreement ever reached". The ensuing Senate Foreign Relations Committee inquiry, published as *The "October Surprise" Allegations and the Circumstances Surrounding the Release of the American Hostages Held in Iran*, agreed that "the credible evidence now known falls far short of supporting the allegation of an agreement between the Reagan campaign and Iran to delay the release of the hostages". And yet, as journalist Robert Parry has pointed out, Congress received one crucial report too late for inclusion. It came from the Russian government, who disclosed that their own intelligence files confirmed the tale of an October Surprise deal.

Also "too late" to be included in the inquiry was material from journalist David Andelman's biography of Alexandre de Marenches, the legendary director of France's intelligence agency SDEC (now renamed the DGSE). According to Andelman, De Marenches acknowledged helping Casey to set up hostage talks with Iranian officials – in Paris, in October 1980. Similarly, Palestinian leader Yasser Arafat told President Carter that the Palestine Liberation Organization (PLO) was also approached by Republican emissaries for a brokerage role. Of course, Arafat and De Marenches may have had their own reasons for spreading the rumours. Or perhaps, as a US government spokesman said of the Russian report, their ideas were "based largely on material that has previously appeared in the Western media".

A matter of faith

John Barry's *Newsweek* cover story of November 11, 1991, "Making of a Myth", commented that the October Surprise theory "reflects back at your own political biases. If you revile the Reagan-Bush epoch, you'll find an administration founded on ultimate treachery. If you admire Reagan's reign, these tales come across as the hallucinations of crazed publicity hounds." Such partisan interpretations of news events were to become the hallmark of the Clinton presidency. The truth, Barry said, had "become so complicated and so hideously detailed that no reasonable person can say with absolute certainty that there was no conspiracy and no deal." A feeling that anyone trying to pin down the truth about conspiracy theories will find horribly familiar…

The evidence for the October Surprise doesn't stand up to close scrutiny – some of the witnesses, especially, could hardly be less reliable. On the other hand, the timing and the coincidence of the Iran–Contra scandal absolutely stink. As journalist Craig Unger, in an October 1991 *Esquire* article, reported a congressional staffer as saying: "You'd have to be the village idiot to believe Iran released them at that time without talking to the Republicans." Another Unger source, Scott Thompson – a Tufts University professor who worked with Bill Casey in the 1980 Reagan–Bush campaign – puts it even more forcefully: "So people finally figured it out. What the fuck did they think was going on?"

SOURCES

Books

Barbara Honegger October Surprise (1989). A former researcher for the Reagan–Bush campaign team, Honegger claims to have heard a senior figure on Reagan's team boasting that the Republicans had "cut a deal" to prevent Carter's October Surprise. Her principled resignation and her detailed investigations soon followed.

Robert Parry Trick or Treason (1993). Gutsy, persuasive book written by a campaigning journalist and true believer in the October Surprise theory. Lots on the gaps in the schedules of the prime suspects.

Gary Sick October Surprise: America's Hostages in Iran and the Election of Ronald Reagan (1992). The best-researched and most convincing version of the October Surprise conspiracy, from an expert on US policy in the region. Lots of fascinating context on the background to the Iranian situation.

Websites

Ⓦ **archives.cjr.org/year/92/2/october.asp** Fascinating analysis of the sourcing of a trio of pieces of investigative journalism into the October Surprise affair. Reveals how conspiracy theories can be created and sustained by journalists.

Ⓦ **www.consortiumnews.com/archive/xfile.html** Links to a series of pro-October Surprise articles by journalist Robert Parry, plus one or two others.

Satanic owls at Bohemian Grove

The Bohemian Grove began in 1872 as a private club for San Francisco journalists and businessmen – along with a few self-professed "bohemians" like Mark Twain, to give some alternative flavour. Members would meet up every summer to drink, relax, network and do some hearty male bonding by pissing on trees and staging silly plays symbolizing how they had put aside the cares of the political and business worlds. The club's defenders would say that, in spirit, it hasn't changed all that much since then. Admittedly, its headquarters has shifted to a group of summer camps among a grove of Californian redwoods. And yes, the membership is rather more exclusive and less bohemian: the 2000-strong list is said to include every Republican president since Calvin Coolidge, along with political luminaries such as David Rockefeller Sr, Henry Kissinger, Donald Rumsfeld and Dick Cheney (all men well known for their liberal and artistic leanings). The club's critics see a different story. For them, the Grove is the dark centre of a conspiratorial web – the furtive meeting-place for the world's most powerful globalizers. The obscene rituals that are performed at the Grove, meanwhile, are proof of the occult forces that propel and guide the arch-conspirators.

Weaving spiders

Outwardly, the Grove is anxious to stress that it is not, in fact, a cabal. Performed annually on July 14, the chief ritual, the "Cremation of Care", features the burning of an effigy of "Care", symbolizing that this is a place for holidaying, not for politicking or advancing business interests. Furthermore, the club's motto is "weaving spiders come not here", indicating that overzealous glad-handing or deal-making is frowned upon. That said, the club has little reason to exist, if not for networking – leaving aside the opportunities for self-congratulation by surrounding oneself with the rich and powerful, of course. The one hundred or so permanent camps at the Grove are even associated with various industrial sectors, from Mandalay – the choice of presidents, intelligence goons and major defence contractors – down to the humbler Sempervirens, which attracts Californian businessmen.

Despite the mottos and ceremonies, some important deals have been made at the Grove. Members boast of a crucial meeting in 1942, at which key details of the Manhattan Project were fixed. (Conspiracists like to claim that the project was actually conceived at the Grove, but in fact, it had been up and running long before that summer.) In 1989, at one of the group's lakeside talks, General John Chain of the Strategic Air Command successfully lobbied for congressional funding for the B2 Spirit "stealth" bomber. Most significantly, the Grove has acted, according to conspiracist legend, as a kind of pre-primary for presidential candidates. In his own memoirs, Herbert Hoover recalls being besieged at the Grove in 1927, after President Coolidge announced he wouldn't be standing again. "Within an hour", he wrote, "a hundred men – publishers, editors, public officials, and others from all over the country who were at the Grove – came to my camp demanding that I announce my candidacy."

In the run-up to the 1968 presidential elections, Nelson Rockefeller dropped his bid for the White House after his fellow Grovers gave him a lukewarm reception; Richard Nixon, by contrast, went all out for the presidency after his far warmer welcome – and after Ronald Reagan promised not to challenge him for the nomination. Nixon later remembered his lakeside speech of July 1967 as "marking the first milestone on my road to the presidency". Nixon is also said to have sent the Bohemians a brown-nosing wire fatuously declaring that "Anyone can be president of the

A performance by the lake at Bohemian Grove, 1924, with the forty-foot concrete owl cleary visible in the background.

United States, but few have any hope of becoming president of the Bohemian Club."

Mary Moore, the chief campaigner behind California's Bohemian Grove Action Network, has said that something isn't right about all this. "This close-knit group determines whether prices rise or fall (by their control of the banking system, money supply, and markets)", she claimed, "and they make money whichever way markets fluctuate." More worryingly still: "They determine what our rights are and which laws have effect, by appointing judges. They decide who our highest officials shall be by consensus among themselves, and then selling candidates to us via the media which they own … Is there true democracy when so much power is concentrated in so few hands?"

Secrecy and infiltration

Moore's complaint is valid enough, but it's more an indictment of American inequality in general, rather than the Bohemian Grove specifically. However, she does rightly point out that the meetings, talks and lectures at the Grove are closed to outsiders and go unreported, even by members, who are supposed to preserve strict confidentiality. A statue of John of Nepomuk, the patron saint of Bohemia in the Czech Republic who legendarily died rather than break the seal of the confessional, stands by the shore of the Grove's lake. To underline the point, the statue's fingers are on its lips. Often-repeated allegations that "you won't even find the Grove on public maps" aren't strictly true, although its 2700 acres are rarely shown in any detail. Still, with thousands of high-powered executives driving down the well-marked Bohemian Avenue every summer, the accusation of secrecy is hard to sustain.

As at other elitist clubs that attract conspiracist attention, like the Bilderberg Group (see p.250) and Chatham House (see p.141), what's said at the Grove stays at the Grove. Detailed accounts from the inside are rare. A *Time* magazine reporter penetrated the Grove in 1982, but his story never saw the light of day. When Dirk Mathison of *People* magazine inveigled himself into the Grove in July 1991, he was spotted by two executives from Time Warner – which owned *People*. There was no question of divided loyalties: Mathison was asked to leave. His story was never published because, according to his managing editor, "he hadn't been there long enough to get a complete story" and was "technically trespassing".

The Grove has only been convincingly infiltrated on two occasions. The first person to do so was Philip Weiss, of *Spy* magazine. Disguised in "conservative recreational wear – a pressed plaid shirt, PermaPrest chinos, Top Siders, a sport jacket" with a copy of *The Wall Street Journal* under his arm, he simply strolled right in. His ensuing article, of November 1989, dismissed claims of high conspiracy and went for a satirical mode. Inside the Grove, he wrote, "The mood is reminiscent of high school. There's no end to the pee-pee and penis jokes, suggesting that these men, advanced in so many other ways, were emotionally arrested sometime during adolescence." British humourist Jon Ronson, who went undercover at the Grove in July 2000, took a similar line. Ronson was persuaded that these were men – albeit powerful men who actually do rule the world – who were emotionally "trapped in their college years".

Satanic owls

Jon Ronson's companion on that night in July 2000 was the "highly strung" Texan arch-conspiracist Alex Jones, the mastermind behind the high-profile commercial conspiracy site, www.infowars.com. The two men saw the "Cremation of Care" ceremony in radically different terms. The procession which, for Ronson, resembled "posh Klansmen or the cast of a Broadway musical" became, in Jones's eyes, "thirty priests in black robes, their faces painted up like death". When Ronson saw a "papier-mâché effigy" of "Dull Care" being carried across a beautiful, dry-ice bedecked lagoon, Jones found himself wondering "whether it was an effigy or real, we do not know". Where Ronson heard the crowd shouting "hooray", and then, once it was over, murmuring things like "could you possibly help me up?", Jones was assailed by the "hateful shouts of the old men", and the incessant "whispering and smacking" of their lips.

The centrepiece of the Cremation of Care ritual is a forty-foot concrete owl which stands on the lake shore. According to club historians, and the ceremony's script, this statue symbolizes wisdom – just as it did in Ancient Greece, when it was associated with the goddess Athena. However, Jones sees darker associations with night and evil – qualities also long-associated with owls. The high-falutin' references in the ceremony's script to Tyre and Babylon, and its sacrificial symbolism, allow Jones to take a further leap of interpretation, and to associate the owl with none other than Moloch, the god to which the Hebrews accused their enemies of sacrificing children. Moloch is, in fact, usually associated with worship of a sacred bull – quite how Jones works in the owl isn't entirely clear.

For Ronson, the ritual sacrifice of "Dull Care" was a way to help these politicians and bankers "enjoy their bloody summer holiday". For Jones, "This is not the Hollywood devil with red pajamas – this is the real deal, Babylon mystery religion-style." The sacrifice symbolized not Care as in "troubles", in the more old-fashioned sense of the word, but Care as in "compassion". Jones believed that he was witnessing a ritual designed to reinforce the single-minded and cold-hearted pursuit of their goals by the power brokers of the New World Order (see p.141).

Low jinks

Even if you don't buy Jones's satanic interpretation of the owl ritual, there is something undeniably creepy about thousands of wealthy, old, white men running amok in a Californian forest. Especially if they're also attending lectures on topics – to quote from the 2006 programme – ranging from "Global Financial Warriors" (courtesy of John Taylor, professor of economics at Stanford), to "The Parallelism and Ultimate Convergence of Science and Religion" (Nobel-prize-winning scientist, Charles Hard Townes) and "From Battlefields to Playing Fields: Economics, Energy and Education" (General Colin Powell).

The Bohemian Grove's traditions also haven't helped its reputation. They include free outdoor urination against the swelling, soaring trunks of the redwood trees, nude bathing in the Russian River and breakfast gin fizzes. The Grovers also take part in "Low Jinks", a comic cabaret heavy on *double entendres*, penis gags and men in drag flashing their knickers. It apparently takes place in a field located between the Pink Onion and Cave Man camps. Journalist Philip Weiss noted the homosexual undertones in both the cabaret and the club in general. One sketch refers to "fairy unguents" that allow men to seek warm fellowship with their fellow Grovers. Standard frat-boy sex talk, you might think, but Nixon called the Grove "the most faggy goddamn thing that you would ever imagine", and rumours of gay cruising at the Grove were widespread in the 1970s. Since then, the club has reportedly purged itself of its more sexually liberated Californian element, but talk of homosexual activity continues to attract the wrath of both left-wingers – furious that politicians should cruise in private and attack gay rights in public – and right-wingers, who object to homosexuality, period.

At the extreme end of allegations of sexual impropriety is the "Franklin Cover-up" conspiracy theory, which alleges that prominent Republicans were involved in a male child-prostitution and drug-mule racket in the 1980s. Acccording to former Nebraskan senator John DeCamp, child porn and even snuff movies have been filmed at the Grove. Unnamed witnesses claim, from the safety of online anonymity, to have seen underground chambers (spelled, apparently, U.N.derground), with rooms entitled Dark, Leather and Necrophilia. A grand jury decided in 1990 that the Franklin story was a hoax, but a handful of people continue to claim they were the victims of organized abuse. One such person, Cathy O'Brien, believes she was brainwashed in a CIA mind-control programme (see p.212), and served as a sex slave to the elite, including more than one Republican president. "Slaves of advancing age or with failed programming", she wrote, "were sacrificially murdered at random in the wooded grounds of Bohemian Grove and I felt it was only a matter of time until it would be me." Luckily, she got out in time to publish her story.

SOURCES

Books

John W. DeCamp The Franklin Cover-Up: Child Abuse, Satanism, and Murder in Nebraska (1996). This lurid, upsetting tale of ritual sex abuse and political corruption shades into extreme conspiracism.

Mike Hanson Bohemian Grove: Cult of Conspiracy (2004). Mike Hanson was Alex Jones's co-conspiracist on the night they attended the Cremation of Care ceremony. This book gives all the lavish detail.

Jon Ronson Them: Adventures with Extremists (2001). British journalist Jon Ronson's account of his visit to Bohemian Grove with Alex Jones and Mike Hanson forms the hilarious coda to his superbly dry book on travels with conspiracists.

Films

Alex Jones Dark Secrets Inside Bohemian Grove (2000). Hyped-up film of Alex Jones's "infiltration" of the Grove, complete with scary red-filter footage of redwood trees and dramatic music. Padded out with Jones's own rants to camera.

Harry Shearer Teddy Bear's Picnic (2002). Satirical film sending up the Grove courtesy of comedian Harry Shearer – he of *The Simpsons* and *This is Spinal Tap* fame.

Websites

Ⓦ **www.infowars.com/bg_story_template.html** Alex Jones's transcript describing his visit to the Bohemian Grove in high-octane terms, along with frequent plugs to buy his video.

Ⓦ **www.pehi.eu/organisations/Bohemian_Grove.htm** British-based Project for the Exposure of Hidden Institutions includes a detailed timeline on the club, lists of alleged members and approximated maps.

Ⓦ **www.sonomacountyfreepress.com/bohos/bohoindx.html** "An online community dedicated to peace, justice, and sustainability for all". This page is devoted to Mary Moore's Bohemian Grove Action Network and includes the full text of Philip Weiss's article for *Spy*.

Ⓦ **www.trance-formation.com/index.htm** Homepage of Cathy O'Brien, former White House sex slave and victim of MK-ULTRA. "What do you REALLY know about minDControl?"

MK-ULTRA

The notion of a programmable agent who robotically carries out assassinations for the CIA, and then has no memory of who told him to do so, has cropped up in speculative theories about the killings of many prominent people. However, it has its roots in a real-life programme, MK-ULTRA, which was worked on by the CIA and the US Army Chemical and Biological Weapons division for two decades.

Origins

Congressional investigations and the declassification of archives have revealed that US military and intelligence agencies have been dabbling in mind control ever since the end of World War II. Project CHATTER was instigated by the US Navy in 1947, following news of successful Soviet experiments with truth drugs. The CIA's mind-control experiments began with Project BLUEBIRD, which evolved into Project ARTICHOKE. This involved the use of hypnosis to induce amnesia in subjects, with the aid of magician John Mulholland. MK-ULTRA, the largest and most infamous such programme, was created when CIA director Allen Dulles amalgamated the various projects in April 1953, and set aside six percent of CIA funds to pay for it.

MK-ULTRA was given added impetus by reports of the Chinese and Koreans "brainwashing" US prisoners during the Korean War. It was feared that such brainwashing might have re-programmed certain POWs to defect or to come back as communists or "sleeper" spies who could be activated by trigger words or signals to carry out some heinous task – hence the 1959 novel and subsequent film *The Manchurian Candidate*.

It's been suggested that the term "brainwashing" was actually invented by a magazine writer-cum-CIA agent who was aiming to introduce the concept to Americans, but to make it appear to be a cruel commie invention. Be this as it may, the fear of what the enemy might do was enough to spur the CIA to try to do it too. As well as seeking the ultimate interrogation techniques and truth serums to use on enemy spies, the CIA wanted to be able to programme its own agents under altered states of consciousness. Not only could they then be activated by a click of the fingers, but their knowledge couldn't be tortured out of them, and ultimately, their memories could be wiped clean.

Experiments

Many of the experiments carried out under MK-ULTRA were performed without the knowledge or consent of their subjects, who ranged from CIA employees to prostitutes and ordinary citizens. Some were supposedly coerced into "volunteering" by being entrapped in brothels set up by the CIA. Dr Sidney Gottlieb, a Bronx biochemist who was supposedly the inspiration for the mad scientist in Stanley Kubrick's film *Dr Strangelove*, was at the helm of MK-ULTRA during its first eleven years.

Gottlieb oversaw some truly bizarre experiments. Subjects were hypnotized and given drugs such as LSD, ketamine, psilocybine, heroin, marijuana, scopolamine, mescaline and alcohol, as well as being subjected to electro-convulsive shocks, implanted electrodes, lobotomies and radiation. They were locked in sensory deprivation chambers, or had their "therapy" sessions recorded and played on a loop through headphones, all while doped on LSD. One subject was given LSD for 77 days straight. Another technique involved pumping someone first with barbiturates, and then with amphetamines, yanking the subject from near-sleep to consciousness.

Sometimes the human guinea pigs "talked" and revealed everything they knew; sometimes they just died. Experiments with heat and cold, and atmospheric pressure – uncannily reminiscent of similar experiments by the Nazis – were also conducted, on around 150 subjects in total. Programme officers "tested" LSD on each other by spiking one another's drinks at parties – one such incident is said to have resulted in the suicide of Dr Frank Olson (see p.14) – and Gottlieb "experimented" with LSD by taking copious amounts himself, when working at Fort Detrick and Edgewood Arsenal (see p.296).

Applications

Even as the recreational use of LSD flourished during the 1960s, Major General William Creasy, the chief of the Army Chemical Corps, was advocating its use to poison the water supplies of enemy cities, as a kinder alternative to nuclear weapons. MK-ULTRA drugs, administered via poisoned cigars or handkerchiefs, were considered as weapons for assassinating Cuba's Fidel Castro (see p.19), Congo's Patrice Lumumba and Iraq's Abd al-Karim Qasim (aka Abdul Kassem) – both of the latter were ultimately dispatched by other means. Although there's no published evidence that any MK-ULTRA-programmed agent had any success, the project has also been linked to the killings of Robert Kennedy (see p.36) and John Lennon (see p.47), as well as the shooting of Ronald Reagan in 1981 and the events of the Jonestown massacre (see p.195).

Most of Gottlieb's records were destroyed, possibly on his own orders, after the programme finished in 1972, a well-timed pre-emption of the congressional Church Committee and the Rockefeller Commission, which investigated the CIA's domestic activities and uncovered MK-ULTRA not long after. President Gerald Ford formally prohibited further mind-control activities in 1976.

Mengele and Montauk

So far, so factual. However, conspiracy theorists of a more luridly imaginative bent have inevitably thickened the plot, speculating that the evil genius behind MK-ULTRA was none other than Nazi doctor Josef Mengele (supposedly brought to the US under the legendary Operation Paperclip). The story goes that Mengele perfected his mind-control techniques by working on tens of thousands of kidnapped children, who were kept in iron cages stacked floor to ceiling in his secret underground base. Many, it's claimed, were enslaved for tasks from sex to assassinations, but just as many were slaughtered in front of the other children for Mengele's pleasure.

The largest of perhaps as many as 25 underground bases used by MK-ULTRA is said to have been at Montauk, on Montauk Island (see p.297), where around 250,000 teenage boys were allegedly brainwashed under the so-called "Montauk Project" from 1976 onwards. (Some believe that the project also involved setting up a time-portal to receive the sailors teleported aboard the USS *Eldridge*, see p.283). Many of these "Montauk Boys" supposedly went on to lead normal and indeed successful lives as journalists, radio and TV personalities, businessmen, lawyers and judges, unaware that they were just agents of a higher power. There are, in fact, still children's summer camps around Montauk on Long Island. Unsurprisingly, though, it's not been reported in the mainstream press that any of these camps are part of a crypto-fascist plot to create a race of brainwashed Americans.

MK-ULTRA victims

Candy Jones, a well-known model during the late 1940s and 50s, claimed in her book *The Control of Candy Jones* to have been one of the first to be programmed under MK-ULTRA. Her claims, however, pale in comparison with those of Brice Taylor, the pseudonym of Susan Ford, who purports to be an MK-ULTRA subject who recovered her senses in 1985, after an "accidental" car crash failed to kill her and instead reawakened dormant memories. In *Thanks for the Memories*, Taylor states that she is the survivor of a NASA–CIA programme of "ritual abuse and government mind control", instigated for both business and pleasure by shadowy governmental figures who were involved in bringing about the New World Order (see p.141). Her handler, comedian Bob Hope, supposedly loaned her out to every president from Kennedy to Clinton, and others besides, sometimes as a favour and sometimes to ensnare them in the bigger Illuminati trap. She also says that she was a drugs courier and part-time human computer for Henry Kissinger, no less, and that her children were "taken to parties where the elite or anybody who wanted to have sex with them was able to".

Another mind-control slave, who claims to have known Taylor, was Cathy O'Brien, who was supposedly "rescued" in 1988 by Mark Phillips, a self-styled intelligence insider. Together, O'Brien and Phillips have released a shelf-load of books, videos and CD-ROMs about the programme of brainwashing slaves for courier work, pornography and prostitution. By their account, Ronald Reagan's trigger word for O'Brien to perform sex acts was "kitten", while deviant sexual practices are also attributed to George H.W. Bush, Dick Cheney and Hillary Clinton (presumably not together). According to her posts on www.amazon.com, Ms Kathleen A. Sullivan knew O'Brien "as a fellow government mind-control victim",

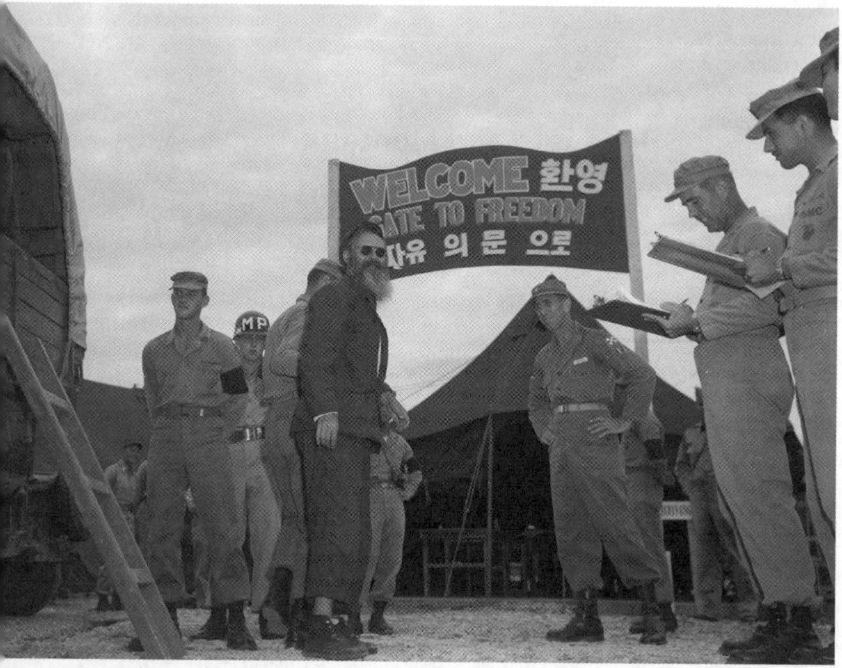

Manchurian candidate? A US POW is released in Korea in 1953.

and worked with Phillips to de-programme her. As she puts it: "I am reasonably certain Cathy's recollections … are probably valid."

Messing with the mind

It has also been alleged that many prominent advocates of LSD, including Ken Kesey (author of *One Flew Over the Cuckoo's Nest*), Timothy Leary, Allen Ginsberg and Baba Ram Dass (Richard Alpert), not to mention future "Unabomber" Theodore Kaczynski, were introduced to the drug under the MK-ULTRA programme. The book *Acid Dreams* suggests that LSD was deliberately allowed to spread among the rebellious youth of the 1960s, in order to space them out and melt their minds into submission. When the programme backfired, and turned out to encourage critical thinking and the questioning of authority, "bad trips" and bad tabs were used to scare users away. The full truth of MK-ULTRA is unlikely to be revealed any time soon. In the meantime, conspiracy theorists, many of whom claim to have been under the programme's influence, will no doubt continue to provide their own accounts – or hallucinations, as the case may be.

SOURCES

Books

Richard Condon The Manchurian Candidate (1950). The Cold War paranoia novel that penetrated – or perhaps inspired – the dark heart of MK-ULTRA.

Bruce Shalin and Martin A. Lee Acid Dreams (1985). The history of LSD in the US, from the social effects on the hippy scene to the literary genius unleashed and the whole sinister CIA plot behind it all.

Films

John Frankenheimer The Manchurian Candidate (1962). The 2004 remake hasn't displaced this chilling film as the classic adaptation of Condon's novel. Suffused with the paranoia of its time, this film looks fantastic, features a fine cast all on top form and includes an incredibly effective brainwashing/garden party dream sequence.

Websites

Ⓦ **mdma.net/mk-ultra/sidney-gottlieb.html** Gottlieb's obituary from the *LA Times*. RIP, Dr LSD.

Ⓦ **www.mindcontrolforums.com/radio/ckln23.htm** An interview with the aforementioned Brice Taylor. Either incredibly imaginative fantasy or even more incredible fact.

Ⓦ **www.trance-formation.com** The website of Cathy O'Brien and Mark Phillips not only gives you a glimpse of their stories, but also include many opportunities to buy materials on MK-ULTRA in book and audio forms.

The White Alliance: the CIA, the Contras and cocaine

Rumours that the CIA keeps a hand in the international drugs trade have circulated for decades, ever since the agency's alleged cooperation in Southeast Asia's opium "Golden Triangle" during the Vietnam War, and its backing for Afghani drug-warlords who fought for the Mujahedeen against the Russians. But the rumour vultures are thickest in the air closer to home, over Central America, where a trail of corpses and cocaine-stained banknotes leads back to the shady narco-regimes and coca-guerillas who were the recipients of generous US government support in the 1980s. Scratch a freedom fighter and you'll find a drug baron; scratch the drug baron, and it seems you'll see the CIA disappearing out of his back pocket.

The Contras and the CIA

On the face of it, allegations that the CIA was in cahoots with cocaine traders are absurd. The US government spends billions of dollars every year on drug suppression, with the Drug Enforcement Administration (DEA) heavily involved in coca-crop eradication and the pursuit of traffickers across South and Central America. Why would one hand of the government palm off what the other was trying to smash with an iron fist?

The answer, say critics, goes back to 1983 and the Boland Amendment, which banned federal funding of the Contras, the Nicaraguan militias dedicated to the overthrow of their country's left-wing Sandinista government. The CIA responded by devising the so-called Iran–Contra scheme (see p.201), swapping weapons for Iranian cash and backhanding the proceeds to their Nicaraguan terrorist friends. But the money wasn't enough, and the Contras had to rely on drugs for their funding as well. Depending on which conspiracist, journalist or politician you ask, the CIA helped the Contras maintain their coke-fuelled campaigns either by not worrying unduly about their allies' finances, or by failing to pass on evidence of trafficking to the DEA, or even by facilitating cocaine shipments. Hardline conspiracists say knowledge of the programme supposedly went right to the top. Seems it's not called the White House for nothing…

Mercurial news

According to the most extreme theorists, the CIA made use of so-called "rogue agents" to actually import cocaine into the US. The agency, they charge, had a taste for two-birds-one-stone schemes like Iran–Contra. Just for the sake of a little powder on its hands, it could fund the Contras and simultaneously guarantee a cheap supply of a debilitating drug that would keep the downtrodden masses – inner-city black communities in particular – nicely in their place.

If this kind of outright evil plotting seems unbelievable now, it might have felt more credible in South Central Los Angeles in the early 1980s. Communities literally came under attack as lethal addiction and violent crime took over the streets, under the influence of crack cocaine. It seemed implausible that a drug with such destructive effects had just rolled in out of the blue. Conspiracy theories that crack cocaine was a new kind of weapon of mass destruction joined the theories about the malevolent hands behind KFC and Snapple, or the AIDS virus (see p.290). None were given mainstream credibility by reporters until August 1996, when investigative journalist Gary Webb published a three-day series of articles under the headline "Dark Alliance" in the *San Jose Mercury News* – a respected paper with Pulitzer prizes under its belt.

Webb didn't claim that the CIA was actually flying crack into LA, but he did trace a process of policy decisions and dubious activities that, he believed, had allowed the cocaine explosion to occur. LA's drug supplies, he said, could be traced back to Nicaraguan drug producers with close links to the Contras. And those Contras were being protected by their CIA handlers. The article caused a blizzard of protest and vehement denial. By May 1997, *Mercury News* executive editor Jerry Ceppos was calling the story "oversimplified" – while claiming he'd never read it – and protesting that the newspaper had always been worried by a lack of corroborating sources. But the genie was out of the bottle. Inevitably, a bunch of government committees began trying to force it back in. And, just as inevitably, a crowd of "witnesses" and "ex-CIA assets" began coming forward, laying claim to key roles in the affair.

The heroin angle: Bo Gritz and Prof McCoy

Surely the most glamorous and controversial figure to take the stand against the US government was Bo Gritz. A highly decorated Vietnam vet, he became the inspiration for "Rambo" as the hero of (failed) missions to find fellow veterans missing in action. He later became a fierce anti-government campaigner and Christian Identity fundamentalist. While Gritz's experience didn't exactly relate to Central America, it did suggest that federal agencies were not averse to a bit of drug trafficking. According to his sensational account, as part of a secret mission to northern Burma, he held talks with the warlord Khun Sa, who controlled the Golden Triangle opium trade, and hence most of the heroin flowing towards the Americas. Khun Sa told Gritz that his main client was… the US government, working through regular conspiracy suspects such as Santos Trafficante, boss of the Florida Mob, and Richard Armitage, the bodybuilding veteran of Vietnam, Iran and the State Department.

Flanking Bo Gritz is the incongruously academic figure of Alfred McCoy, professor of Southeast Asian history at the University of Wisconsin-Madison and author of *The Politics of Heroin*. He too had made an investigative trip deep into the heroin jungle. As a graduate student, he had discovered that French intelligence had funded itself by selling opium during the colonial wars in Indochina. After that, in his own words: "It was basically pulling a thread and keep tugging at it and a veil masking the reality began to unravel." The reality he uncovered was that the CIA routinely recruited upland warlords as allies in the war against Communism, from northeastern Burma in 1950, through Laos during the Vietnam War, to the Afghan resistance to the Soviet invasion. Coming under the wing of the CIA allowed these allies to operate without fear of investigation, and their role in the heroin trade followed the same pattern each time, mushrooming from smaller-scale local production to massive international trading.

Nothing could be allowed to come between the CIA and its fight against the Red menace. The DEA would always concede priority to the bigger campaign. In Honduras, for example, a DEA agent called Tomas Zepeda gathered evidence that the military were corruptly allowing drug barons to fly shipments to the US. His reports threatened a Contra supply line and he was withdrawn. "Faced with the choice", McCoy says, "the United States government chose the cold war over the drug war." It wasn't difficult to arrange: as McCoy points out, the DEA and CIA had their origins with the same personnel and their "institutional relationship" remains close.

DID NOT SNORT: COCA-CLINTON AND THE "MENA" AFFAIR

With Iran–Contra and the CIA–cocaine allegations, the liberal Left pretty much had a monopoly on political mud to chuck around. On the drugs turf, the best right-wing conspiracy theorists could come up with was the Mena scandal. Piggybacking on CIA drug-flight theories, the Mena scandal involved claims that drug-smuggling Contra pilots regularly used the Intermountain Regional Airport at Mena, Arkansas. Based on the dubious statements of characters such as the notorious drug smuggler and DEA informant, Barry Seal, and Richard Brenneke, of October Surprise fame, Mena emerged as the centre of a multimillion-dollar drug smuggling network.

The twist in this tale is the location: Arkansas. "Patriotic" conspiracy theorists would have it that the whole operation must have been overseen, protected and covered up by the then-governor of Arkansas, Bill Clinton, in league with various state banks. The Left came back with a counter-conspiracy: the whole Mena conspiracy theory, it's said, is the result of an actual conspiracy by Richard Mellon Scaife and other right-wing figures to discredit Clinton, and a very well-funded conspiracy at that. At this point, the arguments go round in circles. The least that can be said is that next to known conspiracies such as Oliver North's Enterprise (see p.201) and the downfall of BCCI (see p.252), "Mena" simply doesn't cut the mustard.

Whistleblowers: Castillo, Palacio

The most ubiquitous witness – his testimony is pinned up all over the Internet – is Celerino "Cele" Castillo, a former DEA field agent. He has unusually impressive anti-drugs credentials, and makes a convincing witness. His stints in Central America even brought him face to face with Hector Antonio Regalado, aka "Dr Death", the death-squad specialist and supposed henchman for Roberto D'Aubuisson, the alleged murderer of Archbishop Romero. He also met the infamous Felix Rodriguez, who supervised the execution of Che Guevara and carried the revolutionary's Rolex as a souvenir. While stationed in El Salvador in the late 1980s, Castillo recorded a number of suspicious flights taking off from Ilopango. This remote airfield was used by the CIA to covertly ship weapons to the Contra rebels in Nicaragua, the operation coming under the command of Lientenant Colonel Oliver North, of Iran–Contra fame. Disturbingly, the same facilities appeared to serve known drug traffickers – some with CIA-authorized visas – making their way back to the US.

Castillo claims that he tried to file reports, but was repeatedly warned off investigating further. One CIA agent allegedly told him: "Cele, how do you think the Contras are gonna make money? They've got to run dope, that's the only way we can finance this operation." A month before the Iran–Contra hearings, Castillo says he was told that the operation was protected by the White House. He was instructed not to close his files on the Contras so that they could continue to be active, and thus protected from Senator John Kerry's investigative Subcommittee on Terrorism, Narcotics and International Operations. Castillo was not treated as a whistleblowing hero. He was warned that the DEA would try to get rid of him discreetly and, sure enough, he was soon persecuted over a number of technical infringements of DEA operational rules – including "Failure to Follow Written Instructions". He was temporarily suspended before eventually agreeing on a discharge on grounds of disability.

Another "eyewitness" was FBI informant Wanda Palacio, previously with Colombia's notorious Medellin cartel. She claims she was standing beside Colombia's drug supremo Jorge Ochoa in 1983, as cocaine was loaded onto a Southern Air Transport plane. The company had previously been owned by the CIA, and Palacio says she was told that it was still being used by the CIA to exchange Contra drugs for guns. Senator Kerry passed Palacio's statement on to William Weld, the assistant attorney general for criminal affairs, who reportedly laughed and passed the story off as a rumour, or the work of "bum agents", later comparing Palacio's credibility to "a wagonload of diseased blankets". When, in October 1986, the famous plane was shot down by the Sandinistas over Nicaragua – the so-called Hasenfus incident, named after the pilot that died – Palacio claimed she recognized the co-pilot that survived, Wallace "Buzz" Sawyer, as one of the men she'd seen loading cocaine three years before. President Reagan denied any connection between the government and the Hasenfus plane, but within a month, the Iran–Contra scandal had broken. Was there a drugs angle to Iran–Contra? Or was Palacio taking the chance to give her story a little credence?

Public investigations

Witnesses could be ignored, but the revelation that Iran–Contra was a real, CIA-backed scheme galvanized a few politicians into action. In 1987, Vietnam veteran turned Democratic senator John Kerry headed a subcommittee of the Senate Foreign Relations Committee under the brief of "Narcotics, Terrorism and International Operations". The "Kerry Committee" reported in December 1988. While it didn't state that US officials ran drugs, it did conclude that Oliver North had set up a privatized network to supply the Contras, and that this had been used by drug barons as a cover for smuggling. North's network turned a blind eye to such an extent that it had blithely worked with known drug traffickers. But as with Iran–Contra, the buck stopped with Oliver North. It was left to conspiracy theorists to trace the white lines upwards towards the top.

Kerry's report was deeply critical of the CIA, but many smelled whitewash anyway. The *San Jose Mercury News* furore sparked a new wave of investigations, including three inquiries by the Office of the Inspector General – one at the Department of Justice and two at the CIA. In October 1998, the CIA's report on itself again denied the allegation that it had been involved in drug smuggling, or that its employees had "conspired with or assisted Contra-related organizations or individuals in drug trafficking to raise funds for the Contras or for any other purpose". At least, that's what the summary said. As journalist Robert Parry has pointed out, the detail of the report painted a subtly different picture – more murky grey than white-washed. Frederick Hitz, the CIA's inspector general, made it clearer than ever that the Contras were deeply involved in drug trafficking, and that the CIA had frequently failed to pass on their knowledge of this to the Justice Department or Congress. It had even blocked drugs investigations that threatened intelligence work.

But the CIA argued that this was quite proper. CIA director Bill Casey had actually negotiated an exemption from the legal requirement to report drug smuggling by agency assets to the Justice Department – "in view of the fine cooperation the Drug Enforcement Administration has received from CIA", as the Memorandum of Understanding puts it. Casey's request was granted in February 1982, two months before Reagan authorized CIA support for the Contras. It's not just that the War on Drugs ceded place to the War on Communism, it seems, but that the War on Communism allowed drug barons to operate without having to worry about squads of Special Forces helicopters suddenly descending on their ranches, or their freight planes being shot down.

In the second year of his investigation, Kerry turned to BCCI – the utterly discredited Bank of Credit and Commerce International (see p.252). By the time he submitted his report in 1992, Kerry had exposed an utterly corrupt institution that the CIA had routinely used for secret payments. The bank's web of complicated connections extended from the bin Ladens to the Bushes, and from Saddam Hussein and Manuel Noriega to Richard Helms and William Casey.

White lines and shining paths: the Vladimiro Montesinos case

The coke trail doesn't stop on the north side of the Panama canal. On September 14, 2000, Peruvian TV viewers were amazed to see a leaked video of their intelligence chief bribing an opposition politician to join President Alberto Fujimori's ruling coalition. The resulting mega-scandal saw Fujimori sacked by a Congress that declared him "morally unfit" to govern, and intelligence chief Vladimiro Montesinos going on an eight-month fugitive-run across Central America. It also saw yet more evidence emerge that the CIA tolerated the drug trade. Montesinos, it transpired, had been paid $1 million a year as a CIA asset to fight narcotics trafficking. Did the CIA not know that he had profited to the tune of tens or possibly hundreds of millions of dollars from skims off arms and drug deals, and grand-scale abuses of his office?

The DEA certainly had their suspicions. Government files declassified and released in 2001 show that the agency was investigating Montesinos for taking bribes from drug barons to give them the insider track on anti-drug operations – the very operations funded by the CIA. Montesinos had been cultivated by the CIA since 1974, and rose steadily to become head of the SIN, the Peruvian intelligence service, in the early 1990s. International criticism of his methods – including sponsorship of death-squad killings – was always tempered by CIA and DEA support. Critics of US policy have long suspected that the real reason for this backing was Montesinos' bloody, ruthless campaign against Peru's Maoist guerilla movement – the Sendero Luminoso or "Shining Path" – a twenty-year war that, the Peruvian Truth and Reconciliation Commission concluded in August 2003, had killed an estimated 69,280 people.

US policy-makers also favoured Montesinos' support for the right-wing counter-insurgency in Colombia. Some commentators believe that it was only after the CIA discovered, in August 2000, that Montesinos had double-crossed them (by smuggling ten thousand AK-47 rifles from Jordan to the Colombian rebel group FARC – the very rebels that Washington was funding him to suppress) that they pulled the plug on his operation. Peruvians certainly haven't failed to notice that the leaked video came at a suspiciously useful time for the CIA, which suddenly wanted to get rid of a liability. Other critics, including the Jordanians, claim that the shipment couldn't have happened without CIA support. An anonymous Peruvian judicial source was widely quoted as saying: "How can people doubt that the CIA is capable of something like this? Did the Iran–Contra scandal teach you nothing?"

At the time of writing, Montesinos was languishing in a naval base near Lima, slowly accumulating more and more years to his sentence. Convicted of conspiracy, embezzlement and corruption, he has yet to answer the drugs charges. More shocking revelations seem likely to emerge, though his defence team's appeal for ex-CIA director George Tenet to testify fell on deaf ears.

In the early 1990s, Bill Clinton encouraged US immigration officials to deport gang members back to their home countries – at the height of the programme, hundreds of young El Salvadoreans were arriving every month in San Salvador alone. Some Central American conspiracists have called it a deliberate campaign by the US to destabilize the region. Others believe that the gangs are funded and supported by Colombian cartels, keen to flex their muscle in the US's backyard. The end of the era of CIA-protected narcotics regimes certainly created a gap in the market for an alternative network of distributors…

The upshot

In 2000, a House Intelligence Committee investigation set up to report on the truth of the *San Jose Mercury News* articles declared that "the CIA as an institution did not approve of connections between Contras and drug traffickers, and, indeed, Contras were discouraged from involvement with traffickers". (One wonders what this discouragement involved.) The committee was headed by Porter Goss, a CIA employee whom George W. Bush rewarded with the post of director of the CIA in September 2004. The report added a caveat. "CIA officers on occasion notified law enforcement entities when they became aware of allegations concerning the identities or activities of drug traffickers", it said, while admitting that, in some cases, "CIA employees did nothing to verify or disprove drug trafficking information, even when they had the opportunity to do so. In some of these, receipt of a drug allegation appeared to provoke no specific response, and business went on as usual."

As for allegations that the CIA was responsible for the crack explosion in LA, the House report concluded that the traffickers and dealers named by reporter Gary Webb were not CIA agents or assets. The two most significant, Norwin Meneses and Danilo Blandon, were sympathetic to the Contras, it said, and had made donations of thousands of dollars, but their role was not significant. To sum up, there was "no evidence that any other US intelligence agency or agency employee was involved in the illegal supply or sale of drugs in the Los Angeles area". Gary Webb died in 2004. He had been shot twice in the head – wounds that the coroner established were self-inflicted.

Perhaps the theory of a CIA-inspired eugenic campaign to force-feed drugs down the necks (or up the noses) of US citizens is a little paranoid. The social and economic costs of drug use are so appalling that it seems preposterous that any government agency would knowingly promote the drug trade. Encourage a criminal, violent, volatile and – worst of all – untaxable, underclass? Talk about shooting yourself in the foot. But then if the whole Contra debacle showed one thing, it's that during the Reagan era the CIA would have sold its soul if it would have helped it fight the Reds. Assuming it had a soul in the first place, of course.

SOURCES

Books

Celerino Castillo and Dave Harmon Powderburns: Cocaine, Contras and the Drug War (1994). "Cele" Castillo's ghostwritten testimony asks some serious questions of the CIA–cocaine affair, and tells a terrifying story of life on the front line of the war on drugs.

Michael Levine The Big White Lie: The CIA and the Cocaine/Crack Epidemic – An Undercover Odyssey (1993). Former DEA agent Levine acts as both witness and prosecutor in this fictionalized, highly personal story detailing CIA complicity in the drug trade.

Alfred McCoy The Politics of Heroin: CIA Complicity in the Global Drugs Trade (2003). A serious history of CIA involvement in the heroin trade in Southeast Asia. Some of the material is twenty years old, but new chapters cover Afghanistan and Central America. A virtual conspiracy bible.

Robert Parry Lost History: Contras, Cocaine, the Press and "Project Truth" (1999).One of the foremost journalists writing on the Iran–Contras–CIA–cocaine connection, Parry has also been accused of being a leading conspiracy theorist. Well written and researched.

Peter Dale Scott and Jonathan Marshall Cocaine Politics: Drugs, Armies and the CIA in Central America (1998). At the political and serious end of the scale – co-written by a UC-Berkeley professor and an economics journalist. Updated with a preface covering the *Mercury News* story.

Gary Webb Dark Alliance: The CIA, the Contras, and the Crack Cocaine Explosion (1999). The exposé that launched a thousand others – but it's six hundred pages long, and now a little out of date.

Websites

Ⓦ **www.cia.gov/library/reports/general-reports-1/cocaine/contra-story/pilots.html** The CIA's response to claims by Castillo and others. More reports can be found by searching under "Contra" on the CIA's homepage.

Ⓦ **www.consortiumnews.com/archive/crack.html** Robert Parry was one of the journalists who broke the Iran–Contra story for Associated Press. This is the archive of his articles on the crack cocaine angle.

Ⓦ **www.csun.edu/CommunicationStudies/ben/news/cia/main.html** Dated but satisfyingly huge database of CIA/cocaine-related news articles. Comes under the banner "Cocaine Import Agency" – in case you were wondering which side of the fence this site's author was on.

Ⓦ **www.documentaries.ws/1/e107_plugins/content/content.php?content.220** Documentary featuring Celerino Castillo and John Kerry, among others.

Ⓦ **www.fas.org/irp/cia/product/cocaine/** The official answer to Gary Webb's news articles, aka the Office of the Inspector General of Investigations Staff's report on "Allegations of Connections Between CIA and the Contras in Cocaine Trafficking to the United States" (January 29, 1998). For Volume II "The Contra Story" (October 8, 1998), see www.cia.gov/cia/reports/cocaine/

Ⓦ **www.gwu.edu/~nsarchiv/NSAEBB/NSAEBB37/** Declassified US government files on "Fujimori's Rasputin": Vladimiro Montesinos.

Ⓦ **www.usdoj.gov/oig/special/9712/** "The CIA–Contra–Crack Cocaine Controversy: A Review of the Justice Department's Investigations and Prosecutions" (December 1997).

The Clintongates: a vast right-wing conspiracy?

"I do believe that this is a battle." So said First Lady Hillary Clinton, on NBC's *Today* show, on January 27, 1998. Instead of covering her husband's peccadilloes and misdemeanours, she said, journalists should be writing about "this vast right-wing conspiracy that has been conspiring against my husband since the day he announced for president", a conspiracy designed "to undo the results of two elections." Those two elections, in 1992 and 1996, had really hurt the Right. Bill Clinton was not just a Democrat, he was a liberal-leaning, saxophone-playing, glad-handing scumbag. His wife was worse. Practically a feminist. They had to be stopped.

Fostergate

The first attack came right at the start of President Clinton's first administration. In the "Travelgate" scandal, seven White House travel office workers were fired on the pretext of minor corruption – allegedly so that they could be replaced with travel agents from Little Rock, Arkansas. As deputy White House legal counsel, Arkansas lawyer Vincent Foster investigated the issue. After a hostile *Wall Street Journal* editorial attacked him for alleged complicity in a cover-up, Foster apparently became depressed. On July 20, 1993 – six months after Clinton's inauguration and a day after Foster had contacted his doctor for treatment – he was found dead with a gunshot wound to the head. A week later, a resignation letter was discovered in his briefcase. "Ruining people", it said, "is considered a sport."

Conspiracy theorists pounced. Some said the letter was a forgery. It was widely claimed that Foster had shot himself with the wrong hand, that his body had been moved, that he'd been drugged, that there wasn't enough blood on the scene – the usual allegations that circle round every celebrity corpse. But the most baroque theory behind Foster's death does in fact hold that he killed himself.

The so-called "Norman-Grabbe" or "Fostergate" theory emerged from the pens of journalists James R. Norman and J. Orlin Grabbe. A former editor at *Forbes* magazine (which rejected his story), Norman claims that Vince Foster killed himself because he was about to be unmasked as an Israeli spy. By this account, Foster had been working for the National Security Agency (NSA) on behalf of Systematics Inc, the company behind the infamous PROMIS software (see p.270), which supposedly allows the NSA to hack into the world's banking transactions. Norman contends that Systematics was really a global money-laundering operation, and that Foster was working for Israel, possibly on the acquisition of US nuclear codes. Using a Cray supercomputer, CIA hackers had broken into a Mossad database, found Foster's name and traced it to a Swiss bank account that they covertly emptied and repaid to the US Treasury. Apart from the obvious plot holes – hackers use Crays? Mossad keep their NOC-lists online? Swiss bank accounts can be accessed with a password and a double click? – Norman and Grabbe have a problem with their sources, all of whom are prolific conspiracy theorists themselves.

THE CLINTON BODY COUNT

During the summer of 1998, an email and Web-based list of some fifty suspicious deaths of people said to have been associated with Bill Clinton appeared as if from nowhere. It seems to be an expanded version of a list compiled by an Indianapolis lawyer, pro-gun activist and conspiracist called Linda Thompson, which was circulated to congressmen by former California representative William Dannemeyer in 1994. Thompson admitted to having "no direct evidence" that Clinton had anyone killed – but that scarcely mattered. *The Clinton Chronicles*, a video version of the list compiled by arch Clinton-hater and religious conservative Jerry Falwell, is no more rigorous in its sourcing. The anonymous, silhouetted journalist giving "evidence" on the tape was later revealed to be the video's producer.

Clinton was not the first US president to be attributed such a Machiavellian record – which either shows that politicians are a bunch of murdering maniacs, or that if you trawl widely enough, you can make up a list of this kind for anyone with enough high-profile connections. Take name number thirty: Dr Stanley Heard, a high-flying chiropractor who treated Clinton's mother, stepfather and brother. His private plane caught fire and crashed, killing him outright. Maybe Clinton's stepdad let something slip while his back was being manipulated...

However dubious each death appears individually, after you've waded through fifty suicides, plane crashes and "mysterious" accidents, you'll be tempted to lean towards the latter part of the list's usual subheading: "Coincidence or the Kiss of Death?" But two questions do spring to mind: if Clinton's allies are such psychos, how come they never took out Gennifer Flowers, or Paula Jones, or Monica Lewinsky? And if Clinton could be impeached for getting a blow job in the Oval Office, why did no one ever think of trying him for multiple murder?

Whitewatergate

Some theorists allege that the Norman-Grabbe theory is itself a conspiracy, a deliberate disinformation leak to hide the fact that Foster was murdered by his former friend, Bill Clinton. With the president under increasing pressure to come clean about the so-called Whitewater affair, they say, Foster knew too much. Following every rapid of the Whitewatergate story is a painfully dull paperchase. It's a tawdry tale of Arkansas land deals, bank loans and transactions between the Clintons and their business partners, the McDougals, in which the basic charge is that Clinton abused his position as Arkansas governor to advance his own business interests. By January 1994, the affair had become a right-wing cause célèbre, and Clinton was forced to request that a special prosecutor investigate. Attorney General Janet Reno appointed one Robert B. Fiske, who concluded in June that Foster's death was suicide, and that the White House had not broken any laws. But that wasn't enough. By July, Whitewater was the subject of both House and Senate Banking Committee hearings, and in August Kenneth Starr was appointed as a new special prosecutor. The big dog was off the leash.

The Senate Whitewater probe drew to a close in June 1996. Republicans alleged suspicious obstruction by the Clintons, but could find no smoking gun; Democrat senators separately concluded that the Clintons' water was whiter-than-white, and that they were victims of a Republican smear campaign. Pick a side. Either way, Whitewater was a damp squib – but Kenneth Starr kept going. On October 10, 1997, he released a new report on Foster's death. He found the death to be suicide, and declared the reports of funny business with the corpse – wrong hand, no blood, faked note, you name it – to be untrue. And if Kenneth Starr thinks Foster killed himself, surely the rampant Right can be satisfied.

Monica Lewinsky

Despite everything, the Starr juggernaut kept rolling on. On January 12, 1998, government worker Linda Tripp contacted the special prosecutor directly to let him know that she had tape-recorded her conversations with White House intern Monica Lewinsky. (Tripp, it transpired, had been prompted to make the tapes by her literary agent friend, Lucianne Goldberg – a name familiar to Watergate buffs, as Goldberg had worked as a writer for Democrat George McGovern during his presidential campaign against Richard Nixon, while secretly reporting to Nixon aide Murray Chotiner.) Tripp said the tapes proved that Lewinsky and Clinton had an affair, and that a Clinton aide had told Lewinsky to lie about it in Paula Jones's unsuccessful sexual harassment lawsuit against Clinton. By January 16, Kenneth Starr had obtained permission from Janet Reno to expand his enquiry into examining whether Clinton had lied under oath. That news emerged just a day later on the Drudge Report, a contentious Internet news-sheet. Had Starr's office deliberately leaked the story? Was Starr a tireless campaigner for standards in public life? Or was he simply out to hang Clinton for whatever could be pinned on him?

In August, after earlier denials, Clinton admitted that he'd misled the American people, perjured himself, and had indeed had an "inappropriate" relationship with Lewinsky. Finally, after more than four years and at a cost of almost $40 million, *The Starr Report* was released on September 9, 1998. On December 11, Starr's recommendation that Clinton be impeached was approved by a House Judiciary Committee vote that split straight down party lines. Congress duly sent the case to the Senate. In February 1999, ten Republican senators joined the solid mass of Democrats in voting that Clinton had not committed perjury, while five Republicans stood behind Clinton in rejecting the charge that he had obstructed justice in the Paula Jones case. In both instances, that was a long way from the two-thirds majority required to remove Clinton from office.

A vast right-wing conspiracy?

Hillary Clinton's allegation of a "vast right-wing conspiracy" sounds like the words of someone who is under siege and feeling the pressure. It could equally be a political smokescreen, an attempt to turn media attention around. She could also have been entirely serious. Even Attorney General Janet Reno apparently considered investigating the Whitewater affair as a campaign to smear the Clintons. Was Kenneth Starr a pawn of the Right? A Texan minister's son, Starr had worked under Ronald Reagan's first attorney general, and had gone on to become solicitor general in the first Bush administration.

Hillary and Bill Clinton: who wears the trousers in this relationship?

Although friends called Starr dogged and honest, perhaps his thoroughness was manipulated by a well-funded campaign to bring down Clinton? Multimillionaire and deep conservative Richard Mellon Scaife was a significant force behind the anti-Clinton campaigns – the so-called Arkansas Project. As the owner of the *Pittsburgh Tribune-Review*, he was able to push the Fostergate story. He also helped finance the *American Spectator*, which was the first media outlet to publicize Paula Jones's accusations. Scaife himself has always been open about his campaigning. Similarly, the conservative Rutherford Institute is known to have funded Paula Jones's case against Clinton, while the right-wing Citizens for Honest Government paid for the video version of the "Clinton body count" list (see p.220).

More troubling are the accusations, countered by denials, that the Arkansas Project was behind other projects to fund David Hale, the key Whitewater witness, and to promote the absurd Mena "scandal", in which Clinton was supposed to have profited from a CIA–Contra cocaine-for-arms deal operating out of the Mena airfield in Arkansas (see p.215). But Clinton's enemies might not have needed to pay for bad press. Ever since Watergate (see p.190), a part of every American political journalist has wanted to be a Woodward or a Bernstein. In June 1997, the Clintons' Whitewater lawyer, David Kendall, accused the Starr office of an outright "leak-and-smear" campaign to damage his clients, a campaign that he alleged even broke grand jury secrecy rules. But leaks can't survive on their own, and papers like *The Washington Post* and *The New York Times* played their part in propagating stories that once would have barely made it onto scandal sheets or scurrilous websites.

Some commentators tried to turn Hillary Clinton's words right back on her, claiming that the whole Foster-Whitewater-Lewinsky affair was, in fact, a left-wing conspiracy to obscure a secret agenda. Bill Clinton was a communist! Didn't he make a trip to Moscow as a student? Bill Clinton was a would-be Hitler! He planned to bring the country's political system to its knees and then proclaim martial law – just as the Y2K bug struck. Or perhaps Hillary Clinton is the real prime mover, bringing down her own husband to set herself up for the presidency. According to the Conspiracy Nation Newsletter, Hillary was – perhaps, still is – a member of a powerful but shadowy Feminist Intelligence Network, a movement that counts Linda Tripp, Monica Lewinsky, Madeleine Albright and Maya Angelou among its members.

The dust settles

There's no question that a lot of powerful people believed that Clinton had to be unmasked. The question is, when does a negative political campaign become outright skulduggery? When the facts are blatantly cooked? When the campaign can't wait to have its chance at the next election? Many liberals have an enduring sense of outrage. After miles of newsprint, millions of dollars and endless lawsuits and hearings, all that was officially found wrong with Clinton's presidency was a few blow jobs and a misplaced cigar. Even though Clinton survived impeachment, however, the Republican campaign in 2000 successfully leveraged conservative, "moral" issues to the forefront. George W. Bush was in the White House, and Hillary Clinton was out of the picture. For the time, at least…

Mud had stuck, maybe, but it was also left all over the hands of its slingers. An ABC News poll found that 56 percent of Americans thought Kenneth Starr had been more interested in damaging the president than discovering the truth, and half the population believed a right-wing conspiracy had tried to discredit Clinton. Some of the leading Republican lights behind the impeachment campaign lost their seats at the next election. There may have been no stains on their interns' dresses, but manhandling Lewinsky's hadn't looked good.

2008: the dust rises

Democrat Hillary Clinton's campaign for the presidency in 2008 turned old news into new news once more, as the vast right-wing conspiracy rose again to confront the would-be dictator of a socialist-fascist state. Old muck was raked over, and over. Hillary herself was never one to let sleeping dogs lie. Confronted in 2002 by the proven conspiracy to jam Democrat phone lines in New Hampshire (which resulted in Republican activists being jailed), she advised supporters that "if anybody tells you there is no vast right-wing conspiracy, tell them that New Hampshire has proven it in court". Sympathizers could also draw on the memoirs of David Brock, a former "Conservative Hit Man", in his own words, and the journalist who broke the Paula Jones story. In something resembling a Damascene conversion, Brock turned liberal and confessed his role in a wide-ranging conservative campaign to smear high-profile liberals, a campaign he dubbed the "Republican Noise Machine".

In January 2008, that machine's anti-Hillary noise was unexpectedly muffled. A federal court ruled that *Hillary: The Movie*, a feature film produced by the conservative pressure group Citizens United, could not be aired unless it attached a disclaimer and revealed the donors who backed it. Citizens United tried to argue that their film was a documentary, and thus not covered by campaign regulations on political advertisements – a move which, at one hearing, caused the judges to laugh out loud.

SOURCES

Books

Sidney Blumenthal The Clinton Wars (2004). This memoir from the assistant to the president puts you right inside the White House at the time of the impeachment. Sympathetic but not entirely uncritical.

Hillary Clinton Living History (2003). A thousand pager, but there's only a couple of pages that anyone wants to read – except extreme conservatives, of course, who have taken to this book like historians to *Mein Kampf*.

Joe Conason and Gene Lyons The Hunting of the President: The Ten-Year Campaign to Destroy Bill and Hillary Clinton (2000). Two veteran hacks from the *New York Observer* and *Arkansas Democrat-Gazette* breathlessly tell the story of the characters (and dollars) behind the campaign to discredit Clinton. It wasn't a conspiracy as such, they say, more a "loose cabal".

Ann Coulter High Crimes and Misdemeanors: The Case Against Bill Clinton (1998). Arch-conservative lawyer and liberal love-to-hate-figure Ann Coulter mounts a rampantly aggressive and highly partisan attack on Clinton, hoovering up the same old controversy canards and a bunch of new ones – Wampumgate, anyone?

Carl Limbacher Hillary's Scheme: Inside the Next Clinton's Ruthless Agenda to Take the White House (2003). Investigative journalist claims Hillary has plotted for the top job for decades. So what's new? Ah, her underhand methods.

Richard Poe Hillary's Secret War (2004). Noble, courageous, public-spirited Internet journalists expose the truth about Hillary "Blofeld" Clinton's Stasi-style infiltration and intimidation of the courts and media. Somehow her reach didn't extend as far as stopping this book.

Mark W. Smith The Official Handbook of the Vast Right-Wing Conspiracy (2004). Or, what you should think if you're a deep conservative.

Kenneth Starr The Starr Report (1998). Also published as *Clinton: The Starr Report*, this is the definitive article, comprehensive and scrupulously footnoted. With a few years' hindsight, however, it seems oddly over-comprehensive and perhaps a little too full of scruples.

Websites

ⓦ**archive.salon.com/news/1998/03/cov_17news.html** The *Salon* article linking Richard Mellon Scaife to the Whitewater investigation.

ⓦ**www.citizensunited.org** Includes trailers for *Hillary: The Movie* – "If you want to hear about the Clinton scandals of the past and present, you have it here!"

ⓦ**mediamatters.org** Organization founded by David Brock dedicated to "correcting" conservative disinformation.

ⓦ**www.snopes.com/inboxer/outrage/clinton.htm** Utterly sceptical investigation of the body-count list.

ⓦ**thomas.loc.gov/cgi-bin/query/z?c105:h.res.611.rh:** Congress's original articles of impeachment.

Waco

April 19, 1993: a huge, spellbound TV audience watched as the 51-day siege of the rural compound of Mount Carmel, near Waco, Texas, ended in a hellish inferno. At least 85 people perished in the blaze, including 21 children. Such an horrific end to a siege that had received massive daily media coverage left many unanswered questions, ultimately leading to allegations of conspiracy and cover-up.

The standoff was between Mount Carmel's occupants – men, women and children of the Branch Davidians, a Christian group formed by Seventh Day Adventists in the 1930s – and agents from the FBI and the Bureau of Alcohol, Tobacco and Firearms (ATF). It had begun on February 28, when ATF agents attempted to raid the Carmel compound in search of illegal stashes of firearms and other weapons. But the Davidians, led by their charismatic preacher David Koresh, fought back. Four ATF agents were killed and sixteen wounded, while half a dozen Davidians were left dead.

The FBI took over and began prolonged negotiations with Koresh. At first, everything seemed to be going well and a few Davidians were let out, but the negotiations soon turned sour. Mount Carmel's power, water and food supplies were cut; bright lights and deafening noise tapes were beamed at the buildings at night; no more Davidians were released, and as the days turned into weeks, it seemed the federal side at least was pushing harder and harder for resolution. On April 19, FBI tanks rolled into the compound and started knocking holes in the main building, and firing CS or tear gas inside. Then around midday, the deadly fire broke out, rapidly engulfing the compound's buildings.

Investigations

The US government and its agencies contended that Koresh had ordered the fire to be started as an act of mass suicide – or mass murder, seeing as many of those who died in the fire had no choice in the matter. In October 1993, the Justice Department's investigation into both the FBI's role and its own role in the affair concluded that Koresh wanted his flock to die on a martyrs' pyre. Koresh was portrayed as a fraud, a failed rock star and a predatory sex fiend who had brainwashed his followers into believing that he was the "Lamb of God", sexually exploiting their daughters as he preached apocalypse.

It was reported that FBI bugs had picked up conversations of Branch Davidians in the compound discussing plans to set it on fire hours before the blaze. Arson investigators found traces of gasoline, lighter fluid and stove fuel around the compound. Davidians were said to have shot at agents and firefighters trying to approach the blaze, and to have prevented anyone inside the compound from getting out alive. Investigator Edward Dennis concluded that FBI agents had exhibited "extraordinary restraint" and acted with "great professionalism" throughout the siege. An investigation into the ATF demonized the Branch Davidians as "cold-blooded killers" who "knew ATF agents were coming" and "prepared a deadly ambush". Attorney General Janet Reno told congressional hearings that she took responsibility for ordering the CS gas to be fired, but didn't admit to making any mistakes and stayed in her job. Two federal agents were suspended as a result of the investigations, but were later reinstated.

Things don't add up

In September 1995, top FBI investigator Robert Matthews called the Waco investigations a "whitewash." Some Davidians who left Waco before the siege began testified that Mount Carmel was a peaceful Bible study centre, and according to one survivor, Koresh was a "serious religious scholar", who only prolonged the siege in order to finish a tract on the Book of Revelations.

The first assault on Mount Carmel certainly seemed ill conceived. The ATF stressed that the mission needed to be a "surprise" to work. Yet not only did the Davidians know that the ATF agents were coming, but the ATF knew that they knew – because they had an agent, Robert Rodriguez, inside the compound. As a weeping Rodriguez later admitted in a congressional hearing, he had told his ATF superiors that the Davidians knew about the impending raid after his cover had been blown and Koresh had asked him to leave. Any remaining element of "surprise" had been destroyed by helicopters flying over the compound hours beforehand and by the numerous local TV camera crews outside Mount Carmel.

There was also doubt as to who shot at who when the fire started. Former attorney general Ramsey Clark told a Waco memorial gathering in April 1996 that infrared video from the FBI helicopters showed agents firing heavily into the compound as the blaze began – exactly when anyone inside might have been trying to escape. Despite media reports to the contrary, Clark said that the Davidians did not shoot at the FBI tanks; it was the FBI, not the Davidians, who had prevented the fire department from approaching the compound to put out the blaze. The FBI later said that they had been forced to keep everyone back because of the "million rounds of ammo" waiting to go off in the compound. This did not, however, prevent the still smouldering remains of the compound from being bulldozed within a matter of days, with the result that – as at Oklahoma City (see p.228) – any remaining evidence was destroyed.

It was widely reported that many of the children died of "blunt force trauma", having been beaten to death by their parents. But pathologist Dr Rodney Crowe told the *Maury Povich Show* in late 1993 that the children and their mothers were either crushed to death or suffocated by falling concrete after a tank rammed the bunker they were hiding in. Medical examiner Nizaam Peerwani concurred with Crowe's reports, and the charge was repeated in the documentary *Waco: The Rules of Engagement*.

As London newspaper *The Times* reported, the FBI had bugged the entire compound, so it would have known where the women and children were hiding, as an FBI agent later confirmed. The 1995 congressional hearings were shown video of a tank repeatedly ramming the compound wall where the bunker was. The purpose of this, the Justice Department claimed, was to inject CS gas inside the main building and create exits for the Davidians to escape. That the dead women and children were found in that concrete-enforced room isn't disputed. That Koresh would have herded the most vulnerable people into the toughest, most flame-resistant room doesn't fit with the picture of a man apparently bent on mass murder.

The Branch Davidians' Waco compound is engulfed by flames on April 19, 1993.

The media

A local man, Ken Fawcett, has claimed that TV stations misstated the time of the raid on February 28 by two hours, so that the ATF could edit the tapes. He also said that as the agents climbed into the building that day, some of their weapons misfired. Other agents thought they were under attack and let rip, while a helicopter bombed the room. The agents essentially killed themselves and a few Davidians by using "spray and pray" tactics of firing blindly through walls – the last resort if one man is being pursued, but if dozens of children's lives are at stake?

Many of the charges and other powerful questions over the siege were brought to bear in William Gazecki's documentary, *Waco: The Rules of Engagement*. Every Waco-related website refers to the film, but Gazecki was incensed by the total indifference he received in Hollywood when trying to get backing and distribution for it. Dr Alan A. Stone wrote in the *Boston Review* that Gazecki "seemed not to realize that in the jungle of Waco the liberal establishment was his natural enemy". Stone, a Harvard professor of psychiatry who sat on the government's investigative panels on Waco, added that he himself was assured that his services would "never again be needed in Washington". The reason being that he thought that the investigations didn't add up either.

Stone rounded on the psychological-war tactics used at Waco, which mainly consisted of sleep deprivation by means of bright spotlights being beamed onto the compound and all-night loudspeaker broadcasts of rabbits being slaughtered, teeth being drilled and Tibetan prayer chants. That these methods may have only reinforced the Davidians' solidarity and unwillingness to come out, and could also produce nerve deafness in the children, wasn't something the Justice Department or FBI were aware of, Stone reported. (One conspiracy rumour is that microwave antennas were deployed around the compound, subjecting the Davidians to mind-control techniques that bade them to react violently and ensure their own destruction, to all appearances by their own hands.) It was also the cutting of their electricity supply that forced the Davidians to use stoves and lanterns, hence the presence of liquid fuel drips around the compound.

CS gas cover-up

Stone also objected to CS gas being fired into buildings with unprotected children in them. CS gas can kill in confined areas, which is why it's usually only used outside to disperse rioting adults. Toxicologist Dr William Marcus told the congressional hearings that CS gas converts to hydrogen cyanide when burned. CS particles are often dispersed with kerosene or methyl chloride, which are both highly flammable. Yet CS gas was fired into the confined, wooden interiors of Carmel over a period of six hours, with only a muzzle flash needed to ignite the lot.

The government, however, blamed Koresh for the fires. Attorney General Janet Reno, FBI director Louis Freeh and their subordinates repeatedly told congressional committees, federal courts and the public that the federal government used nothing capable of starting a fire on April 19, something Reno was repeating up until July 1999. Then the following month, former FBI official Danny Coulson told *The Dallas Morning News* that pyrotechnic grenades had been used. The Texas Rangers also had evidence of M-651 CS tear gas grenades, set off by a burning explosive capable of sparking fires, being fired at the compound on April 19. Coulson and the FBI insisted that the grenades were fired at dawn "in a direction far away from the compound", while the fire started around noon, as arson experts verified – although their conclusion was in part based on FBI assurances that no pyrotechnic devices were used.

On the basis of this evidence, Reno ordered a new investigation, headed by Missouri Republican senator John Danforth. In his 2000 report, Danforth criticized the FBI's false statements about the grenades, saying that "the result ... is that people who want to believe the worst about government say, 'Aha! This is something that's really bad'" – hence a 1999 poll showing that 61 percent of Americans blamed the government for the fire. Danforth concluded, however, that there had been "no massive conspiracy or cover-up" and that "the government did nothing evil".

The bigger picture

For many conspiracy theorists, Waco is part of a wider plot. One theory is that Koresh was a neo-Nazi aiming to resurrect the Third Reich, and some theorists believe he deserved to die, as he posed a threat to liberty. Members of the National Rifle Association, on the other hand, have suggested that Waco was deliberately pushed into a calamitous bloodbath to swing public opinion behind the tightening of gun laws. Many right-wing fringe groups take this argument a stage further, seeing Waco as the first phase in a conspiracy to impose the New World Order (see p.141), which seeks to destroy US sovereignty and bring the world under the control of the UN. The federal government, they believe, provoked Waco to justify a strong clampdown on arms ownership and civil liberties, leaving Americans defenceless in the face of this assault.

Rumblings

Murmurs about misdeeds at Waco also rumbled behind General Wesley Clark's nomination as a Democratic presidential candidate in 2004. Clark commanded the III Corps Cavalry Division at Fort Hood when the fort supplied tanks to the FBI, and his officers advised both Texas governor Ann Richards and Reno on raiding Waco before April 19. What substance, if any, there was to these later dark mutterings about General Clark's possible involvement at Waco never materialized; Clark was out of the 2004 race early on.

In the same month that the Danforth investigation reached its conclusion, Ramsey Clark led about a hundred Davidian survivors and relatives in a $675 million suit against the US government over charges that federal agents used excessive force to end the siege. A Texas jury cleared the government of blame. The BBC's Washington correspondent reported that the finding probably wouldn't silence America's "many conspiracy theorists and anti-government activists". These include Clinton-haters, the National Rifle Association, and religious and political right-wingers who, in print and on air, stir up fears of a federal war on US citizens.

BBC Online, however, omitted to mention that the second anniversary of Waco was marked by the blasting to smithereens of the Alfred P. Murrah federal agency office building in Oklahoma City (see p.228). The man convicted and executed for the bombing, Timothy McVeigh, cited Waco as one of the reasons for his rage against the state.

SOURCES

Films

William Gazecki Waco: The Rules of Engagement (1997). This documentary features footage of David Koresh not as a wild-eyed hellfire and brimstone preacher, but as a mild-mannered man explaining the Book of Revelations to his followers.

Neil Rawles Inside Waco (2007). A joint Channel 4–HBO production piecing together the siege from both sides.

Websites

www.salon.com/news/feature/1999/09/09/waco/print.html A Davidian talks about life in Waco.

www.serendipity.li/waco.html The editorial content sometimes alarms (George W. Bush is described as a "psychopath" and the "insane" John Ashcroft as "Bush's Himmler", with no reference to Waco), but this website is continually updated and has copious links to mainstream news websites reporting criticism of Waco and unfolding investigations.

OKC: the Oklahoma City bombing

On the morning of April 19, 1995, two years to the day after the deaths at Waco (see p.224), a Ryder hire-truck pulled up outside the Murrah Federal Building in Oklahoma City, home to offices of the FBI, Drug Enforcement Administration (DEA) and the Bureau of Alcohol, Tobacco and Firearms (ATF), among others. Inside the truck, thousands of pounds of fertilizer were mixed with motor-racing fuel to make a crude, but very lethal, bomb. When it exploded at 9.02am, it destroyed a third of the building, including the federal employees' creche on the second floor. A total of 168 people were killed, victims of what was then the most serious terrorist act ever committed on US soil.

Two hours later, former soldier and alleged paramilitary Timothy McVeigh was pulled over seventy miles from Oklahoma City for driving without number plates. At gunpoint, he calmly handed over a hidden Glock pistol. Traces of explosive were later found on his clothing, and his fingerprints were discovered on a receipt for two thousand pounds of fertilizer. Not a shining example of covering one's tracks. Two days later, an accomplice and militia-member called Terry Nichols gave himself up. Investigators found detonators, fertilizer and a number of guns at his farm; the guns were later revealed to have been stolen from a man named Roger Moore. Strangely, Nichols also stole Moore's quilt. On May 23, 34 days after the bombing, the remains of the Murrah Federal Building were bulldozed.

McVeigh was tried by a federal court in the spring of 1997. His sister, Jennifer, testified that he had boasted shortly before the bombing that "something big is going to happen". At first, McVeigh publicly pleaded his innocence, telling *Time* magazine in 1996: "I enjoy guns as a hobby, I do gun shows and I follow the beliefs of the Founding Fathers. If that means I was involved in the bombing, then … about a billion other Americans were involved in the bombing as well." After he had been found guilty of eight counts of murder in June 1997, however, he confessed in letters sent from prison that "the bombing was a retaliatory strike: a counter-attack, for the cumulative raids (and subsequent violence and damage) that federal agents had participated in over the preceding years (including, but not limited to, Waco)".

McVeigh was killed by lethal injection in 2001 – the first time that the federal government had (officially) executed one of its citizens since 1963. Terry Nichols escaped the death sentence, but Judge Richard P. Matsch sentenced him to life in prison in January 1998, calling him "an enemy of the constitution". At a subsequent state trial in 2004, Nichols reportedly confessed during plea bargaining that "McVeigh told me what to do", which didn't go down any better in court than it does in most infant schools. He also denied that there were any co-conspirators. The jury found him guilty of 161 counts of murder, but could not agree to impose the death penalty.

Doubts: John Doe 2

Following the federal trial, Judge Matsch stated that "there are many unanswered questions. It would be very disappointing to me if the law enforcement agencies of the United States government have quit looking for answers in this Oklahoma bombing tragedy." There seemed to be too many loose ends. The FBI's case was built largely on McVeigh and Nichols' phone records. But were there accomplices? A number of witnesses claimed to have seen another man with McVeigh on the morning of the crime. The FBI spent millions of man-hours chasing the suspect, dubbed "John Doe 2", before finally concluding that he probably didn't exist. Former grand juror Hoppy Heidelberg, thrown off the case for talking to the media, claims some witnesses were never called at the trial in order to conceal the identity of John Doe 2 – a government agent or informant.

Could there have been John Does 3, 4 and 5, as well? Charles Farley, a witness testifying for the defence, claimed to have seen a second truck and a brown car parked with the Ryder truck at an outdoor recreation centre a day or two before the bombing. Five men, he claimed, were handling bags of fertilizer. A Kansas deputy sheriff called Jake Mauck claims he firmly identified the John Doe 2 sketch as being a local "patriot" whom some have linked to previous FBI sting operations against paramilitaries.

Explosive evidence

Suspicions about federal involvement in the bombing focused on the bomb itself. Various explosives experts, would-be experts and supposed experts expressed their doubts as to whether the fertilizer bomb described by the authorities could have been put together by McVeigh and Nichols, or whether it would have worked if they had managed to do so. The conspiracists' star witness is Brigadier-General Benton Partin (USAF, retired), expert witness on munitions to the Oklahoma City Bombing Investigation Committee, a pressure group run by an Oklahoma state representative. His report claims that the damage to the building must have been caused by demolition charges placed on the internal structural columns. But as one conspiracy website ponders, if it's demonstrably true that the truck bomb couldn't have done the damage, why didn't McVeigh's lawyers make this the cornerstone of his defence?

The two-bomb theory

Early media reports that other bombs were found inside the ruins of the building were later withdrawn. If you don't believe that those reports were simply checked and rejected, you could see that as evidence of government coercion. David Hall, part-owner of KPOC-TV in Oklahoma and a campaigner against the alleged government conspiracy at Waco, believes that firefighters found a second, unexploded bomb in the rubble. But he also reckons he heard the original arrest call for a "1978 Mercury, no license plate, involved in OK bombing" while he happened to be listening to a local police scanner.

A more authoritative source of what has become known as "the two-bomb theory" was the University of Oklahoma's

Geological Survey, which was initially puzzled as to why seismographic records seemed to show a second explosion following roughly eight seconds after the first. But as the survey's director, Dr Charles Mankin, later reported, "the second shock was from the same occurrence that caused the first, which had travelled through a different and more dense layer of the earth".

More evidence of a conspiracy supposedly comes from the Ryder truck. CCTV footage showed a UPS truck parked where the Ryder truck should have been – it turned out that the camera's clock was wrong. A photograph by a sergeant from the County Sheriff's office was hailed as an incriminating "before and after" shot – in fact, they're just two similar pictures from very different dates stuck together. An aerial photo supposedly showed the Ryder truck parked in a military facility – it looks suspiciously fake. The truck axle found at the site is alleged to have been moved or planted, or to have had its vehicle identification number doctored to implicate McVeigh.

Federal Bureau of Misinvestigation

Rumours circulated in Oklahoma that the FBI had warned the fire department, or ATF employees, or local judge Wayne Alley, who was originally assigned to the trial before it was moved to Denver, to take "special precautions" shortly before the bombing. The Feds' alleged sluggishness in hunting down John Doe 2 is seen as proof that they were hiding one of their own men. By that account, this supposed agent was the prime mover behind an elaborate sting operation that went tragically wrong when McVeigh et al actually succeeded in setting off the bomb. Others – like McVeigh, still angry about the Waco killings – blame the Bureau of Alcohol, Tobacco and Firearms (ATF). Was the bomb designed to destroy records of the ATF's role in the Waco affair? Supposedly, no ATF staff were in the building at the time – in fact, five were killed.

Some have turned the spotlight on Oklahoma governor Frank Keating. As a former FBI man and a Bush loyalist, he couldn't fail to have had a finger in the pie, surely? And the fact that his brother Martin Keating wrote a thriller called *Final Jihad* about terrorist attacks on the US homeland just proves it. Supposedly written before the Oklahoma bombing, the novel was, in fact, published a year after the event, while the claim that its hero is called "Tom McVey" is simply false.

More genuinely disturbing documents emerged just days before McVeigh's scheduled execution in May 2001, when the FBI let slip that it had "accidentally" withheld some three thousand pages from the defence team, blaming both a "computer glitch" and staff who thought them "irrelevant". Attorney General John Ashcroft immediately postponed McVeigh's execution and ordered an inquiry. In September, Gore Vidal wrote a *J'accuse*-style article in *Vanity Fair* criticizing Right, Left and sundry, and the FBI in particular. However, the inquiry concluded that while there were "serious deficiencies" in the FBI's handling of the case, the missing paperwork could not have affected McVeigh's conviction.

Hardline anti-government activists believe the government deliberately destroyed the Murrah Federal Building as the perfect smokescreen for the introduction of laws cracking down on "patriot" militias. Comparisons were made with the Nazi's Reichstag fire of 1933, which allowed the Nazis to assume control of Germany. McVeigh, they claim, was nothing more than a patsy. Or possibly a CIA agent. Or even a Manchurian candidate, controlled by a microchip implanted during his time in the army. The clincher? That he was strangely cold and subject to mood swings.

9/11 rehearsal?

Perhaps the most disturbing theory stems from Jayna Davis, a reporter for KFOR-TV in Oklahoma City at the time of the bombing. Citing witness statements and intelligence reports, she claims that "olive-skinned" John Doe 2 was a former member of the Iraqi Republican Guard. KFOR-TV showed a digitally blurred photo of the man during a news broadcast, whereupon he stepped forward and sued for defamation of character. The court ruled for KFOR-TV, and the plaintiff supposedly upped sticks and went off to work at Boston's Logan International Airport – from where Mohammed Atta took off on 9/11. Whether or not, as Davis goes on to allege, a Middle Eastern terrorist cell operated in Oklahoma City, and whether or not Terry Nichols had made contact with Islamic Filipino terrorists linked to Osama bin Laden, no court has yet tried to determine. Was this just an angry city turning on the foreigners in its midst?

The sword of justice

On April 24, 1996, almost a year to the day after the Oklahoma bombing, President Clinton signed the Anti-Terrorism and Effective Death Penalty Act. It allowed the State Department to label organizations as "terrorist", and the FBI to launch criminal investigations of people who gave them financial support. Immigrants could be deported without the need for public hearings of evidence, and federal review of state death penalty cases was eliminated.

Web-based rumours that liberal congressman (now senator) Charles Schumer's 1995 bill HR 2580 would have imposed a prison sentence for "publishing or transmitting by wire or electronic means baseless conspiracy theories regarding the Federal government of the United States" turn out to be exaggerated. The bill did indeed blame paramilitary violence on "baseless conspiracy theories regarding the government", but it didn't actually suggest sending people to jail for speculating.

The final word has to be that of the Oklahoma County grand jury investigation, which concluded in December 1998. "We have observed a tremendous amount of journalistic overlap in a number of magazines, books, talk radio shows and Internet websites", it observed. "The same misprinted information is repeated over and over again without anyone validating its veracity. Sadly, these organizations and individuals have glorified those convicted in federal court by vilifying the federal government and increasing the public's distrust of its government by providing half-truths, uncorroborated, and oftentimes outright false information … As Americans we do not want to believe that fellow Americans could plot, scheme and carry out such a cowardly act in the name of protest. Tragically this is the current reality of the world in which we live."

SOURCES

Books

Jayna Davis The Third Terrorist: The Middle Eastern Connection to the Oklahoma City Bombing (2004). Davis pushes the Islamic terrorist thesis, suggests that McVeigh and Nichols had shadowy backers and asks why the FBI shut down the investigation.

David Hoffman The Oklahoma City Bombing and the Politics of Terror (1998). Five hundred pages of hearsay evidence leads Hoffman to conclude that it can't have been a fertilizer bomb, and that neo-Nazis, and possibly Middle Eastern terrorists, were behind McVeigh and Nichols.

Stephen Jones and Peter Israel Others Unknown: Timothy McVeigh and the Oklahoma Bombing Conspiracy (1998). Jones was chief defence counsel for McVeigh, and he holds the torch for those still looking for John Doe 2 – possibly an Islamic extremist.

Kenneth S. Stern A Force Upon the Plain: The American Militia Movement and the Politics of Hate (1996). From one of the influences behind Charles Schumer's anti-militia law. Written as a wake-up call not just to the threat of the militias to the United States, but to right-wing conspiracizing itself. Currently out of print, which says a lot about the agenda shift towards international terrorism.

Gore Vidal Perpetual War for Perpetual Peace (2002). Collection of virtuoso essays attacking the US government from a liberal, but original, perspective. Two fascinating pieces on McVeigh suggest that he cannot have worked alone. Interesting to see the possible links between liberal and right-wing libertarian thinking.

Websites

Ⓦ **www.greatdreams.com/john-doe-2.htm** Huge collection of newspaper articles, many conspiracy-minded, speculating on the identity of the mysterious "John Doe 2".

Ⓦ **www.okcbombing.net** The home of the sceptical, conspiracy-minded Oklahoma Bombing Investigation Committee.

Ⓦ **www.oklahomacounty.org/treasurer/GrandJuryBombingReport.htm** Scotches almost all the theories, but leaves the door open to John Doe 2. If you don't believe Oklahomans, who do you believe?

Ⓦ **www.terrorisminfo.mipt.org/pdf/forensicengineering2.pdf** Engineers' assessment of the blast; conclusion: one truck bomb.

The elections of George W. Bush

On the night of the US presidential election, November 7, 2000, exit polls showed that with three states too close to call – Florida, New Mexico and Oregon – George W. Bush could count on 246 electoral college votes to Al Gore's 255. In total, Gore had received almost half a million more individual votes across the US than Bush, but the presidency is determined not by popular vote, but by votes received in the electoral college, delivered as a block from each state. To win in 2000, either candidate needed 270 electoral college votes; thus, whoever won Florida's 25 votes would also win the overall race. On the basis of exit polls that predicted a Gore victory in Florida, several TV networks that night "called" the presidency for Gore.

Ultimately, the vote in Florida was close enough to force a machine recount – which, on November 10, put Bush ahead by just 327 individual votes. Gore called for a manual recount in four largely Democrat counties, and the process immediately started in hotly disputed Volusia and Palm Beach. Bush's team countered by applying to a federal court to block the recount. At this point, Florida's secretary of state, Katherine Harris – a Republican – stepped in, declaring that she would set a deadline of November 14 for any hand recounts. She also applied to Florida's Supreme Court to block manual recounts entirely.

By November 16, almost thirty separate court cases were underway. It was legalized chaos: some courts ordered recounts, others ruled that for selective recounts to be held in a few largely Democratic counties would be unfair. Eventually, the most significant cases were combined at the US Supreme Court, which decided on December 12, by seven votes to two, to stop recounts on the grounds that different counties shouldn't have different voting standards. On the issue of whether or not new recounts should be ordered, however, the court was split five to four – right down party lines. The five conservative judges decided that to impose a standard on Florida would be to change rather than interpret Florida law – a constitutional no-no for the Supreme Court. They were sorry, but their hands were tied. Katherine Harris, therefore, gave Florida's 25 electoral college votes to George W. Bush, who became America's first Republican president in eight years.

The super-bright spotlight of media and legal attention in November and December 2000 ensured that the slightest molehill in the road to the presidency threw a mountain-sized shadow back onto TV screens and newspapers. And there were plenty of molehills. Some dug up by pretty scary moles.

Butterflies, chads and spoiled votes

The voting systems in a few Florida counties in 2000 were seriously flawed. The infamous "butterfly ballot" in Palm Beach County was designed so badly – albeit by a Democrat – that over 5000 votes were cast for the surprising cross-party duo of Al Gore and Reform Party candidate Pat Buchanan. It was also Florida that gave us the word "chad", as courts debated whether punch-card votes still counted if those itsy bits of paper were left hanging from the card, rather than being punched right through.

Gadsen County, where the population has a particularly high proportion of African-Americans, suffered from a strange excess of spoiled ballots. Papers there were machine-read by an optical "Accuvote" system that rejected any that were wrongly completed – for instance, any that had extra marks on them. Unfortunately for Gadsen voters, the machines recording the vote had a tendency to leave just such marks. Worse still, the "reject" mechanism telling a voter that they'd accidentally spoiled their own ballot

> **THE GREAT ELECTION ROBBERY OF 1876**
>
> The 1876 presidential race between Rutherford B. Hayes (a Republican) and Samuel J. Tilden (a Democrat) makes Bush–Gore look lily-white. Like Gore, Tilden won the popular vote – by some quarter of a million votes. He was just one electoral college vote short of the 185 then needed for victory when Republican-controlled election boards in Florida, Louisiana and South Carolina started disqualifying Democratic votes in numbers big enough to swing the result back to Hayes. Tilden wouldn't back down, so in January 1877 Congress set up a special Electoral Commission to decide the outcome. It was made up of eight Republican senators and seven Democrats. The result? 8:7 for Hayes.

was switched off. As a result, one in eight ballot papers in Gadsen County failed to pass muster. In Tallahassee County, by contrast, the (largely white) voters were warned to try again if they accidentally spoiled their ballot. One in a hundred was spoiled in Tallahassee. According to the US Commission on Civil Rights, over half of the spoiled ballots in Florida 2000 belonged to African-Americans, who make up just eleven percent of the population. Most media commentators blamed that statistic on "lack of education"...

Scrub lists: the crime of being a black voter

During the run-up to November 2000, the politicos knew that the results were going to be close, and that any advantage could be crucial. Luckily for George W. Bush, his brother Jeb was governor of Florida, while two successive secretaries of state, Sandra Mortham and Katherine Harris, were political associates. They commissioned a company called DBT (whose parent company ChoicePoint specialized in conducting manhunts for the FBI) to prepare a "scrub list" of criminals who, under Florida law, would not be eligible to vote. Florida paid DBT $2.3 million – just $2,294,300 more than the last company that did the same job. Statistics show that roughly nine out of ten felons prefer Democrat – and, quite legitimately, the Republicans didn't want to lose the state thanks to the illegal votes of a bunch of criminals.

What looks a whole lot less legitimate is how the list was drawn up. Florida voters' names were matched with known felons by comparing names, birthdays and genders. Crucially, near-matches were included, and never cross-checked – Florida officials told DBT it wasn't necessary. Campaigning journalist Greg Palast claims to have found a handwritten note in Katherine Harris's files saying "DON'T NEED", right next to DBT's proposals for checking.

It didn't help that middle initials were excluded from the computer matching process. A felon called George V. Bush, for example, could be matched with a Florida voter called George Bush, whatever his middle name actually was. And, because racial ID is included on voter rolls in Florida, if George V. Bush was African-American he could knock African-American George Bushes off the rolls – but not white George Bushes. Palast even found 325 names with conviction dates in the future. In all, 57,746 people were listed as felons and were, therefore, denied the vote; a disproportionate number of them were African-American or Hispanic. At least fifteen percent of the list, it seems, was incorrect – enough to have swung the election. The one county that independently cross-checked its felons list found that it could only confirm 34 out of 694 names as those of people genuinely ineligible to vote. That's an error rate of 95 percent.

For the 2004 presidential election, the state of Florida once again commissioned a "potential felon" list, or as it was popularly known, a "black purge" list. The second time around, media pressure forced officials to abandon the plan.

The early call

Some of the stories circulating about the 2000 election are more "theory" than "conspiracy". On election night, the big news channels relied on the Voter News Service (VNS) to report early results and exit polls. At the conservative-minded channel Fox News, an analyst called John Prescott Ellis was working on the VNS's results. He owed the "Prescott" part of his name to his grandfather, Prescott Bush – whose other grandson was up for president that night… Conspiracists allege that it was Ellis's sole responsibility to call the Florida result for Fox. He spoke to both George and Jeb Bush on election night. "It was just the three of us guys handing the phone back and forth – me with the numbers, one of them a governor, the other President-elect", Ellis told *The New Yorker*. "And everybody followed us."

Fox News was indeed the first network to call the election for George Dubya, at 2.16am, and the other networks soon followed. Did Ellis single-handedly swing the election analysis in favour of Bush, thus leaving the future president in a strong position in the legal fight for the White House that followed? Republicans point out that Ellis worked on just one team, on one news channel; that Fox had also been the first to call it for Gore, before retracting the announcement; and that, in any case, the decision was based on real figures from the VNS. No one, they say, "made the call" for Bush.

The age of the machine

In 2000, electronic voting machines were relatively newfangled and uncommon. One of the few counties using them was Volusia, Florida. According to Bev Harris, campaigning author of *Black Box Voting*, it was the announcement by the computers there, during the early hours of November 8, of a huge Bush lead of 51,000 that prompted the networks' early call of a Bush victory in the state. That figure was later corrected, giving Bush some 16,022 fewer votes. The manufacturers blame a faulty memory card for the inaccurate early result. But how often does bad memory selectively alter a few numbers on the data it stores? Harris claims to have found official voting records in the trash at Volusia County's offices, as well as official voting tapes designated for shredding, and memory cards just lying about. Confusion? Or collusion?

Volusia County's machines were manufactured by Diebold Inc. On November 9, 2003, *The New York Times* quoted one Walden W. O'Dell as saying in a letter to fellow Republican loyalists, each of whom had raised over $100,000 for the Bush campaign, that "I am committed to helping Ohio deliver its electoral votes to the president next year". Mr O'Dell's talents were not restricted to fund-raising; he was also chief executive of Diebold, the second largest company providing voting machines in the US.

The largest voting-machine company, responsible for roughly half of US polling stations, was ES&S, which grew out of American Information Systems. One of AIS's first financial backers, Howard Ahmanson, also helped to finance the Chalcedon Institute, dedicated to "restoring the Christian Faith and Biblical law as the standard of all of life", and guiding Christians "in the task of governing their own spheres of life in terms of the entire Bible: in family, church, school, vocation, arts, economics, business, media, the state…" Another controversial ES&S figure is Chuck Hagel, a former chairman who subsequently ran for the Senate as a Republican candidate in Nebraska in 2002. After 24 years of Democratic senators, Hagel won his seat in a landslide. ES&S had supplied vote-counting machines for around eighty percent of those Nebraskan votes.

Perhaps Hagel just ran a great campaign. So perhaps did the Republican candidate for the governorship of georgia, in 2002. After 130 years of Democratic governors, and months of opinion polls in favour of the Democratic candidate, Republican Sonny Perdue marched into office with the help of a sixteen percent swing in the four days leading up to the election. Georgia's touch-screen voting systems, in use for the first time, were made by Diebold. Mysterious software patches were reportedly downloaded onto the systems shortly before the election; afterwards, conspiracists protested that the computers' memory cards had been formatted. And, of course, there could be no recount. Unlike their ATMs and other electronic data systems, Diebold's DRE (Direct Record Electronic) voting machines leave behind no messy paperwork, no "paper trail".

Suppress the vote 2004

Although the election of George W. Bush in 2004 was not as controversial as that of 2000, allegations of a conspiracy to suppress the Democratic vote weren't lacking. Most notoriously, Michigan Republican state representative John Pappageorge was quoted in the *Detroit Free Press* as saying, "If we do not suppress the Detroit vote, we're going to have a tough time in this election." Detroit is almost 85 percent African-American. Pappageorge later clarified that all he'd meant was that the Republicans needed a good campaign in order to win Democrat votes.

In Ohio, the key swing state for 2004, some voters reported receiving phone calls or letters telling them to vote on a different day or at a different location; others were told that they could register their vote there and then on the phone. When it came to election day, Democratic areas were alleged to have been poorly supplied with voting booths or voting machines, causing long queues to form. In the pouring rain of a wet November day in Ohio, this was a major disincentive to vote. Republicans were filmed waiting by the booths to challenge voters' legitimacy. The Republicans pointed out that they were simply stopping non-registered or fraudulent voters; Democrats complained that they were only doing so in black or Democratic areas, and that amounted to intimidation. As Jesse Jackson put it, "suppose five hundred black folks came into a white neighborhood to challenge votes. It would be totally unacceptable."

In the final result, the Democratic turnout in Ohio was well below the Republican figure. In Franklin County, precincts won by John Kerry had an average turnout of fifty percent, whereas those won by Bush registered sixty percent. Some turnout figures seemed even more surprising. Ohio's secretary of state, J. Kenneth Blackwell

George W. Bush and his brother Jeb, the governor of Florida, celebrate the results of the presidential election in November 2000.

– who combined his electoral role with a position as co-chair of the Bush-Cheney campaign in the state – certified turnouts of 124 percent in two precincts of Republican-leaning Perry County. The figures were explained as statistical anomalies caused by the difference between electoral districts and county boundaries. Blackwell had been busy before the election too, challenging 35,000 new voter registrations – before the move was blocked by a federal judge – and attempting to ban registrations made on the wrong weight of paper. He also allegedly targeted presumed-liberal universities and colleges for provisional ballot voting, setting rules so that the slightest error on these ballots would result in their being automatically rejected. Ohio's exit polls had predicted a Kerry victory, by a figure that exceeded their margin of error. But when the final results came in, Bush had won. What had changed?

Politics as usual?

In 2001, news organizations including CNN, *The New York Times* and *The Washington Post* commissioned the University of Chicago's National Opinion Research Center (NORC) to examine what would have happened had the Supreme Court allowed various recount scenarios. The NORC concluded that Bush would actually have won if the partial recounts wanted by Al Gore had gone ahead. A full statewide recount, however, would have given Florida to Gore. But as liberal film- and troublemaker Michael Moore put it in *Fahrenheit 9/11*, it doesn't really matter "just as long as all your daddy's friends on the Supreme Court vote the right way". In 2003, Moore refreshed his reputation for infamy by calling Bush a "fictitious president" while picking up an Oscar.

One result of the 2000 controversy was the Help America Vote Act of 2002, which led to billions of tax dollars being spent on voting machines. Was this a decent, fair-minded attempt to consign chads permanently to the trashcan? Or did a few Republican legislators expect a payback from the companies who made the machines?

SOURCES

Books

Vincent Bugliosi The Betrayal of America (2001). Trial lawyer Vincent Bugliosi argues that the Supreme Court's 5:4 decision to stop the Florida recount was "treasonous" and a "judicial coup d'état".

Ann Coulter Slander: Liberal Lies about the American Right (2003). For Coulter, the conspiracy is that the liberal media stifles real debate by screening out radical, conservative voices like hers. Unfortunately, the fact that Coulter's face is all over the news channels undermines her own argument.

Bev Harris Black Box Voting: Ballot Tampering in the 21st Century (2004). This clarion-call alert to the problems of electronic voting systems, not to mention the vested interests behind them, was published just too late for the 2004 election, but in time to get a lot of people talking about the next one.

Greg Palast The Best Democracy Money Can Buy (2002). Subtitled "An Investigative Reporter Exposes the Truth about Globalization, Corporate Cons, and High Finance Fraudsters", Palast's all-encompassing attack covers Bush scandals such as Enron and the revelation of the Bush family's Saudi Arabian connections, as well as the 2000 election.

Websites

Ⓦ **www.blackboxvoting.org** The leading campaigning website, run by the profoundly energetic Bev Harris, including a well-used chat forum.

Ⓦ **www.countthevote.org** Website campaigning against paperless voting machines, gunning for Diebold in particular.

Ⓦ **www.fair.org/index.php?page=2932** Fairness and Accuracy in Reporting's rundown of how challenges to voter fraud were marginalized in the press as "conspiracy theories".

Ⓦ **www.gregpalast.com** "George Bush's nightmare" and "New Labour's Public Enemy Number One", Palast has acquired plenty of epithets in the course of his combative, anti-establishment reporting career. His coverage of the Bush election itself achieved news-item status.

Ⓦ **www.norc.org/projects/florida+ballots+project.htm** The official site of NORC's Florida Ballot project – with enough "what if" stats to boggle a Supreme Court judge.

Ⓦ **www.verifiedvoting.org** Mainstream campaign for a paper trail – look under "2004 Theories and Counter-theories".

Skull, Bones and Bush

When lantern-jawed senator John Kerry won the Democratic nomination for the 2004 presidential election, conspiracy theorists could hardly believe the evidence of their online news reports. The contest would pit one "Bonesman" – or member of Yale's Skull and Bones fraternity – against another, George W. Bush. To most observers, the society's existence is powerful evidence of a disturbing truth: that expensively educated, emotionally immature private schoolboys are liable to grow up to be expensively educated, emotionally immature college frat boys. These kind of clubs – and there are scores of them at campuses all over America – exist to provide a reassuring sense of elitism for rich kids struggling to come to terms with the levelling, meritocratic atmosphere of higher education – and an excuse to drink a lot. Period.

Others see the Skull and Bones – aka "Chapter 322", aka the "Brotherhood of Death" – as visible proof of a sinister, conspiratorial network of the rich and powerful. Even though it has been around since 1832, the society only achieved its current high profile after the elections of George H.W. Bush (he of the "New World Order", see p.141) and, later, his son George W. Bush. The Internet is now crawling with conspiratorial lists of Bonesmen. Early twentieth-century president William Howard Taft is a prominent name, but otherwise most lists simply feature a smattering of banking-dynasty scions and high-fliers in US intelligence – pretty much what you'd expect of Yale – as well as scores of wealthy lawyers and accountants of whom you've never heard.

Reports of ghoulishly absurd initiation rituals are just as ubiquitous. Ceremonies are held in the campus building of Jonathan Edwards College, nicknamed "The Tomb" – for once the media has a theory it can back up with real pictures. These initiation ceremonies reportedly centre on heavy doses of quasi-Masonic flimflammery involving a skull supposedly looted from the grave of Apache warrior Geronimo by Prescott Bush (George H.W.'s father) in 1918. Following Native American demands for its return, however, tests revealed that it was no such thing. Other rituals are, predictably, heavily sexualized, involving an acted-out murder, the nude confession of previous sexual misdemeanours and masturbation while lying in a coffin.

The more profoundly stupid their actions, the less likely initiates will be to confess to them, it seems. Or is there a darker edge? Is the adoption of cod-Masonic or satanic symbolism proof of real links to Masonic or satanic societies? In *America's Secret Establishment*, author Anthony Sutton traces the society's links back to the mythical Bavarian Illuminati (see p.93), through the popularity of German-style secret societies in 1830s America. But then, Sutton also claims he started his research after he was mysteriously sent bound volumes of the membership list, which – sadly for anyone wanting to check his evidence – he had to give back within 24 hours. Those Masonic lending libraries are so strict about returns…

Some people point out, quite reasonably, that the connotations of the Skull and Bones motif are more than a little sinister. Is it linked to the "death's head" *Totenkopf* sported by the Waffen-SS? Is it a sign that Skull-and-Bones members will "take no prisoners" in their future careers – careers helped along by an alleged "donation" to graduating members? Are members ideologically committed to militaristic notions of death before dishonour? Or is it all just boyish posturing?

SOURCES

Books

Alexandra Robbins Secrets of the Tomb: Skull and Bones, the Ivy League, and the Hidden Paths of Power (2003). The supposed inside story, from a photogenic Yale graduate.

Antony Sutton America's Secret Establishment (1986, updated 2002). Before you buy this, check out the interview with Sutton at www.freedomdomain.com/secretsocieties/suttoninterview.html.

Films

Rob Cohen The Skulls (2000). Frat-boy movie relying heavily on conspiracist thinking.

Websites

Ⓦ **www.bilderberg.org/skulbone.htm** Giant scrapbook of news articles and opinion pieces, with lots of Web links too.

Ⓦ **politicalgraveyard.com/group/skull-bones.html** Purported "very incomplete" list of Skull and Bones members.

Ⓦ **www.yalealumnimagazine.com/issues/2004_09/old_yale.html** From the horse's (or the skull's) mouth: Yale alumni tell the story of their secret societies.

CORPORATE CLAMPDOWN

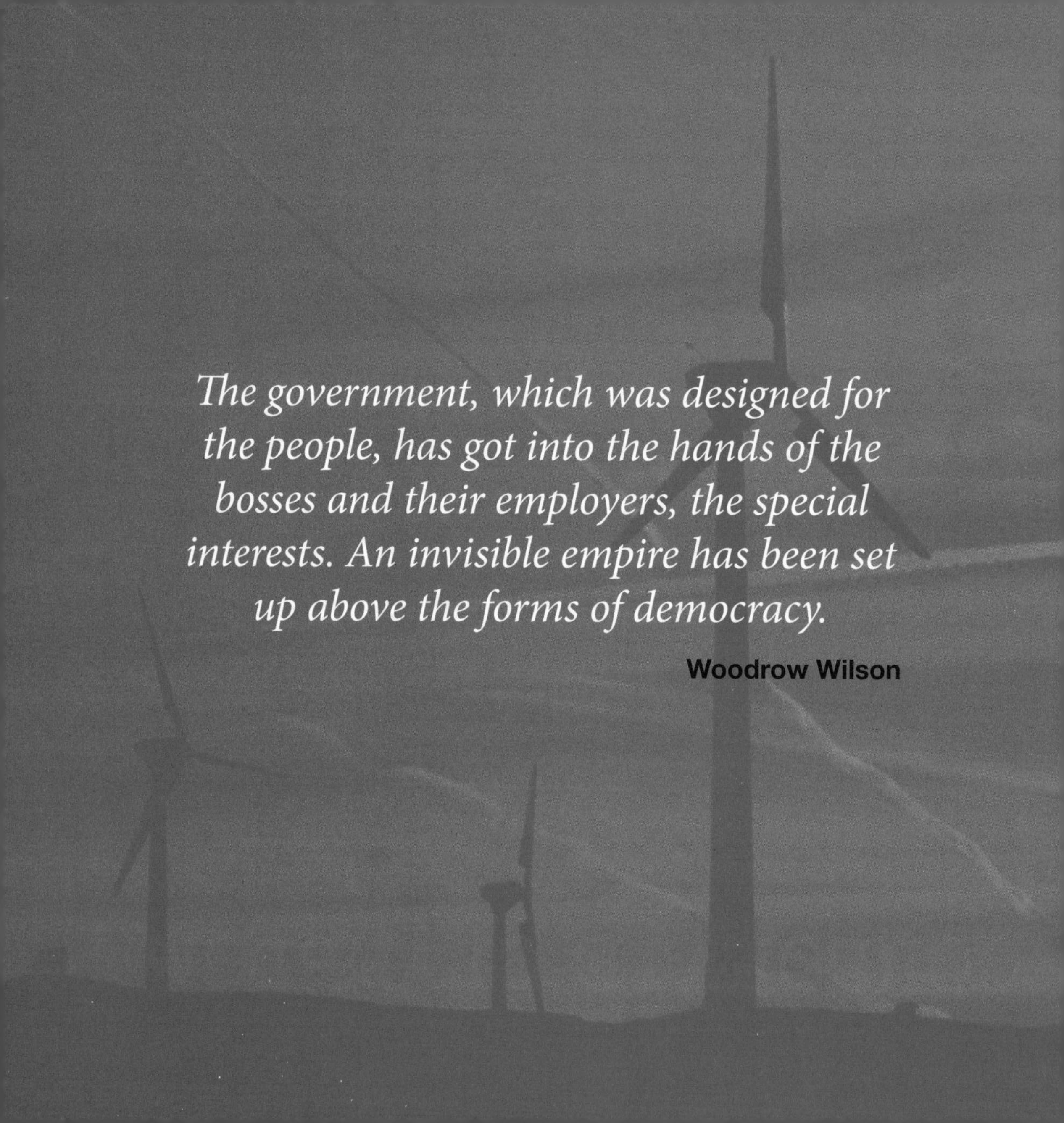

The government, which was designed for the people, has got into the hands of the bosses and their employers, the special interests. An invisible empire has been set up above the forms of democracy.

Woodrow Wilson

CORPORATE CLAMPDOWN

Two truisms of our modern world might be that practically nothing functions, nay, comes into existence, without money, and that nothing will function, or be brought into being, without the prospect of money being made. The world is too complex a place to direct investments by ethics, morality, national interests, democracy or general human wellbeing – there's too much room for cultural disagreement – so let's just have a world governed by the law of profit, where everything starts and ends with banks and big business.

So simple, so powerful; yet some people believe that banks are desperate to keep their true omnipotence quiet, fearing that will reveal the amorality that governs their actions. In the case of the now defunct BCCI – the global bank of choice for those predisposed to murderous subterfuge and law-breaking, from drugs traffickers to the bin Ladens – the banks' critics may have a point. Some conspiracists allege that the banks' evil intentions have more to do with the fact that many international bankers are Jewish – but these sorts of anti-Semitic, hate-fuelled allegations originated from some of the most right-wing and barbaric movements in history, notably Nazism. And it was the Nazis who filled the coffers of knowing, yet otherwise reputable, international banks with confiscated gold, including the melted spectacles, wedding rings and dental fillings of Holocaust victims.

With all that money and our collective global genius for technical advancement, why are the world's great corporations still unable to solve some of the biggest problems of our age? Almost every aspect of our lives needs energy, so why hasn't anyone found a way to create a clean, endlessly renewable soure of energy? Surely designs to create perpetual energy at low cost – be it from the wind, waves, plants, or some kind of "free energy generator" or "overunity machine" – exist? It must be a conspiracy! Critics accuse the oil industry of keeping the lid on clean, efficient technologies – like the Elsbett engine that runs on vegetable oil or the EV1 electric car – to ensure that the world remains dependent on their expensive, filthy product. A similar charge is made of greedy light-bulb manufacturers. For years, conspiracy theorists have insisted that somewhere in the world exists the design for an eternal bulb that will never pop, but how would the manufacturers stay in business after everyone has bought their indestructible light bulbs? They must be suppressing the patent.

Even greater than the pursuit of eternal energy or eternal light is the pursuit of eternal life. It's suspected that the pharmaceutical companies make such a mint out of treating sick people that the last thing they want is for them to get better – or, even worse, for them not to get ill in the first place. One of the most common charges in conspiratorial circles is that a miraculous cure for cancer has already been found, but that it has been suppressed by the drugs companies, because curing the disease would eliminate the need for expensive ongoing treatments. But what if the development of drugs and other medical advances to fight disease, was one of the contributing factors causing disease? That drug companies might actively seek to make people ill is a heady charge, but the pollution caused by the chemical industry and Big Pharma to make medicines, may also be creating the need for them.

A classic example of this is fluoridation – the process of adding fluoride to public water supplies because it's said to prevent tooth decay. Fluoride's backers see it as a wondrously abundant chemical that will keep children's teeth dazzlingly clean, but to its detractors, it's a filthy industrial by-product of the aluminium industry that actually rots teeth, and is suspected of causing untold other ailments. This notorious conspiracy theory is decades-old, sustained – like the cancer controversy – because there is little definitive proof that factor X causes disease Y.

Most of these anti-corporate theories, and many other conspiracies, are rapidly disseminated by that most cutting edge of inventions, the Internet, which so successfully broadens people's minds by connecting them in endless spirals of paranoia. When, that is, this sophisticated piece of kit isn't on the brink of a meltdown due to a simple binary oversight, like the "Millennium Bug". Perhaps the world's computers didn't all break down on December 31, 1999 because the Y2K phenomenon was just a money-making hoax concocted by computer geeks? Then again, with the Internet being tracked by the global monitoring system ECHELON and the ever-friendly and increasingly omniscient search engine Google, perhaps a little distrust of these ultimate surveillance facilities wouldn't be misplaced. Powerful people and powerful organizations – who are probably even more paranoid than you are – use these systems to watch you, as you use the Internet to try to find out more about them.

There are so many different threads, sources, benefactors and beneficiaries to all these conspiracies – surely such plots couldn't be hatched and pursued in isolation? Not within such a vast and increasingly complex world economy? There must be opportunities for all the interested parties – industrialists, bankers, media moguls, business leaders, generals and politicians – to get together to discuss covering up their dirty deeds and to conceive new plans for the future. This is where groups like the secretive Bilderberg Group and the more open and media-friendly World Economic Forum come in, arranging annual conferences in swanky hotels to discuss how they're going to continue running every big bank, corporation, industry, government… the world?

The international banking conspiracy

Reginald McKenna, one-time British chancellor of the exchequer and former chairman of the Midland Bank, once said: "They who control the credit of the nation direct the policy of governments and hold in the hollow of their hands the destiny of the people." That alone is enough for Web writer Christopher Mark to fulminate that the Bank of England, the Bank of France, the World Bank and the International

Monetary Fund are all "bastard siblings" of that "hideous constitutional monster" the Federal Reserve. With the UN as "the ultimate front for international banking interests", the international bankers' mission is "to enslave the entire population of the planet". And all through loans, too. This is the world of the international bankers' conspiracies.

The central banks

According to Gerry Rough, a prolific debunker of banking conspiracies, "The Bank of England holds a special place in the hearts of New World Order conspiracy theorists." He goes on to discuss the "idea that the conspirators had enormous power even as far back as three hundred years ago, and have been gaining power and global influence ever since".

Charging interest on money loans has offended people since long before Christ (when it was simply deemed usury). For some, however, the more recent phenomenon of privately owned banks charging governments interest on loans is even more insidious. According to R. Robertson's *The New World Order*, the bankers struck their first decisive blow in 1694, when Scotsman William Paterson set up a joint stock company to loan £1.2 million at eight percent interest to King William III, so that he could wage war against Louis XIV. When Paterson then won the charter for the Bank of England, he effectively won power over England's monetary systems, with the result that the country's tools of monetary policy were now in private hands. The English government, having been suckered into debt by "international bankers", was then obliged to establish income tax to pay it off. The rot had begun.

Revolution

But England's bankers let greed cloud their judgement, according to Mark. He writes that Britain's American colonies didn't use British sterling, but their own paper money known as "colonial scrip", printed locally as required to keep the economy in tick. It wasn't a currency issued with interest charged on it, and more to the point, England's bankers weren't profiting from it. So the Bank of England pressurized Parliament to outlaw it and make the Bank's interest-bearing monies the currency of the day – reverting monetary control back to England while causing a sharp downturn in colonial economic fortunes, thus precipitating the American Revolution. According to Alexander Hamilton, one of the founding fathers of the US: "The Colonies would gladly have borne the little tax on tea and other matters had it not been for the poverty created by the bad influence of the English Bankers on the Parliament, which has caused in the Colonies hatred of England and the Revolutionary War." For Mark, the reason why this isn't the version of history taught in American schools is the bankers' continuing control of the media.

Assassinations

President Andrew Jackson later called bankers "vipers and thieves!" and sought to undermine the single national, privately owned bank. It's said that it was these anti-bank moves that led to an assassination attempt on Jackson, and that the bankers then did their best to denigrate his character. "Wildcat banks" joined in by creating bad debts, hyperinflation and high interest rates that would tip Jackson's presidency into an economic depression. As Abraham Lincoln was to comment, banking "denounces as public enemies all who question its methods or throw light upon its crimes".

President Lincoln himself sought to pay for the Civil War by issuing "greenbacks" on the same basis as scrip. As Christopher Mark tells it, the distribution of greenbacks was so incendiary to Europe's banks, who would otherwise have happily funded the Civil War, that it provoked France and Britain to mass their troops in Mexico and Canada. Their intervention was only averted, the story goes, by Lincoln's appeals to the Russians: "I have two great enemies, the Southern Army in front of me and the bankers in the rear". Lincoln, of course, was subsequently assassinated, as was President Garfield, who also opposed the international moneychangers and noted, "Whoever controls the volume of money in any country is absolute master of all industry and commerce". A century later, a plan by John F. Kennedy to pay off the federal debt using "US Notes", a US government-printed currency that the Federal Reserve must supposedly accept, also apparently led to his assassination.

Wars and debts

In his 1971 rant *None Dare Call It Conspiracy*, Gary Allen argues that the bankers' battle in the US is just part of a bigger plot. He quotes Carroll Quigley's *Tragedy and Hope* – cited by many as "proof" of conspiracies to take over the world – as saying that "the heads of the world's chief central banks were ... the technicians and agents of the dominant investment bankers of their own countries, who had raised them up, and who were perfectly capable of throwing them down", by means of coup d'état or war.

This theme has been developed by Professor Stuart Crane, who argues that the biggest profits are derived from making interest-bearing loans to governments – and that the largest loans of all tend to be for arms and wars. But how can a bank ensure that it collects on a loan, when it's dealing with a well-armed, sovereign government? Its most obvious recourse if a government defaults is to lend more money to another foreign power, again of course at a profitable rate of interest, to finance a war against the defaulter.

Crane says that the architect of this system was Frankfurt banker Meyer Rothschild, who dispersed his sons to Paris, London, Vienna and Naples to finance wars between the governments of Europe during the eighteenth and nineteenth centuries. The House of Rothschild was the first and most prominent of several European banking families who were granted state monopolies over their respective nations' central banks. The Rothschilds financed the North during the US Civil War, while their relatives, the Erlangers, financed the South (which flies in the face of Christopher Mark's contention that European banks weren't able to fund the North because of Lincoln's "greenbacks").

Minister Muhammed of the UK-based Islamic group Final Call to Prayer, alleged to his followers in 2004 that the Rothschilds and Warburgs financed England and Germany in World War I, whereas historian Antony C. Sutton claimed that Winston Churchill colluded with banker J.P. Morgan to embroil America in the war by arranging for the liner *Lusitania* (see p.323) to be sunk. Sutton argues that the Korean and Vietnam wars were not about fighting communism, but about generating multi-billion-dollar arms contracts, and that Wall Street bankrolled both the US and the USSR. Sutton charges that "the financial elite knowingly and with premeditation assisted the Bolshevik Revolution of 1917 in concert with German bankers", who financed Lenin in order to end Russian involvement in World War I. The subsequent default on Russian debts led all of Wall Street to back the Allied war against the Bolsheviks in 1919 and 1920; similarly, some allege that the hottest spells during the Cold War came when the USSR defaulted on later loans, causing banks to double their lending for US armaments.

Sutton further alleges that Wall Street engineered and profited from Germany's 1923 hyperinflation and the 1929 Wall Street Crash, while the Depression of the 1930s was a bankers' plot that put tens of millions of people into poverty and bankrupted nations, but pushed land and assets into the possession of the banks. Wall Street supposedly backed Franklin D. Roosevelt in the US and Adolf Hitler in Germany; according to Muhammed and Allen, the Warburgs and the Rothschilds financed Hitler, a charge spun by one Internet writer to suggest that Hitler was simply their agent. By that account, both Roosevelt's New Deal and Hitler's Four-Year Plan were near-identical "plans for fascist takeovers of their respective countries". Accordingly, Wall Street also wanted war between France and Germany, which Hitler delivered, and war between the US and Germany, which Roosevelt and Hitler provided.

Harvard professor Richard Pipes has called Sutton's research too "uncomfortable", and it's regularly either ignored or dismissed as "extreme". That said, although Sutton is written off by many as the arch-conspiracy theorist, he's not alone in depicting Wall Street as a cabal of banking families. In 1899, M.W. Walbert's *The Coming Battle: The International Monetary Conspiracy Against the United States* described how European banking families were attempting to siphon away America's riches, by controlling the Treasury via the banks. Allen outlines a detailed, nearly incestuous series of marriages around 1900 between the Warburgs, the Loebs (of Khun, Loeb & Company), the Schiffs (who'd shared digs with the Rothschilds) and their US agent, J.P. Morgan. There was also John D. Rockefeller, who married the daughter of Senator Nelson Aldridge, and whose grandson, also named Nelson, was to become both vice president and governor of New York. Warburg backed Aldridge to set up the Federal Reserve in 1913, and writer Michael Edwards claims that eight banking families own about eighty percent of the Fed to this day (the Rockefellers being the biggest holders). The top seven families at the Fed are European in origin, says Mark.

The Jews

Of course, where some write "European", others write "Jewish", and pick out the Rothschilds, Warburgs, Schiffs and Loebs over the Rockefellers and Morgans. The association of Jews with banks and insidious activities has been one of the most enduring, pernicious conspiracy theories, called by the Anti-Defamation League a "timeworn, classic" anti-Semitic myth, which nonetheless still reappears across a swathe of sources.

Jewish bankers figured prominently in Hitler's hate propaganda. Of course, he also hated the Bolsheviks, who Sutton claims were lent $20 million in 1917 by Jacob Schiff. This has, in part, given rise to theories that the Bolshevik Revolution was in fact a Jewish plot, and hence that the international bankers were Jewish communists engaging in a "bigger conspiracy to control the world". In a somewhat analogous situation, it's been said that more recently stirred-up fears about the threat of Islam are just a cover for the potential economic threat of an Islamic finance bloc stretching from the Middle East to Malaysia, as pioneered by Malaysia's ex-premier Mahathir Mohammed. Yet, in another scarcely ironic twist, the Simon Wiesenthal Center says that Mahathir's diatribes about Jewish finance "would have made Hitler and Goebbels proud".

A pervasive anti-Semitic conspiracy theory in the US alleges that Jews control the Federal Reserve. In his 1931 book, *The Truth About the Slump*, A.N. Field claimed that "the Money Power that rules the world" is a "German-Jew engine of control", which enslaved the US by controlling the Federal Reserve. In *Called to Serve*, James Gritz, who was the

Gold, bearing the stamp of the Nazis, found in the Bank of England.

Populist Party's presidential candidate in 1992, charged that "eight Jewish families control the Fed". Three years later, the Nation of Islam's Louis Farrakhan concurred, adding that the Rothschilds "financed both sides of all the European wars".

Eustace Mullins, in 1983, and Gary Kah, in 1991, both claimed that the Federal Reserve is controlled by those who own and control its largest regional branch, the New York Federal Reserve Bank. Kah's "Swiss and Saudi Arabian contacts" told him that the NY Fed is owned by the banks of Rothschild, Lazard, Israel Moses Seif, Warburg, Goldman Sachs, Lehman Brothers and Kuhn-Loeb – it's easy to see where this is going – while Mullins

NAZI GOLD

Since 1945, legions of treasure hunters have plumbed the depths of Lake Toplitz in Austria, hoping to find the truckloads of Nazi gold supposedly dumped there during the closing days of World War II. Many have died in the process, and the lake had to be sealed off, with only occasional, officially sanctioned dives permitted. However, the Nazis hid away a lot more gold than that, and some of it is much easier to find. Vast sums were deposited in the banks of those countries that remained neutral during the war, countries which, by accepting bullion from the Third Reich, helped the Nazis to fund their war effort. In 1997, the World Jewish Congress and the US Senate Banking Committee uncovered a sordid saga of wartime transactions. Gold from all kinds of sources – looted from invaded countries, or taken from the bank deposits, jewellery, spectacle frames or dental fillings of the millions of people who were exterminated in Nazi concentration camps – was melted down into bullion, and stamped with false pre-war dates to make it appear legitimate.

About $400 million worth of gold, in 1945 terms, went into the Swiss National Bank, and more into the Switzerland-based Bank for International Settlements. Both served as conduits through which $500 million in assets and $300 million in gold were channelled into central banks in Portugal, Spain, Argentina, Turkey and Sweden, as payment for trade. As William Clarke tells it on www.bigeye.com, while the Allies monitored these triangular deals, they either did not, or could not, do anything to close them down.

Although the Swiss National Bank denied taking any "tainted gold" in 1945, the directors of the Reichsbank and the US Military Government in Germany disagreed. The latter concluded that "the Bank for International Settlements accepted looted gold ... [and] was dominated by Axis interests". In 1998, a Swiss government report confirmed that the country's central bank made no effort until late in the war to ensure that the gold paid in had not been taken from Holocaust victims. Swiss bankers also initially denied, then severely understated, "heirless deposits", that is to say accounts held by those who fell victim to the Holocaust, which should, by rights, have passed to their families after the war. According to one estimate, made in 1997, the Swiss held between $6 and $20 billion worth of Nazi gold. Faced by class action suits launched from the US, and the threat that Swiss assets would be frozen and Swiss banking licences in the US revoked, the Swiss government set up a $5 billion fund to pay annual compensation to the victims of all human catastrophes, including the Holocaust.

Not that the Swiss had all the Nazis' gold. The governments of the US, Britain and France set up the Tripartite Gold Commission after the war to reimburse captured gold. However, only around two thirds of it was claimed. That leaves some three and a half tons of gold in the Bank of England, and two tons in the Federal Reserve Bank of New York. In 1999, the US undertook its own efforts to restore assets stolen during the Holocaust to their rightful owners or heirs. Clinton's Presidential Advisory Commission on Holocaust Assets (www.pcha.gov) listed property worth hundreds of millions of dollars, including looted books that had found their way into the Library of Congress, a painting in the National Gallery of Art and several thousand dormant bank accounts. Much of this may have been acquired and/or neglected in all innocence.

But there was one spectacular exception. In 1945, the US Army in Austria appropriated 24 boxcars of paintings, sculptures, gold and possessions that had been stolen by the Nazis, and were then valued at up to $200 million. In 2001, tens of thousands of Hungarian Holocaust survivors brought a class action suit against the US government, charging that the goods had been falsely classified as unidentifiable or enemy property. Survivors were told lies about the fate of their possessions, which in many instances had ended up in officers' homes. The US government settled in 2004.

cites a cabal called the "London Connection" which controls the NY Fed by owning its eight biggest shareholders, and thus makes "the most powerful men in the US answerable to ... the House of Rothschild". However, both writers ignored the fact that the NY Fed has only one vote out of twelve on the board of the Federal Reserve, and that the Federal Open Market Committee must also approve any changes to interest rates. Kah lists mostly foreign or investment banks, which cannot own Fed stock by law. The Anti-Defamation League has called Mullins an "anti-Semitic propagandist" (www.adl.org/special_reports/control_of_fed/print.asp).

The Federal Reserve

The Federal Reserve is the regulatory agency that governs the US banking industry, setting monetary policy and influencing the business cycle through changing interest rates, issuing currency or purchasing government bonds. However, it's alleged that the Fed was also created in conspiracy. Gary Allen alleges that J.P. Morgan created a series of banking panics such as the "Panic Circular" of 1893, which read "You will at once retire one-third of your circulation and call in one half of your loans...", as well as spreading rumours of insolvency at the Knickerbocker Bank and the Trust Company of America in 1907.

Paul Warburg and Senator Nelson Aldridge used such "panics" to lobby for a single national bank, which was set up in the 1913 Federal Reserve Act under President Woodrow Wilson. An attempt to pass a similar act had been made under the previous administration of President William Howard Taft, but Taft had it defeated. So, the theory goes, international "banksters" backed Woodrow Wilson for office and split the Taft vote by backing ex-president Teddy Roosevelt to run. With the Wilson administration successfully installed, the Federal Reserve Act was passed, albeit with most of the opposition on Christmas vacation. Congressman Charles A. Lindbergh Sr called it an act that legalized "the invisible government by the money power". New York mayor John Hylan echoed that claim in 1922, when he decried the Federal Reserve as an "octopus" headed by Rockefeller-Standard Oil and powerful banking houses.

The IMF and the World Bank

Michael Edwards charges that the "big money" that finances both the Republican and Democrat parties in the US is controlled by "a collection of mostly banking family reps known as the Bilderberg Group" (see p.250), who all belong to what's effectively an exclusive club that also dominates the Council on Foreign Relations and the Trilateral Commission (see p.140 and p.143, respectively). Rear Admiral Chester Ward complained that the Council on Foreign Relations is dominated by "Wall Street international bankers" who "want the world banking monopoly from whatever power ends up in the control of global government". That government is the infamous "New World Order" (see p.141), and among the large, venerable institutions often accused of being mere instruments of this global conspiracy are the World Bank and the International Monetary Fund (IMF).

Both the World Bank and the IMF were set up in the aftermath of World War II, with their headquarters in Washington DC. Their aim was to oversee the reconstruction and development of the worldwide economy, the IMF by steering monetary policy and setting the conditions for loans, and the World Bank by alleviating poverty. However, by 2004, some 85 countries owed $97 billion to the IMF, despite the fact that since 1996 the IMF and World Bank have supposedly been working, via the Heavily Indebted Poor Countries (HIPC) Initiative, to ensure that "no poor country faces a debt burden it cannot manage".

Which poses the question: what were the lending policies during the preceding fifty years, which led to so many countries staggering under debt, instead of being kick-started into capitalist prosperity by judicious lending? According to John Perkins, in *Confessions of an Economic Hit Man*, the World Bank and IMF served as channels through which huge loans were directed to poor countries

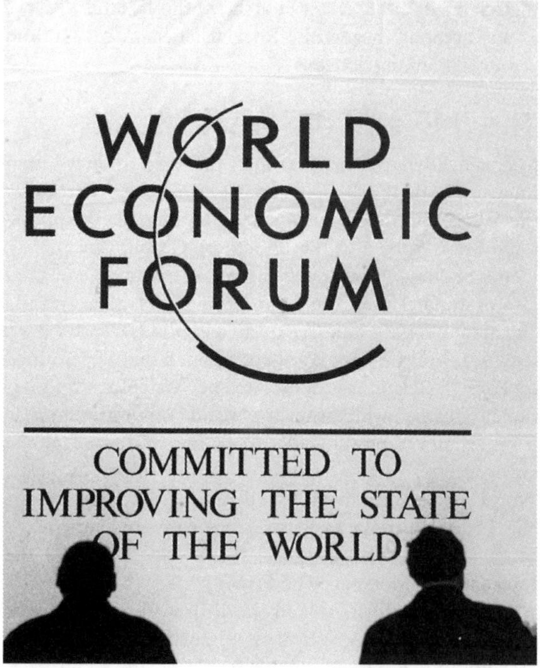

The World Economic Forum at Davos, Switzerland in 2005.

by the CIA and National Security Agency (NSA), to fund grand but utterly useless infrastructural projects. The loans were made conditional on the relevant contracts being awarded to US corporations, which ensured that the loan capital was returned straight to the US, while the debtors were never expected to repay the loans. The point was that when, inevitably, they defaulted on the loans, the World Bank or IMF could step in, and dictate that country's spending on everything from social to military security, and even how it voted in the UN. Resistance would get the country's leadership "removed". Failing that, a war would be engineered so that US forces could go in as bailiffs and reclaim control of the capital.

Perkins claims that this strategy, in which "economic hit men" such as himself worked through civilian consultancies like the Boston-based Chas T. Main, enabled the creation of a new US empire. Thus because half of Ecuador's GDP is owed in debt, the US can say, as Perkins put it to *Democracy Now* in 2002: "Look, you're not able to repay your debts, therefore give our oil companies your Amazon rain forests, which are filled with oil." He added: "We literally have them over a barrel." He alleges that Ecuador's president Jaime Roldes was assassinated over non-payment of debt, while President Omar Torrijos of Panama was killed for awarding a canal contract to a Japanese company rather than a US corporation.

Perkins concedes that he may be derided as a conspiracy theorist. Even so, it does seem strange that so many developing countries have somehow contrived to be so consistently inept for so long under the aegis of capitalism that "austerity measures" have to be imposed by the World Bank and IMF. Over 140 countries, including Brazil, Mexico and Argentina, can only receive continued credit if they lower their subsidies to producers of domestic staples and export commodities, devalue their currencies and demolish their social welfare programmes, utterly irrespective of what their governments were voted in for. Almost two decades after the Cold War ended, over 850 million people worldwide remain malnourished and, according to the UN's Food and Agricultural Organization (FAO), 16,000 children die from malnutrition every day. UN-Habitat reported in 2007 that a billion people live in slums and double that number will do so by 2020.

The main beneficiaries of stable economic prosperity from this system seem to have been the US, Europe and Japan, which all have permanent directors at the World Bank. Meanwhile China and India have gone through decades of development and have now reached the threshold of becoming global economic powers by deliberately shielding their economies from the tentacles of these financial institutions and other alien influences. By a long-standing informal agreement, the president of the World Bank is always an American (former under-secretary of defense Paul Wolfowitz was succeeded as president

THE WORLD ECONOMIC FORUM

Although likened to the Bilderberg Group (see p.250) and mentioned almost as often in conspiratorial contexts, the World Economic Forum is, in fact, a Swiss-based non-governmental organization (NGO) that describes itself as the "foremost global community of business, political, intellectual and other leaders of society committed to improving the state of the world". Business does seem to be the main means – and beneficiary – of these improvement aims, with representatives from the world's top thousand companies making up half of the average 2500 participants at the WEF's annual meeting in Davos, Switzerland, along with heads of state, NGO chiefs, academics and journalists.

The WEF board arranges everything, staffed by luminaries ranging from Peter Sutherland, the chairman of Goldman Sachs International, and Henry McKinnell, the former chair and CEO of the world's largest pharmaceutical research company, Pfizer, to Queen Rania of Jordan and George Carey, the former archbishop of Canterbury. There are few specific theories about the WEF, but it certainly attracts some of the world's top guns. Regular attendees in recent years have included former US president Bill Clinton, former UK prime minister Tony Blair (as president of the G8), European Commission president José Manuel Barroso and UN chief Kofi Annan. Celebrities such as Bono of U2, Angelina Jolie, Michael Douglas, Mohammad Ali, Sharon Stone, Lionel Richie and Pele have also added some bling, if not brains, to the proceedings.

The likes of Bill Gates and the CEOs of Citigroup and the New York Stock Exchange rub shoulders with Pakistan's dictator Pervez Musharref and the US secretary of state Condoleezza Rice, in rooms abuzz with the great and the good from ChevronTexaco, Coca-Cola, Dell, Nestlé, Nike, PricewaterhouseCoopers, Saudi Aramco, Unilever, Sony, Google, Hong Kong's Star Group and many other large corporations. Directors from charitable organizations such as Amnesty International, Human Rights Watch and World Vision International mix with presidents and deans from Harvard University, the London School of Economics and Peking University, while the chairs and editors-in-chief from Agence France Presse, Al Jazeera, BBC News, *China Daily*, the *India Today* group, Novosti, Reuters and *Time* ensure that everything is reported with balance.

The WEF's annual discussions include issues such as equitable globalization, global governance, Islam, United States leadership, and weapons of mass destruction, as well as seminars with themes such as "Shaping the Global Agenda: The Shifting Power Equation". Debates about how the WEF should address the "particular challenges" of the current period of "rapid globalization" in an "increasingly schizophrenic" world have led to some conspiracists wondering if there exists some over-arching plan of globalization that has not yet been fully divulged. Perhaps the WEF is simply another vassal in some elitist plot to create a singular global government?

The WEF also runs a forum of Young Global Leaders, a group of 1111 – a number of unknown significance – people aged under 40, "who share a commitment to shaping the global future ... [and are] destined for future greatness". As well one might be if deemed so by the WEF and asked to engage in the "2020 Initiative" to formulate the "roadmap" to "spearhead change" (see www.weforum.org or www.younggloballeaders.org to find out who these youthful movers and shakers are). Although there isn't necessarily anything sinister in all this, there's nothing remotely democratic about it either: the WEF's projection of the balance of world power in 2020 has identified more Young Global Leaders in Europe and North America than in Africa, Asia, Latin America and the Middle East put together. No change there then.

in mid-2007 by another neocon and self-styled "Vulcan", Robert Zoellick), while the IMF chief is European.

Don't bank on any of it

The phrases "invisible government" and "money power" recur throughout anti-banking literature, as do explicit references to Jews. Anti-Semitism is often so clearly bubbling beneath the surface that you have to wonder whether bigots use the label "European" as a code word to make their views seem more acceptable in public. Are some writers reproducing ancient slurs in new disguises, perhaps unwittingly, or are extremists hijacking ideas that do not deserve to be dismissed on those grounds alone? Gary Allen argues

THE BILDERBERG GROUP

During the early 1950s, with post-war Europe divided and the Cold War turning violent in Korea, prominent Americans such as John J. McCloy (the head of the Office of Strategic Services, the predecessor of the CIA) and C.D. Jackson (the chief of President Eisenhower's unit on psychological warfare) felt that economic and security issues of joint concern to Western Europe and America were not getting enough attention. Backed by the CIA and the Rockefeller and Ford foundations, they decided to instigate informal, unofficial top-level meetings that might foster prosperity and help to avert wars.

Prince Bernhard of Holland hosted the first meetings at the Hotel de Bilderberg in The Hague in 1954, and the Bilderberg Group was born (although subsequent meetings have varied in location, Bilderberg's headquarters are still in The Hague). As the BBC described it in 2004, Bilderberg is an "elite coterie of Western thinkers and power-brokers". The cream of North Atlantic statesmen, royals, bankers, industrialists, pressmen and generals, the Bilderbergers continue to meet annually to discuss world issues, and to select and invite favoured individuals for membership. According to Reuters, both Tony Blair and Bill Clinton came to international attention as speakers at Bilderberg meetings before they achieved power, as did former World Bank president James Wolfensohn. The list of American big-hitters is impressive. Of George W. Bush's neoconservative clique, Richard Pearle, Richard Armitage, Paul Wolfowitz and Colin Powell are all Bilderbergers.

One prevalent theory, originating in the early 1960s from books like right-wing American Phyllis Schlafly's diatribe *A Choice Not an Echo: The Inside Story of How American Presidents Are Chosen*, is that membership of the Bilderberg Group is key to getting into the White House. By extension, it's said that George W. Bush's Bilderberg backers secured him the presidency in 2000 over non-Bilderberger Al Gore. George H.W. Bush lost in 1992 to Bilderberger Bill Clinton, while another member, Gerald Ford, managed to become vice president and president without being elected for either job.

However, the theory of omnipotent Bilderberg power doesn't always hold up. Ford lost the presidency in 1976 to non-Bilderberger Jimmy Carter, who was a member of the Trilateral Commission (see p.143), which is the target of its own secret clique conspiracy theories. Although not a Bilderberg member, George H.W. Bush won the presidency in 1988, while Bilderberg members John Kerry, John Edwards, John McCain and Gary Hart have all been stymied. In any case, many Bilderbergers are also Trilateralists, as well as members of the Council on Foreign Relations (see p.140) and the World Economic Forum (see p.249), so which group has more power and how that ultimately matters is a blurry subject with different spins coming depending on who's having a go at who on any given day. The catch-all theory is that they're just different names for the same old gangs colluding behind closed doors, funded by conspiracy theorists' favourite David Rockefeller, Exxon, IBM and the Carnegie Endowment Fund.

While the real significance of Bilderberg membership is debated, however, the theories about its power can have an impact. Schlafly's book surfaced during the presidential campaign of fellow-Republican Barry Goldwater in 1964. Schlafly ranted that many Republicans were part of the northeastern

that the "anti-Semites have played into the hands of the conspiracy", in that by portraying the banking conspiracy as being the work of Jews they've made it an unacceptable topic for historians to tackle, and that the backlash from the Anti-Defamation League has served to distract attention from the fact that J.P. Morgan and the Rockefellers, for example, were white Christians. At this level of logic, snakes eat their own tails, and as Gerry Rough repeatedly points out, conspiracy literature about banking can be a hideous web of misinformation and politically malign scholarship.

Yet in monetarized economies, the moneymen do have great power, as US founding fathers Madison, Jefferson and Hamilton were all too aware. No one can do much without financial backing of some kind, but banks are rarely accountable to anybody. Within a week of taking office following the 1997 UK election, New Labour handed monetary policy back to the Bank of England (a decision taken by Chancellor Gordon Brown, a Scotsman, in a coincidental sop to the Paterson conspiracy), to keep it "free of politically motivated decisions"– effectively establishment and were just puppets of Bilderberg's godless communists. That dissent in the party's ranks may have contributed to Goldwater's defeat. Over thirty years later, William Rees-Mogg wrote in *The Times* of American evangelist Pat Buchanan's belief that his presidential bid was finished when he snubbed Bilderberg membership. But that may all be another conspiracy…

Right-wing writer Chip Berlet has argued that to devise conspiracy theories about the Bilderberg Group merely distracts from a systematic analysis of how wealthy elites control both politics and the world's economy. Economist and Bilderberger Will Hutton says that the Group does exactly that, likening the group to the World Economic Forum, where "the consensus established is the backdrop against which policy is made worldwide". (Indeed, Goldman Sachs chairman and WEF board member Peter Sutherland presided over the 1999 Bilderberg meeting.) According to Lord Denis Healey, former UK Labour chancellor and one of the founding members of the Bilderberg Group, however, Hutton's idea is "crap".

Others hold the Bilderberg Group responsible for creating the 1957 Treaty of Rome, which formed the first building block of the European Union and the Euro zone. Serbian news agencies reported in May 1999 that the war in Kosovo, which ultimately brought down Serbian president Slobodan Milosevic, was plotted as a "Balkan Vietnam" at Bilderberg's 1996 meeting in Scotland by a "supra government" that included Margaret Thatcher, Helmut Kohl, Valéry Giscard D'Estaing, Henry Kissinger, David Rockefeller and Baron Rothschild. They wanted Serbs to be tried for war crimes at The Hague, and also, according to the Serb press, war with Russia (although the benefits of such a war weren't fully explained).

It's easy to find a more positive spin on Bilderberg's work. Senior editors and correspondents from CBS, ABC, the *Financial Times*, *The Wall Street Journal*, the *LA Times*, *The New York Times* and *Time* all attend meetings, though they're not permitted to report on them, and the minutes of the meetings – which aren't publicly available – do not state who said what. The venues are kept secret, there is no website (which explains how a conspiracy website came to have the auspicious address, www.bilderberg.org), and the telephone line is a terse answerphone. The meetings are serviced by the group's own barracks of cooks, bodyguards and police.

All of this adds to the mysterious aura that helps to fuel the myth of the Bilderberg Group's omnipotence. This in turn, according to the BBC, has proved potent enough for the likes of Timothy McVeigh and Osama bin Laden to point at Bilderberg in their violent rages. Bilderberg has also been called the ultimate club for the architects of the New World Order (see p.141), and a talking shop for liberal Zionists plotting world domination – although for some theorists the two ideas are interchangeable.

You can find out more about the group (and how to join it) by writing either to Bilderberg Secretariat, 1 Smidswater, The Hague, or to Bilderberg Meetings, Amstel 216, 1017 AJ Amsterdam. By a curious coincidence – or perhaps not – its US base was once next door to two other institutes of ill-boding for conspiracy theorists, the Trilateral Commission and the Carnegie Endowment, but it's now at 477 Madison Ave, 6th Floor, New York 10022.

removing whatever UK government control it had in the first place. Indeed, as Robin Ramsay wrote in *The Rise of New Labour*, Tony Blair, Gordon Brown and the rest of the New Labour team were intellectually in awe, and financially in hock, to London's city bankers long before taking office, perpetuating everything the Tories had set in motion long before.

To believe, however, that banks deliberately conspire to manipulate national economies to their own ends, by allowing or even forcing them to go broke, requires you also to believe that they're omniscient or omnipotent enough to do so. What's indisputable is that they're in the business (and usually it's a very successful business) of profiting from the time-honoured practice of lending money and charging for it, often irrespective of the morality or legality of the borrower. The banks continue to profit while their actions power economies from boom and bust to boom and bust, over and over again. Busts that remove families from their homes, and governments from power.

SOURCES

Books

Gary Allen None Dare Call it Conspiracy (1995). As the title suggests, this is an excitable tome, packed with fascinating detail (especially if it's true), and liberally sprinkled with block capitals and exclamation marks.

John Perkins Confessions of an Economic Hit Man (2004). The grubbiness of the title denotes the murderous, fetid squalor of the world of 1960s and 70s international finance that Perkins toured for too long.

Carroll Quigley Tragedy and Hope (1975). A set text in the conspiracy theorists' curriculum.

Robin Ramsay The Rise of New Labour (2002). As pithy as it is damning, Ramsay's book argues that the party that took over the UK in 1997 had, like its predecessor, already been taken over by the banks.

Pat Robertson The New World Order (1992). One of the more recent must-reads to become intellectually conspiratorial.

Websites

Ⓦ **www.antonysutton.com** Links to many of the works of Antony C. Sutton, a prolific writer on banking conspiracy theories.

Ⓦ **www.floodlight.org** A site dedicated to debunking conspiracy theories of a far-right bent, with writer Gerry Rough clinically demolishing banking theories.

Ⓦ **www.imf.org** Official website of the International Monetary Fund.

Ⓦ **iresist.com/cbg/battle.html** The webpage for Michael Edwards' "The Battle America Lost in 1913", an interesting if rather sprawling piece on the rise of the banks.

Ⓦ **www.prisonplanet.com/analysis_mark_022803_deception.html** Christopher Mark's passionately expressed views on international banking and "The Grand Deception and the Theft of America".

Ⓦ **www.worldbank.org** Home of the World Bank, a self-described "vital source of financial and technical assistance to developing countries".

The BCCI scandal

The Bank of Commerce and Credit International SA saga is one case where reality outdoes the most paranoid of conspiracy theorists' imaginings. The short career of this infamous bank began in 1972, when it was founded in Pakistan by Agha Hasan Abedi with backing from sheikhs in Abu Dhabi. Presenting itself as a "Third World Bank" with the remit to invest and foster prosperity in corners of the globe usually beneath the interest of Western capitalism, BCCI ended up with over a million depositors, using four hundred branches worldwide, on every continent except Antarctica, and at one point claimed assets of $25 billion. Such was the claim, but the gargantuan scale of its criminal operations and the bank's tentacular reach were real, and really quite awesome.

Throughout the 1970s, the bank grew speedily, pursuing asset growth over profits – seeking high net-worth individuals and regular large deposits, splitting holdings between Luxembourg and the Grand Cayman, and acquiring other banks in Switzerland. (This, according to conspiracy theorist Lyndon LaRouche's magazine *Executive Intelligence Review*, brought BCCI into the orbit of Rothschild Bank AG.) By then, it's thought, BCCI was already teetering on the edge of bankruptcy, and using deposit cash to fund operations instead of investing, but that didn't stop its expansion into Africa and Asia, and in 1977 it arrived on the shores of the US (although, as the *Review* tells it, BCCI was originally conceived with the connivance of the CIA and the Bank of America). There, BCCI swiftly, secretly and illegally used nominees and friends in high places to buy four banks, which operated in seven states and the

District of Columbia, and included the First American Bank. But BCCI largely restricted its US operations to laundering drug money.

Drug money and turf wars

By early 1985, the US Drug Enforcement Administration (DEA), IRS and CIA were all separately pointing to BCCI involvement in laundering heroin money from BCCI branches in Colombia, Central America and Southeast Asia. Even so, the CIA used both BCCI and First American for its own operations. The 1992 report, *The BCCI Affair*, generated by a Senate subcommittee investigation led by Senator John Kerry, stated that former CIA directors Richard Helms and William Casey, together with other CIA luminaries, "float in and out of BCCI at critical times in its history". Helms and Casey were also involved in critical episodes such as the Camp David peace talks and the Iran–Contra affair (see p.201). Saudi-CIA intelligence agents, meanwhile, worked in BCCI's commodities affiliate, Capcom, which laundered billions of dollars from the Middle East to the US.

Kerry's investigation, however, didn't begin until the late 1980s. Although the CIA told the State, Treasury, Commerce and Justice departments about the drug-money laundering in 1985 and 1986, no investigations were launched at that time. *The BCCI Affair* later slated the belated intra-departmental investigations as being confounded by incompetence, inter-agency turf wars and obstruction by members of various government departments with something to hide. Federal prosecutors in Florida, US Customs, the Federal Reserve, the State Department, the Treasury and the Justice Department all contrived or conspired to obstruct outside investigations.

All the while, BCCI remained reputable enough for Texan oil company Harken Energy, of whom George W. Bush was then a director, to borrow $25 million from its joint ventures in 1987. Around this time, however, it was revealed that Manuel Noriega, the disgraced president of Panama, used the bank to launder drug money, and the Senate Subcommittee on Terrorism, Narcotics, and International Operations instigated Kerry's investigation. With assistance from New York district attorney Robert Morgenthau, the subcommittee uncovered a criminal enterprise of breathtaking scale and reach.

Friends in high places

BCCI, the report stated, boasted an impressive roster of allies who had a "material impact" on its ability to operate, including lawyers and government officials who lobbied to keep the bank afloat, diverted investigations and impugned the motives and integrity of investigators. Among those on the list were former secretary of defense Clark Clifford, former senators and congressmen Stuart Symington, John Culver, Mike Barnes, federal prosecutors, State Department, White House and Federal Reserve officials, and even Jimmy Carter and the Reverend Jesse Jackson. One former BCCI director, James Reynolds Bath, was part-owner of Arbusto Energy, which was co-founded by his National Guard friend, George W. Bush. Bath also purchased Houston Gulf Airport on behalf of Salem bin Laden, one of Osama bin Laden's cousins. Kerry was repeatedly pressured to close the investigation, not just by the Foreign Relations Committee but even – according to a *Washington Monthly* piece by David Sirota and Jonathan Baskin – by Jacqueline Kennedy Onassis.

In 1990, the Bush administration admonished, but didn't close down, BCCI over its involvement in money laundering (the net was closing in on BCCI as its covert CIA purpose to fund the Mujahedeen against the Soviets had been completed, according to LaRouche). That same year, a deal between a concerned Bank of England and major BCCI shareholder Abu Dhabi to prevent the collapse of BCCI withheld information from Federal Reserve investigators as well as BCCI's million depositors, most of whom were entirely innocent and ignorant of the bank's extraordinarily broad criminal activities. The deal, which *The BCCI Affair* said exhibited "extremely poor judgement" by the Bank of England, also allowed records and witnesses to escape from British government control to Abu Dhabi.

Dirty money for dirty deeds

Only in July 1991 were Kerry's committee, US and UK regulators and the Federal Reserve finally able to close BCCI down and indict the group for grand larceny, bribery and money laundering. By then, the bank had laundered money in most of the 73 countries in which it operated, using shell companies, banking secrecy laws and bribes to facilitate its operations. It had also worked with Iraqi arms dealer Sarkis Sarkenalian, with arms traffickers and terrorists in Syria and Palestine, and with drug traffickers in Syria, Afghanistan, Pakistan, Burma and Panama. BCCI was also involved (with the connivance of the CIA) in funnelling heroin trafficking proceeds to fund the Mujahedeen's fight against the Soviet Union in Afghanistan, and had financed and trafficked technology for Pakistan's nuclear programme. The bank had also been implicated in the 1980 "October Surprise" (see p.199), when the release from Iran of 52 American hostages just so happened to coincide with the inauguration of Ronald Reagan as US president – Reagan having defeated President Jimmy Carter largely over his failure to get the hostages released.

According to the Senate report, BCCI had also had its fingers in "prostitution, income tax evasion, smuggling, and illegal immigration", while the CIA later discovered that its customers included Osama bin Laden, members of his extended family, dozens of his comrades and companies thought to have funded Al Qaeda. The great irony, of course, was the extent to which the bank, for all its American friends in high places and collaboration with the CIA, was actively funding anti-Western groups. Indeed, its only limits, said the report, were in the "imagination of its officers and customers" – or at least a few of them. Shutting down BCCI closed off an extraordinary international conduit for dirty money to fund equally dirty deeds, but hundreds of thousands of innocent customers and employees suffered as a result.

SOURCES

Books

James R. Adams and Douglas Frantz A Full Service Bank: How BCCI Stole Billions Around the World (1991). Described as "penetrating" by *The New York Times*, this is a decent overview of the affair by two US journalists.

Jonathon Beaty and S.C. Gwynne The Outlaw Bank (1993) and **Peter Truell and Larry Gurwin False Profits: The Inside Story of BCCI** (1993) also attempt to reveal the inner workings of BCCI.

Websites

Ⓦ **www.fas.org/irp/congress/1992_rpt/bcci** Senator Kelly and Senator Brown's draft 1992 report to the US Senate, *The BCCI Affair*.

Ⓦ **www.larouchepub.com/other/1995/2241_bcci.html** "The real story of the BCCI" according to Lyndon LaRouche's magazine *Executive Intelligence Review* (October 13, 1995).

Ⓦ **www.washingtonmonthly.com/features/2004/0409.sirota.html** "Follow the Money", David Sirota and Jonathan Baskin's *Washington Monthly* article (September 2004).

Perpetual war on perpetual energy

The industrialized world needs energy, energy for which many people expect to be paid a lot of money. But what if energy suddenly became free, or available in quantities boundless enough to threaten one of the big suppliers? Perhaps conspiracies really are afoot to ensure that the world remains dependent upon the filthiest, most expensive and most violently sought-after fuels.

Tesla

Croatian electrical genius Nikolas Tesla (see p.301) registered numerous patents for free energy devices, power sources, propulsion systems and weapons from the 1890s until his death in 1943. Most of them, and the "free energy" sources in particular, failed to attract investors; it's said that J.P. Morgan and John D. Rockefeller sought to suppress any such threats to their own industries. According to conspiracy lore – and lore it is – Tesla invented an on-board electro-propulsion system, using the globally present force of "ether", which was powerful enough to propel machines such as flying saucers with incredible speeds and manoeuvrability.

By this account, the Nazis developed practical applications of Tesla's system during the 1930s. The US managed to keep abreast of these developments through German scientist Werner von Braun, who supposedly secretly visited the US in the late 1930s (he certainly came to the US at the end of World War II). The thousands of flying saucer sightings since then, it's claimed, are real enough, but UFOs are built and flown, not by aliens, but by earthlings.

American physicist and author William Lyne, who has written extensively on the alleged suppression of Tesla's work, describes in baffling scientific detail a power source that's small and cheap enough for everyone to have one, but a world of individuals zipping around in personal flying saucers would be a world without roads or borders. (It would also be a world with a lot of flying saucer crashes, but hey...) This would destroy the oil and automobile industries – among others – in one fell swoop, and also fatally damage the ability of governments to control their own people. The CIA and NASA have, therefore, quashed any dissemination of the technology, using tactics developed by the Gestapo's Reichssicherheitshauptamt (Reich Security Central Office).

To Lyne, the scale of the conspiracy is immense. Academics and universities suppress Tesla's ideas, and instead propagate conventional theories in physics and engineering that sustain the industrial status quo, with the media in on this "misinformational conspiracy" to keep Tesla's plans quiet. Most of the talk of aliens and extraterrestrials is just a ploy to distract the public, while UFO-logists and paranormalists are government agents, coming up with ludicrous ideas for other government agents posing as sceptics to shoot down. Anyone who really does have an interest or belief in UFOs, let alone actual proof, can thus then be written off as a crank.

Lyne claims that another power source, developed by American physicist Thomas Townsend Brown in 1921, has also been suppressed. Brown discovered what was later called the Biefeld-Brown effect, in which a vacuum tube with two asymmetrical electrodes produces an x-ray-based force when powered with high voltage. During his career in the military, Brown made flying discs up to seventy centimetres wide, powered by this strange force. He believed that this power source could be what was propelling UFOs, and Lyne and others say he was right. However, if – as Lyne argues – the information is out there, and certain people not only know about it, but have the know-how to build such a machine, then why haven't they? Such super-fast craft couldn't be intercepted as they flew over the world's cities, showing everyone on the planet what they'd been missing.

Garabed's hoax

In contrast to the alleged conspiracies to keep Tesla and Brown down, Armenian-born Garabed T.K. Giragossian's "free energy generator" was a conspiracy to wind the US government up. Garabed claimed in 1917 that his generator was a machine that would "perform the miracles of the Arabian Nights" and "revolutionize the world's affairs and lift civilization to a higher plane".

A machine born of twenty years of toil and no engineering knowledge whatsoever, it was "intuition" alone that inspired Garabed to create in his little Massachussetts shop an engine that was run by a "mysterious and hitherto unknown force ... waiting to be utilized". He declared that a 48-acre field could provide enough free power "to drive all the industrial machinery in the world", as well as locomotives, ships and even ungainly aircraft. Without any proof of this whatsoever, Garabed somehow persuaded the US government of the feasibility of his project.

In 1918, President Woodrow Wilson signed a bill from the House and Senate which offered Garabed protection from conspiracy, on condition that he "[could] demonstrate the practicability of his discovery" to a panel of scientists. And what was this incredible energy source finally revealed to be? A giant flywheel, which charged up over several minutes and then spat back out its kinetic energy in a second. The project was swiftly killed off.

Unseen powers

The Japanese Mafia, or Yakuza, is said to have kept at least three Japanese-developed "overunity systems" off the market. An overunity magnetic motor not only powers itself but also produces excess energy to power other loads, achieving the Holy Grail of perpetual energy. Japanese engineer Tuero Kawai reportedly invented a system that was confirmed to be workable by Hitachi engineers, and in 1996 a US company in Huntsville agreed to develop and market his engine globally. Within a day of the agreement, however, Yakuza gangsters arrived and scared Kawai's men into scrapping the deal.

In 1972, Texan bulldozer-operator Richard Clem unveiled a vegetable-oil turbine capable of driving a car 115,000 miles on eight gallons of chip fat. As a local newspaper reported, "that might come as a shock to Detroit and the petroleum industry". Ford Motors objected when Clem installed his prototype engine in his Ford Falcon, which should have tipped him off to the possibility that some people wouldn't take kindly to his invention. Soon enough, some big men arrived and told Clem that his next drive would be in the back of a hearse if he didn't ditch his fat-fuelled engine. He died of a heart attack shortly afterwards, and only the efforts of his daughter have kept the story alive.

Elsbett

The fate of Clem's engine bears an uncanny resemblance to the rumours that surround the Elsbett diesel engine. This was patented in 1977 by German engineering company Elsbett AG, to run on either fossil diesel fuel or biodiesel – vegetable oil. (For that matter, the first diesel engine of all, patented by Rudolf Diesel in 1893, ran on peanut oil.) Most diesel engines run exclusively on one or the other, and can be converted from one to the other, but the Elsbett engine can run on both. Biodiesel is carbon neutral and a fraction of the price of fossil diesel, so why isn't the world powered by Elsbetts? Because, the theory goes, oil companies who don't want their fossil-fuel monopoly upset by biofuel vehicles have run the Elsbett into the ground with unfair practices.

Elsbett's website charts the glittering career of engineer Ludwig Elsbett and his company, including over four hundred patents filed, countless corporate and government awards, engineering partnerships with Volkswagen and Scania, design licences from Malaysia to Russia and a $6 million Citibank-backed conversion project in Brazil. Not bad for a firm with six employees, and no mention of any conspiracy. Admittedly, few companies would promote themselves with stories some might consider to be paranoid fantasy. But amid all the self-promotion and success, Elsbett AG's site cryptically mentions one fact that the site says pertains to the date Herr Elsbett was born: "On September 29th, 1913, Rudolf Diesel disappears overboard from a ferry between Antwerp and Harwich" – a startlingly incongruous mention.

Elsewhere, *Forbes* magazine speculated that Diesel was "probably bumped off by the German secret service", as he was heading for talks with the British Admiralty, even though his engine was "key to the new German weapon, the U-boat". Pondering alternatives to petrol, Forbes asked: "Is there a message here for us today? … Just remember what happened to Rudolph when he tried to share his knowledge." So what might Elsbett be referring to?

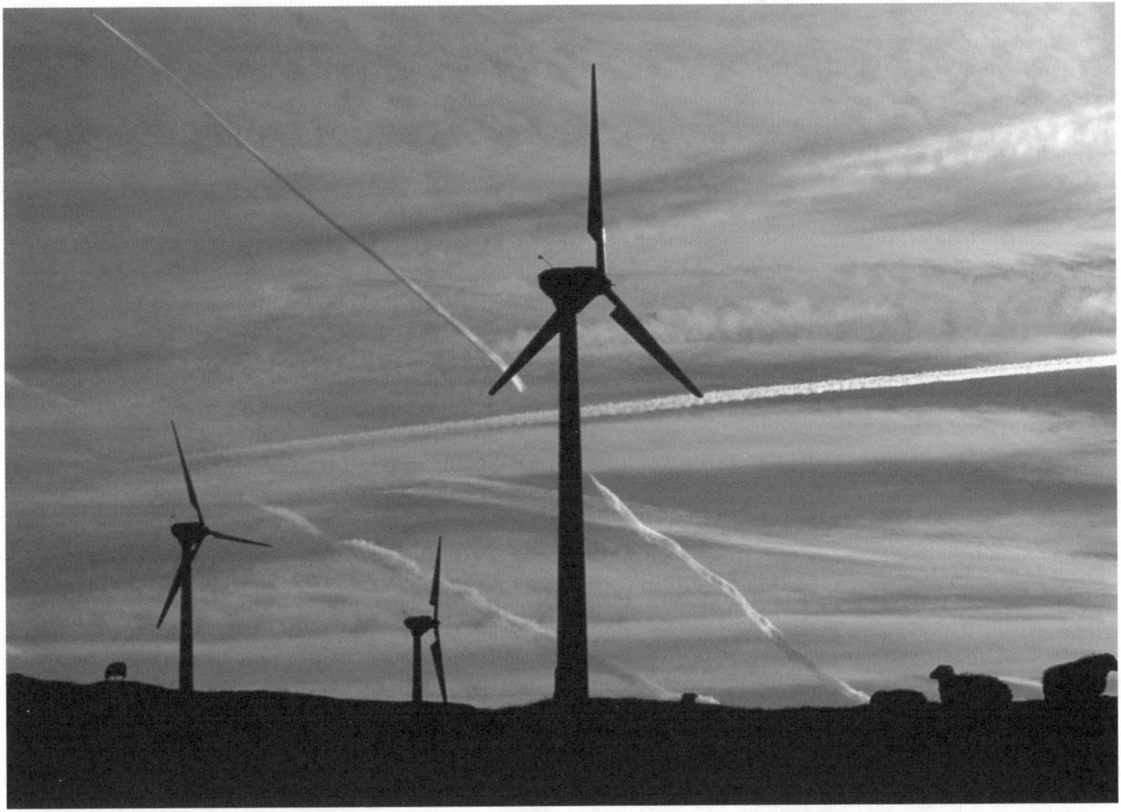

Wind farms: an alternative, green energy source – perhaps not as glamorous as Tesla's ether-powered flying saucers.

Killing the electric car

Industry insiders and deniers can, and have, always argued that these wonderful new gizmos and power sources do not fly commercially because, in reality, they just don't work as well as the fossil fuel alternatives. Cars have long been a case in point; each year sees a new concept car being rolled out, running on solar power, batteries, fuel-cells and the like. But the accompanying promise from the designers that they are about to revolutionize the way cars are powered always seems to remain a distant dream.

The 2006 documentary *Who Killed the Electric Car?* looked into General Motors' electric vehicle, the EV1, which was sold in California in the mid-1990s after the state passed a zero-emissions mandate. The oil companies did not want to lose their monopoly of the transport industry, and they bought patents so they could prevent modern batteries being used in electric cars. The manufacturers did not want to sell vehicles that would be less profitable because they would require fewer repairs than petrol-powered cars. The film even suggested that General Motors attempted to kill off their own product. They cited negative consumer interest in a weird car with a limited driving range – but that lack of interest was allegedly partly due to GM's own less-than-lukewarm efforts to drum up interest. Citing the EV1's lack of success as evidence, the oil companies and manufacturers lobbied the Californian government – and managed to get the zero-emissions mandate reversed. And EV1 drivers were compelled to return their cars to GM for crushing.

Powering on

Since then, hybrid cars, which use both petrol and electric power sources, have become much more widespread in the US (although they are largely imported from Japan). This trend will likely continue as oil prices hit historic highs, due to global oil production beginning to peak, while demand also increases, not just in industrialized countries, but also in East Asia (led by China), India and Latin America, which are all industrializing at a staggering rate. These long-term factors, already in evidence, are adding to the oil-price highs stemming from the Iraq War (see p.417), discord in Iran and related Middle East turmoil.

These economic and political pressures, combined with increased fears about climate change (see p.305), have created a great green bandwagon and driven the development of alternative energy sources, such as biofuels and solar, wind and tidal power, which had previously been considered too expensive in comparison to oil. Ironically, from that perspective, the actions of George W. Bush's White House – chided and lambasted as the most anti-environmental, pro-fossil fuel administration ever – could ultimately combine to become the harbinger of the greatest shift to "green" energy in history.

Despite the tales of a "conspiracy" against the Elsbett engineering company, biodiesel is starting to take off in the US, but in the very sector that actually makes the stuff, and stands to make a fortune from it – farming (where it is making dramatic growth as a fuel for farm machinery). Biodiesel is commercially available in most oilseed-producing American states – the "red" farm states that always vote Republican – and the Republican Party has moved to make biofuel production even more profitable through numerous tax credits. Between 1997 and 2002, biofuel output increased 35-fold to 3.5 million gallons, and it is expected to hit 1 billion gallons by 2010.

Meanwhile, as *Forbes* points out, forty percent of cars in Western Europe run on diesel, which suggests a huge potential market for carbon-neutral conversion. In the UK, a handful of car owners seeking to evade fuel duty by filling up at chip shops has been replaced by great corporate fleets, such as Tesco, switching to biofuel-powered vehicles. It may not be quite as glamorous or thrilling as "ether" power, x-ray propulsion or a perpetual energy motor, but biofuels could become a significant source of energy.

The question now being asked is whether that would be a good thing or a bad thing. Would a rise in biofuels really lead to the reduced use of other fossil fuels? Or any reduction in carbon-dioxide emissions (not least because farming is one of the largest CO2-producing industries, and biofuels simply recycle carbon, they don't absorb it)? Biofuels are mostly being pushed as mixers with petroleum, principally to allow the established oil-based infrastructure and investments to remain intact. And, in the longer term, to sustain the market so that the high-cost extraction of oil from areas such as the Arctic wilderness and Siberian forests becomes economically viable.

Additionally, in 2007, the Bush administration signed a major trade deal with South America to encourage their Latin neighbours to farm maize, soya, rapeseed and sugar-beet for biofuel. The deal is intended to reduce US reliance on unstable Middle Eastern oil supplies and to lessen its dependence on Venezuelan oil (thereby also curtailing the latter country's efforts to fund its neighbours in any anti-American stance). However, it also condemns huge swathes of the world's forests to destruction for farmland and places great pressure on global food production (which is already threatened by climate change and its own fossil-fuel dependence) because it's fuel that's being farmed, not food. The *Financial Times* has already issued warnings about markets linking bread prices with petrol prices, but that's another story.

SOURCES

Books

William Lyne Occult Ether Physics (1998). An outline in sometimes mind-numbing detail of the theories and mathematical problems that lie behind perpetual energy, together with some interesting pages of conspiracy insight.

Films

Chris Paine Who Killed the Electric Car? (2006). A pithy film that seeks to find out why the 1996 EV1 – a car with speed, range and reliability that was loved by its few drivers – failed to take off. Was it made to fail?

Websites

Ⓦ **www.hsv.com** "The Master Principle of Overunity and the Japanese Overunity Engines: A New Pearl Harbor?" by Tom Bearden, who specializes in micro-energy sources, from the *Virtual Times*, January 1996.

Ⓦ **keelynet.com/energy/clem1.htm** The somewhat apocryphally-told story of Richard Clem and his vegetable-oil engine.

Ⓦ **www.nuenergy.org/alt/garabed_fraud.htm** Garabed T.K. Giragossia's "free-energy generator" hoax.

The eternal light bulb and the Phoebus cartel

The suppression of an "eternal" light bulb that never burns out is one of the most widely held conspiracy theories. The fact is that light bulbs are pretty low-tech devices, involving a strip of metal (the filament), sitting in an airtight glass bulb filled with an inert gas, being heated to glowing point by electric current. But while millions of bulbs are made every day, your average household 100-watt shines for only one thousand hours. Surely something so simple could be made in such a way that it lasted forever? The problem, of course, is that an "eternal bulb" would mean that people only need to buy light bulbs once, putting light-bulb manufacturers out of business. So, the theory runs, the manufacturers have bought up and sat on all the world's patents for eternal bulbs to protect their profits.

The Phoebus cartel

Unless someone delves into the vaults of the world's light-bulb makers and finds eternal bulb designs in a file marked "suppressed", the theory will remain just that – a theory. There is, however, a kernel of truth to the thinking behind it. The US did, in fact, have a light-bulb price-fixing cartel from the late nineteenth century, when six light-bulb makers formed the Incandescent Electric Lamp Manufacturers, whose purpose, according to social scientist Patrick Gaughen, was to "fix prices, set output, and divide markets".

The biggest manufacturer, General Electric, shared the Edison patent for light bulbs with its main competitor, Westinghouse Electric Company, and agreed with light manufacturing equipment makers to buy their goods and charge GE's competitors inflated prices. GE soon bought out the other association members and eighteen rivals, and controlled eighty percent of US light-bulb output before moving on to Europe.

There, the short-lived Internationale Glühlampen Preisvereinigung price-fixing cartel collapsed in 1924, but some chicanery from International GE led to its resurrection as the Swiss-based Phoebus SA Compagnie Industrielle cartel, with leading bulb-makers such as Osram, Philips, Tungsram and Associated Electrical Industries. Phoebus divided the world into three markets, and companies dominating particular regions colluded to fix prices locally. Members also had sales quotas depending on their usual market share, and profits were redistributed to companies that hadn't met their quotas, skewing production to quotas instead of demand. As Westinghouse observed in 1937: "The goal … is to make as much money as possible out of those units we are permitted to sell. It is much more advantageous for us to make a profit of 5 cents per unit on 4,000,000 units than 2.5 cents on 8,000,000 units."

Although the eternal light bulb had yet to be invented, Phoebus also had industry-wide "quality control standards". One GE engineer cast light on what this meant in 1932: "The battery manufacturers went part way with us and accepted lamps of two battery lives instead of three … We have been continuing our studies and efforts to bring about the use of one battery life lamps … [which] would result in increasing our flashlight business approximately sixty percent." So the industry conspired to make shoddier bulbs with shorter lives, increasing sales and turnover. GE's participation in Phoebus ended in 1939, when the Justice Department broke the company's domestic US monopoly in the US vs General Electric case. The Phoebus cartel subsequently played a significant role in the plot of Thomas Pynchon's novel *Gravity's Rainbow* (1973).

The upshot

Could an eternal bulb be built? Subjected to continual, random cycles of being heated to several hundred degrees centigrade in a split second, the simple structure of blown glass and metal would most probably always break in the end. What's not clear is how much the current design and materials would need to be improved to create light bulbs that last significantly longer without being substantially more expensive. However, it is possible to extend the lifespan of incandescent light bulbs. A five percent cut in operating voltage, reducing wattage by a fifth, can double a bulb's life. So, a 100-watt, 1000-hour bulb lit at half voltage could glow on for nearly 7000 years – albeit with a dingy 15-watt glow. Light bulbs may be made to blow rather than glow to the end of time, but a little TLC can help them shine long and fine.

Yet, all this now seems to be becoming a moot point, as conventional light bulbs are being phased out in favour of longer-life, lower-watt, energy-efficient bulbs. Although more expensive than their incandescent predecessors, energy-efficient bulbs have become much cheaper in recent years – and government initiatives are keen to remind consumers that they are more affordable in the long term because they use less electricity and last much longer. In 2007, the UK instigated a voluntary agreement for all shops to stop selling conventional bulbs by the end of 2011, as part of a broader EU initiative to make low-energy bulbs the norm. Meanwhile, the Australian government went one step further, saying it would prohibit the sale of incandescent bulbs after 2010. Yet, not long after, reports began to surface stating that low-energy bulbs can blow up, leak mercury, cause migraines – perhaps, the light-bulb conspiracy isn't quite dead and buried after all…

SOURCES

Books

Patrick Gaughen **Structural Inefficiency in the Early Twentieth Century: Studies in the Aluminium and Incandescent Lamp Markets** (1998). Despite its dreary academic title, this book sheds some interesting light on a murky episode from Europe and America's industrial past.

Fluoride

Since the mid-twentieth century, putting fluoride into city water supplies, the process of fluoridation, has been a policy proposed by countless municipal governments and national health authorities. It's said to be good for teeth because it helps to prevent decay. But some people aren't convinced, claiming that fluoride is bad for bones, human reproduction and overall health. Others have claimed that fluoridation is a Nazi-Communist-CIA, malevolent government or industry conspiracy, leading to counterclaims that the anti-fluoridation lobby is a bunch of crackpots and right-wing loonies. Yet, in the US, in the six decades that fluoridation has been carried out, sixty percent of voters have been against it and less than two thirds of America's cities have fluoridated water – which suggests either a frightening number of crackpots, or that the story is more complicated than commonly presented.

The obstructers of progress

"Fluoridation is the most monstrously conceived and dangerous Communist plot we have ever had to face! … A foreign substance is introduced into our precious bodily fluids without the knowledge of the individual – certainly without any choice. That's the way your hard-core commie works!" So said foaming nut General Jack D. Ripper from Stanley Kubrick's 1964 satire, *Dr Strangelove*.

Forty years later, San Diego's civic authorities fluoridated the city's water only after California governor Arnold Schwarzenegger indemnified them from prosecution for it. San Diego's inhabitants previously voted against fluoridation "amid conspiracy theories about plots to poison the water", said the *San Diego Union Tribune*, which also reported without concern that fluoridation was backed by a "local fluoridation coalition and the California Dental Association offering a large grant to San Diego". When fluoridation cropped up in local elections in Connersville, Indiana, in November 1999, CNN chortled: "It's a fluoride conspiracy … Conspiracy theories are flying [while] teeth are decaying."

The American Dental Association claims to have "continuously endorsed the fluoridation of community water supplies". US public health agencies, including the Environment Protection Agency, the American Medical Association and the National Academy of Sciences, all endorse the National Research Council fluoride review "Health Effects of Ingested Fluoride", which is cited by doctors, dentists, researchers and public health officials, and which underlines the safety of fluoride and the benefits of fluoridation.

For Phoebe Courtney, author of the 1971 *How Dangerous is Fluoridation?* pamphlet, fluoridation was a ploy by the confectionery industry to allow children to "eat all the candy and sweets they want". This was despite, according to Courtney, fluoride's ability to kill rats and cockroaches and eat through car engine pipes. As such, fluoridation was also a Communist plot, Courtney said: "Anyone who promotes and supports fluoridation can be considered a 'radical'". When fluoridation came to Wichita, Kansas, in the mid-1970s, leaflets went out entitled "Fluoridation: A Tool of the Communists", which asked: "Shall we give the communists the machinery and the materials to destroy us by simply opening a valve in our water supply?"

Communists like fluoridation, suggests Ian Stephen in *Nexus* magazine, because "repeated doses of infinitesimal amounts of fluoride will in time reduce an individual's power to resist domination by slowly poisoning and narcotising a certain area of the brain, making him submissive to the will of those who wish to govern him". This effect, he claims, also attracted the Nazis, who used fluoridation to subdue the populations of the countries they

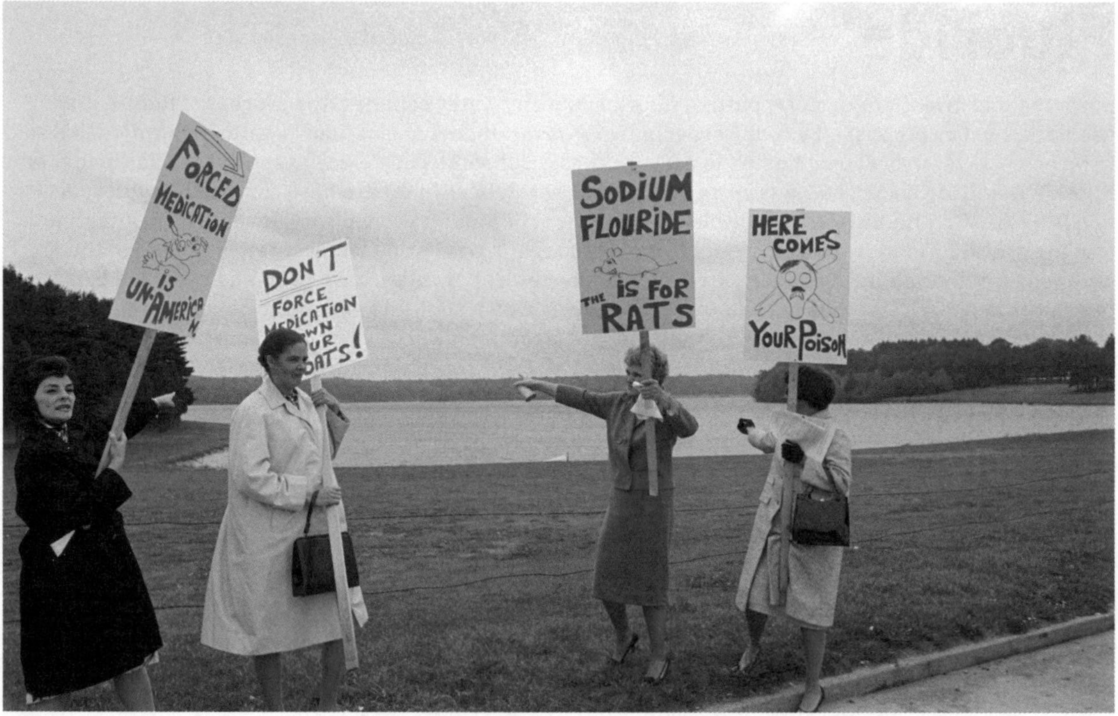

Protestors oppose the "poisoning" of New York City's water supply with fluoride in 1965.

occupied during World War II; it also had the added bonus of sterilizing people, preventing inferiors and undesirables from reproducing. According to some theorists on the Internet, the American Aluminum Company (Alcoa), which produced kilotons of sodium fluoride as a by-product of aluminium manufacture, transferred technology to Germany's IG Farben chemical company, whose Frankfurt headquarters miraculously escaped damage from Allied bombing in World War II. After the war, the US Army and the CIA's MK-ULTRA programme (see p.210) showed much interest in behaviour-controlling drugs, and brought over pro-fluoridation Nazi scientists to pick their brains.

Would the CIA's interest in mind and population control extend to fluoridating the country's water supplies? Why would the lawmakers on Capitol Hill drink only unfluoridated, bottled water? The person who should be asked is Dr George Estabrooks, apparently a one-time adviser to the US government on hypnotism, who later chaired the Department of Psychology at Colgate University (yes, Colgate, the world's biggest producer of fluoridated toothpaste). Furbies, electronic bear-like toys that mutter to their child owners, have also been linked to the mind-control plot, standing accused of being tools for indoctrination by the State. One theory has it that the kids of US government employees have been banned from owning Furbies (as well as from drinking fluoridated water) to prevent them from succumbing to their subliminal messages.

Nuclear teeth

Some conspiracists allege there may have been an even more poisonous plot afoot. In a 1998 *Nexus* magazine article, medical journalist Joel Griffiths and BBC and ABC reporter Chris Bryson told the history of how fluoride had been promoted as a "safe" by-product that was of great benefit to the nation's dental health. The allegation is that the evidence for fluoride's dental benefits came from that unlikely source of good health, the atom bomb programme and a certain "Program F".

The story goes that, in 1944, industrial company E.I. DuPont de Nemours in New Jersey was producing bomb-grade uranium for the Manhattan Project. A major by-product of the process was the pollutant fluoride, which was producing death and disease on nearby farms. The farmers set out to sue DuPont, but this could have closed the company down and meddled with America's destiny of A-bombing its way to global power. No way, said DuPont, the Food and Drug Administration, Agriculture and Justice departments, the Manhattan Project, the US Army and the War Department. While the US Army's Chemical Warfare Service undertook fluoride testing around New Jersey, Manhattan Project directors convinced the farmers, including those suffering from fluoride poisoning, of the government's good faith, before the government spiked their lawsuit by concealing how much fluoride DuPont had let fly: "Disclosure would be injurious to the military security of the United States."

Meanwhile "Program F", set up under Dr Harold Hodge, was spreading the word that fluoride was great, benefiting children's bones and teeth. The information was sourced from the Manhattan Project's fluoride toxicology studies and from a Rochester University study of the toxicity of uranium, plutonium and fluoride – both of which were chaired by Hodge. "Program F" was further supported by evidence from a ten-year study (cut short halfway) into fluoridated water around Newburgh. This was used by the Manhattan Project to fight litigation, and was chaired by none other than… Harold Hodge. Documents pertaining to "Program F", the DuPont trial and others have since "left" national archives.

From industrial pollutant to a world of healthy teeth

Or perhaps it wasn't uranium after all, but aluminium. In 1992, *Covert Action Quarterly* asked "Fluoride: Commie Plot or Capitalist Ploy?" and claimed that fluoridation was simply the aluminium industry dumping toxic fluoride waste at a profit (a view also supported by the UK's National Pure Water Association). Who was it, in 1939, that reported an "amazing sodium fluoride/dental caries prevention discovery" (in rats, at least)? The Mellon Institute. What was the Mellon Institute? Like the Rockefeller, Carnegie and Ford Foundations, which all allegedly investigated population control methods, it was a "philanthropic" research body. Who had founded the Mellon Institute? The Mellon family, who happened to have made their millions as founders of Alcoa, the American Aluminum Company.

And that's not all. In 1941, the United States Public Health Service licensed fluoride dumping in rivers. Who headed the Service at that time? One-time treasury secretary Andrew Mellon (yes, from the same family). Who, when he succeeded Mellon, had the water of 87 cities fluoridated? Oscar Ewing, who also happened to be a lawyer for… Alcoa. The Water Works Association, meanwhile, likened fluoride's toxicity to that of lead and arsenic. In 1951, the American Dental Association reported that dental fluorosis, an unsightly mottling and cracking of teeth enamel caused by excessive fluoride intake, required extensive and expensive correction work. (While, at the same time, Procter & Gamble were comparing Crest toothpaste with the discovery of penicillin.)

A setback was hydrogen fluoride gas being linked to the 1947 Donora Death Fog in Pennsylvania, which killed 17 people and left 6000 ill, and to London's Great Smog of 1952, which killed thousands. So, in US cities where industrial fluoride pollution was found (including Pittsburgh, Chicago, Philadelphia, San Francisco and Oklahoma City), the US Public Health Service backed water fluoridation, spinning "pollution" into "health benefit" – with the aluminium industry supplying the medicine. After the abandonment of a social medicine programme, Oscar Ewing got Congress and the American Medical Association to support nationwide fluoridation, which became a global issue in 1953 when it was pushed for by a World Health Organization committee. Who was the US representative on the WHO committee? Blow me if it wasn't our old friend, Dr Harold Hodge.

Fluoride isn't that safe

Both accounts of the hidden history of the push for fluoridation are pretty dark tales of industrial companies seeking to spin their toxic dumping into a profitable health benefit. Yet the UK's National Pure Water Association, like the New Zealand Pure Water Association and Fluoride Action Network, has multitudes of links to esteemed publications casting doubts on the veracity of fluoridation's healthiness, and lists of well-qualified supporters don't shout "wild-eyed paranoiacs".

In the UK, water fluoridation was first implemented, in the Midlands, in the 1950s. But by 2008, only ten percent of the country's population (around six million people), had access to fluoridated water. In 1995, Yorkshire Water refused to fluoridate, not because they agreed with the opposition, but because, in their own words, they "know which way public opinion rides". Welsh Water has also refrained, calling fluoride a "toxic and potent chemical", as has UK Water. In 2002, the Medical Research Council reported to the Department of Health that while fluoridation benefited teeth, "much of the current evidence on the benefits of fluoride comes from research conducted several decades ago ... Little high quality research had been carried out on the broader question of fluoride and health".

In the face of that report, and others, the UK government mandated the fluoridation of all water in the UK in 2003. However, five years later, the government was still adopting a very piecemeal approach to "enforcement", presumably not seeking to stoke wholesale opposition. In February 2008, Health Secretary Alan Johnson called for all England's water to be fluoridated – a similar pledge by the Scottish Parliament had already aroused stiff opposition, as had suggestions brought before the Welsh National Assembly. More piecemeal attempts to fluoridate water supplies in Northern Ireland, the Isle of Man, Bedfordshire, Cumbria and beyond met with opposition from the public, press, local councils and even the water companies. UK opponents have cited the practice as the cause of illnesses as diverse as cancer and Down's Syndrome – not to mention its being in contravention of the basic human right to refuse compelled medication.

The war continues

In 1971, the year of Phoebe Courtney's diatribe, US Green Party spokesman Ralph Nader said: "There are better ways to cut down the dental caries in the subject population [namely, children] without exposing eighty or so percent of the population to it." Any new elements should be introduced into the ecology only with "awfully good reason", a position he still supported in 2000. Environmental group the Sierra Club is also concerned by fluoridation. The US National Research Council has said that up to eighty percent of children may have dental fluorosis. Some doctors have paralleled the symptoms of "chronic fatigue syndrome" – fatigue, memory loss, mental dullness and apathy – with those of fluoride poisoning. A 1989 National Toxicology Program study for the Environmental Protection Agency (EPA) linked fluoride with bone and liver cancer, but when senior adviser William L. Marcus exposed this, he was fired. A court ruled that he had "publicly questioned and opposed EPA's fluoride policy".

The John Birch Society (JBS, see p.188), deemed by some to be a hotbed of foaming anti-communist sentiment and placed by others as behind the paranoid Wichita leaflet campaign, has complained that mass fluoridation is simply an involuntary mass medical treatment that violates individual rights. In 1992, the JBS-affiliated magazine *The New American* railed against fluoride as a "highly toxic and probably carcinogenic substance". And while the report "Health Effects of Ingested Fluoride" found that, overall, current concentrations of fluoride do not have clear effects on cancer rates or birth rates, it also noted that fluoride accumulates in bones and that more research is needed. As for the effect on teeth, the report states that there has been an increase in the prevalence of dental fluorosis. So, in the US at least, the process of fluoridation inexorably grinds on, but on a case-by-case basis, because – although the detractors of fluoridation may be portrayed as cranky and mad – a lot of people believe them.

SOURCES

Articles

Ian E. Stephen "Fluoridation: Mind Control of the Masses?" (*Nexus* magazine, Aug/Sept 1995). Why would there suddenly be such global concern about having bright and shiny teeth? This article suggests the more sinister reasons for mass fluoridation.

Websites

Ⓦ **www.aislingmagazine.com/aislingmagazine/articles/TAM26/Fluoridation.html** A view from Down Under, from *Australian Fluoridation News*.

Ⓦ **www.fluoridealert.org** Website of the Fluoride Action Network, a sober, well-sourced site about what the problem with fluoride is.

Ⓦ **fluoride.oralhealth.org/papers/1999/cnncom110199.html** *San Diego Union Tribune* article that sums up the view that opposition to fluoride is a concern of the paranoid, even today.

Ⓦ **www.npwa.freeserve.co.uk/** The National Pure Water Association's critique of fluoridation: "They poison children, don't they?"

Cyberdisease and Y2K

A widely held conspiracy theory among computer users – more an entrenched belief, really – is that software companies deliberately build in obsolescence and invent problems simply so they can make a profit out of "solving" them. Thus while computer viruses may wipe billions of dollars from the global economy, they also generate huge revenues for PC fixers and virus-killing programs. Is the computer industry simply a large-scale version of the old scam in which glaziers smashed windows by night and fixed them by day? Major software firms make a show out of employing former hackers – even Bill Gates started out as a hacker – to test out their products, so why don't these poachers-turned-gamekeepers do it better, and actually make software bugproof before it's sold? The prime example of the artificial creation of a digital disease – or at the very least, of an overhyped panic – has to be Y2K. Remember the so-called "Millennium Bug", which threatened to take down every computer on the planet on the stroke of midnight, December 31, 1999?

Where Y2K came from

The first computers were simple things with limited memories. As a shortcut to maximize the space available for data, many used only the last two digits of a year to store the date: thus the year 1999 was stored as "99". As 2000 AD approached, the fear began to grow that computers with this system would not be able to distinguish between 2000 and 1900, and that the world would be swept away by a tsunami of digital nervous breakdowns. The havoc that this

"Y2K" bug might wreak was thought to be stupendous: it might cause the international banking system to crash; airplanes to fall out of the sky; power stations to blow up; and thousands of nuclear missiles to launch themselves spontaneously.

An International Y2K Co-operation Centre (IY2KCC) was set up, supported by the UN and 190 countries. The estimated cost of preparing for Y2K, including spending on new software, hardware and debugging facilities, came to $250–600 billion. As the great day grew nearer, governments around the world announced that they had cleansed their networks of Y2K, and were ready for the new millennium.

An impending apocalypse

In October 1998, the BBC reported that thousands of Americans were stockpiling food, weapons and ammunition to resist the coming of the New World Order (see p.141), which they believed would be ushered in by the anarchy caused by the collapse of the global computer system. UN troops were said to be planning to move in to disarm the US population and restore order. Various state militias were up for the fight.

Meanwhile, talk in Internet chatrooms described Y2K as an Illuminati plot (see p.93) to create mass chaos and make people beg for a police state. Joseph Farah, the editor of *WorldNetDaily*, detected the hand of the White House at work. In the John Birch Society magazine, *New American*, he asked: "Much like the Reichstag fire, could the Millennium Bug provide an ambitious president with an opportunity to seize dictatorial powers?"

Bible literalists and Christian fundamentalists had a field day with Y2K. In 1993, twenty percent of Americans are said to have believed that the Second Coming would occur around 2000. Y2K was written up in lurid apocalyptic terms in books such as Gary North's *Y2K and Millennial Pinball* and Michael Hyatt's *The Millennium Bug: How to Survive the Coming Chaos*.

According to the website Y2K Storm Watch, set up to monitor the storm of activity to deal with Y2K as much as any actual damage wrought by the glitch, 11.59pm on December 31, 1999 marked a unique moment in world history. For once, the mysterious step into the unknown was enough to cause "New Age Prophets, Fundamentalist Christians and Agnostic Computer Geeks to actually agree on something!"

World Wide Windup

The trouble is, nothing happened. In the US, the world's most computer-dependent nation, a handful of power stations had to reset their clocks, a few hundred slot machines seized up, and a customer in a New York video store was billed $91,000 because the store computer thought his video had been loaned out since 1900. Hardly Armageddon. If the problem of omitting "00" had been known about since the dawn of computing, why, conspiracy theorists wonder, was nothing done about it before? And why had the bug continued to be left in millions upon millions of new machines? Perhaps it was because that's the way the computer industry wanted it: designers and manufacturers knew that the bug would generate an avalanche of profits at the turn of the century.

Hysteria or just hysterical?

John Koskinen, who was in charge of the Y2K debugging effort in the US, claimed that the campaign was a victim of its own success. The US government spent $8 billion on the problem, including a $50 million command centre for Koskinen's team. But was the problem overstated? Koskinen dismissed such speculation: "Corporations don't naively spend hundreds of millions of dollars."

According to top conspiracist Jim Marrs, Y2K did have one notable effect. As Marrs reported, "congressional testimony [in 1999] revealed that none of our oil refineries would be ready for the Y2K rollover", and indeed a worldwide series of refinery fires, explosions and broken pipelines brought production down and forced prices up. The subsequent and predictable rise in oil prices boosted the oilmen's profits several times over (most OPEC countries had ordered US-made computer chips en masse).

World Wide Waste of money

In the event, notwithstanding a few billion hangovers, the world of January 1, 2000, was much the same as that of December 31, 1999. Had Y2K been cooked up by spotty, bespectacled computer geeks as a desperate ploy to make themselves appear heroic? By some accounts, the global campaign on Y2K was a success story on the scale of the eradication of smallpox. By others, the world fell victim to its own propensity for hysteria, or rather, its propensity to believe hysteria whipped up by the very industry that stood to profit the most from it. Over half a trillion dollars was spent on Y2K that could have gone on Millennium celebrations – just ask the Y2K de-programmers how much champagne that can buy.

SOURCES

Books

Sherman S. Smith Lie-2K: Why the Alleged End-of-the-World Year-2000 Computer Crisis is Really Just a Hoax (1999). And doesn't it all seem so obvious now?

ECHELON and the World Wide Web

The World Wide Web is a wonderful tool, linking tens of millions of computers and enabling the citizens of the world to communicate – for commercial, academic, scientific, political, military or criminal reasons, or just plain fun. However, the Web was developed by the US military, who (together with all governments) remain very much "online" and interested in what we do on the Web and say in our emails.

Dark origins

The phenomenal growth of the Web during the 1990s served to obscure its murky origins. It was created on the back of the pre-existing Internet (short for "interconnected network") developed from the 1960s onwards by the US Department of Defense, which wanted a communications network impervious to nuclear attack. The DoD's Advanced Research Projects Agency Net (ARPANet) connected university and military computers and sites, before being divided in 1981 into ARPANet and a purely military network.

Alarmed especially by the involvement of every conspiracy theorist's favourite multinational, the RAND Corporation, more than one writer has put forward – on the Web, naturally – the view that the World Wide Web is a prime component of the "Technopoly Conspiracy". That, according to writer Neil Postman, is a society in which "culture seeks its authorization in technology, finds its satisfactions in technology, and takes its orders from technology". Those who thrive in a technopoly exalt technological achievement above all else, while society itself becomes technology's slave.

Operation Prometheus, and the truth about ECHELON

The military roots of the Web have prompted some to allege that the Google and Yahoo! search engines are both spin-offs of a National Security Agency (NSA) plan, Operation Prometheus. Supposedly, this monitors online activity to detect any user or data that could harm the US, and tracks the details of users who enter particular "keywords" in their searches. The theory continues that search engines deliberately ignore certain sites so that users will never see them,

BAR CODES

Bar codes – those odd little grilles of bars and numbers on the sides of shop goods – were, the masses are led to believe, invented for the purpose of price scanning and stock control. When a product is passed over the trapezium of red laser lights at the checkout, the price is registered and a computer takes note that another one needs to be ordered. But for the conspiracy theorist, such an explanation is far too simple. According to the website www.davidicke.com, bar codes are but one major step to the mass monitoring of everyone on the planet.

Post offices also use bar codes to track mail, and can do so, it's said, from satellites in space. Similarly, it's argued, bar-coded goods can be tracked from purchase to consumption, or from the store to your home, meaning that someone somewhere may well know exactly what's in your cupboards. Credit cards can already log what you buy, where and when, and on the day that cash is finally dropped in favour of smart cards, the government will know the very contents of your shopping bags.

Bar codes also supposedly have a Satanic significance, with the lines of varying thickness somehow being computed to give the number 666, the mark of the Antichrist, and the trademark of the backers of a cashless economy: "He also forced everyone, small and great, rich and poor, free and slave, to receive a mark in his right hand or in his forehead, so that no one could buy or sell unless he had the mark, which is the name of the beast or the number of his name ... His number is 666" (Revelation 13:16).

One step on from smart cards is smart chips implanted directly under your skin – and they could become reality sooner than you might think. Microchips are already being inserted into military personnel, the children of the elite, criminals and sufferers of Alzheimers' disease. Cashless payments via swiped credit cards, store cards, Internet banking and the like are becoming widespread, and private data about everything from your spending habits and emails to your fingerprints and DNA is being demanded, collected, shared and stored on databases all over the world (not to mention lost…). With biometric passports already widespread and ID cards looking likely, perhaps it won't be long before everyone has smart chips implanted under their skin, and the Antichrist's hell on earth will begin. So when someone cute eyes you up at the bar, perhaps you'll have to start asking if they like your smile or your Verichip (see p.304). Either way they want your number…

perhaps firewalling or deleting them, or even attacking their hosts with viruses. This makes search engines surveillance, censorship and propaganda machines rolled into one.

In fact, the Operation Prometheus story is a hoax. But even so, the Internet *is* monitored, on a global scale. Every email, as well as, for that matter, every fax and phone call, whether via landline, cell, microwave, fibre-optic cable or satellite, is monitored by a vast global system known as ECHELON. While there are monitoring bases in Canada, the UK, New Zealand, Australia, Germany and Japan, the hub is the US, where ECHELON is maintained and overseen by the NSA. Originally established to monitor Soviet communications traffic, and supported when militarily necessary by countless submarines and satellites, the programme's remit has been extended to monitor rogue states and anything or anyone deemed of interest – be they civilians, senators, Amnesty International, Greenpeace or Christian Aid. Massive computers using voice-recognition and optical character dictionaries filter for keywords, and messages are flagged up, recorded and transcribed for analysis. In 1998, the European Union released a report that gave details of ECHELON; in response to the extensive monitoring of its citizens and corporations, it invested millions of euros in encryption software.

The military-industrial complex and PROMIS

ECHELON couldn't pay for its upkeep simply by pursuing terrorists. Instead, it's said, many of the corporations that helped to build it have benefited from intelligence that it has picked up, forwarded via a liaison office in the Department of Commerce. Thus journalist Patrick S. Poole has alleged that in 1990, AT&T received a cut of a $200 million deal between Indonesia and Japanese satellite-maker NEC Corp, thanks to ECHELON-derived intelligence and the help of President George H.W. Bush. Similarly, the giant Raytheon corporation got a slice of a $1.3 billion radar deal between Brazil and a French radar company, courtesy of the CIA and NSA intercepts, while US car-makers benefited from CIA information on Japanese makers of zero-emission vehicles. The NSA and FBI are said to have bugged the entire Asian-Pacific Economic Conference in Seattle in 1997, to learn more about hydroelectric dam deals in Vietnam.

As *The Economist* reported in 2000, ECHELON is indeed a favourite of "conspiracy theorists". The magazine claimed that "concrete examples of companies that have gained – or lost – because of this surveillance system are rarely offered", but one German MEP has charged that European businesses have so far lost over $20 billion. The French press has accused ECHELON of involvement in Boeing winning contracts over Airbus, while Tom King, former UK defence secretary and chair of the Commons intelligence committee, has blamed ECHELON for "bad blood" between the Americans and the French over industrial espionage. According to the UK Foreign Office,

The huge "golf balls" at RAF Menwith Hill, Yorkshire are considered by many conspiracists to be part of ECHELON.

the interception of the kind of data on which ECHELON snoops is permitted for "economic well-being".

As for its anti-terrorism brief, ECHELON is said to have "played a key role" in the arrest of the alleged 9/11 mastermind Khalid Sheikh Mohammed in Pakistan in March 2003 (together, according to *The Guardian*, with an $18 million bribe to an "Al Qaeda foot soldier"). ECHELON monitored Mohammed's dozen-odd mobile phones; just the sort of tracking that the 9/11 hijackers hoped to evade by using pre-paid Swiss cellular phones not registered in any name.

The ECHELON facility has been ascribed to the "brainstorm" version of the software programme PROMIS, developed by Inslaw for the US Department of Justice to coordinate and track disparate data on separate systems, on- and offline. Rumour has it that PROMIS can also track submarines, and even predict stock market movements. It's not known if ECHELON is empowered to predict individuals' thoughts and actions – but then that isn't the extraordinary sci-fi goal of a group of mad military scientists, but the openly declared, soon-to-be-realized aim of our friendly Web browser, Google.

ECHELON? The future's Google

ECHELON isn't the half of it. One facet of social networking sites like Facebook and MySpace is the amount of data users freely upload – reams of demographic material, including opinions, tastes and personal identity information, that's invaluable for advertisers, finks, hackers and crooks. Even the online store Amazon has a database of information going back to 1999, which the FBI is entitled to retrieve, without probable cause – and without your knowledge – in their battles against crime and terrorism. Most Western governments have legislated, or are in the process of legislating, for the mass storage of *all* Internet data, and social networking sites are a voluntary en masse extension of this. This is leading to the selling of all kinds of personal data to private intelligence and law enforcement agencies, as well as to marketing and polling companies; not forgetting the use of questions typed into search engines as evidence in court cases.

As online techie writer Nick Douglas opined on the somewhat sardonic blogboard valleywag.com, the search engine Google has already patented methods to observe online games and record and infer as much as possible about the wants and motives of online players. The ultimate dual uses of this technology are targeted advertising and the gauging of political bias and criminal intent. Search engines and servers like Microsoft's MSN, Yahoo! and AOL have already capitulated to US and Chinese government demands to hand over user records. Google's refusal to comply with one such request from the US Department of Justice was derided, particularly by ex-CIA man Robert Steele.

Google is the conduit for more than half of the global traffic on the Web, and is the world's finest, most personalized catalogue of human wants, habits and inquiries. It also hosts satellite imagery of homes and businesses around the world, and will soon include real-time footage of any and everyone in any outdoor public space. In 2007, Google's new "Street View" feature added thousands of on-the-ground images of US cities to its Google Maps facility, with photos taken by its own camera teams. While legal concerns regarding privacy laws, particularly in Europe, have so far prevented Google Street View from going global, it has already been proven technically possible to access live CCTV through Google platforms. All too soon, you'll probably be able to Google yourself and find yourself watching you, being watched, all the day long.

In May 2007, Google "admitted" that it did not yet "know enough" about its users and would increase its efforts to collect their personal information, in what CEO Eric Schmidt described as "the most important aspect of Google's expansion". Ultimately, Internet users would not use Google just to search for their wants, but to ask far more personal questions, such as "What shall I do tomorrow?" and "What job shall I take?" Schmidt has said that, within "five years", Google will have software that can verify the truth of statements made by politicians. How long will it be before this can be extended to everyone, everywhere, in real time?

Further out in the wilder sci-fi regions of conspiracy theorizing is the idea that Google will one day have amassed so much data and have been so well-infused with computing power, data mining, data tagging, self-teaching capabilities and artificial intelligence that it will become a "self-aware" entity. With the ability to tag and upload data on every person from every page on the Web by tapping into power systems, communications, banking, surveillance, any and every operating system, it would be omniscient and omnipresent – God. It's theoretically possible, albeit extremely far off in the future, or so mere human programmers believe. What Google thinks is another matter…

SOURCES

Websites

- Ⓦ **fly.hiwaay.net/~pspoole/echelon.html** Patrick Poole sums up the powers and the perils of ECHELON.
- Ⓦ **www.googlewatch.org** Watching us, watching you – the website dedicated to watching the ultimate stealth-watcher.

A cure for cancer

In the West, at least, cancer is the biggest natural killer. "A cure for cancer" is the Holy Grail of medical research – assuming that a catch-all cure existed, whoever found it would save millions of lives and make tens of billions of dollars in the process. Some people suspect, however, that numerous cancer cures have already been found, but are being suppressed by drug companies and other bodies who have a vested interest in continuing to provide their own particular (and expensive) treatments. There are claims that some of these companies and bodies prefer palliative treatments to cures or preventions, because their profits would suffer as a result.

Every year six million people die from cancer. One in three Westerners will contract some form of the disease in their lives, and one in four will die from it. Of the scores of known cancers, breast and cervical cancer are the biggest killers of women, while stomach, lung and prostate cancer figure highly in male cancer rates. It's certainly not down to lack of research. Since President Nixon launched his "War on Cancer" in 1971, US government funding on cancer research has increased more than tenfold from $223 million to over $3 billion in 1998, a fraction of what medical companies themselves spend. Meanwhile, in the US at least, incidence rates for stomach and cervical cancer have declined by almost eighty percent since 1975. Lung and breast cancer rates have also fallen since the late 1970s, seeming to suggest that on some fronts at least, the war against cancer is gradually being won.

In the case of lung and breast cancer rates, however, that decline is from all-time peaks. In 1940, the death rate for breast cancer was one in twenty women. Now it's one in eight. From 1973 to 1990, overall cancer death rates in the West rose by 7.5 percent. Worldwide, over ten million people are diagnosed with cancer annually, but the World Health Organization (WHO) estimates this will rise to fifteen million new cases by 2020. With all this money, research and increased awareness of health risks, how can cancer incidence be rising? Some theorists have said that it's no coincidence that Nixon's War on Cancer was launched at Fort Detrick (see p.298), a place usually associated not with benign public health programmes, but with bio-warfare developments. This has led to speculation that some cancers have been developed by government scientists and are being used as weapons on the unsuspecting public (AIDS has been seen as a similar, though more targeted weapon, see p.290). In most cancer conspiracy theories, however, it's financial and professional – rather than political – interests that are said to be behind it all.

The heretics of cancer will burn

One theory is that new treatments are being held back because of the threat they pose to the medical establishment. Dr Alan Cantwell, an American doctor best known for proposing the existence of an AIDS conspiracy, believes that the massive investment – both financial and psychological – in conventional treatments has led to a "cancer conspiracy" to discourage research into possible bacterial causes of the disease. In *The Cancer Microbe* (1990), Cantwell claims that the "recognition of microscopic cancer bacteria at this late date would be an embarrassment to the medical profession", leading to "expensive and questionable radiation and chemotherapy" being dumped.

Cantwell cites two earlier researchers into cancer-causing bacteria as victims of this "cancer conspiracy": Dr Virginia Livingston-Wheeler, whose 1984 book *The Conquest of Cancer* led to her being labelled a quack, and the Freudian-trained psychoanalyst Dr Wilhelm Reich. Both claimed to have found bacterial microbes in cancers, though Livingston-Wheeler's professed ignorance of Reich's earlier work in the field has been questioned. Having outlined his theory that cancerous cells had lower levels of "orgone energy" than healthy cells in his 1948 book *The Cancer Biopathy*, Reich was successfully prosecuted in the 1950s for manufacturing and selling "orgone accumulators". His books and papers were burnt by the Food and Drug Administration (FDA), and he died in prison.

According to "alternative newspaper" publisher Barry Lynes, an even worse fate befell Dr Raymond Rife, who posed a similar threat to "organized medicine". In the 1930s, Rife not only claimed to have discovered cancer-causing viruses with his self-made microscope, but also invented an electromagnetic energy device, the "Rife Ray Tube", to kill them. As Lynes tells it, the University of Southern California proved the worth of Rife's Ray Tube by curing sixteen terminally ill patients, but his adulation was short-lived. Pro-Rife doctors were murdered and their laboratories burnt, as drug and insurance companies, and hospitals and doctors, facing ruin, colluded in "deep, criminal activities". (Rife, it's alleged, was murdered by an "accidental" overdose of Valium and alcohol.) Lynes unearthed the story in 1985, but found that no one in Congress wanted to know. Still, Lynes claims that his own books have successfully brought Rife's treatments to thousands of cancer sufferers, despite a "virulent" counteroffensive from science, government and "mysterious private interests".

One problem with Cantwell's conspiracy theory is that finding a bacterial cause for cancer would actually open up a whole new area of research funding and profitable treatments. Nor can Cantwell speculate that any breakthrough in this area would render chemotherapy redundant, because different cancers need different treatments. Lynes' view that Rife's treatments are so cheap that they would threaten industry is also a bit odd. If Rife's devices cost so little to manufacture, surely this would only help to increase profit margins: the $64,000 question is whether Rife's treatments really work. Lynes says they do, and that the problem was caused by Rife's refusal to sell the designs to a certain Morris Fishbein who, he claims, went on to destroy Rife's instruments, career and life.

Harry Hoxsey and the Fishbein connection

Morris Fishbein's name crops up regularly in the conspiracy literature of the medical establishment versus alternative medicine. Perhaps that's because Fishbein – who, apparently, originally studied to be a clown – ended up as the head and sole stockholder of the powerful American Medical Association (AMA), despite never having treated a patient in his life. Drug advertisements helped make the AMA's journal one of the most profitable publications in the world, but another leading advertiser was tobacco giant Philip Morris, whose ads boasted that "More doctors smoke Camels than any other cigarette". As AMA chief and editor of the journal, Fishbein became the "voice of American medicine" for four decades.

"Of all the ghouls who feed on the bodies of the dead and the dying", declared Fishbein in a 1947 editorial (repeating a phrase he had already used in a *March of Time* newsreel), "the cancer quacks are the most vicious and most heartless." Fishbein's principal target was "cancer charlatan" Harry Hoxsey, an American alternative healer who became rich and famous in the 1920s for his various tonics and poultices for cancer, but who was hounded by Fishbein, AMA journalists and the Food and Drug Administration (FDA) for years. In 1950, the FDA got the courts to stop Hoxsey's interstate shipments and, in 1956, put up 46,000 "Public Warning Against Hoxsey Cancer Treatment" posters in post offices across the US. "Organized medicine" forced the Hoxsey clinic to relocate to Mexico, and in 1964 the FDA spent millions having Hoxsey's treatments banned nationwide.

What caused officialdom to pursue Hoxsey so vigorously was the dark brown liquid, "Hoxsey's Tonic", used to treat internal cancers. For decades Hoxsey – a former coal miner with no medical training – wouldn't reveal what was in the tonic, before finally divulging that his great-grandfather had developed the formula after one of his horses had apparently cured itself of cancer by eating a particular combination of plants. For bodies like the AMA and FDA, naturally enough, this proved their case.

The real question, however, is whether "Hoxsey's Tonic" actually worked. Even if it wasn't the product of conventional scientific research, this needn't have stopped the AMA and FDA from carrying out their own. In fact, the tonic contained many traditional herbal ingredients, such as pokeweed, barberry, buckthorn and Stillingia root. As *The Lancet*, *Pediatrics* and *Nature* journals, and researchers in Japan, the US and Germany have since reported, all of these ingredients have effective anti-tumour properties. Was Hoxsey, then, a case of the medical establishment getting the government to gun down alternative treatments?

If Hoxsey's defenders – including Kenny Ausubel, who has written a book and made a film on the subject – are to be believed, it would certainly seem so. According to Hoxsey, a "senior member of the AMA" tried to muscle in on his business, in a deal that would have given Fishbein and his cronies all of the profits for the first ten years, and Hoxsey a small percentage thereafter – but only if they were satisfied that it worked. This implied either that Fishbein was sufficiently vicious and heartless himself to exploit what might turn out to be another quack remedy for all it was worth – or that he knew all along that Hoxsey's concoction wasn't just snake-oil.

When Hoxsey (unsurprisingly) refused the deal, Fishbein had him arrested more than a hundred times in a period of sixteen months for practising without a licence. Not only were the charges consistently thrown out of court, but Fishbein himself was also finally forced to admit that Hoxsey's herbal cancer remedy worked, on skin cancer at least (because there have never been proper tests, the jury is still out on its effectiveness in treating internal cancers). Eventually, multiple scandals forced Fishbein to resign, but not before his campaign against an unlikely, but potentially effective, alternative treatment had succeeded.

"I know these guys, they would not do something like that"

According to cancer sufferer Michael Higgins, any "workable alternative cures would be adopted without cover-up". Higgins writes that he knows, "there isn't any cancer conspiracy" on www.cancertreatmentwatch.org (a site whose main purpose is "to debunk ineffective methods marketed as 'cures'"), because it would require hundreds of thousands of compassionate medics to systematically lie about possible cures. That pharmaceutical companies could control medical knowledge and their employees is "ridiculous", states Higgins – governments would welcome having cheaper cancer treatments and fewer people to treat.

The money that governments and tobacco companies make from cigarettes is countered by the money spent on public education about smoking hazards, according to Higgins. Tobacco companies were wrong to suppress research linking smoking and cancer, but despite the fortunes at stake, he says, "the truth was not suppressed for long". However, with no disrespect to Higgins, the millions spent by governments on persuading people not to smoke is a drop in the ocean compared with the billions earned in revenue from tobacco. And when he says that "the truth was not suppressed for long", he's talking about a period of more than thirty years.

A rather different view is given by Dr Jeffrey Wigand, research director at US tobacco giant Brown & Williamson, who earned $300,000 for the privilege of researching "safer" cigarettes. In 1994, he went public, telling CBS's *60 Minutes* that B&W, and their partner British American Tobacco, had known since the mid-1960s that smoking could cause disease (emphysema, heart disease, lung cancer…) and that nicotine was addictive. References in B&W research to making "safer" cigarettes were removed by company lawyers, as it implied that the company knew its products were unsafe – a fatal admission in any future product liability suits. B&W's CEO Thomas Sandefur told a US Senate subcommittee in 1994: "I believe that nicotine is not addictive."

The *60 Minutes* episode was almost never aired because CBS's parent company Westinghouse objected. Meanwhile Dr Wigand was subjected to a horrendous smear campaign led by B&W and picked up by much of the US media, down to the last parking ticket. The story was grittily depicted in Michael Mann's 1999 film *The Insider*, which gave many Americans their first opportunity to hear Wigand's explanation of why millions of people had died. Thanks to the mainstream media's obsession with the O.J. Simpson trial, that bit of the story had been largely – and for the tobacco industry, conveniently – overlooked.

"Don't ask why they're ill, just make them better"

The best way to reduce the incidence of the various cancers associated with smoking (lung, mouth, throat…) is, of course, to dissuade people from smoking in the first place. Indeed, no less an authority than the former US National Cancer Institute director Samuel Broder has declared that prevention is "the most cost-effective way to deal with any disease". It might be thought, then, that every effort would be concentrated on prevention rather than cure. As far back as the 1950s, the World Health Organization estimated that eighty to ninety percent of cancers could be environmentally caused, and today states that enough is known "to prevent at least one-third of all cancers". Yet the WHO also estimates that cancer rates will increase by fifty percent by 2020, mostly in industrializing countries.

So where is the prevention? In a special 1998 issue of *The Ecologist*, Ross Hume Hall and Dr Samuel Epstein argued that a "medical-industrial" complex – including the "cancer establishment" of the American Cancer Society and (despite the views of its ex-director Samuel Broder) the National Cancer Institute (NCI) – are set on discouraging research into how industrial pollutants cause cancer by contaminating food, water and air.

In 1999, Hall and Epstein pointed out, 99 percent of the NCI's $3.2 billion budget went on diagnosis and treatment. Although industrial chemical output increased five-hundred-fold between the 1940s and 1980s, less than ten percent of new industrial chemicals have been tested for their carcinogenic properties and only five percent of the five hundred carcinogens found in animals have been studied by the NCI. The same chemical industries supplying pharmaceutical companies also benefit from zero-cost chemical waste dumping, and the scientific research justifying the "safety" of dumping pollutants is skewed by the chemical industry paying for the research.

The same issue of *The Ecologist* cited the work of doctors and missionaries over centuries in noting the absence of cancer among the locals in Gabon, Senegal, northern Canada and Alaska. As Zac Goldsmith asked, "how can it be, by anyone's logic, that while breast cancer today afflicts one in eight women in the US, there has been virtually no sign of it among traditional people living traditional lives?" There again, who knows for certain what factors are involved?

No single problem, no single answer

That is the problem with cancer. There is no single form of cancer, and no single cause for the West's biggest "natural" killer – be it dietary, environmental, genetic, viral or (as some claim) bacterial. It follows, therefore, that there is no single cure. The complexity of the diseases collectively known as "cancer" is reflected in the range of different approaches to finding their causes, then treating – or preventing – them. Personal actions, genetic predispositions and environmental influences combine to form an exceedingly complex morass of variables and any number of combinations resulting in enhanced effects.

If there is a "cancer establishment" crushing numerous avenues of research and treatment, it has failed to stop the research that the WHO's estimates about preventable cancers are based on, or the research at Columbia University that, in 2000, linked Polycyclic Aromatic Hydrocarbons (PAHs, or compounds found in soot and fossil fuel fumes) to genetic damage leading to breast cancer, as the Breast Cancer Fund reported. There seems little doubt, however, that treatment gets better funding than prevention. This may partly be because treatment is, for want of a better term, sexier (compare your grey-suited fire safety officer with your muscled, smoky, sweat-beaded, hose-wielding fireman).

How things are reported also makes a lot of difference. In August 2007, Cancer Research UK released figures indicating soaring increases in rates of "good life" cancers, or "cancers of affluence": smoking and drinking had caused increased rates of mouth cancer, up from 3700 in 1994 to over 5000 ten years later; obesity had helped bump incidence of womb cancer up by twenty percent in ten years; smoking had pushed the rate of kidney cancer up by ten percent; and cases of malignant melanoma had risen by fifty percent betwen 1995 and 2004, which the report put down partly to the rise in cheap flights. But the biggest killers, according to statistics reported later that month, were lung, bowel, breast and prostate cancer, for which Britain had the worst survival rates in Europe, despite spending the most on treatment. Drinking and smoking are also among the causes of bowel and lung cancer – but not the exclusive causes – yet the mainstream media cited no cause for any of these diseases.

Dr Ronald Finn, a consultant physician, described cancer as "essentially a disease of industrialization". He told a House of Commons committee that in pre-industrialized nations "cancer rates are far lower", and its spread is more notable due to its rapidity. The Chinese press reported in 1999 that one single river in the Jiangsu province contained 93 different carcinogens; the province is also China's most industrialized region and home to twelve percent of its cancer sufferers. The (heavily censored) press of this rapidly industrializing nation writes freely about "cancer villages" near polluting factories or waterways. In 2006, the *Journal of Nutritional and Environmental Medicine* reported research from the University of Liverpool that exposure to even small amounts of environmental contaminants, carcinogenic or hormone-disrupting chemicals, or organochlorines found in pesticides and plastics, could be a major factor in causing hormone-dependent malignancies such as breast, prostate and testicular cancers.

As with measures to protect the environment, cancer prevention means radically changing the behaviour of both individuals and industries – perhaps the whole Western lifestyle – and, as with smoking restrictions, it could take a long time to achieve the critical mass of opinion needed to make the necessary changes. In the meantime, prevention may be better than cure, but treatment remains the more popular and profitable option. Focusing on genetic predisposition to cancer is proving the next great profitable field for pharmaceutical firms and biotech researchers (as well as health insurers targeting likely sufferers with higher premiums). It's also a field of research that further personalizes the causes of cancer, moving the focus even further from the industry itself.

SOURCES

Books and articles

Alan C. Cantwell The Cancer Microbe (1990). A friend of Dr Livingston-Wheeler defends her controversial and unorthodox theories (and those of Wilhelm Reich). Worth reading to get a measure of the opposition faced by doctors who take on the medical establishment.

Robert Lynes The Cancer Cure that Worked: 50 Years of Suppression (1987). Lynes sets out to save the world by championing the cause of the Rife Ray Tube.

Various "Cancer: Are the Experts Lying?" (*The Ecologist*, Vol.28, No.2, March/April 1998). A disturbing special issue with well-documented arguments, suggesting there is a conspiracy by the "cancer establishment" – largely funded by the chemical, nuclear and pharmaceutical industries – to direct research away from environmental pollution as the main cause of cancer and towards financially profitable treatment. (See edwardgoldsmith.com/page23.html)

Films

Michael Mann The Insider (1999). An excellent *film noir*-ish treatment of research scientist and whistleblower Dr Jeffery Wigand's decision to spill the beans on his employer, tobacco giant Brown & Williamson. With Russell Crowe as Wigand and Al Pacino as the TV producer responsible for getting the story aired on CBS's *60 Minutes*.

Websites

Ⓦ **www.cancer.gov** and **www.who.org** The "official" viewpoint on cancer, its causes and treatment is given by the US government and the World Health Organization respectively.

Ⓦ **curezone.com/art/read.asp?ID=91&db=5&C0=779** "When Healing Becomes a Crime", a 2001 article by Kenny Ausubel on the Hoxsey case, which he turned into a book and film of the same name.

Ⓦ **www.jeffreywigand.com/insider/60minutes.html** Videoclip and transcript of Wigand's extraordinary TV revelations.

Ⓦ **www.rense.com/general19/enemy.htm** "Morris Fishbein: AMA Enemy of American Health", Bob Wallace's attack on Fishbein, discusses the Rife case in some detail and brings in the Hoxsey affair.

REAL WEAPONS OF MASS DESTRUCTION

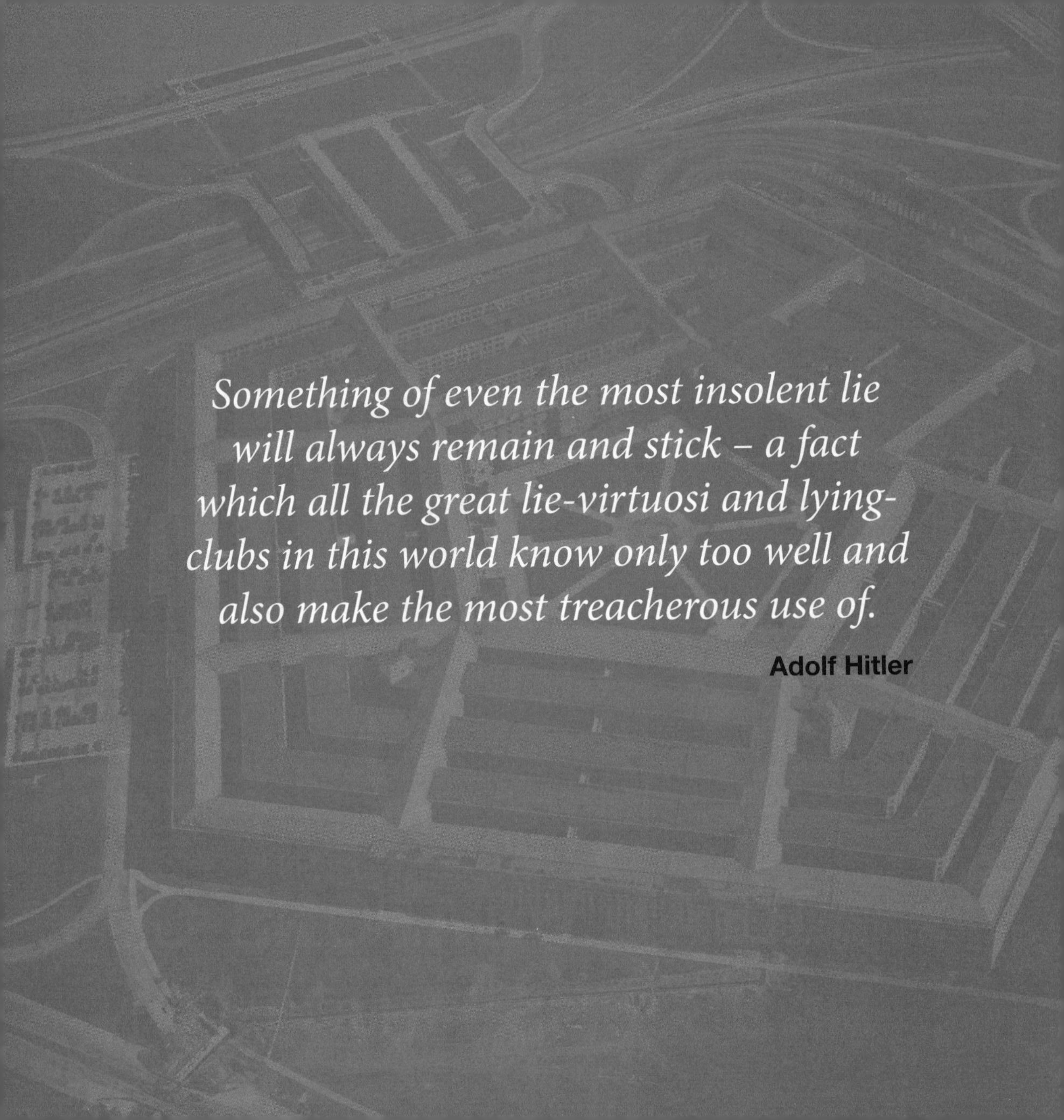

Something of even the most insolent lie will always remain and stick – a fact which all the great lie-virtuosi and lying-clubs in this world know only too well and also make the most treacherous use of.

Adolf Hitler

REAL WEAPONS OF MASS DESTRUCTION

With all the talk of the threat of "weapons of mass destruction" – whether biological, chemical or nuclear – falling into the hands of terrorists or rogue states, it's easy to forget just how long such weapons have at least been believed to exist. It was a familiar tactic in medieval sieges, for example, for attacking armies to hurl anything and everything, including disease-ridden beasts, into the besieged camp. When the plague, or Black Death, hit Europe in the mid-fourteenth century, the belief – sometimes stirred up by cynical governments – that some malign "foreign" influence was responsible led to even more deaths than might otherwise have occurred.

Imperial Japan's Unit 731 really did inflict plague, as well as anthrax, botulin and typhoid, on Chinese and Korean villages and US prisoners of war during World War II. If this has received less publicity in the West than contemporaneous Nazi medical experiments, it may be because many of the Japanese involved ended up being employed in the US's own bio-warfare programmes, co-ordinated by the Pentagon and carried out in secret bases such as Fort Detrick or Edgewood Arsenal.

The fruit of these dastardly projects, some believe, was what they suspect to be the most cunningly designed biological weapon yet – AIDS. While conspiracy theories about the origin of AIDS extend from Moscow to the US Army to "Big Pharma", belief in some of the theories is having a palpable effect on the battle against the disease, with AIDS drugs being blocked because recipients are seen as "guinea pigs" in a big race-based conspiracy (other people said similar things about SARS). The explosion at Port Chicago in 1944 is suspected of being not only the world's first atomic bomb blast, but also a case of the military carrying out hideous experiments on its own personnel, though ironically the more fantastical Philadelphia Experiment – to make ships invisible – was stopped because of the horrible effects it had on servicemen.

There are also questions over the real purpose of HAARP, a massive Alaskan-based field of antennae supposedly built to monitor the upper atmosphere and make phone calls less crackly, but which has been blamed for everything from US power cuts to the Asian tsunami of 2004. Some have blamed HAARP for fomenting Hurricane Katrina in 2005, although many more put the blame for the devastation on the feigned ineptitude of the governing bodies and emergency management services responsible for anticipating, coping with and clearing up after the hurricane.

Following the UK floods in the summer of 2007, the British government were also accused of incompetence. Few, however, linked them to any greater or more sinister schemes – unless it was to wonder whether the flooding might not be related to the great issue of the day: climate change. Some very powerful and persuasive people quickly entered the debate, murmuring words of reassurance and trying to convince everyone that climate change was not only unrelated to weather disasters, but that it wasn't really happening at all. Curiously, some of those sceptics are the very same interested parties who make huge profits from the oil, energy and automobile industries – the industries that have so much to lose if the world attempts to combat climate change by lowering its carbon emissions. And to complete the circle of suspicion, some of those same names also crop up in theories about who profited the most from the flooding and rebuilding of New Orleans.

False threats being used to justify real weapons; false threats leading to self-destructive violence and mass murder; real stories of genocide being covered up; real stories of imminent disasters being ignored or denied; secret bases hiding sinister secrets – some real, some probably not; microwaves being used to kill, track or control; friends becoming foes overnight (and vice versa); the enemy abroad and the enemy within – all are part of the rhetoric of WMDs.

The Black Death

Although bubonic plague has swept through Europe many times, the most devastating outbreak, in terms of both the total number of deaths and the proportion of the population who died, was in the mid-fourteenth century. The "Black Death" is estimated to have killed some 25 million people in Europe alone. As a contemporary German historian wrote: "In some lands everyone died, with the result that no one was left." Ships were found adrift at sea, still laden with cargo but with the crew all dead – and it was ships such as these, coming from the East, that are thought to have found their way into Mediterranean ports, carrying the plague with them. The disease spread into France, Spain and Britain by mid-1348, then into northern Europe and Russia in 1351. Curiously, Poland and Flanders were largely spared.

In a continent that was – not surprisingly – gripped by panic, stories spread that the Black Death was the deliberate work of some enemy, what would now be called biological warfare. From a modern perspective, such an interpretation seems like paranoia, but it provides an object lesson in how irrational fears can be whipped up into hatred and used to justify genocide.

An act of war over trade?

According to contemporary speculation, the various princedoms of India, which had recently been increasing their trade with numerous European states, had become disgruntled at the terms on which they were obliged to operate. They, therefore, placed plague-laden rats on

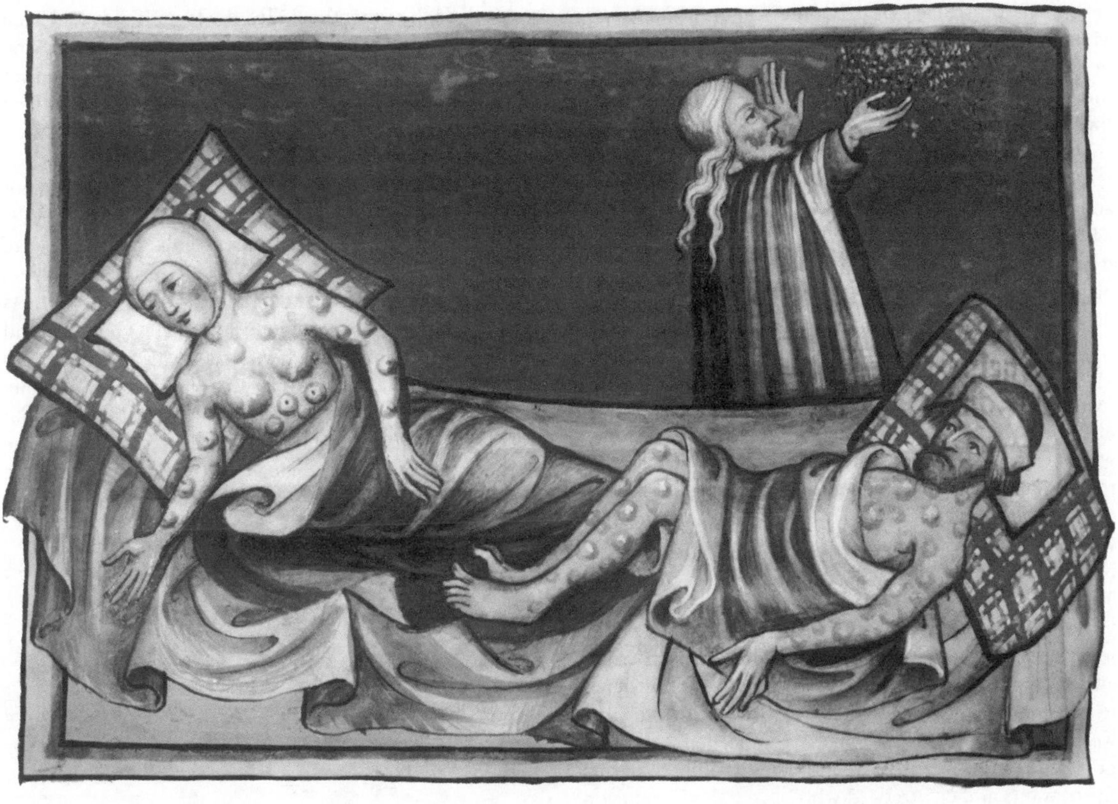

Fifteenth-century illustration of bubonic plague victims covered in buboes, or swollen lymph glands.

Europe-bound ships, hoping to inflict massive depopulation, especially near the major Mediterranean ports. Meanwhile, an Indian army would be heading that way, to take over if not the whole continent, then at least large swathes of it.

It's certainly true that areas of northern India were succumbing to plague at the time, and it may have spread to Europe from India aboard European ships. The bio-warfare theory doesn't bear much scrutiny, however. There's a world of difference between seeking to redress trade grievances and attempting to wipe out most of your export market. And Indians were as prone to the disease as anyone else, so for them to infect the land their army was supposedly seeking to take over might well have proved counterproductive. In any case, an Indian invasion never materialized.

Enemies without and within

One invading force that actually turned up on Europe's borders around that time did come from the East. In the aftermath of the Black Death, some accounts blamed the Mongols for carrying the disease west from an outbreak in the central Asian steppes, while others write that the Mongols catapulted plague-ridden corpses into the besieged Crimean city of Kaffa, which was under Genoese control. From there, the plague was inadvertently shipped to Genoa itself in 1347, whence it spread across Europe.

By the autumn of 1348, however, the rumour spread through Europe – much like the disease itself – that the plague was the work of the Jews. They were said to be deliberately infecting wells, springs and other water sources used by Christians. The Count of Savoy took it upon himself to investigate, and ordered the arrest of Jews living around Lake Geneva. One such arrestee, Agimet of Geneva, "confessed" under torture to having poisoned wells in Venice, Calabria, Toulouse and elsewhere around the Mediterranean. He said that he had been bidden to do so by Rabbi Peyret of Chambéry, who had sent other well-poisoners to France, Switzerland and Italy, as part of a bigger plot hatched by Jewish elders in the enclave of Toledo.

The story is steeped in anti-Semitic superstition: the Jew as scapegoat. In Strasbourg, which had yet to be afflicted, two thousand Jews of all ages were murdered to pre-empt the threat they allegedly posed to the city's wells. All debts owed to them were cancelled, and their possessions and wealth seized and redistributed among the peasants and city traders, who passed their profits on to the Church. A contemporary account – thought to be by Strasbourg historian Frederick Closener – was quite blunt about the real motive for the slaughter: "The money was indeed the thing that killed the Jews. If they had been poor and if the feudal lords had not been in debt to them, they would not have been burnt." If you have a creditor and a debtor, who gains from the death of the other? Plus, it makes no sense for city-dwellers to poison their local well: it's simply suicidal. In any case, Strasbourg's pre-emptive strike failed: the plague came and wiped out sixteen thousand inhabitants.

As news of the supposed confessions spread, tens of thousands of Jews, young and old, were tortured, stabbed, drowned or burned in hundreds of towns and hamlets around the Mediterranean, and in France, Germany and Switzerland. Sometimes there was a "trial", sometimes not. The message was clear. It was the enemies of white Christian Europe who were responsible for the plague; it was "them", whether that be Indians, Mongols or Jews. The disease itself, of course, made no distinction as to whom it killed, wiping out millions across Asia and Africa, as well as Europe.

SOURCES

Books

John Kelly The Great Mortality: An Intimate History of the Black Death, the Most Devastating Plague of All Time (2005). Kelly richly details the squalor of life in Europe's medieval cities and shows what prime venues they were for disease to spread. No conspirators; you just had to be there to get the sniffles and watch your skin fall off. Grim reading about Europe's greatest visit from the Grim Reaper.

Websites

Ⓦ **www.fordham.edu/halsall/jewish/1348-jewsblackdeath.html** Paul Halsall's comprehensive account of how the Jews came to be blamed for the plague.

The Philadelphia Experiment

Many people believe that the US military has led from the front in pushing the frontiers of science. However, if the Philadelphia Experiment is to be believed, it is one case in which even the US military went too far, meddling with forces it couldn't control.

The story of the experiment – for there are few facts as such – runs something like this. During World War II, the US Navy sought to discover the ultimate camouflage for its warships: invisibility to radar, achieved by generating an intense magnetic field around a ship. The operation, known as "Project Rainbow", aimed to utilize new theories of physics that involved "magnetic resonance". Experiments were conducted at the Philadelphia Naval Yard, Pennsylvania, where the destroyer USS *Eldridge* was equipped with an array of electronic gadgetry that, according to the outlines of Albert Einstein's "Unified Field Theory" – which neither Einstein nor anyone else has ever proved – would make it invisible. The switch was flicked in June 1943. Engulfed by a mysterious green mist, the *Eldridge* remained invisible to both radar and the naked eye for a good fifteen minutes. However, the crew of the *Eldridge* fell sick, and some of those aboard reported seeing some other port during the experiment. Evidently some unknown frontier had been crossed. The navy resolved to ensure that it obtained radar invisibility and nothing more.

When the rejigged *Eldridge* was tested again in October, it once more disappeared from radar screens and normal vision in a green fog (though a green fog is not exactly invisible), with its hull still imprinting the water. Then, with a blinding blue flash, the ship completely disappeared, and teleported from Philadelphia to Norfolk, Virginia, over two hundred miles away. There it sat for some minutes, in view of men aboard the merchant ship SS *Furuseth*, before returning to Philadelphia in another flash. This time, *Eldridge* crew members were not just ill but crazed into the bargain, while a handful were fused to the ship's metal and some were even missing altogether. Surviving sailors suffered bouts of invisibility, spontaneous combustion and "freeze-framing" into positions for days on end. Suitably frightened, the project scientists and its military backers concluded that they were meddling with forces they didn't understand, and abandoned all hope of finding a crock of gold at the end of "Project Rainbow".

The navy denies everything

The US Navy has always rebuffed questioning about the Philadelphia Experiment. The Office of Naval Research (ONR) stated in September 1996 that "ONR has never conducted investigations on invisibility, either in 1943 or at any other time". Pointing out that the ONR was not even established until 1946, it denounced the story as "science fiction". The master of the *Furuseth*, Lieutenant Junior Grade William S. Dodge, has written that neither he nor his crew saw anything strange going on in Norfolk. The Naval Historical Center has added that the *Eldridge* wasn't launched until late July 1943, so it couldn't have been experimented on in June (though conspiracy theorists respond that the ship's paperwork could have been faked so that it could be used for experiments). And the ship wasn't in Philadelphia at the alleged time of the second test either, being on convoy duty in the Atlantic in October. The *Eldridge* was in Norfolk on November 2 and 3, but the *Furuseth* was not.

Moore to the story

The best-known source for the story, *The Philadelphia Experiment: The Truth Behind Project Invisibility*, was first published in 1978 by Charles Berlitz and William

Moore. (Moore, a "relentless researcher", subsequently had to "retreat to a remote area of the United States to live quietly".) They drew heavily on the work of UFO investigator Morris K. Jessup. His 1955 book, *The Case for the UFO*, attracted reams of fan mail, including a series of letters from a mysterious figure called Carl M. Allende, who claimed that he'd seen the *Eldridge* appear and disappear from on board the *Furuseth*.

Although Allende's letters claimed to have come from Texas, they were post-marked from Pennsylvania and elsewhere. He stressed his points by the liberal use of multicoloured pens, writing whole texts in upper case, with much underlining and total disregard for grammar and punctuation. He also went by several different monickers in the letters, calling himself Carlos Allende, Carl Allen and other variations thereof. After the Office of Naval Research received a copy of Jessup's book in early 1957 replete with scribbled ideas about teleportation and Philadelphia, they invited Jessup to Washington. The scribbles in their copy of the book matched the handwriting on Allende's letters to Jessup, and a couple of dozen photocopies were circulated around the ONR. At that point, however, the openness and interest of the ONR abruptly stopped, and Jessup's investigations were stonewalled. Puzzled into a mental breakdown, Jessup committed suicide in 1959. Others involved in the investigation are said to have died in "freak" accidents, disappeared or told their stories only on pain of total anonymity.

Sailors' stories

According to Berlitz and Moore, there's one slither of fact in Allende's account: he cites a story from a Philadelphia newspaper about a brawl that involved *Eldridge* sailors in the Seamen's Lounge bar. Berlitz and Moore say that "presumably still exhibiting the effects of the field", the sailors vanished into thin air mid-fight! They supposedly found the relevant newspaper clipping after a long and tortuous search, although they fail to include a photo of it in their book, and its date and source remain unknown.

A source not cited by Berlitz is a sailor called Edward Dudgeon who told UFO investigator Jaques Valle that he was at that bar fight, but being a minor, was pushed out the back by staff fearing a bust for underage drinkers – hence the "disappearing" sailors. He adds that the *Eldridge* did indeed disappear that night, but only to Newport, not Norfolk, along the Chesapeake-Delaware channel, and that it returned the next day. Dudgeon also contended that the project's quest for invisibility was really about making ships "invisible" to magnetic torpedoes.

Neither the colourful presentation of the multi-monickered Allende's theories, nor Jessup's subsequent mental collapse, adds much to the credibility of Berlitz and Moore's case. Their book is not exactly convincing either, and it concludes after 192 pages that "perhaps, as the Navy has so insistently contended, the entire incident is a legend and never took place". Finally, some people have drawn connections between Berlitz and Moore's work and the science-fiction novel *Thin Air*, by George Simpson and Neil Burger, which came out the year before.

Montauk

One theory that's been put about since is that the *Eldridge* teleported not just in space, but also in time. After disappearing through a "time-hole", it's claimed that the ship reappeared in 1983 off Montauk, Long Island (see p.297). Sailors who swam ashore were greeted by Dr John von Neumann, the original director of "Project Rainbow", who had waited forty years just to say "I've been expecting you". After a few tests, he sent them and their ship back to 1943. However, he hadn't used the intervening decades to address the problems of the men being killed, driven mad or welded to the ship.

A story shrouded in fantasy

The whole saga appears to be a bizarre case of fact and fiction becoming confused and conflated. Berlitz and Moore's book remains widely known and is still in print, and the story has been expanded upon in numerous Discovery Channel documentaries, the feature film *The Philadelphia Experiment* (1984) and an episode of *The X-Files*, "Dod Kalm". The 1980 movie, *The Final Countdown*, gave it another spin, with Kirk Douglas commanding an aircraft carrier that teleports back to Pearl Harbor in 1941, where a couple of the carrier's F-14 jet fighters shoot down the Japanese air force.

SOURCES

Books

Charles Berlitz and William Moore The Philadelphia Experiment: Project Invisibility (1998). A vaguely entertaining exercise in imaginative rhetoric, inevitably short on substantive evidence.

Morris K. Jessup The Case for the UFO (1955). A pioneering work for its day, arguing for the existence of extraterrestrials on Earth.

Films

Stewart Raffill The Philadelphia Experiment (1984). A fun faction-drama adaptation of Charles Berlitz and William Moore's book.

Port Chicago

The propensity for the military forces of various countries to test out new weapons on human guinea pigs is well established. UK scientists tested nerve gas on conscripts at the Porton Down miltary research base (see p.289); the Japanese tested bio-weapons on hundreds of thousands of Chinese and Korean civilians and soldiers; and the US got GIs to stand and watch atomic explosions. However, the story of Port Chicago hints at an even greater zeal for such tests, suggesting that the US may even have nuked one of its own towns.

An explosion of unprecedented power

The port of Port Chicago was constructed in haste after 1941 near the town of the same name, 35 miles north of San Francisco. It served as a major ammunition transit point for US forces fighting in the Pacific during World War II. Every day, thousands of tons of bombs, bullets, mines and lethal explosives were transferred from trains to ships. Just before 10.20pm on the evening of July 17, 1944, as two merchant ships, the SS *EA Bryan* and the SS *Quinault Victory*, were being loaded, a cataclysmic blast wiped the whole place out. The *Bryan* and a train on the pier were vaporized, while pieces of the *Victory* were blown five hundred metres away. A twenty metre deep, two hundred metre long crater was blasted out of the river bottom. A total of 320 people were killed instantly, and 400 more were injured. Body parts were found a mile away. Buildings in Port Chicago town, two miles distant, and across fourteen counties were damaged. Locals thought the blast was an earthquake; indeed, tremors measuring 3.5 on the Richter scale were recorded in Nevada.

Newspapers reported a "dazzling", "sun-like flash" and a "mushroom-like cloud". A few days later, an army pilot told a US Navy court of inquiry that he had seen a white flash, a smoke ring and a "ball of fire" that reached 12,000 feet, with white-hot pieces of metal as large as houses flying past. It appeared that there had been two explosions. The first was on the pier next to the *Bryan* – loaded with 4600 tons of munitions, half being high explosives – which held several thousand tons of diesel and 429 tons of munitions, in 16 boxcars. A distinct sound and brilliant flash suggested that

The remains of the two merchant ships destroyed in the Port Chicago disaster.

a second bomb, a cluster or depth bomb, detonated the explosives on the pier, which in turn caused everything aboard the *Bryan* to explode.

After 39 days, the court of inquiry said that the explosion probably happened because "a supersensitive element [i.e. some explosive] was detonated in the course of rough handling by an individual or individuals". Other possible causes mentioned included bad loading procedures, defective munitions and the neglect of safety procedures to speed things up. With all the evidence blown to smithereens, it was easier to blame the workers – predominantly black enlisted men – who were dismissed as "poor quality … poor material". Their white officers, by contrast, were praised for making the port work. The inquiry's conclusion remains the only official verdict on the event.

No ordinary blast, and maybe no accident?

The army pilot who saw chunks of the town flying past two miles up had been ordered aloft "to observe Port Chicago". What exactly was there to observe, as the port went about its usual business in the darkness of the evening? Later A-bomb explosions under water produced a condensation cloud, or "smoke ring", much like that he had observed at Port Chicago. Then there was the sun-like flash, the tremor, the scale of the devastation… Did Port Chicago fall victim to the world's first atomic bomb?

That theory derives from the diggings of investigative journalist Peter Vogel, who in 1980 made a Hollywood-esque find at a jumble sale in New Mexico. He came across a box from Los Alamos Laboratories, where the atomic bomb was created, which contained photographs and a paper labelled "History of 10,000-ton Gadget", and dated

September 1944. Drawings on the paper resembled the workings for an A-bomb, and included the note: "ball of fire mushroomed out at 18,000 feet in typical Port of Chicago fashion." Port Chicago? Embarking on a twenty-year quest, Vogel reported his findings in the online book *The Last Wave from Port Chicago*, which unearths a lot of curious pointers. Vogel himself had studied physics under Dr Edward Teller, the so-called "Father of the Atomic Bomb". But when he interviewed Teller, and asked him to explain the markings on the paper, Teller replied that the interview was over, and that he would forever deny seeing it.

On visiting Concord Naval Weapons Station, as Port Chicago was renamed, Vogel was informed that there was a film of the blast, but that it was a re-creation made by Hollywood filmmakers in the 1960s for the benefit of the military. Unfortunately, he was told, the footage was on fragile nitrate-based film, and therefore could not be viewed – which is strange, because nitrate film hasn't been used since 1950. Vogel did eventually get to see the film, which he was convinced showed a real atomic blast, but the navy subsequently destroyed it.

Los Alamos scientists did indeed take a great deal of interest in Port Chicago. Thus Captain William Parsons – who later became bombing officer on the *Enola Gay* B-29 bomber, and, as a rear admiral, oversaw the Bikini nuclear bomb tests – submitted a report on Port Chicago within a week of the disaster. His main concern in September 1944 was that the war would finish before the A-bomb could be tested in anger. Desert demonstrations would be an expensive "political and military fizzle", he wrote, but "Such a demonstration … would not be held one thousand feet over Times Square, where the human and material destruction would be obvious". Anything other than the kind of carnage seen at Port Chicago would be an "intense disappointment". While Parsons may have been gung ho – perhaps almost psychotically so – he didn't say, "let's test another bomb, this time on New York". And perhaps his enthusiastic interest in the Port Chicago blast is only to be expected from someone working on the ultimate bomb a couple of states away.

Just a few kilos of uranium

The earliest A-bomb prototypes were small affairs known as "gun-bombs". The director of the Manhattan Project, James Conant, suggested shelving the Mark II gun-bomb to concentrate on the next model, following an unidentified test in July 1944. The damage reported for this test parallels the damage assessment at Port Chicago. But there are no records of any such test, so what was Conant talking about?

Although the US government claimed, referring to Port Chicago, that it didn't have enough bomb-grade uranium in 1944 to test A-bombs, a gun-bomb only needs fifteen kilos of uranium. Department of Energy records show that 93 kilos of uranium were available in 1944. Los Alamos destroyed the contents records for two of the boxcars at Port Chicago. Did they contain a gun-bomb? What's more, the *Bryan* was bound for Tinian, in the Mariana Islands, which is where the *Enola Gay* took off from in 1945 on its way to drop the A-bomb on Hiroshima.

The Concord Naval Weapons Station – Port Chicago, as was – lies in a county that, even today, has one of the highest cancer rates in the US. Given that the base cleaned and decommissioned ships that were exposed to other Pacific test blasts, a high level of radioactive contamination might be expected. As Vogel contends, however, that might also mask its earlier contamination by an A-bomb.

An A-bomb or just any bomb?

Was it a deliberate A-bomb test? The first official atomic test took place in July 1945 in the heart of the New Mexico desert – a remote location, difficult to spy on, with nothing valuable to be damaged; in short, ideal test conditions. A port located on an ocean brimming with enemy spotter craft, on the other hand, would make a very public testing ground for such a major new weapon. Vaporizing a major munitions hub also makes little strategic sense, to say nothing of the mass of other explosives around the port that would have distorted the results of any "test".

So was an A-bomb accidentally discharged in transit? That seems unlikely too. Shipping a workable yet untested bomb towards an enemy who could capture it intact, if they didn't sink the little merchant ship transporting it – which was also carrying a load of volatile explosives – seems unnecessarily rash. When the Hiroshima bomb "Little Boy" was carried across the Pacific, it was entrusted to the towering battleship USS *Indianapolis*. And even that was sunk as it returned home, when the war was basically over.

Vogel believes that the damage inflicted on Port Chicago could only have been caused by a nuclear blast, saying that the cited quantity of conventional explosives just wasn't sufficient. In November 1944, however, four thousand tons of explosives were accidentally detonated in an underground bunker at RAF Fauld in the UK. That explosion left a twelve-acre crater, while the ground shock was recorded by seismographs as far away as Casablanca.

A blast in the past

The reason why neither the US Navy nor the US government has bothered with any further investigations or denials is largely because there's been little public clamour for them to do so. Port Chicago has not seized the public imagination, and it's not even big in conspiracy circles. However, the theory has been cast in a new light by Vogel's work with Robert L. Allen in *The Black Scholar*, a journal of black studies and research. They have reminded the world that the worst wartime blast in the US was swiftly followed by the largest mutiny. By September 1944, many survivors from Port Chicago were re-billeted to Mare Island to load ammunition, but 258 men refused to carry out what they regarded as lethal work – 208 of them were summarily court-martialled, and the rest tried for mutiny.

SOURCES

Websites

Ⓦ **www.portchicago.org** Peter Vogel's handsomely presented, exhaustive site – the home of his book *The Last Wave from Port Chicago* – benefits from a wealth of behind-the-scenes documents from the Manhattan Project.

Ⓦ **www.theblackscholar.org** The site of African-American journal *The Black Scholar*. Robert L. Allen and Peter Vogel's article about Port Chicago was published in Vol. 13 (No. 2 and 3), in spring 1982.

Chemical cover-ups

Gas was, of course, used as a weapon in the trench warfare of World War I, but one of the Nazis' most hideous innovations in World War II was to use it to exterminate millions of innocent civilians in the death camps of occupied Europe. Nazi doctors also conducted countless vile medical experiments on human guinea pigs, a practice that still elicits worldwide opprobrium. Outside China and Korea, however, the comparable activities of the Nazis' counterparts in Imperial Japan have been barely remarked upon – indeed, for many years, these crimes have been actively hushed up. History may be written by the victors, but the victorious Americans seem to have agreed with the vanquished Japanese not to mention what the latter did both before and during the war.

Unit 731

The Japanese Imperial Army first revealed its enthusiasm for biological warfare in experiments conducted by Unit 731 between 1932 and 1945 in Japanese-occupied Manchuria and beyond. Much of the testing was carried out in a prisoner camp at Ping Fang, near Harbin in northeast China, where Unit 731 operated under the name of the Water Purification Bureau. Up to three thousand Chinese and Korean nationals are thought to have died here, infected with diseases ranging from anthrax, cholera, typhoid and tuberculosis to bubonic plague. Human vivisections were performed along with such psychopathic experiments as freezing prisoners' limbs to observe the progress of frostbite.

Unit 731's commanding officer, Lieutenant-General Ishii Shiro, also experimented on US POWs at a camp at Mukden. In addition, Japanese planes dropped plague-infected fleas onto several Chinese cities in 1940, and attacked hundreds of hamlets with germ bombs. Japanese troops also dropped cholera and typhoid cultures into wells and ponds, killing an estimated two hundred thousand Chinese and Korean civilians. Unit 731 was stockpiling botulism and anthrax when the war ended, and has fittingly been described as the Asian Auschwitz.

Post-war whitewash

The work of Unit 731 was raised only once at the Tokyo war crimes tribunal in 1946-48, and that was by surprise, when the treatment of US prisoners was brought up. When the presiding judge asked "How about letting this item go?", the US lawyer replied "Well, then, I'll leave it". The Soviets carried out their own war crime trials in Khabarovsk, but neither Ishii Shiro nor his co-officers were ever tried. That was because the US military found their research just too fascinating to give up, describing their data on humans as "invaluable".

Dr Norbert Fell and Lieutenant Colonel Arvo Thompson, both members of General Douglas MacArthur's intelligence team at Fort Detrick, offered Ishii and his men immunity from prosecution if they assisted the US's own bio-weapons programme. That immunity also saw certain doctors from Unit 731 return to handsome positions in post-war Japan's medical community. Ishii's successor as commander, for example, Dr Masaji Kitano, became head of Japan's largest pharmaceutical company, the Green Cross.

Masking the trail

During the Korean War, the Chinese and Korean governments accused the US of using chemical and biological weapons on North Korea in 1951, charges that the International Scientific Commission said had a strong basis. B-29 pilots are said to have launched from Okinawa, while Ishii was allegedly in South Korea orchestrating bio-weapons for the US Army. Ishii's men went on to lecture for the US Army and to form the basis of President Kennedy's Project 112, which evaluated chemical and biological weapons for "limited war applications". However, Ishii's own involvement has always been denied.

In his 1981 article, "Japan's Biological Weapons 1930–1945: A Hidden Chapter in History", American journalist John W. Powell alleged that there had been a US government cover-up, only for the relevant chapter to be cut from the US edition. Author Sheldon Harris made similar charges in *Factories of Death*. It seemed that only Japan's right-wingers dared mention Unit 731, and even then only in the context of complete denial. Unlike the horrors of Germany's past, which the country's children learn about in school, Japan's bio-warfare programme is not taught in schools or mentioned in history books.

A 2002 trial in a Tokyo court acknowledged for the first time that Unit 731 – and other units – had engaged in "cruel and inhumane" biological warfare in China. However, the judges decided that the 180 plaintiffs' claims for compensation were without legal foundation. Meanwhile, Ishii's legacy continues: in late 2003, 29 Chinese people were hospitalized after buried chemical shells were uncovered in Heilongjiang.

Porton Down

Such conspiracies were by no means confined to the US or Japan. One of the longest-running Cold War cover-ups in the UK centred on the testing of chemical weapons on unwitting Britons at Porton Down in Wiltshire (where Dr David Kelly once worked, see p.61). The base had been testing poison gas since 1916, but thousands of military personnel, or "live guinea pigs", were exposed to nerve gas, mustard gas and other chemicals during the 1950s and 60s. One soldier, twenty-year-old Ronald Maddison, died in May 1953, after Sarin nerve gas was dripped onto his arm in an experiment presented to volunteers as seeking a cure for the common cold. A secret inquest held weeks later ruled that his death was an "accident". Only in December 2004, when the inquest was reopened, did a jury unanimously rule that Maddison was unlawfully killed.

But old habits die hard, and the UK government still sought to have the ruling overturned, insisting that the Porton Down scientists had done no wrong. Resistance ultimately proved futile, however, and the Maddison family were granted £100,000 in compensation. In January 2008, the Ministry of Defence announced that the government accepted there may have been "shortcomings" with regard to "aspects" of the experiments, which may have put the lives or health of the participants at risk. They agreed to pay out £3 million in compensation – "not even half the price of a tank by today's standards", as one survivor put it to the BBC. The money was to be divided among the 360 surviving veterans of Porton Down's experiments, working out at about £8,000 for each of them, some of whom had suffered lifelong ill health.

SOURCES

Books and articles

Sheldon H. Harris **Factories of Death: Japanese Biological Warfare 1932–1945 and the American Cover-up** (2002). The best-known (and best-received) book on Japan's bio-warfare experiments.

Robert Gomer, John W. Powell and Bert V.A. Roling **Japan's Biological Weapons 1930–1945: A Hidden Chapter in History** (*Bulletin of the Atomic Scientists*, Oct 1981). This survey of the complicity between the US Army and the Japanese war criminals is a faster read than Harris's book.

Websites

Ⓦ **www.fas.org/nuke/guide/japan/bw/** This is an easy-to-read summary of Japan's bio-weapon crimes and the US's post-war complicity in cover-up and development.

Ⓦ **www.theage.com.au/articles/2002/08/28/1030508070534.html** Shane Green's article from Australian newspaper *The Age* outlines how the Japanese authorities continue to deny and dismiss the charges of bio-warfare crimes laid against their empire.

AIDS

AIDS, or Acquired Immunodeficiency Syndrome, is the final, fatal – though not inevitable – stage of infection for people with Human Immunodeficiency Virus (HIV). Sufferers die as a result of having their immune systems wiped out, which makes them susceptible to conditions that are normally either extremely rare or not serious. Pneumonia, tuberculosis and Kaposi's sarcoma, a form of skin cancer, are common in the end stages.

AIDS was first identified by doctors in the US in 1982, when previously healthy, young homosexual men began dying of obscure cancers and pneumonia. Shortly afterwards, two distinct HIV viruses were discovered – HIV-1 and HIV-2 – and it was established that HIV could be contracted by sexual intercourse, direct contact with infected blood, or perinatal transmission. The first drug to treat AIDS to be approved by the US Food and Drug Administration (FDA) was AZT in 1987, but although various treatments can slow the growth of HIV and thus stave off AIDS, no cure has yet been found.

UNICEF has called AIDS "the worst catastrophe ever to hit the world". Figures from the Joint United Nations

Programme on HIV/AIDS (UNAIDS) say that from 1981 to 2006, AIDS killed 25 million people, while the World Health Organization (WHO) reported that in 2007 alone, some 33.2 million people were estimated to be living with HIV, 2.5 million people had become newly infected and 2.1 million people had died. Sub-Saharan Africa was grossly over-represented in all of those statistics – the region is home to just 10 percent of the global population, but had 68 percent of all the world's HIV cases in 2007. AIDS remains the primary cause of death in Africa. Elsewhere, the number of people living with HIV in Eastern Europe and Central Asia has increased by over 150 percent, while the estimated number of people living with HIV in Vietnam more than doubled between 2000 and 2005, and Indonesia has the fastest growing epidemic in Asia.

SARS

AIDS and Ebola are not the only contagious diseases suspected of being man-made. The precise cause of Severe Acute Respiratory Syndrome, or SARS – which caused death, panic and mayhem across East Asia and beyond in 2003 – hasn't been discovered, but the line supported by the Chinese government, for one, is that it may be a variation on a virus carried by cat-like creatures called civets.

One local theory, however, is that SARS was deliberately manufactured to slow the region's prodigious economic growth and power. The death toll from SARS in 2003 was a few hundred people, most of whom were in China, where the health system is relatively basic. The real impact of the disease was economic, in that the attendant fear and disruption caused financiers and businessmen to steer clear of the region. According to the financial services company J.P. Morgan, SARS caused greater damage to Asia's economy than the 2004 tsunami. Some Chinese find it suspicious that SARS did not appear to return during the warmer months of 2004. One rumour has it that this is because anyone suspected of having SARS is simply whisked away by the Chinese police and shot.

Where did it come from?

The precise origin of HIV remains unknown. According to one broadly accepted scientific theory, the disease originated among green monkeys in Africa, and somehow became transmitted to people, possibly because they hunted and ate the monkeys as "bush meat". However, not everyone goes along with this explanation. Many link the higher prevalence of HIV and AIDS in Africa and among homosexuals to something more sinister.

In conspiracist circles, two documents are often cited as proof that darker forces were at work. The first is a July 1969 Department of Defense appropriation request for funding from the US Senate for $10 million to develop synthetic biological agents, or bio-warfare weapons. US Army bio-warfare expert Dr Donald MacArthur told the Senate: "Within the next five to ten years, it would probably be possible to make a new infective micro-organism [that] … might be refractory to the immunological and therapeutic processes [depended upon] to maintain our relative freedom from infectious diseases" – in other words, a virus that would kill the immune system. The second document is National Security Memorandum 200, "Implications of Worldwide Population Growth for US Security & Overseas Interests", dated December 10, 1974 and declassified in 1989. In it, National Security Adviser Henry Kissinger is reported as arguing that "Depopulation should be the highest priority of US foreign policy towards the Third World", to secure mineral supplies for the US. How this depopulation was to be achieved was not specified.

The WHO: vaccinations that spread disease

In 1986, Dr Robert Strecker alleged that the US military distributed its HIV bio-weapon by means of the World Health Organization's smallpox vaccination programme, under which tens of millions of Africans were vaccinated by injection during the late 1970s. HIV was then introduced into the US population via Public Health Service hepatitis B vaccinations on gay and bisexual men, carried out between 1978 and 1981 in New York, Los Angeles, San Francisco, St Louis, Denver and Chicago. Those cities subsequently developed the country's highest AIDS rates.

Time magazine denounced Strecker's theory, but it has since been supported by various doctors, including Dr Alan Cantwell, author of *AIDS and the Doctors of Death*, and Dr Robert Gallo, who is credited with having been the first to isolate HIV (at Fort Detrick in 1984). Gallo commented in 1987 that the smallpox–HIV link was "interesting and important", adding that "live vaccines such as that used for smallpox can activate a dormant infection such as HIV". Dr Johnathan Mann of the WHO's AIDS programme responded that the smallpox–HIV link just doesn't fit, while the *British Medical Journal* sardonically commented that the theory came from the same source as the "Hitler Diaries", i.e. it was bogus.

Charges that the disease may have inadvertently been spread by vaccinations resurfaced in February 2003. A team of US doctors, led by Dr David Gisselquist, wrote in the *International Journal of STD and AIDS* that only around thirty percent of pre-1988 AIDS cases in Africa resulted from sexual transmission, not the ninety percent usually claimed, and that over half were spread by unsterilized needles. The team says that the evidence was discounted because of "preconceptions about African sexuality and a desire to maintain public trust in healthcare". However, UK newspaper *The Times* quoted Professor Michael Adler of UCL medical school as being "extremely doubtful" that needles could have caused so much damage. The WHO estimates that unsafe injections are responsible for five percent of HIV infections. Experts point out that if dirty needles were responsible, then hepatitis B would be growing faster than AIDS in Africa and Asia, and also that dirty needles would affect all age groups, whereas AIDS overwhelmingly affects sexually active age groups.

Cold War or big business?

According to Dr Boyd Graves, AIDS is a joint US-USSR plot to obliterate blacks and homosexuals. The plot, known as the "Special Virus Program", was apparently first hatched in 1960, although a joint agreement to implement it was only made in 1972. Graves links Gulf War Syndrome to AIDS, saying that both were spread by giving contaminated vaccines to soldiers. He also claims that he himself contracted AIDS and cured it with "colloidal silver", but that this and other known cures are being suppressed (significantly, he singles out an Israeli medical institute and an Israeli pharmaceutical company for criticism, hinting at a Zionist conspiracy).

Similarly, the unfortunately named Dr Gary Glum writes in *Full Disclosure* that liquorice extract, essiac tea and an olive-leaf extract are viable treatments, but that they are being suppressed by pharmaceutical companies. He argues that AIDS was concocted at Cold Spring Harbor, New York, in around 1978 as part of a plot by the Olympians, a pro-eugenics sect of the Illuminati (see p.290), to wipe out non-whites. For that matter, he also says that AIDS can be transmitted through kissing, mosquito bites and "casual contact", in which case nearly all of us should be dead by now. Such nonsense doesn't disprove his other theories, but hardly makes them more plausible. Neither is it clear why a company would suppress a highly lucrative AIDS cure, unless there's more money to be made in continuous, long-term care than there is in a cure (a theory also suggested in relation to a cure for cancer, see p.271).

Kissinger, Rockefeller, Mengele and Malta

In *Emerging Viruses: AIDS and Ebola: Nature, Accident or Intentional?*, Dr Leonard Horowitz alleges that the twin co-funders and inventors of AIDS were Fort Detrick, home to the National Cancer Institute, and the Rockefeller Institute for Medical Research. With the aid of defence companies such as Litton Bionetics, they set out to target Jews, blacks, Hispanics and gays. Horowitz suggests that Kissinger's 1974 memo arguing that the US should actively seek to depopulate the Third World was based on the plans of various prominent individuals at the Council on Foreign

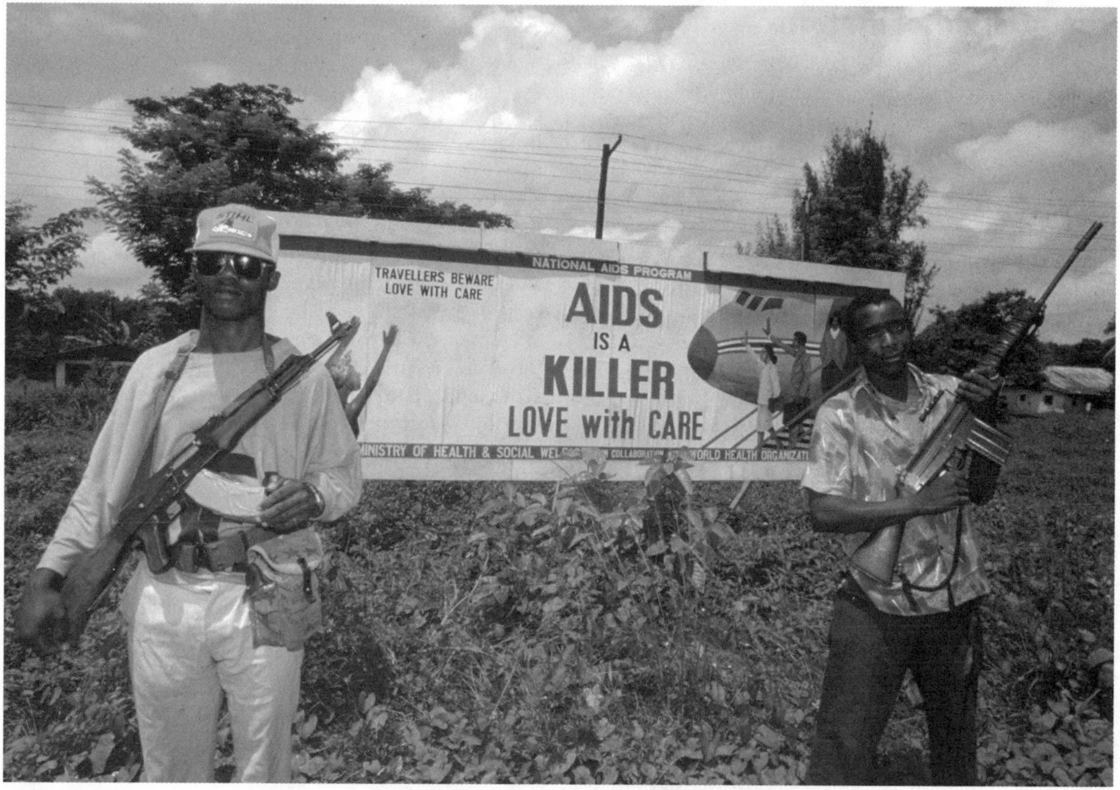

AIDS epidemic in Africa: the World Health Organization warns people to "love with care".

Relations (see p.140). He argues that various parties had already carried out their own cancer tests on Puerto Rican patients, so such eugenics-based work would be nothing new. As Nazi scientists had been brought to the US under Operations Paperclip and Sunshine, US taxpayers were funding Dr Mengele's protégés to concoct genocidal diseases. The flesh-eating disease Ebola was another example.

Horowitz rather loses his thread when he traces the US eugenics programme back to the quasi-Masonic Sovereign Military Order of Malta. However, his contention that Gallo may have actually discovered HIV back in the early 1970s, but that his work was suppressed, is echoed by Richie and Rosalind Chirimuuta in *AIDS, Africa and Racism*. They argue that much of the literature about AIDS in Africa is racially biased, and they wonder why the possibility that AIDS was a lab construct has not been more fully investigated. They also note the similarity between HIV and the sheep virus Visna, hinting at some lab-induced mutation.

Soviet disinformation

In his 1986 pamphlet *AIDS: USA Home-Made Evil*, Jacobo Segal, biology professor at Humboldt University in East Berlin, suggested that HIV was created at Fort Detrick in 1977, when the sheep virus Visna was spliced together with HIV-1. The resulting concoction was tested on "volunteer" prisoners, in exchange for early release, and HIV then spread to the population through the gay community. Fort Detrick promptly denied Segal's theory, while KGB defector Vasili Mitrokhin subsequently denounced it as a KGB disinformation programme. According to Norman Covert's book *Cutting Edge*, Mikhail Gorbachev himself apologized to Ronald Reagan for the rumours. In March 1992, then-intelligence chief and later prime minister of Russia, Yevgeni Primakov, admitted that the KGB had made up the story that AIDS was a "crafty" American plot.

Jews against blacks

Both Louis Farrakhan of the Nation of Islam and the New Black Panther Party have charged that AIDS is a Jewish plot to wipe out blacks. The Anti-Defamation League's director Abraham Foxman replied that Farrakhan was "a relentless racist and anti-Semite" who has accused Jewish bankers of financing the Holocaust, Jewish doctors of infecting black babies with the AIDS virus, and has claimed that the Jewish community controlled the African slave trade. According to Nation of Islam lore, whites are "blue-eyed devils" created in a failed laboratory experiment.

The Vatican fails to help

In late 2003, the Catholic Church instructed people in AIDS-stricken countries not to use condoms, because they're not impermeable to HIV. The head of the Vatican's Pontifical Council for the Family, Cardinal Alfonso Trujillo, told the BBC that HIV was small enough to pass through the "net" formed by condoms. The WHO countered by stating that correct condom use reduces HIV infection by ninety percent, and that while condoms can break or slip, they're impermeable to the virus.

Bush and "Big Pharma"

In January 2003, President George W. Bush announced a five-year, $15 billion aid package to fight AIDS in Africa and the Caribbean. However, Oxfam has criticized the Bush administration's refusal to allow poor countries to import low-cost generic drugs to treat HIV and AIDS, and some say that the aid programme is a massive bung to major US pharmaceutical companies, intended to squash attempts elsewhere to produce cheaper, generic versions of the drugs. It's also been alleged that the money was made provisional on the acceptance of Christian-sourced education and agreement to pro-US trade rules.

Further connections

South Africa's president, Thabo Mbeki, has claimed that the CIA is part of a conspiracy to promote the view that HIV causes AIDS, which allows Big Pharma to sell useless – but highly profitable – anti-retroviral drugs to control AIDS. Having "exposed" the scam and said that AIDS is really caused by poverty, Mbeki also claims to have been the target of a broader CIA–Big Pharma plot to undermine his position. The South African government has interfered with AIDS drug distribution programmes, and the African National Congress (ANC) party has accused the country's HIV/AIDS treatment advocacy group, Treatment Action Campaign, of plotting "to market unsafe drugs". After massive protest, in 2003 the ANC allowed the distribution of AIDS drugs, but it has still accused the US of treating Africans like "guinea pigs", and "entering into a conspiracy" with drug makers over AIDS treatments that may have caused deaths.

In 2004, reports appeared stating that there was a resurgence of polio in numerous African states, despite a sixteen-year, $3 billion WHO campaign to eradicate it. As *The Baltimore Sun* reported, Muslims in northern Nigeria were refusing polio vaccines, believing them to be contaminated with either an anti-fertility agent or AIDS, in "an American plot to depopulate the developing world". One WHO doctor explained that the war in the Middle East had aggravated the situation. "If America is fighting people in the Middle East, the conclusion is that they are fighting Muslims." During and after the wars in Afghanistan and Iraq, the number of polio cases in Nigeria rose from 3 incidents in 2001, amd 54 in 2002 to 74 in the first eleven months of 2003. Three predominantly Muslim Nigerian states banned the vaccines for periods in 2004, prompted, said *The Baltimore Sun*, by "doctors, imams, political leaders and professors who endorse the conspiracy theory". New polio outbreaks in Benin, Cameroon, Togo, Chad and the Ivory Coast, all once Africa's leading polio-free countries, were traced back to Nigeria, according to *The New York Times*. Nigerian polio cases increased fivefold to 259 new cases in 2004, while global cases reached 339, double that of 2003. Ultimately, however, to the dismay of conspiracy theorists, the immunization programme did indeed stem the polio outbreak.

No end in sight

While the origins of HIV may never be discovered, it seems all too conceivable to many people that the virus could have been made in a laboratory and then released, whether deliberately or not. But there's more to the destructive power of AIDS than its effect on individuals. Whether or not the disease is a bio-weapon being used for eugenic purposes, it's certainly being used as a rhetorical weapon, to stir up hatred between people of different races, religions or sexualities, or to promote moral agendas.

In early 2005, *The Washington Post* published the results of a survey of five hundred African-Americans that had been carried out by Oregon University and the RAND Corporation. Over half of those questioned believed that HIV was man-made; over a quarter said they believed that AIDS had been produced in a government laboratory; and more than a tenth believed that it had been created, and spread, by the CIA. The survey also reported that many believed that cures for AIDS were being withheld from the poor, and that those who took new HIV medicines were government guinea pigs, while some said that AIDS was genocide against blacks.

That same year, the US State Department saw fit to issue a riposte to the charges that AIDS was a US-made bio-weapon. They argued that "false rumors and misinformation naturally arose" because there was no obvious explanation as to the cause of the disease, which was further exploited by Soviet disinformation specialists and the "musings of conspiracy theorists". The theory the State Department seemed to back was that the main HIV-1 virus originated in monkeys and probably became established in human beings in around 1930, as was suggested by research done by scientists at the Los Alamos National Laboratory on "powerful supercomputers".

SOURCES

Books

Alan Cantwell AIDS and the Doctors of Death: An Inquiry into the Origin of the AIDS Epidemic (1992). In this and in his *Queer Blood: The Secret AIDS Genocide Plot* (1993), Cantwell makes some interesting – if excitably written – arguments.

Richard and Rosalind Chirimuuta AIDS, Africa and Racism (1997). The authors blame a pernicious combination of imperial ambition and racist attitudes for the notion that AIDS originated in Africa and that the continent is ravaged by the disease (although parts of it undeniably are).

Leonard G. Horowitz Emerging Viruses: AIDS and Ebola: Nature, Accident or Intentional? (1996). Horowitz seemingly manages to interview every expert and cite nearly every theory on AIDS in this grittily detailed (if at times flailing and over-personalized) polemic, which insists that AIDS was manufactured.

Websites

Ⓦ **www.boydgraves.com** Dr Boyd Graves expounds his views on the genocidal function of AIDS as a weapon, with a fascinating chart on the origins of AIDS, which he traces back to the nineteenth century.

Ⓦ **www.unaids.org** The home of the Joint United Nations Programme on HIV/AIDS.

Ⓦ **usinfo.state.gov/media/Archive/2005/Jan/14-777030.html** The State Department's official denial that AIDS was created by the US.

Ⓦ **www.who.int** The World Health Organization's website is host to numerous reports and statistics covering the global AIDS epidemic.

Secret bases

Conspiracy literature is permeated with references to scores, if not hundreds, of "secret bases" scattered around the world. These include government bunkers, command centres, test sites and depots for awful, yet spectacular, weapons, and hide-outs and bases for desperadoes from this world... and others. The same names keep recurring, showing the powerful grip these places have on the imagination of conspiracy theorists. And every now and then, as in the case of Fort Detrick for instance, there really is a lot of dark history for the imagination to feed on. What follows is a handy primer to the most (in)famous secret bases.

Heart of darkness: the Pentagon

The iconic Pentagon, located just outside Washington DC in the American state of Virginia, was constructed during World War II to house the War Department, the Office of Strategic Services (the predecessor of the CIA) and other ministries previously dotted around the US capital. Its main proponent, John McCloy, who was also, at various times, chairman of both the Council on Foreign Relations (see p.140) and Chase Manhattan Bank, ensured that it was built despite opposition from President Roosevelt. These days, 23,000–29,000 employees of the CIA and Department of Defense work in the Pentagon (depending on your sources). It's an ugly, but tough building, strong enough on September 11, 2001, to absorb the Boeing 757 that crashed directly into it (see p.399).

The Pentagon: a symbol of Freemasonry or something more sinister?

Officially, the Pentagon is pentagonally shaped due to the constricting layout of the surrounding roads on the original design site. However, the Pentagon can be seen as being shaped around a five-pointed star – the symbol of Freemasonry (and of the fifty states on the US flag). Most of the Founding Fathers were Freemasons (see p.82), and the entire city of Washington is said to have been laid out along Masonic symmetries by architect Pierre Charles L'Enfant (see p.91). The five-pointed star is also Satanist, and the Pentagon is built on a marsh called Hell's Bottom. To some conspiracists, that suggests that it's actually a huge ringpiece or anus, which in turn alludes to sodomy, the favourite sexual practice of Satanists. It's certainly an evil enough place for some people to believe it required an exorcism. In 1967, as part of a 70,000-strong peace demonstration, some hippies sought to rid the building of the evil spirits within by singing and chanting until it levitated and turned orange (because it's a nice colour?). It didn't work.

The building is allegedly full of symbolism reflecting numbers that have a Masonic meaning, such as five (for the star), seven (it doesn't take longer than seven minutes to get from any point in the building to another) and eleven. According to www.freemasonrywatch.org, eleven also puts the Pentagon in the frame for 9/11, as construction of the Pentagon began on September 11, 1941 – exactly sixty years before 9/11. (For more on the numerical coincidences of 9/11, see box on p.404.)

The Pentagon is apparently mathematically appealing to Pythagoreans and Majestic-12 (see p.345), and the latter is also suspected of operating from there. Others claim that the base played a role in Operation Paperclip, under which former Nazi scientists were brought to the US during the Cold War, before continuing their experiments to develop weapons at the Edgewood Arsenal base. It's even been claimed that the Pentagon was built at the request of several Nazis who came to Washington in the 1930s, and wanted a base for their eventual return after the war – a request said to have been backed by rocket scientist Jack Parsons and his spiritual mentor, Aleister Crowley.

Crowley and Montauk

Crowley is also said to have worked (in an undisclosed capacity) with Nazis who ended up at the mysterious mega-lab of Montauk Point, Long Island. This takes its name from its original inhabitants, the Montauk Indians, who according to the courts no longer exist as a tribe, though they themselves continue to insist that they do. Supposedly a defunct air force base, Montauk was rumoured to be reopening as a New York state park, but that didn't happen. Instead, people have apparently seen high-power and high-capacity phone lines being taken into the sealed-off underground complex – which suggests to some theorists that electromagnetic experimentation is continuing. Montauk is allegedly where the time-travelling navy ship USS *Eldridge* reappeared in 1983 (see p.283), and it's indubitably near the area where TWA Flight 800 crashed into the ocean in 1996 (see p.336). Theorists have also pointed at Montauk in relation to the downing of flights SwissAir 111 in 1998 and EgyptAir 990 in 1999. All those incidents are said to be the joint work of a Masonic sect from the National Security Council and Nazis who were left behind after U-boat operations during World War II.

Give the Nazis a home

Some conspiracy theorists also believe that Nazis are still living in parts of Antarctica. Two German expeditions to the continent were made in 1938 and 1939, allegedly in the hope of finding Aryans (who had kicked out the previous inhabitants, the Knights Templar) living under the ice. A U-boat base was built there, and U-boats were supposedly spotted heading in that direction after the war. The US is said to have sent a task force of 1400 men in pursuit, under "Operation High Jump", who were ostensibly searching for coal deposits. The theory continues that the leader of the mission, Admiral Byrd, succeeded in meeting with Aryan representatives, and agreed to keep their secret safe. The man behind the plan, Navy Secretary James Forrestal, was outraged, but he was "retired" to a psychiatric isolation ward, where he killed himself. All this, it's said, explains why drilling on the continent is banned – it's so that the civilization beneath it won't be discovered. Some say that Nazis shot down Kiwi airliner TE 109 in 1979 for spying. Although Antarctica is not usually prone to the vagaries of tectonic shifts, an earthquake was detected there in 1998 that measured 8.1 on the Richter scale. This has been attributed to massive nuclear blasts as part of Aryan subterranean construction work.

America's underground government

Apparently, the Nazis aren't the only ones who are big on bunkers. As part of the US's "Continuity of Government" programme, which was set up during the 1980s to prepare for the possibility of nuclear war or some other calamity, the US government has built a network of deep underground nuclear-proof bases. The programme falls under the aegis of the Federal Emergency Management Agency (FEMA), which certainly exists, and apparently had the tunnels built in cooperation with the RAND Corporation and the Mining Bureau.

The "Continuity of Government" plan calls for the president, cabinet and entire executive branch to relocate in the event of some major disaster to a self-sustaining underground base beneath Mount Weather, Virginia, sixty miles from Washington DC. Under the Joint Emergency Evacuation Plan, special teams equipped with war plans and military codes would accompany several dozen designated constitutional successors to the president to a hundred secret command posts across the country, in locations including Pennsylvania, West Virginia, Maryland, North Carolina and Napa County, California. All are linked via satellite, ground-wave and microwave relay systems.

That much is known. What some conspiracy theorists speculate, however, is that FEMA also has over six hundred prison camps across the US, all ready to receive prisoners following the imposition of martial law. The camps are all said to be connected by road and rail, and some have mini-airstrips. Most can apparently house twenty thousand prisoners, but one in Fairbanks, Alaska, can take two million. These camps were built under the Rex 84 Program, designed to deal with a mass exodus of illegal aliens (from Mexico, rather than outer space). However, they're now claimed to be part of two conspiracies run by FEMA – Operation Cable Splicer and Operation Garden Plot – which will enable the government to control the population when the New World Order (see p.141) begins, abetted by fleets of hidden United Nations tanks.

Forts and weapons centres

A military base that undeniably exists and has attracted the attention of a lot of conspiracy theorists over the years is Fort Detrick, located in Frederick County, Maryland, only an hour's drive from Washington DC. Fort Detrick is now home to the US Army Medical Research and Materiel Command, the National Cancer Institute (NCI-Frederick) and other biomedical organizations. It has also been home to population control research, and was where Dr Frank W. Olson fell victim to the Special Operations Division's experiments with LSD and other incapacitating drugs (see p.14). Until 1969, Fort Detrick was the US Army's main base for research into chemical and biological weapons, a programme that was then, officially, destroyed. It was reopened by President Nixon in 1971 as the Frederick Cancer Research Facility.

Detrick's dirty past was revealed by the 1977 congressional report, *US Army Activities in the US Biological Warfare Program*. The fort's website openly describes the army's experiments with dispersing bacterial spores into the Pentagon, San Francisco and the subways of New York. Detrick's work has been associated with Dugway Proving Ground, Utah; Edgewood Arsenal, Maryland; Pine Bluff Arsenal, Arkansas; Rocky Mountain Arsenal, Colorado, and others. It has also been suggested that Detrick is where HIV/AIDS and the strains of anthrax that hit the US in the wake of 9/11 were developed. In addition, the fort has been linked to Porton Down laboratories in the UK, where nerve gas was tested on "volunteer" soldiers during the 1950s (see p.289) and where the military use of gas had been investigated since World War I. The various projects undertaken at Detrick may just have been too evil – or idiotic – to have ever received publicly supported funding. But then that's what the infamous "black budgets" are all about – secret flows of money with no public trail.

It's these "black budgets", according to conspiracists, that fund astounding new weapons in the US outback. It's reported that electronic weapons systems are developed at places such as Nellis, Las Vegas, an airbase and munitions facility where two hundred nuclear warheads are stored. The Nellis complex incorporates the Tolicha Peak Electronic Combat Range and the Tonopah Test Range, where the Department of Energy tests artillery shells, bombs, cruise missiles and rockets, and it was home to the first squadron of F-117 stealth fighters. These were developed around Antelope Valley, California, home to research facilities for aircraft industry giants Lockheed, McDonnell Douglas and Northrop – companies that the conspiracy theorists say have all dabbled in testing anti-gravity propulsion systems and other exotic engine designs.

It's said that Lockheed has its own hothouse in Plant 42 at Groom Lake, Nevada, where strange new breeds of stealth and hypersonic aircraft use two two-mile runways. Air force transporters fly in and out with cargoes during the night, while base workers – supposedly told to deny that they work at Groom Lake – are flown in from Las Vegas by day. Northrop Corporation's equivalent is the Tejon Ranch below the Tehachapi Mountains, in Lancaster, California. No livestock is visible on this supposed "cattle ranch", which Northrop admits is an "electromagnetic research facility" – as shown by the large radar and microwave dishes on its surface – and which has 42 levels underground. There are also said to be tunnels to other nearby installations, including Edwards Air Force Base, a hundred miles northeast of Los Angeles.

Aliens among us

You might think that with Russia out of the arms race and other contenders left trailing behind, there would be little need for the US to keep on developing ever more sophisticated weaponry. As UFO-inclined theorists see it, however, the US military is preparing to repel space invaders – with friendly aliens helping to upgrade weaponry they regard as primitive.

Although the command centre for US Space Command is at the Peterson base in Colorado, the space weapons being built for the SDI programme – to defend Earth from alien attack – are apparently being developed at the Kirtland base in Albuquerque. The Wright Patterson base, near Dayton, Ohio, is where the US Air Force allegedly investigated UFOs under Project Blue Book, logging up over seven hundred yet "unidentified" sightings. But sightings aren't

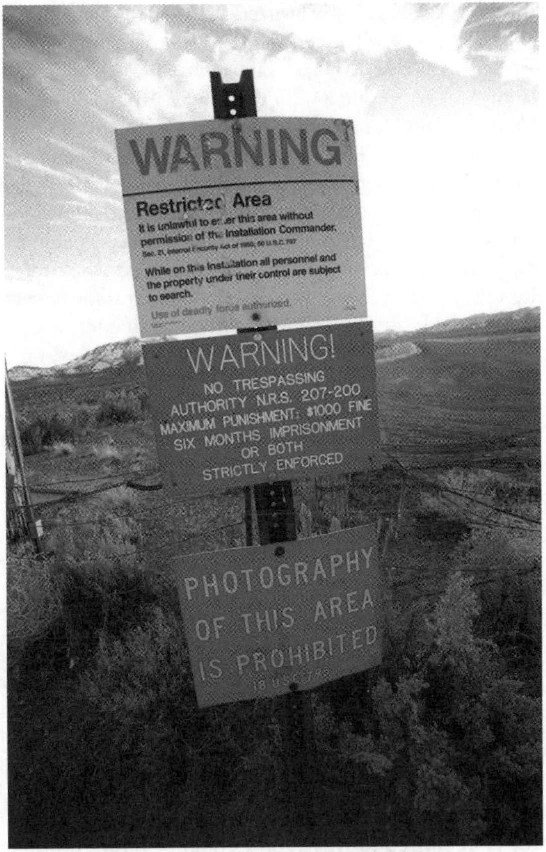

Area 51 in Rachel, Nevada: visitors are clearly not welcome.

the only activity going on there. Wright is also said to be an aviation research centre that holds UFO wreckage from the Roswell incident (see p.342), and it is linked – in the conspiracist's mind – to the most famous "secret" military base of all, Area 51 in Nevada. Supposedly, aircraft that incorporate designs pilfered from crashed UFOs are built and flown at Area 51 using the world's longest runway –

the base itself is as big as Switzerland – while signs outside say "trespassers will be executed".

Alien spacecraft are also said to be housed ten miles from Area 51 at Site S4, hidden under Mount Shasta in California near a base that's home to an alien race called the Lemurians. (The Lemurians are not to be confused with another group of underground-dwelling interstellar migrants, the Terras, who it's said prefer to live a thousand miles beneath the Earth's crust.) More UFOs are thought to be garaged two miles beneath the Jicarilla Apache Indian Reservation near Dulce, New Mexico, which some believe is the world's first joint Earth-alien bio-genetics laboratory. A similar co-stellar project is said to be based on a French Polynesian island, where the Bilderberg Group (see p.250) and the Council on Foreign Relations have apparently allowed the aliens to maintain a base to observe earthlings since the 1950s, and vice versa. Finally, it's been claimed that aliens have also marked out and built their own Middle Eastern kingdom, Kuwait, the borders of which were drawn to ensure that, from space, the country bears the profile of the Lord of the Sith, Darth Vader. Which explains, of course, why the Pentagon stepped in so valiantly to rescue Kuwait in 1991.

SOURCES

Websites

- **www.abovetopsecret.com** This charts allegations of what FEMA's true purpose may be; compare it with the official site, www.fema.gov.
- **www.boblazar.com** One man's own collection of places you couldn't visit, even if you knew they existed.
- **www.detrick.army.mil** Fort Detrick's website is adamant that the fort has a benign influence on its neighbourhood, being Frederick County's largest employer and helping it be "the third fastest growing county in Virginia".
- **www.mod.uk/issues/portondownvolunteers/history.html** The official Ministry of Defence version of what happened to the volunteers at Porton Down.
- **www.mutanex.com/reconalpha.html** "Six State Tour of Secret Bases & Secret Technologies Bases" – this fascinating reportage of one man's odyssey around the US's alternative arsenals steps into the unknowns of UFOlogy.
- **www.secret-bases.co.uk** Alan Turnbull's absorbing tour of secret bases in the UK, written with a tinge of wide-eyed wonder.

HAARP

Completed and operational since 2007, HAARP, or the High Frequency Active Auroral Research Program, is an array of 180 antennae neatly lined out across 33 acres. Officially this massive transmitter is designed to watch and observe happenings in the ionosphere, the great layer of sky that starts thirty miles above the Earth's surface and stretches for six hundred miles into space. That needs a lot of power, and HAARP needs 10 megawatts to deliver its 3.6 million watts of radio frequency power and 1 gigawatt of electro-radioactive pulse power.

As well as being the largest such transmitter in the world, HAARP is one of the most remote, being located eight miles north of Gakona, Alaska. There is a broad range of ionospheric conditions in the area, which is also suitable because HAARP's transmitting and observing gadgetry needs a quiet electromagnetic location away from cities. Managed by the Air Force Research Laboratory and the Office of Naval Research, HAARP enjoys scientific and research input from the University of Alaska, UCLA, Cornell, Stanford and the universities of Maryland, Massachusetts, MIT and Tulsa,

THE ORIGINS OF HAARP

HAARP is said by some theorists to be an updated version of the inventions of Croatian-born engineer Nikolas Tesla, who features in several engineering-related conspiracy theories (see p.255). An electrical genius, Tesla moved to the US in 1884, where he worked for Thomas Edison and Westinghouse Power. By the time he died in 1943, he had amassed over seven hundred inventions, ranging from fluorescent lights and alternating current generators to power systems and flying machines.

In 1900, with private backing, Tesla set about building the hideous 187-foot Wardenclyffe Tower on Long Island. An octagonal pyramid, spearing up into something that resembled a huge, sagging fly's eye, it was designed to broadcast electricity worldwide from surrounding power stations. Financier J.P. Morgan, one of its principal backers, withdrew when it occurred to him that Wardenclyffe might damage his own electricity monopoly. Even so, the structure was finished by 1904.

What Tesla was up to at Wardenclyffe over the next few years isn't clear, but in April 1908, something vast exploded in Tunguska, Siberia, wiping out half a million acres of forest. The official theory – and it's still no more than that – is that a piece of Encke's Comet rammed into the Earth. However, some say the blast was a misfiring from Wardenclyffe, beaming trillions of watts of power into the wrong area. The tower was demolished in 1917, as German U-boats were reportedly using it for navigation.

Tesla returned in 1934 with what *The New York Times* called a "death beam", which could melt enemy bomber engines 250 miles away and cause armies of millions to "drop dead in their tracks", while also powering flying machines to defend the homeland and bomb the enemy. However, the paltry $2 million needed to build the beam didn't materialize. Indeed, many of Tesla's designs were never constructed and he died in poverty. Fifty years later, however, Tesla's "death beam" concept resurfaced in the weapon patent taken out by Dr Bernard Eastlund, which referenced Tesla's earlier works on wireless energy transmission.

among others. According to Alaska University, HAARP exists "to further advance our knowledge of the physical and electrical properties of the Earth's ionosphere which affects our military and civilian communication and navigation systems". The ionosphere is of interest to science, business and the military because it disrupts ground-to-satellite signals, mangles radio and radar signals, and can induce power surges and outages. HAARP's work could lead to improvements in communications, for example with submerged submarines, according to Alaska University.

That HAARP is being backed by the US Department of Defense, the air force and the navy doesn't lend much conviction to the idea that it's solely a "civilian" project. Why are quite so many academic bodies involved? What is such a device doing in the middle of nowhere? Is HAARP something more than just a big experiment involving the upper atmosphere? Is the Alaskan-based antenna, in fact, a weapon of mass destruction, able to manipulate the planet's meteorology to the malign ends of its masters? Whatever it is, it's got a lot of conspiracy theorists very excited indeed.

A mega-weapon of the modern age?

According to theorists like Jerry E. Smith (author of *HAARP: The Ultimate Weapons of the Conspiracy*), HAARP is anything but a grand exploration of the atmosphere for the sake of science and better phone calls. An offshoot of the Strategic Defense Initiative (SDI), it's uncannily similar to a weapon designed by Texan physicist Bernard Eastlund – US Patent 4,686,605 – which could "alter" the upper atmosphere by "transmitting electromagnetic radiation", enabling one to eavesdrop, interfere with and destroy an enemy's communications without interfering with one's own. What's more, Eastlund claims, the device can be used in "missile or aircraft destruction", and its long-range Electro Magnetic Pulses (EMP) can knock down power grids.

The patent for Eastlund's invention is owned by ARCO Power Technologies Inc, a subsidiary of defence contractor ARCO-Atlantic Richfield – the company contracted by the Pentagon to build HAARP. The patent claims that "weather modification is possible". Alaska University, however, insists that "HAARP will not affect the weather", possibly in response to rumours that it could fundamentally affect agriculture by fostering crop growth on previously barren land, but inflicting drought and famine elsewhere. The university states that HAARP's transmitted energy has practically no effect on the weather-producing troposphere or the stratosphere. Electromagnetic interactions only occur in the ionosphere, the size and capricious magnetic stability of which reduce the effect of HAARP to the level of an "immersion heater in the Yukon River". HAARP's operations are not meddlesome but "strictly passive".

However, a 1996 paper by US Air Force officers entitled "Weather as a Force Multiplier: Owning the Weather in 2025" outlined the military's efforts to pursue weather-altering weaponry. Interestingly, the paper did not cite the outlawing of weather modification systems by the UN in 1970 and 1976 as the primary obstacle to developing effective weather weaponry. Indeed, it only briefly mentioned "extreme and controversial examples of weather modification" – such as "climate modification" or "steering storms" – because the technical obstacles to such ideas were considered "insurmountable within 30 years".

In 1998, Congress increased funding for HAARP to examine "the utility of the ionospheric modification", to be used in "military, intelligence, counterproliferation, counterterrorism and counter-narcotics missions ... [supporting] military and intelligence requirements identified in the Joint Vision 2010 Defense Science and Technology Strategy", involving "Full Spectrum Dominance and the Joint Warfighting Capability", to "assess initial capabilities of Stochastic Resonance for Defense and intelligence applications." Whatever all that means in practice, it hardly sounds passive. And as for the weather, a paper given at the 1997 Intersociety Energy Conversion Engineering Conference declared that "the effects of HAARP on the weather are completely unknown", adding that "heating the jet stream over Alaska could have profound results on the weather in Denver or Miami".

The following year, the European Parliament's Committee on Foreign Affairs, Security and Defence Policy said that it considered HAARP "to be a global concern" and called for its "legal, ecological and ethical implications to be examined by an international independent body", while also stating disappointment at the US's refusal to give evidence about the device's environmental risks. However, any follow-up was dropped because of the EU's lack of clout over US military policy, and to avoid a Washington–Brussels showdown – proving to some that resistance is indeed futile.

Earthquakes and tsunamis

And then there's the whole business of "stochastic resonance". Eastlund's patent had its roots in the work of Nikolas Tesla, whose experiments with stochastic resonance in New York around 1900 are said to have nearly destroyed several buildings. Is HAARP an attempt to harness the same technology on a global scale?

Some conspiracy theorists suspect that HAARP may be able to peer deep into the Earth and spy on the underground secrets of enemies. And if earthquakes can disrupt the ionosphere and magnetosphere, could radio waves blasted through the Earth have the same effect? It has even been suggested that HAARP was behind the massive earthquake in the Indian Ocean in December 2004, which caused a devastating tsunami. This not only struck the major East Asian economies – burgeoning competitors to the US – but gave the Bush administration the chance to ride to the rescue in a region that's simmering with anti-American sentiment.

Rohan Gunaratna of the Institute of Defence and Strategic Studies in Singapore has pointed out that in both the worst-hit areas, Aceh and southern Thailand, Islamic separatist groups are fighting their respective governments. He told CNN that with the terrorist groups literally washed away, the tsunami afforded "a golden opportunity" for the US to step in and win the war of ideas. Secretary of State Condoleezza Rice concurred, telling the US

Senate in January 2005: "I do agree that the tsunami was a wonderful opportunity to show not just the US government, but the heart of the American people, and I think it has paid great dividends for us." Democrat senator Barbara Boxer reminded her that the tsunami "was one of the worst tragedies of our lifetime".

Professor Ali Hassan of the University of Malaysia suggested that earthquakes could be provoked by submarine nuclear tests conducted by the superpowers. Britain's *Big Issue* magazine reported, in February 2005, that oil corporations in Southeast Asia had been continually firing huge "air shots" into the ground in the days preceding the quake, in order to chart the underlying geology. Whether the air shots had caused the quake, no oil company or geological surveyors would say, the magazine added.

Power cuts, mind control and the New World Order

On August 11, 2003, power cuts blacked out eastern Canada and the northeastern United States, bringing chaos and darkness to New York, Detroit, Toronto and Ottawa – a total of fifty million people. The Canadians blamed a fire at a power plant near Niagara, the US blamed a power transmission problem from Canada. The University of Tokyo, however, recorded a testing of HAARP that began at 4.00pm, just eleven minutes before the blackout began. Was HAARP flexing its muscles? Concerned citizen Michael Kane wrote to the Department of Energy, but received no reply, so he put his fears on the Web.

While HAARP is officially a high-frequency research device, theorists like Jerry Smith say it can use the same electromagnetic low-frequency (ELF) radiation and radio waves that both Western and Soviet researchers have reportedly shown to be the frequencies at which the human brain operates – thus enabling it to be tapped into from a distance. Carrying no ionizing radiation and low heat, and having no visibly grotesque manifestations in terms of physical deformities or vicious diseases (at least, not in any immediate sense), ELF signals cannot be detected. As Smith argues in his book on HAARP, this makes them "ideal for covert use".

Smith claims that the US government is researching the use of ELF signals "as a handle on mind control". He isn't alone in claiming that many former Soviet scientists were involved in setting up HAARP and are engaged in its research, which taps into the "one world" theory of the New World Order (see p141). According to Smith, HAARP is the ultimate, largely untraceable, weapon of mass destruction, able to smite troublesome countries with floods and droughts (as seen in China and North Korea) or earthquakes (as in Japan, Iran and Southeast Asia). HAARP thus forms the biggest part of the Strategic Defense Initiative, which might appear to be a feeble missile defence system, but is actually – according to some conspiracy theorists – a raft of weaponry to control people on every front.

Some theorists also blamed HAARP for Hurricane Katrina (see p.311), which devastated New Orleans in 2005. They claim it was part of a grand scheme to send oil prices through the roof and to use the profits to buy up Gulf Coast real estate on the cheap. One blogger claimed that Katrina was intentionally created to give the Bush administration a reason to introduce a bill that would allow them to set up an "official" weather control agency using HAARP and chemtrails (chemical-laden aircraft contrails) – although that bill was actually introduced in March 2005, several months before Katrina hit. Chemtrails are suspected of containing metals or other chemical elements which, when strafed in lines into the high skies, can further HAARP's radar and climate-meddling range. Said to be notably thicker than normal contrails, the chemtrails' patterns are also allegedly worth noting – with the various grid or parallel line formations apparently signifying whether they are being used for climate control, mind control (an aerial offshoot of MK-ULTRA), or simply to poison people. The 2001 Space Preservation Act sought to list chemtrails as an "exotic weapons system", in order to get them banned – but it didn't succeed. Still, the US Air Force has called the idea a hoax.

MICROWAVES

Conspiracy theorists claim mini-tech mind control now lies well within the capacity of earthling inventors. Fillings, spectacle frames, pencils, earrings – all have been cited as the carriers of tiny "silent radio" transmitters. Just like dog whistles, these transmitters are said to work on high frequencies that lie beyond normal human hearing, but can still vibrate into the subconscious, and make victims act according to their instructions. Ultra-paranoid conspiracists warn that street and traffic lights are really surveillance cameras in disguise, while the worst offender of all is your TV. You think you're watching it, but in fact people are using it to watch *you*. Never mind, have some cereal – just not Kellogg's Lucky Charms or General Mills' Count Chocula, because the CIA apparently conceals millions of sub-molecular nanite chips in the marshmallows in order to implant children.

A more convenient system of control, and a major tenet of conspiracy theories, is that human behaviour can be affected from a distance using pulse-modulated electromagnetic radiation, or microwaves. By this reckoning, microwaves mimic the extremely low frequency electrical waves that occur as part of the brain's natural function. Thus, by duplicating the waves, you can alter someone's state of mind. Radiation as a form of mind control was experimented with as part of MK-ULTRA (see p.210), which it's said identified 450 MHz as the optimum control frequency. Thus some theorists view mobile phone networks as strategic mind-control devices, for use against the population as necessary. Certainly, mobile phones do seem to force people to talk loudly about incredibly dull or personal things, causing mass irritation and embarrassment, though it's hard to be sure whether that's a conspiracy.

MI5, the UK's counterintelligence agency, supposedly possesses mobile microwave units, which it can beam at homes or offices to induce cancer, strokes, heart attacks or nerve damage, as well as mental breakdowns and suicide. That makes microwaves the ultimate traceless murder weapon, cited for example in the deaths of 25 Marconi scientists who worked on the Strategic Defense Initiative (SDI). Other victims who proved bothersome to the British establishment, such as David Icke, Princess Diana and Bill Clinton, were simply induced into humiliating public behaviour.

In the US, the Ground Wave Emergency Network (GWEN) was constructed in the 1980s, ostensibly to maintain communications in the event of nuclear Armageddon. However, its eighty sites across the continent are said to emit high levels of dangerous electromagnetic radiation, and their locations are well known, so they'd presumably be targeted in any attack. That leads conspiracist Jerry Smith to suspect that GWEN's real purpose is "producing behavioural alterations in the civilian population". Smith is an expert on HAARP (see p.300), which theorists believe is a mega mind-control machine. Both GWEN and HAARP are said to have their roots in designs by Nikolas Tesla (see p.301), from whose notebooks the Soviets plundered their own microwave beam, which they fired at the US embassy in Moscow, inducing an inordinately high cancer rate among workers there. By the 1970s, the Russians were reportedly using a short-wave beam nicknamed the "Russian Woodpecker" to interfere with global radio signals. Somehow that long-range mind-control device was not effective enough to stop the citizens of the USSR abandoning the Communist enterprise in 1991.

It's been claimed that chips were inserted into Gulf War soldiers to monitor their brain waves; frequencies could then be changed remotely to affect their nervous systems and fighting ability. During the Vietnam War, soldiers were supposedly implanted with a "Rambo chip" that increased adrenaline flow into the bloodstream, while Timothy McVeigh is said to have claimed that a chip implant commanded him to bomb Oklahoma City (see p.228). Prisoners in Sweden were supposedly implanted with mind-control chips during the early 1970s, and it's certainly true that many convicts on remand or probation are "tagged" to keep their whereabouts known.

Is that all so implausible? After all, identity chips are commonly implanted into pets, while firms such as Sematech and Hughes Identification Devices already supply the US Army, and make transponders or "tags" small enough to be inserted under the skin. The US company Applied Digital Solutions manufactures the "Verichip", which provides medical, financial and personal information for rapid identity verification. Its "Digital Angel" combines bio-sensor technology and Web-enabled wireless telecommunications, enabling its wearers to be located anywhere, have their physiological health check remotely and be cleared for ecommerce. Marking the crossing of yet another sci-fi frontier, the BBC reported in 2005 that a Massachusetts hospital had developed a brain chip that can read thoughts and send them to a computer to decipher – in this case, enabling a paralysed man to control appliances around him.

The end of days

If HAARP really is some kind of mega-weapon harbinger of the Apocalypse, none of us would know about it until it were truly too late. We can only hope that when we've eaten the last of our crops by candlelight, our minds will be melted before the floods come to wash our cities and corpses away. On the other hand, the HAARP programme is unclassified, its Environmental Impact Process documents are in the public domain, and the facility is even open for tours for two days at the end of each summer. And if your communications are interfered with by HAARP, you can always report it to the Federal Communications Commission, on +1 907 822 5497.

SOURCES

Books

Leonard Horowitz Death in the Air: Globalism, Terrorism and Toxic Warfare (2001). A lot of familiar conspiracy theory ground is retrod by the good doctor as he outlines the forthcoming medicine of the New World Order's global Apocalypse.

Jerry E. Smith HAARP: The Ultimate Weapon of the Conspiracy (1998). An entertaining, "fact"-packed account of HAARP's allegedly dubious history and sinister purpose.

Websites

Ⓦ **www.bariumblues.com/haarp_patent.htm** Bernard Eastlund's original weapon patent.

Ⓦ **www.haarp.alaska.edu** Alaska University's summary of HAARP's official, civilian work.

Climate change: convenient untruths

The world is warming: Earth's average surface air temperature has increased by roughly 0.8°C in the last century. The rate of change is picking up too – it's currently some 0.2°C per decade. And Greenland, for instance, has warmed by some 0.2°C every century since the last Ice Age. Every year now seems to break a new record. In 2007, there was less sea ice in the Arctic than ever before recorded – and a man actually swam at the North Pole. At the same time, unprecedented amounts of carbon dioxide are being released into the atmosphere. And, as everyone is now all too well aware, more carbon dioxide equals more heat, thanks to the greenhouse effect. In fact, there is now so much evidence that human activity causes climate change that only a tiny minority of people on the scientific and political fringes now dispute as much. These disputatious contrarians are, however, a very noisy few. They call themselves climate-change sceptics. Their opponents call them climate-change deniers.

Scientific consensus or scientific conspiracy?

Reading the newspapers or browsing the Internet, you could be forgiven for thinking that scientists disagree about climate change. In fact, experts almost universally agree – as shown by the respected journal *Science*, which surveyed 928 peer-reviewed papers on climate change in 2004, and found that "none disagreed with the consensus position". Where there is disagreement, it only concerns the exact scale of the warming we can expect. A rise of 2°C now seems inevitable, even with the help of the international (but not quite global) Kyoto Protocol, which attempted to put caps on carbon emissions from 1997. Whether or not 4°C or even 6°C – and Armageddon – is just over the ever more shimmery horizon, it's hard to say. But it's certainly possible. There are, of course, one or two dissenters. But, for the most part, they've either dropped out of the public debate or radically changed tack in recent years. (Not that this stops their old work from being endlessly recycled.)

Faced with such an overwhelming scientific consensus, climate-change deniers have had to find a new line of attack – and they've focused on consensus itself. It is the result of a "drive to conformity", say the doubters, if not quite a conspiracy. Only studies that reflect the current mainstream notions, they claim, make it past the filter of peer review into leading scientific journals. As thriller writer (and hero of climate-change denial) Michael Crichton put it: "If it's consensus, it isn't science. If it's science, it isn't consensus." In the hands of shriller journalists, this becomes a matter of "shutting down debate".

Similarly, public funding is pulled towards projects that don't go against the prevailing currents. As right-wing British columnist Melanie Phillips puts it, "the surest way to obtain research funding is to produce yet another study confirming global warming theory – and the surest way to academic ostracism is to deny it." Ostracism is putting it mildly. According to sceptical atmospheric physicist and "hero/outcast" Richard Lindzen (in *The Wall Street Journal* in April 2006) scientists standing outside the alarmist "feeding frenzy" have seen "their grant funds disappear, their work derided, and themselves libeled as industry stooges, scientific hacks or worse."

It is true that consensus doesn't necessarily equate with truth. The average parish in the rural Midwest would probably find consensus in the idea that evolution doesn't describe how humans came into being. Members of the average scientific common room in the nineteenth century would, no doubt, have agreed that you could trace criminal tendencies in the shape of a person's skull. But if you can't turn to climate scientists for answers about climate change, who can you turn to? To journalists like Melanie Phillips? To governments?

Whiting out the evidence

Scientists have protested that, if anything, the chief pressure put upon them is to conform to the party political line rather than the scientific consensus. In 2006, the independent, non-profit, US Union of Concerned Scientists found that nearly half of their respondents had "perceived or personally experienced pressure to eliminate the words 'climate change', 'global warming' or other similar terms from a variety of communications".

That pressure, it appears, came from the very top. In 2002, a political appointee of George W. Bush, Phil Cooney – who had previously worked as a lobbyist for the American Petroleum Institute – edited the Environmental Protection Agency's report to Congress on climate change. The report became the "dodgy dossier" of the climate-change debate. Cooney's changes were so significant that the EPA eventually disowned the entire section on climate change. After the scandal broke in 2005, Cooney resigned – but he wasn't left stranded. Within days, he was offered a new job with the oil mega-corporation, ExxonMobil. A few months later, Vice President Dick Cheney's energy plan became law; it subsidized coal-fired power to the tune of $9 billion, and oil and gas energy production by a further $6 billion.

The Bush administration also attempted to exert unusual control over which federal scientists were allowed to speak to the media on climate issues – especially after Hurricane Katrina (see p.311). In 2006, leading climate-change scientist James Hansen claimed that NASA officials were interfering with his media relations: "they feel their job is to be this censor of information going out to the public", he fumed. He said he had been threatened with "dire consequences" if he didn't clear all requests for interviews. In 2007, the congressional Committee on Oversight and Government Reform concluded that "the Bush Administration has engaged in a systematic effort to manipulate climate-change science and mislead policymakers and the public about the dangers of global warming."

A similar incident was exposed in the UK in 2004. After

voicing the opinion that "climate change is the most severe problem we are facing today – more serious even than the threat of terrorism", the government's chief scientific adviser, Sir David King, was asked not to give interviews. The request – or was it a politely worded order? – came from Tony Blair's chief private secretary, Ivan Rogers.

Big business, big lobbies

If the Bush White House was a powerful voice in climate-change denial, it was more than matched by the panicked squealing of the energy corporations. The most prominent business to "combat climate-change alarmism" was ExxonMobil, also known as Esso. A survey conducted by The Royal Society in London – the world's oldest scientific academy – concluded that ExxonMobil had given almost $2.9 million in grants to groups that had "misinformed the public about climate change", many of them denying the evidence outright. The Union of Concerned Scientists later concluded the figure was actually nearer $16 million over seven years.

When The Royal Society publicly asked ExxonMobil to stop funding lobbyists engaged in climate-change denial, right-wingers fumed about "censorship" and infringements of "freedom of speech". ExxonMobil's own reply was to protest that "the recycling of this type of discredited conspiracy theory diverts attention from the real challenge at hand". It's true that climate campaigners' methods are, at times, disconcertingly similar to outright conspiracism. A classic conspiracist technique is to use chains of acquaintance to suggest that these players are, in fact, conspirators. To websites like the Greenpeace-funded www.exxonsecrets.org, for instance, if a scientist or opinion-maker can be linked with a group funded by ExxonMobil, it is virtual proof that their ideas and opinions are for sale – or they were until ExxonMobil bought them. ExxonMobil points out, not unreasonably, that corporate contributions to "public policy groups" for research on policy issues "should not be confused with management of their policy recommendations. The only organization that speaks on behalf of ExxonMobil", says ExxonMobil, "is ExxonMobil." Others think money speaks louder than words.

Climate conspirators

Unfortunately for activists, the same conspiracist techniques can be used by both sides. To take one example, in the words of rebellious-minded journalist Alexander Cockburn, Al Gore is not just a would-be US president and global spokesman for climate-change action, but also a "shill for the nuclear and coal barons from the first day he stepped into Congress entrusted with the sacred duty to protect the budgetary and regulatory interests of the Tennessee Valley Authority and the Oakridge National Lab". To unravel this particular climate conspiracy, all you have to do is follow the money. Who stands to benefit from carbon regulation? Businesses burning "clean coal", the nuclear industry, bioscience companies, universities. Cockburn believes that "the best documented conspiracy of interest" is not between ExxonMobil and the White House, but between "the Greenhouser fearmongers and the nuclear industry".

In the UK, deniers' fears focus less on the corporations and more on the government. Professional contrarian Melanie Phillips believes that the Treasury "thinks it can impose eye-watering new taxes by proclaiming that this is the only way to save the planet". Yes, global warming was cooked up at No. 11 purely to justify taxing "modern life until the electoral pipsqueaks turn green". There was, of course, the side benefit that the virtual market in carbon trading could produce vast profits. Phillips also noted that the World Bank (where, suspiciously enough, senior Treasury official Sir Nicholas Stern used to work) is "heavily involved in the trade". "Is it any surprise", she wonders, that Stern's 2006 report on the economics of climate change gave the idea of carbon trading "an enormous boost"?

Smoke and mirrors in the lobby

Just as big tobacco companies once tried to discredit the links between smoking and cancer, energy companies

LORD MONCKTON: VOICE OF REASON

Christopher Monckton is one of the most prominent "sceptical" voices in the UK – in fact, he is far more influential than his qualifications might suggest. His credentials are not exactly scientific: he is a former journalist with a degree in classics, a one-time Conservative Party press officer, inventor of the Eternity puzzle and, as Viscount Monckton of Brenchley, a hereditary peer (albeit one without a seat in the House of Lords).

According to the website of the Competitive Enterprise Institute, which lists him as an associated expert, Monckton is also an officer of the Order of St John of Jerusalem and a Knight of Honour and Devotion of the Sovereign Military Order of Malta – an extremely well-connected Catholic, in other words.

Monckton has previously applied his unique journalistic insights to other threats to global stability, such as the AIDS crisis. In 1987, he proposed putting all people with HIV in quarantine – a solution he has since rejected as unworkable on the humanitarian grounds that there are now too many sufferers. But climate change is now the Monckton hobby-horse. He even rode it all the way to the UN's Bali conference in December 2007 – though, unfortunately, people he described as "sinister bureaucrats" didn't accept his credentials as a journalist and he was refused entry.

Monckton could be said to stand for the old-fashioned, Tory view: that all this nonsense about climate change is an outrage to common sense and free thought, while the plans to deal with carbon emissions amount to nothing less than an attack on free enterprise and freedom of action, probably orchestrated by socialistic European bureaucrats conspiring together in their taxpayer-funded mega-offices.

Few doubt the purple-faced sincerity of people making this kind of argument, but the use the media makes of it is more suspect. Climate-change denial is a topic that some editors will pay good money to see recycled until the paper falls apart and the ink runs dry. The maverick voice of a Monckton is inevitably heard above the quiet and serious murmur of consensus.

have long tried to undermine the links between human activity, carbon-dioxide emissions and global warming. Interestingly, the methods of denial used for the two disparate issues are often remarkably similar – perhaps because the very same lobbyists were employed for both. One of the most scandalous discoveries of the "big tobacco" lawsuits was an internal memo circulated within the cigarette manufacturer Brown & Williamson. "Doubt is our product", it noted, "since it is the best means of competing with the 'body of fact' that exists in the mind of the general public. It is also the means of establishing a controversy".

This was exactly how some right-wingers chose to handle climate change. In 1994, political strategist Frank Luntz advised the Republicans to "make the lack of scientific certainty a primary issue in the debate". If this had been the strategy, it wouldn't have been much of a conspiracy – it would have been misguided politics, but not exactly secret or nefarious. The energy industry, however, chose to go about its campaign by quietly setting up or funding scores of quasi-autonomous research and campaigning organizations. Some were little more than front organizations with scientific-sounding titles.

In 1991, the US's National Coal Association, Western Fuels Association and Edison Electrical Institute backed an all-new "Information Council on the Environment" (ICE) with $500,000. Its strategy was to "reposition global warming" as "theory rather than fact", according to a leaked memo. It produced one advertisement pointing out that: "Some say the earth is warming. Some also said the earth was flat." The ICE was quickly disbanded amid accusations of scientific dishonesty, but, in 1998, the American Petroleum Institute – the chief US trade association for oil and gas – was said to have tried a somewhat similar tack. According to *Newsweek*, a dozen "people from the denial machine", including rebel environmental scientist Fred Singer and officials from ExxonMobil, met to draw up a secret Communications Action Plan. "Victory will be achieved", it stated, when "average citizens 'understand' uncertainties in climate science" and when "recognition of uncertainties becomes part of 'conventional wisdom'." The proposed $5 million publicity campaign was only scuppered by a leak to the press.

Until it was "deactivated" in 2002, the most successful lobbying group (or "corporate conspiracy", depending on who you ask) was the Global Climate Coalition. Formed in 1989 in response to the threat of international action on climate change, it brought together many of the biggest corporations with an interest in oil, including the car manufacturers General Motors and Ford, and the energy giants BP, Shell and ExxonMobil. The coalition lobbied hard against the Kyoto treaty in the US and abroad, even taking out adverts warning consumers that "Americans would pay the price" for any emissions regulation. Undersecretary of State Paula Dobriansky eventually sent the group a congratulatory memo, describing how George W. Bush had refused to sign the Kyoto agreement "partly based on input from you".

Europe vs America

Another successful lobbying group is the Competitive Enterprise Institute, which, until 2006, counted ExxonMobil as one of its major donors. The head of its climate-change scepticism wing is Myron Ebell. He was caught up in the Phil Cooney scandal (see p.306), but achieved true notoriety among climate-change activists by claiming on BBC Radio 4's *Today* programme in 2004 that European scientists, unlike American ones, could not be independent because they were funded by governments. Asked whether European countries were "out to get America", Ebell agreed that this was "pretty obviously and explicitly the programme of the EU Commission".

The comment is a classic piece of bullishly nationalist US conspiracism. Back home, many other people took a similar view. Senator and arch anti-environmentalist Jim Inhofe asked himself whether the "phoney science" that human activity caused warming was "the second-largest hoax ever perpetrated on the American people" (the largest being the separation of Church and state), because, he assured himself, "it sure sounds like it". British journalist Melanie Phillips seems to agree. She believes that there is an "ideological agenda at the heart of the green movement which is anti-capitalism, anti-big business and anti-America". She may be right about that, but is global warming "ideological propaganda" and a "global fraud", as she puts it? Is it really "one of the greatest scientific scams of the modern age"?

A new conspiracy theory about American climate-change denial emerged in February 2007. According to certain left-leaning British newspapers, the American Enterprise Institute (AEI) – a prominent neoconservative think-tank whose links to ExxonMobil were helpfully pointed out in a number of articles – had offered $10,000 to academics willing to criticize the Intergovernmental Panel on Climate Change's Fourth Assessment Report by writing essays that "thoughtfully explore the limitations of climate model outputs". Replying to these outrageous transatlantic slurs, *The Wall Street Journal* pointed out that payment is usual for commissioned work, that ExxonMobil contributed less than one percent of AEI's budget, and that the scholars were asked not to deny climate change, but to present a "range of policy prescriptions that should be considered for climate change of uncertain dimension." The *Journal* fingered Greenpeace as the source for the "smear campaign" and huffily concluded that "the environmental left and their political and media supporters now believe it is legitimate to quash debate." Identifying a sinister "green lobby", and investing it, by association, with all the legendary powers of the so-called Israel Lobby, became the new way for deniers to attack climate change.

Governors of the world

American right-wingers may mistrust the European Commission, but it's surely a bit-player when compared with its global, Geneva-based cousin. After all, only the UN has black helicopters and aspirations for a New World Order (see p.141). And only the UN, according to conspiracists, has a powerful enough motive for fostering the climate-change scam. In a classic broadside for his muckraking magazine *Counterpunch* in May 2007, climate sceptic Alexander Cockburn described how the UN sees climate change as "the horse to ride to build up the organization's increasingly threadbare moral authority". He also likened global warming to Iraq's weapons of mass destruction: "Months and years later", he speculated, will come "the qualifications and the retractions, long after new contracts and grants have been awarded, and fresh legions hired to staff the ever-expanding empires of the threatmongers."

Similar fears of unaccountable mega-bureaucracy were echoed by Christopher Monckton (see box on p.308), another flag-bearer for climate-change denial, writing in *The Sunday Telegraph* in November 2006. He called the IPCC a "transnational bureaucracy" and accused the UN of having "undervalued the sun's effects on historical and contemporary climate, slashed the natural greenhouse effect, overstated the past century's temperature increase, repealed a fundamental law of physics and tripled the man-made greenhouse effect." Monckton generally refrained from speculating as to whether the UN's actions were sinister or merely incompetent, although according to his article in *The Sunday Telegraph*, the climate change "scare" was "less about saving the planet than, in Jacques Chirac's chilling phrase, 'creating world government'." (Former French president Chirac proposed setting up a new United Nations for the Environment – another bureaucracy, admittedly, but not exactly a fascist mega-state.)

Supporters of the IPCC's scientists, however, claim that the conspiracy actually works the other way. The UK's House of Lords, for instance, expressed "concerns about the objectivity of the IPCC process, with some of its emissions scenarios and summary documentation apparently influenced by political considerations" – suggesting that their lordships thought the UN was leaning on its scientists not to talk up the potential damage of climate change, but to downplay it. As environmental journalist George Monbiot observed in *The Guardian*, the IPCC's 2007 report was oddly "shorn of the warning that 'North America is expected to experience locally severe economic damage, plus substantial ecosystem, social and cultural disruption from climate change related events'." It doesn't take a huge leap of the imagination to guess which country was doing the shearing.

SOURCES

Books

Christopher Booker and Richard North Scared to Death (2007). Libertarian-minded exposé of the "age of superstition", by the authors of *The Great Deception: The Secret History of the European Union*. Unfortunately, their analysis of climate change isn't one most scientists would accept, to put it mildly.

Michael Crichton State of Fear (2004). This thriller, by the author of that faithful-to-genetic-science novel *Jurassic Park*, portrays global warming as an evil plot perpetrated by environmental extremists. Like *The Da Vinci Code*, it claims to be based on real facts…

Ross Gelbspan Boiling Point (2004). Steam-powered excoriation of climate-change scepticism.

Robert Henson The Rough Guide to Climate Change (2006). Clear, readable and thoughtful overview of all the issues.

Bjørn Lomborg Cool It: The Skeptical Environmentalist's Guide to Global Warming (2007). Lomborg's 2001 book, *The Skeptical Environmentalist*, was the bible for those who couldn't quite bear to deny climate change is happening, but preferred not to do anything about it; this 2007 effort updates and pre-digests for a popular audience. The website www.lomborgerrors.dk challenges his calculations and assumptions.

George Monbiot Heat (2006). Monbiot is the UK's foremost environmental journalist, and he wields a nicely sharpened pencil. This is mostly about "how to stop the planet burning", but it includes an "exposure of the corporations trying to stop us from taking action".

Films

Davis Guggenheim An Inconvenient Truth (2006). This award-winning documentary of Al Gore's climate-change campaign is more gripping than the average thriller – but then it's all real.

Websites

Ⓦ **www.climatesciencewatch.org** "Promoting integrity in the use of climate science in government".

Ⓦ **www.exxonsecrets.org** A Greenpeace-run site naming and shaming 124 organizations that are either funded directly by ExxonMobil or work closely with Exxon-funded groups. Includes a nifty interactive map that allows you to follow the money.

Ⓦ **www.ipcc.ch** Homepage of the Intergovernmental Panel on Climate Change (IPCC) – the running dogs of the New World Order.

Ⓦ **www.junkscience.com** A gaping mouthpiece of right-wing denial. George Monbiot claims to have "lost count of the number of correspondents who, while questioning manmade global warming, have pointed me there."

Ⓦ **www.monbiot.com** If you want to learn how to counter the deniers, George Monbiot's website is the place to start.

- **www.newsweek.com/id/32482** Full text of Sharon Begley's *Newsweek* story from August 13, 2007: "The Truth About Denial".
- **www.realclimate.org** Counters all the sceptical or denial theories ever put forward, drawing on peer-reviewed papers. A full refutation of Michael Crichton's "argument" can be found in the 2007 archives.
- **www.stopclimatechaos.org** The UK's main campaigning group.
- **www.telegraph.co.uk/news/main.jhtml?xml=/news/2006/11/05/nosplit/nwarm05.xml** Christopher Monckton's controversial article of misfaith in climate change. You can download the "references and detailed calculations" – printed out, they make excellent kindling.
- **www.whitehouse.gov/ceq/foia/cei/2_ceq_14.pdf** Facsimile of Myron Ebell's memo to Phil Cooney concerning the infamous "dodgy dossier" of the climate-change controversy.
- **www.zmag.org/debatesglobalwarming.html** Read and relish one of the greatest journalistic rows on climate change – a series of articles and counter articles by provocative *Counterpunch* journalist Alexander Cockburn and arch-environmentalist George Monbiot.

Hurricane Katrina devastates the "Big Easy"

From August 23, 2005, it took just five days for a tropical depression over the Bahamas to develop into a top-of-the-scale, hand-of-God, category-five hurricane. Named Katrina, the hurricane scythed its way across the US Gulf Coast, with winds that reached 175mph throwing ships on land, oil rigs on their heads and hacking down anything vertical in Mississippi, Alabama and Louisiana. The eye of the storm missed New Orleans, steering away at the last minute, but the city known as the "Big Easy" was far from spared. Early on the morning of Monday, August 29, reports started filtering out of the city of water sloshing over the levee walls of the 17th Street and Industrial canals, spilling the waters of Lake Pontchartrain and the Mississippi River into downtown New Orleans. Soon, the levees began breaking (over fifty failings were ultimately counted), and the areas of Lakeview and the Lower Ninth Ward were the first and worst hit by flooding that eventually engulfed eighty percent of the city, at depths ranging from a couple of feet to a couple of stories.

What the world saw, through the lenses of the news helicopters buzzing over the city, was a disaster zone comprising thousands of murky, stinking canals awash with floating debris and bobbing bodies (some flushed out of graveyards), not to mention sewage, petrol, chemicals and various bacteria. The Louisiana Superdome became the prime venue for almost 30,000 of the city's refugees (although US news channels refused to refer to them as such, being a term reserved for Bangladeshis or Kosovans, not Americans). They had gone to the sports' arena seeking shelter, but it quickly became a horrific hothouse of Hell, bereft of adequate food and water supplies, with blocked toilets overflowing into corridors and sleeping areas, and rumours of assaults, rapes and murders running rife.

In the days and weeks that followed, search and rescue teams found both survivors and bodies trapped in attics, hospitals, nursing homes and prisons. Some 25,000 body bags were sent to Louisiana, but the final death toll for all the affected states was closer to 1830. Katrina was,

An African-American family seeks refuge in the Louisiana Superdome from New Orleans' rising flood waters.

Bungling Bush and a predicted catastrophe

On September 1, as the crisis reached its height, President George W. Bush stated on *Good Morning America* that "no one anticipated" the levees failing. However, it later emerged that in July 2004, over a year before Katrina hit, a Homeland Security department drill involving fifty organizations had envisaged the fictional "Hurricane Pam" deluging Louisiana, blasting through New Orleans' levees, trashing half a million buildings and forcing a million people out of their homes. The Federal Emergency Management Agency (FEMA) also warned the government that a hurricane hitting New Orleans was the most likely potentially catastrophic threat facing the US homeland. In the words of British newspaper *The Guardian*, Hurricane Katrina was "the most widely predicted catastrophe in American history".

In 2004, the Cuban government had managed to successfully evacuate 1.5 million people from the path of a 160-mph hurricane, with no loss of life. So, is it any wonder that, in the wake of Hurricane Katrina, some people began to cry conspiracy? It was pointed out that the US could afford to spend $300 billion fighting wars in Iraq and Afghanistan, but did not have enough money to help its own people, many of whom had lost everything in the flood. The US could apparently reach across the world's biggest ocean to help tsunami-smashed Indonesia in 2004, yet struggled to rescue the New Orleans residents stranded much closer to home (many of whom remained

nevertheless, the deadliest US hurricane in almost a century and, with the damage estimated at over $80 billion, it was certainly the costliest.

in the Superdome until September 3). As one New Orleans journalist pondered: "How do you aid tsunami victims instantly and only three or four days later get to New Orleans?"

Bush, who was on holiday in Texas when the crisis began, flew over the stricken city on his way back to Washington on August 31 – with all the accompanying disruptions to air traffic (including rescue operations) that the presidential cubic mile cordon requires. Meanwhile, Al Gore, the man he "beat" to the White House in 2000 (see p.232), managed to charter a plane and fly a couple of hundred refugees out of the devastation. Even President Lyndon B. Johnson had managed a more noteworthy response back in 1965, when Hurricane Betsy struck New Orleans. He apparently headed to the city the very next day and yelled into the darkness of a blacked-out shelter in the Ninth Ward, "This is your president! I'm here to help you!" Perhaps President Bush takes after his mother, Barbara, who said that it was "scary" that so many New Orleans refugees billeted in Houston wanted to stay in Texas.

Divine retribution

One of the first reactions to the hurricane was every religious pundit and his dog declaring it as some kind of divine retribution. As with countless other natural disasters in the past, they saw Katrina as the hand of God smiting godless sinners not just from the city, but from the South, the government, the entire US. New Orleans mayor Ray Nagin said, "God is mad at America … [for] being in Iraq under false pretenses". Others, such as Israeli rabbi Ovadia Yosef, cited the pressure the US was putting on Israel to pull out of Gaza as inciting God's wrath, while in one simple statement, Reverend Bill Shanks encompassed all the various strains of hateful glee that the disaster unleashed: "New Orleans now is abortion free. New Orleans now is Mardi Gras free. New Orleans now is free of Southern Decadence and the sodomites, the witchcraft workers, false religion."

Racism, inequality and exploding levees

But what vice would cause God to send a deluge against the poor, black community of the Lower Ninth? One of the most frequently cited statistics in the aftermath of the hurricane was that prior to Katrina, 67 percent of New Orleans' population was African-American, but after the hurricane, it was just 40–50 percent. (However, no accurate counts seem to be available to verify these statistics.) Many people believe that blacks were worst hit by the floods and least served by the rescue operations, while conspiracy theorists claim that the subsiding waters left behind a whiter, richer city. Private homes and large city housing projects, which were once home to tens of thousands of black residents, remained off-limits and boarded up, with former occupants prohibited from returning. As one resident put it, "we black folks ain't no tourist attraction". The leader of the Nation of Islam (NOI), Louis Farrakhan, told *Time* magazine that "the feeling is that race played a part".

Not all the claims about race- or wealth-related conspiracies have since been borne out, however. Those that wondered why the Lower Ninth was flooded while the wealthier, whiter French Quarter and Garden District remained dry miss the fact that both of the latter regions were on higher ground, above the flood levels. Large neighbourhoods of high-value real estate, including the central business district and houses belonging to high-income earners, were also flooded. A report by the Knight-Ridder media company also concluded that Katrina victims "weren't disproportionately African-American". But concerns about racism and inequality in New Orleans were not simply the paranoid pathology of poverty, or the reiteration of age-old conspiracies about whites plotting to wipe out blacks (adding to a list that includes AIDS, see p.290, and cocaine, see p.214). Countless mainstream news sources carried similar accusations, with Britain's *The Observer* declaring: "When Hurricane Katrina devastated New Orleans it was the city's poor – almost exclusively African-Americans –

FLOODING IN THE UK: THE THAMES GATEWAY CONSPIRACY

It's often said that whatever happens in the US will shortly after come to the UK. Not two years after Hurricane Katrina, the classic wet British summer turned into something bigger – not quite a Biblical flood besetting a decadent city, but a serious soaking nonetheless. In late June 2007, while the national media paid only passing interest to accumulated heavy drizzle flooding out a few thousand homes and businesses in western England, nationwide public and media interest remained, by and large, focused on the attention-seeking and newly appointed prime minister, Gordon Brown, and his new cabinet's collected composure in responding to some failed car bombings in London and Glasgow. However, the rains continued, and continued, and continued throughout July, and the number of affected homes and firms rose with the rapidly rising waters into the scores of thousands. Roads, railways and power lines were cut, water supplies were contaminated, and crops were soaked and destroyed. Insurance claims lapped up to £2 billion amid reports of shops being looted and panic buying.

Then, just as with Hurricane Katrina, stories started floating about ignored weather warnings, lack of government preparation, and flood defences suffering from years of neglect and spending cuts. It emerged that only 57 percent of the UK's flood defences were in "good condition", while the UK's largest insurers – who had been vainly lobbying the government for years for extra spending on flood defences – were being denied critical information about those same defences. It was also revealed that the Environment Agency's staff responsible for flood defences were about to suffer the worst culling in the Agency's forthcoming staff redundancies – caused by the government cutting £15 million from its budget. This revelation coincided with the prime minister pledging £14 million in emergency aid for the worst hit regions. The Met Office's warnings to ministers about very wet weather due to the El Niño phenomenon were ignored, while the government pressured water companies not to spend money on bigger drains and flood defences in order to prevent politically damaging higher water bills in the short term. At least £1 billion a year was said to be needed to beef up flood defences against climate change – the government promised just an extra £200 million a year, then didn't pay up.

What's more, who was in charge of coordinating the rescue, the air deliveries, the clean-up operation, and so on? The Home Office? The ministries of the environment and defence? Local councils and communities? All, none or some of the above? John Redwood, the Conservative MP for Wokingham, Berkshire, said, "There were no sandbags, no pumps and no ditches had been cleared" and asked "Why wasn't the army mobilized?", only to find out that the army was already stretched to breaking point fighting foreign wars – hence the small, piecemeal mobilization of the army, to some, but by no means all, of the affected areas. Then there

who were left to fend for themselves as the city drowned in a lake of toxic sludge."

Various media organizations and blogs also carried accounts of what sounded like explosions being heard immediately after the storm had passed. A levee wall blasting open due to the weight of tons of water and debris pressing upon it would sound explosive, but New York talk-radio host Hal Turner summed up the suspicions of sabotage that were on many people's lips. He reported that a diver with the US Army Corps of Engineers had found burn marks on levee debris, but was told to ignore them by a FEMA official. However, the diver snuck out a chunk of the wall for testing at the US Army Forensic Laboratory, and it was found to include traces of explosives. A year after the disaster, "They bombed that sucker", was also very much the conclusion of "A Closer Look" on ABC's *World News with Charles Gibson.*

Accusations about the deliberate destruction of the levees led, inevitably, to heated political debate. Summarizing many people's views of Washington's response to the flooding, film director Spike Lee quoted rapper Kanye West, who said "George Bush doesn't care about black people", and himself declared, "You have a large population who happened to be poor, and if they did vote they didn't vote Republican anyway." In a somewhat bitter televised debate, during which he was derided as were the profiteers: the Ministry of Defence sought guarantees of payment for food and sleeping bag deliveries, and one council ransomed sandbags at £20 a sack as they were found to be in desperately short supply, as were pumps and other basic equipment.

In yet another mealy-mouthed British aping of the Katrina debacle, many of those worst afflicted by the floods were living in new, lower-cost housing that had been built on cheap flood-prone land in response to the UK's chronic shortage of affordable housing – not the poorest of the poor, just the most common. And therein lay the crunch: sitting gloriously at the top of Gordon Brown's new political agenda was the plan to build 200,000 new homes in Britain every year – with a total of three million by 2020 – many of which would have to be built on flood plains. Despite reports that this new plan would "worsen" flood risks and make deluges like that of July 2007 even more probable, the plan got the go-ahead, for, in the words of one Labour spokesman, "this country is desperately short of new homes ... To simply say we stop the house-building programme is not on."

By far the biggest part of this grand house-building scheme is to build tens of thousands of new homes on the vast mudflats of the Thames Estuary, stretching from London's Isle of Dogs out to Kent and Essex: the great Thames Gateway project. The new houses will be cheap – and despite the claims of recent publicity drives – they will probably be energy inefficient, but most significantly, they are primarily being built on the wrong side of the Thames Barrier. Built in the 1980s to protect London against rapidly increasing flood tides, the barrier won't provide any protection to the majority of the new houses Brown is planning to build. There have been suggestions, reported by the BBC, that the government was considering the construction of a bigger £20 billion barrier further upstream, but moves to build hundreds of thousands of new homes appear much further advanced than any plans to build a new barrier to protect them.

The question soon being asked was: is all this a cock-up or a conspiracy? In late 2005, the investigative, satirical magazine *Private Eye* (which also reported the emerging crisis over the flood defences several months before the summer 2007 floods) published a letter about the "real" plan behind the Thames Gateway project. The letter said that the project was a deliberate plot to use a great deluge to get rid of poverty altogether. Build a load of dirty, polluting housing, fill it with poverty-stricken common folk, and just sit back and wait for the big wave to come and sweep it all away. Literally overnight the problems of environmentally unfriendly housing, poverty and housing shortages would simply be washed away. With all the evidence of ignored weather warnings, budget cuts and poor flood defences in the wake of the summer 2007 floods, perhaps all this doesn't sound quite so incredible after all.

a "conspiracy theorist", Lee exclaimed: "As an African-American in this country, I don't put anything past the government."

Lee also referred to the heavy flooding caused forty years before by Hurricane Betsy hitting New Orleans. Back in 1965, the poor old Ninth Ward was again engulfed by breached levees, leading to 9-foot water levels, 81 deaths and 250,000 people being evacuated. Rumours suggested that the then-mayor Victor Schiro intentionally blew the levees to protect his own wealthier district, Lake Vista. It was also alleged that doing so could have tipped the forthcoming election in his favour if all the blacks, who were likely to vote for his opponent, were drowned.

When the Levees Broke, Spike Lee's 2006 documentary about the destruction wrought by Katrina, also pointed out that there was a proven precedent for destroying levees to save one area at the expense of another. During the Great Mississippi Flood of 1927, levees in rural Louisiana were blown in order to save New Orleans from flooding, but doing so also washed out hundreds of thousands of poor rural blacks (ultimately precipitating the Great Migration of southern blacks to northern cities).

All rot, cried the political Right. The Internet news blog NewsBusters, whose *raison d'être* is "exposing liberal bias", laid into ABC's *World News with Charles Gibson*, declaring that the programme "recycled wild black conspiracy theories about how the levees were blown up". Blogger Winston Smith added that the media's criticisms were typical anti-Republican race-mongering, "standard practice" during election years. Evidence of this counter-conspiracy was declared to be the widespread coverage of the Rodney King beating during the 1992 presidential election, which reputedly got the black vote and swung the result for the Democrats. Right-wing political commentator Rush Limbaugh said he would not believe "a damn thing" from this "Katrina media" until he saw "10,000 bodies".

In 2007, an investigation by the American Society of Civil Engineers finally decided that multiple, fatal "design flaws" had caused the levees to fail – for which they blamed the US Army Engineer Corps. However, that conclusion is unlikely to sway *all* of the conspiracists who trust the explosives "evidence" of the unnamed Engineer Corps diver and believe that the levees were intentionally blown.

Weather weapons

Internationally, several people, including the UK's deputy prime minister John Prescott and Germany's environment minister Jurgen Tritten, wondered if Katrina could have been caused by global warming (see p.305). Others considered whether more active weather-related aggression could have played a part. Blogger William Thomas suggested that the hurricane was being used as an excuse to give more federal funding to military weather experiments, such as HAARP (see p.300), chemtrails and other gizmos that affect cloud formation and the like (despite this being banned by the UN in the 1970s). But on websites such as portland.indymedia.org, some people took this even further, suggesting HAARP may have been actively used to create Katrina or steer it towards New Orleans. One site, www.abovetopsecret.com, featured a chart apparently showing that extreme HAARP-like magnetic variations in the atmosphere were recorded between August 24 and 25 – Katrina's formation period.

Conspiracy theorists have come up with countless reasons why the powers that be might have wanted to control the weather and trash New Orleans. Some suggested that the incident may have been contrived to distract voters from other disasters, such as the Iraq War (see p.408), George W. Bush's crashing poll ratings, the burgeoning Plame scandal and the weakening economy. But the disastrous management of the post-Katrina clean-up operation probably cast the government in an even worse light.

Other theories proposed that the hurricane may have been created for reasons of profit, rather than diversion. Articles on conspiracist website www.rense.com said that "new Scalar technology" (based on the ideas of Nikolas Tesla, see p.301) was being used to "create weather weapons of mass destruction". They claimed that Katrina was part of a "destroy and rebuild" plan that would generate massive profits for "the Illuminati and their government agents" through stratospheric oil prices, cheap real estate and tax-funded reconstruction. The Republicans' "blind faith" in the free market has also been cited as contributing to the devastation of New Orleans – with the privatization and outsourcing of FEMA's emergency rescue services, and the cutting of funding to the army engineers responsible for levee maintenance, receiving much of the blame.

A conspiracy to fail?

The biggest question asked in the aftermath of Katrina, however, was why were the government's rescue efforts such a failure? FEMA was seen as failing so badly in its response to the disaster that its chief, Michael Brown, resigned just days after the crisis passed. Among numerous other complaints, FEMA was criticized for stopping the Red Cross and the National Guard from accessing the worst-stricken areas with relief aid. Indeed, law enforcement officers and soldiers were even reported as saying that they had been ordered not to provide citizens with food, water or medical aid.

On September 5, *The New York Times* wrote "FEMA

prevents Coast Guard from delivering diesel fuel", while the agency's own website reported "FEMA [told] first responders not to respond". Journalist and conspiracy theorist Mike Whitney even claimed that people at the Convention Center were denied water in order to make them leave. As Dr Lance Hill commented on the website for the New Orleans-based Southern Institute for Education and Research, the US is signed up to the Geneva Convention's human rights treaty, which prohibits governments from blocking humanitarian aid to the victims of natural disasters. "At a minimum, our nation's own laws should forbid using food and water as [a] weapon against our own people", Hill added.

Rumours that the US Navy was jamming all communications in New Orleans, including emergency radios, proved untrue, but sources such as the news programme *Democracy Now* and the Green Party warned people that the city had become "Iraqified", with military control zones, weakened human rights protection and corporate profiteering. The streets were also said to be patrolled by all manner of private and government security teams, ranging from the US Marines and the Coast Guard to private Blackwater security contractors and Scientology Disaster Relief teams.

One conspiracy theory states that FEMA's poor response was due to deliberate, systematic underfunding, the intention of which was to create a pared-back, incompetent agency that would need rescuing by the military. The armed forces could then intervene and create a de facto state of martial law. Mike Whitney wrote on the website www.informationclearinghouse.info that the White House, FEMA, the Department of Homeland Security and the Pentagon conspired not to lift a finger for four days after the hurricane, in order to force Louisiana governor Kathleen Blanco to surrender control of the local police and National Guard. Whitney claimed that Katrina was part of the Bush administration's strategy of "fear and anarchy to advance their global agenda" by dismantling America's regional defences and leaving no resistance to federal military takeover. He said that allowing a ring of steel to encircle the city would clear away local resistance to redevelopment plans, and enable a "massive ethnic cleansing operation" to displace tens of thousands of poor, black residents. Whitney went on to declare that New Orleans had become the "first domestic beachhead" of the New World Order (see p.141).

No law led to martial law

The conservative Internet forum Free Republic dismissed all of these conspiracy theories as classic liberal whining – whatever people might say about the plight of the poor black residents of New Orleans or about federal plots to take control of the city, the disaster was solely Kathleen Blanco's fault. The Louisiana governor was accused of ignoring all warnings about the approaching hurricane, leaving long-standing disaster plans redundant and refusing to officially request federal help (unlike the governors of Alabama or Mississippi), as it might have highlighted her own incompetence. At that time, the Posse Comitatus Act prevented the president from sending federal troops into any US state unless directly requested by its governor. However, the breakdown of law and order in New Orleans compelled Bush to instigate the Insurrection Act and federalize the National Guard, so that he could get rescue forces in despite Blanco's opposition.

In order to avoid any further president–governor political two-stepping in future, it was decided that the Insurrection and Posse Comitatus acts would need revising. On the same day that Bush signed the Military Commissions Act (allowing for the torture and detention of US citizens abroad), he also signed the 2006 John Warner Defense Authorization Act. This new law enables the president to declare a "public emergency" and put troops anywhere in the US to suppress "any insurrection, domestic violence, unlawful combination, or conspiracy" should he – and he alone – decide that state authorities are incapable of maintaining public order. As Democrat senator Patrick Leahy warned, it means that the president could declare martial law far more easily, and that federal authority could override state sovereignty. Hurricane Katrina was, perhaps unwittingly, the first step towards what political activist and writer Frank Morales called "a rapidly consolidating police state".

SOURCES

Films

Spike Lee When the Levees Broke: A Requiem in Four Acts (2004). Lee's HBO documentary looks into how and why New Orleans' levees broke, but its focus is the appalling scale of the human tragedy, much of it due to the ineptitude of the rescue operations.

Websites

Ⓦ **www.abovetopsecret.com** Search for HAARP and Hurricane Katrina on this site to see the magnetometer chart that apparently shows a spike in magnetic variations just before Katrina hit Florida.

Ⓦ **www.cnn.com/SPECIALS/2005/katrina** CNN's rolling news version of the disaster, plus special reports, photos, videos and victims' stories.

Ⓦ **www.hhs.gov/katrina** The government's "official" version of events.

Ⓦ **www.informationclearinghouse.info/article10182.htm** In "The Siege of New Orleans", Mike Whitney reveals the "true story" about the Bush administration's conspiracy to take control of the city.

Ⓦ **www.katrina.house.gov/full_katrina_report.htm** The House of Representatives' investigation into the preparation and the aftermath.

Ⓦ **newsbusters.org/node/7282** The right-wing Internet news blog attempts to expose the "liberal media bias" of ABC's reporting of racial tensions in New Orleans after the hurricane.

Ⓦ **www.newyorker.com/fact/content/articles/051003fa_fact** David Remnick's "High Water" from *The New Yorker* is a fascinating blend of history, on-the-ground reportage and reflection on the disaster.

Ⓦ **www.southerninstitute.info/commentaries/?p=29** Civil Rights specialist and New Orleans' resident Lance Hill expounds his views of racism and incompetence at the New Orleans Convention Center.

Ⓦ **www.whitehouse.gov/reports/katrina-lessons-learned** The White House also took a look at what it could have done better.

CONSPIRACIES OF SEA, SKY AND SPACE

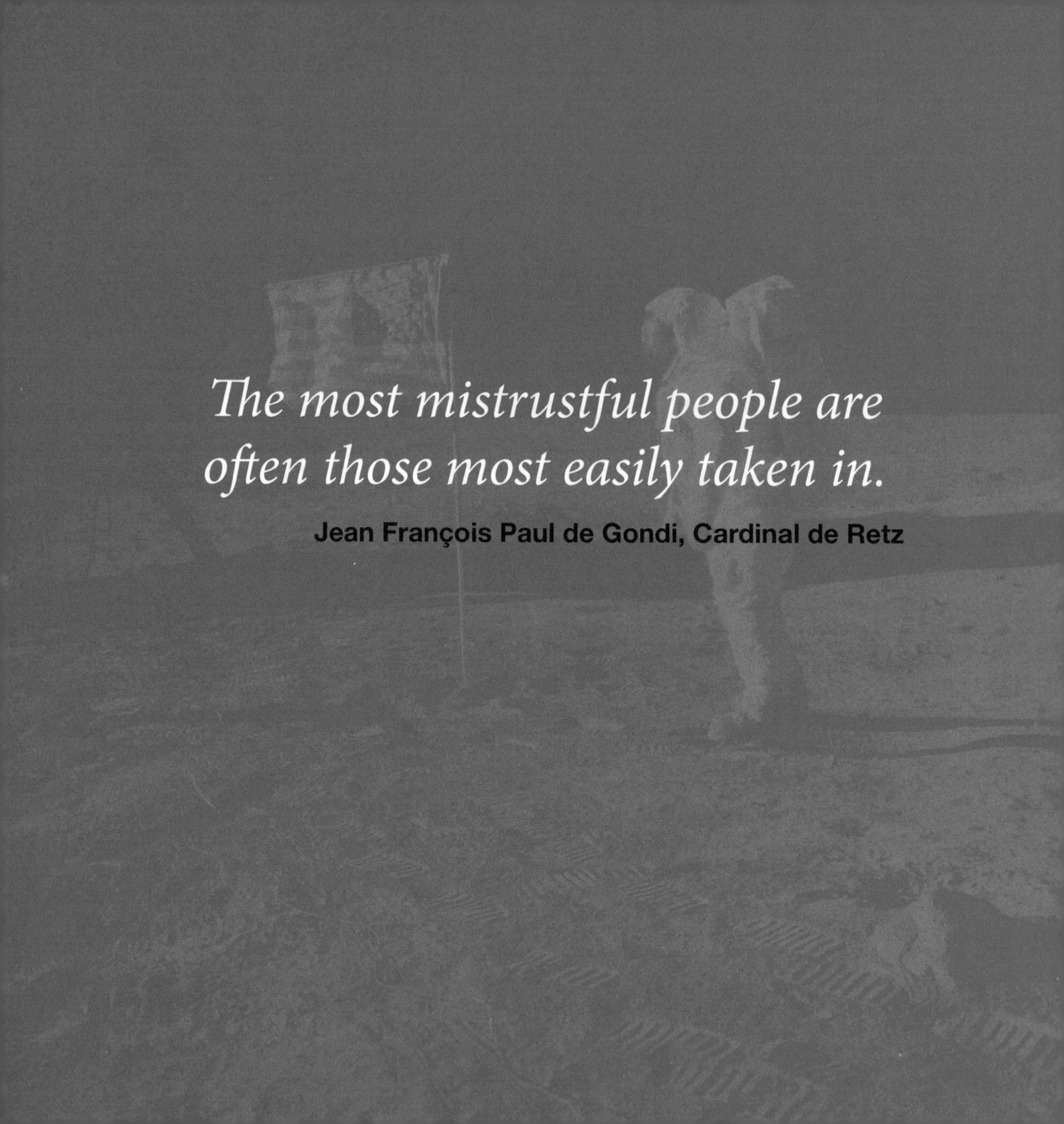

The most mistrustful people are often those most easily taken in.

Jean François Paul de Gondi, Cardinal de Retz

CONSPIRACIES OF SEA, SKY AND SPACE

Sea, sky, space: the big blue bits that surround the continents and the world, and on and through which people and goods are propelled in carriers both large and small. But their routes from A to B aren't all that's plotted. If some theorists are to be believed, there's also many a mean conspiracy that has been carried out in these vast, cold arenas. To put it another way, there's scarcely an accident that hasn't provoked an accusation: disasters hide dastardly plans, while calamities are masked by cover-ups.

It's said, for example, that the *Titanic*'s fatal collision with an iceberg was actually an insurance fraud that went horribly wrong, with more than 1500 people losing their lives instead of being rescued as planned. Just three years later, in 1915, the *Lusitania* was sunk by a German torpedo. But again, some suspect that this was what the perfidious Brits wanted, because the loss of the ship and its American passengers might have sparked sufficient anti-German resentment to bring the US into World War I. If that was the plot, however, it didn't work – not immediately, anyway. (A similar conspiracy surfaced in 1941 when the Japanese attack on Pearl Harbor drew the US into World War II, but that's another story, see p.360.)

Towards the end of the century, ocean liners had been supplanted by airliners, and torpedoes had evolved into missiles. A trio of incidents in the 1980s and 90s involved huge Boeing 747 passenger planes, filled with civilians, being violently scythed from the night skies. At the height of the Cold War, Soviet fighter jets shot down Korean Airlines Flight 007 over the USSR, having apparently mistaken it for an American spy plane. Poor evidence, secretive governments and various inconsistencies led to all manner of theories regarding cover-ups and conspiracies, from claims that the plane had deliberately strayed off course because it was working for US intelligence to allegations that the surviving passengers were being held in Siberian labour camps.

Five years later, in December 1988, Pan Am Flight 103 was blown up by a bomb in a suitcase over Lockerbie, and the previously obscure Scottish town became the centre of a web of intrigue involving the CIA, MI6, Mossad and other covert organizations. Libya was ultimately blamed, tried and punished, but despite paying a substantial fine, still denies any involvement in the incident. It has long been forgotten that the prime suspects initially included

Syria, Palestinian freedom fighters, Iran and a few well-connected Americans.

Another US passenger flight met with disaster in 1996. On July 17, TWA Flight 800 exploded and crashed into the dark waters of the Atlantic, twenty miles off the coast of Long Island – but this time there was no international enemy to blame. The US government spent considerable time and money insisting that it was an accident and trying to prove that the plane had, in effect, fallen apart, but others claimed it was a victim of "friendly fire", shot down by a US Navy missile during a training exercise. However, there was a change of tack after 9/11, and in the build-up to the war on Iraq, with both theorists and high-ranking politicians attempting to embroil Iraqi terrorists in the disaster.

Like the Cold War, the space race also had its fair share of conspiracies and cover-ups. It's thought, for instance, that Russian cosmonaut Yuri Gagarin wasn't the first man into space, but rather the first man to make it back alive... As for the first ever moon landing, by the US *Apollo 11* mission in 1969, there are plenty of people who believe that it was a massive hoax. It's alleged that the astronauts apparently walking on the moon were really filmed out in the American desert – a case of one small step for man, but one giant step for special effects. If the allegation is true, it must be the biggest con trick ever.

A different sort of obsession is displayed by the UFOlogists who believe that aliens crash-landed a spaceship at Roswell, New Mexico, in 1947, an incident they claim has been covered up by the US government ever since. Officials have always claimed that the "flying saucer" was just a weather balloon – but then they would say that, wouldn't they?

Titanic hubris

For sheer symbolism, as well as scale, the tragedy of RMS *Titanic* can hardly be surpassed. A massive luxury ship embarks on its maiden voyage, carrying thousands of passengers – ranging from the obscenely rich to the abjectly poor – from the Old World to the New, only for most of them to die in the freezing waters of the black Atlantic. The incident has inspired countless novels and many films including James Cameron's 1997 box-office titan starring Kate Winslet and Leonardo DiCaprio. The film's tagline was "Collide with destiny". But was fate really the culprit, or was the *Titanic* disaster the result of epic hubris, utter folly or a conspiracy to commit an almost unimaginable fraud?

When the RMS *Titanic* was launched in early 1912 from Belfast shipbuilders Harland & Wolff, it was, at 852 feet and 46,329 tons, the largest ship in the world. It had been commissioned by the White Star Line to ply the highly competitive Atlantic route between Europe and America, and for first-class passengers at least it was said to offer the last word in luxury. It was said to be "practically unsinkable" (rather than simply "unsinkable", as later accounts suggested) because its hull had a series of virtually watertight bulkheads, four of which could be filled without sinking the ship.

On April 10, 1912, the *Titanic* left Southampton for New York under the command of Captain Edward J. Smith, with 2224 passengers and crew on board. Four days later, just before midnight on the night of April 14, 1912, the ship struck an iceberg around four hundred miles south of Newfoundland; the iceberg tore through the *Titanic*'s starboard side and ruptured five of its

THE LUSITANIA

The British passenger ship SS *Lusitania* was sunk off the coast of Ireland by the German submarine U-20 on May 7, 1915, with the loss of 1198 lives. Although Britain and Germany had been at war for some months, transatlantic passenger services like the New York–London route being plied by Cunard's liner had continued. This was despite warnings from Germany, published in American newspapers (and on May 1, when the *Lusitania* sailed), that England-bound ships were fair game for their submarines. So the US public couldn't say they weren't warned, and the sinking of the *Lusitania* bloodily underscored the danger. There was righteous outrage in the US, not only that the filthy Huns would sink a civilian ship, but that they would dare to kill the 128 Americans aboard.

The *Lusitania*, hit by one torpedo, sank in just eighteen minutes. (By contrast, the *Titanic*, hit by an iceberg, had taken two hours to sink.) What kind of damage had the torpedo done to make the ship sink so quickly? Suspicion turned on the idea that the *Lusitania* had been carrying a huge consignment of contraband munitions that neutral America shouldn't have been supplying to Britain. But then another suspicion arose: did the Brits conspire to have the ship sunk in order to sting the US into entering the war with Germany?

The key event cited by conspiracist historians is an Admiralty conference on May 5, attended by then first lord of the Admiralty, Winston Churchill, at which the destroyer meant to escort the *Lusitania* into harbour was ordered to be withdrawn. While the Admiralty War Diary doesn't record who ordered the destroyer's withdrawal, it notes that four other destroyers in the Bristol Channel were assigned to escort duties instead. But that never happened, and the *Lusitania* sailed unprotected into U-boat infested waters. Was Churchill hoping for the ship to be sunk and the US to be spurred into war?

The problem with this theory is that it rests on some big assumptions. First, that Churchill could be pretty sure that the *Lusitania*, going full speed and zigzagging to avoid subs, would indeed be sunk by one of the handful of U-boats in the broad, rough seas of the Atlantic. Second, that he could also be sure that the US would be provoked into war as a result – a provocation that, in the event, President Woodrow Wilson resisted. As for the possible presence of contraband munitions, US secretary of state William Bryan had made it clear that Germany was entitled to stop contraband reaching the Allies, writing that a "ship carrying contraband should not rely upon passengers to protect her from attack". And, surely, if the *Lusitania* had been carrying munitions, the British would not have wanted it to be sunk en route? In any case, Wilson went on to win re-election in 1916 on a neutrality platform, and he kept the US out of the war as long as Germany kept its U-boats well away from the US's coast and ships. When the Germans started sinking US ships again in early 1917, however, the US entered the war on the Allies' side.

bulkheads. By 2.20am, the ship had sunk with the loss of 1503 lives.

Incompetence and ill fortune

The Cunard liner *Carpathia* arrived on the scene eighty minutes after the *Titanic* sank, a fatally long time in near-freezing waters. Inquiries in both the US and the UK revealed that another ship, the *Californian*, was sitting less than twenty miles away from the *Titanic* the whole time. However, its radio operator was not on duty to hear the *Titanic*'s SOS, which was not, in any case, sent out until 35 minutes after the collision. The *Titanic* was categorized in the same group as ships weighing just 10,000 tons, so it was equipped with a mere 16 lifeboats, enough to carry just 962 people – even though it was built for 3511 passengers and crew. It also had 4 collapsible lifeboats, increasing capacity to 1178. But the first boat wasn't launched until ninety minutes after the collision, a fatal delay. Why did the first SOS and the first lifeboat launch take so long? And what was the *Californian* doing in the middle of the Atlantic?

It later transpired that the *Californian* was owned by the financier J.P. Morgan, who in part owned White Star Line. The ship was also said to be carrying some three thousand thick woollen jumpers and blankets, and had allegedly been dispatched to that very spot. A curious mission, especially during a coal strike that curtailed all but the most essential or profitable shipping. It was widely reported that Morgan himself had been due to travel on the *Titanic*, but had cancelled his trip because he was "ill" (although this excuse was later revealed to have been just that: an excuse). Furthermore, why did five hundred crewmen from Belfast refuse to rejoin the *Titanic* at Southampton, despite the coal strike that had put thousands of them out of work?

A Titanic insurance fraud...

Clearly, something was up. If a shipyard worker nicknamed "Paddy the Pig" was to be believed, the *Titanic* never sank at all – instead, its slightly older sister ship, the *Olympic*, was sunk as part of a huge insurance scam. The design differences between the *Olympic* and the *Titanic* were minuscule, so the *Olympic* was disguised as the *Titanic*, and then deliberately sunk. Where the plan went awry was in the tragic deaths of so many people.

The main proponent of this theory is Robin Gardiner, who has written three books on the subject, including *The Titanic Conspiracy*. He argues that the *Olympic* had collided with a Royal Navy cruiser, HMS *Hawke*, in Southampton a few months earlier, which damaged the *Olympic*'s starboard hull enough for the liner to be written off. However, the navy's inquiry, not surprisingly, absolved the navy of any blame. The *Olympic* was, therefore, both unsailable and uninsurable, and White Star would remain uncompensated. That would ruin the company, which was already struggling in its battle with the leaner, faster Cunard liners.

So, shortly before the *Titanic* was launched, the *Olympic* was taken to the same Belfast shipbuilders and spent a week in dry dock, ostensibly for repairs to its propeller (which should only have taken two days). That's when, the theory goes, the switch was supposedly made, after a few minor cosmetic alterations, name changes and a bit of paperwork – even the linen and plates aboard weren't ship-specific, all being labelled "White Star". The two ships were so alike that, to this day, many of the images and films that purport to show the *Titanic* are actually re-labelled footage of the *Olympic*. Besides, no one was paying much attention. The *Titanic* received its seaworthiness certificates after just half a day of tests, instead of the usual, mandatory, two full days. And it passed those tests despite smoke pouring from every porthole due to a fire in one of its coal bunkers!

Apparently, the plan was to dispatch the *Olympic* disguised as the *Titanic*, sail it close to an iceberg, then blow a hole in its hull using explosives. The hole would be blamed on a collision with the iceberg, and the ship would slowly sink, giving the nearby *Californian* plenty of time to rescue everyone on board. However, on the night, the *Titanic* did, in fact, hit an iceberg, which caused the ship to sink far faster than planned. Captain Smith and his crew then panicked for half an hour, before finally launching a real SOS.

...or Titanic blarney?

The insurance story only surfaced in 1995, ten years after the wreck of the *Titanic* (or *Olympic*) was found two and a half miles down on the ocean floor, in two huge pieces. But then maritime researchers Steve Hall and Bruce Beveridge set out to debunk Gardiner's theory in *The Olympic and the Titanic: The Truth Behind the Conspiracy*. The *Olympic*'s ship number was 400 and the *Titanic*'s was 401, and it was the latter number that was found on one of the propellers on the Atlantic floor. The number and location of the portholes on the two ships differed, and those on the wreck conformed to the arrangement on the *Titanic*. The front of the wheelhouse on the *Olympic* was bowed, but the *Titanic*'s was straight – and the wheelhouse on the wreck was straight, too. Besides, if it was known that the *Titanic* would be sending out an SOS, why didn't the *Californian* have anyone on duty to pick it up? Finally, the theory requires fifteen thousand people who worked on the ships to have kept quiet about the switch, with the single exception of "Paddy the Pig", whose real name was nowhere to be found on the workmen's records for either vessel.

The *Titanic* and *Olympic* being built side by side in the Harland and Wolff shipyard, Belfast, in 1910.

However, the evidence that Hall and Beveridge say proves that the ship on the ocean floor is the *Titanic* – like the portholes, propeller and bridge – are all essentially cosmetic details, just the kind of minor alterations that Gardiner contends were "fixed" when the ship was in dry dock. And fifteen thousand shipbuilders wouldn't have needed to be involved. Only a few would have been employed to make the cosmetic alterations, and unless they were *au fait* with the *Olympic*'s insurance problems, which is highly unlikely, the sinister significance of filling in a porthole here or there, wouldn't necessarily have occurred to them. That's not to say Gardiner's theory is true, but *The Truth Behind the Conspiracy* doesn't completely sink it either.

The reckless racing myth

A longer-standing theory holds that the *Titanic* was racing to reach New York in record time, and that it sank because caution was sacrificed for speed. J. Bruce Ismay, chairman and managing director of the White Star Line, is said to have ordered Captain Smith to "make a record crossing". Ismay, who was aboard the ship, was also singled out for cowardly behaviour, it being claimed that he pulled rank to get himself into one of the first lifeboats. However, Smith, who was the highest paid commander in the mercantile marine and was on the final voyage of his career, would have been unlikely to defer to Ismay on navigation. And it was Smith who failed to heed the warnings of ice, and allowed partially filled lifeboats to leave the sinking ship. In fact, Ismay helped to fill the boats, and was among the last to leave the *Titanic*.

In any case, White Star competed on bulk, not speed: the top speed of the *Titanic* was still five knots slower than that of the Cunard liners, and not all its boilers were lit. Ironically enough, it was taking the longer southern route precisely to avoid icebergs. The charges of reckless racing stemmed from the newspapers of William Randolph Hearst, who is said to have had a personal antipathy for Ismay, and prosecuted a "vicious" campaign against him. According to BBC Online in 2002, "stories were invented and witnesses, wishing to strengthen exorbitant insurance claims for lost baggage against the company, declared that Ismay ordered Smith to make a record crossing".

Horrible Huns and creepy clairvoyance

In the light of the fact that World War I broke out a mere two years after the sinking, some have charged that the Germans wanted to test out their U-boat submarine designs, and expose the myth that the *Titanic* was unsinkable. Thus a U-boat torpedoed the *Titanic* as it passed the iceberg – the iceberg took the blame, while the U-boat slipped away.

In 1898, meanwhile, clairvoyant and novelist Morgan Robertson had written a disaster novel about a luxurious British liner, "the largest craft afloat", plying the Atlantic route. Kitted out with "water-tight compartments", the three-propeller, multiple-bulkhead 800-foot ship was "unsinkable", and embarked in April with its full complement of three thousand passengers. But days into the maiden voyage, at around midnight, it hit an iceberg that cut through its starboard side like a tin-opener. Thousands died as a result of its inadequate provision of lifeboats. The ship's name? The SS *Titan*.

A century later

As things stand, the insurance-scam theory has received little coverage beyond the small community of *Titanic* enthusiasts. And to most of them, it's an amusing oddity of a story, not something to be seriously entertained. However, serious changes did result from the *Titanic* tragedy. Maritime laws were changed in 1913, requiring ships to have lifeboat space for everyone on board, to hold lifeboat drills every voyage and to maintain a 24-hour radio watch. A warning system about icebergs in North Atlantic shipping lanes was also set up. But it's the fate of the *Titanic* itself that continues to grip the imagination.

SOURCES

Books

Robin Gardiner The Titanic Conspiracy (1998). This builds on two earlier books by Gardiner: *The Ship That Never Sank* and *The Riddle of the Titanic*.

Steve Hall and Bruce Beveridge The Olympic and the Titanic: The Truth Behind the Conspiracy (2004). An efficient, but not entirely conclusive, debunking of Gardiner's claims.

Websites

Ⓦ **www.encyclopedia-titanica.org** This aptly named website is full of all things *Titanic*.

KAL 007: a spy shot from the sky?

Korean Airlines Flight 007, bound for Seoul, South Korea, took off from Anchorage, Alaska early on September 1, 1983. The Boeing 747, which had first flown in from New York, carried 246 passengers, mainly Korean and Japanese, and 23 Korean crew. It should have been an easy 3800-mile flight south over the friendly seas of the Pacific Ocean, but the plane veered into the eastern edge of USSR airspace. As KAL 007 flew over the Kamchatka Peninsula, Soviet fighter planes were scrambled to intercept, only for the Boeing 747 to re-enter international airspace, before returning again to Soviet skies over Sakhalin Island. Two Soviet Sukhoi-15 fighters were sent up to meet and greet the Korean plane. After some clumsy attempts to get Flight 007 to leave, Soviet air command ordered the plane shot down. One of the Soviet fighter pilots, Major Gennadie Osipovich, fired two air-to-air missiles at the 747, hitting it at 3.26am local time."The target is destroyed", he reported, as the plane fell from the sky.

There was international uproar. "Straying off course is not a capital crime by civilized nations", the US ambassador to the UN railed, as tens of thousands of South Koreans protested on the streets of Seoul and at various Soviet embassies, and the families of the 63 American victims demanded answers. The shootdown was a "crime against humanity", said President Reagan. "The borders of the Soviet Union are sacred", the Soviet defence minister replied. Within a week, the Soviet chief of staff Nikolai V. Ogarkov claimed that KAL 007 had been mistaken for a US spy plane in the area, before adding that KAL 007 was itself a spy plane, and that it had sheared through Soviet airspace in "a deliberate, thoroughly planned intelligence operation". However, there was no evidence to back up Ogarkov's claim or anything else. With no survivors or witnesses of any kind able to come forward, most people's hopes rested on the aircraft's black box recorders, but the Soviets insisted that these had not been found in their waters. In fact, in all the searches carried out by Russia, the US and Japan over several weeks, very little evidence was found, including plane debris, luggage and other belongings, and the remains of passengers and crew.

One of the earliest questions asked in response to the incident was how on earth KAL 007 could have strayed nearly two hundred miles off course, when there were three internal navigation systems aboard, all separately programmed and powered in order to prevent just such a tragedy? How had Captain Chun Byung-in, who had accumulated 10,000 hours of flying time (6600 hours in Boeing 747s), and his crew managed to ignore the internal navigation systems and ground-radar, which would both have shown land below them, where there should have been sea? The Koreans would also have been well acquainted with the perils of stumbling across the borders of this particular paranoid superpower: only five years before, Korean Airlines Flight 902 had flown a course almost exactly opposite its true path, and was hit by a Russian missile for its error. KAL 902 was damaged, but not destroyed, and the pilot managed to land at Murmansk in northwest Russia – which Ogarkov cited as the precedent for alien invasion of Soviet airspace.

An American spy plane?

KAL 007 was not lost, R.W. Johnson argued in *Shootdown: Flight 007 and the American Connection*. He said that the plane was working for US intelligence, and had been deliberately sent into Soviet airspace to trip, and expose, Soviet defences. This trick of a civilian aircraft, without any spy gadgetry, "drifting" into Soviet airspace, so that the Russians' reactions could be monitored from afar by high-tech spy aircraft, had been going on for decades. Johnson contended that the US subsidized the Anchorage–Seoul route in return for this drifting and spying technique being added to the flight's duties. US–Soviet tensions were already very high at that time, with the US bullishly announcing its Strategic Defense Initiative (SDI) anti-missile programme just a few months before, as well as carrying out a series of exercises of the Pacific fleet, which involved boats and planes encroaching on Soviet territory in provocation missions. Johnson also claimed that KAL 007's captain, Chun Byung-in, commented that he would not fly another "mission" for the US because they were too dangerous – it looks as though he was right.

In *The Target is Destroyed*, journalist Seymour Hersh also placed the tragedy in the context of the period's high Cold War tensions and the massive US military exercises in the region, and referred to the "Cobra Ball" intelligence-gathering missions, which saw large, four-engined RC-135 American spy planes loitering along Soviet air borders. However, Hersh argued that the KAL 007 passenger plane was not a US military scapegoat, but was simply, and unfortunately, mistaken for an RC-135 spy plane by the Soviets. He further added that Major Osipovich's Sukhoi-15 fighter, running out of fuel and time, was bade to shoot down the Boeing 747 in near panic.

Following the dissolution of the Soviet Union in 1991, the Russian newspaper *Izvestiya* agreed with Hersh's assessment – panic in the Soviet defence command had brought down the plane. Responding to US government figures like Senator Jesse Helms who were still asking for answers, Russian president Boris Yeltsin also used the early 1990s period of rapprochement to admit that they had, in fact, found KAL 007's black box flight recorders. The cockpit voice recorder, according to *The New Yorker*, portrayed the crew sitting around talking idly about nothing and chatting, with no consternation, to the crew of the follow-on flight KAL 015 right up to missile impact. With the flight-recorder data and other information emerging, the International Civil Aviation Organization (ICAO) concluded that the crew failed to engage the inertial navigation systems (INS) aboard the plane, and had almost slept their way into being shot down over Russia. The Aviation Safety Network, rather generously towards the Soviets, blamed the crash on "flightcrew navigational error".

However, some people remained unconvinced that pilot and crew error were the only reasons for the tragedy. KAL 007 had been making deliberate turns within Russian airspace, and James Gollin and Robert Allardyce put forward the theory, in the article "Desired Track: The Tragic Flight of KAL Flight 007", that the plane was carrying out a "great circle" route under direct pilot control, and could not have been on some kind of mistakenly programmed autopilot. The authors concluded that, whatever the pilot was doing, he was doing it for a reason – and that reason was spying. Indeed, David Pearson notes in his book, *KAL 007: The Cover-Up*, that the aircraft's flight path passed over various Soviet missile, radar and submarine sites and bases on the Kamchatka Peninsula and Sakhalin Island and, ultimately, over a "Soviet military center at Vladivostok".

Or a dogfight?

Another possible theory about exactly what brought down KAL 007 arose from the transcription of one of the air traffic tapes recorded by Tokyo air traffic control that night. During one conversation between KAL 007's crew and Tokyo, someone apparently says "gonna be a bloodbath, real bad". But, as pilot and aeronautical engineer Michel Brun reported in *Incident at Sakhalin: The True Mission of Flight 007*, various examinations of the recording over the years have failed to identify who that "someone" actually was. Did the comment come from KAL 007's co-pilot, or perhaps from some unknown person in another aircraft nearby? A group of Japanese octopus fishermen nearby also reported seeing and hearing an explosion, and even smelling burning aviation fuel, and to Brun this and the "bloodbath" comment are commensurate with a massive air battle involving a number of planes.

Brun's story depicts a score of US reconnaissance and fighter aircraft invading Soviet airspace around Sakhalin

Island that night, precipitating a two-hour dogfight that saw a dozen US aircraft scythed from the skies by Soviet fighters. He says that KAL 007 had escaped to the south when the fighting began, only to be shot down over the Japanese island of Honshu an hour later – probably by the US armed forces. Fearing that the battle could have led to World War III, the US and USSR apparently agreed to focus on the destruction of the Korean airliner, instead of the dogfight.

The main problem with Brun's theory is that it seems unlikely the USSR would have passed up the opportunity to announce to the world that they had successfully repelled a wilful US air invasion, and even more unlikely that they'd take the blame for the only US kill that night – of a civilian aircraft. However, the Cold War was never black and white. And it wasn't just war at stake, but a chance at peace too; a new US–Soviet missile control treaty was being negotiated in Geneva at that time, so perhaps the Russians agreed to a cover-up in order to preserve that?

Congressman McDonald

One of the passengers onboard KAL Flight 007 became the only US congressman to be killed by the Soviets during the Cold War: the vociferous anti-communist and chairman of the John Birch Society (see p.188), Democrat congressman Lawrence McDonald of Georgia. He was almost joined by North Carolina senator Jesse Helms, Idaho senator Steve Symms (both Republicans) and Kentucky congressman Caroll J. Hubbard, but they all changed flights due to other commitments. Rather predictably, several theories have suggested that McDonald may have been the intended target of the Russian missiles.The CIA reported that the Soviets could have intercepted telexes indicating that McDonald and other "tempting targets" were on the plane. But the State Department countered that nothing indicated that the Soviets knew or even cared about McDonald.

The congressman, however, had undoubtedly made enemies on the home front. His extreme anti-communism had seen many top US politicians exposed as "Reds", he despised "one world" organizations like the Trilateral Commission (see p.143), and he had been involved in a book exposing the secret financial dealings of the Rockefeller dynasty. McDonald had also been seen as a potential opponent to presidential hopeful George H.W. Bush for the 1988 election. Some conspiracists have alleged that the State Department's investigation into KAL 007 was wrapped up in a mere ten weeks because McDonald's death so relieved the Republican government.

One potential twist in the McDonald theories comes from the fact that he had been sponsoring the publication of a book, *Nicaragua Betrayed*, about the South American country's former president, Anastasio Somoza, who had been toppled in a grotesque coup backed by the CIA (see p.201). If the CIA suspected that telexes giving McDonald's whereabouts may have been intercepted, why didn't it try to keep them – or him – more secure? Perhaps the beleaguered Agency, which was battling behind the scenes to keep the Iran–Contra scandal under wraps, wanted the Soviets to know who might be straying into their skies?

The real question to ask about the McDonald theory, however, is would the Soviets really shoot down an entire aircraft of innocent men, women and children just to get at one relatively minor US politician? It would surely be better to take him alive and beat some information out of him – but then perhaps that's just what they did? Unfortunately, it has never been conclusively proven whether McDonald is dead or alive, as his body was never found – nor, for that matter, was anyone else's.

Nothing to be found...

The enduring problem with confirming exactly what happened to KAL Flight 007 has always been the dearth of bodies, luggage and wreckage found at the "wreck" site. R.B. Cutler, in his self-published 1986 book *EXPLO 007: Evidence of Conspiracy*, cited one US Air Force intelligence officer as saying that the US blew up the plane using a radio-control device, and that it is now at the bottom of the Kuril Trench deep in the Pacific Ocean.

Other theories have it that the plane hit the water with such impact that most of the evidence was, in effect, vaporized – an unprecedented event – while another theory states that the nose and tail were shot off by the Russian missiles and the wind-tunnel-like fuselage blasted the plane's contents over a vast area.

In 2001, Lieutenant General Valeri Kamenski, who was involved in that night's adventure in his role as commander of the Soviet Air Defence Force for that area, told a Ukrainian newspaper that the fate of the passengers and crew remained "a mystery". Perhaps giant crabs ate all the bodies, one explanation ran, although crustaceans do not eat bones, nor luggage for that matter. Certainly the US and Japan were frustrated by the Russians' search for the downed plane. As Admiral Walter Piotti, commander of the US operation, concluded, the aircraft stood a "good chance" of being found, if his force had been permitted to search for it "without restriction". In late 2003, Mikhail Prozumentshchikov, deputy director of the Russian State Archives, was quoted as saying that the Soviets knew where KAL 007 had come down, but had pretended otherwise, doing all they could to impede and "disinform" the US and Japanese search operations. He also added that the defence minister, the head of the KGB and even the Soviet leader, Yuri Andropov, were all in on the plan.

An even more sinister conspiracy was suggested by the Russian newspaper *Izvestiya* in 1990, which claimed that the lack of bodies, luggage and wreckage was due to the fact that there were none to be found. The few body parts and pieces of debris that washed up were a decoy. KAL 007 never crashed, but landed intact on one of Sakhalin Island's numerous airfields, or it ditched into the sea, with everyone onboard being rescued by Soviet ships and helicopters. This theory was backed up by Seymour Hersh noting that, in the first few hours of KAL 007's disappearance, CBS News had reported that it had landed on Sakhalin, and a Korean Airlines official told anxious relatives at the airport in Seoul that they were going to negotiate the return of the passengers.

Furthermore, while most reports say the plane "exploded" and "plummeted uncontrollably" into the ocean, US secretary of state George Schultz verified that Russian and Japanese radar showed KAL 007 took nearly twelve minutes to reach sea level, having first descended steadily to a safe oxygen level of 16,400 feet. The Boeing 747 was acting like an airworthy plane that was under control, whereas a plane falling uncontrollably from 35,000 feet would have hit the water in just two minutes. Analysis by the International Civil Aviation Organization (ICAO) from 1993 said that the time between the sound of the impact and the point at which the depressurization alarm activated, as heard on the black box recordings, was eleven seconds, which suggested a very minor hole in the plane, only a maximum of one square foot in size.

Given the apparent reputability of these sources, Bert Schlossberg, director of the International Committee for the Rescue of KAL 007 Survivors, finds this version of events highly credible. But if the plane did manage to make a controlled, safe landing somewhere, with most of the passengers surviving, where did they all go? The website belonging to Schlossberg's organization www.rescue007.org suggests that the mostly Korean survivors were claimed by North Korea, a Soviet ally, who sent them to work in the Siberian labour camps. Incredibly, several such camps were reported to be still in operation in 2001 by the Western press, and they may still be. The camps are said to be staffed by tens of thousands of North Korean labourers – could any of them be the survivors of KAL Flight 007?

A cold case from the Cold War

Despite all the different conspiracy theories, it's still widely believed that no one aboard KAL 007 survived when the plane was shot down in what was a senseless, cold-blooded killing. And there is currently little pressure to re-investigate this Cold War catastrophe. But what the two superpowers said at the time and since still doesn't quite add up, and some people remain suspicious of the official investigations. From Russia keeping quiet about finding the plane's black boxes to all the rumours about US intelligence operations in the area, there do seem to be reasons not to trust either government's version of events.

Mistrust of the US was further fuelled in 1995, when Alvin Snyder, who was involved in the US's presentation to the UN on KAL 007, said in his book, *Warriors of Disinformation*, that the National Security Agency (NSA), State Department and White House had conspired to delete five critical minutes of conversation between the Russian fighter pilots and ground control from transcripts of the incident. Moreover, in 2007, Bert Schlossberg suggested that KAL 007 was diverted off course at least partly due to the antics of RC-135 American spy planes in the area. Worse still, it was claimed that this information was suppressed by the US law courts so as not to compromise intelligence operations, and to prevent the US government from being sued by the victims' families.

When the Cold War was at its height, there was a true and terrible danger that innocent people all over the world could become the victims of some proxy battle between the two combative superpowers. And the accumulation of secrets, lies and suspicions, plus the division of truth meant that whatever tragedies did occur, the reality would likely be lost under avalanches of political point-scoring – as was the case in the shootdown of KAL Flight 007.

SOURCES

Books and articles

Robert Allardyce and James Gollin **Desired Track: The Tragic Flight of KAL 007** (*A Review of General Semantics*, Dec 1997). The article that suggests Captain Chun Byung-in was a CIA stooge deliberately sent into Soviet airspace to trip their defences.

Michel Brun **Incident at Sakhalin: The True Mission of KAL Flight 007** (1996). Brun contends that KAL 007 was brought down in the aftermath of a mighty US–USSR air battle in an interesting, if sometimes awkwardly written, book.

Seymour Hersh **The Target is Destroyed** (1986). This concentrates on the lethal military and political point-scoring between the US and USSR that made the demise of KAL 007 a tragically inevitable sideshow.

R.W. Johnson **Shootdown: Flight 007 and the American Connection** (1986). Johnson's main argument is that the plane was on a US spying mission, and therefore that much of the blame for its loss lies with the duplicitous Reagan administration.

David Pearson **KAL 007: The Cover-Up** (1987). Pearson focuses on Congressman McDonald's presence on the flight and its route over highly sensitive Soviet defence sites.

Films

History Channel **Secrets of the Black Box: KAL 007** (2005). A retread of the story that the Soviets shot down a civilian airliner, having mistaken it for an American spy plane.

Websites

Ⓦ **www.rescue007.org** The site of the International Committee for the Rescue of KAL 007 Survivors features documentary evidence, such as interviews, "secret" memos, *Izvestia* articles and Bert Schlossberg's *Rescue 007: The Untold Story of KAL 007 and Its Survivors*.

Pan Am 103 to Lockerbie

Officers from the RAF, CID, Scottish police and the CIA spent the Christmas of 1988 combing the bleak lowlands around Lockerbie, Scotland. They were looking, over 850 square miles, for remnants of Pan Am Flight 103, which had left London's Heathrow airport on the early evening of December 21. The Boeing 747, the *Maid of the Seas*, had 259 passengers and crew aboard, 189 of whom were Americans, and was on the Atlantic leg of a Frankfurt–London–New York–Detroit flight.

Just after 7pm, the *Maid* had entered Scottish airspace at around 30,000 feet, out of sight and sound as it approached the small town of Lockerbie. Then, at 7.03pm, 38 minutes into the flight, a bomb had exploded in the forward luggage hold. The disintegrating plane hurtled earthward, with the fuel-laden wings exploding onto Lockerbie's homes, killing eleven townsfolk. Although it's thought that some 150 passengers survived the initial explosion, everyone on board was killed on impact.

Police and intelligence services from the US, UK, Germany and the Middle East joined in the search for the killers, focusing on Syria, Libya, Germany, Scotland, London, Beirut and Washington. But it was not until November 14, 1991 that two Libyan intelligence officers, Abdelbaset Ali Mohmed Al Megrahi and Al Amin Khalifa Fhimah were indicted for blowing up PA 103 by the Scottish Crown Office and the State Department. Then it was another ten years before a Scottish court, which Libya insisted should be set up in neutral Holland, could try the two men for murder and conspiracy to destroy an aircraft.

In January 2001, after an eight-month trial with three judges but no jury, Al Megrahi was found guilty and Khalifa Fhimah was cleared. The case took so long to come to court because the Libyan government persistently denied the charges, and for seven years, refused to hand over the pair, despite the imposition of punitive UN economic sanctions in 1992. These sanctions were finally lifted in August 2002, after the Libyan government offered to pay $2.7 billion in compensation.

However, Libya's president Mohammed Qaddafi has always insisted that Al Megrahi didn't do it, as has his prime minister, Shokri Ghanem, who told BBC Radio 4 in February 2004 that Libya had paid the compensation in order to get the sanctions lifted, not because it accepted guilt. The payout was the "price for peace", as Ghanem put it, and it resulted in the sanctions being suspended and diplomatic relations with Britain restored. Evidently, those who thought Libya's official statement accepting responsibility "lacked remorse" were right. But the Libyan government isn't alone in protesting its innocence, and many believe that the country was the victim of far bigger conspiracies.

The case against the Libyans

The prosecution had charged that Al Megrahi and Khalifa Fhimah had placed a Samsonite suitcase containing a Toshiba radio filled with plastic explosive onto an Air Malta flight to Frankfurt. There, it was alleged, the case had been transferred onto PA 103. The bombing was said to be an act of revenge for the April 1986 US air attack on Tripoli, itself revenge for Libya's supposed involvement in the bombing of a Berlin nightclub frequented by US marines. Under the mercurial Colonel Qaddafi, Libya was considered perfectly capable of such outrages. By the mid-1980s, he was seen in the West as a madman who had turned his oil-rich country into the world's number one terrorist state (an image sufficiently familiar for Libyan terrorists to feature in the 1985 comedy film, *Back to the Future*). Qaddafi's delusions of pan-Arabian grandeur and of breaking the West's hold over the Middle East marked him out as an international troublemaker.

Libya wasn't the first, or biggest suspect

During the trial, the Arab news network Al Jazeera reported that former Iranian intelligence official Ahmad Behbahani claimed responsibility for international attacks carried out by the Iranian government, including Lockerbie. The news agency's notion that this might "have an impact on the current trial in the Netherlands" wasn't borne out, and Al Jazeera suggested that Behbahani might have some desire for revenge against the Iranian government. Both the Organization of African Unity and Nelson Mandela, however, have questioned the validity of Al Megrahi's conviction, with the latter visiting Al Megrahi in his Glaswegian prison in 2002. During the trial, both of the Libyans had pleaded not guilty, and blamed Syrian-backed Palestinians.

Most tellingly, the German government refused to back the US and UK indictment of the Libyans. Investigations by the then-West German police into the Frankfurt link had pointed to an offshoot of the Palestinian Liberation Organization (PLO), the Syrian-backed Popular Front for the Liberation of Palestine–General Command (PFLP-GC). Police raids on PFLP-GC cells in West Germany prior to the bombing had uncovered radio bombs and barometric (altitude-triggered) fuses. One of the seventeen suspects arrested during the raids, Mohammed Abu Talb, had a calendar on which he had circled December 21 – the date PA 103 had crashed. But Talb, who was placed in Malta at the time of the bombing, ended up as a key witness for the prosecution, for which he was granted lifelong immunity. However, in 2005, Lord Fraser of Carmyllie, who presided over the Lockerbie investigation and issued the two arrest warrants, told *The Sunday Times* that Talb was "unreliable", and "an apple short of a picnic".

The fact was, by late 1989, there was "virtually no disagreement" among investigators and intelligence agents that the PFLP-GC was responsible, as David Johnston reported that year in his book *Lockerbie: The Tragedy of Flight 103* – a claim repeated in Steven Emerson and Brian Duffy's *The Fall of Pan Am 103*. The supporting theory was that the PFLP-GC had been co-sponsored by the Iranians, in revenge for the erroneous shooting down, in July 1988, of an Iranian airbus by the US Navy ship USS *Vincennes*, killing 290 people aboard. Iran's Ayatollah Khomeini had vowed that the skies would "rain blood" in revenge. Indeed, Brigid Keenan, the wife of a British diplomat, wrote in her 2005 book *Diplomatic Baggage: The Adventures of a Trailing Spouse*, that a former Interpol agent told her at a party that the bombing was Iran's revenge, and that Iran had paid £5.9 million into the West German PFLP-GC cells' Swiss bank account after the attack.

An unlikely coincidence over the Gulf War and Western hostages

In early 1991, US president George H.W. Bush asked British prime minister Margaret Thatcher for the PFLP-GC investigation to be "toned down". Days after the Libyans were indicted that year, Bush said that Syria – which had backed the US in the First Gulf War – had taken a "bum rap" over PA 103; meanwhile, the US State Department said that Libya – which had condemned the Gulf War – had tried to frame Syria and the PFLP-GC by planting false leads. The UK Foreign Office chimed in by stating that Libya was the sole and prime suspect for the bombing. In the following days, as this shift in blame was being digested, the last Western hostages in Beirut were released.

This pretty neat coincidence was picked up on by the BBC's 1993 documentary, *Silence Over Lockerbie*, which debunked the case against Libya and blamed Syria and Iran. Libya, it concluded, had been framed in favour of the US's Gulf War "allies". The documentary feature *The Maltese Double Cross*, which was withdrawn from the 1994 London Film Festival and investigated by the FBI, was based on the same theory. *The Maltese Double Cross* was aired on Channel 4 the following year, with the support of Dr Jim Swire of the PA 103 victim support group UK Families Flight 103, Labour MP Tam Dalyell and Tory MP Sir Teddy Taylor. It's quite something, one journalist wrote, when "a right-wing Tory MP openly accuses his own government and the USA of conspiring to cover up the truth". The FBI, meanwhile, attacked the film's objectivity, saying that it was part-financed by Libyan money and that key witnesses were "known fabricators", with some of them being criminals indicted by the US government for fraud and drug-dealing.

Syria, the CIA and a case of drugs

References to drug-dealing hit on an interesting fact about flight PA 103. Among the debris scattered across the moors, searchers found $500,000 in cash and a case containing cannabis and heroin. These were taken away by a helicopter-borne troupe of CIA agents, who also removed an unidentified body. One tagged body was also moved from one area of the crash site to another, and another body disappeared altogether.

The CIA had arrived at Lockerbie within just two hours of the crash, looking for members of a CIA team who had been on the flight after working in Beirut to secure the release of American hostages being held in that war-torn city. British soldiers had found a map locating two such hostages, and the map, together with other papers, was being carried on the plane by US Army Special Forces major Charles McKee. CIA officers took the papers, along with McKee's suitcase, but their "disregard for the rules" of investigation meant that the case had to be returned.

Aviv's investigation

The possible significance of the CIA's involvement was brought out by an investigation that Pan Am commissioned from Juval Aviv, a former agent of the Israeli secret service organization Mossad (see p.149). The investigation suggested that "rogue" CIA agents had allowed a Syrian arms dealer to smuggle heroin into the US on PA 103, in exchange for the release of US hostages in Beirut. McKee's team were couriering the drugs, but the drugs were switched for a bomb during a stopover in Frankfurt – not Malta – a bomb meant specifically to take out McKee's team. As Al Jazeera reported years later, Aviv was able to find this out because Mossad had helped to set up the Syria–drugs–CIA triangle.

The Syrian drugs link in Aviv's report was leaked to the press via an Ohio congressman, and was given a further twist in a *Time* magazine piece, "The Untold Story of Pan Am 103", published in April 1992, after the indictment of the Libyans. *Time* portrayed McKee's team not as dirty-dealing spooks, but as the good guys trying to expose the link between the Syrian drug trafficker and a rogue CIA unit, and being killed by the PFLP-GC for their pains. The magazine suggested that McKee's team weren't from the CIA, but the DIA (Defense Intelligence Agency), and that the CIA blew up the DIA before the DIA could blow the CIA's operation.

An alternative (and unsourced) Internet theory explaining the presence of drugs on PA 103 is that Pan Am's Frankfurt–US flights were a regular drug trafficking route for a London-based criminal gang that enjoyed high-level protection from US and UK intelligence. The Samsonite suitcases were said to be marked with symbols to assist their identification and passage by baggage handlers at airports. An investigation into all this by British authorities was then, supposedly, covered up.

Was it ... President Bush?

In *Cover-up of Convenience: The Hidden Scandal of Lockerbie*, published in 2002, John Ashton and Ian Ferguson also backed the theory of an Iranian revenge attack, suggesting that the Syria-backed, Germany-based PFLP-GC group was brought in to carry out the bombing because of its experience in that area. The Libyans were blamed later out of geopolitical expediency. They imply, however, that it wasn't just the CIA who would have been embarrassed by the exposure of the Syria–drugs–CIA ring.

In 1986, the Iran-Contra scandal (see p.201), which also involved arms, drugs and hostages, had nearly sunk President Reagan and his vice president, ex-CIA director George H.W. Bush. Bush survived Iran-Contra to be elected president in 1988, just weeks before Lockerbie. How desperate would he and his old agency have been to avoid another humiliating exposure? Desperate enough to blow up an airliner? Predictably, the CIA denounced the Syria–drugs–CIA explanation as "rubbish", and have dismissed subsequent variations on it as "conspiracy theories". As far as is known, there has been no State Department or Senate investigation into the allegations.

Some warnings were heeded, others were not

In 1989, a US State Department ambassador told a Senate subcommittee that if there had been any foreknowledge of an attack, the Beirut team would not have taken the flight. Yet despite the fact that many Americans were going home for Christmas at the time, the ill-fated PA 103 was only two-thirds full. This was because, victims' relatives alleged, many State Department employees had cancelled their reservations and flown on other airlines.

An anonymous call had been made to Helsinki's US embassy on December 5, 1988, warning that within two weeks an American airliner from Frankfurt to New York would be bombed. The State Department and the UK government said that, at the time, the warning had been considered a hoax. A researcher for a House Transportation subcommittee, however, found that the State Department hadn't considered the warning to be a "hoax" until after Lockerbie, and that it had been circulated to numerous US agencies and embassies, suggesting a retrospective cover-up.

The House Transportation researcher, Sheila Hershow, and her boss were later fired, but her investigation also unearthed a 1986 report by security consultants KPI Inc, which stated that Pan Am's luggage and passenger security were "vulnerable to most forms of terrorist attack". This vulnerability had not been addressed, despite a battery of bulletins from the Federal Aviation Administration (FAA) in November and December 1988, which relayed vague concerns about hijackings and possible terrorism after the West German police raids on PFLP-GC cells. As one State Department official said: "What sort of security officer is not going to phone his wife and say 'take the kids off the flight' or phone his buddies and pass on the warning to them?"

Somehow, the warnings that so many US government employees seemed to act upon didn't translate into saving PA 103 from being bombed. The presence of the McKee team on the plane may have been an uncanny coincidence that exposed other nefarious CIA dealings by chance, or the plane may have been deliberately targeted by the CIA, which would mean that some CIA agents had the reach and the PFLP-GC contacts to get that exact flight bombed. As for blaming Libya, it's said that the policy of pre-arranging groups to blame for heinous deeds was developed in the early 1980s by CIA agents as part of the groundwork for the alleged Iran-Contra operations. Hatching such a conspiracy is one thing, but actively pursuing it over more than a decade is another.

A P2 connection? Or a compensation conspiracy?

Some parts of the Italian press linked the bombing to the quasi-Masonic group P2 (see p.134), claiming that P2 had teamed up with the CIA in an extended effort to frame Libya and make Qaddafi pay compensation for seizing Italian assets (Qaddafi had thrown the Italians out of Libya – once an Italian colony – in the 1970s).

Another Internet rumour says that the oil-rich Libyans were blamed and had sanctions imposed on them to force them to pay compensation far in excess of the paltry $75,000 per person Pan Am would otherwise have paid (had the airline not gone bust). The only people to benefit from such a scheme, however, would have been the victims' relatives – hardly the most likely candidates for a conspiracy.

The aftermath

It's odd that the Libyans would endure ten years of economically painful sanctions, then give up the suspects and pay a $2.7 billion fine, yet still protest their innocence. Obviously, they were acting out of self-interest in taking the "reward" of economic and diplomatic rehabilitation in return for accepting responsibility for Lockerbie, but having done so, you might think that they would prefer not to risk rocking the diplomatic boat by reviving the controversy.

Just think what a difference an hour can make. Had Pan Am Flight 103 taken off on time, the bomb aboard would have detonated over the Atlantic, sending the plane and all its evidence irretrievably to the bottom of the sea. Instead, it blew up over land, and so began a terrible, twisted tale involving Washington, Tripoli, Frankfurt, Beirut, Damascus and the hitherto obscure Scottish town of Lockerbie.

From another point of view, the passing of almost two decades since the bombing has seen some remarkable changes, and yet also a sense of things staying the same. At the time of the bombing, Lockerbie sealed the notoriety of Colonel Qaddafi's Libya as the world's worst terrorist state, and President George H.W. Bush stood allied with

President Hafez al-Assad of Syria. At the time of writing, Qaddafi is still in charge of Libya, but the country is treated like an international paragon, enjoying close diplomatic ties with the West and an influx of investment for its oil and gas, with the UK and Italy leading its diplomatic "rehabilitation". Now it's Syria, under the leadership of Hafez's son Bashar al-Assad, and Iran that are regarded by the US as the world's top terrorist states.

In June 2007, Hugh Miles wrote a riveting update to the Lockerbie saga, "Inconvenient Truths", in the *London Review of Books*. The article listed a litany of problems with Al Megrahi's trial: key evidence about luggage and freight movements at Frankfurt airport was taken by the Crown Office and not shared with the defence, a move that the Privy Council's judicial committee condemned; members of the US Department of Justice present at the trial seemed to "guide" the prosecution, according to criticism by UN observers; and the prosecution repeatedly insisted that the bomb was planted at Malta and not at Frankfurt. Miles also quoted Robert Black QC, the emeritus professor of Scottish law at Edinburgh University who helped set up the court. Black said before, during and after the trial that "no reasonable tribunal, on the evidence heard ... should or could have convicted" Al Megrahi, and that his conviction was an "absolute disgrace".

Al Megrahi's lawyers filed a second appeal to have his conviction overturned in 2007; the appeal was ongoing at the time of writing. One move by his lawyers was to petition for access to secret documents pertaining to the massacre that prosecution lawyers had seen during the trial, but defence lawyers had not, as they were said to relate to matters of "national security". In March 2008, the Court of Appeal refused the request, but allowed the petition to continue to the High Court.

SOURCES

Books

John Ashton and Ian Ferguson Cover-up of Convenience: The Hidden Scandal of Lockerbie (2002). The authors book-end their account by going back over the first suspicions and investigations, and ending with disquieting questions about the Libyans' convictions.

Steven Emerson and Brian Duffy The Fall of Pan Am 103 (1990). A detailed investigation of the goings-on at the Lockerbie crime scene, in West Germany and elsewhere, which also makes some disturbing revelations about efforts to stymie the truth.

David Johnston Lockerbie: The Tragedy of Flight 103 (1989). An early, slightly salacious account of the then-ongoing investigation and its controversies, but noting much incompetence on the US side and notably pointed suspicion pointing nowhere near Libya.

Films

Allan Francovich The Maltese Double Cross (1994). This controversial documentary posits that Libya was framed for the bombing and looks at the CIA's drug-running operations in Beirut.

Frontline Scotland Silence Over Lockerbie (1993). Casting doubts over the case that laid the blame at Libya's door, this current affairs programme looks again at the Syria–Iran connections.

TWA Flight 800

On the evening of July 17, 1996, Trans World Airlines Flight 800 left New York's JFK airport for Paris, carrying 212 passengers and 18 crew. About twelve minutes after take-off, at around thirteen thousand feet, a catastrophic event caused the Boeing 747 to disintegrate and explode over the northern Atlantic. The blazing bulk smashed into the ocean twenty miles southeast of Long Island, at about 8.30pm. Debris and bodies showered the dark, cold water over three miles. There were no survivors.

Three agencies and four years

In the course of several months, over ninety percent of the shattered aircraft's remains were recovered and reconstructed in a hangar at Calverton, Virginia. Separate investigations by the FBI, Federal Aviation Administration (FAA) and the National Transportation Safety Board (NTSB), led to several pronouncements that some kind of electrical short circuit had caused a fire and explosion in the aircraft's central fuel tank, making a hole in the 25-year-old 747 beneath seat rows 17 to 28. Half a minute later, the tank blew up and destroyed the plane. In August 2000, the NTSB's open hearing delivered what it considered the most likely, but still unconfirmed, conclusion: "The 230 men, women and children on board TWA 800 lost their lives not as a result of a bomb or a missile or some other nefarious act but as a result of a tragic accident."

Or was it a missile?

That same month, however, the two hundred-strong TWA 800 Eyewitness Alliance group ran a full-page ad in *The Washington Times*: "We the eye-witnesses, know that missiles were involved … for some reason our government has lied and tried to discredit all of us to keep that question from being addressed", it declared, adding that the FBI, CIA and NTSB were involved in a cover-up. According to the FBI, these were mostly "credible" witnesses, who had seen a "missile" or "streak of light" heading towards TWA 800.

Evidence in favour of the theory included a photo taken that night, which showed something bright heading skyward, and the fact that luggage from the plane was strewn across the ocean earlier on its flight path than the main explosion could have thrown it – meaning that something must have made a hole big enough for suitcases to be sucked through. What's more, the very first reports of the crash, from the Pentagon no less, suggested a missile. And only four days later, *The Jerusalem Post* reported speculation from French military defence experts saying that if a missile was responsible for TWA 800's doom, it could only have been a US military missile, adding "it is unlikely that the US army will admit it".

The NTSB explicitly attempted to rebut the notion that flight TWA 800 was shot down by a US Navy missile. Theorists charge that neither the navy nor the government could admit that a missile was behind the crash without risking massive public wrath. Likely consequences would include curbs on the military's right to carry out exercises wherever they wanted, the cancellation of an expensive new missile system and a mountain of lawsuits. The NTSB responded to the missile theory with a "zoom climb" theory, saying that while the main fuel tank blew at 13,000 feet and blasted off the cockpit and first-class section, the remainder of the fuselage continued to climb for another half a minute, a further 3200 feet. They said that this would have created a rising, flaming blur which would have looked like a missile's tail-flame to distant eyewitnesses.

In August 1996, retired United Airlines pilot and former crash investigator Richard Russell wrote a memo in which he suggested – apparently on the basis of information received from a friend who had attended a high-level briefing on the crash – that "friendly fire" had downed the 747. As he later told *The New York Times*, he emailed the memo to some friends, mostly air accident investigators like himself. The problem was that Russell's memo subsequently found its way onto the Internet, and gained international attention in November 1996 when it was cited as a crucial piece of evidence for the navy missile theory by former White House press secretary and ABC News correspondent Pierre Salinger.

Salinger claimed that a French intelligence source with good US official contacts had told him that TWA 800 had been accidentally shot down by a US Navy missile, and had given him a document describing what had happened. Unbeknown to Salinger, however, this turned out to be Russell's memo, rather than an official report, and when both men refused to reveal their sources, Salinger's allegations lost credibility. The fact that Russell's memo had previously been posted on the Internet (which, it was widely believed, was where Salinger had found it) even led to the christening of the "Pierre Salinger syndrome", defined as the tendency to believe that everything published on the Internet is true.

Salinger, however, returned in March 1997 with radar images and hearsay reports of navy personnel lamenting their roles in the shootdown. Claiming that Russian satellites had filmed the incident, he cited a secret 1996 presidential commission as reporting that missiles had destroyed 26 planes since 1978, killing 600 people (a vital report even without the context of TWA 800's destruction, but no other news channel has reported on it and its existence hasn't been corroborated). The NTSB responded that claims of "some massive government cover-up" were "irresponsible", the FBI said that no radar images showed any missiles, and the Pentagon called Salinger's work "bunkum". CNN took it upon itself to say that Salinger's report was "littered with errors and misinformation ... and lacked legitimate attributions". Nonetheless, both Salinger and Russell stand by their charges.

What wasn't denied by any of the official organizations was that huge swathes of the Atlantic Ocean were zoned off for US military exercises, and that the multi-billion dollar AEGIS missile system was being tested in zone W-105, perilously close to TWA 800's flight path. Salinger argued that an unarmed Stinger missile had been launched to hit a target drone, but had instead locked onto a far bigger target – TWA 800. The Stinger lanced through the Boeing 747, clipping the central fuel tank and starting the fire that led to the fatal explosion.

That same story appeared weeks later in journalist James Sanders' *The Downing of Flight TWA 800*. The book contained photos showing a reddish-brown crust, the colour and chemical composition of missile fuel, on seat-foam taken from rows 17, 18 and 19, where the missile had supposedly impacted. According to Sanders, those photos earned his publishers a subpoena from the FBI. He claimed that the FBI had scoured the Calverton hangar and the ocean floor during the winter of 1996 for missile parts, and had impounded FAA radar tapes showing what the FAA called an "unexplained blip" around TWA 800. One FAA source said that there was a "remote possibility" that the blip was a missile. The NTSB, having been initially prevented from seeing the radar tapes, later rejected this possibility – but they didn't say what the blip was either.

Different investigations drew different conclusions. A January 1997 report by the BATF supported the idea that an electrical short circuit was responsible, the FBI said in June that a missile, bomb or mechanical problem were still possible causes, while the NTSB couldn't rule out that a "projectile" had struck TWA 800, without elaborating on what kind of projectile knocks down jumbo jets at ten thousand feet. CBS News speculated that the "streak of light" was flaming jet fuel, while the FBI and CIA said that it was probably the 747 breaking up. When the FBI finally closed its sixteen-month probe, it found "no evidence" of any criminal act and endorsed the short-circuit theory. But FBI agents told a 1999 Senate subcommittee that the investigation was "sloppy" and "inept".

Outside experts also got in on the act. Ex-US Navy commander and crash investigator William Donaldson scorned the NTSB's findings and presented the House Aviation subcommittee in 1998–99 with evidence supporting the Stinger-missile theory. The subcommittee, however, agreed with the NTSB. The conclusions drawn by the NTSB and FAA led them to recommend design changes to fuel tanks, wiring and associated hardware, as well as changes in inspection and maintenance. Donaldson's group and the eyewitnesses continued to press their case from the sidelines.

An Iraq connection?

During the build-up to the 2003 Iraq War (see p.408), the destruction of TWA 800 was reinterpreted to make a link between Iraq and 9/11. In *Study of Revenge: Saddam Hussein's Unfinished War Against America*, Laurie Mylroie

The reconstructed fuselage of TWA Flight 800 in an aircraft hangar in Calverton, New York.

wrote that on July 16, 1996, Iraq's terrorist front group the Islamic Change Movement (ICM) said that it would "deliver the ultimate response" to US threats. The next day, the anniversary of his 1969 Ba'athist Party coup, Saddam Hussein railed against the US and the sanctions imposed against his country, while on July 18, the ICM claimed responsibility for "the plane attack of yesterday".

Also on July 17, alleged Iraqi agent Ramzi Yousef was tried in New York for plotting to blow up US airliners over the Pacific in "Operation Bojinka", which involved using airplanes filled with TNT as flying bombs. Colonel Robert Patterson wrote in *Dereliction of Duty* that the navy accidentally shot down TWA 800 when trying to hit one such airplane flying ahead of it. Authors Jack Cashill and James Sanders posited a similar scenario, with Baghdad being responsible for the plane the navy tried to shoot down, in the book *First Strike: TWA Flight 800 and the Attack on America*. *First Strike* gave Sanders' pet subject an updated, fresh spin, while somewhat undermining his earlier work. Cashill and Sanders contended that the then-president Bill Clinton knew it was a terrorist attack – hence the heavy naval and air-force presence in the area – but that he had sought for the FBI and NTSB investigations to conclude anything but. The book alleged that this was so Clinton could maintain his "peace and prosperity" platform and keep his comfortable lead over the Republican contenders for that year's presidential election, whereas an Arab attack would require a military response – a riskier position come the election.

In addition, the authors alleged that Hillary Clinton was in on the truth, which they contended could destroy her bid for president in 2008. However, if the incumbent Republicans could beat Hillary with this stick, surely they would have done so by now. Moreover, despite all the White House's dubious claims to justify the invasion of Iraq, it never suggested that Saddam Hussein had been involved in the downing of TWA 800.

Kerry vs Gore

Jack Cashill also contrived another theory in the aftermath of 9/11. After the World Trade Center attacks, some politicians speculated that terrorists had also destroyed TWA Flight 800. Senator John Kerry did so on *Larry King Live* and on MSNBC's *Hardball*, without identifying who the "terrorists" might have been or how they might have brought the plane down. Meanwhile, certain newspapers alleged that Vice President Al Gore had failed to implement the recommendations of his 1996 commission on airline and airport safety, because the costs to the aviation industry's big players would have "forced" them to curb donations to the Democratic Party. The basic charge was that Gore's corruption and/or negligence had left the airports unguarded, and thus made 9/11 possible.

Cashill claimed that Kerry's public speculation about possible terrorist involvement in the downing of TWA 800 was an oblique way of pointing the finger at Gore – his only serious opponent for the 2004 Democratic presidential nomination – for his alleged failure to implement the airline safety commission's recommendations. Given sufficient coverage, it was an allegation that could scupper Gore's nomination bid. "Just by hinting that he knows the story," Cashill suggested, "Kerry may be able to put Gore out of the race even before he gets in." Gore, who had won more votes in 2000 than any previous Democrat, dropped out of the race before the primaries even began. By August 2004, the Democrats had chosen John Kerry.

Montauk? Who said anything about Montauk?

In 2000, *The New York Review of Books* reported speculation that TWA 800 was brought down by an electromagnetic radiation beam, possibly fired from the top-secret experimental base at Montauk, Long Island (see p.297). In itself, there was no compelling reason to take the theory seriously, but the same article made connections that appeared to link TWA 800 with two later plane disasters, SwissAir 111 and EgyptAir 990.

Atlanta Olympics

Cashill put yet another spin on it all in July 2006, when media interest in the disaster was reignited by the tenth anniversary. Writing on www.worldnetdaily.com in a ten-part feature special, Cashill posited that the White House did not want to acknowledge a terrorist attack that could have shut down East Coast aviation right on the eve of the Atlanta Olympics. "Accordingly, all missile talk ceased", particularly in *The New York Times*, Cashill charged. At first, the paper had led the way in reporting stories about a "mysterious radar blip" and eyewitness sightings of "a bright light" homing in on the 747, only to later become the vanguard of printing the "official" version of events.

A costly cover-up?

Whatever the truth, the NTSB, FAA and Senate all publicly concluded that the TWA 800 disaster was an accident. If they did indeed conspire to cover up the accidental shooting down of TWA Flight 800, it was an extraordinarily elaborate deception, which led to reams of detailed and costly recommendations to change aircraft design and maintenance procedures – a hell of a lot of work to make the official explanation seem more plausible. That said, the FAA and NTSB did, in fact, drop their recommendations in 2001, saying that they were "too expensive" for dealing with risks that were "too remote".

That was still the case upon the tenth anniversary of the disaster, when the CNN Presents programme *No Survivors: Why TWA 800 Could Happen Again* gunned for the "certainty" that ageing planes were vulnerable to fuel tank explosions. CNN executive Mark Nelson slammed the airlines for lobbying against the FAA's additional safety equipment because "it's too expensive and unnecessary". However, the programme also touched on the shootdown theories, quoting Jim Kallstrom, the former chief of the FBI in New York, as saying "I would have bet my rather meager government paycheck that it was an act of terrorism".

At the time of writing, there had been no change in the airline industry's resistance to making the recommended safety changes, and as *Newsday* reported, the FAA "still does not require commercial jetliners to carry devices to make the fuel in their tanks inert". In July 2007, the US government proposed a new airline safety device – an anti-missile laser defence kit that could be installed on all airliners (at a cost of $6 billion) to misdirect shoulder-launched missiles. However, a Congressional Research Service report that said that such missiles had shot down 24 aircraft and killed 500 people, also noted that "no plane in the US has ever been attacked".

While victims' families and independent investigators continue their quest for information, no further government inquiry is underway and no one has sought to curb the military's rights to exercise as it sees fit. It's ironic that, according to the missile theory, a significant part of the danger that threatens civilian aircraft in US skies derives from the activities of the massive forces charged with their protection. Changing an aircraft's design, or tripling the guard at airports, does nothing to stop a missile accidentally fired by your own side.

SOURCES

Books

Laurie Mylroie **Study of Revenge: Saddam Hussein's Unfinished War Against America** (2000). An interesting work, if only for how much emphasis it places on Hussein as the architect of most terrorist attacks on the US. Mylroie also chastises the Clinton administration for ignoring an overarching terrorist network called Al Qaeda...

James Sanders **The Downing of Flight 800** (1997). A rapid account of the unfolding controversy and conflicting stories by a journalist whose significant scoops outweigh the somewhat personalized tone. In the later *Altered Evidence*, Sanders charged that his investigations led to him and his wife being framed by the US government.

Websites

Ⓦ **aviation-safety.net/specials/twa800** Collates various official reports.

Ⓦ **www.twa800.com** The website of the late William Donaldson, whose colleagues and supporters continue to investigate and press the theory that TWA 800 was shot down.

Ⓦ **users.erols.com/igoddard/TWA800/** Although he was later misleadingly reported as having retracted his "friendly fire" theory, Ian Goddard marshalled an impressive array of eyewitness, circumstantial and physical evidence to support his scrupulously documented case.

Ⓦ **www.worldnetdaily.com/news/article.asp?ARTICLE_ID=24734** Jack Cashill's interpretation of why Senator John Kerry was beating the terrorist drum – significant for suggesting that Kerry's aim was to obtain political benefit from a totally unsubstantiated theory.

Roswell and Majestic-12

On June 24, 1947, a pilot called Kenneth Arnold was flying over Washington State's Cascade Mountains when he saw what he later described as bat-winged craft that looked like "saucers skipping over water". Unfazed by the odd choice of image (since when did saucers skip about on water?), the news media all over the US seized on Arnold's report. The ground had been well prepared by similar stories in the science fiction of the 1930s and early 1940s. By the first week of July 1947, "flying saucers" were on everyone's minds.

The Roswell Incident

On July 8 that year, Lieutenant Walter G. Haut, the public information officer at Roswell air base, in Chaves County, New Mexico, told local press that the actual remains of just such a flying saucer, or "disc" as he described it, had been found by local rancher Mack Brazel the previous week. The press release may have been intended as a joke or, as some claim, as a crude cover story for some military research or nuclear accident. Many UFOlogists believe, however, that the report was genuine. Whichever, it was quickly retracted in a second press release issued the following day, and the debris was dismissed as the remnants of a weather balloon.

Although that explanation satisfied most people, from September 1947 onwards the air force began to secretly collate data regarding UFO reports as part of what later became known as "Project Blue Book". Roswell itself was largely remembered only by UFO folklorists. In 1978, however, UFO researchers Stanton T. Friedman and William L. Moore announced that a certain Major Jesse A. Marcel, an intelligence officer who had been based there in 1947, maintained that he had discovered some very strange material at Roswell, which was like indestructible aluminium foil. "I still don't know what it was", Marcel recalled. "It could not have been part of an aircraft, [or] any kind of weather balloon or experimental balloon". Marcel added that he'd seen rockets before, and "it definitely was not part of an aircraft or missile or rocket".

Marcel also claimed that he had been sent to show samples of debris to General Roger Ramey, the commanding officer of the Eighth Air Force. He spread out the material on Ramey's desk, then went with the general to the map room to talk him through the site location. When they returned, however, the debris was gone, and pieces of a weather balloon had mysteriously taken its place. At this point, press officers took the famous photo of Marcel with his supposed findings.

As discussion of the "Roswell Incident" gathered pace once more during the 1970s and 80s, other witnesses started to come forward. Most notably, a mortician named Glenn Dennis, who had worked at a funeral home near Roswell, claimed that he had been called up by airfield technicians who wanted child-sized coffins and advice on how to stop bodies putrefying. On visiting the base, he'd seen strange engravings on some bits of wreckage before being threatened by military police and escorted off the base. A nurse he met – who has never been traced – described an autopsy she had witnessed being performed on horrific-smelling alien corpses that looked distressingly like "100-year-old Chinese".

Area 51 and alien technology

Major Marcel's story, more or less backed up by various "eyewitness" memories like those of Glenn Dennis, established the basic Roswell story – that an alien craft had crash-landed and that there had been a military cover-up. Speculations as to exactly what the military knew remained

ALIEN ABDUCTIONS

Do you suffer from dreams about being beamed aboard UFOs? Are you harassed by aliens at night and men in helicopters by day? Do you act impulsively against your will, while suffering memory lapses and horrific flashbacks of alien or army interrogation? Do you have muscle pains, panic attacks and nosebleeds, or find that streetlights turn off when you walk past them? Have you ever found weird bits of metal in your teeth, nose, ears or deep within your rectal chamber? Do your children look suspiciously non-terrestrial? Then you may be in the same boat (or ship) as up to two million others – nearly all American, if only because the relevant poll was carried out by the US-based Alien Abduction Research Center (AARC) – who claim to have been abducted by aliens.

Alien abduction has formed the theme of many an episode of *The X-Files*, as well as the hit TV series *Taken* and *The 4400*. In the real world, abductees can get help and support via endless conventions, Internet chatrooms and even the cable TV show *UFO-AZ*. The AARC publishes its own handbook, *Alien Abduction: Can it Happen to You?*, to help those keen to avoid unpleasant extraterrestrial kidnappings. If they can't help, there's also the International Center for Abduction Research, headed by Dr David M. Jacobs. He has made alien abductions his life's work for more than forty years, writing books such as *The UFO Controversy in America*, *Secret Life: Firsthand Accounts of UFO Abductions*, and conducting almost nine hundred hypnotic regressions with abductees since 1986. He is not, he earnestly assures us on his website, a crazy.

Gail Seymour, a pioneer of interstellar medicine on the UFOlogy and holistic healing circuits, advertises that she can remove and deactivate alien implants, be they of Grey, Zeta or Reptilian origin. (Greys, we're told, are into abduction and observation, whereas Reptilians like rape and torture. Both engage in vivisecting animals and humans and use Earth women to breed their offspring.)

So what kind of implant does Seymour mean? According to the UFO Folklore Center, one model of alien implant, first identified in the late 1950s, is a "stimoceiver", which receives and transmits electronic signals via FM radio. *UFO Magazine* investigated one such device in 1997, found by a British man named James Basil. After a series of problems including encountering weird humanoids in his neighbourhood, being bothered aboard spaceships and seeing "strange lights" outside his home, Basil claimed that aliens had "implanted a small object in his mouth". The problem, as the magazine's journalist pointed out, is that such implants often disappear, perhaps getting lost in the carpet, while nasal "implants" often turn out to be "of earthly biological origin" – bogies, to you or me. So it was with some excitement that Basil's dullish grey implant, suspected of being "miniaturized alien technology", was taken to the author's university colleagues for analysis. Scanned by a stereo light microscope, then an electron microscope, then an Energy Dispersive X-ray Microanalysis system, the implant proved to be a mysterious mix of calcium, silicon, mercury, tin and silver – a tooth filling.

It remains unclear exactly who is behind the alleged abduction plots. Abductees' piecemeal recollections of being aboard spaceships are often interspersed with interrogations by earthlings in army uniforms or black suits (the so-called "Men in Black", see p.125). But are these earthling interrogators trying to find out what the abductees saw, or are they trying to delete their memories, to cover up the awful truth of humans colluding with aliens? (Unfortunately, the mysterious human conspirators seem to be using memory-wipe techniques that don't quite work.) Worse still, are abductees' memories of aliens actually fake memories, implanted to cover up whatever super-secret project they may have accidentally stumbled across? Perhaps these fake memories are made deliberately ridiculous, so that the abductees will seem crazy to the world at large?

In fact, delusions of alien abduction, and suspicions that anything and everything may be an instrument of mind-control, sound like classic symptoms of paranoia. Many victims find their hallucinations are actively entertained and supported, and provide an entrée into a world of like-minded people. Their extremes of loneliness and misery may only seem explicable in terms of a great terrestrial or extraterrestrial conspiracy to oversee their lives, and imagined attention from aliens seems preferable to the pain of remaining anonymous even to their closest neighbours. In that sense, tales of implants and microwaves are a way to avoid responsibility on a chronic scale. Thus one of Gail Seymour's patients told her of a "long string of motorcycle and automobile accidents" over twenty years that he put down to an alien implant – not down to his lack of earthly driving skills.

General Ramey and Colonel Dubose examine debris from the 1947 Roswell crash, and declare it to be a "weather balloon".

just that until 1989, when a certain Bob Lazar revealed on Las Vegas local television that he had worked at the notorious Lake Groom military installation in Nevada, better known to conspiracists as "Area 51" (see p.299). As a physicist from the elite Massachusetts Institute of Technology (MIT), Lazar said he had been employed to "reverse engineer" extraterrestrial spacecraft, i.e. to work out the principles of alien science by examining their technology. One of the spacecraft he studied – and, yes, there were many – was the "disc" found at Roswell.

There are many, many holes in Lazar's story. For a start, only a fairly naïve non-physicist would take him on his own account. Scientifically speaking, tales of his discovery of "Gravity B" – a force created by manipulation of the nuclear force-field of a new element called "ununpentium" – ring very hollow. And there is no record of Lazar studying physics at MIT (or anywhere else, for that matter). Lazar had the answer to that, of course: his name was scrubbed from the university rolls as part of a government conspiracy to discredit him. The fact that the base at Groom Lake wasn't used between World War II and 1955 (when it was seemingly brought back into service for the testing of prototypes of Lockheed's U2 spy plane), was another problem – and in any case, Lazar himself was only born in... 1959. (Of course, the Roswell disc could have been stored elsewhere until Lazar was summoned to examine it.)

Despite Lazar's feeble credibility, the concept of a government with access to alien technology was suddenly fully "out there" in both mainstream and UFOlogist media. So too was the idea that Area 51 was the ultimate secret base, an all-American version of a master criminal's lair. Ultra-right-wing "patriot" organizations were delighted to acquire yet more evidence that the federal government was malignant and manipulative. According to conspiracy lore, Area 51 rapidly acquired a massive underground facility and elaborate protection systems, ranging from motion sensors that could also "smell" intruders to black "stealth helicopters" – supposedly developed on site with the help of reverse-engineered technology. The existence of armed, private security guards, at least, was real, as was the new name for the nearby State Highway 375 – it was grandly named "The Extraterrestrial Highway" by a Nevada state government eager to cash in on the burgeoning UFO-tourist market.

The Roswell autopsy film

Possibly even less credible than Bob Lazar's Area 51 story was the infamous film that surfaced in early 1995 purporting to be original grainy footage of an autopsy conducted on the bodies of the Roswell aliens. Even before the film was aired, things didn't look good. No "witness" had ever mentioned a film of the autopsy before, and the British company promoting it had previously handled Disney movies. When Ray Santilli's film was aired on the Fox network in August 1995, the quality was found to be atrocious – both cinematically and surgically. Film experts thought it strange that the close-ups of the aliens' organs were uniformly out of focus, while medical specialists found the techniques of the "doctors" amusingly amateurish. It was clearly a hoax.

Official conclusions

Such was the public pressure for information that, in September 1994, the US Air Force finally published an official report into the Roswell incident. It concluded that the famous debris had, in fact, come from a balloon – one that was part of a research project codenamed MOGUL, which had used high-altitude balloons to monitor atomic tests in the desert. Following widespread complaints that witness statements had been swept under the carpet, a second report was issued in 1997. It concluded that "these witnesses are mistaken about when the events they saw occurred, and they are also seriously mistaken about details of the events". Reports of alien bodies were blamed on crash-test dummies recovered from the balloon, and Glenn Dennis's tale was explained away as a confusion of two separate events that occurred several years later: a burning air force tanker incident from 1956, and an accident involving a manned balloon from 1959.

The US government had always denied the existence of Area 51, but after satellite pictures were published on the Internet in 2003, Assistant Secretary of Defense Kenneth H. Baconfelt was forced to respond. Asked what he could say about what went on at the facility, he replied "Darn little". He added: "We have a right, as a sovereign nation – in fact, a responsibility to the citizens of the United States – to develop various weapons from time to time. Sometimes these weapons are developed in classified locations". Probed further, he clarified, "I think I can say beyond a shadow of a doubt that we have no classified program that relies on aliens from outer space".

Majestic-12 and the Aviary

In 1984, photographs of a supposed "briefing paper" prepared for President Eisenhower on November 18, 1952 were mailed to a producer of television documentaries called Jaime Shandera. The paper discussed the Roswell incident, letting slip that "news reporters were given the effective cover story that the object had been a misguided weather research balloon". The paper also confirmed that alien bodies had been found; it called them "Extraterrestrial Biological Entities", or EBEs for short, and noted that "although these creatures are human-like in appearance, the biological and evolutionary processes responsible for their development has apparently been quite different from those observed or postulated in Homo sapiens". Without going into any detail, the briefing paper speculated that Mars was a possible origin for the Roswell spacecraft, "although some scientists, most notably Dr Menzel, consider it more likely that we are dealing with beings from another solar system entirely".

An attached memo from Harry S. Truman agreed that the "Majestic-12" group would be established to preside over the whole affair, and a higher-than-top-secret security classification "MAJIC EYES ONLY" would apply to all relevant documents. Meanwhile, Shandera and his research partner, UFO writer Bill Moore, were apparently receiving communications from disgruntled sources in the military and CIA who wanted to expose the "shadow government" of "Majestic-12" and publicize the truth about alien encounters such as Roswell. To protect their sources' identities, Moore and Shandera gave them bird names, such as "Falcon" and "Condor", and they slowly built up a significant network of contacts, which they dubbed "the Aviary".

The Majestic-12 documents were finally published by UFO writer Stanton Friedman in 1986. For credulous conspiracists, this was the perfect proof of the theory they had long cherished: that the government knew much more than it was letting on. Unfortunately, the "briefing paper" was an obvious fraud. Aside from its simplistic content, it was riddled with anachronisms, notably the words "media" and "impacted", which only came into use in the 1950s. It also failed to follow the standard formulas for editorial style – the format for giving dates and so on – and was even stamped with the "Top Secret Restricted Information" security classification, which was only introduced under President Nixon. Sceptics also alleged that Bill Moore had suggested to colleagues back in 1982 that fake UFO documents might be published to help flush out military sources who hadn't yet revealed their secrets; that same year, Moore had even worked on a novel called *MAJIK-12*.

Aliens, abductions and arms

The air force's official debunking reports and the exposure of both Majestic-12 and the Roswell autopsy film only served to fuel further speculation. The presupposition is that these are all part of a massive government cover-up, a conspiracy to dupe the world into believing that there has never been any alien contact. Meanwhile, the government – in hock to the military-industrial complex (see p.121), obviously – reverse engineers its way to superior military technology, while keeping secret the more peaceful technological benefits of alien science.

Some suggest that since Roswell the government has actually made contact with live aliens. The spate of abduction claims is seen as further evidence of government–alien collusion, with US citizens being traded for ever more futuristic weapons. All of which is a long way from the bits of tinfoil and rubber found by Mack Brazel in 1947. As he told the Roswell *Daily Record* in the immediate aftermath of the incident: "I am sure what I found was not any weather observation balloon. But if I find anything else besides a bomb they are going to have a hard time getting me to say anything about it."

SOURCES

Books

Charles Berlitz and William L. Moore The Roswell Incident (1991). The original book that set the whole Roswell research circus in motion; these are true believers, in full rumour-chasing cry.

Thomas Carey and Donald R. Schmitt Witness to Roswell: Unmasking the 60-Year Cover-Up (2007). You wouldn't think that new witnesses could still be emerging in 2007… but they are. And they say they saw one alien alive.

Philip J. Corso with William J. Birnes The Day After Roswell (1997). Corso retired from the US Army as a Lieutenant Colonel in 1963, after working in the Pentagon's "Foreign Technology Division". His analysis of the alien debris from the Roswell crash apparently allowed the army to develop everything from Kevlar and Stealth technology to SDI, and to win not just the Cold War, but the war against invading aliens too. Full of holes, but a bestseller nonetheless.

Stanton T. Friedman Top Secret/Majic: The Story of Operation Majestic-12 and the United States Government's UFO

Cover-up (1997). A long-term UFOlogist "exposes" half a century of government cover-ups, and the appalling "truth" behind Majestic-12.

Kal K. Korff The Roswell UFO Crash: What They Don't Want You To Know (2000). For once, "they" refers not to alleged conspirators, but to the Roswell conspiracy theorists. This is a detailed, well-researched debunking, with lots on high-altitude balloon research – it's widely decried as government disinformation, of course.

James McAndrew The Roswell Report: Case Closed (1998). The more detailed "second report" published by the US Air Force; includes stories of heroic experimentation in the early days of USAF research.

Charles B. Moore, Benson Saler and Charles A. Ziegler UFO Crash at Roswell: The Genesis of a Modern Myth (1997). The cultural anthropologist authors treat the Roswell incident as folklore, examining its relation to mythology and religion, and observing how the narrative only becomes clearer and more detailed as time passes. Moore, a physics professor who actually worked on Project Mogul, adds a chapter on the scientific research of the period.

Karl T. Pflock Roswell: Inconvenient Facts and the Will to Believe (2001). A UFO researcher finds his own "will to believe" collapsing in the face of the evidence.

Kevin D. Randle The Roswell Encyclopedia (2000). Four hundred pages of everything you could ever want to know about Roswell – and more.

Websites

Ⓦ **www.abduct.com/news/n46.htm** The photo of Major Jesse Marcel with the debris.

Ⓦ **www.bluebookarchive.org/** An online archive of over 56,000 pages on "Project Blue Book", and counting…

Ⓦ **www.gl.iit.edu/wadc/history/Roswell/Report/index.html** Links to downloadable PDF versions of the USAF's Roswell reports.

Ⓦ **www.majesticdocuments.com** Hundreds of PDF files of "Majestic" documents, "evidence that we are not alone", including assessments of the documents' authenticity – usually positive.

Ⓦ **www.mufor.org/majestic.html** Facsimiles of the "original" Majestic briefing for President Eisenhower.

Ⓦ **www.truthseekeratroswell.com** Includes lots of archive photos of the key players etc.

Ⓦ **www.ufoevidence.org /topics/Roswell.htm** "In-depth, quality and scientific research on the UFO phenomenon", i.e. lots of pro-UFO evidence, including links to "Majestic" documents.

The Apollo moon landing

On July 20, 1969, astronaut Neil Armstrong stepped onto the moon and proclaimed: "That's one small step for man, one giant leap for mankind." Minutes later, Edwin "Buzz" Aldrin joined him on the surface, while Michael Collins orbited overhead in the *Apollo 11* command module.

The Apollo landing was the culmination of President John F. Kennedy's vow to "have men on the moon by the end of this decade". It had required a workforce of over 400,000 people and a budget of $30 billion. Kennedy made his pledge at a time when the US was being thrashed in the so-called "space race" by the USSR. The Soviets had been the first to get satellites into space; live animals into space; live animals back from space; a man into space; a woman into space; and, finally, to complete a multi-crew mission. However, the Americans came back with the Apollo programme, which launched seven manned flights to the moon by 1972 – although *Apollo 13* failed to land, due to equipment malfunction. As Armstrong unfurled the billowing Stars and Stripes flag, the watching world was agog.

But to some observers, the notion that three men could fly a quarter of a million miles to the moon and back without a hitch was inconceivable. Armstrong himself only believed that there was a fifty percent chance that the moon landing would go as planned. And so the doubts crept in:

none of the photos taken from the surface of the moon shows any stars in the sky, when there should have been a dazzling sea of them over the atmosphere-less planet. And why didn't the lander module's thrusters blast out a large crater on landing? And why was the US flag waving, when surely there's no wind on the moon?

A hoax of astronomical proportions

Precisely where the idea that the moon landings had been faked came from is unclear. However, it was clearly circulating around Hollywood while the Apollo project was still underway – James Bond stumbles across a fake moon-landing set in *Diamonds Are Forever*, which was released in 1971. While rumours circulated, former aerospace writer Bill Kaysing, who worked for an Apollo engine manufacturer, was asked to write a satire on the moon-hoax theories. His 1976 book, *We Never Went to the Moon: America's Thirty Billion Dollar Swindle!*, which was presented as a work of nonfiction, described how NASA had defrauded the world with its Apollo Simulation Project.

In collaboration with the Defense Intelligence Agency, the landings were supposedly filmed in a vast mock-up of the lunar surface in the empty Nevada desert, in the region where the Atomic Energy Commission carried out atomic tests. On launch day, an empty Saturn V rocket took off from Florida, and then fell back into the sea. Meanwhile, the *Apollo* crew interspersed lunar filming with parties in Mob casinos in Las Vegas, where they gorged on showgirls, booze and roulette. They also attended "guilt therapy" sessions to cope with lying to everyone on the planet. As the *Apollo* craft supposedly returned to Earth, the astronauts were put in a space pod, pushed out of a cargo plane into the ocean, and hailed as heroes.

By Kaysing's account, astronaut Gus Grissom had been about to expose the whole Apollo programme as a charade in 1967 when he was killed with two others in a mysterious launch pad fire aboard *Apollo 1*. Grissom is known to have been aggrieved with NASA because it held him responsible for "sinking" his *Mercury* spacecraft on splashdown, and he therefore received little of the acclaim he felt was his due. Kaysing later contended that the *Challenger* space shuttle was blown up in 1986 to silence the squealers aboard. The reason why *Apollo 13* "failed" – after all, why have a hoax fail? – was to revive public interest, and with it future funding.

It's debatable whether or not Kaysing lost the plot in writing his "satire". As proof that his own publishers were in cahoots with NASA to suppress the book, he submitted a letter from his editor saying that the manuscript wasn't written well enough for publication – but both book and letter were published. "Evidence" for the astronauts being in girlie bars included a full-page spread of an exotic dancer. In 1997, Kaysing also tried to sue astronaut Jim Lovell for calling him "wacky", but the case was thrown out. However, his book may, in part, have inspired the 1978 film *Capricorn One*, which recasts the theory to a doomed Mars mission, which leads to a costly and murderous hoax lasting several months.

Fox versus Plait

Bill Kaysing resurfaced in 2001 on Fox TV's *Conspiracy Theory: Did We Land on the Moon?*, hosted by *The X-Files* actor Mitch Pileggi. Kaysing asserted that NASA was technically incapable of reaching the moon, but the race with the USSR forced them to fake the whole thing at Nevada's Area 51 (see p.299). The programme certainly scored an own goal by alleging that the moon-landing filmmakers borrowed special-effects technology from the film *Capricorn One*, which was made much later. But this was offset by an interview with Grissom's son Scott and his widow Betty, both of whom concurred with Kaysing's suspicions that the *Apollo 1* fire was no accident. They had no proof, but that's what they believed.

NASA responded to the programme with an article by astronomer Dr Tony Philips that used "rocks and common sense" to prove that *Apollo* had reached the moon. The rocks – all 841 pounds of them – were peppered with tiny meteoroid hits and cosmic ray isotopes, which Philips said could neither be found nor simulated on Earth (to which Kaysing replied that they could have been made by anyone with a special kiln). As the subject for a future conspiracy theory, Philips jokily suggested: "Did NASA go to the moon to collect props for a staged moon landing?"

Philips's article also pointed readers towards www.badastronomy.com, a NASA-approved website run by Phil Plait, an astronomer for Sonoma State University. Plait rejects the Fox programme's contention that a breeze on set caused the flag to wave. The flag may look as though it's waving, but it's just being jiggled as it's twirled into the ground. Any breeze to make the flag wave would also have blown dust around, of which there's no sign.

Plait goes on to discuss a number of other objections. Why don't the photos show the stars that should be dazzling everyone? And if the sun is the only source of light, and there is no air to scatter that light, then the shadows on the moon should be black, but they're not. In addition, photos show objects on the surface with long shadows that aren't parallel, which they should be if the sun is the only light source. Also, the lunar photos are suspiciously well taken and composed, although the cameras were mounted on the front of the astronauts' spacesuits, with no viewfinder. What's more, in some photos, the black crosshairs on the camera's lens appear to be behind the objects being photographed – an impossible feat, unless the photographs have been faked in some way.

Predictably, Plait can offer an explanation for each of these points. The stars are competing with the brightly lit grey-white lunar landscape and the visitors dressed in white next to a shiny spacecraft. The rapid exposure time needed for decent quality photos would not take in even the brightest starlight. Equally, the lunar surface and objects are bright enough to reflect light all over the place – you don't need an atmosphere to do that. Perspective and wide-angle lenses make parallel objects appear not to be so. And if there are multiple light sources, where are the multiple shadows? Everything, including the taking of photos, was rehearsed endlessly, and the photos we're familiar with are the best of thousands taken by the astronauts. And any subject that is bright enough overwhelms the film and the imprint of black crosshairs on it.

COMMIE COSMONAUTS

While the Russians offered public congratulations to the US on the Apollo moon landings, the Soviet press ran a grumbling campaign claiming that they were faked. Many in high places confirmed that view, with cosmonaut Boris Volynov still saying so in 2000. But they may just have been jealous. Their own remarkable lead in the space race had included sending the first man into orbit – Yuri Gagarin, who went up in a tiny Vostok spacecraft on April 12, 1961. However, Gagarin's true feat may have been that he was the first man to return from space alive, and to the right country. According to an article by the Russian newspaper *Pravda* in 2001, cosmonauts Alexis Ledovsky, Serentyi Shiborin and Andrei Mitkov, flew into space in 1957, 1958 and 1959 respectively, but all three died in the process. A documentary on the UK Horizons TV channel, *Cosmonaut Cover-up*, further claimed that cosmonaut Vladimir Ilyushin orbited Earth three times five days before Gagarin's flight, only to crash-land in China, where he was held for a year. Gagarin, crucially, landed back in the USSR.

Gagarin was killed in 1968 when the fighter plane he was flying spun into the ground. The official story runs that he could have ejected, but he stayed aboard so that he could steer the plane away from a school. However, some say that the Communist Party bumped him off, over a public slanging match he had with General Secretary Nikita Khrushchev. Supposedly, despite Gagarin's uncomradely womanizing and drinking, his huge popularity was putting the party's own bigwigs into the shadows. On the other hand, if Gagarin was really killed for arguing with Khrushchev, the confrontation must presumably have taken place when Khrushchev was still president, prior to 1964; for him to have had Gagarin bumped off four years later would seem like a long time to hold a grudge.

Apollo 11: Buzz Aldrin on the surface of the moon? Or an actor in a film studio at Area 51?

So what about the lack of a blast crater under the lander's rocket? There is a crater: it's just very small. On Earth, any gas discharge displaces the surrounding air, which displaces more air and so on; on the moon, where there's no air, only the dust directly touched by the exhaust gas gets displaced. Another charge the programme made was that the astronauts would only have needed to shift in the cabin to alter the lander's centre of balance and cause it to crash, and that the top half of the lander produced no visible flame from its rocket when it took off from the lunar surface. Plait retorts that the lander's exhaust and booster rockets could move to counter shifting weights, while its fuels, hydrazine and dinitrogen tetroxide, burn with a transparent flame.

When viewed at double speed, according to the Fox programme, film of the astronauts walking and driving (in a lunar rover) looks like Earth movements at normal speed. So it would, says Plait, but the film also shows dust thrown up by the rover's wheels travelling in a perfect parabolic arc rather than billowing about, as you'd expect in a vacuum. Surely, the Fox programme said, radiation in the Van Allen Belts, and in deep space, would have killed the astronauts, while the searing sunlight on the moon would have baked them. Yes, Plait agreed, if unprotected men had gone up for long enough, they would have died, but the spaceship's metal hull blocked most of the radiation. These scientists have an explanation for everything.

Tricky Dicky and the Vietnam War

In his 2001 movie *A Funny Thing Happened on the Way to the Moon*, Nashville filmmaker Bart Sibrel argued that the *Apollo 1* fire demonstrated that the NASA programme was in such a shambolic state that it couldn't possibly have reached the moon two years later. The faked landings were just a distraction from the Vietnam War, he says, pointing out that the man in the White House at the time of *Apollo 11* was cover-up king Richard Nixon – even if he had only been in office for six months. Sibrel's own profile was raised in September 2002, when he buttonholed Buzz Aldrin outside a Beverly Hills hotel and demanded that he "swear on the Bible" that he'd gone to the moon. Aldrin smashed Sibrel in the face, saying later that the filmmaker had similarly harassed other Apollo astronauts. "He has a good punch", Sibrel told Reuters.

Masonic lunacy

Whether or not the moon landings actually happened, some suggest that the whole Apollo programme was the ultimate expression of Masonic power. All the astronauts were Freemasons (see p.82), and the head of NASA during Apollo, Kenneth Kleinknecht, was a member of the 33rd Degree of Scottish Freemasons. A photograph in the House of the Temple in Washington DC is said by one website to show Neil Armstrong on the moon holding his Masonic apron. By this reckoning, Apollo is also "Lucifer", while the Scottish Rite of Freemasonry flag is the United Nations Flag with the nations of the world encircled by the laurel of Apollo.

Meanwhile the website www.theforbiddenknowledge.com links the space shuttles' names to the Illuminati (see p.93) with the phrase, "A Colombian Enterprise to Endeavor for the Discovery of Atlantis ... and all Challengers shall be destroyed" – its source isn't made clear. What this Illuminati plot is really about, it's claimed, isn't the exploration of space, but conveying to the general public that space travel is possible. Once people believe that, they can more easily believe that aliens are capable of reaching Earth, and because that prospect is both terrifying and unprovable, people can be scared into submissive order, leaving the Illuminati's reign unchallenged. The only people, however, who claim that aliens could come to Earth, or indeed have already arrived, aren't the government, but true believers like David Icke (see p.116).

China heads for the moon

Somewhere between six percent (according to Gallup) and twenty percent (according to Fox) of Americans believe that the moon landings were faked. Even so, President George W. Bush has directed NASA's sights towards a manned mission to Mars. Meanwhile, the Chinese, as part of their move towards global superpower status, are pursuing their own manned moon mission. Thus NASA could silence its detractors by asking the "taikonauts", as they're called in Chinese, to bring back pieces of the Apollo vehicles that were left on the lunar surface. On the other hand, the Chinese could claim that they'd found no evidence that the US had ever been there. But then how long would it be before the world started to doubt whether the Chinese had been there either?

SOURCES

Books

Bill Kaysing and Randy Reid We Never Went to the Moon: America's Thirty Billion Dollar Swindle (1999). The satire that backfired, this is the first and funniest exposé of the greatest "hoax" ever.

Films

John Moffett Conspiracy Theory: Did We Land on the Moon? (2001). Fox's televised run-through of Bill Kaysing's theories; easier to assimilate, but with less humour.

Bart Sibrel A Funny Thing Happened on the Way to the Moon (2001). Sibrel's amusing, irreverent take raises some not completely invalid questions over the landings (see also www.moonmovie.com).

Websites

Ⓦ **www.BadAstronomy.com** Astronomer Phil Plait's retort to the Fox programme. *Bad Astronomy* is also the title of his book on the subject.

Ⓦ **www.redzero.demon.co.uk/moonhoax/** A useful site with links to the more obscure details supposedly proving or disproving the moon landings.

Ⓦ **science.nasa.gov/headlines/y2001/ast23feb_2.htm** This is NASA's "rocks and common sense" piece, but it's somewhat undermined by Dr Tony Philips harping on about what a terrible impact the Fox TV programme had on his mother.

WARPLAY

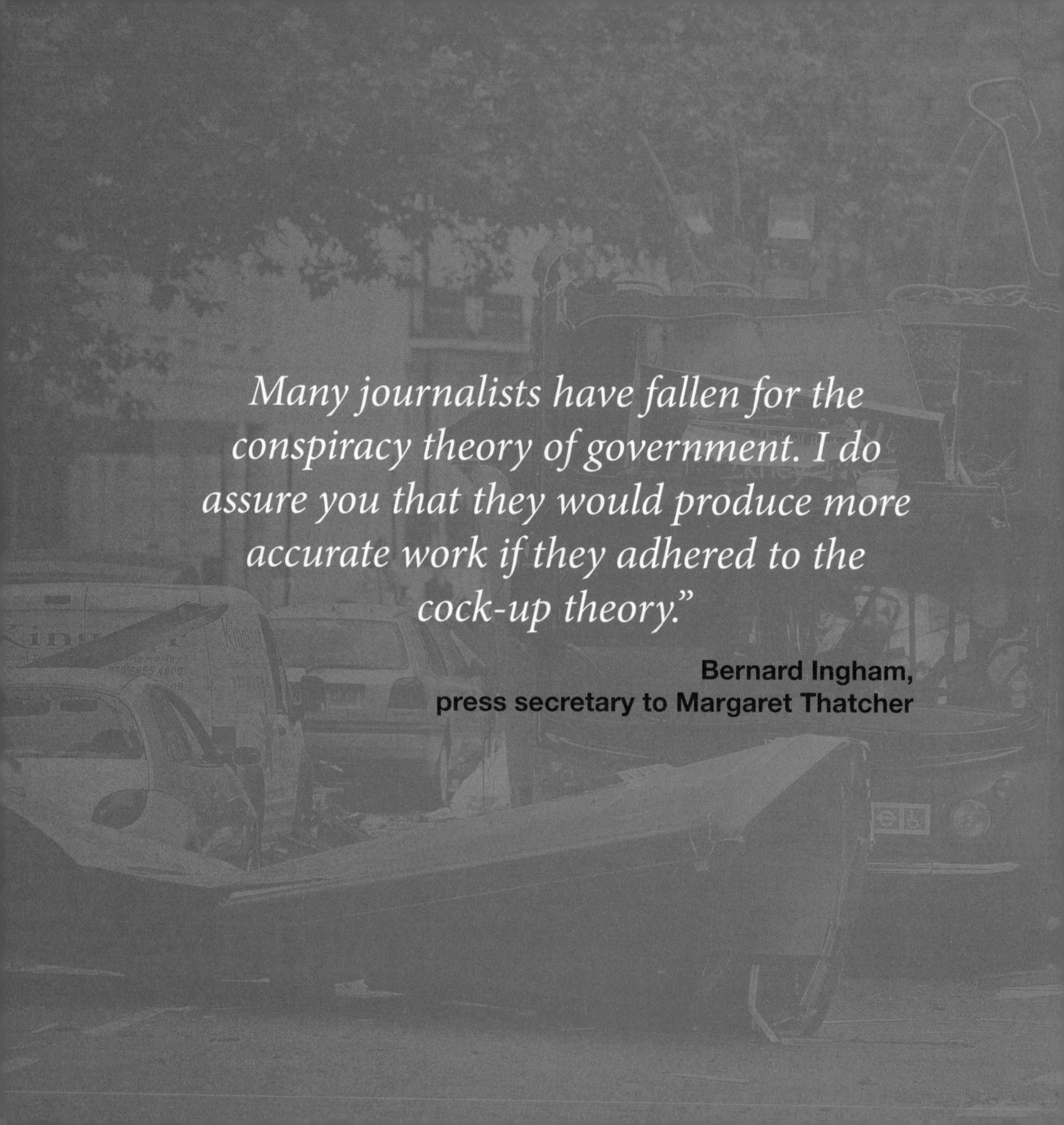

Many journalists have fallen for the conspiracy theory of government. I do assure you that they would produce more accurate work if they adhered to the cock-up theory.”

Bernard Ingham,
press secretary to Margaret Thatcher

WARPLAY

The term "gunboat diplomacy" refers to the practice of dispatching a warship to some far-flung outpost of the empire when it looks as though simmering problems might be about to boil over. An intimidating piece of weaponry can do wonders to remind the locals just who's boss. Diplomacy is, however, a multi-faceted art, and sometimes you can't help suspecting that gunboats have been sent in not so much to keep the peace, but to provoke an attack that might justify a war.

Such instances form part of a long-established tradition: no one likes to be seen as actually wanting a war. Even blatant aggressors often cast themselves as victims, prompted to fight only in "self-defence". Thus Hitler, for example, found it necessary to stage fake attacks from Poland in order to justify his "counter-invasion" of the country in 1939. That incident became a prime example of how complete fictions can lead to holocaust. Similarly, in Rwanda in 1994, a terrible genocide arose from an accumulation of lies, intolerance, racism and fear being taken to their most murderous conclusion.

Between the dictators and the chaotic states sit democracies which, despite popular myth, do start wars – all the time. It is easier for democratically elected leaders to win popular support for taking their countries to war if they can persuade the citizens that they have fallen victim to an unprovoked attack. In two classic examples – the sinking of the USS *Maine* in Cuba in 1898, and the Gulf of Tonkin incident in 1964 – it's unlikely that American vessels were attacked at all, but both led the US into full-scale war, against the Spanish and the North Vietnamese respectively. Some conspiracy theorists have even charged President Franklin D. Roosevelt with having deliberately failed to defend Pearl Harbor against an anticipated Japanese attack in 1941, in order to embroil the US in World War II.

After World War II, the Western powers sought to save the world from Communism and its mighty Marxist military machine, but it's often said that the Red menace was somewhat exaggerated by US politicians and defence specialists, together with their major benefactors – the arms companies. These days, the Russians are seen as more friendly, capitalist types, but have themselves been accused of exaggerating the threat posed by their enemies and of conducting their own false-flag operations. Many conspiracists have suggested that the Moscow apartment bombings that provoked Russia into invading Chechnya in 1999 were, in fact, the work of the Russian secret services. The bombings also allegedly gave the Russian government the excuse it needed to become far more authoritarian domestically.

An almost identical parallel has been drawn regarding the 9/11 attacks on the US. Al Qaeda may have carried out the attacks, but conspiracists suggest that they did so with the foreknowledge, if not outright connivance, of certain right-wing elements in the US government, military and security services (a modern incarnation of the never-executed Operation Northwoods, perhaps). The 9/11 attacks were used as the pretext to start wars in Afghanistan and Iraq, and to close down civil liberties at home in the US. Similar – but less widespread – accusations followed the London underground bombings of July 7, 2005 and the Madrid train bombings of March 11, 2004.

In the current political climate, however, it seems that physical attacks falsely attributed to the "enemy" are no longer required; it's enough to simply persuade the populace that the enemy is so capable of perpetrating some dastardly onslaught that it would be suicidal not to attack them first. As George W. Bush put it on June 1, 2002, preparing the way for the 2003 invasion of Iraq, "If we wait for threats to fully materialize, we will have waited too long."

Granted that war is an expensive business, why would anyone be so keen to get involved? Conspiracy theorists love to cite the profits to be derived from oil as the principal reason for conflicts such as the Gulf Wars, the Iraq War, Chechnya and even the Vietnam War. Iraq, Iran and North Korea were allegedly demonized as the "Axis of Evil" not because of their weapons of mass destruction programmes or unpleasant regimes, but because they switched from dollars to euros.

Theorists go on to argue that when not fought for profit, wars tend to be fought for stark, Machiavellian reasons of power politics, perhaps to knock out an irritating opponent or imperial competitor. That kind of project appeals to big-money interests far more than to ordinary voters, which makes it necessary to concoct some other excuse – even when such ends as the destruction of Imperial Japan or the toppling of Saddam Hussein also happen to be morally desirable.

Particularly paranoid conspiracy theorists see the state as benefiting from fear itself. Every conflict is dependent on munitions and financing, so arms manufacturers and banks love war. Appearing to be forever on the brink of conflict with the Soviets, or terrorists, or some part of the Islamic world, is part of a huge money cycle; ruling parties spend generously on equipping national armies, while the industries that benefit from their largesse support them, in turn, for as long as the money keeps rolling in. What's more, fear not only deters foreign aggressors, but also keeps your own people in line and prepared to pay the necessary price for their safety, not only in terms of taxes and votes, but even as cannon fodder.

The USS Maine and the Spanish–American War

Fifty years have passed since Fidel Castro came to power, sparking a new round of tensions between the US and Cuba. But it's easy to forget that the first major intervention by the US into the island's affairs was triggered by the destruction of the American warship USS *Maine* a good half-century before that. There's no question that the ship sank, but the issue still remains, who or what was responsible: the Spanish? The Cubans? The Americans? Or simply fate?

As the end of the nineteenth century approached, Cuba still formed part of Spain's overseas empire, but the Spanish grip on the island was loosening, as more and more Cubans took up arms to fight for independence. The guerrilla war in Cuba alarmed not only Spain but the US as well, which had considerable investments there. An American warship, the USS *Maine*, was dispatched to Cuba in January 1898, to keep an eye on events and evacuate US citizens should the situation deteriorate. The *Maine* anchored in Havana harbour, in Spanish waters, on January 25. Three weeks later, at 9.40pm on February 15, 1898, a massive explosion blasted the 6680-ton *Maine* out of the water. Of the 354 sailors and officers aboard, 262 were killed.

A US Navy court of inquiry was set up by President McKinley the very next day, and it concluded on March 15 that the *Maine* had suffered an external explosion on the port side bow, which set off a larger internal explosion in the ship's ammunition magazine. Whether the external explosion was caused by a floating mine or a torpedo, the inquiry did not determine, and although it cleared the navy of any "fault or negligence", neither did it explicitly blame the Spanish or the Cubans.

Among certain members of McKinley's administration, however, there was no doubt as to Spanish guilt. Assistant Secretary of the Navy Theodore Roosevelt, who had declared the day after the sinking that "the *Maine* was sunk by an act of dirty treachery on the part of the

The USS *Maine* goes down in Havana.

OPERATION NORTHWOODS

Six decades after the USS *Maine* exploded in Havana harbour, the memory of how its sinking sparked the Spanish–American War remained vivid in the minds of a new generation of American politicians. According to former deputy CIA director Robert Cline, at the start of the 1960s, the CIA, the out-going Eisenhower administration and the fledgling Kennedy administration were "obsessing" over removing the communist Fidel Castro from Cuba.

After the failure of the Bay of Pigs invasion in 1961 – planned under Eisenhower but instigated under JFK – the Kennedys set up Operation Mongoose (see p.19), to "stir things up" in Cuba via espionage, sabotage and general disorder. However, such far-fetched CIA schemes as using flaming cats to burn down sugar fields or sending Castro an exploding cigar, achieved little beyond outraging Robert Kennedy, who dumped the plan in February 1962. By then, the chairman of the Joint Chiefs of Staff, General Lyman Lemnitzer, was drawing up Operation Northwoods, a plot that – but for the fact that it was real – might sound like the paranoid ramblings of a conspiracy theorist. Its aim was to trick public opinion in the US and around the world into supporting a full-scale invasion of Cuba. "We could blow up a US ship in Guantanamo Bay [yes, *that* Guantanamo Bay] and blame Cuba", Lemnitzer proposed, "casualty lists in US newspapers would cause a helpful wave of national indignation".

Further suggestions included creating public ill-feeling towards Cuba by having US armed forces disguised as the Cuban military hijack and harass civilian aircraft and boats around the Gulf of Mexico, or by flying a pilotless drone passenger plane over the island, transmitting Mayday recordings as if under attack by Cuban jets, and then blowing it up by remote control. If war could be provoked between Cuba and its neighbours, a US invasion could be justified as deposing the alleged aggressors. Perhaps something involving the Commonwealth states of Jamaica or Trinidad and Tobago could persuade the UK to attack? Or US planes disguised as Cuban bombers could raid Dominican Republic sugar fields, and "Cuban" messages and arms to the Dominican Communist underground could be "uncovered"?

As well as considering blowing up one of their own ships, Lemnitzer's team suggested that stooges in Cuban Army fatigues could attack the US naval base in Guantanamo Bay, and *faux* "saboteurs" inside the base could blow things up, probably killing a few hapless US servicemen in the process. Reconnaissance planes could also be sent over for the Cubans to shoot down. It was even suggested that astronaut John Glenn's rocket could be blown up as he prepared to become the first American to orbit the Earth, and Cuba could be blamed. Worst of all were the schemes to set off bombs in Miami and Washington and arrest Cuban patsies, planting documents that proved they had Castro's support.

Fortunately, Operation Northwoods was never activated, being comprehensively rejected by Secretary of Defense Robert McNamara and President John F. Kennedy in March 1962. Lemnitzer, however, continued to stoke up rage among his generals, for which behaviour he was transferred to Europe to become the head of NATO. He later made it back onto President Ford's Foreign Intelligence Advisory Board, but after Lemnitzer lied to a Senate committee about Operation Northwoods, Senator Al Gore called successfully for him to be sacked. The existence of the operation was finally confirmed after author James Bamford sued the National Security Agency (NSA) for documents on the Cuban Missile Crisis and wrote up his findings in his book, *Body of Secrets*. Published in early 2001, the revelation that the US military had considered unleashing terror attacks on the American people came just six months before 9/11.

Spaniards", pressurized the wavering McKinley into asking Congress to support a declaration of war. It duly did so on April 25.

The US did very well indeed out of the war with Spain, taking control of Cuba, Puerto Rico, the Philippines and Guam, and supplanting Spain's position and power not only in the Caribbean but also over much of Latin America and the western Pacific. Roosevelt himself did even better: he resigned his political post to serve in Cuba as lieutenant colonel of the so-called "Rough Riders", the 1st US Volunteer Cavalry, and parlayed his resultant fame into becoming first McKinley's vice president in 1900, and then America's youngest-ever president when McKinley was assassinated in 1901.

Picking a fight

According to conspiracy-minded historians, the US was already determined to fight Spain, and the sinking of the *Maine* simply provided the pretext for which it had been searching. While it's easy to trace the bellicose spirit in the US, there are fewer signs of any Spanish desire for war. The Spanish Empire was in terminal decline, and in no position to provoke conflict with the youthfully muscular United States. The Spaniards had agreed to the *Maine*'s visit to Cuba, greeting it with diplomatic niceties and friendliness, and Spanish officers had dined aboard the ship, but the Americans were suspiciously quick to point the finger of blame after the explosion. William Randolph Hearst's newspapers had already been stirring up anti-Spanish sentiments, and well before the inquiry reached its conclusion, one such paper echoed Roosevelt's charge of Spanish treachery by roaring: "The Warship *Maine* Was Split in Two by an Enemy's Secret Infernal Machine!"

A Spanish investigation, which was denied access to the wreck of the *Maine*, attributed the internal explosion to mechanical failure, but that theory was discounted in the US as a whitewash concocted by the guilty party. Admiral Hyman Rickover, who carried out another investigation for the US Navy in the 1970s, concluded that the explosion was probably caused by the spontaneous combustion of coal dust in a storage bunker, which then ignited the ammunition magazine. Some historians dispute whether such spontaneous combustion is possible, others whether it could go undetected.

There's obviously a big difference between saying that the US capitalized on the explosion and alleging that it actually blew up its own ship. Irrespective of what destroyed the *Maine*, however, it's clear that the US raced to blame Spain and declare war. Thus the real conspiracy might centre on deliberate attempts to keep the truth behind the sinking from ever reaching the public. In 1912, with the war over some years before, the *Maine*'s damaged bow was cut off and replaced with a wooden one, so the ship could be floated out to sea and re-sunk amid great ceremony. But the removal of its damaged exterior destroyed any hope that the true cause of the explosion might be found.

Was it the Cubans?

Some US historians have asserted that Cuban insurgents were responsible for blowing up the *Maine*, in the hope of forcing an American intervention from which they might benefit. It's certainly true that Cuban rebels repeatedly burned American-owned properties and sugar plantations, which might have served to provoke US action to protect its own interests, and perhaps depose the inept Spaniards in the process. However, no evidence of Cuban involvement in the *Maine* explosion has been unearthed, and to ascribe any such motives to the rebels is purely speculative. They were fighting for independence, not to provoke heavy-handed intervention by another regional power, and the rationale behind attacks on US assets in Cuba need have been no more sophisticated than the desire to weaken the resources available to the colonial occupier.

The press on the warpath

It was the US press that was responsible for arousing sufficient public anger to demand war from Congress. The *Maine* incident, and virulent anti-Spanish coverage, precipitated massive increases in newspaper sales. The "yellower", more jingoistic and more bellicose the journalism, the greater the profits. Was the prospect of war so profitable to press barons such as William Randolph Hearst that they engineered their coverage to that end?

The power of public rage is mentioned at Arlington Cemetery, where the mast of the *Maine* is interred. The memorial there describes the sinking as the "seminal event" leading to the Spanish–American War, acknowledging that: "Although the cause of the explosion (whether a Spanish torpedo or an internal mechanical malfunction) has never been definitively determined, the event enraged American public opinion."

RCES

Louis A. Perez Jr The War of 1898: The United States and Cuba in History and Historiography (1998). A quick history of the conflict, which also covers a couple of conspiracy theories.

Websites

www.history.navy.mil/faqs/faq71-1.htm One official account of the *Maine*'s destruction and the mayhem that ensued can be found in the US Navy's online history file.

Pearl Harbor

The US Defense Department calls the 1941 Japanese attack on Pearl Harbor "one of the greatest military surprises in the history of warfare". In 2002, President George W. Bush, in his presidential proclamation on National Pearl Harbor Remembrance Day, said that the attack had come "without provocation or warning". There are those, however, who believe that not only did then-president Franklin D. Roosevelt have forewarning of Pearl Harbor, but also that he deliberately provoked the attack.

In 1941, the Hawaiian island of Oahu was home to five airfields and the port of Pearl Harbor, the largest US naval base in the Pacific. On Sunday morning, December 7, 1941, most of the Pacific fleet, including 8 battleships, 9 cruisers and 31 destroyers, were in dock. The ships were aligned in positions highly vulnerable to attack, but then the port, like the US, was at peace. However, as dawn broke, just 200 miles northwest, wave after wave of Japanese bomber and fighter aircraft swooped off the aircraft carriers of Japan's First Fleet.

At 7.55am, the first of over 350 planes hit Pearl Harbor, strafing, bombing and torpedoing the American fleet. It was carnage: 21 ships, including all 8 battleships, were sunk or damaged, some 300 aircraft destroyed, over 2400 people killed, and nearly 2000 wounded. All for a total Japanese loss of 29 aircraft, 6 submarines and 100 men. December 7, President Roosevelt told the nation, was "a date which will live in infamy", and on December 8 Congress declared war on Japan.

Warnings

One of the Japanese flight leaders, Commander Fuchida, had yelled "Tora, Tora, Tora!" – code for the US being caught by surprise. It would seem, however, that it was not a total surprise. There were warnings of an attack.

Japan's diplomatic correspondence was encrypted under a code that the US military called "Purple". Since the summer of 1940, every Japanese dispatch had been read by the US through its decryption system "Magic". Thousands of intercepts that revealed Japanese preparations for some big hit, somewhere, flowed in during the months preceding Pearl Harbor, including many from US, Dutch and French outposts in the Asia-Pacific region. The War and Navy departments in Washington sent out war warnings on October 16 and November 24, while the secretary of state told the military chiefs on November 27 that negotiations with Japan had failed and that further action would be the responsibility of the military.

On November 27, the Navy and War departments dispatched a warning that war was imminent: "Negotiations with Japan looking toward stabilization of conditions in the Pacific have ceased … an aggressive move by Japan is expected within the next few days." On December 6, 1941, the US intercepted a Japanese communiqué that stated that the US and UK were "obviously hostile" and that "the

THE INVASION OF POLAND

It's well known that World War II broke out in Europe as a consequence of the Nazi invasion of Poland on September 1, 1939 – the UK and France declared war on Germany two days later. However, it's often overlooked that Adolf Hitler was not prepared for his own people to see him as the aggressor. Thus he told a shocked Reichstag (German parliament) on September 1 that Polish forces had invaded Germany, and that the Wehrmacht (German armed forces) had been returning fire since 5.45am. Indeed, it was claimed that the bodies of a dozen slain Polish soldiers had been found, proving the reality of the invasion, and that radio commands, in which the Polish forces revealed their intent, had been intercepted. Germany's armed forces were counterattacking with great success.

It was all a lie. The SS had taken twelve prisoners out of Buchenwald concentration camp and ordered them to don Polish Army uniforms, whereupon they were shot dead. An SS officer announced in Polish over the radio that the Poles were invading, then the SS left the bodies as "evidence". The ensuing invasion of Poland followed the plan known as *Fall Weiss*, or Case White, which had been devised earlier in 1939 after the Nazis took Czechoslovakia. The antiquated, outnumbered Polish armed forces were routed, although Warsaw endured eleven days of shelling before falling; the end came with another surprise on September 17, when the Soviets invaded from the east. Polish resistance ended two weeks later. An improbable non-aggression pact between Germany and the USSR had been unexpectedly announced in late August, but the part about dividing up Poland between them hadn't been revealed.

Germany's problem with Poland was that the Poles had been given a corridor to the sea after World War I, which incorporated the German city of Danzig and divided Prussia from the rump of Germany. Also, Hitler sought a face-to-face border with the USSR, ready for Germany's invasion of the Soviet Republic in 1941. He had written in *Mein Kampf* that the Poles were "inferior", and that they were only useful as slaves of the German Empire. Six million Poles, including three million Jews, were to die under the Nazi occupation. But the shock for Hitler was that the UK and France finally put their foot down. Having let the Führer spend the latter part of the 1930s retaking Rhineland, annexing Austria, stealing Sudetenland and invading Czechoslovakia without a shot being fired, they gave him the final surprise by declaring war on Germany on September 3, 1939.

American government … may be said to be scheming for the extension of the war". The military build-up was "perfecting an encirclement of Japan … which endangers the very existence of the Empire". East Asia had endured Anglo-American imperial dominance for a century, something that "the Japanese government cannot tolerate the perpetuation of". Further negotiations were unacceptable. As FDR put it, "this means war".

The intelligence was there, it just wasn't disseminated

But somehow no one told Hawaii. The November 27 and December 6 messages became the twin focuses of eight successive, high-level wartime investigations into the Pearl Harbor attack, which pointed the finger at one top official after another, up the chain of command to the White House.

The Roberts Commission, set up eleven days after the attack at the behest of FDR, was a stitch-up. Commission member Admiral Standley deemed it "crooked", in that it served only to keep the prestige of the Roosevelt administration "fully preserved in the public mind", and Admiral Robert A. Theobald agreed with that assessment in his 1954 book *The Final Secret of Pearl Harbor* (Theobald was the commander of the destroyers at Pearl Harbor in 1941, and he also attended the commission). In January 1942, Justice Owen Roberts cleared everyone in Washington and blamed the Hawaiian commanders, Admiral Husband E. Kimmel and General Walter C. Short, for dereliction of duty. They'd failed to confer over warnings and failed to implement war plans preparing for outside attack.

However, those plans were the responsibility of the Washington-based War and Navy departments, overseen by General George C. Marshall and Admiral Harold

The burning battleship USS *Arizona* goes down following the Japanese attack on Pearl Harbor.

R. Stark. In 1944, the Army Pearl Harbor Board slammed Marshall and the War Department for not keeping Short "fully advised" of rising tensions with Japan, not forwarding intelligence to Hawaii, and particularly for not sending the December 6 communiqué until after the attack.

The concurrent Naval Court of Inquiry rebuked Stark in similar terms. Stark coolly observed in 1945 that everything he did before Pearl Harbor, including refusing to forward key Japanese intercepts to Hawaii, he did on "higher orders" – which could only have come from FDR. The president did receive censure, but only after the war was over and he was dead. In May 1946, the Joint Congressional Committee castigated FDR, Stark, Marshall, the secretary of the navy Frank Knox, Kimmel and Short, while also lamenting that the information it had was glaringly incomplete.

Itching for a fight

Each investigation centred on the fact that intelligence pointing to an imminent attack existed, but that thanks either to incompetence or conspiracy, it was rendered redundant by inaction. With the steady deterioration of US–Japanese relations, some kind of military showdown had been brewing for a long time. Japan's Asian empire was by then threatening the Dutch East Indies, the Philippines, Burma, Singapore and Australia. The US restricted shipments of airplane fuel, scrap metal, machinery and wheat to Japan throughout 1940, and Anglo-American support prevented the Dutch East Indies falling into Japan's economic clutches. Filipino exports of raw material to Japan were halted, and the US, British and Dutch stopped trade and froze Japanese assets following the Japanese seizure of French Indochina. The US oil embargo was enlarged in mid-1941 to become a petrol embargo.

Some of the US moves were justifiable responses to Japanese actions. But some also tally with an "eight-point plan" drawn up for FDR by Lieutenant Commander Arthur McCollum on October 7, 1940. (The plan was later found in navy archives by former navy officer Robert B. Stinnett, who cites it in his book *Day of Deceit.*) Beginning with the words "The United States desires that Japan commit the first overt act", McCollum set out a series of deliberately provocative steps. These included using and aiding British military bases and forces; deploying US ships in Japan's Asia-Pacific sphere; and financially and militarily supporting China to fight the Japanese, while recalling British, US and Dutch citizens from the region. The trade embargoes and freezing of assets were also McCollum proposals.

During late 1941, the US and Japan were engaged in protracted diplomatic negotiations, but on November 25, Secretary of War Henry Stimson met with FDR to predict war by December 1. On November 26, the US proposed that peace could be sustained if the Japanese withdrew from China and Indochina, guaranteed not to threaten other Western interests, accepted the economic encirclement, and gave up its tripartite alliance with Germany and Italy. It was this proposal that was cited in Japan's December 6 communiqué as the cause of the breakdown in negotiations – negotiations that the US Navy and War departments said had "ceased" on November 27.

Even the press knew

Another shocking revelation made by Stinnett concerned a secret press conference held on November 15, 1941, at which Marshall told correspondents from *The New York Times*, *Newsweek*, *Time* and Associated Press that the US had broken Japanese codes – "We know what they know and they don't know we know it" – and that an attack was expected in the first ten days of December. The press, presumably, was required to say nothing at the time. If, however, reporters knew that Pearl Harbor wasn't the surprise that it was claimed to be, how come they didn't spill the beans later? Perhaps they kept quiet out of a sense of patriotic duty – or perhaps they were muzzled after the event as well.

A Red in the White House

Another theory is that Pearl Harbor was precipitated by Communist agents working for the USSR, who wanted the US in the war not so much to fight Japan as to fight Nazi Germany, which by late 1941 was invading Russia with terrifying speed. The ultimate extension of this theory, as advocated by Mark Emerson Willey in *Pearl Harbor: Mother of All Conspiracies*, is that FDR himself was a communist. Playwright George Bernard Shaw once said that "Roosevelt is a communist but does not know it", which Willey translates into "Franklin Roosevelt was a hard-core Marxist".

Willey argues that Roosevelt's Marxist beliefs were revealed when his administration re-established trade

…lomatic ties with the USSR in 1933, ties that had …vered since the 1917 Russian Revolution. FDR …imself an "internationalist", and set up the Lend-Lease programme to supply arms, minerals and credits to the Soviets to fight the Nazis. He overruled Winston Churchill's request to invade Europe through the Balkans to stop Stalin taking Eastern Europe. And at Yalta in 1944, says Willey, FDR "gave over to Communist enslavement 725 million people", from Germany to Korea.

For Willey, all this "treason" proves that FDR "always worked for Stalin's interests". What Willey overlooks, however, is the fact that, whatever else he may have done, FDR did a superb job in serving the interests of the US, taking it from economic depression to the status of global superpower (and Russia's only rival) in little over a decade, and winning four consecutive elections while defeating two major fascist powers.

Some historians who have always backed the sneak attack story at least agree with Willey and Stinnett's suggestion that war with Japan made it possible for the US to deal with the real threat: the Nazis. As Gordon Prange argues in *At Dawn We Slept*, the US military and State Department saw the possibility of a German victory over Britain as a danger to US security. Britain's industries, bases and navy would fall to Germany, and the Nazis would further cement their Atlantic power through economic and political links with Latin America. The problem was that US polls showed ninety percent of Americans wanting nothing to do with "Europe's war" – a view publicly supported by the likes of Charles Lindbergh, Henry Ford and Joe Kennedy (JFK's father). In 1940, FDR himself had been re-elected on an isolationist ticket.

When the time came, however, the tripartite agreement that Hitler had signed with Japan and Italy came into effect. Four days after Pearl Harbor, Hitler declared war on the US, and within a week, America was facing war on two fronts. Not that it was so unprepared. In January 1941, FDR submitted the huge peacetime military budget of $10 billion, to expand the army to one million men with fifty thousand planes and the navy to two hundred thousand men, fifteen thousand planes and a fleet fit for two oceans. If not for war, then for what?

Mother of all myths

If a war with Japan was sought, if only as a means to war with Germany, it seems odd to start out by knowingly letting your major naval forces be hammered on day one. Warning Pearl Harbor of the attack wouldn't have stopped the attack itself, nor removed the justification for war – it would only have limited the damage, so the surprise may have been one of location. But only of location. It was no surprise when an attack came, and war was arguably something that both sides wanted. The need for the US government to still downplay its active will to war before Pearl Harbor may be part of sustaining the myth that the US is never the aggressor (even in pre-emptive wars), even when – in the case of Hitler and the Japanese emperor Hirohito, at least – there might be strong grounds for doing so.

And then there is the myth of Roosevelt himself. Even Stinnett says that his own revelations "do not diminish FDR's magnificent contributions to the American people" and that his "legacy should not be tarnished by the truth". The US entry into a global war saw it emerge by 1945 as a true global superpower. If Stinnett's reaction to what he himself calls FDR's awesome duplicity is any indication, then it doesn't matter that a few Americans question the perception held by the overwhelming majority of their fellow countrymen – that Pearl Harbor was a sneaky surprise, not an incident predicted and possibly provoked by their own president.

Hollywood is certainly keen to perpetuate the myth of a "surprise" attack, as seen in the 2001 blockbuster *Pearl Harbor*. Although the film portrays FDR as so incandescent over Japan's betrayal that he hoists himself out of his wheelchair in rage, this was not among the many historical inaccuracies for which it was lambasted. Ironically, the flag-waving story of how Americans responded with unquenchable resolve against aggressors was a hit with cinema-goers, if not with critics, and with near-perfect timing, it was released only weeks before foreigners launched another sneak air attack on the US seaboard: 9/11.

SOURCES

Books

Robert Stinnett Day of Deceit: The Truth About FDR and Pearl Harbor (2001). With new access to archives through the Freedom of Information Act, ex-US Navy officer Stinnett argues that FDR knew Pearl Harbor was coming, because it was what he had wanted all along. A soberly written book, and all the better for it.

Robert A. Theobald The Final Secret of Pearl Harbor (1988). Theobald's case (first published in 1954) – that Pearl Harbor was something FDR actively sought – is all the more surprising considering the seniority of his naval command in 1941 and his attendance at subsequent government inquiries/cover-ups.

Mark Emerson Willey Pearl Harbor: Mother of All Conspiracies (2001). Willey's argument that Pearl Harbor was a set-up becomes almost incidental to his frenetic attempt to prove that FDR was the architect of a global communist plot. A good read, if only to see the tortuous, twisted arguments that support Willey's conclusions.

Websites

Ⓦ **www.apfn.org/apfn/pearl_harbor.htm** The American Patriotic Friends Network has a stab at denouncing FDR for his murderous duplicity. A concise summary of the case against the US government.

ODESSA and the Org

In September 2000, the CIA admitted something that scores of journalists, authors, human rights groups and politicians worldwide had been claiming almost since 1945: that after the German defeat in World War II, the CIA and British intelligence had hidden, funded and rehabilitated thousands of Nazis in a huge counterintelligence operation against communism. The idea that a vast, secret network of Nazis were not only at large but working with the CIA, MI6 and even the Vatican had been given scope in numerous conspiracist accusations, novels and films – but, as is surprisingly often the case, it had a basis in fact.

In May 1945, SS general Reinhard Gehlen, Adolf Hitler's chief of Eastern intelligence, surrendered to US forces advancing into Germany. With some insouciance, he insisted on speaking only to the American Counter-Intelligence Corps (CIC). Considering Gehlen was wanted by the USSR for war crimes, he risked nothing but the harshest treatment before being thrown to the Russians. However, he had something to offer the CIC – all his organization's intelligence about the Soviets (safely stashed in the Alps), and about the agents and spy networks in Soviet-dominated areas.

Gehlen offered all this information to the US in return for immunity from prosecution, the recruitment of some of his persecuted colleagues and the right to continue running his networks. With a massive fight against communism in the offing, the CIC agreed. Dressed as a US Army officer, Gehlen was flown to the US, and at Fort Hunt, Maryland, he dined with officers and directors of the OSS, the forerunner of the CIA. Future CIA director Allen Dulles was particularly taken with Gehlen, and the CIA would eventually channel over $200 million into Gehlen's Bavaria-based organization, aka the Org. (According to conspiracy theorist Mae Brussell, Dulles had been running his own Org-esque programme, Operation Sunrise, since 1942.)

OSS WLTM ex-Nazis for mind games and love rocketry

In return for fighting communism, thousands of Gestapo, Wehrmacht and SS veterans, many indicted for war crimes, had their pasts whitewashed and were given their freedom. Big names on the CIA payroll included SS commander Karl Wolff, who dispatched three hundred thousand Jews to Treblinka, and the notorious SS officer Klaus Barbie, the "Butcher of Lyon", who was wanted by the French for sending Jewish children to Auschwitz. Barbie ultimately "escaped" to South America, but was handed back to the French courts by Bolivia in 1983. Dulles justified the programme with the words: "[They're] on our side, and that's all that matters." So respectable did the Org become that it was openly incorporated into the West German government's intelligence organization, the Bundesnachrichtendienst, in 1955.

The Org tapped into underground fascist networks to become NATO's main intelligence source within the Warsaw Pact. After all, countries like Hungary, Bulgaria and Romania had been led by fascist governments dependent on Nazi Germany, and had contributed militarily to the Nazis' 1941 invasion of the USSR. Early Org successes included providing information about Soviet jet fighter development and tip-offs about the remilitarization of East Germany. The Org also apparently helped the CIA to bring about the 1953 coup in Iran, deposing the democratically elected premier Mohammed Mossadegh (who had unwisely nationalized Iran's oil industry) and reinstalling the pro-Nazi Pahlevi family. As the shah of Iran, Mohammed Reza Pahlevi remained a major US ally for almost three decades.

The programme also brought technological benefits for the US. Under Operation Outcast (later Operation Paperclip), the army's Field Intelligence Agency Technical unit (FIAT) sought out the Nazis' finest scientists to boost US economic development – in effect, a form of war reparations. The most famous of the Nazi boffins to have his wartime CV rewritten by the Pentagon, and to be given employment in the US, was Werner von Braun. Having led the development of the V2 missiles that bombed London and Antwerp, von Braun was rewarded with the leadership of US rocket programmes at NASA. Other Nazi scientific research that continued in one form or another in the US included work salvaged from Germany's atomic bomb programme, and experiments on humans involving gas, varying atmospheric pressures, sterilization and mind control. These became the basis of research at Edgewood Arsenal (see p.297) and MK-ULTRA (see p.210).

Reds, rats and the Vatican

It's not clear whether the notorious shadowy counterpart to the Org known as ODESSA – the Organization der Ehemaligen SS-Angehörigen, or the Organization of former SS officers – ever actually existed. According to rumour, ODESSA was an escape route set up by the Nazis during the final days of World War II and run by Hitler's top SS commander, Otto Skorzeny, from Lisbon or Buenos Aires. It supposedly helped notorious Nazis such as Adolf Eichmann, Martin Bormann and Dr Josef Mengele to flee to Latin America. Dedicated Nazi-hunter Simon Wiesenthal certainly believed in ODESSA, and acted as a consultant to Frederick Forsyth on his novel *The Odessa File*, in which ex-Nazis help Egypt to develop plague-laden missiles to fire at Israel. In *Blowback: The First Full Account of America's Recruitment of Nazis*, however, Christopher Simpson says that ODESSA was not so much an organization in its own right as a gaggle of extra-Org networks, which obtained gainful employment for ex-Nazis as "security advisers" in the Middle East or in various Latin American death squads.

According to Mark Aarons and John Loftus's book *Unholy Trinity*, in the first years after World War II, the Vatican was so afraid of communist clampdowns on Catholicism in Eastern Europe and Latin America that it used churches and monasteries to funnel fascist war criminals to places where they could serve as "freedom fighters" against communism. These included Treblinka commandant

Franz Stangl, "mobile gas chamber" inventor Walter Rauff, and Croat dictator Ante Pavelic. The scheme was overseen by Pope Pius XII, directed by Giovanni Montini (later Pope Paul VI) and aided by British and US intelligence under the codename Operation Ratlines. The Vatican also channelled Nazi gold and looted treasures into Swiss banks (see p.246), with the full awareness of Allen Dulles, while the "ratlines" served as the working template for the Iran-Contra system (see p.201).

The journals *Covert Action Information Bulletin* and *The Rebel* describe an even murkier version of the story, in which the Vatican used its Pro Deo intelligence network in Portugal and OSS-funded branches in New York and Rome to assist ODESSA. By this account, Gehlen, OSS director Bill Donovan and the improbably named future CIA director James Jesus Angleton were all linked through a quasi-Masonic sub-sect, the Sovereign Military Order of Malta; its chief, Pope Pius XII, awarded the trio the order's highest honour.

Employing ex-Nazis was never exactly a risk-free scenario. To what extent Gehlen deliberately fuelled Western fears of communist domination to justify the existence of the Org, and how much the Org simply passed on Soviet disinformation, may never be known. According to Simpson, Org-supplied intelligence that Soviet forces were massing to attack in 1948 nearly started a calamitous war. It's also claimed that the Org was the source of the Soviet disinformation that led to the "missile gap" scare of the 1950s and 60s (see p.369). Some Org agents were simply Soviet double agents who hated democracy more than communism, and used the Vatican's ratlines to penetrate Western intelligence. Gehlen's ultimate game may simply have been to save his Nazi comrades, employing some and distracting the CIA from finding the rest. Mae Brussell, on the other hand, attributed the shooting of John F. Kennedy to a powerful Nazi cabal.

The sheer horror of not only enabling former Nazis to evade justice, but actually re-employing them in jobs that, in some cases, were no less evil than their war careers, was justified as being necessary in the fight against the greater global threat of communism. It was all in the name of freedom, even if the fight paradoxically involved the creation and sustenance of fascist networks. By a bitter irony, it may have been these fascist war criminals that exaggerated the threat of communism in the first place.

SOURCES

Books

Mark Aarons and John Loftus Unholy Trinity: The Vatican, the Nazis and Soviet Intelligence (1998). A depressing but fascinating exposé of the depths to which the Cold War could descend.

Christopher Simpson Blowback: The First Full Account of America's Recruitment of Nazis and its Disastrous Effect on our Domestic and Foreign Policy (1988). The title says it all: a seminal work, charting the birth of the Org and its often malign impact on its US sponsors.

Websites

Ⓦ **dir.salon.com/news/feature/2000/05/03/nazi/index.html** "Our Nazi Allies", by Ken Silverstein. A fascinating article that details Silverstein's efforts to trace Nazis in the US, and the years of indifference he encountered from the CIA and FBI.

The Cold War conspiracy

For nearly fifty years, the US and its allies waged a Cold War against what President Reagan called the "Evil Empire". That war extended from the polar icecaps to the equatorial jungles of Southeast Asia, from submarines at the bottom of the ocean to satellites in space, from the bleak expanse of Greenham Common to the urban monstrosity of the Berlin Wall, and even to the cosy surroundings of America's libraries and film studios. It was a colossal scrap. But was it a real one?

Reds under the bed

On February 9, 1950, Wisconsin senator Joseph R. McCarthy unveiled what he claimed to be a massive communist conspiracy. He triumphantly revealed to the Republican Women's Club in Wheeling, West Virginia, that he had a "list" of 205 individuals who were "either card-carrying members or certainly loyal to the Communist Party", mostly in the State Department. Over the following fortnight, as the numbers on McCarthy's list plummeted to 57 then nudged back up to 81, he hammered on, insisting that the Truman administration was rife with communists.

McCarthy didn't mention that the "list" was drawn from "loyalty boards" set up by Truman to screen communists from federal employment, and neither did he heed a Senate investigation that found no communists in the State Department. Indeed, on June 14, 1951, he railed to the Senate that chief of staff General George C. Marshall and Secretary of State Dean Acheson were "marching side-by-side with Stalin", helping the communists to take over the world as part of "a great conspiracy", that was immense enough to "dwarf any previous such venture in the history of man", a "world-wide web ... spun from Moscow", with Truman "their captive". The allegations were truly outrageous and unfounded, but at first they were hardly questioned. People believed them.

Stalin had tried to blockade West Berlin; Eastern Europe and China had turned Communist; and Chinese- and Soviet-backed North Koreans were slugging it out against US-led UN forces in Korea. What was worse, the USSR had the atom bomb, thanks to secrets supplied by Americans Julius and Ethel Rosenberg (who were later executed as spies, although debate continues as to their guilt, see p.147). The House of Representatives' Un-American Activities Committee (HUAC) set out to find so-called "Reds" in libraries, schools, colleges, the Church and Hollywood, and thousands of professionals, some well known, were sacked, blacklisted, or pushed either abroad or to the point of suicide. Senior State Department official Alger Hiss was tried by HUAC for spying for Russia, and was ultimately convicted of perjury.

McCarthy's Government Operations Committee, supplied with information by Red-hating J. Edgar Hoover's FBI, effectively gave the government employees it interrogated the choice of either naming "communists" or losing their jobs. Any senators, usually Democrats, who denounced the charges as smears were simply smeared themselves as communists, which cost a few their re-election and scared others into silence. As historian Elmo Richardson later put it, "Americans believed charges that the Democrats had allowed communists to gain high government posts".

Dwight Eisenhower, the Republican presidential candidate in the 1952 election, campaigned on the theme "Korea, communism and corruption", and handsomely defeated Democrat Adlai Stevenson. And while President Eisenhower lamented McCarthy's desire to burn "communist" books, he didn't publicly criticize the senator. This bitter era of paranoia and distrust in the government, based on cavalier accusations of treasonable crimes, came to be termed "McCarthyism". McCarthy, however, never made his list public, and of the thousands of federal employees he accused, not one was identified as a communist.

The real conspiracy was McCarthy's. Before the 1950 elections, the senator, worried on account of his lacklustre career in the Senate, flimsy war record and bribery charges, held a dinner with allies. According to his biographer, "McCarthy talked with his guests for a while before bringing up the subject of the need for an issue. The group discarded quite a few before choosing communism, suggested by [Father Edmund] Walsh, an ardent anti-Red. 'That's it,' McCarthy said. 'The government is full of communists. We can hammer away at them.'" Only when McCarthy accused the army of "coddling communists" in 1954 did his public support evaporate, and the Senate took the chance to vote him down for "conduct unbecoming a senator". When he died three years later, one young senator from his Government Operations Committee admitted that he would have voted down McCarthy, if he hadn't been "ill" that day. His name was John F. Kennedy.

The "missile gap"

During the late 1950s, there were widespread fears that a so-called "bomber gap" had left the Soviets with more long-range nuclear bombers than the US. After this was disproved by U-2 reconnaissance flights over the USSR, the notion arose instead that there was a "missile gap". Furthered by US Air Force reports and the Congressional Gaither Committee in 1957, it became a hot potato in the 1960 election. Senator Kennedy was campaigning as the voice of vigorous youth to replace the avuncular but ineffective President Eisenhower. During televised debates with Vice President Richard Nixon, Kennedy blamed Eisenhower for the supposed disparity between US and Soviet weapon stockpiles. "I believe there is a missile gap between the United States and the Soviet Union", he declared. He believed it, the voters believed him, and he became president.

There were indeed missile and bomber gaps – but they were in favour of the US, several times over. As Kennedy oversaw the greatest expansion of US military might since 1945, reaching the level of 220 intercontinental ballistic missiles (ICBMs) and 3000 intercontinental bombers, the disparity with the Soviets' 100 missiles and 200 bombers increased still further. Then, however, the new-fangled spy satellites and a National Intelligence Estimate dramatically reduced the accepted counts of Soviet ICBMs. On December 5, 1962, shortly after the Cuban Missile Crisis, Kennedy and his advisers complained that they had been duped. With both sides possessing enough nuclear warheads to wipe out life on the planet, Kennedy commented, "I don't see quite why we're building as many [ICBMs] as we're building."

When Defense Secretary Robert McNamara presented Kennedy with the 1964 defence budget – set at an unprecedented $54.4 billion, 48 percent of discretionary government expenditure – he expressed concern. He suggested that the Pentagon might, to prevent any slowdown in spending, concoct some harmful story about US military weakness, just as they had over the missile gap: "A myth … created by, I would say, emotionally guided but nonetheless patriotic individuals in the Pentagon." Laughing, Kennedy replied that he himself had been "one of those who put that myth around – a patriotic and misguided man!"

The intelligence that originally supported the "missile gap" had come through agents, possibly in the so-called "Org" intelligence organization of ex-Nazi Reinhard Gehlen (see p.365). According to CIA spy Victor Marchetti, as quoted in Colin Simpson's *Blowback*, "Gehlen provided us [the CIA] with specific reports on the Soviet ICBM program … He said, 'We have two reliable reports confirming this, and they [the Soviets] have just installed three missiles at that site', et cetera, claiming that they had contacts among the German scientists captured by the Russians at the end of the war."

It was a story that the Pentagon and the press were all too ready to believe. The US missile industry, headed by former SS rocket scientist Werner von Braun, secured further funding in 1955 after another former Nazi, missile-maker Walter Dornberger, published an article about Soviet sea-launched missiles – it wasn't true, but it was part of the currency at the Pentagon. Did the Org make up the information to justify its existence, or did it simply pass on Soviet propaganda designed to deter attack? Some say that by late 1963, Kennedy was inclined towards both disarmament and disengagement from Vietnam. After Kennedy's assassination, however, President Lyndon B. Johnson rejected both policies, stressing the need for war to counter the "threat" of Vietnamese communists (see p.373).

A lack of evidence doesn't prove anything

Whatever Kennedy's intent concerning ICBM production, missile output flourished under his successor, and the Soviet–US nuclear missile race reached fever pitch. By the time Richard Nixon was elected president in 1969, people were getting worried that the expanding stockpile of bigger and bigger weapons was making war by accident all the more likely. Nixon abandoned ideology in favour of *détente* with the USSR and China, accepting political differences in the interest of achieving a balance of interdependent peace. A brake on missile development was applied in 1972, when Nixon and USSR premier Brezhnev signed the Anti-Ballistic Missile treaty.

However, as Adam Curtis argued in the 2004 BBC documentary series, *The Power of Nightmares*, the neoconservative disciples of the political philosopher Leo Strauss were waiting in the wings. Paradoxically, Strauss – a German-Jewish émigré who lectured at Chicago – had been influenced by the anti-Semitic political philosopher Carl Schmitt, a Nazi, as early as 1933. Schmitt believed that politics was – and should be – a life-and-death power struggle: political parties and countries became strong by fighting an enemy. Applying this principle to America, Strauss believed that if the US was to avoid descending into liberal decadence, it had to have such an enemy, even if it were a mythical one. That enemy, of course, was the Soviet Union.

As the smoke of trauma from the Vietnam War and Watergate (see p.190) still swirled across the US, President Gerald Ford's neocon defense secretary Donald Rumsfeld, his chief of staff Dick Cheney and analyst Paul Wolfowitz began preaching the new gospel – which was, of course, a revival of old American fears of communist plans for world domination. In 1976, Rumsfeld declared that the Soviet Union had been secretly building newer and better weapons in greater numbers than ever before. A neoconservative group, Team B, was organized to prove this hidden threat to the US. Its chairman, Richard Pipes, was convinced that Soviet statements and weapons were meaningless. What mattered was "the Soviet mindset", which was bent on conquering the US.

Just because there was no evidence of illegal, aggressive weapons procurement, that didn't mean they didn't exist; it just meant that the Soviets were hiding them very well. Dr Anne Cahn of the Arms Control and Disarmament Agency summarized Team B's approach like this: "'We can't find evidence that they're doing it the way that everyone thinks they're doing it, so they must be doing it a different way. We don't know what that different way is, but they must be doing it.' No evidence didn't mean it didn't exist, it just hadn't been found." While the CIA insisted that Soviet air defences, like the Soviet economy, were heading for collapse, Team B argued that this was just a ruse, and that their air defences worked perfectly – it said so in the Soviet training manual.

The supposed Soviet threat was further extended to terrorist groups such as the PLO, Hezbollah and the IRA, which the neocons said were not fragmented units fighting their own causes, but part of a secret network coordinated from Moscow. Neocons cited Clair Sterling's book *The Terror Network* to convince CIA chief William Casey, even though his CIA subordinates were sure there was no such network. The CIA's former Soviet affairs chief, Melvin Goodman, said of Sterling's work that "very clear episodes where CIA black propaganda – clandestine information that was designed under a covert action plan to be planted in European newspapers – were picked up and put

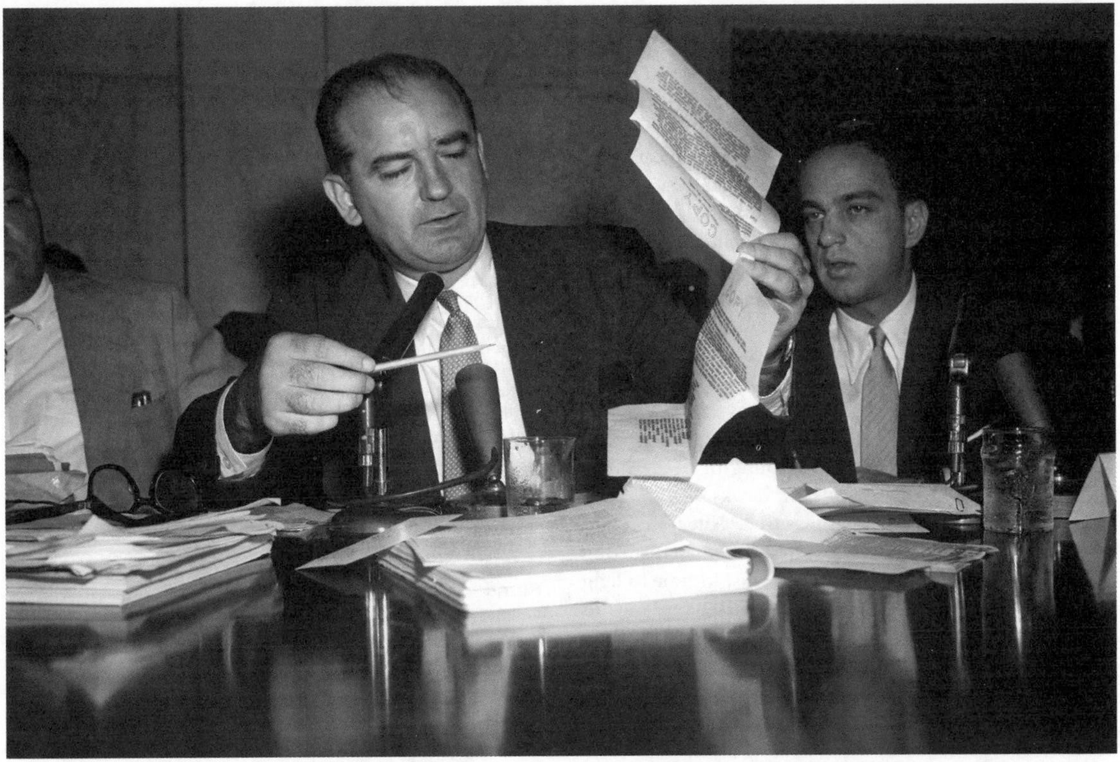

Red-hunter Joseph McCarthy at a hearing of the House Un-American Activities Committee (HUAC).

in this book". In other words, the CIA knew the book was nonsense because they had written the lies themselves.

Casey, however, became a believer. Armed with Pipes' dossier on the hidden terror network, he persuaded President Reagan to implement a new policy of covert wars abroad in 1983. A huge increase in funding and arms for military dictatorships soon followed. "Death squad paramilitaries", trained at the US's School of the Americas, murdered and tortured supposed "left-wing terrorists" in Colombia, Chile, Honduras and El Salvador. Grenada was successfully invaded. The Sandinista government of Nicaragua, which President Carter had supported against the previous Somoza dictatorship, was still fighting Somoza's Contras. But Reagan saw the Sandinistas as communists, and backed the Contras through such murky means as the Iran–Contra conspiracy (see p.201). Around fifty thousand civilians died in a war the World Court denounced as "unlawful".

Reagan also praised Afghanistan's Mujaheddin guerrillas as "freedom fighters" and gave them billions of dollars in arms and funds to fight the Soviet occupiers. (In fact, as Steve Coll outlines in his 2004 book *Ghost Wars: The Secret*

History of the CIA, President Carter's security adviser Zbiginiew Brzezinski had engineered US aid to the Afghan government to begin in mid-1979, hoping that it would provoke a Soviet invasion and get the USSR into an unwinnable war – a war that would eventually cost 1.8 million Afghan lives.) Ironically, the Soviets' ultimate defeat in the CIA-supported *jihad* in Afghanistan enabled the extremist elements in the Mujaheddin to establish the Taliban regime, and attracted followers to such political mavericks as Osama bin Laden.

After the USSR collapsed in 1991, President George H.W. Bush gloated to the Senate: "We won the Cold War!" Years of warnings from the likes of Mikhail Gorbachev and Melvin Goodman that the USSR was heading for economic implosion were conveniently overlooked, as was the fact that the US was about to fall into a recession that would cost Bush the 1992 election, thanks to the tripling of the national deficit. Instead, the reputations of hawks like Cheney, Wolfowitz and Rumsfeld were assured. After an eight-year interlude of Democrat rule, the neocons returned to power under George W. Bush in 2001, just in time to fight the evil terrorist mastermind Osama bin Laden and his worldwide terror network, Al Qaeda. The neocons are now allegedly behind the Proactive, Preemptive Operations Group (P2OG), which mounts covert missions to "stimulate reactions" from militant groups, i.e. to incite them to violence in order to justify a US "counterattack".

Conspiracy to exaggerate?

The Cold War was all about mutual paranoia. To suggest that the communist threat was exaggerated by the US, however, is not to say that it did not exist. Nor is it to deny the terrible totalitarianism of most communist regimes (though the right-wing dictatorships of a great many of the US's anti-communist allies were equally appalling in their own way). But in overestimating the communist menace, the US expended vast resources and blighted millions of lives by attacking states and people, at home and abroad, who actually posed no threat at all.

SOURCES

Books

Edward S. Herman The Real Terror Network: Terrorism in Fact and Propaganda (1982). An eloquent, impassioned rebuttal of Clair Sterling's *The Terror Network* and the role of propaganda in "creating" terrorism (and keeping people terrified).

David M. Oshinsky A Conspiracy So Immense ... The World of Joe McCarthy (1985). A witty attack on the life and lies of Joe McCarthy.

Richard H. Rovere Senator Joe McCarthy (1996). A work of its time, written shortly after McCarthy's death, that still divides its critics in its reprinted edition.

Films

Adam Curtis The Power of Nightmares: The Rise of the Politics of Fear (2005). An edited version of the award-winning BBC documentary series (the original can be downloaded – with Curtis's blessing – from various websites). A brilliantly told, compelling story of how US (and latterly UK) politicians tightened their grip on power, not by selling dreams of a better future, but by playing on people's fears – first of communism, then of an international terror network.

Websites

Ⓦ **hnn.us/articles/1204.html** An interesting piece by Don B. Kates on the power of conspiracy theories.

Ⓦ **www.jfklibrary.org** The official site of John F. Kennedy's library hosts a growing archive of materials from his presidency.

The Gulf of Tonkin incident and the Vietnam War

A so-called "incident" in the Gulf of Tonkin in August 1964, in which North Vietnamese vessels allegedly fired on US warships, provided the pretext for the US to step up its involvement in Vietnam. Up to that point, US personnel in Vietnam were officially described as "military advisers" to the South Vietnamese government, but from then on, the Americans were engaged in a full-scale conflict – though never, technically speaking, a war. The incident merits close examination, not merely because it was so obviously fabricated, but also because it swiftly became clear to the conspirators that they had bitten off much more than they could chew.

Communism dominoes across Asia

By early 1964, the US government was becoming worried that its ally, South Vietnam, was losing its fight against communist Vietcong guerrillas, supported by Ho Chi Minh's government in North Vietnam. President Lyndon B. Johnson and Defense Secretary Robert McNamara were concerned that if South Vietnam fell to the communists, it would precipitate a "domino effect" under which further regimes across Asia might succumb to the Reds. Therefore, they provided the South Vietnamese with fast patrol boats and the necessary training to operate them. Ostensibly these boats were for defensive purposes only, but in practice – under Operation 34A, coordinated in Washington and Saigon – they were used to attack North Vietnamese radar stations, ships, bridges and other military targets. US ships, tacking along the North Vietnamese coast in international waters, provided the intelligence to direct these attacks.

On August 2, 1964, the USS *Maddox* destroyer was carrying out just such operations in the Gulf of Tonkin when it was attacked by three North Vietnamese torpedo boats. The *Maddox* was hit by two machine-gun bullets; in response, the North Vietnamese boats were shelled and strafed by fighter-jets. The destroyer USS *Turner Joy* was dispatched to support the *Maddox*, and during the night of August 4, the two warships reported that several fast craft fired almost a dozen torpedoes at them. The Pentagon declared this to be a second attack by North Vietnamese PT boats. Calling the two attacks an "outrage", Johnson went on national TV to denounce North Vietnam's "open aggression on the open seas". Air strikes against North Vietnam were announced, with carrier planes from the Seventh Fleet bombing oil facilities and ships that very day.

"They started it!"

According to the *LA Times*, "the communists, by their attack on American vessels in international waters, have themselves escalated the hostilities", while a headline in *The Washington Post* described the air strikes as a "Move Taken to Halt New Aggression". With impressive speed, the Gulf of Tonkin Resolution was written and passed by Congress on August 7, opposed by only two senators. It authorized the president "to take all necessary measures to repel any armed attack against the forces of the United States and to prevent further aggression", and "to take all necessary steps, including the use of armed force, to assist any member or protocol state of the Southeast Asia Collective Defense Treaty requesting assistance in defense of its freedom". Although this did not constitute a declaration of war, a sustained campaign of heavy bombing was instigated almost immediately, and by early 1965, the first of hundreds of thousands of US combat troops began arriving in South Vietnam.

"Shooting at whales"

The North Vietnamese attacks were hardly unprovoked, as Johnson readily acknowledged. He described the coastal raids as something "I imagine [the North Vietnamese] wanted to put a stop to". Yet neither of the US ships sustained any damage or casualties from the August 4 attack. Was there even a "second attack" at all?

The US Navy Historical Center now concedes that "North Vietnamese naval forces did not attack *Maddox* and *Turner Joy* that night". Even at the time, there were doubts. The captain of the *Maddox* spoke of "freak weather conditions" messing with the radar, while before Johnson's TV announcement, Admiral Grant Sharp of the Pacific Fleet sent word back to the White House that "many of the reported contacts and torpedoes fired appear doubtful". Citing the weird weather, and hyped-up personnel aboard the US ships, Sharp said: "A lot of these torpedo attacks were from the sonar operators!"

Squadron commander James Stockdale, a navy pilot who later became a POW and Ross Perot's 1992 vice-presidential candidate, said he had "the best seat in the house" that night. In his book *In Love and War*, he wrote that "our destroyers were just shooting at phantom targets – nothing there but black water and American fire power". President Johnson admitted in 1965 that "for all I know, our Navy was shooting at whales out there", while McNamara went much further in the 2001 documentary *The Fog of War*. Declaring with surprising contrition that "we initiated the action", he reflected that the geopolitical intentions of the North Vietnamese had been "misjudged", and the dangers to the US "exaggerated". That same film revealed a phone conversation between Johnson and McNamara, some weeks before Tonkin, in which Johnson expressed the desire to manipulate the North Vietnamese government into doing something provocative, declaring "I want to be able to trap these people".

As for Congress's speedy resolution, it clearly had its origins in a resolution drawn up in May 1964 by Undersecretary of State George Ball, who oversaw Operation 34A. His draft endorsed "all measures, including the commitment of force", to defend South Vietnam and Laos, should their governments seek help. The National Security Council responded at the time by suggesting that it would fare best in Congress after the 1964 civil rights bill had gone through in July. According to Daniel Hallin in *The Uncensored War*, the shoddiness of the case for war was clear. Journalists had "a great deal of information" contradicting the official Gulf of Tonkin account, but it simply wasn't used. Hanoi had complained about boat and aircraft attacks on August 1, but was ignored.

Oil, the Kuomintang and Kennedy

McNamara and Johnson's inflated perceptions of the threat of communism may have meant that, for them, the end of war justified the means. However, in his 1972 book *The War Conspiracy*, Professor Peter Dale Scott argued that a more complex web of arms and oil corporations had pushed the US government into war in Vietnam, seeking control of the "considerable offshore oil deposits in the South China Sea", which were mainly south of South Vietnam.

Also involved, apparently, were elements of Chiang Kai-shek's Kuomintang (KMT) dictatorship in Taiwan, who were eager to regain the lost Chinese mainland. According to Scott, "The only way the KMT imagined they could get back into China would be if they somehow involved America in a war in that area" – provoking turmoil in Indochina through the diaspora of Chinese exiles, linked and funded by drug trafficking, as well as through Chinese dissidents in the CIA.

Scott highlighted two National Security Action Memorandums: NSAM 263, signed by President Kennedy in early October 1963, was to withdraw 16,000 US military personnel from Vietnam by 1965; NSAM

273, signed by Johnson just three days after Kennedy's assassination (see p.22), purported to continue the withdrawal policy by referring to the previous memo, as *The New York Times* and *The Washington Post* reported. However, it actually referred to a separate, non-binding adviser's report, while escalating US military assistance to South Vietnam. The timing of the NSAMs was alarming. Scott remarked that "the Kennedy assassination was itself an important, perhaps a crucial, event in the history of the Indochina war conspiracy", and claimed that pressure from the CIA blocked the distribution of his book for several years. On the other hand, it seems bizarrely indirect for the Taiwanese to start trouble simply to get the US "into the region". If the hope was to divert mainland China and keep its expansion plans in check, it has to be noted that the US defeat in Vietnam didn't lead to a Chinese invasion of Taiwan.

Scott's speculation as to the profit motive behind the war might seem to be supported by the action of the South Vietnamese government in 1973, just as the US Senate refused to fund further military operations in Indochina, in awarding oil exploration contracts (never fulfilled) to Mobil, Exxon, Shell and others. But that's hardly a smoking gun, and it seems a bit belated considering the war had already been going for a decade. It is true, however, that the South China Sea holds enormous oil and gas reserves, with proven oil reserves estimated at 7.5 billion barrels – a significant amount, if not as high as the 210 billion barrels proposed by some Chinese estimates. Since the early 1970s, arguments as to who controls its islands have led to increasingly frequent naval clashes between Vietnam, China and the Philippines. Six countries contest ownership of the Paracel and Spratly Islands, none of whose claims are recognized by the US. American historian Howard Zinn has also pointed to the chain of US bases in the Philippines, Taiwan, Japan and South Korea that were rendered "precarious" by increasing communist control, as was the US hold on tin, oil and rubber from Indonesia and Malaysia.

Bankers backing losses and unlikely communists

Some theories circulating on the Internet are clearly bonkers. These include the notion that the Vietnam and Korean wars were deliberately lost, in order to scare other non-communist states worldwide into supporting the US and NATO, and to rope them into the US dollar economy and international banking system. Given the uncertainty of the desired outcome on the one hand, and the huge loss of men, money and prestige on the other, this hardly seems cost-effective, to put it mildly.

Another suggestion, put forward by the *New American* magazine, is that the Vietnam War was never intended to be won, because McNamara, Henry Kissinger and President Nixon, all members of the Council on Foreign Relations (see p.140), were communists who wanted communist victories in Indochina. If this was the case you have to wonder why they had a war at all.

An enduring legacy

Around 58,000 US military personnel and 1.25 million Vietnamese soldiers from both sides were killed during the Vietnam War, together with hundreds of thousands of Vietnamese civilians who died as a result of either direct action or the attendant chaos. In addition, 750,000 Cambodians perished following Richard Nixon's illegal bombing of their country. Although the calamitous costs of the war, and the resultant domestic unrest in the US, led Lyndon Johnson not to seek re-election in 1968, he was never called to account for the fabricated "Tonkin incident" that started it all. In 2001, journalist Larry Berman's book *No Peace, No Honour: Nixon, Kissinger and Betrayal in Vietnam* argued that the 1968 election was, in effect, sabotaged by Nixon's team, who secretly passed information about the US Democratic administration's negotiations with North Vietnam to the Republicans and the South Vietnamese, who promptly withdrew from the talks.

Vietnam – a poor, predominantly agricultural country – had more bombs dropped on it than Nazi Germany, along with a massive dose of dioxin-laden defoliants that still cause hideous birth defects today. To rub salt in the wound, the US then subjected it to a further twenty years of economic sanctions. Cambodia, meanwhile, was taken over by the genocidal Khmer Rouge regime, which was overthrown in 1979 when the Vietnamese invaded after several years of murderous Khmer incursions. This prompted the US and UK governments to send arms and SAS instructors to aid Pol Pot's Khmer forces on the Thai border.

Cambodia's plight was famously depicted in Roland Joffe's film *The Killing Fields*, based on the experiences of US journalist Sydney Schanberg and his Cambodian friend Dith Pran. During the First Gulf War, Schanberg recalled the Gulf of Tonkin fabrications and warned: "We Americans are the ultimate innocents. We are forever desperate to believe that this time the government is telling us the truth."

SOURCES

Books

Daniel Ellsberg Secrets: A Memoir of Vietnam and the Pentagon Papers (2003). This book by an insider who decided to blow the whistle begins with the Gulf of Tonkin incident. Ellsberg worked in the Defense Department and, later, on the top-secret McNamara study of US decision-making in Vietnam, later known as the Pentagon Papers.

Peter Dale Scott The War Conspiracy: The Secret Road to the Second IndoChina War (1972). An angry if not always persuasive diatribe against the larger forces that, Scott claims, conspired to make war in Southeast Asia.

Films

Errol Morris The Fog of War: Eleven Lessons from the Life of Robert S. McNamara (2002). Morris's Oscar-winning documentary is based on interviews with McNamara, the charismatic US defense secretary 1961–68, and covers Vietnam and the Cuban Missile Crisis. Don't hold your breath for a sequel starring Donald Rumsfeld.

Websites

ⓦ **www.eia.doe.gov/emeu/cabs/schinatab.html** Detailed documentation on energy reserves in the South China Seas.

The Israeli attack on USS Liberty

The gains made by Israel during the June 1967 Six Day War were truly remarkable. Within less than a week, the Israelis attacked and comprehensively defeated the armed forces of Jordan, Syria and Egypt, quintupling its territory by retaking the Golan Heights, the Gaza Strip, the West Bank and the Sinai Peninsula. What's more, those victories were won single-handedly, with no direct military support from the US.

But that's not the whole story. In what's largely a forgotten footnote to the conflict, Israeli military forces actually attacked the US Navy intelligence ship USS *Liberty*, killing 34 servicemen and injuring 174 more. This mysterious incident, which eight successive US presidents, from Lyndon Johnson to George W. Bush, have publicly acknowledged to have been a mistake, is regarded by some as evidence of an intricate conspiracy at the highest levels of the US and Israeli governments.

It was on June 8, three days after the start of the war, that the USS *Liberty* of the Sixth Fleet found itself under attack a dozen or so miles off the Sinai coast. At about 2pm Sinai time, as the *Liberty* was gathering radio intercepts from the chaos ashore, Mirage jet planes appeared, circled the ship, and then began to bomb and strafe it. They were later joined by Israeli torpedo boats, in a protracted attack that lasted over an hour and inflicted enough death and destruction that the blood-spattered lower decks were said to look like a "meat locker".

"It was a mistake"

Although both Egypt and the USSR were initially suspected of carrying out the attack, Israel took responsibility within days, claiming that its aircraft and boats had mistaken the *Liberty* for an Egyptian vessel, the *El Quseir* – a civilian cargo ship a quarter of the size of the *Liberty*. Among the barrage of reports that backed the story were the Israelis' Ram Ron Commission of Inquiry, which said on June 16 that the attack was "a bona fide mistake", and a US Navy Court of Inquiry, which concluded two days later that it was a case of "mistaken identity". A month later, the Clifford Report for the Foreign Intelligence Advisory Board said that "information thus far available" suggested that the attack was not knowingly carried out against a US vessel. But despite the admission of error, no one was charged or court-martialled for the attack.

The "mistake" version fails to hold water

In his 1976 book, *Assault on the Liberty*, a survivor of the attack, Lieutenant Commander James Ennes, argued that the *Liberty* was obviously American, and that it was located in international waters. He suggested that the Israelis deliberately attacked the US intelligence ship in order to stop the Americans learning about a surprise assault on Syria. This theory was further expanded on Ennes's USS *Liberty* memorial website (www.ussliberty.org), and by the History Channel's 2001 documentary, *Cover Up: Attack on the USS Liberty*.

The Israelis alleged that the *Liberty* was not flying a flag, and that no identifying markings were discernible to the Israeli pilots and boat crews. However, the US Navy Court of Inquiry, the Clifford Report and the Salans Report (which was written at the request of Secretary of State Dean Rusk by his official legal adviser) all agreed that a five-foot by eight-foot flag was visible, as were hull markings on the bow and stern. James Ennes additionally stated that there was enough wind to blow the flag aloft. Attacking unidentified ships in neutral waters would, in any case, be considered a war crime. It's also claimed that one of the Israeli planes recognized the ship as being "possibly American or Soviet", and non-hostile, before the main air attack began. According to Ennes, witnesses aboard the *Liberty* reported that the Israeli planes were so close at times that the pilots could be seen in their cockpits, and that they had waved at the planes. The *Liberty*'s crew were supposedly told to stay quiet or face court martial, at the very least.

The CIA replies

In August 1977, accusations that the assault on the *Liberty* was being covered up prompted the CIA to declassify its own conclusion, reached five days after the attack, that the attack had been accidental, and caused by the resemblance between the *Liberty* and the *El Quseir*. That September, CIA director Stanfield Turner appeared on ABC's *Good Morning America* to say that the Israeli government had no knowledge of the *Liberty*'s existence prior to the attack, and he further wrote in 1978 that the attack "was not in malice".

Operation Cyanide

The USS *Liberty* Veterans Association (LVA), formed in 1982, claimed that the attack was deliberate. Concocted between the US and Israel, it was a ruse designed to blame Egypt and justify a massive, nuclear retaliation by the US on the Arab world, thereby ensuring (eternal) victory for Israel. This was also the case argued by a former *Sunday Times* journalist, Peter Hounam, in *Operation Cyanide: How the Bombing of the USS Liberty Nearly Caused World War III*, and in the BBC documentary *Dead in the Water*. Hounam stated that the *Liberty* was in international waters, flying its flag, when attacked by unmarked planes. Only because it failed to sink, and didn't carry all the evidence and witnesses to the bottom of the sea, was Israel forced to admit to the attack. Supposedly, LBJ knew all about it in advance, the White House twice recalled rescue planes heading for the *Liberty*, and Secretary of State Dean Rusk said it was no accident.

Judge Cristol defends the "mistake" theory

US civil judge A. Jay Cristol, a former navy pilot and lawyer who wrote *The Liberty Incident: The 1967 Israeli Attack on the US Navy Spy Ship*, has become the most prominent advocate of the "mistake" case. His view, reported at length by both the *Jerusalem Post* and the Anti-Defamation League, is that the *Liberty* was marked on the Naval Intelligence map board at Haifa, only to be removed shortly before the attack. That decision was made at a "tactical level", while Israel's defence minister, General Moshe Dayan, was at lunch in the countryside. Israeli torpedo boats were seeking a "grey ship" suspected of shelling Israeli forces, which had been spotted heading for Port Said.

Air strikes began just after 2pm, but after fourteen minutes the flight leader noticed that the ship's hull markings were not in Arabic, and stopped the attack. When Israeli torpedo boats arrived soon afterwards, signals from the *Liberty* were unfortunately obscured by smoke. The order to "hold fire" was interpreted as "open fire", and the boats replied with torpedoes. The *Liberty* was identified first as Egyptian, then Soviet and then Egyptian again, before an Israeli helicopter pilot finally confirmed it as American at 3.12pm.

In 2003, Cristol sued the National Security Agency (NSA) to obtain transcripts of communications between Israeli helicopter pilots, intercepted by an EC-121 aircraft flying nearby between 2.30pm and 3.27pm. These transcripts, drawn from before, during and after the attack, reveal the same confusion he'd previously reported. No tape has been found to confirm the claims of conspiracy theorists that Israeli pilots identified the ship as American before they attacked it. Senator John McCain, whose father took part in the navy inquiry of June 18, 1967, and Senator Bob Graham of the Senate Select Committee on Intelligence, concurred with Cristol's findings. Cristol states that a total of ten US and three Israeli investigations have now concluded it was a case of mistaken identity.

The battle gets ugly

According to Internet writer William Hughes, the helicopter pilots' view of the incident as a case of mistaken identity is irrelevant, because they arrived after the attack. The NSA intercepts released in 2003 show one helicopter hearing at 2.30pm that the ship was "unidentified", and then ground control telling them all at 2.42pm that it was an Egyptian cargo ship, without mentioning the name *El Quseir*.

For the pilots to appear to be so comfortable attacking the ship despite the doubt as to its identity is frightening. That would be against international law, and surely common sense. And it does seem strange that they could tell that the ship's name, written in two-foot high letters, was not in Arabic, but were unable to discern that the writing was in English, notwithstanding the six-foot high identification numbers on the ship's sides. In addition, the fact that the *Liberty* was removed from the Israelis' war map shows that at some point they knew the ship existed, which contradicts the version of events given by the CIA in 1977.

Something to hide

In his 2000 book *Body of Secrets*, former ABC TV *World Tonight* reporter James Bamford wrote that radio intercepts gathered by the EC-121 show that the Israeli pilots saw the American flag. Bamford suggested that US servicemen were not the only ones being murdered, and that the *Liberty* was attacked in order to stop it from learning that Israeli forces on Sinai were massacring Egyptian prisoners. If that's the case, Israel would have had to weigh the possible consequences of attacking a major ally, and perpetrating a war crime, to cover up a war crime that was taking place somewhere else.

Cristol countered in the *Jerusalem Post* that while Bamford quoted linguist Marvin Nowicki, aboard the EC-121, about the intercepts, he failed to quote a letter from

Nowicki to Bamford stating that the intercepts proved the accident theory. Arguing that "Mr Bamford's writings are much closer to fiction than to history", Cristol questioned how any electronic intelligence ship could overhear murders happening miles over the horizon. Furthermore, no supporting evidence, such as graves or even allegations from Egypt, has ever appeared. Cristol added that the USS *Liberty* Veterans Association was "very active" in supporting conspiracy theories, and was co-founded by Congressman Paul Findley of Illinois, a politician sympathetic to the Palestinian cause.

The Moorer inquiry indicts Israel

Despite Cristol's rebuttal, Bamford's interpretation of the radio messages was taken seriously by the Liberty Alliance investigation in October 2003, which was led by the former chairman of the Joint Chiefs of Staff, Admiral Thomas Moorer, and backed by Marines general Raymond Davis, Rear Admiral Merlin Staring and ex-ambassador to Saudi Arabia, James Akins.

According to the Moorer inquiry, Israel wanted to blame Egypt for the sinking of the *Liberty*, and thus provoke the US into joining the war. It concluded that the movements of the *Liberty* were watched for eight hours, before it was attacked by a dozen Mirage jets using napalm, 30mm cannon and rockets. As Israeli vessels subsequently unleashed their torpedoes and machine guns, distress messages were jammed. According to Captain Joe Tully of the carrier USS *Saratoga*, and Rear Admiral Lawrence Geis, the White House withdrew a Sixth Fleet intervention to rescue the *Liberty*.

Captain Ward Boston, counsel to the 1967 Navy Court of Inquiry, added that Secretary of State John McNamara and President Johnson instructed the inquiry to reach the conclusion that it was a case of mistaken identity, and compressed the necessary six months into a mere ten days. Boston also claimed that Admiral Kidd, the chairman of the inquiry, privately admitted that his hand had been forced. Dean Rusk, former CIA director Richard Helms, and two former NSA directors agreed. While Moorer arguably prejudiced his own inquiry by stating back in 1993 that "I can never accept the claim that this was a mistaken attack", this does nothing to impugn the testimony of the various senior notables who supported his conclusion.

The Anti-Defamation League (ADL) responded to Moorer's charge by arguing that Israel didn't need the US to intervene in the war. The Israelis had already destroyed the Egyptian air force, and were racing across the Sinai, with victory just hours away. Neither did Israel conceal its responsibility for attacking the *Liberty*. Both the ADL and Judge Cristol refer to Admiral Kidd's remarks as "alleged", and argue that because he's dead they're not valid testimony. They suggest that the *Liberty*'s radio was not jammed, but tuned to the wrong frequencies, with its cables and antennae damaged by gunfire, and finally, that if the Israelis had really wanted to sink the *Liberty*, they would have succeeded.

Insults and arguments

At a January 2004 State Department hearing, Bamford and Cristol clashed in person, trading arguments and insults. Protestors, who shouted "whitewash" and "cover-up" when the hearing concluded that the attack was a "mistake", had to be forcibly removed. In June 2004, the ADL described the *Liberty* issue as "popular among anti-Israel conspiracy theorists" seeking to undermine Israel. That same month, the *Jerusalem Post* published "exclusive transcripts" from the Israeli jet pilots, claiming that they proved that the attack was a "tragic mistake". The highlights of the new transcripts centred on what ground controller Colonel Mushuel Kislev told the jet pilots (all timings are in local Sinai time).

At 1.50pm Kislev says: "If it's a warship then screw it." At 1.54pm a weapons officer asks: "What is this? Americans?" – but his guess is dismissed. At 1.56pm a pilot queries: "What is it? What is it? A destroyer? A patrol boat? What is it? … I can't identify it, but in any case it's a military ship." He then begins strafing with 30mm cannon, before other pilots enter the affray with bombs and napalm.

At 1.58pm Kislev is surprised that the ship isn't returning fire, and at 2.02pm he advises that "if there is a doubt, don't attack". After a colleague gives the go-ahead, he concludes at 2.03pm "you can sink her". Then his colleagues change their minds again, and at 2.04pm the attackers are told to hold back because the navy "want to get close and have a look". Kislev suggests at 2.09pm that they should "look for a flag if they can see one", but the pilots then misread the *Liberty*'s identification letters. Only at 2.14pm, amid serious alarm that the ship may be "apparently American", does Kislev order the air attack to be stopped.

Neither the transcripts nor the *Jerusalem Post* mentioned that the boat attacks continued after Kislev stopped the air attacks, and neither did the *Post* mention the *Liberty*'s exact location. The transcripts don't fully fit the events laid out by either Ennes or Cristol's NSA transcripts, which report doubts on the ship's identification at 2.30pm and then call it "Egyptian" at 2.42pm.

A controversy without end

After four decades and dozens of books, documentaries and inquiries, the bitterness of the arguments over the *Liberty* seems only to have increased. There has still been no congressional-level investigation, and a lot of very senior US political and military figures believe that a conspiracy of some kind took place. Quite what the purpose of that conspiracy may have been, however, remains unclear – contradictory theories suggest that the aim was either to embroil the US in the war or to keep it out of it. Some also argue that whether the attack was deliberate or not, Johnson and successive presidents have publicly accepted it as a "mistake" in order not to antagonize the Jewish vote in the US.

The 2002 BBC documentary *Dead in the Water* suggested a more likely reason for the official silence: that the placement of the *Liberty* spy ship off the coast of Egypt was proof of US complicity, if not outright backing, for Israel's attack on Egypt. Hence, any attempts to keep the matter under wraps at the time would have been less about covering up some ruse that had gone wrong, and more about ensuring US involvement was kept quiet in order to prevent an even greater political backlash in the Middle East. However, that does assume that the Arab states did not otherwise suspect that US involvement in the Six Day War was a foregone conclusion.

Debate as to the precise facts of the case has become increasingly incidental to some of the nastier arguments. Cristol is not alone in believing that the incident has been stirred up by enemies of Israel. Michael Oren, author of *Six Days of War*, argues that conspiracy theories about Israel and the Jews are "immortal" because "they tap into the notion or belief of an international Jewish cabal, the Protocols of the Elders of Zion thing" (see p.109). The Liberty Alliance has accused powerful pro-Israeli interests of thwarting proper congressional investigation, while the USS *Liberty* memorial website prints comments from "its critics and certain self-hating Americans". This war looks set to continue for some time to come.

SOURCES

Books

James Bamford Body of Secrets (2002). Bamford analyses radio transcripts in immense detail in a bid to prove Israel's culpability.

A. Jay Cristol The Liberty Incident: The 1967 Israeli Attack on the US Navy Spy Ship (2003). Judge Cristol, a stalwart proponent of the "mistake" theory, reports on his personal fifteen-year investigation.

Peter Hounam Operation Cyanide: How the Bombing of the USS Liberty Nearly Caused World War III (2005). Perhaps the most paranoid of all *Liberty* literature, this books sees the attack as an attempt to bring about nuclear war.

Films

Christopher Mitchell Dead in the Water (2002). A useful documentary reconstructing the events of the attack (albeit events obviously open to much dispute), including high-level interviews with Defense Secretary Robert McNamara and Israel's former naval chief.

Websites

www.adl.org/Israel/uss.asp The response of the Anti-Defamation League to the ongoing controversy.

www.ussliberty.org The definitive "conspiracy" site on the *Liberty*, detailing most of the theories and offering links to even more.

The Rwandan genocide: who started it?

The outwardly placid waters of Lake Kivu, on the western border of Rwanda, Central Africa, have witnessed two kinds of terrible explosions. One is a natural phenomenon: huge quantities of methane are dissolved in the water, and they are thought to explode once every thousand years or so, with devastating effect. The other explosion was man-made, but no less destructive. The Tutsi are Rwanda's main ethnic minority and, until 1994, some 70,000 of them lived around the lake's eastern shore, in the province of Kibuye. Between April and July 1994, however, over three-quarters of the province's Tutsis were murdered: some 40,000 people were hacked down with machetes or clubs; another 10,000 were killed with guns or grenades; thousands more were drowned, buried or burnt alive, hanged, stoned or even mown down by tractors. Across Rwanda, the number of murder victims – both Tutsis and moderate Hutus who opposed the extremist Hutu Power government – reached close to one million people. In just one hundred days, one in ten Rwandans were killed. Today, the identities of the killers are, for the most part, well known. Who fired the first fatal shot, however, remains a source of conspiracist speculation.

The mysterious Falcon: shot down in flames

Shortly before 8.30pm on April 6, 1994, two – some say three – ground-to-air missiles seared their way upwards from the smoke-scented darkness of Kigali, the Rwandan capital. A fraction of a second later, a fireball lit up the sky as the missiles struck their target: a Mystère Falcon 50 private jet, just coming in to land. Fragments of burning metal came tumbling down over the city; mixed up among the debris were the corpses of the presidents of both Rwanda and neighbouring Burundi. The body of Rwandan president Juvenal Habyarimana, by ominous chance, fell into his own back garden.

The two premiers were returning to Kigali after renewing a shaky commitment to end the civil war between Rwanda's Hutu-dominated government and the rebel army on its borders, the Tutsi-led Rwandan Patriotic Front (RPF). Peace, however, was not the outcome: for tens of thousands of pre-armed and pre-warned extremists from the Hutu ethnic group, the attack was a long-expected signal. From radio loudspeakers across the country – all tuned to Radio Mille Collines, the voice of Hutu extremism – came the harsh call: "the Tutsis have killed our president! … Let us begin the annihilation of the cockroaches!"

Over the next one hundred days – while the UN floundered, the US, UK and France obfuscated, and the rest of the world stood by – somewhere between 750,000 and one million Rwandan Tutsis and moderate Hutus were murdered by Rwandan soldiers and death squads of Interahamwe militias. Most of their victims were killed by hand, with machetes. A lucky few bribed their killers for the luxury of a bullet to the head. Meanwhile, hundreds of thousands of women were raped or mutilated – and often both.

Did the Tutsis fire the missile?

We'll probably never know who really fired the missiles that downed the Mystère Falcon, but allegations aren't thin on the ground. Within minutes of the plane coming down, Radio Mille Collines was laying the blame at the door of the

Tutsi rebels – under the banner of the Rwandan Patriotic Front. The RPF's motive was supposedly to derail the peace effort so that they could begin their invasion of Rwanda. The rebels certainly had the military capacity to launch the attack – and Hutu extremists claimed they had assistance from mercenaries supplied by the former colonial power, Belgium. (Ten Belgian soldiers were murdered by Rwandan government soldiers within hours of the plane coming down.) Whether or not the RPF could have successfully penetrated the area around Kigali airport, however, isn't certain. It was swarming with government troops linked to the Hutu extremists, after all. Some Hutu apologists claim that hundreds of RPF soldiers in civilian clothes had infiltrated the area, but the RPF maintains that its 600 troops in Kigali were confined to the old parliament building.

One theory posits not Belgian, but US assistance in bringing down the plane. But, like so many conspiracy theories, it is built chiefly on a lack of evidence. The

Refugees fleeing the Rwandan genocide find relative safety in a camp in neighbouring Burundi.

Mystère Falcon's black box is missing – supposedly smuggled away by the UN and kept secret under pressure from the US government. (Quite why a black box would reveal anything about who fired the missile that destroyed the plane carrying it is never explained.) The US allegedly has satellite and surveillance evidence revealing when the genocide began – but again, that evidence has apparently been withheld. It is also claimed that the US issued a "non-combatant evacuation order" to pull its citizens out of Rwanda very early on, apparently suggesting that they had foreknowledge of what was about to happen. Another mystery troubling conspiracists is the failure of the UN's International War Crimes Tribunal to investigate events that took place before the plane was brought down. The reason its remit was restricted to events after the crash is supposedly because the evidence it was amassing was starting to point in an awkward direction: at a US-backed RPF. This unspecified evidence is also rumoured to link the RPF with European mercenaries who had leased warehouses near Kigali airport, and to link those mercenaries with – who else? – the CIA.

... or was it the Hutus?

The RPF, predictably enough, blames Hutu extremists within the Rwandan Army (Forces Armées Rwandaises, or FAR). The plane was brought down, say the RPF, to stop the Rwandan president reaching a compromise power-sharing deal with the Tutsi rebels – and to create the conditions of insecurity and chaos necessary to allow the genocide to take place. It's a plausible theory, and there's some evidence for it. Colonel Theoneste Bagosora of the Rwandan Army took control quickly and efficiently after the attack, and the first killings by Hutu extremists seemed planned and timed rather than improvised in response to a surprise attack. They also began within hours of the president's plane being shot down. So the prosecutor alleged at Bagosora's still unconcluded trial, where Bagosora maintains his innocence. The prosecution also pointed out that the colonel had previously commanded an anti-aircraft battalion and knew the flight paths of approaching aircraft. Furthermore, according to an air traffic controller who claims to have been in the tower at the time of the attack, another Hutu Power leader was the only person who knew the exact arrival time of the presidential jet. When the Canadian commander of the UN peacekeeping force UNAMIR, Lieutenant-General Roméo Dallaire, sent his troops to locate the plane's wreckage, they were prevented from reaching it by the most extreme Hutu faction in the Rwandan Army, the Presidential Guard.

Liberté, égalité, complicité

The US State Department somehow heard that it wasn't just the Presidential Guard that blocked Dallaire's peacekeepers. "Unconfirmed reports", a declassified document claims, say that French military officials were also involved, perhaps as part of their efforts to secure the airport and rescue the bodies of the plane's French aircrew. The current Rwandan government – the heirs of the RPF Tutsi rebels – claim that the French military's actions at the airport were sinister. Were the French involved in the missile attack? And were they to some degree responsible for the genocide that followed?

No one is saying that French troops manned the genocidal barricades, machetes in hand. It's rather that the French government supported the Hutu-dominated regime, providing it with arms, training and political support before the genocide began. Kigali was awash with French weapons at that time – twenty tons of arms were arriving each day in February 1993, and French grenades sold for less than $2 in Kigali market. The very plane in which President Habyarimana died was a gift from the then-president of France, François Mitterrand. Before the genocide began, French troops had fought on the front line against the RPF rebels, providing technical support for artillery gunners and helicopter pilots. More controversially, RPF and foreign diplomatic sources claim that French troops trained not just the government army, but also the extremist youth militia, the Interahamwe, who were the shock troops of the genocide. Around fifty French troops were still working within the Presidential Guard when the genocide began – and it was the Presidential Guard that were responsible for eliminating the moderate Hutu opposition on the morning of April 7, 1994. It's hard to believe that France had no idea of the genocidal conspiracy that was brewing; harder still, perhaps, to imagine that France suppressed news of the massacres in the bloody weeks that followed – but that is exactly what France did in the corridors and meeting rooms of the UN.

France may well have backed a regime that turned genocidal, but specific proof of French toleration or even support for the killings is very hard to find. One of the key pieces of supposed "evidence" is that some white men were seen in the Masaka Hill area of Kigali when the missiles were fired. (The conspiracist is inevitably reminded of the legendary tramps spotted on the "grassy knoll" when JFK was killed, see p.24.) According to a mysterious letter sent to Belgium's leading newspaper, *Le Soir*, these white men were French soldiers providing training to the Rwandan Army, and it was they who fired the missiles. The letter further alleges that the French soldiers were wearing stolen Belgian uniforms.

Even if anonymous letters were to be trusted, the detail about the stolen uniforms seems too neat, too much like counter-propaganda, to be believed. But there is more. A well-connected French mercenary, Paul Barril, had worked for Habyarimana, setting up intelligence operations in Rwanda. Barril had also worked for François Mitterrand, and with Mitterrand's national security adviser, François de Grossouvre – who committed suicide on April 7, the day after the plane was brought down. Barril himself has claimed that de Grossouvre was murdered, observing that there were two bullets in his head. This would seem suggestive: for suicide, one bullet is normally enough. Grossouvre's death was widely interpreted as being linked to his alienation from Mitterrand during French corruption scandals, but the timing is curious.

Black furies, white liars: the Brugière inquiry

France hasn't been content to sit still and take the criticism. A French parliamentary commission into the allegations against France concluded, in 1998, that France had made "errors of judgement", but that the international community in general, and the UN and US in particular, were most to blame. In his 2005 book *Black Furies, White Liars*, the investigative journalist Pierre Péan claimed that the RPF Tutsi rebels had engaged in a counter-genocide against the Hutus. This anti-RPF theme was soon taken up in judicial circles, when French magistrate Jean-Louis Brugière opened an inquiry into the deaths of the French aircrew aboard the Mystère Falcon.

Brugière cuts a high profile. Early in his career, he hunted down the left-wing terrorist Carlos "the Jackal" and, with FBI help, was instrumental in causing Libya to take the fall for the Lockerbie bombing (see p.331). In 2007, he joined Nicolas Sarkozy's right-wing party, the UMP, but he failed to win a seat. His 2006 inquiry into the Mystère Falcon caused enormous controversy by stating that it was the Tutsi RPF, led by the current Rwandan president Paul Kagame, which launched the missiles that brought down the plane. Chillingly, this was the same accusation used by the Hutu extremists as an excuse to murder thousands of innocent Tutsis. Brugière even issued arrest warrants for nine officials in Kagame's Rwandan government.

Critics found numerous flaws in Brugière's report, from misspellings of key names to the use of evidence rejected by the earlier parliamentary enquiry. Few thought he had built a convincing case against Kagame and the RPF. A key witness, Emmanuel Ruzigana, was quoted as admitting he had been a member of a secret "Commando Network" set up by Kagame in order to bring down the plane. As soon as the report was published, however, Ruzigana was on the phone to the Rwandan newspaper *The New Times* to deny he had said any such thing. "I told [Brugière] that I was based in Umutara province", Ruzigana expostulated, "and didn't see who shot down the plane." Inevitably, French legal sources responded that Ruzigana had only withdrawn his testimony after receiving death threats – the implication being that these threats emanated from Rwanda.

Rwanda's response was to cut diplomatic ties with France. In the battle to establish control over which version of events will survive – ultimately, a battle over history itself – neither side looks willing to back down. With responsibility for genocide at stake, there's every reason to believe that the argument will continue.

Tutsis, Hutus and Anglo-Saxons

The most puzzling aspect of the anti-French allegations is why France would have been so involved with the Habyarimana regime in the first place. Rwanda hadn't even been a French colony – it was Belgian. There's no oil there, either. (Lake Kivu may have its methane resources, but that hardly stacks up against the oil reserves of Iraq, for example.) Some analysts think Habyarimana may have helped launder arms shipments for Mitterrand, allowing France to evade embargoes. They claim that France thus began to see his government as a key regional ally, and to see Rwanda as a kind of giant military staging post, a strategic base from which to pursue its political – or rather, mineral – interests in neighbouring Congo. Rwanda's foreign minister, Charles Murigande, had a different theory. France wanted to blame his government, he fumed, because "they cannot face their own guilt". And France supported the genocidal regime because it had "this obsession with Anglo-Saxons".

Clearly, these Anglo-Saxons are not the Dark-Age invaders of the British Isles. Thanks to Belgian colonization, Rwanda was part of *la Francophonie*, the loose grouping

THE TUTSI–HIMA WORLD-DOMINATION MEGA-PLOT

Just like the Nazis, Hutu extremists used racial conspiracy theories to prepare the ground for slaughter. Among Hutu nationalists, the historic dominance of the "aristocratic" Tutsis in Rwanda is often read as part of a broader struggle for racial ascendancy, with native "Bantu" Africans on one side, and alien "Hamitic" people from the Nile region on the other. The idea has its roots in colonial-era theories of migration, in which the Tutsis were thought to have their origins in Ethiopia or Sudan. Such "tribal" divisions were artificially exacerbated by the colonial powers to implement policies of divide and conquer.

Today, racial divisions are deeply rooted. On the one hand, the stereotypically taller, paler Tutsis are accused of considering themselves a neo-Aryan master race, and of plotting regional domination on a Nazi model. Even today, leaders such as Rwandan president Paul Kagame and Ugandan president Yoweri Museveni are regularly accused of conspiring to revive a supposed Hamitic or "Hima" empire in the Great Lakes region. In defending the eastern part of the Congo against a combined Ugandan–Rwandan invasion in 1998, even the Congolese president Laurent Kabila resorted to this kind of rhetoric.

In the same breath that they're accused of master race ambitions, the Tutsis are also reviled as subhuman aliens, much as the Nazis slurred European Jews. In a clear echo of European anti-Semitism, Tutsis are described by their enemies as insect-like or reptile-like, and sometimes as practitioners of evil with a particular thirst for human – and non-Tutsi – blood. In the late 1990s, a high-level source in the Congolese government was quoted as broadcasting an appeal to Congolese forces to "smash the vermin, the scraps, the microbes". The Tutsi, he said, risk "living the same sad experience as the Jews did. They are perfidious, rancorous and bloodthirsty. Vermin – yes, I call them vermin – who spoil and poison the body of our nation, which we must eradicate." Hitler himself could hardly have attained such flights of intemperance.

With further echoes of neo-Nazism, the very same people who advocated the killing of Tutsis now claim that the Rwandan genocide was itself the result of a further, Machiavellian Tutsi conspiracy. Like Holocaust deniers (see p.101), the extremists state that the Rwandan genocide never really happened, or that only a few thousand Tutsis were killed, or that the RPF (Rwandan Patriotic Front) murdered many more Hutus when they invaded. The so-called "Rwandan genocide", they say, is a fabrication aimed at furthering the Tutsis' imperial schemes.

of French-speaking African nations. France tends to view these countries as satellites of the mother ship. But while Habyarimana and his Hutu-dominated government had the expected ties with France, Paul Kagame and his RPF rebels were based across the border in Uganda – a former British colony whose key links were with the UK. This all meant that Kagame himself was part of what the French call the "Anglo-Saxon" world.

Scarred by the losses of its North African and Indochinese colonies, France was determined not to lose its toehold in Central Africa as well. High-ranking French soldiers even referred to the RPF rebels as the "Black Khmers", bringing back uncomfortable memories of the fall of French Indochina and its subsequent sufferings under the communist Khmer Rouge (or "Red Khmers"). Telegrams and memos published in the French press reveal that President Mitterrand feared that if Rwanda was lost to the barbarians, other Francophone countries might follow suit. (Immediately after the Rwandan genocide, this is precisely what happened in the Democratic Republic of the Congo, where the dictatorship of former French ally Mobutu Sese Seko was brought down by English-speaking Laurent Kabila, with the help of Paul Kagame and others.) A French president who reportedly commented "in such countries, genocide is not too important" might not be too choosy about the methods taken to ensure Rwanda stayed within the fold.

UNhelpful: Booh-Booh and Boutros Boutros

The darkest allegation of all in relation to the genocide is that the international community knew what was coming and decided not to do anything about it. The only alternative explanation is negligence and incompetence of the highest order. Lieutenant-General Roméo Dallaire, the commander of UNAMIR, the United Nations' peacekeeping force in Rwanda, has said he repeatedly warned UN headquarters of the approaching dangers in early 1994. He appealed for the doubling of his forces, arguing that this could avert the impending catastrophe. In fact, UNAMIR's numbers were slashed from 2500 to just 270 during the course of the genocide.

Dallaire's harrowing memoir of the genocide, *Shake Hands with the Devil*, is not kind to the head of the UNAMIR mission, former Cameroonian foreign minister Jacques-Roger Booh-Booh. According to Dallaire, Booh-Booh played down the crisis to UN chiefs in New York and had links to ministers in Habyarimana's government. Such contacts are the essence of diplomacy, but suspicious minds construe bias or even collusion from them. The RPF, for example, has claimed to have intercepted messages between Booh-Booh and Hutu military chiefs. Booh-Booh, for his part, asserts that Dallaire was far too close to the RPF, to the extent of providing it with military intelligence and concealing details of its last offensive.

Booh-Booh's very appointment caused some firebrands to claim that the UN was actually complicit in the genocide – if only by turning a blind eye. Booh-Booh owed his job to the UN secretary general, Boutros Boutros-Ghali, who was an experienced Rwandan observer. (As Egypt's deputy foreign minister, Boutros-Ghali had worked on a multimillion dollar arms deal with Rwanda in the early 1990s.) Dallaire's cables to the Security Council went through Boutros-Ghali, and some council members have claimed that the much-disputed "genocide fax" – allegedly detailing the precise dangers Rwanda was imminently facing – never made it through. But then, the Security Council had many reasons to claim ignorance. How else could its inaction be excused?

In fact, many institutional forces were conspiring, with varying degrees of passivity, to paralyse the Security Council and ensure that action wasn't taken to avert the genocide before it happened. Booh-Booh and Boutros Boutros-Ghali were only pieces in a larger game. In the countdown to the genocide, influential Rwandan Roman Catholics, many of them linked to the Hutu extremists, were vociferously arguing that fears of impending catastrophe were exaggerated – as were the governments of France, Belgium, the US, Canada and the UK.

The genocidal mega-war

The most extreme conspiracy theories see a controlling hand behind the international community's blindness to Rwanda. The genocide was, they say, the result of a long-established colonial policy of reducing the world's population. Poor people and black people were the prime targets – so Rwandans ideally fit the bill. In this genocidal mega-war, Rwanda was merely one campaign; AIDS was another (see p.290). Conspiracists disagree on the identity of the conspirators behind this master plan, but the top candidates are the Club of Rome and the Bilderberg Group (see p.250), working through agencies such as the UN, World Bank and IMF (see p.247) – not forgetting, of course, the sinister World Wildlife Fund (see p.114).

According to the January 1995 issue of the LaRouchite magazine *The New Federalist*: "the entire Rwandan genocide had nothing to do with tribal or civil warfare. It was a British-orchestrated assassination and invasion program. And the WWF administered parks played a pivotal role in the slaughter." One only has to look at the suspicious proximity of the supposed "gorilla protection programmes" in neighbouring Uganda and Congo. These wildlife parks were, it seems, nothing less than disguised military bases, launching points for an invasion by the army of the Ugandan president and "British puppet" Yoweri Museveni who, at the time of the genocide, was being "run" by Britain's overseas development minister, Baroness Lynda Chalker.

SOURCES

Books

Roméo Dallaire **Shake Hands with the Devil: The Failure of Humanity in Rwanda** (2003). This eyewitness account of the genocide from the commander of the UN's peacekeeping troops is, by turns, grimly realistic and so appalling that it beggars belief. An essay in compassion, shame and sheer terror.

Philip Gourevitch **We Wish to Inform You that Tomorrow We Will Be Killed with Our Families: Stories from Rwanda** (1998). A journalist's politically sophisticated and compassionate account of the genocide, and the international policies that failed to prevent it.

Linda Melvern **Conspiracy to Murder** (2004). Conscientious exposé of how meticulously the genocide was planned by Hutu extremists within the Rwandan government. Melvern had unique access to sources such as the International Criminal Tribunal for Rwanda and the UN's own peacekeeping archive, and she reveals the prominent role of John Major's UK government in the international "conspiracy of silence" that allowed the killings to continue unchecked.

Pierre Péan **Black Furies, White Liars** (2005). This hyper-revisionist account accuses the RPF of initiating a counter-genocide, and labels Paul Kagame a war criminal. It also posits an Anglo-Saxon conspiracy to undermine French interests in Africa.

Gérard Prunier **The Rwanda Crisis: History of a Genocide** (1995). The first major treatment of the genocide is now dated, but still acute and superb on Rwanda's history.

Dina Temple-Raston **Justice on the Grass: A Story of Genocide and Redemption** (2005). Focusing on the war crimes trials of three journalists, this powerful book highlights the crucial role of the Rwandan media in stoking the flames of the genocide.

Films

Michael Caton-Jones **Shooting Dogs** (2005). This British feature uses documentary techniques – it was shot on location using many local actors – to powerful effect. It dramatizes Rwanda's abandonment by the outside world by putting two idealistic Europeans at the centre of the events. The US release title was *Beyond the Gates*.

Terry George **Hotel Rwanda** (2004). Often called the African *Schindler's List*, this film is sentimental but justifiably so. It tells a version of the true story of Kigali's Hotel des Mille Collines, which sheltered hundreds of refugees from the genocide.

Websites

Ⓦ **www.assemblee-nationale.fr/dossiers/rwanda/rapport.asp** The French parliamentary commission report, from December 1998.

Ⓦ **www.francewatcher.org** Edited by African exiles, this site exists "to expose France, which has so far done an excellent job of being a thug at night and an enlightened sophisticate during the day ... and to explore and to implement non-violent strategies for weakening and terminating the French Empire in Africa."

Ⓦ **www.hrw.org/reports/1999/rwanda/Geno1-3-11.htm#P774_296641** The enormous 1999 report by Human Rights Watch, *Leave None to Tell the Story*, exposes how France, Belgium, the US and the UN all failed to act on what they knew about the impending genocide.

Ⓦ **www.lindamelvern.com** The investigative journalist's page includes online versions of key articles on Rwanda.

The Kremlin and the Chechen rebels

"Kremlinology", the old-fashioned art of divining which way the wind was blowing in Russia from almost imperceptible clues, was supposed to have died with the collapse of the USSR. Arguably, however, the philosophy that underpinned Kremlinology long predated the Soviet Union; indeed, it may have shaped the twilight-grey shades of Communist politics, rather than vice versa. Former KGB chief, former prime minister and former president Vladimir Putin is a man widely considered to.be an *éminence grise* of the Kremlin's black arts. In May 2008, President Putin was succeeded by his anointed successor, Deputy Prime Minister Dmitry Medvedev. In a game of musical thrones, Putin is set to become prime minister again, but many suspect he will remain very much the presidential puppeteer. His time as prime minister and president were characterized by a series of bloody disasters and terrorist atrocities, several of which were linked to Chechnya. Some observers, however, claim to discern an appalling conspiracy of terror, and trace the chain of events back to Putin himself. Whether such events will continue remains to be seen.

A Russian conspiracy in the Caucasus?

During the summer of 1999, Vladimir Putin, then Russia's new acting prime minister, was confronted by renewed conflict in the unstable mass of mini-republics in the Caucasus region, in southern Russia. Militant Muslim forces from Chechnya – the tiny breakaway republic that, during its fight for independence between 1994 and 1996, fought the Russian Army to a standstill and caused President Boris Yeltsin to hit the vodka bottle even harder – were raiding next-door Dagestan.

That August, BBC Online reported a rumour that the Dagestan incursion was a "well-orchestrated conspiracy involving senior figures associated with the Kremlin". By that reckoning, the leader of the insurgency, Chechen warlord Shamil Basayev, was acting on Kremlin orders to create trouble. The incursion served to justify a state of emergency, and the postponing of Russian parliamentary elections in December, while also providing a chance for Putin to blood himself by driving the insurgents back into Chechnya. The BBC's Dagestan correspondent gave more credence to the notion that militant Islamic forces were broadening their *jihad* against "infidel" Russians, and that the incursion was the first phase in building an Islamic republic of states through which Chechnya could gain access to the Caspian Sea. Three years after fending off the Russians at horrific cost, he suggested, Chechen separatists were harbouring suicidal delusions of grandeur.

Someone's bombing Moscow

Then the bombings began. On September 4, 1999, a bomb destroyed an apartment building in the southern Russian city of Buinaksk, killing 62 people. Two more apartment blocks were blown up, this time in Moscow, on September 9 and 13, killing 222 men, women and children in their beds. Finally, on September 16, a further 17 people were killed by a blast in the southern city of Volgodonsk. With impressive speed, the Russian secret service, the FSB (the successor of the KGB), posted a computer-generated picture all over the capital of a Chechen man, Achimez Gochiyaev, who had rented ground-floor space in the Moscow blocks. According to the FSB, Gochiyaev was working for Chechen warlords Shamil Basayev and Khattab.

On October 1, 1999, Putin ordered a wholesale "anti-terrorist operation" in Chechnya, and the Russian Army moved in en masse. Overnight, Putin's public image changed from being a grey nonentity handpicked by Yeltsin to a powerful macho leader. Promising to restore stability to Chechnya, he won the presidential election in March 2000 with over half the vote. His Communist opponent and runner-up, Gennady Zyuganov, accused the government of falsifying the results.

A fifth bomb is foiled

The Russian authorities, however, never produced any significant evidence that Chechen terrorists were behind the Moscow bombings. No terrorist group claimed responsibility, and no one has been brought to trial. Some men have been arrested, but none of the alleged "ringleaders". Respected British journalist John Sweeney reported that bulldozers obliterated the second bombsite just three days after the blast, destroying any remaining evidence.

The strangest detail of all was the "thwarting" of a fifth bomb in the southern city of Ryazan. A resident of an apartment block there saw a car with a Moscow licence plate, containing a Russian-looking couple who drove off when approached. The police were called, and in the building's basement they discovered three sacks of hexogen powder – the explosive used in the other four bombings – and a timing device. The building was evacuated. FSB men confiscated the sacks, and announced the next day, a hundred miles away in Moscow, that the whole thing was an "exercise" and that the sacks contained sugar. Two Russians were arrested and then released.

Considering the fact that real bombs were blowing up real people, that's a hell of an "exercise". The Ryazan police were adamant that the timer and hexogen they discovered were real. If it was just a drill, why were the two Russians arrested at all? One resident said that he didn't know who was behind the foiled attack, but pointed out that "the government started bombing Chechnya the next day".

War damage in the Chechen capital, Grozny, April 1995.

Pointing the finger

The mystery of the "fifth bomb" was reported by John Sweeney, the *LA Times* and author David Satter, who argued in *Darkness at Dawn* that it made absolutely no sense for Chechens to blow up apartment blocks. In March 2002, exiled ex-oligarch and former Putin ally Boris Berezovsky told the press in his new home of London that the FSB had carried out the bombings, with Putin's complicity, in order to justify a second Chechen war and boost Putin's profile. As evidence, he presented documents showing that the Russian Explosives Conversion Centre had, in 1999 and 2000, purchased large quantities of hexogen from military units, and shipped it all over Russia.

Berezovsky repeated his charges in the film *Assassination of Russia*, while the Russian newspaper *Novaya Gazeta* quoted GRU agent Alexei Galkin as saying that the FSB and GRU (Russia's military intelligence service) were behind all the blasts. According to an Agence France Presse report in July 2002, the chief suspect, Achimez Gochiayev – who comes not from Chechnya but Karachayevo-Cherkessia, and remains in hiding – claimed that a school friend thought to be an FSB agent had advised him to rent the premises in the apartment block. Former KGB colonel Konstantin Preobrazhensky commented that "Chechen rebels were incapable of organizing a series of bombings without help from high-ranking Moscow officials".

The FSB, however, denied all involvement in the bombings. Berezovsky, for one, had an axe to grind. He had fled from Putin's Russia to the UK, finding himself wanted for "economic crimes" despite having used his TV stations to help Putin become president. From his London base, Berezovsky criticized both Putin and his government, which, he argued, had made covert KGB killings an overt state policy. Claims that the bombings were the work of the FSB were fleshed out in greater detail in *Blowing Up Russia: Terror from Within*, written by Yuri Felshtinsky and a certain exiled ex-FSB lieutenant-colonel, Alexander Litvinenko (see p.65). The book, published with Berezovsky's help in London (but banned and burned in Russia), essentially put almost every woe to befall post-Soviet Russia down to some nefarious FSB plot. In particular, it claimed that the Moscow bombings "conspiracy theory" (as *The Times* called it) was used as the justification for a new Chechen war and for the replacement of Yeltsin's decadent democracy with a strong, authoritarian Putin presidency. Yet another former FSB officer, Mikhail Trepashkin, who was a lawyer in Moscow by 2003, also uncovered FSB links to the bombings, but he was arrested under questionable circumstances in October 2003, just before he was due to present his findings in court.

In September 2004, a *Financial Times* article by Martin Wolf argued that "we make common cause with Putin at our peril", because "the bombings that preceded his first election and then as conveniently ceased gave him the presidency". The British Helsinki Human Rights Group responded that "Boris Berezovsky's well-funded conspiracy theory" overlooked the fact that the Chechen separatists' invasion of Dagestan had already happened.

The Moscow siege

On October 23, 2002, a 41-strong gang of Chechen rebels took over Moscow's Dubrovka theatre. The hostage-takers, armed and strapped with explosives, were seeking to focus the world's attention on the plight of Chechnya. The siege ended when Russian security services pumped a mysterious gas into the theatre, knocking out everyone inside, and then stormed the building. They refused to disclose what kind of gas it was, even to the hospitals treating the hostages. A total of 129 civilians, plus all the rebels, died in an incident that the Russians called their own 9/11.

Although all the hostage-takers were among the dead, they were not killed by the gas, which had successfully immobilized them. Instead, according to British Conservative MP Dr Julian Lewis, they were shot in cold blood. As he asked the House of Commons in June 2003: "If those people were so incapacitated … that they could not explode their devices, why did the Russian authorities not act [to take them alive], if not from any sense of simple humanity, then from the common-sense desire for the intelligence that might be gained from interrogating captives who had mounted such a damaging, dangerous and destructive operation … Why were those considerations put aside and the people executed on the spot while unconscious?"

That question was prompted by former Soviet dissident Vladimir Bukovsky and allegations reported by Agence France Presse and *Novaya Gazeta* that April which were quoted by Lewis in Parliament. A Chechen rebel leader and former Russian spy had claimed that former Chechen journalist Khanpach Terkipayev was among the hostage-takers and that he had been placed there by Russian security services. Moscow supposedly needed the siege because Western governments were promoting the idea of negotiating with Chechnya's separatists. Dr Lewis warned dissenters that "all I would say is that that is not just my conspiracy theory", adding that the Moscow apartment bombings "conveniently" provided the perfect *casus belli* for the second Russian invasion of Chechnya.

Murder and mayhem – and the mysterious Basayev

The Caucasus region seemed to be calming down, until on August 28, 2004, two Tupolev passenger jets on internal Russian flights crashed within hours of each other, killing ninety people. Two female Chechen suicide bombers, one aboard each plane, were officially blamed, and when a bomb subsequently exploded at a Moscow metro station, Chechens were blamed once again.

Then came the worst atrocity of all. On September 1, 2004, 32 men and women, armed with guns and home-made bombs, took over an elementary school in Beslan in the state of North Ossetia, which bordered Chechnya. A thousand hostages, most of them children, were held for three days before the siege ended amid explosions and gunfire. Over half of the 330 people killed were children. According to a website that says it serves as his official mouthpiece, www.kavkazcenter.com, the Chechen warlord Shamil Basayev claimed responsibility for the plane crashes and the Beslan school seizure. Holding the Russians accountable because of their war in Chechnya, he promised more to come.

Vilified in the Russian media for his alleged links to Al Qaeda, Basayev was called "Russia's homegrown version of Osama bin Laden" by CBS News. He first came to prominence when he seized control of a Russian hospital in 1995. Although a hundred hostages died in the ensuing battle with security services, Basayev and his men managed to escape. He was also said to have claimed responsibility for the Moscow theatre siege and for the killing of Kremlin-backed Chechen president Akhmad Kadyrov in 1999, but Basayev blamed people from Dagestan for the Moscow bombings.

Although Basayev was thought to have left Chechnya just a couple of times in a decade, the Americans were sufficiently worried about him for Secretary of State Colin Powell to have called him, in August 2003, a "threat to US national security", as well as to the American people, policy and economic interests. Tall, often depicted with a peaked cap, a hedge of a beard and a massive cigar, Basayev resembled a youthful Fidel Castro. His most distinctive feature being that he had only one leg, having lost the other while escaping Russian forces who chased him through a minefield in 1999.

Before his death in 2006, the Russian authorities had repeatedly failed either to catch Basayev or to forestall his attacks, despite offering a $10 million reward. Some liberal Russian political figures alleged that the Russian government didn't really want to capture Basayev at all, as his presence and antics justified continued fighting in Chechnya. Anatol Lieven of the Carnegie Endowment for International Peace dismissed such rumours as similar to suggestions that President Bush's administration was behind 9/11 (see p.395). As he told the Associated Press news agency: "You can oppose these conflicts without yielding to irrational conspiracy theories." Ultimately, however, Basayev was taken out by Russian agents. In July 2006, he and his cohorts were travelling in convoy in Ingushetia, when they were blown up by a truck bomb – a pretty nifty hit job on the second most elusive terrorist of the decade.

A third force

Despite Basayev's claim, and despite the widespread assumption that Chechens were responsible, Russia's defence minister Sergei Ivano admitted that there were no Chechens among the hostage-takers at Beslan. Former Chechen president Aslan Mashkadov's envoy Akhmed Zakayev denied

THE GREAT GAME: AFGHANISTAN AND CASPIAN GAS

In October 2001, a US-led military force invaded war-torn Afghanistan in order to overthrow the cruel, oppressive Taliban regime, which had refused to hand over Osama bin Laden, the mastermind behind 9/11. By Christmas, the Taliban had been brought down, and a new UN-backed government installed. Instead of being the first victory in George W. Bush's "war on terror", however, perhaps this was just the latest round in what Rudyard Kipling called the "Great Game" – the secret struggle to dominate Central Asia.

Some conspiracy theorists argue that Afghanistan was invaded not because it was a haven for terrorists, but because it was an invaluable transit route for oil and gas from the huge reserves in the landlocked Central Asian states of Azerbaijan, Kazakhstan, Turkmenistan and Uzbekistan. Rather than pipe their fuel through such undependable countries as Iran and Russia, Western oil companies suggested building pipelines to Pakistan, via Afghanistan. For that to be a viable proposition, however, the Taliban would have to be removed. And removed they were, with such alacrity that one has to suspect that the forward planning was in place before 9/11 provided the excuse to move in.

In a BBC report broadcast just before the invasion of Afghanistan, analyst Malcolm Haslett attacked this hypothesis as being "flawed" and favoured by those with "a fondness for conspiracy theories". While "the importance of Central Asian oil and gas has suddenly been noticed", he declared, Afghanistan is not the only potential route. Thus, a pipeline has been built from the Caspian Sea in Azerbaijan through Georgia to the Mediterranean coast of Turkey. In any case, Haslett argued, Afghanistan still isn't stable enough for a pipeline, and Western powers have rendered pipeline deals considerably less likely with their criticisms of "human rights abuses" by Central Asia's authoritarian regimes.

In fact, Central Asian fuel reserves had hardly been "suddenly noticed". In December 1997, for example, Taliban officials met in Texas with oil corporation Unocal to discuss the construction of a gas pipeline from Turkmenistan across Afghanistan to Pakistan. Unocal announced that it had agreed with Turkmenistan to sell its gas and with Pakistan to buy it, and had begun training Afghan staff to build and maintain the line. A BBC correspondent described the deal as part of an "international scramble" to profit from developing the rich Caspian Sea energy resources.

An April 1998 paper from the James A. Baker III Institute for Public Policy at Rice University reported: "Senior Administration officials have delivered well-publicized policy declarations on the importance of Central Asia and the Caucasus to the United States. And a US military exercise in the region, though long-planned and small in scope, has been cited both there

Chechen responsibility, blaming "a third force that brought Russian president Vladimir Putin to power" for all three incidents. Their motive was supposedly to destabilize the North Caucasus by creating animosity between the Christians of North Ossetia and the Muslims of Chechnya, thereby justifying the continued presence of Russian soldiers.

In Internet chatrooms, a story circulated that the Beslan hostage-takers were not "international terrorists", but local mercenaries let into the school by local police who knew them. Once inside, they dug up arms from under the gymnasium floor, where they had been buried by builders months before. By this reckoning, the ensuing massacre was simply a mistake. A bomb detonated by accident, bringing down the roof and panicking parents and police into storming the building.

In late January 2005, British newspaper *The Independent* reported that hundreds of Beslan residents were blocking roads to protest about what they called "official apathy" over the atrocity, and to denounce suspected Russian complicity in the attack. On January 28, Interfax News and the BBC reported that Aleksandr Torshin, the deputy speaker of the Federation Council (upper house) and the chairman of the Russian parliamentary commission investigating Beslan, told journalists that "a terrorist atrocity on a scale such as this could not have been committed without accomplices". He stated that the accomplices must have held ranks higher than major or lieutenant colonel.

According to Vladimir Kulakov, another senator and commission member, the terrorists had accomplices not only in Beslan, but also at federal (i.e. Russian) level, and

and here as a signal of our strategic interest in the region." According to some observers, the paper noted, that interest was seen as compelling enough for the region to require "a new and more assertive US policy towards it ... Why? Oil and gas. The Caspian Basin is rich – perhaps very rich – in both."

As for the need for stability, it was originally felt that if the Taliban regime could deliver it, that would be good enough. Pakistan's prime minister Nawaz Sharif argued that if the US recognized the Taliban and Unocal was permitted to build the pipeline, this would create a virtuous circle of investment and stability. Things began to go wrong when President Bill Clinton authorized the bombing of Al Qaeda terrorist camps in Afghanistan in late 1998, in response to the bombing of US embassies in Tanzania and Kenya. World opinion turned decisively against the Taliban when they started blowing up historic Buddhist statues, and 9/11 completed the process.

Post-Taliban, the first US envoy to Afghanistan was former Unocal risk analyst Zalmay Khalilzad. An Afghan émigré, Khalilzad had previously been employed by the Reagan administration and Unocal to work with the Taliban in connection with their anti-Soviet activities and the proposed pipeline respectively. (A founding member of the Project for the New American Century, see p.418, he subsequently served as George W. Bush's special envoy to post-war Iraq and was finally named US ambassador to Afghanistan in September 2003.) As envoy to Afghanistan, Khalilzad worked hand-in-glove with interim president Hamid Karzai, himself a former oil industry analyst, as feasibility studies for oil and gas pipelines were drawn up. Karzai met with Turkmenistan's President Niyazov and Pakistan's President Musharraf in 2002 to approve a gas pipeline from Turkmenistan's Dauletabad gas field to the Pakistani port of Gwadar.

Present-day Afghanistan remains deeply troubled. The pipeline was given the go-ahead in late 2002, when its projected $2.2 billion cost was worth over ten percent of the country's GDP and more than all foreign aid contributions combined. Achieving peaceful stability was apparently so close at hand that the deal was struck, although US and UK troops were still hammering away at pockets of Al Qaeda resistance and tribal groups battling for territory in what was viewed as the post-Taliban aftermath. But the Taliban never really went away. The pipeline's construction was supposed to start in earnest in 2006, but two years later, large areas through which it was supposed to run were still under Taliban control. In early 2008, suggestions appeared in the US and UK media about possibly negotiating with the Taliban; after all, if they can't be gotten rid of, then surely their presence shouldn't be allowed to forfeit the fossil-fuel fortunes of others in Kabul, Islamabad and Houston?

that the latter were "still in their posts". Meanwhile, an amateur video was given to CBS TV apparently showing talks in progress between the ex-president of Ingushetia, Ruslan Aushev, and the terrorists. How a US TV channel had acquired this video was not made clear. Various investigations into the atrocity drew widely different conclusions: Russian prosecutors concluded, in late 2005, that the security services were not at fault for triggering the mass murder, whereas another report by a Russian MP said they had gone into the school with all guns blazing.

Putin refused any public inquiry into Beslan lest it become too much of a show, instead opting for a parliamentary commission, which, in December 2006, directed blame at the local police. However, the *Sunday Herald* reported that two MPs involved in the inquiry denounced the investigation as a "cover-up", saying that it served only to back up the Kremlin's "fabricated" version of events. Grass-roots efforts demanding further investigations or alleging official incompetence and recalcitrance over the event and its aftermath have fared badly. As of 2008, the "Mothers of Beslan" activist group had been sidelined, while a bid by the "Voice of Beslan" group to have an international investigation culminated in the group being charged with "extremism".

Putin blames the US

On September 4, 2004, responding to the Beslan school siege, Putin told Russia that the country's borders were no longer safe "from East or West". He accused the US of supporting terrorists, trying to disarm Russia's nuclear capabilities and scheming to diminish its territory. "Some would like to cut a juicy piece of our pie", as he put it; "terrorism is just one instrument they use". The allegation seemed strange in view of the official US stance depicting Basayev as being in cohorts with Osama bin Laden, and the fact that, at that same moment, the siege was being cited at the Republican National Convention as the kind of Islamic extremism that justified the global "War on Terror".

The conspiracist magazine *The Insider*, on the other hand, depicted Beslan as forming part of the "terror" war that enabled Putin to become even more authoritarian, diverting attention from the economic liberalization that privatized medicine, closed schools, worsened unemployment and failed to deliver pensions. Putin was also busy reinforcing the powers of the FSB, creating an anti-terrorism ministry, tightening the grip of the Security Council, and reinstating the "vertical" rule of the Communist era by appointing regional governors instead of having them elected.

There's oil in them there mountains

So what makes Chechnya and the other tiny fragmented mountain states of the Caucasus – like Ossetia (north and south), Ingushetia, Kabardino-Balkaria and Karachaevo-Cherkessia – so important to the Russians? The Chechens themselves are in no doubt. After Dzhokar Dudayev was elected president of Chechnya in 1991, on a constitution based on "US principles" of government, his administration suffered a dozen assassinations and coup attempts, which he claimed were Russian-backed. Then came the first Russian invasion, from 1994 to 1996. Dudayev wrote in *The Washington Post* in 1995 that "the lure and importance of the Chechen oil and pipeline [through the Caucasus states] have prompted Moscow to use brutal force … to seize control of our capital Grozny".

Putin was clearly alarmed by the increasing US military and economic presence in the independent ex-Soviet states of Azerbaijan and Georgia, just south of the Russian Caucasus – which constitute a critical route for oil and gas pipelines from the Caspian Sea and Iran – and by further NATO encroachment into former Soviet satellites. Both Russia and the US have described Azerbaijan's Pankisi Gorge as a hotbed of Islamic militancy that justifies intervention from both countries.

The poison of power

In retrospect, Putin's complaint that territories were being encouraged to secede from Russian influence was given an eerie resonance by events on September 5, 2004, in the former Soviet state of Ukraine. With Beslan still dominating the headlines, Ukraine's opposition leader Viktor Yushchenko was invited to dine with the chiefs of the country's security service. In a grisly assassination attempt, he was fed soup containing dioxin, which swiftly turned his handsome face into a ghoulish mask. Yushchenko survived, after treatment in Austria, but "lost" Ukraine's presidential election in November. Worldwide attention then focused on Kiev, as demonstrators poured into the streets. It was eventually declared that the first ballot had been rigged in favour of the incumbent pro-Putin prime minister, Viktor Yanukovich, and Yushchenko won a re-run in January.

Had Yushchenko died as planned, in September, would the wider world have noticed? And who stood to gain the most from a pro-Putin premier in Ukraine? According to the official Russian perspective, the US has been exerting too much untoward influence in the country. Thus, in 2003 and 2004, the Americans spent $65 million in Ukraine subsidizing democratic institutes and meddlesome NGOs – such as the Poland–America–Ukraine Cooperation Initiative – that the Russians see as "blatantly" favouring Yushchenko. Moscow's incandescence over Kiev's courting of the West has been stoked by continuing moves to have Ukraine join NATO. In April 2008, US president George W. Bush reiterated to Yushchenko the benefits of Ukrainian membership of NATO. Meanwhile, Yushchenko's presidency became most notable to the wider world for a series of bad-tempered confrontations with Russia, as the latter used its gargantuan gas supplies through Ukraine as a political weapon.

A war without end

Estimates for the total number of Chechen men, women and children who have died either directly or indirectly since 1994 from the two Chechen wars have reached as high as 250,000. Tens of thousands of Russian soldiers have also been killed in campaigns that have proved more costly than the Soviet invasion of Afghanistan. While questions may have been raised among the international community, however, neither the governments of Yeltsin nor Putin have received any significant censure or opprobrium. What concerns have been expressed have focused principally on the threats Putin's centralizing reforms pose to Russian democracy. Thus, in January 2005, US Secretary of State Condoleezza Rice described "the concentration of power in the Kremlin to the detriment of other institutions in Russia" as "a real problem", saying that "the path to democracy" was uneven and far from assured.

Alarm has also been voiced about diminishing media freedoms, the persecution of Russia's oligarchs and Russian attempts to influence Ukraine's elections. Meanwhile, the country's GDP has been growing fast, thanks largely to rising sales of oil and gas. Russian foreign minister Sergei Lavrov has dismissed all such criticisms, arguing that critics merely hated the idea of Russia becoming economically strong and independent, and that they wanted a new Cold War. Nevertheless, within three months of each other in 2006, three of Putin's principal opponents and critics of the Chechen war – separatist leader Shamil Basayev, journalist Anna Politkovskaya and exiled ex-FSB lieutenant-colonel Alexander Litvinenko (see p.65) – were dead. Many questions were also raised – and remain unanswered – about the conduct and veracity of the vote in Russia's 2008 general election, which resulted in a "shoo-in" for Putin's chosen successor, Dmitry Medvedev.

SOURCES

Books

Anna Politkovskaya Putin's Russia (2004). Since her tragic murder in her apartment block in 2006, Russian journalist Politkovskaya has been remembered not just for her bravery in exposing the darker side of her government's policies, but also for her ability to be in the right place at the right time. As well as witnessing atrocities in Chechnya, she was a negotiator at the Moscow siege, and she might have made it to Beslan, had she not been nearly fatally poisoned en route.

Websites

- **eng.terror99.ru/publications/072.htm** The place to look for all the latest theories about the Moscow bombings.
- **www.theinsider.org/mailing/article.asp?id=575** Interesting piece on the political capital Putin gained from the Beslan school siege.
- **www.truth-and-justice.info/theater.html** A selection of alternative perspectives on what really happened in the Moscow theatre siege.

9/11: picking over the rubble

In August 2004, the Reuters news agency's polling company, Zogby International, found that just under half (49.3 percent, to be exact) of New York City residents believed that senior officials in the Bush administration knew about the 9/11 attacks in advance and had "consciously failed" to act. Others thought that President George W. Bush and his team were behind the attacks themselves. By May 2006, despite a stream of official (and unofficial) investigations, the proportion of Americans who believed that their

government and its 9-11 Commission "concealed or refused to investigate critical evidence that contradicts their official explanation", Zogby found, was 42 percent. As *Time* magazine put it, "This is not a fringe phenomenon. It is a mainstream political reality."

Like the assassination of John F. Kennedy (see p.22), the terrorist attack on New York's "Twin Towers" on September 11, 2001 delivered a massive, epoch-making shock to the US. It wasn't only America's sense of security that had been punctured, but its sense of self. Conspiracy theorists' response to 9/11 was also disturbingly similar to their response to JFK. When a second event of the magnitude of "JFK" came around, theorists just followed forty years of training. They pored over the tiniest minutiae of the attacks, chipping away at the timing, questioning the motives, and cross-referencing the words and actions of government officials. Each finding was released back into the churning conspiracy media – now swollen by the Internet and innumerable TV channels. Even the government seemed to be obeying the JFK rules, when it set up the 9-11 Commission to answer public doubts. Like the 1963–64 Warren Commission, of course, its 2004 report was dismissed as a whitewash. Perhaps its strongest charge was that the Clinton and Bush administrations had "not [been] well served" by the FBI and CIA.

The morning of September 11

At around 8.15am on September 11, 2001, American Airlines Flight 11 went off course shortly after it had taken off from Boston. Within five minutes, the plane's identification transponder beacon was switched off and a flight attendant alerted a colleague on the ground that hijackers had taken control. Almost twenty minutes later, at 8.38am, Boston air traffic controllers alerted North American Aerospace Defense Command (NORAD). At 8.42am, the transponder of United Airlines Flight 175 also blinked off, and at 8.46am, two F-15 fighter jets were scrambled from Otis Air National Guard base near Falmouth, Massachusetts.

At 8.46am, Flight 11's Boeing 767 ploughed into the North Tower of New York's iconic World Trade Center (WTC) building, striking on the north side, just fourteen stories from the top. Within a minute, a third plane, American Airlines Flight 77, changed its course and started heading

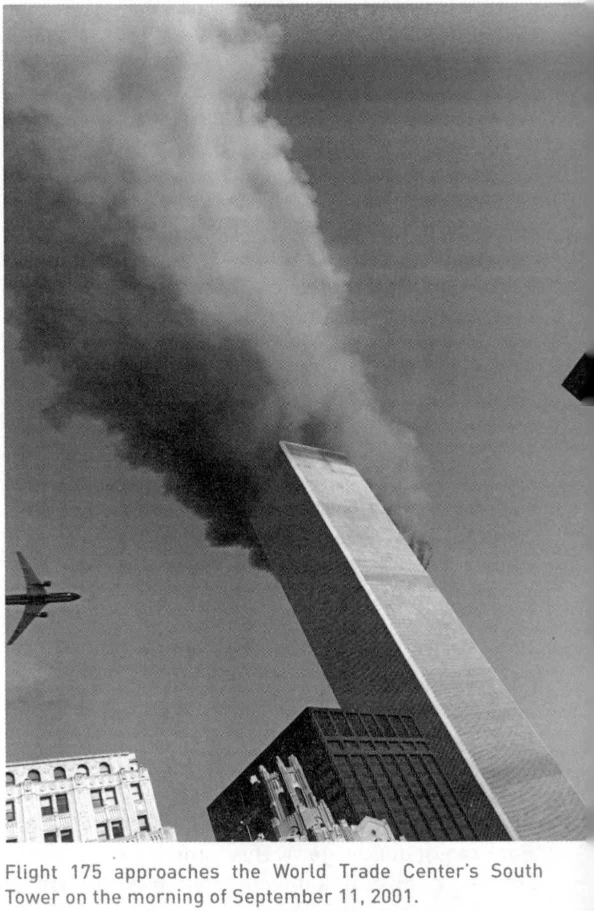

Flight 175 approaches the World Trade Center's South Tower on the morning of September 11, 2001.

back east. Meanwhile, confused and excited reporters were trying to make sense of the image of a burning North Tower on news networks around the world. Evacuations had already begun in the WTC's South Tower when, at 9.02am, it was struck in turn by another Boeing 767, as Flight 175 smashed into the corner of the building at the eightieth floor, causing a massive explosion of fuel and debris. It was watched by an audience of millions. Most were horrified; some cheered at this obviously symbolic blow against US hegemony and world capitalism.

At 9.06am, while President George W. Bush was sitting in on a second-grade class at a school in Florida, his chief of staff went over and whispered in his ear: "A second plane hit the other tower, and America's under attack." Bush continued with the now notorious "pet goat" reading lesson until 9.11am, when the two F-15s arrived over New York. At 9.30am, two F-16s were scrambled from Langley, Virginia, and five minutes later Flight 77 began a spiralling descent before smashing into the side of the Pentagon. At 9.59am, the South Tower of the World Trade Center pancaked down on itself, sending giant clouds of ash and smoke across Manhattan. Three minutes later, a fourth hijacked plane, United Airlines Flight 93, plunged into the ground near Shanksville, Pennsylvania. And at 10.23am, the North Tower of the World Trade Center finally collapsed.

Responsibility

In all, 2749 people were confirmed dead or missing as a result of the four hijackings and the WTC collapse. The Bush administration very quickly blamed the Al Qaeda network of extremist Islamic terrorists, and the charge was soon supported by a video discovered in Afghanistan in November 2001, on which Al Qaeda's chief, Osama bin Laden, admitted full knowledge of the attacks. Final confirmation only came in April 2002, however, when Khalid Sheikh Mohammed told Al Jazeera reporter Yosri Fouda: "I am the head of the Al Qaeda military committee … and yes, we did it." Tapes released in May 2006 featured Osama bin Laden proudly stating, "I was responsible for entrusting the nineteen brothers … with those raids."

Some felt he'd missed a trick. If he'd said instead that Al Qaeda had nothing to do with 9/11, conspiracy theorists would have had a field day. Even as early as April 2002, the Web was crawling with allegations of sinister conspiracies. Some even struggled out of the online mire onto the relative dry land of print. At the simplest level, some conspiracy claims seemed to stem from sheer disbelief. As millionaire's son and arch-9/11 conspiracy theorist Jimmy Walter bluntly announced: "It wasn't nineteen screw-ups from Saudi Arabia who couldn't pass flight school who defeated the United States with a set of box cutters." Or as Moroccan-born Canadian Adil Charkaoui put it, just after he was released from two years' detention on suspicion of being a terrorist: "I'm not an expert but from what I read some guy living in a cave doesn't have the means to plan an attack against the most powerful nation in the world."

Asked who he thought was responsible, Charkaoui told Federal Court Justice Simon Noël: "Maybe it was done by ultra-conservatives in the United States for economic gain. It was the world's biggest conspiracy." This was the classic "insider" theory, in which 9/11 is seen as a "false-flag operation" – a covert action carried out in order to be blamed on the enemy. There are plenty of alleged precedents – from the Reichstag fire of 1933 to Pearl Harbor (see p.360), and from Operation Northwoods (see p.358) to the Gulf of Tonkin incident (see p.373) – but relatively few commentators, however cynical, could bring themselves to believe that the Bush administration was warped (or still less brilliant) enough to actually plot the 9/11 attacks. The more common claim, therefore, was that Bush's team knew about the plan in advance, and for broad strategic reasons allowed it to go ahead.

The hijackers

The weakest link in the official version of events concerned the hijackers themselves. So little was known about them, and so much of what was known was classified. Why had they been allowed into the country, when it was discovered that only four out of the nineteen involved had managed to fill in a proper visa application form? Why had they enrolled in flight schools in the US when they could have learned more cheaply and more safely elsewhere? Was it true that this group of "religious extremists" had celebrated on the night of September 10 by calling up prostitutes and drinking in bars? Why had the ringleader, Mohamed Atta, tried to take incriminating documents with him in his luggage? (In the event, a delay meant his bags never made it onto the plane.) Why did Atta's instructions to his comrades include prayers whose content, according to journalist and Middle East expert Robert Fisk, "mystified every Muslim friend I know in the Middle East"? How had the hijackers managed to board the planes without showing up on CCTV cameras? And if they had used aliases, how had the FBI managed to track some of them down to their flight schools within a day of the Twin Towers' collapse? Were they already being watched? And allowed to proceed?

The Twin Towers collapse

Harder-core conspiracy theorists believe the Bush administration was more deeply involved. It didn't simply let the hijackers do their work, it actually caused, or assisted in, the collapse of the Twin Towers. Innumerable pundits, few with any expertise, claimed that the burning aviation fuel was not hot enough to melt the WTC's steel support structures. Scientific-minded conspiracists pointed out that the smoke was "sooty" and therefore not the product of a super-hot inferno. Firemen were quoted as saying that they had thought the fires could be controlled, and photos of workers looking out of gaping holes in the tower were used to demonstrate that the temperatures inside must have been tolerable. There were even reports of explosions and seismic tests showing that bombs had gone off just before the buildings collapsed, leading some to allege that the collapse was the result of a controlled demolition – either to save the rest of Manhattan, or to bury the evidence of an inside job. (Curiously, these bomb reports echo similar allegations made about the Oklahoma City Bombing, see p.228.)

Tales of jumpy seismic readings later turned out to be urban myths, but tapes of scared, dust-spattered witnesses describing "explosions" in the immediate aftermath of the attacks are now endlessly recycled as evidence. Some conspiracists see "squibs" of smoke puffing out below the collapsing levels in video footage of the collapse, which they read as proof of lower-level detonations. Naysayers interpret these puffs as airborne detritus being forced down lift-shafts or out of windows ahead of the main collapse. The supposed "free-fall" speed of the towers' collapse is seen as further evidence of a demolition job. A job which, presumably, must have involved charges being laid on every single floor. In fact, the falling building's kinetic energy would be of the same order as a small nuclear weapon – easily enough to cause it to collapse.

For questions related to exactly how and why the towers collapsed, it's hard to say definitively who is right. There just aren't any parallels. (In fact, engineers around the world have picked over the fine detail of the disaster to work out how they can build skyscrapers to withstand a similar catastrophe.) The National Institute for Standards and Technology answered many questions in their 2005 report. The fire, they found, was hot, very hot: some 1000°C, in fact. This, combined with impact damage, was enough to weaken the core columns and cause the floors to sag, which, in turn, weakened the perimeter columns. Eventually, the floors effectively unzipped themselves from their supports, before pancaking downwards in a catastrophic collapse.

The remaining questions are for the conspiracy theorists to answer. How were demolition charges inserted throughout the towers without anyone noticing? Why were no explosive remains found by clear-up teams? The theorists' answer, it seems, is simple: the towers' maintenance workers and administrative staff, as well as all the firefighters and volunteers involved in clearing up the site, were part of a truly mega-scale conspiracy.

Pod people

There's surprisingly little video footage of Flight 11 crashing into the North Tower, but every last frame has been picked over. In one version, a white-hot fireball or "mysterious burning object" visibly shoots ahead of the plane, trailing black smoke. Was this debris launched by aviation fuel exploding under pressure? Or is it evidence of the use of depleted uranium? Is a mysterious "pod" visible under Flight 175 in one photograph, as conspiracy theorist Dave vonKleist alleges? Experts in digital imagery have scornfully asserted that the famous "pods" and "whatzits" in the images are, in fact, "compression artefacts", or distortions inherent to digital imagery. When low-resolution images are hugely magnified, they're all the more noticeable. It's the twenty-first century version of Victorian fairy-hunters getting over-excited about a bit of lens flare. Conspiracists who take this kind of line are called "pod people" by their critics – especially those within the 9/11 truth movement. This kind of amateurish speculation, they mutter, detracts from the seriousness of their own suspicions.

The Pentagon under attack

VonKleist's 911inplanesite.com website, and associated video and DVD, are typical of post-disaster conspiracy theorizing. Photographs and video and audio footage – even seismographic readings – are ripped out of context and given a speculative forensic examination, and the inevitable "anomalies" revealed to an eager public. Few have tried it on with the World Trade Center, given the abundant film footage of a jetliner visibly slamming into the South Tower. When it comes to Flight 77 and the Pentagon, however, the field is wide open: all the relevant video and CCTV footage was initially confiscated by the FBI.

The notion that "there was no plane at the Pentagon" was bubbling away on conspiracy newsgroups within weeks of the disaster. However, the story hit the big time in April 2002, when French writer Thierry Meyssan published *L'eFfroyable imposture* or "The Horrifying Deception", (though the English title was *The Big Lie*). In Paris, the book sold out its initial print run of 20,000 within two hours of going on sale. Meyssan's theory sprang from photos of the Pentagon taken by a computer worker called Steve Riskus and posted in the immediate aftermath on the (now defunct) criticalthrash.com. The hole made in the outer wall looked bizarrely small for one punctured by a dive-bombing Boeing 757. As one French aviation expert commented: "It's like imagining that a plane of this size could pass through a window and leave the frame still standing." The grass in front of the building looked green and unscorched, and there were no signs of any wreckage. Meyssan's answer? The damage was not caused by Flight 77, but by a missile. Shot by the Pentagon at itself.

Pentagon theories

Partly in response to public pressure, the Pentagon finally released five frames of the attack. The effect was like pouring aviation fuel on a smouldering fire. Conspiracy theorists asked why only five frames. Why, if the Pentagon had lots of good footage, which it surely must, were these five frames so ambiguous? Why were workers at the site shown wearing full body suits? Did they know that there was depleted uranium lying around in the wreckage? Surely the bits of airline debris weren't what the Pentagon said they were? What had happened to the plane's wings? Why was there no footage of the actual crash?

Photos of what appeared to be a wrecked jet engine were not, it was claimed, the auxiliary power unit of a Boeing 757, but the remains of a Rolls Royce Allison AE3007H jet, which had (about) the same diameter. And this engine was used on the Global Hawk, a futuristic drone or unmanned aerial vehicle. Awkward eyewitness accounts of an American Airlines jetliner were explained by the alleged addition of red and blue stripes.

If it wasn't Flight 77 that had smashed into the Pentagon, sceptics asked, then where had Flight 77 (and all its passengers) gone? And what about the phone calls relatives received from terrified hijack victims? Pentagon officials

September 11, 2001: the Pentagon burns.

described exactly how the airliner had bounce-crashed into the ground right in front of the building, how the wings had snapped, and either burned up or been driven into the building. The photos were confusing because they were taken with super-long lenses, creating a distorting sense of distance, and they were partly concealed by smoke or the water from fire hoses. Aerial photos showed that the plane had done far more damage than the hole visible in the initial snapshots, slamming its way through the newly reinforced outer wall and on into the first five "rings" of the building.

Undeterred, conspiracy theorists now asked how a mere 757 had done so much damage. They seized on a new picture of the inside wall of the second-to-innermost ring, punched through by an almost perfectly circular, heavily scorched hole. A missile's exit wound? No, Pentagon officials said, it was damage from an aircraft engine that had broken free of its moorings, creating an air hole that sucked the firestorm through it.

A more troubling allegation was based not on "I'm not an expert but that's how it looks to me" analysis, but on reports of the extraordinary manoeuvre that brought Flight 77 down from the air and into the Pentagon. The hijacker pilot, Hani Hanjour, had pulled off an amazing descending-spiral turn before successfully flying the 757 so low over the ground that it decapitated exterior light stands as it approached the Pentagon. Some stunt. And this from a rookie pilot whose skills were so weak that he had been refused permission to rent a small plane a month earlier. That said, Hanjour did have the help of the 757's flight control computer, and he was actively trying to bring the plane down. Whether or not that's a tough job is difficult to say – few people have tried it. In any case, it would be rather hard for a cruise missile to sever street lamps on its way in...

Pulling down WTC7

Outside the conspiracist world, or maybe Manhattan, few people know that a third tower collapsed on September 11. At 5.20pm, the World Trade Center 7 building came down in a now-familiar cloud of smoke and debris. It fell in just under seven seconds, collapsing neatly in on itself. WTC7 was right next to the Twin Towers. To some, it was amazing that it was the only neighbouring building to collapse that day. This was evidence, surely, of the destructive power of a major skyscraper fire. It was also good counter-evidence that the Twin Towers were not dynamited – why would anyone have pre-mined a building that was never going to be hit by a plane?

Or perhaps it was a sign of another conspiracy? Larry Silverstein, billionaire property developer and owner of the WTC lease, unwittingly reignited conspiracist fire when he recalled the events of 9/11 in the television documentary *America Rebuilds.* He remembered telling a Fire Department commander, "'We've had such terrible loss of life, maybe the smartest thing to do is just pull it.' And they made that decision to pull and then we watched the building collapse." Conspiracists zoomed in on the words "pull it", saying this was slang for a controlled demolition – and evidence, somehow, that the other buildings were also blown up on purpose – but to "pull" a building actually means to bring it down using cables. Silverstein has since commented that he meant "pull the firefighters out of the building". Exactly how an imagined insurance scam connects with a government conspiracy is rarely made clear.

A preliminary investigation into the collapse by the Federal Emergency Management Agency (FEMA) could only comment: "the specifics of the fires in WTC7 and how they caused the building to collapse remain unknown at this time". This comment fanned the flames of conspiracy, but speculation was soon dampened when the more detailed National Institute of Standards and Technology (NIST) report emerged, along with new photos revealing a huge ten-storey tear in the building's south wall. This was not a photo to which conspiracy theorists had drawn attention. Telling video footage released by CBS revealed that the penthouse area visibly began to crack some eight seconds before the whole structure started to give way – hardly the work of a demolition squad.

Pennsylvania: Flight 93

Flight 93, which crashed relatively unspectacularly into the ground near Shanksville, Pennsylvania, received relatively little coverage until it was announced that the passengers had heard about the events in Manhattan on their mobile phones, and had told relatives that they were going to tackle the hijackers. It was widely reported that they had succeeded, and nobly crash-landed the plane in the countryside to prevent any further loss of life. Only later was it officially concluded that the hijackers had destroyed the plane themselves, albeit under threat from a passenger revolt.

Some doubted that this in fact was the case. It was reported that in the aftermath of the attacks, Vice President Dick Cheney finally ordered the military to shoot down any further hijacked planes, and told Defense Secretary Donald Rumsfeld, "It's my understanding they've already taken a couple of aircraft out" – who "they" were, he didn't say. And in 2004, Rumsfeld told US troops in Baghdad during his Christmas Eve address that "the people who attacked the United States in New York shot down the plane over Pennsylvania". If he was stating that Flight 93 was *shot* down, presumably by the US military, didn't this imply that they had carried out the New York attack as well? Pentagon officials claimed that Rumsfeld "misspoke". Humiliatingly, they also observed that the military did not even know that Flight 93 had been hijacked until four minutes after it crashed.

One Flight 93 theory rested its case on the fact that debris was found a suspicious 6.9 miles away from the Shanksville crash site, in Indian Lake. This would imply that the plane was first damaged in the air by, say, a missile strike, before crashing into the ground. This argument looked promising until someone observed that the distance between the two sites was actually only about a mile. The figure of 6.9 miles came up if you entered the site locations into a road mapping program – giving a seven-mile round trip by car.

Cheney and Rumsfeld: drills and stand-down orders

If Cheney's understanding was correct and Rumsfeld's "slip" in saying that Flight 93 was shot down was true, it would prove that US air defences were not quite as leaden-footed as is often claimed. It would also prove that Rumsfeld and Cheney were not, in fact, arch-villains who had planned the whole thing. In the absence of clarification on this point, however, the apparent failure of NORAD (North American Aerospace Defense Command) to scramble fighter jets early enough to shoot down the hijacked airliners is taken as evidence of the Bush administration's complicity. According to some theorists, even when the jet fighters were scrambled, they must have flown at a fraction of their top speeds to explain the timescales, despite the evocative soundbite from one of the pilots, who said they had flown "like scalded apes". Surely the US could not have been so incompetent as to let 9/11 happen. Surely somebody, somewhere, must have issued a "stand-down order".

According to Michael C. Ruppert, author of *Crossing the Rubicon*, that somebody was Dick Cheney, and the somewhere was the White House Situation Room. With a puppet president conveniently trapped at a schoolroom photo opportunity (and later sidelined on an unprotected Air Force 1 chicken flight), Cheney had free rein to run the whole operation. He was a shadow government of one.

These kinds of allegations received some circumstantial support when it was revealed that the National Reconnaissance Office (NRO) had actually scheduled a war-game-style exercise involving a corporate jet crashing into the NRO's headquarters in Chantilly, Virginia – just a few miles from Washington DC. In 2004, former National Security Council counter-terrorism chief Richard Clarke revealed in his book that this exercise was only part of a bigger war game called "Vigilant Guardian". Bizarrely, it involved all three 9/11 crash sites, and ensured that Clarke and Cheney were already in the White House Situation Room when the terrorist attacks occurred.

Some, including *October Surprise* conspiracy writer Barbara Honegger, believe that Vigilant Guardian must have included hijack scenarios, because the key decision-makers in the White House were not, at first, surprised when they heard the news of the 9/11 attacks. It explains Bush's otherwise unconscionable delay in that Florida classroom. Had the hijackers found out about the war-game plans? Had they been tipped off? One final piece of "evidence" was President Bush's bizarre claim at a press conference that he had seen the first plane hit the WTC. Was this confusion, or posturing? Or had he seen simulations beforehand? Was the hijack scenario the US government's own idea?

Four thousand Jews

One widespread rumour in the aftermath of the attacks was the notoriously racist "4000 Jews" conspiracy theory, which exploded onto the streets of the Middle East, then onto Middle Eastern conspiracy websites before working its way back to the West. It began as a generalized whisper that Israel, or its intelligence agency Mossad (see p.149), was behind the attacks – a conspiracy theory that routinely follows pretty much every disaster or terrorist attack involving Muslims.

On September 14, Major General Hamid Gul, ex-chief of Pakistan's ISI secret intelligence agency was reported in *Newsweek* as declaring that "Mossad and its American associates are the obvious culprits. Who benefits from the crime?" The benefits would be the attacks that the US would feel free to unleash on a "guilty" Muslim population... Confusingly, he also suggested that Israel had masterminded the WTC attacks against its American allies. "The Israelis don't want to see any power in Washington unless it's subservient to their interests", he said, "and President Bush has not been subservient". More cogent theorists alleged that Mossad had known about the attacks in advance, but had failed to pass on the information to the US authorities.

The more specific "4000 Jews" conspiracy theory that Israeli workers were warned to stay away from their offices in the World Trade Center originated from a story in the *Jerusalem Post*'s Internet edition, which said that the Israeli foreign ministry had gathered the names of four thousand Israelis who were thought to have been in the vicinity of the World Trade Center and the Pentagon on the morning of September 11. Through a system of conspiratorial Chinese whispers, the story morphed into the allegation that four thousand presumably forewarned Israelis had failed to turn up for work that morning, as reported by Hezbollah's Al Manar network on September 17. The story was repeated largely, but not exclusively, by Middle Eastern news services in the following weeks. "Israelis" soon became "Jews". In fact, the proportion of Israelis among the victims of the attack was roughly equivalent to the proportion of Israelis in the population of New York – and more than one in ten of the victims was Jewish.

Many Middle Eastern theorists saw the hidden hand of the "Elders of Zion" (see p.109) at work. This was all too easy to connect to the widespread rumour that unusual trading in American Airlines stock had taken place on September 10. This would suggest that traders – or "Jewish bankers" – had been forewarned about the plot, or were even behind it. (No one seemed to think that Al Qaeda associates might have done a little profiteering on the side.) The trades were eventually traced to a newsletter issued on September 9, which had recommended the deals. The assertion of an Egyptian academic, writing in the newspaper *Al-Ahram*, that Jewish holders of airline and insurance company stock had sold their shares ten days before the attacks, and bought them again afterwards, could not be verified. But how could anyone know whether such trades were by Jewish or gentile speculators?

No less racist was the rumour that there were no cabs (many driven by Muslims) near the WTC on the morning of September 11, or that all the (Arab-run) coffee shops and newsstands nearby were closed. The entire Muslim population of New York, these theories suggested, had stronger allegiances to extremist terrorists than to their own city.

Foreknowledge

The conspiracy theory that the Bush administration had known about the attacks in advance actually gained currency as press releases and leaks filtered through from the 9-11 Commission, which was set up in November 2002 – despite initial opposition from President Bush, on the grounds that it would cover "sensitive information". Were these reports evidence of massive incompetence on the part of the FBI and CIA, as the 9-11 Commission would later suggest? Or of a more sinister, orchestrated campaign to shut down investigations that could prevent the 9/11 attacks?

Intelligence reports from April and May 2001 had titles such as "Bin Laden planning multiple operations", "Bin Laden threats are real" and "Bin Laden network's plans advancing". In August, an intelligence briefing for President Bush warned that Osama bin Laden might hijack commercial airliners. It was entitled "Bin Laden Determined to Strike in US" (though administration officials speaking to

9/11 NUMEROLOGY

Viral marketeers must envy the incredible success of one piece of 9/11 theorizing: 9/11 numerology, which regularly tours inboxes around the world and can be found pinned up all over the Internet (in many cases accompanied by debunkings, it must be said). The message takes various forms, and is often interpolated with asides like "this'll make your hair stand on end", but the essence remains the same and is as follows:

New York City has 11 letters.
Afghanistan has 11 letters.
George W. Bush has 11 letters.
New York was the 11th state to join the Union.
The first plane crashing into the Twin Towers was Flight 11.
Flight 11 was carrying 92 passengers: 9+2=11.
Flight 77 was carrying 65 passengers: 6+5=11.
The tragedy took place on 9/11: 9+1+1=11.
The US emergency services telephone no. is 911: 9+1+1=11.
The total no. of victims on the planes was 254: 2+5+4=11.
September 11 is the 254th day of the year: 2+5+4=11.
The Madrid bombings were on 3/11/2004: 3+1+1+2+4=11.
The Madrid bombings happened 911 days after 9/11.
The most recognized symbol for the US, after the Stars and Stripes, is the Eagle. The following verse is taken from the Koran: "For it is written that a son of Arabia would awaken a fearsome Eagle. The wrath of the Eagle would be felt throughout the lands of Allah and lo, while some of the people trembled in despair still more rejoiced: for the wrath of the Eagle cleansed the lands of Allah and there was peace." That verse is no. 9.11 of the Koran.
Open Microsoft Word. Type in capitals Q33NY. This is the flight number of the first plane to hit one of the Twin Towers. Change the actual font to Wingdings.

It all sounds very alluring, but in many cases the numbers just don't add up. Flight 11 had 81 passengers (including 5 hijackers) and 11 crew. OK, that's a total of 92, but Flight 77 had 58 passengers (including 5 hijackers) and 6 crew – which makes 64. In total, there were 265 victims (including 19 hijackers), which can't be made to add up to 11. Unfortunately for the numerologists, the Madrid bombings happened 912 days after September 11 – though 911 days could be said to separate the two events. As for the supposed Koran passage, it is pure concoction. It was presumably concocted by a Westerner, as the language is distinctly biblical, rather than Koranic. In the Picthal translation, sutra 9, verse 11 of the Qu'ran reads: "But if they repent and establish worship and pay the poor-due, then are they your brethren in religion. We detail Our revelations for a people who have knowledge." Other translations are similar. The last, and most amazing piece of number trickery, the so-called "Wingdings message" turns out to be a mendacious bit of anti-Semitism. In Wingdings, Q33NY reads ✈▤▤☠✡. But there is no such flight number as Q33NY.

the press later left out the word "in"). Also in the summer of 2001, George Bush was personally warned that Islamic terrorists were capable of crashing an airliner into the summit building of the Genoa G8 conference, which he was attending. At around the same time, Russian intelligence warned the CIA that suicide pilots were training for attacks on US targets, while Israel's Mossad actually gave the agency a list of terrorists who had infiltrated the US – four of the names on the list were 9/11 hijackers.

Among the most significant dead-end leads was the July 2001 "Phoenix Memo", sent to FBI bosses by agent Kenneth Williams from Phoenix, Arizona. It warned of the possibility that Osama bin Laden might place agents in US flight schools. Later that month, a threat assessment led to Attorney General John Ashcroft refusing to fly on commercial airlines. And on September 10, a group of top Pentagon officials suddenly cancelled their travel plans for the following morning. Rumours that this was due to security alerts were denied. It seems that Pentagon officials travel very frequently, and almost as frequently change their plans. That's why they have first-class tickets.

Whistleblowers

The various intelligence reports of the summer of 2001 were explained away as bits of flotsam in a sea of contradictory intelligence. It was patiently explained that there were thousands of similar reports raising the possibility of terrorist attacks that never happened. But, at the least, they proved that protests by senior officials that the attacks were a total surprise, an event that could not have been foreseen, were disingenuous. National Security Advisor Condoleezza Rice, speaking two weeks before she appeared in front of the 9-11 Commission, said: "We had no specific information." Challenged by FBI translator and whistleblower Sibel Edwards, she clarified: "I made a mistake. I should not have said 'we'. I should say that I personally did not have specific information."

Edwards also alleged that in her role as an FBI translator (in Farsi, Turkish and Azerbaijani) she had seen or heard about evidence that senior US government figures were "directly involved" in the financing of the 9/11 attacks, to the extent that they were financially implicated in drug trafficking and money laundering. Another FBI whistleblower, Coleen Rowley (who later became *Time* magazine's Person of the Year – the magazine was evidently congratulating itself for running her story), accused FBI bosses of deliberately blocking her attempts to investigate Zacarias Moussaoui, the so-called "twentieth hijacker". Edwards and Rowley are far from lone voices, but if the US government really did attack itself, it's strange that no whistleblower has come forward with proof of the massive planning that would have been required.

The closest anyone official came to pointing the finger of blame at the government was the 9-11 Commission itself. The chair and vice-chair raged that they were "set up to fail" because of poor funding, and that they were repeatedly blocked or misled. In August 2006, *The Washington Post* reported that some commission staff were so appalled by the Pentagon's responses to questions about the morning of September 11, that they considered pushing for a prosecution. "Suspicion of wrongdoing ran so deep", the *Post* noted, "that the ten-member commission, in a secret meeting at the end of its tenure in summer 2004, debated referring the matter to the Justice Department for criminal investigation." Of course, the criminality in question was lying to the commission, not orchestrating 9/11. Still, what did the Pentagon have to hide?

Why?

Thrown together in this way, pieces of circumstantial evidence can seem to form a coherent picture of US government complicity in – or even direct responsibility for – 9/11. What's less clear is why the US government would be involved in such a massive conspiracy. There are, of course, plenty of theories. It is correctly pointed out that the WTC attacks swung world opinion behind the neoconservatives' aggressive military agenda, and that they loosened the diplomatic ties that fettered America's hands. As Tony Blair told a House of Commons committee in July 2002, "To be truthful about it, there was no way we could have got the public consent to have suddenly launched a campaign on Afghanistan but for what happened on September 11."

The international, loosely left-liberal view holds that the US needed unrestricted supplies of oil, as well as strategic bases in the Middle East, and that 9/11 allowed it to go get what it wanted, first in Afghanistan and then in Iraq. Someone – the Bush administration, Dick Cheney, the CIA, the military-industrial complex (see p.121), the neocons, the PNAC (see p.418), or a combination of these – must, therefore, have planned the attacks.

From the conspiracist libertarian Right comes the alternative theory that the federal government planned 9/11, or allowed it to happen, as an excuse for tightening its grip on its own country. The same arguments were trotted out in the wake of the Oklahoma City bombing (see p.228). Fears of a declaration of martial law weren't borne out, but the Patriot Act, rushed into law in October 2001, certainly made serious inroads into civil liberties.

In 2002, a former aide of Republican senator Bob Dole, the controversial Stanley Hilton, filed a $7 billion lawsuit on behalf of "hundreds" of victims' families. Hilton was quoted as citing "Bush and his puppets" for being involved "not only in aiding and abetting and allowing 9/11 to happen but in actually ordering it to happen". Hilton had done his senior thesis on how the US could be turned into a "presidential dictatorship" by a bogus Pearl Harbor. And he had been to college with many senior neocons, including Donald Rumsfeld… Maybe they had peeked at his notes? Unfortunately, a federal court threw out the suit, on the grounds that a sitting president had "Sovereign Immunity".

Blood brothers? The Saudi connection

The Saudi "blood-brother" claim was not a new one. Anti-Bush activists have attacked the family's oil and business relations with Saudi Arabia for years. In his vastly popular film *Fahrenheit 9/11*, liberal filmmaker Michael Moore claims that "six to seven percent of America is owned by Saudi Arabians", and he traces numerous links between Saudi Arabian companies and Bush family interests. The same links are painstakingly uncovered by Craig Unger's bestselling *House of Bush, House of Saud*, which alleges "brilliantly hidden agendas and purposefully murky corporate relationships" between the two families. "With the Bush family", the blurb claims, "the Saudis hit a gusher."

Conspiracy theorists attribute the "success" of the young George W. Bush's oil firm Arbusto to Saudi investment. Most notoriously, they allege that George W. Bush's fellow "draft-dodger" in the Texas Air National Guard, James R. Bath, invested not his own money in Arbusto, but money on behalf of various influential Saudi businessmen. White House officials later seemed to attempt to conceal George W's connections with Bath by blanking out his name when they released Bush's military service records.

Despite Osama bin Laden's well-documented status as the rogue or black sheep of his vastly wealthy family, *House of Bush, House of Saud* and *Fahrenheit 9/11* also made a big noise about the movements of the bin Laden family in the wake of 9/11. It was alleged that they had departed the US before national airspace had reopened – and without being interviewed. Who had pulled those strings, if not Bush? The 9-11 Commission countered that while members of the bin Laden family were airlifted to assembly points, they were at least "made available" for interviews with the FBI, and were only actually flown out of the country on September 14, after flights resumed.

It was widely hinted that the claims of FBI whistleblower Sibel Edwards related directly to the involvement of Saudi Arabian government figures in the financing of the 9/11 attacks. Unfortunately, the gag orders imposed on her by Attorney General John Ashcroft – on the basis of "state secret privilege" and "diplomatic relations" – meant that she couldn't name anyone she claimed was involved or their country of origin. The most she could say was that what she knew was connected to BCCI (see p.252) and international securities fraud.

Mega-theories and counter-theories

As ever, there is a lunatic fringe to the 9/11 conspiracy theorizing. Much is made of 9/11 numerology (see box on p.404), which focuses on the number eleven – quite why this number is so sinister isn't explained, except perhaps that the WTC towers could be said to resemble a giant figure eleven. Then there's *The X-Files* conspiracy spin-off series, *The Lone Gunmen*, whose March 2001 pilot featured a plot in which an airliner is hijacked (by remote control, mind you) and the heroes only just save it from … crashing into the World Trade Center. To successfully yoke fiction with fact, conspiracists must somehow link the writers of the series with the dark forces behind the 9/11 conspiracy. Easy – the series was shown on Fox TV, known for its links with ultra-conservatism…

David Icke and his ultra-conspiracy crowd have a mega-theory that traces a real (and non-human) blood connection between the Houses of Bush and Saud. According to Icke, the attacks were "co-ordinated by forces within U.S. borders. Those responsible are possessed by non-human entities and have no regard for human life any more than most humans have regard for the death and suffering of cattle". It's good, but it's beaten by the invention of one online conspiracist, who theorized that Al Qaeda deliberately recreated the "Falling Tower" card from the Tarot deck, and that "maybe" bin Laden was therefore an "evil Masonic sorcerer who just killed the secret spell that has held the US together these many years". Tugging on the same Masonic chain, radical, London-based cleric Abu Hamza al-Masri declared that the "business lobby" wanted World War III. Plenty of people would agree with him, but perhaps not his conspiratorial belief that "most of them are Freemasons loyal to the Zionists".

A number of campaigning groups have complained that the wilder conspiracy theories muddy the waters. Some suspect they are part of a deliberate propaganda campaign. According to the website 911review.com, the 9/11 attack was "a complex psychological operation carefully designed to conceal the truth", relying on the dissemination of *memes* – ideas that, like genes (or germs) can be transmitted from person to person. One of the most important *memes*, the site claims, "is the idea that all people who question the basic tenets of the official story are loony conspiracy theorists, whose ideas are not worthy of consideration".

SOURCES

Books

Nafeez Mosaddeq Ahmed **The War on Freedom: How and Why America Was Attacked, September 11, 2001** (2002). Or how the government knew and did nothing, and why the Bush family got its hands dirty. Ahmed, who is a Londoner, a Muslim and a political scientist, has also written companion volumes on *The War on Truth*, *The War on Terror* and the London bombings.

Noam Chomsky **9/11** (2001). Not Chomsky's best – a hundred-odd-page rush job. Despite conservative allegations, Chomsky doesn't say that the 9/11 attacks were justified, but that they can be explained as a reaction to imperialist US foreign policy.

Richard Clarke **Against All Enemies: Inside America's War on Terror** (2004). Written by a Washington insider who served every president from Ronald Reagan to George W. Bush, this is a fascinating insight into official anti-terror measures, and a harsh indictment of the Bush administration's failure to take Al Qaeda seriously.

Don DeLillo **Falling Man** (2007). The master of the conspiracy novel responds to 9/11 with brittle, fragmented fiction interweaving the traumatized lives of survivors and the story of one of the hijackers.

David Dunbar, Brad Reagan, et al. **Debunking 9/11 Myths: Why Conspiracy Theories Can't Stand Up to the Facts** (2006). A book-length version of *Popular Mechanics* classic articles debunking 9/11 conspiracy theories.

David Ray Griffin **The New Pearl Harbor: Disturbing Questions About the Bush Administration and 9/11** (2004). One of the most balanced presentations of the case against the Bush administration.

David Icke **Alice in Wonderland and the World Trade Center Disaster** (2002). David in fairyland, more like. Icke cashes in with more of the same old conspira-lunacy.

Sid Jacobsen and Erine Colón **9/11: The Illustrated 9/11 Commission Report** (2006). Shrunk to 128 pages, the weighty 9-11 Commission report gets a cartoon, but not superhero treatment, from two comic-book veterans. The chair and vice chair of the 9-11 Commission wrote the foreword, commending the graphic novel's "close adherence" to the original report. Thin pickings for conspiracists but humanizing and original.

Peter Lance **Cover Up: What the Government Is Still Hiding About the War on Terror** (2005). A serious investigative reporter takes the 9-11 Commission to task, detailing the national security failures in the lead-up to 9/11 and the agendas behind the cover-up of the final report. Asks some trenchant questions.

Jim Marrs **Inside Job: Unmasking the Conspiracies of 9/11** (2005). Marrs is one of the US's leading conspiracy theorists. This book is rather unbalanced in tone, but gives a great overview of the details of the main conspiracy theory arguments nonetheless.

Thierry Meyssan **9/11: The Big Lie** (2002). Originally published in France as *L'Effroyable imposture*. Discussed in detail in the main text.

Michael C. Ruppert **Crossing the Rubicon: The Decline of the American Empire at the End of the Age of Oil** (2004). In preparation for "Peak Oil: an economic crisis like nothing the world has ever seen", insiders in the Bush administration – i.e. Dick Cheney and his cronies – pulled off an amazing false-flag operation.

Der Spiegel Magazine **9-11: What Really Happened** (2002). Dated but still electrifyingly vivid and clear-eyed account of events by the journalists of Germany's leading news magazine.

Paul Thompson **The Terror Timeline: Year by Year, Day by Day, Minute by Minute: A Comprehensive Chronicle of the Road to 9/11 – and America's Response** (2004). The title says it all (it's certainly long enough). Gripping.

Craig Unger **House of Bush, House of Saud: The Secret Relationship Between the World's Two Most Powerful Dynasties** (2004). An experienced investigative journalist exposes the "brilliantly hidden agendas and purposefully murky corporate relationships" between the two vastly wealthy families.

Films

Dylan Avery **Loose Change** (2007). This claims to be "the most downloaded film in Internet history", and it's surely the most viewed 9/11 video. Mainstream theorists, however, are said to consider it an embarrassment, partly because of its over-focus on the Pentagon. Free download from www.loosechange911.com.

Paul Greengrass United 93 (2006). Dark docu-thriller dramatizing the (imagined) events aboard Flight 93.

Oliver Stone World Trade Center (2006). Set in the rubble of the WTC, where rescue workers are trapped alive. Patriotic and sentimental, but effectively so – if you don't mind the uniform-worship.

Websites

cooperativeresearch.org This website is a serious research tool: "the Center for Cooperative Research seeks to encourage grassroots participation and collaboration in the documentation of the public historical record using an open-content model." Features the famous "Complete 9/11 Timeline", plus well-attended discussion "phorums".

www.crisispapers.org/essays/911-testimony.htm Hilarious fictional transcript of the Bush-Cheney testimony to the 9-11 Commission.

www.9-11commission.gov/report/911Report.pdf A downloadable PDF version of the 9-11 Commission report. All 585 pages' worth...

www.911review.com One of the best "sceptical" websites – and sceptical cuts both ways. Includes detailed evidence that the Pentagon/missile claims are phoney.

www.911truth.org The gateway to the 9/11 Truth Movement and an excellent place to start further digging. The site campaigns "to educate the public about the Sept 11th cover-up and inspire popular pressure to ... expose the truth surrounding the events of 9/11; namely, that elements within the US government must have been complicit, or worse". Includes excellent links to a host of campaigning groups, as well as official resources.

www.pentagonstrike.co.uk Smartly put-together flash video presenting the basics of the Pentagon/missile theory.

www.questionsquestions.net/WTC/767orwhatzit.html Detailed discussion of the fact that when conspiracy theorists see pods, missiles or what-have-you in low-res images, they're actually seeing compression artefacts, or by-products of digital processing.

www.september11news.com/Mysteries2.htm 9/11 numerology.

www.time.com/time/covers/1101020603/memo.html Coleen Rowley's whistleblowing memo to FBI director Robert Mueller.

usinfo.state.gov/media/misinformation.html Detailed, point-by-point rebuttal. You can even listen to messages left on their home answering machines by crew members on the hijacked planes.

wtc.nist.gov The official investigation into why the towers collapsed, with downloadable reports and regularly updated press briefings.

Iraq: the case for war

On March 20, 2003, a US-led coalition of military forces stormed into Iraq in an invasion codenamed "Operation Iraqi Freedom". The war would swiftly bring down the brutal dictatorship of Saddam Hussein and lead to his capture, imprisonment and eventual execution (on December 30, 2006), while a system of multiparty democratic government was finally established in the country. Although the war officially ended in May 2003, Iraq is, at the time of writing, still occupied by a multinational force, mainly comprising US troops, and is still suffering a brutal, bloody insurrection.

The war has also engendered bitter political opposition across the globe, not because people supported or sympathized with Saddam, but because many believed that the US government, in particular, had a hidden agenda. What follows, therefore, is an examination of the "official" reasons given for going to war, followed by a separate piece (see p.417) looking at the alternative explanations that have been put forward, some of which have been publicly dismissed as "conspiracy theories".

The official version(s)

Although Tony Blair, who was the British prime minister when the Iraq War began, has sometimes talked as though he decided to remove Saddam single-handedly, there is no doubt that the initiative came from the Bush administration, and that Blair, for whatever reason, decided to stand "shoulder to shoulder" with the Americans. In the December 2004 edition of the British magazine

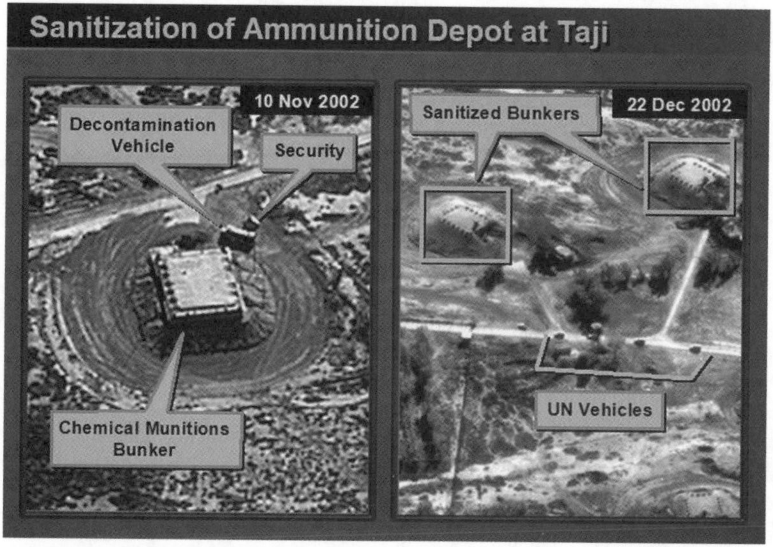

Satellite imagery presented to the UN Security Council in 2003 as evidence of Iraq's WMD programme.

Prospect, Paul Wolfowitz, then US deputy secretary of defense, and the man widely regarded as the architect of the Iraq War, recalled that President George W. Bush made three arguments when he first went to the UN to seek approval for war: "He talked about terrorism, he talked about WMDs and he talked about abuse of the Iraqi people."

Wolfowitz had identified the same three "fundamental concerns" in an interview for *Vanity Fair* in 2003, when he said that "for reasons that have a lot to do with the US government bureaucracy we settled on the one issue that everyone could agree on, which was weapons of mass destruction". In his *Prospect* interview, however, Wolfowitz cited the need to try to gain UN backing as the reason for focusing on WMDs ("The UN was what forced us down the WMD path"). Whatever the case, there was always more than one official reason for going to war.

Weapons of mass destruction

Let there be no doubt about this: Saddam *had* had WMDs, and he had been continuing to develop them. On December 9, 2002, *The Guardian* reported that, prior to their departure from Iraq in December 1998, UN weapons inspectors had destroyed or made unusable "48 long-range missiles, 14 conventional missile warheads, 30 chemical warheads, 'supergun' components, close to 40,000 chemical munitions, 690 tonnes of chemical weapons agents and the al-Hakam biological weapons plant". They had also discovered "evidence of a nuclear programme that was more advanced than previously expected".

To get things into perspective, however, it is worth remembering a number of points about the US's own possession and use of WMDs. First, the US has by far the world's largest arsenal of nuclear weapons, and is the only country to have used them, at Hiroshima and Nagasaki in 1945. Second, although the US ratified the Geneva Protocol in 1975 and the Chemical Weapons Convention in 1997, it still retains large stockpiles of the types of weapons the convention bans: as of May 2004, according to the US Army Chemical Materials Agency, the US had destroyed less than thirty percent of its original declared stockpile of over 30,000 tons of mustard gas and nerve agents, including sarin and VX. During the Vietnam War, of course, the US made extensive use of chemical weapons, most notably defoliants such as Agent Orange.

The position regarding biological weapons is less clear. In 1975, the US ratified the Biological Weapons Convention, having already ordered the destruction of its own biological weapons by 1973. In 2001, however, longstanding international negotiations for a verification protocol broke down when the US insisted that such a protocol would interfere with legitimate research into defence against biological weapons. Meanwhile the US Army Medical Research Institute of Infectious Diseases, located at Fort Detrick (see p.298), continues to produce biological agents for "research" purposes.

Saddam, of course, had used chemical weapons before – not only against the Iranians in the Iran–Iraq War of 1980–88, but also against Kurdish rebels inside Iraq. Indeed, this enabled the Bush administration to link WMDs to the humanitarian issue of Saddam's treatment of the Iraqi people. Thus, in his January 2003 State of the Union speech, President Bush declared: "The dictator who is assembling the world's most dangerous weapons has already used them on whole villages – leaving thousands of his own citizens dead, blind, or disfigured.

What Bush didn't mention was that under Ronald Reagan, the US had supported Iraq during the Iran–Iraq War, despite knowing that – as a declassified November 1983 memo to then secretary of state George Shultz put it – Saddam was using chemical weapons on an "almost daily basis". He also failed to mention that up until 1989, under the Reagan and George H.W. Bush administrations, the US had sent or sold samples of these agents to Iraq. These samples included anthrax, botulism and West Nile virus, some of which were used by Saddam in his biological weapons research programme. The US knew, in other words, that Saddam had biological warfare capability because they – along with France, Germany, Japan and the UK – had supplied him with it.

Halabja

When George W. Bush referred, in his 2003 State of the Union speech, to Saddam using WMDs on his own people, he was referring, above all, to the gas attack on the Kurdish village of Halabja in March 1988, which left more than 5000 dead and has often been cited as an example of Saddam's brutality. Commenting on Bush's speech in *The New York Times*, however, Stephen C. Pelletiere, the CIA's political analyst for the Iran–Iraq War, wrote: "We cannot say with any certainty that Iraqi chemical weapons killed the Kurds." As the Defense Intelligence Agency had reported, recalled Pelletiere, both sides in the war used gas, but what killed the Kurds at Halabja was Iranian cyanide gas – Iraq only had mustard gas.

Oh really? The same month of Pelletiere's article, British journalist Robert Fisk reported in *The Independent* that recently declassified State Department documents revealed that "the Pentagon had pushed US diplomats to blame Iran for Halabja – but not to present details, because the story was a lie". Far from punishing Saddam for Halabja, indeed, both the US and British governments gave him more money: the incoming George H.W. Bush administration doubled Iraq's "agricultural credits" – whatever they were – to $1 billion a year, while the UK approved an extra £340 million of credit.

Furthermore, in July 1988 – just two months after Halabja – the giant California-based Bechtel Corporation won a contract to build a petrochemicals plant near Baghdad, which Saddam planned to use to produce fuel-air explosives and mustard gas. Construction was only halted after the Iraqi invasion of Kuwait. In 2003, Bechtel was awarded contracts worth over $2.5 billion for reconstruction in Iraq.

Selling to Saddam

Just how far the Reagan administration had been prepared to go in assisting Saddam was underlined by a now declassified US State Department memo of May 9, 1984, which said that the US was reviewing its policy "on the sale of certain dual-use [civilian and military] items to Iraq nuclear entities" and that "preliminary results favor expanding such trade to include Iraqi nuclear entities". As regards other WMDs, a Senate committee inquiry into US export policy to Iraq prior to the Gulf War concluded in

1994 that "the United States provided the government of Iraq with 'dual use' licensed materials which assisted in the development of Iraqi chemical, biological and missile-system programs".

According to the report, these materials included "chemical warfare-agent precursors; chemical warfare-agent production-facility plans and technical drawings; chemical-warfare filling equipment; biological-warfare-related materials; missile-fabrication equipment and missile-system guidance equipment". Between 1985 and 1990, in fact, the US Department of Commerce approved 771 licences for exporting $1.5 billion worth of such dual-use items to Iraq. As a later joke put it, the Americans knew that Saddam had WMDs because they still had the receipts.

Humanitarian concern?

After 1990, of course, when Saddam's invasion of Kuwait sparked off the Gulf War (see p.412), everything changed. The UN Security Council imposed a trade embargo on Iraq and passed resolutions for all of Saddam's WMD stocks and facilities to be destroyed. These "sanctions" were turned by the US and UK into a complete economic blockade, including food and medicine, and accompanied by intermittent bombing.

Compounded by the after effects of the Gulf War, the results were devastating. In May 1996, CBS *Sixty Minutes* reporter Lesley Stahl, referring to reports that half a million Iraqi children had died as a result, asked Madeleine Albright, then US ambassador to the UN, whether the cost was worth it. Albright replied: "I think this is a very hard choice, but ... we think the price is worth it." Although the figure of half a million deaths and the apportionment of blame continue to be disputed (see, for example, www.reason.com/news/show/28346.html), UNICEF reported in 1997 that nearly a million Iraqi children were malnourished, while the fact that the UN introduced an "oil-for-food" programme in December 1996 speaks for itself.

Meanwhile UN inspection teams were sent in to inspect suspected weapons sites and ensure the destruction of any WMDs they found. But Saddam frequently refused to cooperate and, after the inspectors pulled out in 1998 complaining of obstruction, there was massive retaliatory bombing by the US and UK. Inevitably, despite the much-trumpeted use of "smart" weapons and supposedly precision targeting, there was significant "collateral damage". According to Amnesty International, a confidential UN report found that over a period of five months in 1999, 41 percent of the victims of US and UK air strikes were civilians. Concern for the Iraqi people would later be cited by the US government as a reason for removing Saddam.

"Things related and not"

In December 2000, George W. Bush was finally declared to have won a presidential election – which has spawned its own fair share of conspiracy theories (see p.232). According to the BBC's *Newsnight* programme and *Harper's Magazine*, secret meetings planning the ousting of Saddam Hussein and discussing likely successors were being held in the US and across the Middle East "within weeks" of Bush taking office in 2001. And then came 9/11 (see p.395).

The reaction of one member of the new Bush administration, in particular, suggests that he saw the terrorist attack on the Twin Towers as an opportunity to put some long-laid plans into operation. "Barely five hours after American Airlines Flight 77 plowed into the Pentagon", CBS News reported in 2002, "Defense Secretary Donald H. Rumsfeld was telling his aides to come up with plans for striking Iraq – even though there was no evidence linking Saddam Hussein to the attacks."

According to notes taken by one of these aides at the time (see www.cbsnews.com/stories/2002/09/04/september11/main520830.shtml), Rumsfeld wanted "best info fast. Judge whether good enough [to] hit SH [Saddam Hussein] at the same time. Not only UBL [Osama bin Laden]". He added: "Go massive. Sweep it all up. Things related and not." Iraq, of course, wasn't related: seventeen out of the nineteen hijackers, like Osama bin Laden himself, turned out to have come from Saudi Arabia – a country that, after the invasion of Kuwait in 1990, the US feared Saddam might attack. According to *Time* magazine, however, Rumsfeld was so set on finding a rationale for attacking Saddam that he asked the CIA to find evidence connecting

THE FIRST GULF WAR

The common perception of the First Gulf War is that, in invading Kuwait, Saddam Hussein failed to take account of the likely US (and world) reaction to Iraq's unprovoked aggression against its tiny neighbour. There are those, however, who believe that the US administration of President George H.W. Bush deliberately encouraged the invasion.

In August 1990, Saddam Hussein ordered the armies of Iraq to annex Kuwait and its oilfields. He claimed that Kuwait was part of Iraqi territory, and that it had been illegally taking oil from the Iraqi portion of the Rumaila oilfield on the Iraq–Kuwait border. The main reason seems to have been that annexing Kuwait would enable Saddam to use its immense wealth to pay off debts accrued during the Iran–Iraq War (during which, ironically, Kuwait had aided Iraq and had been bombed by Iran as a result). If oil prices rose because of the invasion, so much the better.

While Saddam's annexation of Kuwait attracted nearly universal condemnation – the Palestine Liberation Organization (PLO) was a notable exception – the US seemed to have particular reason to feel aggrieved. Throughout the 1980s, the US had supplied Saddam with arms, commodity credits, loans and military intelligence to fight Iran – and this was how he repaid them. In January 1991, a US-led UN coalition of forces from 28 countries, including France, Saudi Arabia, Syria and the UK, bombed Iraq's munitions factories and armed forces into the sand, before sweeping the Iraqis out of Kuwait in February.

It so happened, however, that April Glaspie, the US ambassador to Iraq had met Saddam one week before the invasion, as Iraq's forces were massing on the Kuwaiti border. Excerpts from a document described by Iraqi government officials as a transcript of the meeting, and written in Arabic, were subsequently given to ABC News and published by *The New York Times* (see www.chss.montclair.edu/english/furr/glaspie.html). Glaspie is reported as telling Saddam that "we have no opinion on the Arab–Arab conflicts, like your border disagreement with Kuwait", and that this view reflected the instructions of US secretary of state James Baker.

According to the website whatreallyhappened.com, which gives a different version of part of the document, (unidentified) British journalists got hold of the transcript and a tape of the meeting and confronted Glaspie as she left the US embassy in Baghdad. Glaspie is quoted as saying: "Obviously, I didn't think, and nobody else did, that the Iraqis were going to take all of Kuwait." As one journalist is said to have asked, didn't this imply that she thought he was going to take some of it? Glaspie later said that she was the victim of "deliberate deception on a major scale", and denounced the Iraqi transcript as "a fabrication" that distorted her position, although it contained "a great deal" that was accurate. Iraqi deputy prime minister Tariq Aziz said later that Glaspie had not given Iraq a green light for the invasion.

The Washington Times, however, reported that the conversation had become a central "article of faith" among Arab conspiracy theorists as indicating American willingness to turn a blind eye to the invasion of Kuwait. Although conceding in an editorial that it was more likely to have been simply "inept diplomacy", the paper, usually a staunch Republican Party ally, agreed that relations between Iraq and the US had remained friendly right up until August 2, and that no indication had been given that Saddam's invasion would meet with American disapproval.

According to the late Alistair Cooke on his BBC *Letter from America* radio programme, the US was initially against taking military action. It was only a meeting with former British prime minister Margaret Thatcher, said Cooke, that persuaded President George H.W. Bush that Saddam had to be dealt with, as he now posed a threat to Saudi Arabia. Middle East expert Hugh Roberts and Crown Prince Hassan of Jordan later concurred, however, that a diplomatic solution remained possible even after the invasion, but that this possibility was deliberately sabotaged by the US.

Perhaps the last word should be left to Lawrence Korb, assistant defense secretary under Ronald Reagan, who shortly before the Gulf War started was quoted by the *International Herald Tribune* as saying: "If Kuwait grew carrots, we wouldn't give a damn."

Iraq to 9/11 on ten separate occasions, but to no avail: the evidence simply wasn't there.

An Al Qaeda connection?

This didn't stop the Bush administration from talking up the terrorist threat that Iraq allegedly posed. Before the war, US vice president Dick Cheney spoke of "overwhelming evidence" connecting Al Qaeda and the Iraqi government. Condoleezza Rice said "there clearly are contacts between Al Qaeda and Saddam Hussein that can be documented" and told CNN that "Saddam Hussein cavorts with terrorists" (the mind boggles). Bush declared: "We know that Iraq and Al Qaeda have had high-level contacts that go back a decade … Alliance with terrorists could allow the Iraq regime to attack America without leaving any fingerprint" – which, ironically, would make it impossible to prove Iraq's role in such attacks.

In September 2002, Donald Rumsfeld spoke of "bullet-proof" CIA evidence of an Al Qaeda presence in Iraq. When a journalist pointed out to White House spokesman Ari Fleischer that Al Qaeda operatives were suspected only in Iraq's no-fly Kurdish zone, over which Saddam had no control, Fleischer replied: "Iraq is Iraq". In June 2004, both Bush and Cheney were still insisting there were strong Iraq–Al Qaeda connections.

The US Senate's 9-11 Commission, however, concluded that there was "no evidence" of cooperation between Iraq and Al Qaeda, or of Iraq aiding terrorist acts on the US. CIA analyst Melvin Goodman argued that Iraq's regime didn't support terrorism, and that bin Laden considered Saddam – whose Baa'thist regime was secular rather than Islamic – a "socialist infidel". Other US diplomats have said that Saddam giving WMDs to terrorists was "inconceivable". Bush himself later said that there was "no connection" between Saddam and Al Qaeda and, in October 2004, Rumsfeld told the Council on Foreign Relations: "To my knowledge, I have not seen any strong, hard evidence that links the two." Rumsfeld described US intelligence on the subject as having "migrate[d] … in the most amazing way", a statement he later said had been "misunderstood".

A nuclear threat?

The alleged threat posed by Saddam also included nuclear weapons. Before the war, Bush warned: "The regime is seeking a nuclear bomb and with fissible … fissile material could build one within a year". And in January 2003, he told the US Senate that "the British government has learned that Saddam Hussein recently sought significant quantities of uranium from Africa", and that they had documents showing that uranium oxide, or "yellow cake", had been sold to Iraq by Niger. However, US secretary of state Colin Powell hadn't considered the evidence for this claim "sufficiently strong" to present it to the UN eight days earlier. CIA director George Tenet had also deleted the Niger claim from the draft of a speech Bush had given three months earlier, on the basis that it was unreliable.

UN weapons inspector David Albright said that the photos of Iraq's nuclear sites that Colin Powell presented to the UN as evidence were a decade old, and that the charges were "complete nonsense". The International Atomic Energy Agency (IAEA) repeatedly asked the US and UK for copies of the allegedly incriminating documents, but were only given them in February. On March 7 – just eleven days before the war began – the IAEA director-general told the UN Security Council that the yellow cake documents were "not authentic", i.e. they were forged: dates, titles and the names of government ministers were incorrect and words were misspelled. The US national security advisor Condoleezza Rice, meanwhile, told CBS politics show *Meet the Press* that Tenet's deletion of the Niger claim was something that "people didn't remember" when Bush's State of the Union speech was being put together.

Downing Street: behind closed doors

On May 1, 2005, *The Sunday Times* published the top-secret minutes of a meeting held in Downing Street on July 3, 2002, eight months before the invasion of Iraq. It also quoted a briefing paper for the meeting, which proved that Prime Minister Tony Blair had taken the crucial decision to support the US in April 2002. "When the prime minister discussed Iraq with President Bush at Crawford in April", the briefing stated, "he said that the UK would support military action to bring about regime change." As for the Americans, they just wanted to get rid of Saddam, "whether or not he posed an immediate threat", as *The Sunday Times* put it.

This was confirmed at the meeting itself by Sir Richard Dearlove, the chief of the UK intelligence service MI6. Dearlove – identified by his codename "C" – reported on talks that he had held in Washington with CIA director George Tenet. "There was a perceptible shift in attitude", the minutes record. "Military action was now seen as inevitable. Bush wanted to remove Saddam, through military action, justified by the conjunction of terrorism and WMDs. But the intelligence and facts were being fixed around the policy."

For the UK's foreign secretary, Jack Straw, this presented a problem: "The case [for war] was thin. Saddam was not threatening his neighbours, and his WMD capability was less than that of Libya, North Korea or Iran." He then went on to suggest a solution: Saddam should be given an ultimatum to allow the UN weapons inspectors back in, which would also help with the legal justification for the use of force (presumably on the basis that if he refused, it would provide grounds for war).

The attorney general, Lord Goldsmith, however, told the meeting that "the desire for regime change was not a legal base for military action". He explained that there were three legal grounds: "self-defence, intervention to end an humanitarian crisis and a [new] resolution from the UN Security Council". Only the last might apply to Iraq; to rely on an existing UN resolution would be "difficult".

On July 17, 2002, Blair told the House of Commons, referring to military action against Iraq: "as I say constantly, no decisions have yet been taken". From one point of view, he was correct: the first conclusion of the meeting was that "we should work on the assumption that the UK would take part in any military action", but that a fuller picture of US plans was needed before any firm decisions could be made. As the briefing for the meeting made clear, however, Blair had already signed up to support US military action: all he was doing was waiting for the fine print.

Dodgy dossiers: conspiracy and cock-up

The Bush administration wasn't the only one to fit intelligence and facts around the policy of regime change. In September 2002, the British government presented a dossier on Iraq. Among other claims, it stated that Saddam had plans to use biological and chemical weapons and that "some of these weapons [were] deployable within 45 minutes of an order to use them". A second dossier followed in February 2003, entitled "Iraq: its infrastructure of concealment, deception and intimidation", which claimed to be based on numerous sources, including what was described as "intelligence material".

As Cambridge academic Glenn Rangwala discovered, however, the bulk of the February dossier had been directly copied from three previously published articles (not, as widely reported, a PhD thesis). Two of the articles – one dating from 1997 – were from *Jane's Intelligence Review*, an international journal for threat analysis. The biggest debt, however, was to a piece by postgraduate student Ibrahim al-Marashi, based primarily on Iraqi documents captured in the 1991 Gulf War and freely available on the Internet, from where it had been copied complete with grammatical idiosyncrasies and typographical errors. The only substantive changes to the articles were that numbers had been increased or rounded up and particular words had been replaced to make the claim sound stronger.

The impression, inevitably, was that civil servants – whose identities were revealed in the "properties" section of the computer file – had been given the job of coming up with material to back up a decision that had already been taken. This "dodgy dossier", as it came to be known, was later called "wholly counter-productive" by a House of Commons Foreign Affairs Select Committee. The 45-minute claims of the September dossier were similarly claimed to have been "sexed up" (see p.61) and later found to refer to short-range, battlefield tactical weapons.

The Chalabi connection

Similarly dubious claims about the threat posed by Saddam's WMDs were being made on the other side of the Atlantic. In September 2002, Bush told the UN that Saddam had failed to account for over "three tonnes" of material for bio-weapons production, and that Saddam was expanding production facilities for "stockpiles of VX [nerve], mustard and other chemical agents". In his State of the Union address in January 2003, Bush claimed that Saddam hadn't accounted for biological agents that should have been destroyed – enough to make 25,000 litres of anthrax, 38,000 litres of botulin toxin and 500 tonnes of sarin, mustard and VX nerve agents. Iraq also had mobile biological weapons labs. "We know that", Bush asserted, "from three Iraqi defectors."

Those three defectors, it turned out, had been supplied by the industrious Iraqi exile, Ahmad Chalabi, whom some suspect of having played a colossal confidence trick on the US and UK governments. Chalabi, whose wealthy Iraqi Shiite family had fled Iraq in the 1950s, was educated in the US, where he moved in early neoconservative circles. In 1977, he founded a bank in Jordan, whose collapse in 1989 led to his conviction *in absentia* for fraud. Fleeing to the West once more, Chalabi founded, and became the leader of, the Saddam-opposition group, the Iraqi National Congress (INC). Chalabi was such a smooth talker that, in 1995, he separately persuaded the CIA and Kurdish groups that he had the support of the other to overthrow Saddam. But this lethal wheeler-dealing came unstuck when he tried to convince the Iranians to join in, showing them the CIA "plans" to depose Saddam. When the CIA found out about this leak, they ditched the plan wholesale, while Saddam killed thousands of Kurds.

Undeterred, Chalabi continued to lobby for the INC, which was the chief beneficiary of nearly $100 million of funding given to Iraqi opposition groups under the Iraq Liberation Act in 1998. With the support of influential neocon friends, such as Richard Perle and Paul Wolfowitz, Chalabi effectively became the voice of anti-Saddam opposition in Washington. Most importantly, he played a key role in supplying intelligence on WMDs – especially from a defector codenamed "Curveball", the brother of one of Chalabi's aides – that was used by the Bush administration to justify the war in Iraq, notably in a presentation given to the UN by Colin Powell. Chalabi also told the Pentagon that invading US forces would be greeted as "liberators".

"Heroes in error"

When the US-led coalition invaded Iraq, Chalabi was given a position on the country's interim governing council by the Coalition Provisional Authority, and he even served briefly as its president. It wasn't long, however, before Chalabi's chickens came home to roost. Not only did the occupying forces find themselves facing a bloody insurrection, but also the WMD "intelligence" Chalabi had supplied – and been paid millions of dollars for by the Pentagon and State Department – turned out to be bogus. The Robb-Silberman commission into US intelligence failures later said that there was an overreliance on information from defectors.

Chalabi was unrepentant, telling British newspaper *The Daily Telegraph*: "We are heroes in error. As far as we're concerned we've been entirely successful. That tyrant Saddam is gone and the Americans are in Baghdad. What was said before is not important." After CIA chief George Tenet resigned following a number of high-profile intelligence failures, Chalabi was quick to shift the blame: "[Tenet provided] erroneous information about weapons of mass destruction to President Bush."

In 2004, Chalabi was investigated for currency fraud, grand theft and other criminal charges; he has also been accused of passing US state secrets to Iran (with whom he had been in "continuous dialogue"), and even of being an Iranian double agent. Nonetheless, despite all that and polls that showed him to be one of Iraq's least popular politicians, Chalabi still contrived to become the country's acting oil minister and one of its four deputy prime ministers. While no longer holding these posts, in late 2007, he was put in charge of delivering numerous governmental briefs, from security and energy to health, a position requiring the highest backing from both the Iraqi government and the US forces in Iraq. Chalabi seems to be the kind of guy who can be knocked down, if not hoist by his own petard, yet still come back stronger than ever.

A last-minute change of advice

By the end of 2002, Saddam decided to allow UN weapons inspectors back into Iraq, following threats from President Bush that the US would take military action if he failed to disarm. The ensuing reports from UN weapons inspection chief Hans Blix led to bitter debate as to whether Iraq was in "material breach" of its disarmament obligations. The UN Security Council divided, with China, France, Germany and Russia wanting a diplomatic solution and more inspections. The US and UK governments, however, insisted that Saddam had had enough time, and would only carry on playing games as he had already been doing for twelve years.

On the British side, there was one further obstacle. The attorney general, Lord Goldsmith, continued to argue that regime change could not legally be the aim of war, and on March 7, 2003, he delivered a thirteen-page opinion to that effect. Along with a number of other caveats, this stated that a legal war would probably need a second UN Security Council resolution backing the use of force. But then Goldsmith made a trip to Washington, and on his return to the UK, his advice – now whittled down to one side of A4 – was "unequivocal" in arguing that war was legal, which is what the UK Cabinet were told on March 17, 2003. War began just three days later.

The Bush blitzkrieg

If Saddam did have any WMDs left at the time of the invasion, he didn't use them. US vice president Dick Cheney described the advance of coalition forces as being "dazzling" and "unprecedented" in its speed and lightness of casualties (he also drew a favourable – if rather unfortunate – comparison with the 1940 German offensive in the Ardennes). The corresponding speed of Iraq's collapse, however, prompted rumours in the Arab media of a secret arrangement, or *safqa*, between the Iraqi leadership and the US to finish the war quickly and save lives all round. The Muslim pressure group Media Review Network reported that this agreement had been cooked up by Saudi monarch Prince Abdullah, the only Arab leader to be invited to Bush's Crawford ranch.

A simpler explanation, however, is that Iraq's military was collapsing anyway. In February 2001, Colin Powell had said that Saddam was "unable to project conventional power against his neighbours". In July, Condoleezza Rice claimed "we are able to keep his arms from him" and that since the First Gulf War, "his military forces have not been rebuilt". These statements were, of course, made before 9/11. But if they were true, where was the threat?

It's official: no WMDs, no Al Qaeda links

In September 2006, the US Senate Intelligence Committee published the findings of a three-year investigation that concluded that no evidence could be found of any links between Saddam Hussein and Al Qaeda. The investigation also drew attention to the complete lack of evidence concerning the claims over Iraq's weapons of mass destruction (reiterated once again by inspector Hans Blix in March 2008, upon the fifth anniversary of the start of the war).

For months after the invasion, the Iraq Survey Group – led by former UN weapons inspector David Kay with 1400 scientists, and military and intelligence experts – combed

Iraq for weapons of mass destruction. In September 2004, they concluded that there were no WMDs left in Iraq at the time of the invasion. All of Saddam's stockpiles had been destroyed in 1991, and his facilities and programmes dismantled by 1996 – which is what UN weapons inspectors could have confirmed if they'd been allowed to carry on doing their job. The trouble was that Bush and Blair didn't let them. The question is, why not?

For sources, see p.425.

Iraq: the real reasons for war?

In the run-up to the Iraq War (which began on March 20, 2003) the world was warned over and over again that, in defiance of international law, throttling sanctions and repeated bombing, Saddam Hussein was still in possession of all manner of chemical, biological and possibly nuclear weapons. We were reminded that he was a proven mass-murderer of his own people, and that he had waged war on Iran, Kuwait and Israel. He and his weapons of mass destruction could – and in all likelihood would – strike again, and only the US and their allies could stop him... or, so the story went. Having already looked at the "official" reasons given for going to war (see p.408), it's now time to examine the "alternative" explanations that have since come to light.

The neoconservatives' not-so-hidden agenda

One group of neoconservatives had been planning regime change in Iraq well before George W. Bush came to power, let alone before 9/11. In January 1998, the neocon think-tank Project for the New American Century, or PNAC (see p.418), wrote a letter to President Clinton calling for Saddam's removal. "If Saddam does acquire the capability to deliver weapons of mass destruction", the letter argued, "the safety of American troops in the region, of our friends and allies like Israel and the moderate Arab states, and a significant portion of the world's supply of oil will all be put at hazard".

The first signatory of the letter was Elliott Abrams. Abrams had escaped prison in 1991 by pleading guilty to failing to tell Congress that he had solicited a $10 million contribution for the right-wing Nicaraguan Contra rebels (see p.201) from the sultan of Brunei. He was pardoned by George H.W. Bush in 1992. At the time of the PNAC letter to President Clinton, Abrams was president of… the Ethics and Public Policy Center, and in February 2005, George W. Bush made him deputy national security adviser, with special responsibility for his strategy for… democracy.

The PNAC letter's other signatories included: John Bolton (later George W. Bush's under-secretary of state for arms control, and then US ambassador to the UN); Richard Perle (assistant defense secretary under Reagan, and later chairman of the Defense Policy Board); Donald Rumsfeld (defense secretary under Gerald Ford and George W. Bush, who met Saddam twice as Reagan's special envoy to the Middle East during the Iran–Iraq War); and Paul Wolfowitz (under-secretary of defense to Dick Cheney, deputy secretary of defense to Donald Rumsfeld, and later president of the World Bank).

A further PNAC letter – whose signatories again included all of the above – was sent to the speaker of the US House

THE PROJECT FOR THE NEW AMERICAN CENTURY

Were it not for the fact that it makes no secret of its goals, the Project for the New American Century (PNAC) would be the sort of organization that gives conspiracy theories a good name. A Washington-based foreign-policy think-tank and pressure group, the PNAC describes itself as "an educational organization supporting American global military, diplomatic, and moral leadership". For the likes of former British Labour minister Michael Meacher, former Labour MP Tam Dalyell and many more, however, the PNAC is a sinister and dangerous neoconservative cabal bent on achieving American world domination. The PNAC has also held the George W. Bush presidency in its thrall for years, with the group's members stalking many corridors of power in the White House and beyond.

PNAC's origins can be traced back to a controversial "Defense Policy Guidance" (DPG) paper drafted in 1992 under the supervision of Paul Wolfowitz for then-defense secretary Dick Cheney, during George H.W. Bush's administration. The document's central strategy was to "establish and protect a new order" and to maintain the mechanisms capable of "deterring potential competitors from even aspiring to a larger regional or global role". Scenarios in which US interests could be threatened by regional conflict included "access to vital raw materials, primarily Persian Gulf oil [and] proliferation of weapons of mass destruction". (Examples of possible conflict areas included North Korea and Iraq; the latter had recently been defeated in the Gulf War, but with Saddam's regime left in place.) If necessary, the paper said, the US should act pre-emptively and unilaterally – and yet, in a classic example of double-think, to "promote increasing respect for international law, limit international violence, and encourage the spread of democratic forms of government and open economic systems".

When the DPG paper was leaked to the press, it caused a furore both in the US and abroad. Officials, however, claimed that the document – which described itself as "definitive guidance from the Secretary of Defense" – had not been given final approval by Cheney or Wolfowitz, although they both acknowledged that they had played a substantial role in its creation and endorsed its principal views. A toned-down version was subsequently produced (see www.yale.edu/strattech/92dpg.html).

In 1997, along with Florida governor Jeb Bush (George W.'s brother), former and future defense secretary Donald Rumsfeld and other prominent neocons, Wolfowitz and Cheney signed the Statement of Principles issued by the newly formed PNAC. Harking back to the Reagan era, the statement talked of the need to "shape a new century favorable to American principles and interests", which would require four main actions: significantly increasing defence spending, challenging regimes hostile to US interests and values, promoting political and economic freedom abroad, and accepting responsibility for the US's role in "preserving and extending an international order friendly to our security, our prosperity, and our principles".

The key document for understanding the PNAC's world-view, however, came in September 2000, shortly before George W. Bush became president. "Rebuilding America's Defenses" (RAD) was based on the earlier "Defense Policy Guidance". Describing the DPG as "a blueprint for maintaining US preeminence … and shaping the international security order in line with American principles and interests", the RAD states: "The basic tenets of the DPG, in our judgment, remain sound". It's hardly surprising that one of the report's listed project participants was Paul Wolfowitz.

The report's core missions for the US military included the need to "fight and decisively win multiple, simultaneous major theater wars" and "to perform the 'constabulary' duties associated with shaping the security environment in critical regions" – the US as global sheriff, in other words. To fulfil these missions, the US would need to develop and deploy global missile defences "to provide a secure basis for US power projection around the world", and control space and cyberspace. The report even hinted that the US should consider developing its own biological weapons, suggesting that technological advances "may transform biological warfare from the realm of terror to a politically useful tool".

of Representatives and to the majority leader in the Senate in May 1998. The letter stated: "We should establish and maintain a strong US military presence in the region, and be prepared to use that force to protect our vital interests in the Gulf – and, if necessary, to help remove Saddam from power." This letter was followed, in 2000, by a PNAC report called "Rebuilding America's Defenses" (RAD), which now reads as a blueprint for George W. Bush's foreign policy.

If all that weren't frightening enough, the report describes the process of technological transformation of US military capabilities as "likely to be a long one, absent some catastrophic and catalyzing event – like a new Pearl Harbor". Given the suspicions that a previous US administration deliberately allowed Pearl Harbor to be attacked (see p.360), conspiracy theorists see this as evidence that in 2000, PNAC had somehow already factored 9/11 into its plans.

Its undeniable that Bush's post-9/11 pronouncements on defence policy seem to have been drawn straight from the RAD – and the claimed right to take pre-emptive and unilateral action from the earlier DPG. The "Axis of Evil" to which Bush referred in his 2002 State of the Union address, corresponded exactly to the threats identified by RAD, which had said: "We cannot allow North Korea, Iran, Iraq or similar states to undermine American leadership, intimidate American allies or threaten the American homeland itself." Similarly, RAD had called for the US to withdraw from the anti-ballistic missile treaty, to commit itself to a global missile defence system and to increase defence spending to as much as 3.8 percent of GDP – precisely what Bush did in 2002. The successive years of his presidency also saw historically unprecedented growth in military spending. What the PNAC proposed, the president made policy.

Enacting PNAC policy required the positioning of PNAC members in high places within George W. Bush's administration. Jeb Bush's role in winning the White House for the Republicans in 2000 is well known (see p.232), while Cheney became vice president, Rumsfeld defense secretary, and Wolfowitz deputy defense secretary. Other PNAC members holding offices in high places in military and international affairs included: Cheney's chief of staff I. Lewis "Scooter" Libby, Richard Armitage as deputy secretary of state, Richard Perle as chairman of the Defense Policy Advisory Committee, Francis Fukuyama on the President's Council on Bioethics, and Zalmay Khalilzad as US ambassador to Afghanistan and later Iraq. John Bolton oversaw the most virulent growth in military spending during his time as under-secretary of state for arms control, as well as the cancellation of arms- and missile-control treaties – he was then appointed as US ambassador to the UN.

However, almost without exception, the great neocon enterprises failed. By 2008, seven years after the invasion, the Taliban were still so much of an influence in Afghanistan that it was being mooted that they would have to negotiate with them to secure peace. Five years after the invasion of Iraq, that country remained in a state of almost a daily massacre. Meanwhile, Iran was as defiant as it was undemocratic, North Korea was armed with nuclear weapons, and oil prices were sky-high. The PNAC members also saw their own fortunes crash as violently as they had ascended: the US Senate refused to ratify Bolton's tenure at the UN (he was replaced by Khalilzad); Rumsfeld and Wolfowitz's respective posts at the Pentagon and World Bank ended in humiliating ignominy; Libby's role in the so-called Plame Affair, or CIA leak scandal, would have seen him in jail had not President Bush pardoned him; and Jeb Bush dropped out of further campaigns to govern Florida, let alone the country.

Unfortunately, the PNAC isn't the only neocon think-tank on the block. Other groups include the similarly influential American Enterprise Institute (AEI), which rents office space to the PNAC in its own building. George W. Bush also claimed to have borrowed a score of the AEI's members to work with his administration. Similar organizations include the Heritage Foundation and the Center for Security Policy, with the latter's mission being "to promote world peace through American strength". Another policy group that regularly crops up in conspiracy theories is the RAND Corporation, which has existed since World War II. It is renowned for its handle on statistics and probabilities for war scenarios, and has employed more than a few big guns in US politics. These days, RAND researches everything from how to avoid becoming a terrorist target to how to avoid becoming fat. In comparison, however, the PNAC seems less the stuff of conspiracy theory than of realpolitik fact.

Stating that the US had sought to play a more permanent role in Gulf regional security for decades, the report said: "While the unresolved conflict with Iraq provides the immediate justification, the need for a substantial American force presence in the Gulf transcends the issue of the regime of Saddam Hussein."

The principal author of the RAD report was Thomas Donnelly, who subsequently became director of strategic communications and initiatives at Lockheed Martin, the world's largest defence contractor (see p.123). Among the contributors listed at the end of the report were I. Lewis "Scooter" Libby (formerly George H.W. Bush's deputy under-secretary of defense, and later chief of staff to Vice President Dick Cheney) and Paul Wolfowitz, who supervised the writing of the controversial "Defense Policy Guidance" (DPG) with Libby for then-defense secretary Cheney in 1992. Among other things, this policy guidance stated that the US should use military power to protect "access to vital raw materials, primarily Persian Gulf oil".

Perhaps the last word here should be left to former PNAC co-chairman Donald Kagan, another contributor to RAD. Acknowledging the probable need for a major concentration of forces in the Middle East over a long period of time, Kagan told reporter Jay Bookman in September 2002: "When we have economic problems, it's been caused by disruptions in our oil supply. If we have a force in Iraq, there will be no disruption in oil supplies." For the PNAC, it was as simple as that.

It's the oil, stupid

On January 15, 2003, two months before a coalition of US-led forces invaded Iraq, Labour MP Dennis Skinner put it to UK prime minister Tony Blair that the imminent war was all about "America getting their hands on the oil supplies in the Middle East". Rejecting what he called "the conspiracy theory idea that this is somehow to do with oil", Blair argued that if this were the issue, it would be "infinitely simpler to cut a deal with Saddam, who I'm sure would be delighted to give us access to as much oil as we wanted if he could carry on building weapons of mass destruction". What the war was about, Blair insisted, was Iraq's growing arsenal of WMDs: in the light of 9/11, the madman of Baghdad had to be stopped.

It was the same story on the other side of the Atlantic. Just a month before Blair's rejection of the oil explanation, US defense secretary Donald Rumsfeld was asked by CBS's *60 Minutes* if the coming war was about oil. "Nonsense. It just isn't",

No blood for oil: Iraqi anti-war protest at the Doura oil refinery near Baghdad, March 2003.

he snapped, and called the idea a "myth". Asked the same question on the same programme, however, oil and gas expert Phillip Ellis of Boston Consulting replied, "Of course it is".

The players

The oil theory was lent added weight by the close links between the Bush family and their various administrations and the oil industry. President George H.W. Bush had spent the 1950s climbing the greasy pole in the Texas oil industry, becoming chief of Zapata Petroleum (which, ironically, took its name from a Mexican guerrilla leader). Before beginning his own political career, his son George W. Bush started up the oil company Arbusto (Spanish for "bush"), which was part-financed by Osama bin Laden's brother.

After the largely unsuccessful Arbusto merged with Harken Energy in 1986, Bush's connections paid off, with Harken winning its first overseas oil-drilling contract in Bahrain. (The Bush family also has strong ties with the Saudi royal family, see p.406, and the Carlyle Group.) Bush eventually became governor of the oil state, Texas, and according to the Center for Public Integrity, six of the ten largest contributors to his presidential campaign came from or had connections with the oil business. Meanwhile, Secretary of State Condoleezza Rice, who had been a member of George H.W. Bush's National Security Council, went on to become a board member of Chevron in 1991 and even had a 130,000-tonne tanker named after her.

The biggest player, however, has to be Vice President Dick Cheney, who between 1995 and 2000 earned $44 million as chief executive of Texas-based Halliburton, the world's largest oil and gas services company. (You have to admire Cheney's chutzpah: in his last year at Halliburton, he also served as the head of George W. Bush's vice-presidential search committee, considering various candidates before finally selecting… himself.)

The Cheney–Halliburton connection was well explored in a 2004 article in *The New Yorker* by Jane Mayer. Both in and out of government, says Mayer, Cheney has been a longtime champion of the private sector, arguing that it can supply cheaper and better services than state bureaucracies. As Mayer points out, his arguments seem to have won the day – in 2002, for example, over $150 billion of public money was transferred from the Pentagon to private contractors. These include Cheney's old firm, Halliburton, which is by far one of the largest private contractors for US forces in Iraq, having received contracts worth up to $11 billion for its work there.

This, however, marked the culmination of a process begun ten years earlier, when Cheney was defense secretary under George H.W. Bush. As Peter W. Singer notes in his book *Corporate Warriors*, when the Pentagon decided to contract out its non-military support services for overseas operations to a single contractor, it paid Halliburton $9 million to carry out two studies into this. It came as no surprise that when the US Army awarded a five-year contract for providing all its overseas support services in August 1992, that contract went to the very same firm that had carried out the studies – Halliburton.

Under Cheney's stewardship, Halliburton nearly doubled its government contracts, from $1.2 billion to $2.3 billion. And although Cheney claimed, in 2000, that he had a "firm policy" that Halliburton should not do any business with Iraq, two of Halliburton's subsidiaries signed Iraqi contracts worth more than $73 million while he was CEO. The deals helped to reconstruct Iraq's oil-production infrastructure – the very same infrastructure whose destruction Cheney had supervised while he was defense secretary during the First Gulf War.

As regards the Iraq War, the closest thing to a "smoking gun" is a top-secret National Security Council document of February 3, 2001. This document instructed NSC staff to offer their full cooperation to Cheney's newly formed Energy Task Force during its consideration of what it described as the "melding" of two policy areas: "the review of operational policies towards rogue states" – which naturally included Iraq – and "actions regarding the capture of new and existing oil and gas fields".

The prize

There's a lot of oil in Iraq. It has proven reserves of 112 billion barrels – the world's largest after Saudi Arabia's – and may have up to 220 billion barrels. Global oil reserves, on the other hand, have peaked, while demand (mainly from Asia) is set to soar. By 2025, meanwhile, the Department of Energy estimates that the US – the world's largest consumer of oil – will be importing up to seventy percent of the oil it needs. In September 2002, *The Washington Post* reported that ousting Saddam would herald a "bonanza" for American oil companies long banished from Iraq, while scuppering oil deals Iraq had with Russia, France and China. These three countries – all ambivalent or flatly against the Iraq War – had previously agreed oil concessions with Saddam, to be developed once UN sanctions were lifted.

Faisal Qaragholi, petroleum engineer and London director of the exiled Iraqi National Congress (INC) opposition group, said the INC wasn't bound by these deals. INC leader Ahmed Chalabi (see p.415) added: "American companies will have a big shot at Iraqi oil". An eve-of-war speech by George W. Bush, ironically published on the White House website under a banner bearing the words "Iraq: Denial and Deception", seemed to reflect the order of priorities. First, he warned Iraqis not to destroy oil wells, describing them as "a source of wealth that belongs to the Iraqi people", and then he told them "not [to] obey any command to use weapons of mass destruction", adding that war crimes would be prosecuted.

The Axis of Evil and the dollar/euro switch

There again, it might not be oil as such, but the currency it's sold in. Saddam Hussein switched to selling oil in euros in 2000, which increased Iraqi profits as the euro rose against the US dollar. When the US put Iraqi oil back on the open market in 2003, the *Financial Times* reported, it switched the trading currency back to US dollars. Iran, meanwhile, has sold its oil in euros since 2003, while North Korea ditched dollars for euros in 2002. As journalist Robert Fisk speculated in *The Independent*, Bush's so-called "Axis of Evil" might, in fact, be an "axis of euro", which – in challenging the supremacy of the dollar as the dominant trading currency for oil – poses a threat to the economic well-being of the US itself.

Officially, one of the most important reasons why Iran should be regarded as part of this "Axis of Evil" is its development of enriched uranium, which can be used in both bombs and power stations. Quite why a country rich in oil and gas needs nuclear power stations is not clear, but doubts have been raised about whether Iran has a nuclear bomb programme. In November 2004, *The Washington Post* reported that a "single unvetted source" supplied the intelligence for US secretary of state Colin Powell's accusation of Iranian nuclear bomb-building, while UN weapons inspector Mohamed El Baradei said in February 2005 that the International Atomic Energy Agency (IAEA) lacked "conclusive evidence" of such a programme.

But that lack of evidence did not abate White House rhetoric about attacking Iran, and the war-talk grew in violence and volume throughout 2006. Washington's issues with Iran sounded unnervingly similar to those made against Iraq in the run-up to that war in 2003, with Defense Secretary Donald Rumsfeld describing Iran as having "indicated an interest in having weapons of mass destruction" and as supporting terrorists. In Spring 2006, *The New Yorker* and *The Washington Post* carried journalist Seymour Hersh's top-sourced reports that claimed air strikes on Iran were "beyond contingency planning". And Bush declared that "no options" were off the table with regards to a pre-emptive nuclear strike on Iran. Some top US generals were concerned enough to let it slip, according to *The Times* in February 2007, that they were prepared to quit should any such attacks be carried out. Iran did not help its case by defying calls to allow full inspections of its nuclear facilities, and proclaiming wilful indifference to UN sanctions. But, despite all this, Iran continued to protest its innocence over WMDs, with President Mahmoud

Ahmadinejad reiterating the claim before audiences of university students in the US in late 2007.

Finally, in December 2007, the drums of war were seemingly, and shockingly, silenced, when the US National Intelligence Estimate (NIE), collating the work of sixteen intelligence agencies, concluded that Iran had suspended its nuclear weapons programme four years before, in 2003. The stark discrepancy between Bush's rhetoric and this disclosure caused great disquiet around the world, but Bush nonetheless asserted, "Nothing's changed … I think the NIE makes it clear that Iran needs to be taken seriously as a threat to peace".

But why would the White House be so hellbent on taking on Iran? According to writer William Clark, Iran's supposed nuclear ambitions are just a pretext for attacking the country – the real problem with Iran is its setting-up, in direct competition with the London-based International Petroleum Exchange and New York's Mercantile Exchange, of a euro-based oil trading exchange in 2005. This, Clark argues, will further increase the desirability and purchasing power of the euro while sending the dollar into a tailspin of devaluation and dumping from capital markets, thereby hammering the US economy. A pro-US regime in Iraq, on the other hand, will help to counter the move towards "petroeuros". In the short term, the Iraq War may add to massive US deficits and do nothing to halt the dollar's decline. But, in the long term, the cost of this – borne by taxpayers anyway – is outweighed by the benefits of ensuring that the black stuff continues to be sold in the US's own currency.

Iran's oil stock exchange was not set up as scheduled, but from 2005 to 2007, the country took systematic steps to have most of its oil contracts paid in euros. Then, in February 2008, just weeks after the NIE's conclusions made it very clear that it would be nigh on impossible to justify an attack, Iran inaugurated its exchange. The US dollar became just one of many currencies, including the euro and the ruble, used for oil trading, and it became increasingly sidelined as its value began to drop.

A further twist to this theory was added by the Arab news network Al Jazeera, which reported that the Organization of the Petroleum Exporting Countries' (OPEC) drift towards euros was only stymied by the US's ally Saudi Arabia, something "largely suppressed in the US media". The continued hegemony of the dollar, it would seem, relies heavily on Saudi support. As the euro rises in parity and desirability, increasingly becoming the reserve currency for India, China and Russia, the US, in turn, is becoming increasingly dependent on Saudi goodwill.

An offer Saddam shouldn't have refused

There's another theory that says that the war was really just sour grapes over Saddam's refusal to play ball in what amounted to a political and financial protection racket. According to John Perkins in *Confessions of an Economic Hit Man*, the US helps to keep the House of Saud in power in return for the House of Saud helping to keep oil prices stable and investing or spending a large part of its petro-dollar income in the US, a scheme benefiting both sides handsomely. Thus the Saudis not only invested heavily in US government securities, but also used US firms to build new cities and infrastructure in Saudi Arabia – and then, of course, there are all those juicy defence contracts.

A similar deal, along with some cheap World Bank loans, was apparently proposed to Saddam, only he turned it down, not realizing that it was an offer he couldn't refuse. According to Perkins, refusing such offers leads to CIA-backed "jackals" fomenting a coup d'état or setting up an assassination. Failing this – before his capture in 2003, Saddam had proved a notoriously elusive target – the next stage is, and always has been, war.

Zionist conspiracy

Given the close relationship between the US and Israel on the one hand, and the fact that Iraq is an Arab country on the other, it's hardly surprising that the war has been seen by some as a Zionist conspiracy. In March 2003, *The New York Times* reported the theory that a cadre of pro-Zionist zealots in the White House and the media seeking to oust Saddam and make the Middle East safe for Israel had finally succeeded. Congressman Jim Moran declared: "If it were not for the strong support of the Jewish community for this war with Iraq, we would not be doing this." Similarly, the late Professor Edward Said of Columbia University pointed to the "Zionist lobby, right-wing Christians or the military-industrial complex" in Congress who hate the Arab world. However, given the fact that Saddam had attacked Israel with Scud missiles during the First Gulf War, Israel's support for his removal is hardly surprising, and in itself, provides no evidence of a Zionist plot.

Ongoing grief

The most important official reason given for the war on Iraq was the threat posed by Saddam's alleged WMD capabilities. With the benefit of hindsight (which is a wonderful thing), WMDs were a threat that was not so much exaggerated as nonexistent. As the Iraq Survey Group confirmed, the weapons and facilities in question had been destroyed following UN inspections in the 1990s. In the end, however, it was not Saddam, but Bush and Blair who had stopped the weapons inspectors from carrying on with their job and finding this out. And up to that point, the US and UK governments deliberately exaggerated the scale of the alleged threat. In the UK at least, people weren't fooled: in September 2003, *The Independent* published an opinion poll that suggested that 59 percent of the British public believed that Blair had lied over Iraq.

George W. Bush and Tony Blair were both re-elected following the start of the Iraq War, in 2004 and 2005 respectively – yet Iraq was ultimately a factor in the Republicans' drubbing in the 2006 US midterm elections and in Blair's departure from office the following year. Serious damage was done to public trust in both "intelligence" and political leaders, meaning that the citizens of the US and the UK are less likely to believe their governments if a genuine threat emerges in the future. As the US Robb-Silberman commission put it: "US credibility was put on the line over the existence of an Iraqi WMD programme – and as a result of nothing being found, it has been severely undermined."

On the war's fifth anniversary, in March 2008, the *Financial Times* damningly opined: "These five years have provided the most public demonstration of the limits to American power – watched live on satellite television throughout the Arab and Muslim worlds like a modern version of the Crusades." The same day, top UN weapons inspector Hans Blix called the invasion "a tragedy – for Iraq, for the US, for the UN, for truth and human dignity". Bush, on the other hand, said it was a "noble" war that would become "a major strategic victory in the broader war on terror", having already made the world safer by deposing Saddam. However, a joint poll by ABC and *The Washington Post* found that over two-thirds of Americans considered the war to be no longer worth waging.

International relations have hardly been helped either, not only in the West, but also between the West and the rest of the world, particularly Islamic countries. And the wave of sympathy for the US that 9/11 created (though not everywhere) has, at best, subsided. For some, the US and the UK's willingness to take pre-emptive, bilateral military action – in what they see as blatant disregard of the UN, international law and the centuries-old principles of a just war – sets a dangerous precedent.

In late 2007, the Congressional Budget Office reported that the Iraq War had cost US taxpayers over $400 billion, with $11 billion being added each month – probably leading to a total of more than $600 billion by the end of 2008. The Iraq War and the ongoing tensions in Iran have also helped send oil prices soaring from under $30 a barrel at the time of the invasion to over $110 a barrel in March 2008, making global economic depression even more likely. Such an economic downturn will probably begin in the oil-dependent US, with the country already burdened by massive war-debts and at the centre of a global credit crunch.

Some US construction firms, service providers, defence contractors and oil companies – often with strong Washington connections – seem to be doing very nicely out of the war, thank you, and will probably continue to do so. Meanwhile some unemployed Iraqis are so desperate for work that they're prepared to risk being blown up as they queue for equally dangerous jobs in the police force that pay just a few dollars a day.

The full human cost of the war and ongoing insurrection is impossible to calculate. At the time of writing, at least 4000 US, 175 British and 126 coalition soldiers had been killed (according to an Associated Press count), with contractor deaths estimated at around 1000. Neither the US nor the UK, on the other hand, has attempted to try to keep track of the ever-increasing number of Iraqi civilian casualties, as dozens are killed almost daily in car bombs and shootings in Baghdad alone. The independent Iraq Body Count project estimated civilian deaths in Iraq from 2003 to 2007 at 89,790, but a controversial *Lancet* report extrapolated a far higher death toll of 655,000 civilians from 2003 to 2006. Oxfam reported in 2007 that 28 percent of Iraqi children were malnourished and over two-thirds lacked clean drinking water, both "sharp increases" since 2003. That same year, adult unemployment was figured at at least fifty percent, while at the same time the country's professional classes left in droves – up to eighty percent of doctors from Baghdad's hospitals and universities were reported to have gone by 2008.

Overall, though, surely it can't be denied that Iraq is better off without Saddam Hussein? Well, that's a question for the Iraqi people to answer – and at least they now have the chance to speak for themselves. But to justify the war in terms of regime change is ultimately the equivalent of saying that the end justifies the means. The $64 billion question, however, is what end or ends the Bush and Blair administrations were pursuing through regime change – and in whose interests? Whether we suspected Saddam and Al Qaeda of plotting to use weapons of mass destruction, or Bush and Blair of using weapons of mass deception, we're all conspiracy theorists now.

SOURCES

Books

Ross Carne Independent Diplomat: Dispatches from an Unaccountable Elite (2007). Carne, a rising star in the British diplomatic corps, resigned in the run-up to the Iraq War in protest over the West's right to wage war on Iraq.

Richard Clarke Against All Enemies: Inside America's War on Terror (2004). Clarke advised presidents Reagan, H.W. Bush, Clinton and W. Bush. He castigates the latter for failing to take terrorism seriously, and for then turning on Iraq immediately after 9/11 as the "Vulcans" (Wolfowitz, Rice, Rumsfeld) had been planning all along.

Laurie Mylroie Bush vs the Beltway: The Inside Battle over War in Iraq (2004). Mylroie, an American Enterprise Institute fellow who advised Bill Clinton on Iraq, argues that the CIA and State Department, among others, conspired to discredit vital intelligence about the threat from Saddam and his links with Al Qaeda. In *The War Against America* (2001) – praised by Richard Perle – she claimed that Saddam was involved in the 1993 World Trade Center bombing.

Stephen C. Pelletiere Iraq and the International Oil System: Why America Went to War in the Persian Gulf (2001). A pretty savage indictment of the US government's motives for its continued interference in the Gulf, by the CIA's own analyst for the Iran–Iraq War.

William Rivers Pitt and Scott Ritter War on Iraq: What Team Bush Doesn't Want You to Know (2002). Ritter (a former UN weapons inspector) and Pitt lay into the neocons pushing the US into war, shooting down the Bush administration's arguments about Saddam's WMDs and his alleged connections with Al Qaeda.

Randeep Ramesh (ed) The War We Could Not Stop: The Real Story of the Battle for Iraq (2004). British, American and Arabic-speaking journalists detail the historical context to the Iraq War, from the rise of a neocon cabal in Washington to Tony Blair's efforts to bring the UK onside with fears of Iraq's WMDs.

Geoff Simons Iraq: From Sumer to Post-Saddam (2004). This book lays out the history of a nation created, exploited and invaded in the cynical pursuit of Western interests.

Gore Vidal Dreaming War: Blood for Oil and the Cheney-Bush Junta (2003). Bush (with his curious family connections to the bin Ladens) and Cheney are "corporate oil gunslingers" who were warned that 9/11 was likely but needed an excuse to take on Iraq. A typically pugnacious piece from the vitriolic Vidal.

Bob Woodward Plan of Attack: The Road to War (2004). Journalist Woodward, one of the famous Watergate investigation duo, reports from within the White House in the run-up to the Iraq War, detailing the split between the gung-ho Cheney and Rumsfeld and the more cautious Colin Powell and General Tommy Franks. The influence of Saudi ambassador Prince Bandar emerges particularly clearly.

Films

Robert Greenwald Uncovered: The Whole Truth about the Iraq War (2003). A score of experts weigh in with sober judgements on the "threat" from Iraq, and against the painful paucity of facts coming from the Bush administration and their use of frightening rhetoric.

Websites

- **www.americaforsale.org** Carrying the banner "This is not a conspiracy theory. This is history in the making", this site uses mainstream media sources to counter the kind of misinformation and misunderstanding that has led seventy percent of Americans, according to CNN, to believe that Iraqis attacked the US on 9/11.
- **www.casi.org.uk/discuss/2003/msg00457.html** Cambridge academic Dr Glenn Rangwala's exposure of the UK government's "dodgy dossier", with links to both the original dossier and one of the three articles (not, as commonly thought, a PhD thesis) it plagiarized.
- **globalresearch.ca/articles/CLA410A.html** "The Real Reasons Why Iran is the Next Target" – an article by William Clark that supports the euro vs dollar theory.
- **www.gwu.edu/~nsarchiv/special/iraq/** "The Saddam Hussein Sourcebook: Declassified Secrets from the US–Iraq Relationship" is another invaluable Web publication from the US National Security Archive. Click on "Iraq and Weapons of Mass Destruction".
- **intelligence.senate.gov/phaseiiaccuracy.pdf The US Senate Select Committee's 2006 findings about Iraq's WMDs and links to terrorism – plus how they compare to the pre-war assessments.**
- **www.newyorker.com/archive/2004/02/16/040216fa_fact** "Contract Sport: What did the Vice President do for Halliburton?" by Jane Mayer. *The New Yorker*, famous for its fact-checking, delves into the murky connections between Vice President Dick Cheney and government contracts awarded to Halliburton, his former employer.
- **www.oxfam.org/en/policy/briefingpapers/bp105_humanitarian_challenge_in_iraq_0707** Oxfam's 2007 Iraq policy brief.
- **www.thelancet.com/webfiles/images/ journals/lancet/s0140673606694919.pdf** *The Lancet*'s mortality report, proposing a death toll of at least 600,000 Iraqis since the 2003 invasion.
- **wwww.timesonline.co.uk/tol/news/uk/article387374.ece** "The secret Downing Street memo", i.e. the minutes of the 23 July, 2002 meeting, which was published in *The Sunday Times* on May 1, 2005.

The Madrid train bombings

Madrid, Spain, Thursday March 11, 2004: in the space of three minutes leading up to 7.40am, ten bombs blew apart four packed commuter trains, all trundling along the same line of track towards Madrid's Atocha station during the morning rush hour. In total, 191 people were killed and over 2000 injured in what was the worst terrorist attack in Europe since the Lockerbie air disaster of 1988 (see p.331).

The official line: ETA's responsible

Before the day was out, the Spanish government under Prime Minister José María Aznar and the Partido Popular (PP) was singularly pointing the finger of blame at the Basque separatist group Euskadi ta Askatasuna, or ETA. The charge was, in part, based on early police information that said the suspected explosive used in the bombings was Titadine, a type frequently used by ETA in their attacks. The group had also issued warnings about a big attack being imminent, in response to Aznar's tough, combative, no compromise stance against them. (ETA's battle for a separate homeland in the Basque region of northern Spain had, since the 1960s, resulted in the deaths of more than 850 people in bombings and shootouts.)

"It is absolutely clear that the terrorist organization ETA was seeking an attack with wide repercussions", Interior Minister Angel Acebes declared that same day, and Aznar sought to counter those repercussions by calling for all Spaniards to show solidarity and take to the streets in protest on Friday March 12. The mass protests were also held just two days before the polls opened for Spain's 2004 general election. Pre-election polls had indicated a narrow lead for Aznar's party over their socialist opponents, Partido Socialista Obrero Español (PSOE), led by José Luis Rodríguez Zapatero. And, following the Madrid tragedy, political commentators suggested that hardliner Aznar would see his lead – and his chance of re-election – increase if ETA were deemed responsible for the attack.

However, ETA's political wing Batasuna immediately responded to Aznar and Acebes' accusations by saying they "absolutely rejected" responsibility for the bombings. Others began pointing at Islamic terrorist organization Al Qaeda, and US intelligence agencies reportedly said that multiple, closely timed bombings were "characteristics" of both ETA and Al Qaeda. On the very day of the atrocity, an Al Qaeda-affiliated group called the Abu Hafs al-Masri Brigades claimed responsibility for the attacks in a letter sent to the London-based Arabic newspaper *Al-Quds Al-Arabi*, but its claims were widely considered unreliable. Nevertheless, the scale of the carnage was more typical of Al Qaeda than ETA, which not only usually forewarned of specific attacks, but had also, of late, targeted high-level Spanish officials, rather than groups of civilians.

It could well be either, reported right-wing US think-tank the Heritage Foundation on March 16, 2004 – or even both. The Foundation suggested that the bombing could have been the result of an ETA–Al Qaeda collaboration to shatter the alliance between Spain and the US, "precisely because it has been so effective in combating terrorism". But the think-tank declared that Al Qaeda was the most likely suspect, as Spain was at the "forefront" of the global war on terror. Prime Minister Aznar was such a strong backer of the Iraq War that he had hosted the historic Azores summit on the eve of the war in March 2003, which could certainly have put Spain in line for terrorist retaliation. (Some conspiracists who believed Al Qaeda was responsible noted that the Madrid attack came 911 days after 9/11 – but there were, in fact, 912 days between September 11, 2001 and March 11, 2004.)

As speculation mounted, investigations were already well underway in Madrid, and it soon became apparent that the official line blaming ETA for the attacks was highly unlikely. All four of the trains had departed from Alcalá de Henares station, and the police found a van nearby containing detonators, a tape of Koranic verses, and mobile phones that were thought to have been used to detonate the bombs. The explosives used were also soon disclosed as being Goma-2, not Titadine as first suspected. Just two days after the attack, on Saturday March 13, three Moroccans and two Indians were arrested in connection with the incident, and following a tip-off to a Spanish TV station, the police found a video purportedly created by those behind the attack, in which they declared it to be Al Qaeda's revenge for Spain sending troops to Iraq and Afghanistan.

On the day of the attack, one prophetic pollster had declared that if "the rumours about Al Qaeda gain credence, then things would be perceived in a very different way" – and so they were. With all the evidence pointing to Al Qaeda being released in the run-up to polling day – together with incendiary revelations by Spanish intelligence that they had told the government, on the very day of the bombings, that Islamist militants were probably responsible, but were told to stay quiet – Aznar's Partido Popular saw its early lead fall and the election take a very different direction. The official line remained that it was ETA, ETA, ETA – and Aznar was soon vigorously denounced. He was condemned for using the attacks to justify his government's hardline policy on ETA, with the charges spearheaded by his opponent José Luis Rodríguez Zapatero and given full headline support by socialist-leaning newspapers like *El País*.

With the evidence seeming to suggest that Al Qaeda was responsible for the attack, Aznar was doubly damned, as the bombings were widely perceived as retaliation for Spain's involvement in the Iraq War – a war that Aznar had backed in the face of opposition from ninety percent of the Spanish public and the majority of the Spanish parliament. On March 14, the Spanish people made their feelings clear: Aznar lost the election, Zapatero's socialist party won office, and a major ally in the US-led Iraq War was brought down. Just over a month after winning the election, Zapatero announced the withdrawal of Spanish forces from Iraq. His actions were seen, by some, as surrendering to terrorist threats.

Some blamed the Zionists

Although ETA and Al Qaeda were widely considered the main suspects, other theories, of course, abound. One theory proffered by a few Middle East newspapers suggested that the van-load of Islamic evidence at Alcalá de Henares station was really part of an attempt to frame Arabs for what was really a Zionist attack. A columnist in Kuwait's *Al-Watan* newspaper said: "I claim with certainty that the ones who attributed all evil to the Arabs and the Muslims are the Zionists, those who are closest to carry out such an operation like the other operations." And a Saudi newspaper of the same name chided Arab intelligence services for being "incapable of discovering the hidden Zionist fingers planning many terror operations" that framed Muslims. The Egyptian *Al-Gumhouriyya* went so far as to accuse Zionists of being behind every terrorist attack worldwide.

Neither ETA nor Al Qaeda?

And although Al Qaeda's involvement was generally considered far more likely than ETA's, neither could be definitively proven at that time. On April 3, 2004, police laid siege to an apartment in the Madrid suburb of Leganés, which they suspected was the base of operations for a group affiliated to the terrorist Moroccan Islamic Combatant Group (GICM). The siege ended when the apartment was blown to pieces in an apparent suicide blast, killing all four occupants and one policeman. It was soon found that the blast was caused by the same type of explosive (Goma-2) used in the March 11 attacks (now pithily branded M-11), and the investigations continued in that vein.

A vast left-wing conspiracy?

As the dust settled from the violence of both the bombings and the subsequent political fallout – with the destruction moving from ordinary lives to the national government in such a short space of time – new questions began to surface. Was Aznar's government really misinformed about the bombings? And how did the socialists and their allies in the press manage to discover and disseminate such damning information so quickly? Perhaps they had the duplicitous assistance of the police and security services, wondered Partido Popular-leaning newspapers like *ABC* and *La Razón*.

In the months after the attack, theories unrolling from the radio network Cadena Cope, various talk-show commentators and the newspaper *El Mundo*, as well as Partido Popular (PP) members, began to suggest that there had been some kind of conspiracy. They contended that the attack had been carried out by ETA after all, but that pro-socialist elements in the police and intelligence services had connived to pretend otherwise as soon as Aznar had publicly made the accusation – leading to his fall from grace, and from power.

The PP went on to charge that the socialists and Spanish intelligence services had not only sought to make a quick political deal with ETA after the attack, but that they and Moroccan intelligence had also connived to instigate the attack in the first place. This theory proposed that Moroccan intelligence had helped by providing false intel blaming Al Qaeda-type forces prior to the election, and then assisted in the framing of the Moroccan terrorist group GICM afterwards. All in all, a grand conspiracy theory was unfurling.

A vast right-wing Catholic military conspiracy?

The PP's outrageous charges were given the backing of a right-wing coalition of politicians, militarists and the Catholic Church, and it was in this coalition that some left-wingers saw a counter-conspiracy. They suggested that the accusations about a conspiracy involving the socialists, ETA and the intelligence services were an attempt by right-wingers to not only disrupt the socialists' efforts to negotiate with ETA, but also to bring down Zapatero's left-wing government because it was seeking to give more autonomy to Catalonia, sanctioned gay marriage and favoured limited public funding of private Catholic schools. According to journalist and human rights leader Mariano Aguirre, these were the real reasons behind the "paranoid conspiracy theories" being churned out months and even years later to "poison the public mind" about who was really behind the bombings.

A political maelstrom whipped up by an "impartial" media

Ultimately, a 21-month judicial investigation ruled, in April 2006, that the bombers were a gang of Algerian, Moroccan and Syrian drug traffickers, including two police and Civil Guard informants. The group were said to be sympathetic, but otherwise unconnected, to Al Qaeda or the Moroccan Islamic Combatant Group (GICM), but their actions *were* partly provoked by the Iraq War. ETA was not involved.

It was troubling that some of the 29 suspects indicted for their involvement in M-11 were either known informers or confidants of the police and Civil Guard, and several of these informers had been associated with the bombers before the attacks. However, this did not mean that the intelligence services of Spain or Morocco were in any way involved in directing the bombings or allowing them to go ahead. The investigation concluded that there were tenuous low-level links between the informers and the bombers, but that these links were not monitored enough to have made it possible for the intelligence services to join the dots prior to the attack. Had the available sources been better tapped or the information collated and examined more thoroughly it may have been possible to uncover parts of the plot, but operational failures prevented this.

Despite the evidence, the conclusions of the investigation remained a matter of perspective for some. "There are more shadows than there is light in this case", Partido Popular spokesman Eduardo Zaplana told parliament, indicating just how complex and murky all the accusations, claims, conspiracies and counter-conspiracies had become. Meanwhile, several of the party's MPs alleged that

The wreckage of one of the commuter trains at Atocha station, Madrid, March 11, 2004.

[redacted]drid police had tampered with – or even destroyed nce. It was reported that the Madrid train carriages en destroyed in order to hide evidence – which was also allegedly why the victims were buried without autopsies. However, Spain's supreme court dismissed these allegations as untrue.

Zapatero's interior minister, Alfredo Pérez Rubalcaba, countered these accusations by saying that the PP was still trying to blame ETA for the bombings in order to cover up its own mistakes and to stoke fantasies about a socialist-led conspiracy. The PP denied this and demanded a thorough investigation into the M-11 atrocity – although possibly not one as salacious as that then being conducted by *El Mundo*. That right-wing newspaper had played up the strength of the links between the bombers and the intelligence services, and even alleged that the explosives used in the attack may have come via police informers.

Spain's divided, partisan media showed its true colours through its selective reporting of the evidence and conclusions of the investigation into the March 11 bombings, with some media establishments blowing up some details way out of proportion. Editorial direction seemed to be directed by ownership, rather than objectivity – with *El Mundo* on the Right, alongside the Catholic Church-owned Cadena Cope radio network, and the *El País* newspaper and Cadena Ser radio station, both owned by the pro-socialist media magnate Jesús de Polanco, on the Left. The aftermath of the Madrid bombings soon developed into a battle between broadcasters and broadsheets.

The clash between *El Mundo* and *El País* was illustrated in September 2006, when *El Mundo* published numerous interviews with José Emilio Suárez Trashorras, who was accused of supplying the explosives for the attack. In the interviews, Trashorras claimed that he was "the victim of a [socialist] coup they tried to hide behind a bunch of Muslims". *El País* countered by accusing *El Mundo* of publishing conspiracy theories and claiming that Trashorras was paid for his story, which *El Mundo* fiercely denied. In October 2007, Trashorras was convicted for his role in the attacks.

Caught after the act: vital government files deleted

In pointing the finger of blame at ETA on the very day of the bombings, was then-prime minister Aznar deliberately misled about the evidence, or was he seeking to make political capital just prior to the election out of inaccurate, early information? Was he panicking about the terror attack and the forthcoming election, or was he engaging in reckless, calculated opportunism, thinking that polling day would be over before any untruths could be exposed? Or was he as unwittingly mistaken as everyone else, but ruthlessly denounced as a liar by an opportunist opposition party?

In December 2004, the Spanish Congressional Commission of Inquiry into the Madrid bombings revealed that Aznar's government had ordered that all the computer records in his office dealing with the days between the bombings and the general election be erased. New prime minister Zapatero took this as proof that his rival had deliberately deceived the Spanish people about ETA's guilt, and told the inquiry, "This was the decisive information, evidence, that from that moment there was never an ETA line of investigation". In fact, all records from the former prime minister's office – covering the whole of Aznar's eight years in government – were deleted, as *El País* reported and the inquiry verified. Zapatero accused Aznar's government of a "massive campaign of deception" in the three days between the Madrid bombings and the general election – Aznar retorted that Zapatero had told him by telephone on March 11, that "it made no difference to him whether it was ETA or Al Qaeda".

Whatever the truth, M-11 exposed the many deep, dark, animosities running within and between Spain's political, religious, military and media establishments. The scale of the anger fuelled by the bombings and their aftermath is perhaps exemplified by the words of José Ricardo Martínez, the general secretary of Spain's largest trade union: "the political and social responsibility for the death of 192 people in Madrid on March 11 lies with José María Aznar". Both sides of the political spectrum seemed to be far more interested in making the maximum possible capital out of how scandalous and duplicitous their opponents could be made to appear, rather than in the whys and wherefores of exactly who carried out the Madrid tragedy, and how and why they did so.

Whatever the motivations of the various political figures involved, the aftermath of the bombings saw a vile slur carried throughout much of the Western media. It was claimed that the Spanish electorate had "cowardly" capitulated to terrorism by ousting Aznar and backing the "appeaser" Zapatero, who had campaigned on the promise that he would withdraw the country's troops from what he considered to be an illegal war in Iraq. This theory, which emanated from the "stay the course" wing, simply ignored the political impact of a national leader taking his country into a dubious war – which even the UN declared illegal – and then apparently misleading his own people, for political purposes, about who may have perpetrated a major domestic terrorist attack (whether or not that was the intention of some elaborate plot by his opponents).

SOURCES

Websites

- **www.abc.net.au/news/stories/2004/03/12/1064248.htm** Midway between the blasts and the election, ABC reported the pivotal change in perception that it was possibly Al Qaeda – or at least not ETA.
- **www.elmundo.es/elmundo/2007/06/12/espana/1181678226.html** Doubts about every aspect of the case are illustrated in this *El Mundo* piece, written years after the bombings and even the judicial inquiry.
- **www.guardian.co.uk/world/2006/sep/15/media.pressandpublishing** The bitter battle for "truth" – or what passes for it – over the Madrid bombings is well laid out in this piece concerning the mud-throwing between the *El País* and *El Mundo* newspapers.
- **www.heritage.org/Research/Europe/wm445.cfm** The Heritage Foundation's somewhat prescient piece in the aftermath of the attacks pointing beyond the-then dominant theory that it was ETA alone.
- **www.nationalreview.com/comment/stalinsky200405060835.asp** Writer Stephen Stalinsky compiled a list of the top ten "conspiracy theories" from the Arab press a few weeks after the Madrid bombings, with the usual suspects featuring highly.
- **www.opendemocracy.net/democracy-terrorism/11-M_3341.jsp** Human rights activist and left-wing writer Mariano Aguirre outlines a broad conspiracy that Spain's right-wing elite were furthering a conspiracy theory about the bombings in their path back to power.

7/7: the London bombings

For the first few days of July 2005, the UK – and especially London – was the place to be. Hyde Park held the Live 8 concert on July 2, London beat off Paris to win the right to host the 2012 Olympic Games on July 6, and the G8 leaders were gathering in Edinburgh to talk about saving the world. But suddenly all that glory was shattered. On the morning of Thursday, July 7, 2005, towards the end of the rush hour, the media reported that a series of "power surges" had caused several explosions on the London Underground. The underground network was shut down and the city's public transport descended into chaos. Just after midday, Prime Minister Tony Blair made a statement saying that there had been "a series of terrorist attacks in London". By the end of the day, it was all too clear – these were not power surges, but bomb explosions. Three devices had been detonated aboard London Underground trains and one had exploded aboard a bus; 56 people had been killed and some 700 injured.

Within a week of the attacks, police and press reports had pieced together the following story. The bombings were carried out by four British nationals, Mohammad Sidique Khan, Shehzad Tanweer, Germaine Lindsay and Hasib Mir Hussain, who were all among the dead and who were identified by various forms of ID found on or near their remains. Three of the men had driven a hire car down from Leeds, West Yorkshire (Lindsay had driven himself from nearby Aylesbury, Buckinghamshire) to Luton railway station, where police later found it loaded with explosives and Islamic paraphernalia. The bombers – each carrying a bomb in a rucksack – then caught the 7.40am Thameslink train to King's Cross Station, London, and thereupon split up. Three of them blew themselves up on separate underground trains almost simultaneously at 8.50am, near to Aldgate East, King's Cross and Edgware Road stations. Hasib Mir Hussain's bomb went off 57 minutes later aboard a number 30 double-decker bus, at Tavistock Square. All of the bombs were peroxide-based devices, traced back – by means of one of the bomber's personal items – to a "bomb factory" house in Leeds.

On 7/7 itself, Foreign Secretary Jack Straw commented that the attacks looked like they had "all the hallmarks" of the Islamic terrorist network Al Qaeda, a view corrobo-

The double-decker London bus destroyed by a terrorist bomb on July 7, 2005.

rated by Metropolitan Police Commissioner Sir Ian Blair. Al Qaeda was also reported as having taken credit for the attack in a message issued via a supposedly pro-Al Qaeda Islamic website – although both the message and the Maryland-based website were soon found to be fake. Nevertheless, it was said that the bombers' motives were assuredly related to the fact that they were disaffected young Muslims who had become radicalized and suicidally embittered towards the West – with two of them having made trips to Pakistan and Afghanistan. These motives were proven by the two home-made "martyrs' video" monologues recorded by Khan and Tanweer that were released by the Al Jazeera news network on September 1, 2005 and July 6, 2006, respectively.

Al Qaeda: yes, no, maybe?

The version of events outlined above was essentially the same version put forward in May 2006, when the Home Office published its Report of the Official Account of the Bombings – the official "narrative" (as the government termed it) of the key people and events surrounding 7/7. Home Secretary John Reid told the House of Commons that there was no "categorical" proof linking Al Qaeda to the bombings, but the report interwove details about the four men's lives and movements with information involving various notable figures, methods and locations associated with Al Qaeda.

The report, replete with heavy caveats and acknowledged uncertainties, came instead of the open, independent inquiry that many people wanted, including J7: the July 7th Truth Campaign group, but Prime Minister Blair resisted the demand from the outset. Such an inquiry would prejudice current investigations, divert attention from safeguarding against future attacks and cost too much money, he said, before concluding that a full, transparent investigation into the UK's worst-ever terrorist attack would be a "ludicrous diversion".

However, just weeks after the publication of the official report, Reid had to concede to the House of Commons that its conclusions were wrong on a fundamental point: the bombers could not have caught the 7.40am train from Luton to King's Cross, because – as train operator Thameslink confirmed – it had been cancelled on the day in question. As Reid blithely noted, the bombers had "in fact" caught the earlier 7.25am train. That error was just one of the many anomalies and burning questions regarding the events of 7/7 that journalists, bloggers and campaigners had been asking about over the past year.

"Was it suicide?" *The Daily Mirror* asked on July 16, 2005, pointing out that the bombers had stable homes, careers and families to look after. If they knew they were on a suicide mission and were not coming back, why had the men bought a seven-day parking permit at Luton station, as well as return train tickets? And why were they carrying so much identifying material? Had they been "duped" into suicide by Al Qaeda handlers? Others asked why they had left a trail of evidence to the still-operational bomb factory in Leeds, and even left bombs in their car. Furthermore, why had Hussain tried to call the other three on his mobile phone at King's Cross station if he knew that they would all have died when they set off the bombs? Some people even suspected that the four men were not duped, but actually had nothing to do with the attack at all.

As the Internet documentaries *Mind the Gap*, *Ludicrous Diversion* and several other sources noted, the police said that the bombers didn't fit the "normal" terrorist profile or modus operandi. Furthermore, Mohammad Sidique Khan's martyr's video was old and he neither referred to blowing himself up nor to any specific targets. *The Guardian* reported that one of Khan's cousins described him as having "no obvious interest in politics or radical Islam". Some witness reports said that the bus bomber, Hussain, was ransacking his rucksack in panic just before the bomb went off – was he realizing, too late, that something was wrong? Were the four young men the perfect patsies, asked the producers of the Web-based film *7/7 Ripple Effect*? The film proposed that the four men, seeking some extra pocket money, may have been attempting to prove their patriotism by playing the parts of suicide bombers in a grand, mock-terror exercise in London.

Identical events, yet shifting times and places

One truly bizarre coincidence was that, on the morning of 7/7, a terrorist crisis management "exercise" involving 1000 people was being run in London. Chief among them was Peter Power, a former Metropolitan Police anti-terrorist officer and the managing director of private security firm Visor Consultants. Power exclaimed on ITV News and BBC Radio 5 Live that same day that the real attacks so closely resembled the exercise that it made the "hairs on the back of my neck stand up". Visor's unnamed client had apparently "helped to choose the exact scenario … based on simultaneous bombs going off precisely at the railway stations where it happened this morning". A series of rush-hour explosions on the London Underground was also the scenario at the centre of a 2004 episode of the BBC's *Panorama* programme entitled "London Under Attack", on which Power worked as an expert witness.

Power has since refused to elaborate further on the comments he made that day, but he was the first to say that the bombs were "simultaneous". The blasts at Aldgate East, King's Cross and Edgware Road stations were initially reported as having gone off at 8.51am, 8.56am and 9.17am respectively, and were not widely stated as having been simultaneous until July 9.

It was not just the timings of the bombings that caught the conspiracy theorists' imaginations. Many people also pointed to the apparent anomalies in reports about the exact locations of the bombs. On July 7, journalist Mark Honigsbaum of *The Guardian* reported from Edgware Road that passengers had described how the train's floor coverings and tiles "flew up, raised up" as if blasted from below, suggesting the bomb had been under the train, not inside it. A year later, Honigsbaum lamented that while he corrected his story later that same day and reported that the bombs had, in fact, detonated inside the train, his first report was now ensconced in the "paranoid ether-world" of an online, global "movement of conspiracy theorists". Still, on July 11, 2005, the *Cambridge Evening News* reported an interview with a survivor of the Aldgate East blast, Bruce Lait, who described the hole left by the bomb blast in similar terms: "The metal was pushed upwards as if the bomb was underneath the train." Lait also said that he didn't remember seeing any person or bag being near where the bomb went off. Meanwhile, tube driver Jeff Porter, whose train had been close to the Edgware Road blast, told *The Evening Standard* that on his train "two guys had gas masks on", but he didn't know "where they got them from".

Nothing caught on camera in CCTV capital

Despite the fact that the UK is the most watched nation in the world, being home to more than four million closed circuit television (CCTV) cameras – with Londoners caught on camera an average three hundred times a day – only three CCTV images of the 7/7 bombers were released. Two of the images showed Hussain on his own at King's Cross station, and the third showed all four men walking towards the entrance to Luton station earlier that morning. The latter image curiously roused the ire of many Internet bloggers who asserted that it was "demonstrably fake". Their arguments were summarized on July 26, 2005, in an article on the Social Democracy Now website entitled "The London Bombings Were a Hoax". The article declared that the image was a "PhotoShop creation" riddled with inconsistencies, with the depicted men suffering from odd ailments like "half legs" and being impaled by railings. Odder still was the four men being the only people in the image, despite the fact that they arrived at the station during the rush hour.

The Luton CCTV image was probably just appalling quality, but the thousands of hours of video that the police apparently viewed don't seem to have been much help either. Peter Clarke, the head of the Metropolitan Police's anti-terrorism branch, had to appeal for witnesses to help trace Hussain's movements – "Did you see this man at King's Cross … Do you know the route he took from the station, did you see him get onto a number 30 bus?" – because none of the three CCTV cameras on the bus were working. The Prison Planet conspiracy website reported that the very bus that was blown up in Tavistock Square had undergone "irregular maintenance work" just prior to July 7, and that it was also unique for having allegedly been the only bus to be diverted off its route that day. By sheer chance, it was also blown up just outside the British Medical Association building – where a terror drill was supposedly underway.

Forewarnings and Israel

Was there any connection, the Social Democracy Now article hinted (though very much between the lines), between the lack of useful CCTV images of the attack and the fact that, since 2004, one of the companies providing CCTV "video solutions" for part of the London Underground was Verint Systems, an Israeli-owned firm? Suggestions of an Israeli connection to the London attack had already been made by several different sources. Peter Power had described his terrorist exercise client on 7/7 as being very close to Jewish property in the City and to American banks, which some conspiracy theorists took as the first pointer towards a bigger plot principally involving Israel, if not the US as well.

On July 7, a report from the Associated Press's Tel Aviv office, which was also carried by CBS News and *The Guardian*, said that the British police had warned visiting Israeli finance minister Benjamin Netanyahu not to leave his hotel *before* the first explosion occurred. Later that day, reporters asking Deputy Assistant Commissioner Brian Paddick how much advance intelligence or warning the security services had been given referred to the AP report, but they were given the answer "none". Not long after, the AP report was withdrawn and rewritten to say: "After the first explosion, our finance minister received a request not to go anywhere." These words were apparently taken from a quote by Israeli foreign minister Silvan Shalom to Israel Army Radio. The *Asia Times* also drew attention to an apparent Israel connection by reporting "frantic" telephone traffic between the US and Israeli embassies in London just before the first blasts. On July 10, the German newspaper *Bild am Sonntag* reported that the London office of the Israeli intelligence organization Mossad had received advance warning of the attack, but only six minutes before the first blast – "too late", as one Mossad source put it.

Bush, Blair and the "War on Terror"

On July 10, conspiracy theorist Michael James wrote an article on the Truth Seeker website entitled "Tony Blair Ordered the London Bombings", suggesting that the attack was part of an intricate plot by London, Tel Aviv and Washington to further justify Western warring on Middle East "terrorists". James claimed that Blair had got what he wanted out of the deal, namely the collapse of all resistance to national ID cards, the exacerbation of public rage against Islam in preparation for an attack against Iran or Syria, and a distraction from the continuing, illegal war in Iraq.

In late 2006, the *Daily Express* published a piece ascribing similar motives to alleged American involvement in the bombings. The article claimed that George W. Bush and his entourage may have planned the attack on London in order to disrupt the G8 summit's discussions about climate change (see p.305) and poverty – matters on which Bush's administration took a lot of flak – and instead put the "War on Terror" back at the top of the agenda.Was it a coincidence, the J7 campaign group wondered, that the hero of 9/11, former New York mayor Rudolf Giuliani, was staying at the same hotel as Israeli finance minister Netanyahu on July 7? And what about the fact that London Transport chief Bob Kiley is a member of the US-based foreign policy organization, the Council on Foreign Relations (see p. 000), and a former CIA high-flyer.

Meanwhile, Prison Planet noted another parallel between the 9/11 World Trade Center attacks (see p.395) and the 7/7 bombings: strange fluctuations in the stock and currency markets in the days leading up to 7/7. The fact that the British pound fell in early July was seen by some conspiracy theorists as evidence that some powerful brokers must have had foreknowledge of a significant event that could cause panic in the currency market – such as a terrorist attack on the capital, perhaps?

Police state

So, how much forewarning had there been of a terrorist attack on London? Some evidence seems to suggest none at all. For instance, MI5's Joint Terrorism Analysis Centre (JTAC) reduced the terror threat just a month prior to the events of 7/7, and the security service's director-general, Dame Eliza Manningham-Buller, told MPs on July 6, 2005 – the day before the attack – that there was no imminent terrorist threat to the UK. However, a certain perverted chain of conspiracist logic posited that the security services may have allowed the bombings to go ahead – despite the fact that they showed them to have seriously fouled up – in order to justify the bequeathing of ever greater powers to them and their jackboot-sporting backers.

A few months after 7/7, *The Guardian* columnist Polly Toynbee mockingly wrote of the "several plots a day" sent to her by paranoiacs and conspiracy theorists, most of which pointed towards the government's complicity in the London bombings. "*Cui bono?* Why Blair, of course", she scoffed, explaining that the blasts supposedly "rallied" national support to the prime minister's increasingly authoritarian, yet faltering leadership. However, this notion was being given more serious consideration elsewhere. The J7 group's website carried the article "July 7th as Machiavellian State Terror?", by Professor David MacGregor, which postulated that the attack was an act of violence "perpetrated against the state by elements of the state itself". On the same site, writer William Bowles outlined the theory that although Blair did not plan 7/7, he did seize upon the opportunity it afforded him to push through various security and anti-terror laws. Bowles also noted the uncomfortable similarities between Britain's new "de facto police state" legislation and laws passed by Hitler and Mussolini many years before.

Principal among the advocates of the theory that 7/7 was an MI5 inside job was ex-MI5 agent David Shayler. In his Web documentary *Mind the Gap*, Shayler suggested that the bombing was a "false-flag operation", a covert state-backed attack that could be blamed on the enemy in order to terrify the population into accepting far greater state control and oppression through anti-terror laws. More anti-terror laws were passed in the ten years prior to July 7, 2005 than in the previous century, Shayler noted, listing the dramatic expansion in police and security service powers of arrest, detention without charge, taking biometric data, investigation and snooping through telecommunications, expansion in technology and recruitment, and many other things.

The anonymously produced *Ludicrous Diversion* voiced its suspicions of the police in relation to the events of 7/7, and suggested they knew more than they were letting on. Was it not odd, the film noted, that Metropolitan Police Commissioner Sir Ian Blair referred to "four miserable bombers" on live news early on July 7, before anything had been confirmed, but then quickly corrected himself, "I'm not saying there are four bombers…" *Ludicrous Diversion* also noted that the mobile phone networks had not been disabled on 7/7, thereby apparently "proving" that the police knew the bombs were not being detonated by mobile phone. The police could not be trusted, the filmmakers' argued.

Olympic leaps of logic

Other conspiracy-minded individuals have proposed that there might be a more venal motive behind the JTAC lowering the terror threat in 2005. Security expert Crispin Black asked in his book, *7-7: The London Bombings: What Went Wrong?*, "What kind of pressure was at work on the JTAC when it lowered … its threat level?" Perhaps, some wondered, the pressure to make London seem as safe as possible in the final days of the city's Olympic bid? A *Daily Express* article noted that if the bombers had struck just two days earlier, they would most likely have sunk London's Olympic bid – at a cost of millions of pounds in investment. With this in mind, it has also been suggested that whoever carried out the attack did the UK a "favour" by waiting for the Olympic committee's decision before setting off their bombs – something only an ally with some kind of "special relationship" with the UK might do.

One Internet blogger speculated that the bombings were designed to distract attention from emerging allegations about underhand tactics used in London's Olympic bid, or perhaps to mask the more controversial elements of the Olympic Bill that was passed shortly after July 7. Alternatively, it has been theorized that the attack was deliberately timed to follow immediately after the Olympic announcement, so as to fuse the two in the public psyche, welding the idea of the Olympics with the need for overarching security (as it is, the 2012 Olympics' security budget is growing in leaps and bounds). Taking this theory one giant step further, an actual "false-flag" attack on the games themselves could be seen as the final prelude to compulsory ID cards, increased surveillance and the UK becoming a techno-totalitarian state.

Further links, leaps and loops

Just a fortnight after the events of July 7, the BBC reported that an outside "controlling hand" involved in the bombings could still be at large, pointing the finger of suspicion back at Al Qaeda. Just two weeks before 7/7, a suspected Al Qaeda member named Harron Rashid Aswat had entered the UK, and had apparently left just hours before the blasts. The BBC reported that this man "was not put under surveillance", but did not explain how the information about his movements could be so detailed. It was claimed on Fox News that Aswat was a double agent supported by MI6, who was also wanted by the CIA. Aswat was arrested in Pakistan after 7/7, but then released, before being picked up again in Zambia. The veracity of the allegations made against Aswat and the willingness of the authorities to fill out their case against him have been notably wanting, and whilst he has denied any involvement with terrorism, Aswat was extradited (under protest) to the US in 2006 in connection with investigations concerning terror training camps.

Just two weeks to the day after the July 7 attack, on July 21, another bomb attack on the London Underground was being thwarted. In what appeared to be a copycat attack, three men carried three bombs in rucksacks onto the underground, seemingly planning to set them off simultaneously, and another man boarded a London bus with a bomb in a rucksack an hour later. In the event, none of the bombs were successfully detonated and there were no casualties, while a fifth bomber aborted his mission before it began. Those behind the failed attack were all caught, tried and convicted, but during the two-year process, a befuddling mix of claims and counterclaims emerged in press reports concerning exactly what MI5 knew and when they knew it.

It emerged that Mohammad Sidique Khan, the alleged ringleader of the 7/7 attack, had previously had vague interactions with the 21/7 bombers. MI5 admitted that they had kept Khan under surveillance for a while, and had observed his brief interactions with the 21/7 bombers, but that they had not considered him a threat at the time. The suspected links to Al Qaeda were reinforced when the Crown Prosecution Service (CPS) declared that it had information about how 7/7 bomber Shehzad Tanweer had been "turned" by people in Afghanistan – the CPS said it had been given the information by Scotland Yard. Tanweer was also tracked surfing the Internet for bomb-making tips in June 2005, just two weeks before the attack. Astonishingly enough, MI5 later said that both Khan and Tanweer were put under surveillance back in 2004. However, the security service's claim that the temporary surveillance ended in 2004 was subsequently exposed as untrue, with newspapers reporting that anti-terrorism police had continued investigating Khan in early 2005.

Security expert Crispin Black wondered if Tony Blair's government was so desperate to avoid any associations between the Iraq War and terror threats in the UK that intelligence efforts were actively diverted from pursuing any lines of enquiry linked to anger about the war. As political blogger Guido Fawkes put it in late July 2005: "Jack Straw, Fatty Clarke and John Reid are all over the media repeating the same mantra, 7/7 bombings are nothing to do with British troops in Iraq". But, in reality, Fawkes opined, the bombings were the "backwash", or result, of the war, as had been forewarned by the Foreign and Commonwealth Office (FCO) and top-drawer British think-tank Chatham House. A top FCO official had written to Number 10 in May 2004 saying that British foreign policy was a "recurring theme … especially in the context of the Middle East peace process and Iraq" in creating "anger and impotence" and other negative perceptions among a "younger generation of British Muslims". The JTAC had also warned, a month before 7/7, that "events in Iraq are continuing to act as motivation and a focus of a range of terrorist-related activity in the UK" (despite having itself reduced the terror threat level at around the same time).

An investigation by the Intelligence and Security Committee (ISC) largely exonerated MI5, concluding that the security services' decisions were "understandable" and that MI5 could not have prevented the July 7 attack because of "limitations on … resources" and "other priority investigations". However, no mention of the FCO, Chatham House or JTAC reports appeared in the ISC's report. The shadow home secretary, David Davis, said: "It is becoming more and more clear that the story presented to the public and Parliament is at odds with the facts." Adding fuel to the fire, in October 2007, King Abdullah of Saudi Arabia claimed that the UK "may have been able to avert the tragedy" of 7/7, had it acted upon Saudi anti-terrorist intelligence. Had there been forewarnings from both Israel and Saudi Arabia?

In May 2007, Tony Blair again rejected requests from his political rivals and the families of the victims for an independent inquiry into the 7/7 attack, saying that it would "undermine support" for the security services – but that horse had long since bolted. In June 2007, a Channel 4 poll of 500 British Muslims showed that 24 percent believed that the government and security services were involved in the 7/7 attacks, and over 50 percent thought that the security services had fabricated evidence to convict the four terrorist suspects, particularly the CCTV and martyrs' videos.

SOURCES

Books

Crispin Black 7-7: The London Bombings: What Went Wrong? (2006). A short, crisply written book that gives an overview of a systematic breakdown in British intelligence, which Black, an expert in security affairs, partly ascribes to political meddling.

Films

Anonymous Ludicrous Diversion (2006). This anonymous film, released in 2006 on Google Video but currently available all over the Web, got its title from Tony Blair's assessment that an inquiry into 7/7 would be a "ludicrous diversion".

Anonymous 7/7 Ripple Effect (2007).This film was first broadcast in late 2007 through the website jforjustice.co.uk, but is now available more widely on YouTube, Google Video and so on. With its dull narration, it has received quite widespread criticism and was harshly derided by J7: the July 7th Truth Campaign, but it raises a few interesting points.

David Shayler Mind the Gap (2006). Ex-MI5 agent David Shayler presents a 45-minute argument for the July 7 attack being an "inside job" carried out by British and other security services as a pretext for tightening domestic anti-terror laws and escalating the "war on terror". Available on YouTube, Google Video and elsewhere.

Websites

Ⓦ **www.blogigo.co.uk/socialdemocracynow/THE-LONDON-BOMBINGS-WERE-A-HOAX/15/** Social Democracy Now's article "The London Bombings Were a Hoax" summarizing the alleged problems with the CCTV footage of the bombers.

Ⓦ **fra.europa.eu/fra/material/pub/London/London-Bomb-attacks-EN.pdf** A November 2005 EU report on the impact of the London bombings on Muslim communities within the EU.

Ⓦ **www.julyseventh.co.uk** A well-ordered and comprehensively sourced website set up in the wake of the 7/7 bombings "with the aim of getting to the truth about what really happened on the day". The homepage of J7: the July 7th Truth Campaign, it also features a host of links to sources both official and sceptical.

Ⓦ **www.official-documents.gov.uk/document/hc0506/hc10/1087/1087.asp** A PDF of the UK government's "Report of the Official Account of the Bombings", from May 2006.

- www.order-order.com Guido Fawkes' Right-leaning political conspiracy blog and discussion site.
- www.prisonplanet.com Many a mention and twist on 7/7 and its broader significance in the setting up of a global police state can be found on Alex Jones's brilliant conspiracy website.
- rachelnorthlondon.blogspot.com Rachel from North London is a 7/7 survivor demanding an investigation.
- www.thetruthseeker.co.uk/article.asp?ID=3329 The article "Tony Blair Ordered the London Bombings" by conspiracist Michael James.

Extraordinary rendition

They came at night, small white aircraft landing at cold, windswept airfields across the UK and Europe; their cargo, terror suspects, picked up off city streets and remote hillsides throughout the world by men in black suits, khaki fatigues or turbans. These flights were, the stories ran, continuing on to secret torture facilities dotted across Eastern Europe and beyond. Surely the stuff of the most paranoid conspiracy theorists' worst nightmares, one might hope – or rather, one might have hoped.

The "War on Terror" promises that all over the world lurk terrorists plotting to pull off another almighty attack on the West, à la 9/11 (see p.395). The surest means to prevent these "ticking bomb" terror threats seems to be to go wherever these terrorists hang out, capture a few suspects, take them away somewhere and subject them to some "enhanced interrogation techniques" to find out exactly what they're up to. This had all been reported in the Western media since at least early 2002, and as one US diplomat told *The Washington Post* not long after 9/11: "these sorts of movements have been occurring all the time."

But the big problem for the US and their allies has less to do with identifying and apprehending terror suspects, wherever they are, than it has to do with getting around US and international law. Whichever way you spin it, capturing someone, holding them without trial and inflicting pain upon them in order to obtain information is illegal – it runs just a bit too close to kidnapping and torture in the eyes of the law. So the best solution in this newly globalized world seems to lie in "extraordinary rendition" – ship (or, more likely, fly) the suspect off to the other side of the world where such things are permitted and outsource the dirty work to offshore contractors. As the same US diplomat told *The Washington Post*: "It allows us to get information from terrorists in a way we can't do on US soil." One anonymous intelligence agent allegedly put it even more bluntly to *The Washington Post*, in a quote that has since been reported worldwide: "We don't kick the shit out of them. We send them to other countries so they can kick the shit out of them."

Ghostly tales take flight

Stories of the CIA's extraordinary rendition flights coming to Britain and elsewhere in Europe took off in the press in September 2005. *The Guardian* newspaper reported that, since 2001, there had been some 210 instances of CIA-chartered planes, from Gulfstream jets to Boeing 737s, landing in the UK at RAF airfields and civilian airports (including Heathrow, Gatwick, Stansted and Glasgow) to refuel. These planes were believed to be trafficking terror suspects to countries where they might well be tortured. The official response at the time was, in the words of one UK Foreign Office official, that the story was just "a conspiracy theory".

Undeterred, in November 2005, the UK-based civil rights group Liberty presented its "very real suspicion" to the Association of Chief Police Officers (ACPO) that these "terror rendition flights" had landed on British soil, thereby making the British authorities complicit in offences ranging from aiding and abetting false imprisonment to kidnapping and torture, or at the very least, conspiring to do such things. Unsurprisingly, the matter was raised in the House of Commons the following month, only for Foreign Secretary Jack Straw to respond that it was all "extremely improbable". For one, no records of US requests for such flight stopovers existed, Straw argued, nor had any related papers been found. Therefore, he concluded, these rendition flights could not have traversed UK soil.

The US secretary of state, Condoleezza Rice, had made her assurances to the British government, Straw continued, and so – on the back of these cursory investigations – no inquiry was needed. "Unless we all start to believe in conspiracy theories and that the officials are lying, I'm lying and that behind this there is some kind of secret state in league with some dark forces in the US, and we believe Secretary Rice is lying, there is simply no truth in claims that the UK has been involved in rendition." Unfortunately, such assurances were "worthless", MPs said, countering that no records would exist because, as the Home Office admitted, transit applications are not kept after the transit has been completed, meaning that checking for permission requests was "derisory".

The trouble was, by an uncanny coincidence, on the same day that Straw was making this declaration in the House of Commons, the Council of Europe (CE) had declared "credible" a report from Swiss senator Dick Marty, which detailed CIA abductions and the transportation of terror suspects across European borders, including the UK's. The report was considered so credible, in fact, that by the following February, Germany, Spain, the CE and the European Parliament were all beginning their own inquiries into rendition flights. In Italy things had already progressed much further, with an Italian magistrate issuing warrants to arrest a bevy of CIA agents in connection with the abduction of a Muslim cleric. Abu Omar (aka Hassan Mustafa Osama Nasr) was allegedly hauled off a Milan street in February 2003 and taken to Egypt, where he claimed he had been tortured.

Just a month after the Commons meeting – in response to a leaked Foreign Office memo published in the *New Statesman* detailing the precise legal definition of rendition – Straw admitted that, in fact, four such flights had been requested by the US, two of whch had already been disclosed to Parliament and all of that were back in 1998. But this did little to temper rumours that many more requests and approvals for such flights might be waiting to be "discovered". In May 2006, the UK's Joint Committee on Human Rights (JCHR) said that ministers had not "adequately demonstrated" any proper investigation into "ghost flight" claims. Shortly afterwards the CE published more of Senator Marty's findings, which concluded that UK airspace and airport facilities were freely accessed by CIA flights. By January 2007, the European Parliament, having identified some 1200 suspicious flights across Europe between 2001 and 2005, was singling out the UK as being most uncooperative in its inquiry. The parliamentary commission on extraordinary rendition then approved a report accusing several EU states of complicity with CIA rendition flights.

Brought down by planespotters

Much of the evidence about these rendition flights had been unwittingly compiled by planespotters indulging in their seemingly harmless hobby across the world, from Glasgow and Athens to Karachi. Unaware of the greater significance of these strange planes coming to their airports at odd times of the day and night, they had duly photographed them, logged their arrivals and departures, and – most critically – noted the aircrafts' serial registration numbers and uploaded them to the Web. Journalists and researchers then began connecting the times, locations and aircraft registration numbers detailed on the Web with stories of alleged extraordinary rendition.

No evidence

June 8, 2007 was an important date in the history of extraordinary rendition. On that day, the Association of Chief Police Officers (ACPO) told the British press that "no evidence" to support Liberty's claims had been found. Liberty's press release on the issue stated that Chief Constable Michael Todd had told them that ACPO was refusing "to commence any police enquiry into the allegations", leading them to question whether ACPO had even investigated the claims, and acting as a reminder of Straw's declaration that no inquiry was required. That same day, hearings began in the Milan extraordinary rendition trial of US and Italian intelligence agents in connection with the alleged abduction of Muslim cleric Abu Omar (the US agents suspected of involvement failed to show up).

By another coincidence, ACPO's announcement also came just hours after the conclusion of the Council of Europe's nineteen-month investigation into rendition flights. The CE investigation declared that it was an established fact" that secret CIA gulags had been operating in Eastern Europe, mainly in Poland and Romania. To quote a Channel 4 News report, Senator Marty's charges "weren't conspiracy theories, it turns out". His investigation found that the UK was just one of fourteen European states that were all too aware of what was going on in their airspace and on their soil.

Indeed, all of these states must have known about the flights, because one of the first NATO agreements after 9/11 was to allow the CIA blanket clearance for rendition flights, while the secret CIA prison operators also reported directly to the leaders of the relevant EU states. No less legally culpable – let alone diabolically reprehensible – than their US paymasters, the Europeans were made offers considered impossible to refuse, such as Romania being given "formidable" American support for its bid to join NATO. President George W. Bush had already admitted in September 2006 that the Polish and Romanian prisons were real, but he then ameliorated this revelation by announcing that the inmates had all since been transferred to Guantanamo Bay, the notorious US military prison in Cuba.

No proof

Yet despite all this evidence, the accused European governments still dispatched hasty denials to Senator Marty's reports, saying that there was no "concrete proof" to back up his accusations. Meanwhile, a CIA spokesman claimed that Europe was the source of "grossly inaccurate" allegations about CIA counter-terrorist activities, although he also admitted that he had "yet to see the report".

That "grossly inaccurate" information must have included data uncovered by the separate investigations carried out by individual states' parliaments, the European Parliament, the Council of Europe, Swiss senator Dick Marty, Amnesty International and Liberty. Further reliable evidence was provided by the award-winning book *Ghost Plane: The Untold Story of the CIA's Secret Rendition Programme* by British investigative journalist Stephen Grey, and by *Torture Taxi: On the Trail of the CIA's Rendition Flights* by Trevor Paglen and A.C. Thompson.

The story that came to light through these different investigations included men, women and even children as young as seven being picked up in countries such as Iran, Somalia, Indonesia and Italy, and trafficked via the UK, Ireland, Germany and other EU states to detention camps in Afghanistan, Jordan, Thailand, Syria and Romania (to name but a few), as well as the infamous Abu Ghraib and Guantanamo Bay prisons in Iraq and Cuba. Several of these prisons had formerly been run by the Taliban, Saddam Hussein's Ba'athists and the Soviet Union, and all had become, as Stephen Grey wrote, part of one almighty interconnected gulag, where "enhanced" interrogation apparently includes prisoners spending months in solitary confinement, where they are kept constantly shackled, and often naked, in cramped cells. Other alleged interrogations techniques include prisoners being forced to suffer: extreme temperatures; blinding lights 24 hours a day; deafening rock music; "recordings" of family members being tortured; poor food; no bed clothes; dog attacks; taunts in front of other prisoners and guards; and various forms of physical abuse. Prisoners are also denied access to the Red Cross, other inmates, lawyers or a fair trial. So far, no one has claimed any of that to be a "conspiracy theory".

Some truth be told

In February 2008, the new UK foreign secretary, David Miliband, admitted that US rendition flights carrying terror suspects had indeed touched down on British soil on two separate occasions in 2002, both times on the Indian Ocean archipelago of Diego Garcia (which was still a British dependency, although it had been leased to the US as a bomber base for decades). Previous US assurances that no such rendition flights had ever occurred on British land were declared, by State Department spokesman Sean McCormack, to be an "administrative error", an error for which Miliband apologized to MPs.

Again, Miliband's message was curiously timed with other related news reports that emerged on the same day. According to a report by *The Guardian*, the European Commission duly rebuked the governments of both Poland and Romania for failing to adequately carry out detailed inquiries into their own complicity in extraordinary rendition, as they were told to do in mid-2007. "We have not received a reply from Poland and the information from Romania was not considered complete", a commission spokesman said in February 2008. Instead, both countries have so far continued to deny that they helped the US transfer prisoners or run secret CIA jails.

Extraordinary rendition, or "torture by proxy" as it is sometimes known, is such a murky tale that it looks set to continue unravelling – with or without any official independent inquiry – for some time to come. The sheer scale of global rendition operations is awesome, and Europe is just one part of the puzzle, but that does not mean it should be considered inevitable or taken for granted. It's best to be reminded, as often as possible, of Article 3 of the United Nations' Convention Against Torture of 1984, which was drawn up and signed by the US, UK and numerous other EU countries: "No State Party shall expel, return ('refouler') or extradite a person to another State where there are substantial grounds for believing that he would be in danger of being subjected to torture."

SOURCES

Books

Stephen Grey Ghost Plane: The Untold Story of the CIA's Secret Rendition Programme (2006). Grey's investigative work looks into many cases of rendition, which he was first informed about by CIA chief Porter Goss, who called it "a way of bringing people to a kind of justice".

Trevor Paglen and A.C. Thompson Torture Taxi: On the Trail of the CIA's Rendition Flights (2006). This book charts the operations and consequences of the CIA's "midnight airline", transporting terrorists or hapless victims to torture resorts worldwide.

Films

Gavin Hood Rendition (2007). A fictionalized story of the experience of an ordinary Egyptian-American citizen who is mistaken for a terrorist and subjected to rendition and torture. Reese Witherspoon as his American wife and Meryl Streep as a CIA official give emotional performances throughout this extraordinary film.

Jim Threapleton Extraordinary Rendition (2007). Released the same year as Hood's film, this independent British film is a bleak depiction of rendition and torture, about one man who "disappears" from both the face of the world and his own sanity.

Websites

Ⓦ **www.amnesty.org/en/library/info/EUR45/059/2005** Amnesty International's press reports from December 2005 alleging UK complicity in US rendition.

Ⓦ **assembly.coe.int/Main.asp?link=/Documents/WorkingDocs/Doc07/EDOC11302.htm** Senator Dick Marty's final, complete June 2007 report to the Council of Europe on "secret detentions and illegal transfers of detainees" in Europe.

Ⓦ **www.liberty-human-rights.org.uk/issues/1-torture/11-extra-ordinary-rendition/index.shtml** The UK civil liberties group Liberty's reports and press released on extraordinary rendition, and its campaign for an independent investigation.

CONSPIRACY ARCHIVE

Specific sources and material relating to individual conspiracy theories can be found throughout this book, at the end of each theory. But there is, of course, more to every subject than first meets the eye – and there's a wealth of general conspiracy information out there. Here, therefore, is a careful selection of the most important – or just gripping – conspiracy theory books, films, magazines and websites. Explore further at your own risk...

Books

General reference and theory

David Alexander Conspiracies and Cover-ups (2002). A neat collection of essays on the darker histories and stories of the twentieth century, written with a healthy dose of objectivity. Somewhat dry in tone, however, and maybe a little confused about what it's trying to prove.

Eric Alterman When Presidents Lie: A History of Official Deception and its Consequences (2004). Four presidential lies: Franklin D. Roosevelt on the Yalta accords, JFK on the Cuban Missile Crisis, Lyndon B. Johnson on the Gulf of Tonkin and Ronald Reagan on Central America. Each lie has left a troubling legacy.

Michael Barkun A Culture of Conspiracy: Apocalyptic Visions in Contemporary America (2003). A serious but very readable study of the links between mega-conspiracies (Barkun calls them superconspiracies) and right-wing, neo-fundamentalist beliefs. Thoughtful and alarming in equal measure.

Richard M. Bennett Conspiracy: Plots, Lies and Cover-ups (2003). A compendium of brief historical anecdotes that covers real, acknowledged conspiracies as much as conspiracy theories. There's an excellent spread of subjects, from Nero to 9/11 via Operation Northwoods, but it's not particularly thought-provoking, and the tone is disappointingly bland.

Jonathan Black The Secret History of the World (2007). The subtitle of the American edition, *As Laid Down by the Secret Societies* (which also uses the author's real name, Mark Booth), gives the game away. Peddles the notion that there is indeed an alternative esoteric history of the world that secret societies down the ages, from the Ancient Egyptians to the Rosicrucians, have all been privileged to know. Nicely illustrated, but one wonders how sincere the author can be.

Thom Burnett and Alex Games Who Really Runs the World? The War Between Globalization and Democracy (2007). Enron, Worldcom, the CIA, Martha Stewart – they're all involved. Part of a series from "Conspiracy Books" that also covers Opus Dei, the Illuminati, the space race, the oil wars and surveillance.

Paul T. Coughlin Secrets, Plots and Hidden Agendas: What You Don't Know about Conspiracy Theories (1999). An American Christian attacks right-wing Christian fundamentalist conspiracy theories. Focuses particularly on Waco and Oklahoma, and on the apocalyptic heritage of American fundamentalism.

Nick Davies Flat Earth News (2008). Disillusioned former reporter delivers excoriating exposé of quite how seriously journalism – "a profession corrupted at the core" – is in hock to the PR industry. You'll never read a newspaper in the same way again.

David Brion Davis (ed) The Fear of Conspiracy: Images of Un-American Subversion from the Revolution to the Present (1971). This compendium includes brief essays from historians, but it's really an academic sourcebook for classic cries of "conspiracy!" from America's past, from John Robison's anti-Illuminati "Proofs of a Conspiracy" (1797) and A.J. Warner and H.C. Baldwin's "The British Plot to Enslave the World" (1892) to Senator Joseph McCarthy's astonishing "A Conspiracy of Blackest Infamy" (1951) and Robert Welch's John Birch Society tract "The Truth About Vietnam" (1967).

Mark Fenster Conspiracy Theories: Secrecy and Power in American Culture (1999). Highbrow literary criticism with conspiracy culture as the text. A handful of essays focus on subjects such as Bill Clinton, JFK and Christian militias, but Fenster's main purpose is to analyse political ideology itself, not its manifestations.

Michael Haag and Veronica Haag The Rough Guide to the Da Vinci Code (2005). Okay, we're blowing our own trumpet here, but this is the most readable (and most pocketable) of the many "decoding the code"-style books.

Al Hidell and Joan D'Arc The Conspiracy Reader: From the Deaths of JFK and John Lennon to Government-sponsored Alien Cover-ups (1999). These articles from *Paranoia* magazine cover some of the same ground as this book, albeit with a strong emphasis on pop culture. But the lack of contextualization, an overview or any concerted effort to distinguish fact from fiction can make it feel rather pointless. There's also a second volume from 2004, *The New Conspiracy Reader*.

Richard Hofstadter The Paranoid Style in American Politics, and Other Essays (1952). Hofstadter is one of the leading historians of post-war American politics. This classic essay on conspiracism on the American Right was the first to use the clinical term "paranoid style" for the conspiracists' view of history, which he compares to clinical paranoia. Brief but fascinating discussions of anti-Illuminati and anti-Masonic panics, plus McCarthyism.

Michael Howard The Occult Conspiracy (1989). Howard takes a well-sourced look at the history, motives and power of secret societies, from Ancient Egypt to the present day.

Devon Jackson Conspiranoia! The Mother of All Conspiracies (1999). This is a densely written stream-of-consciousness tome, interspersed with near-impenetrable diagrams and making phenomenal leaps from subject to subject. A good read, nevertheless, offering an insight into how the minds of some conspiracy theorists work.

Jim Keith (ed) Secret and Suppressed: Banned Ideas and Hidden History (1993). A collection of intensely written, tautly argued pieces on everything from the

Jonestown massacre to sexual symbolism in Masonic worship. It's not always clear whether some of the writers believe the wilder edges of their theories.

Jim Keith Mass Control: Engineering Consciousness (1999). Before his controversial death in 1999 (he fell off the stage at the Burning Man festival, and died after surgery), Keith was one of the leading figures in US conspiracism. This charts his belief that alien phenomena are the tip of a techno-conspiratorial iceberg, and traces the emergence of the great conspiracy from early twentieth-century eugenics through to the modern "psychocivilized society".

Peter Knight Conspiracy Culture: From the Kennedy Assassination to The X-Files (2000). Not a book of conspiracy theories, but a book of theories about conspiracy theories. Knight's survey of other academics' thinking is probably the best around, and there are lots of insightful comments on the rise and development of conspiracy theories in American culture, well illustrated by examples from theories about JFK, AIDS, crack cocaine – and even feminism. See also the excellent collection of essays edited by Peter Knight, *Conspiracy Nation: The Politics of Paranoia in Post-war America* (2002).

Peter Knight (ed) Conspiracy Theories in American History: An Encyclopedia (2003). Before it mysteriously vanished from bookstores, this was the last word in conspiracy literature, with 925 pages on over 300 conspiracies. Write-ups come from over 120 mainly academic, specialist contributors; most try to sort the wheat from the chaff. Covers conspiracist culture as much as actual theories, with entries for novelist Thomas Pynchon and "yellow journalism", as well as overview pieces. JFK gets the most detailed coverage, with fifteen pages.

George Monbiot Captive State: The Corporate Takeover of Britain (2000). Britain's leading anti-globalization journalist exposes the pernicious and sometimes malicious influence of corporations on British society, from the imposition of the infamous Skye Bridge and the "economic cleansing" of supermarkets to the role of corporate capital in university research. Angry, but balanced, persuasive and impeccably researched.

Vance Packard Hidden Persuaders (1957). Classic exposé of advertising techniques that occasionally slips into conspiracism. Packard protests that they try to invade the privacy of our minds. All the more fascinating for being very dated.

Jane Parish and Martin Parker (eds) The Age of Anxiety: Conspiracy Theory and the Human Sciences (2001). Ten academic sociologists' essays on conspiracy culture. Topics covered include the New World Order, the Patriot movement, viruses and France's Front National, but the book is theoretical for the most part, trying to define conspiracism as a sociological phenomenon.

Marvin Perry and Frederick M. Schweitzer Anti-Semitism: Myth and Hate from Antiquity to the Present (2002). Scholarly but very readable study of hate-myths about Jews, from them being ritual murderers of Christians to global banking oligarchs. Reveals how these conspiracy theories have profoundly influenced history.

Daniel Pipes Conspiracy: How the Paranoid Style Flourishes and Where It Comes From (1997). Thoughtful overview of conspiracism throughout history, particularly strong on disentangling the various strands of conspiracist thinking and showing how much modern theories owe to the past. Pipes excoriates the ultra-Right, but doesn't miss the chance to lambast the Left.

Daniel Pipes The Hidden Hand: Middle East Fears of Conspiracy (1996). Pipes is a controversial figure with a strong pro-Israeli agenda, but this is one of the best books on Arab conspiracism nonetheless, with lots of examples of conspiracy theories in post-war Middle Eastern history.

Robin Ramsay Conspiracy Theories (2006). Ramsay, who is also editor of *Lobster* magazine, looms large in the conspiracy world as an investigative writer with a pretty sane take on theories, their flaws and their truths. This is a well-argued mini-guide to his preferred conspiracies, with interesting thoughts on what conspiracy theories are, and why they matter.

Jon Ronson Them: Adventures with Extremists (2001). In this insightful and very funny travelogue into the extremes of conspiracy culture, British writer Ronson gets right down into the conspiracy basement with some serious weirdos.

Elaine Showalter Hystories: Hysterical Epidemics and Modern Culture (1997). Showalter's notorious is that modern epidemics – such as chronic fatigue syndrome, Gulf War syndrome, alien abduction and Satanic ritual abuse claims – are classic symptoms of hysteria amplified by modern communications and *fin de siècle* anxiety. Conspiracism, she says, is a psychic problem.

Kenn Thomas (ed) Cyberculture Counterconspiracy (1999). These "Web readers" are republished articles from the Steamshovel Press conspiracy magazine, and are sometimes authoritative, sometimes wacky and almost always distinctly conspiracist. Comes in two volumes – take your pick from the contents list.

Damian Thompson Counterknowledge (2008). Or, "how we surrendered to conspiracy theories, quack medicine, bogus science and fake history". A bit of a rant, with more on medicine than conspiracies, but it will blow away the cobwebs nicely.

Jonathan Vankin and John Whalen The 80 Greatest Conspiracies of All Time (2004). As the title suggests, this US-centred tome is written with a keen eye on the popular market. It's actually quite well written, but many of the accounts of the theories are very thin – some are little more than brief book reviews.

Francis Wheen How Mumbo-Jumbo Conquered the World (2004). Vitriolic, comic and ultimately journalistic rant against UFOs, religion, New Age culture, astrology, self-help… and conspiracy theories.

Robert A. Wilson Everything Is Under Control: Conspiracies, Cults and Cover-ups (1998). The grandfather of conspiracism in an encyclopedic but thoughtful and playful set of essays. Asserts that the usual suspects, such as Jews, the New World Order and patriarchy, aren't real in the way that "basketballs, barking dogs, and baked beans" are.

Fiction

Dan Brown The Da Vinci Code (2003). The book that (re)launched Christian conspiracy theories on the world. Poorly written and clunkily plotted, but there's a reason this book sold tens of millions of copies. It covers everything from the bloodline of Jesus and Mary Magdalene to the heritage of the Templars, with lots of what Brown calls "symbology" thrown in. *Angels and Demons* (2000), which imagines a terrorist standoff between techno-happy Illuminati and the Vatican, is the better thriller, but the subject matter feels more hackneyed.

Ian Caldwell and Dustin Thomason The Rule of Four (2004). A kind of middlebrow *Da Vinci Code*, featuring two Princeton students on a moderately thrilling quest to trace the secret behind the Renaissance manuscript, the *Hypnerotomachia Poliophili*.

Richard Condon The Manchurian Candidate (1959). The satirical political thriller that launched two hit films (see p.210).

Joseph Conrad The Secret Agent (1907). A bomb plot in the heart of London draws in foreign agents, anarchists and unwitting family members. Strange, often absurd and always deeply pessimistic, or as Conrad puts it, "An impenetrable mystery seems destined to hang for ever over this act of madness or despair."

Don DeLillo Libra (1988). Brilliant and very literary conspiracy novel: two CIA agents plan a false-flag operation to fake an (unsuccessful) assassination of JFK and blame it on the Cubans. Unfortunately, the patsy they choose is called Lee Harvey Oswald. While writing *Libra*, DeLillo has said, "there were times when I felt an eerie excitement, coming across an item that seemed to bear out my own theories. Anyone who enters this maze knows you have to become part scientist, novelist, biographer, historian and existential detective."

Craig DiLouie Paranoia (2001). Zeitgeisty, literary-lite novel charting the descent of an orderly working at a mental health hospital into the world of conspiracy, where paranoia becomes a dangerous addiction and scepticism is no longer an option. Draws chiefly on Illuminati, WMDs and presidential assassination conspiracy theories.

Benjamin Disraeli Lothair (1870). A glamorous romp through nineteenth-century European high politics, taking in Roman Catholic conspiracies and Italian secret societies. As British prime minister, Disraeli frequently warned against conspiracies – you'd have thought he knew a thing or two.

Umberto Eco Foucault's Pendulum (1988). The intellectual's *Da Vinci Code*. Eco is the master of the ironic, postmodernist esoteric thriller, and this novel is probably his most challenging and rewarding. It's also drawn straight from conspiracy culture. Three eccentric Italian literary types design their own Templar conspiracy theory and are then horrified to find it appears to be true. Packed with verbal brilliance and abstruse fragments of Renaissance and Jewish occultism.

Giuseppe Genna In the Name of Ishmael (2003). This literary-minded detective thriller tracks two parallel police investigations in Milan, one in 1962, the other in 2001. The two detectives' enquiries converge ominously on a mysterious and powerful figure called Ishmael, whose murky political and sex crimes seem to be at the centre of decades of conspiracies – both Italian and international.

Robert Harris Fatherland (1992). It's 1964 and the Nazis have most of Europe in their grip. Maverick Berlin detective Xavier March starts to uncover clues that lead him to discover the conspiracy buried deep in the Nazi past: the Holocaust. A thrilling, intelligent and fascinating take on alternative history.

Thomas Pynchon The Crying of Lot 49 (1965). At around 150 pages, this is Pynchon at his most accessible, but it's still pretty meaty stuff – a brilliantly chaotic and often darkly comic maelstrom of pop and conspiracy culture, science and occultism. As the executor of her late boyfriend's estate, Oedipa Maas seems to discover a web of conspiracy focused on a bizarre postal system called Tristero. There's more crazy 1960s Americana in *Vineland* (1990), but for truly serious Pynchon, try *Gravity's Rainbow* (1973), set around a World War II quest for the V2 rocket, with plenty of conspirators on the sidelines.

Robert Shea and Robert Anton Wilson Illuminatus! (1975). Inspector Saul Goodman, Homicide, comes across memos that suggest the Illuminati still exist, and sets out on the trail. Much beloved by computer nerds, this high-camp occultist sci-fi trilogy rolls endless conspiracy theories into its magpie-picking at 1960s alternative culture, along with characters such as Padre Pederastia and heavy doses of eschatological humour. The first sentence of part one, *The Eye in the Pyramid*, says it all: "It was the year when they finally immanentized the Eschaton."

Films

Jack Arnold It Came from Outer Space (1953). Easily the most durable of the spate of 1950s sci-fi films about UFOs coming to America. An eccentric amateur astronomer discovers that a meteor crash is, in fact, a downed spaceship. Nobody believes him, of course, until the local townsfolk start to behave seriously strangely. Heavy anti-communist undertones, and a good twist in the plot.

Francis Ford Coppola The Conversation (1974). Gene Hackman plays an obsessive covert surveillance expert whose brilliant technical skills help him to piece together a murderous plot involving a mysterious VIP client. Conceived pre-Watergate and made in the wake of *The Godfather*, this is a superb downbeat study in paranoia.

Costa-Gavras Missing (1981). Based on the true story of Thomas Hauser, this follows the search by one American father for his son in the aftermath of General Pinochet's 1973 coup in Chile. In Costa-Gavras's first US production, the audience accompanies the excellent Jack Lemmon on his journey to the painful realization that his son is as lost as thousands of innocent Chileans in a coup backed by his own government. Condemned by the US State Department, if you need any further recommendation.

Costa-Gavras Z (1969). In an unnamed country under right-wing rule – the story is based on real-life events in Costa-Gavras's native Greece – an outspoken opposition leader (Yves Montand) is fatally injured in a traffic accident. Or was he assassinated? Jean-Louis Trintignant is the magistrate seeking the truth and uncovering the true mendacity of power. Coming so soon after the killings of the Kennedy brothers and Martin Luther King, this Oscar-winning political thriller resonated with US audiences.

Emile De Antonio Rush to Judgement (1967). A documentary from Mark Lane's book of the same name about JFK's assassination, narrated by Lane as he cuts down the Warren Commission's conclusion. Interesting as one of the earliest conspiracy theories on JFK, and for observing what conspiracy documentaries looked like in those days.

Brian De Palma Blow Out (1981). In one of his best roles, John Travolta plays a B-movie sound engineer who accidentally records a car crash that kills a presidential candidate. After rescuing the sole survivor (Nancy Allen), he becomes convinced that the fatal blowout was caused by a bullet, and persuades her to help him unmask the conspiracy. Alludes knowingly both to other films (Michelangelo Antonioni's *Blowup*, Francis Ford Coppola's *The Conversation*) and to theories about JFK's assassination and Teddy Kennedy's "Chappaquiddick incident".

Roger Donaldson Thirteen Days (2000). As the world teeters on the brink of nuclear war during the Cuban Missile Crisis, the Kennedy brothers find that the war-crazies aren't confined to Moscow – a few work at the Pentagon too. A fascinating, taut depiction of real events (although the Pentagon refused to cooperate with filming).

Richard Donner Conspiracy Theory (1997). Mel Gibson plays nervy, paranoid, rambling New York cab driver Jerry Fletcher, who's obsessed with both a government mind-control conspiracy and lawyer Alice Sutton (Julia Roberts). Fletcher starts to think he is going mad himself until the government, in the shape of Patrick Stewart, steps in to shut his mouth. Thrilling, and it plays provocatively with the idea that a conspiracy theory can have a final validation.

Roland Emmerich Independence Day (1996). In this "America Saves the World" extravaganza, aliens come and zap every capital city on the planet. Fortunately, the US military has kept all those alien spaceships at the fabled Roswell airbase nicely tuned-up for just such an occasion.

Theodore J. Flicker The President's Analyst (1967). A zany 1960s spy spoof, with James Coburn as a New York shrink hired to analyse the US president back to sanity, only Coburn nearly goes mad when pursued by the world's finks and spooks seeking to unpick the president's noodle.

Bryan Forbes The Stepford Wives (1975). A paranoid feminist's nightmare. All the men in Stepford have conspired to turn their wives into perfectly submissive fantasy women, but Katharine Ross just won't play ball. Funny and disturbing in equal measure.

John Frankenheimer The Manchurian Candidate (1962). Korean war veteran and ex-POW Frank Sinatra has nightmares about fellow soldiers carrying out missions for the commies. A cunning plot to use brainwashed POWs as sleeper assassins is uncovered. But is it really the Reds who are behind it? In Jonathan Demme's 2004 remake, Denzel Washington and Meryl Streep can't quite match the Sinatra/Angela Lansbury team of the original, but the updating of the North Korean setting and Cold War context to Iraq and the military-industrial complex is clever and successful.

John Frankenheimer Seven Days in May (1964). The sequel to *The Manchurian Candidate*, and every bit its equal. US president "Lyman Jordan" initiates a nuclear disarmament programme alongside the Soviets. Quiet but ruthless General Scott (Burt Lancaster) seems about to launch a military coup to prevent it, but his plans are uncovered by Jiggs Casey (Kirk Douglas), a Pentagon aide who just happens to be a friend and close associate of Scott's. Tensely plays out ethical dilemmas and conspiracy plots in atmospheric White House/Pentagon settings.

William Friedkin Rules of Engagement (2000). Pro-army propaganda that relocates the mass killings of Somalis by US Marines in Mogadishu in 1993 to Yemen. Commander Samuel L. Jackson is framed by a bent State Department and a long trial ensues. Strangely, the closing credits claim that the film is based on fact.

Peter Hyams Capricorn One (1977). Elliot Gould plays a reporter who stumbles across the hoax of the century, with NASA faking an entire six-month manned mission to Mars. But when the spacecraft burns up, the astronauts (still on Earth, on the film set) have to be disposed of…

Stanley Kubrick Dr Strangelove (1963). This seminal Cold War satire sees George C. Scott's lunatic US general taking the world into a nuclear war because of his own paranoid fantasies – including a commie plot to fluoridate America's water. Peter Sellers plays nearly everyone else, including a scientist supposedly modelled on Dr Sidney Gottlieb, the LSD-toking chief of the CIA's MK-ULTRA project.

Barry Levinson Wag the Dog (1997). Political satire featuring a spin doctor (Robert De Niro), a Hollywood producer (Dustin Hoffman) and a White House aide (Anne Heche), who join forces to bury the news of the president's molestation of a young girl – a fortnight before the election. Their solution is a nice, distracting, fake war in Albania. Predates the Clinton–Lewinski saga and the Kosovo War.

Doug Liman The Bourne Identity (2002). Matt Damon washes up somewhere on the Mediterranean coast with his memory erased, but somehow equipped with incredible skills of evasion and survival. As he tries to piece together how he got there, he is pursued around glamorous European locations (notably Paris and Prague) by dodgy Americans with long coats and a host of tracking devices. Based on a Robert Ludlum thriller, this film mixes questions about identity with a high-action plot. *The Bourne Supremacy* and *The Bourne Ultimatum* complete the trilogy.

Richard Linklater Slacker (1991). A genuinely original independent movie, shot for $23,000 on 16mm film. It's basically a collection of semi-comic rants by a long series of quirky counter culture types, on subjects ranging from UFOs to JFK and Elvis conspiracy theories. What could be incredibly dull is made immediate and absorbing by an improvisational feel and a thoughtful take on conspiracist culture.

Sidney Lumet Network (1976). A TV anchorman (an Oscar-winning Peter Finch) has a nervous breakdown and suddenly tells his audience it's all "bullshit". This, of course, only wins viewers and gets Finch his own show – one paranoid man fighting the agenda behind the "real" news. But he is unwittingly compromised by a network bent on winning ratings at any cost – including fabricating its own stories.

David Lynch Mulholland Drive (2001). Lynch's films are famously disorienting and this is the most confusing of them all. As such, it's impossible to summarize, but it's based on the dreams of a suicidal young woman. While it isn't a conspiracy-theory film as such, it's a brilliant riff on how narratives can be twisted by different viewpoints and interpretations, by memories, fantasies and forgetfulness, and it vibrates with a paranoid and deeply conspiratorial style.

John Mackenzie Ruby (1992). Sub-JFK flick focusing on Jack Ruby, the murderer of Lee Harvey Oswald. Conveys a good flavour of the era's seedy mobster glamour, and includes a great reconstruction of the Dealey Plaza assassination, but unconvincing as a conspiracy theory – Ruby is apparently exposing "the truth" of Mafia–CIA collusion.

Fernando Meirelles The Constant Gardener (2005). A shy English diplomat (Ralph Fiennes) in Kenya is drawn into a dangerous conspiracy involving a pharmaceutical company's sinister drug-testing scheme following the death of his feisty political activist wife (Rachel Weisz). Featuring flashbacks that illuminate the early days of their relationship, this film – based on a typically sophisticated John Le Carré novel – is stunningly shot.

Scott Michell The Innocent Sleep (1996). Based on the Roberto Calvi affair, this thriller centres on a down-and-out who witnesses the murder of a businessman, left hanging from a London bridge. He is drawn into investigating the affair and the corrupt policeman involved, but the more he discovers about a major conspiracy, the greater the danger he stumbles into.

David Miller Executive Action (1973). A cabal of rich old white men plot JFK's assassination in this fictional take on the killing that's both colder and far more convincing than Oliver Stone's *JFK*.

Michael Moore Fahrenheit 9/11 (2004). This controversial documentary-style, one-man political roadshow portrays a pernicious post-9/11 Bush administration cynically spreading a message of fear in order to prepare the electorate for a war on Iraq and blind it to abrogations of civil liberties. Michael Moore spins a suggestive web connecting the Bush family to the House of Saud and Osama bin Laden. The film inspired a right-wing backlash against Moore's "conspiracy theories". Gripping, but you know you're being manipulated by Moore too.

Niels Mueller The Assassination of Richard Nixon (2004). As honest salesman Samuel Bicke's life falls apart in 1974, he sees President Richard "Crook" Nixon still occupying the White House. So Bicke (played by Sean Penn) sets out to kill Tricky Dicky in this factually based drama.

Alan J. Pakula All the President's Men (1976). Robert Redford and Dustin Hoffman sweat and snap at each other in this intelligent but wordy depiction of how real-life reporters Bob Woodward and Carl Bernstein battled against newspaper deadlines, editorial jitters and walls of silence to trace the Watergate burglary all the way back to the White House – at considerable personal risk.

Alan J. Pakula The Parallax View (1974). A strange, claustrophobic thriller made around the time of Nixon's resignation, with Warren Beatty's reporter delving into a vast, mysterious, extra-governmental conspiracy following the assassination of a Kennedy-style presidential candidate.

Alan J. Pakula Rollover (1981). The eerily topical premise here is that the power of the dollar depends on Saudi Arabians selling oil in it and funnelling the profits through the world's banks. But what if they suddenly conspired to withdraw their investments? Murdered banker's widow Jane Fonda and Wall Street troubleshooter Kris Kristofferson join forces to battle the Saudis and the government to avert a global economic depression. Too cerebral for a conventional action thriller, but well worth seeing.

Wolfgang Petersen Outbreak (1995). A mutated strain of the Ebola virus is brought to the US by an infected monkey. The truth behind a military WMD experiment and cover-up is revealed. Bog-standard scaremonger thriller just about rescued by good performances from Dustin Hoffman and Rene Russo.

Roman Polanski Chinatown (1974). An Oscar-winning *film noir* thriller in which LA detective Jake Gittes (Jack Nicholson) investigates a murder – and almost drowns in a murky conspiracy involving the water company and local government.

Sydney Pollack The Interpreter (2005). United Nations interpreter Nicole Kidman overhears a plot to assassinate an African dictator. G-man Sean Penn swallows the urge to say "don't worry, love, happens all the time" and mixes in to stop them both being killed in a thriller that has more pace than imagination. Added interest comes from it being shot almost entirely at the UN's HQ in New York.

William Richert Winter Kills (1979). Adaptation of the Richard Condon thriller, with Jeff Bridges and John Huston. Almost twenty years after a Kennedy-style presidential assassination, the heir to the "Keegan" political dynasty starts to uncover the truth. As his father warns him, "They will run you dizzy. They will pile falsehood on top of falsehood until you can't tell a lie from the truth and you won't even want to. That's how the powerful keep their power. Don't you read the papers?"

Phil Alden Robinson Sneakers (1992). Robert Redford's shadowy team of techno-geeks tries to snare evil tycoon Ben Kingsley in his quest to control the world's stock markets with a brilliant gizmo in a box. A pudgy Dan Aykroyd makes a lot of noise as a conspiracy-theory nut in this vaguely amusing caper.

John Schlesinger Marathon Man (1976). An ex-Nazi in Latin America (played by Laurence Olivier), who breaks his cover in New York, and a secret government agency called the Division conspire to make Dustin Hoffman very confused. A thriller of cross and double-cross that will give you nightmares about your next visit to the dentist – especially if he looks anything like Olivier's sadistic Szell. Other, lesser films on similar topics include *The Odessa File* (1974) and *The Boys from Brazil* (1978).

Don Siegel Invasion of the Body Snatchers (1955). People in a small town keep complaining that their spouses aren't their normal selves, the reason being that they've been replaced with alien clones grown from pods. Classic paranoid thriller about the outsiders within, which Philip Kaufmann's 1978 remake adds to with icky special effects.

Barry Sonnenfeld Men in Black (1997). Very silly and sometimes very funny comedy playing up to the mythology of the "Men in Black" alien/FBI conspiracy theory. Will Smith stars as a New York cop recruited to a secretive government agency aimed at suppressing "illegal aliens" – extraterrestrial-style aliens, that is.

Steven Spielberg Close Encounters of the Third Kind (1977). This suggests not only that friendly aliens have been coming to Earth for years, but that they've been up to all sorts of tricks that the government's been aware of all along. Visually impressive, if a fraction overlong.

Oliver Stone JFK (1991). Kevin Costner in one of his best roles, as voice-in-the-wilderness Jim Garrison, a district attorney struggling against all the odds to bring a lawsuit against the conspirators behind the JFK assassination. The unashamedly one-sided account is partly explained by the fact that it drew heavily on the conspiracy theories of Garrison himself and Jim Marrs, and partly by Stone's self-proclaimed desire to create not a documentary but a "fable", an emotional counterpunch to the rationalist approach of the Warren Commission. Long and often rambling, but the "magic bullet" courthouse scene is unmissable.

Oliver Stone Nixon (1995). A discomfiting biopic of Richard Nixon – the chronology is jarringly disrupted – sprinkled with Stone's trademark images and fleeting allusions to far bigger, blacker conspiracies. Surprisingly, Nixon (played by Anthony Hopkins) comes across not so much as an arch-villain as an outsider vainly battling to tame the real beasts that run America.

Jon Turteltaub National Treasure (2004). *Indiana Jones* meets Masonic conspiracy theories. Nicolas Cage stars as a treasure-hunter trying to steal the Declaration of Independence, which conceals a treasure map that will guide him to the Masonic secrets of America's founding fathers. The similarly heavy-footed sequel, subtitled *Book of Secrets*, offers more of the same fare, taking as its starting point the eighteen missing pages of the diary of John Wilkes Booth, Abraham Lincoln's assassin.

Andy and Larry Wachowski The Matrix (1999). Keanu Reeves is a computer programmer by day and a whiz hacker by night, until a series of fortuitous discoveries lead him to realize that the human race is living in a virtual-reality dream world, unwittingly serving as a giant energy cell to power "the Machines". The two sequels add big battle scenes, but little else to the concept.

Irwin Winkler The Net (1995). Hollywood's most successful "cyberthriller" stars Sandra Bullock as a somewhat unlikely computer expert whose identity is stolen. As she attempts to get it back, she is dragged out of her safe life into a world of conspiracy. Hackneyed, but satisfyingly tense.

Websites

Conspiracy theory sites and magazines

www.bilderberg.org One-man campaign, run from Bristol in the UK by a Quaker, which describes itself as a "lobbying organization" against the "power elite". Begins with the Bilderberg Group, but soon spirals out into attacks on globalization and all kinds of conspiracy areas. "It is the facts behind very real groups like the Bilderbergers, the Skull and Bones and the Council on Foreign Relations that must be known before we can best understand how to deal with them on a personal and a global level."

www.carpenoctem.tv/cons Nicely written and generally level-headed list of mini-guides to around forty or so conspiracy theories. Elsewhere on the site you'll find similar pieces on serial killers and haunted hotspots.

www.conspiracyarchive.com The Illuminati Conspiracy Archive believes in "the occult nature of the ruling elite". Lots of professionally presented articles on Freemasonry, the New World Order and the paranormal. According to the authors, the word "conspiracy, in many cases, should be replaced with policy. Likewise, theory is easily interchanged with documented" – which kind of makes it a "documented policy" site.

www.conspiracyplanet.com The Alternative News and History Network describes itself as the "antidote to Media Cartel Propaganda". It borrows a lot from other conspiracy websites and mixes intelligent takes on events with more flagrant fruitcake views.

www.covertactionquarterly.org Formerly the Covert Action Information Bulletin, this is a mixed bag of broadly left-wing, generally well-sourced news and conspiracy articles. Its mission is more to seek out what powers like the CIA or neo-Nazi groups are up to, rather than to indulge in wild-eyed speculation on aliens and Masons.

www.davidicke.com Click on the "headlines" link and scroll down past all the book promos to get to the Icke team's wacky take on the news of the day. Lots of good photos and wildly scurrilous allegations. Icke's more seriously conspiratorial work can be found at www.davidicke.net.

www.deepblacklies.co.uk Author David Guyatt is a former investment banker with a mission to expose the truth about the financing of the international arms trade.

From this tight, serious base, the site spirals into discussion of WMDs, Nazi gold, Vatican corruption and much more. Also includes lots of World War II conspiracy history.

www.disinfo.com Lots of stories, some very well argued, plus videos and links to Disinformation's excellent publications (*Everything You Know is Wrong, The Book of Lies* etc). Includes a discussion site for theorists on the dubious side of current affairs – the "disinformation meebo room".

www.fromthewilderness.com Newsletter and website maintained by former LAPD narcotics investigator and CIA/drugs whistleblower Michael Ruppert, whose main interest is now Peak Oil and the conspiracies that surround it, notably from within the "Bush–Cheney drug empire".

www.larouchepub.com The official site of Lyndon LaRouche's deeply conspiratorial *Executive Intelligence Review*. LaRouche is a man on the fringe of the US political scene – his supporters think he's a visionary, but some think he's a conspiracy theory in his own right who exists to spread disinformation and discredit other theorists.

www.lobster-magazine.co.uk *Lobster,* the Journal of Parapolitics – "as denounced in the House of Commons" – is edited by the tough, sceptical left-winger Robin Ramsay, who has even less time for bullshit than he has for political chicanery. It's a proper magazine: you need to subscribe to get access to the articles.

www.maebrussell.com Lots of articles on contemporary conspiracy theories, but the best thing about this site is the downloadable MP3s of Californian conspiracy commentator Mae Brussell's original radio shows. Mesmerizing.

www.namebase.org Amazing searchable index of historical and political books – mostly conspiracy-related – and the people who appear in them. A great tool for researchers, you can even find out which pages of which books your suspect appears on.

www.newsalliance.com Unusually, a site focusing on British conspiracy theories: Diana, David Kelly, MI5, and the "dangers" of immigration and Muslim extremism.

www.paranoiamagazine.com *Paranoia* magazine has been publishing articles on conspiracy theories, the occult and the paranormal since 1992. It leavens the usual fare with pinches of humour and salt. You can browse online, but have to subscribe to receive the full magazine three times a year. Back issues are now published as a book.

www.parascope.com Although this site was undergoing changes at the time of writing, you can still trawl the archive for articles on conspiracies, aliens and the paranormal. Theories you may not have come across before include "Air Force invades NASCAR race", whatever that's about.

www.pehi.eu The Project for the Exposure of Hidden Institutions focuses on the "old boys' network of low-profile, privately funded and intelligence-ridden institutes" that exert disproportionate influence on government. Writes up the usual suspects, such as Bohemian Grove, but also includes lesser-known groups like Le Cercle, apparently connected with the Vatican, and the 1001 Club.

www.prisonplanet.com A professionally presented rolling news site featuring theories and commentaries. One of many sites linked with prolific, slick US radio host Alex Jones, a libertarian, anti-New World Order commentator. Jones's official, commercial website is www.infowars.com. For an antidote, see www.perrylogan.org/AlexBleef.html for a long list of disturbing and often contradictory beliefs apparently subscribed to by Jones.

www.publiceye.org/conspire The progressive think-tank Political Research Associates maintains a sophisticated site devoted to debunking conspiracy theories. The wry "Conspiracy Theory Generator" shows how "conspiracism as a genre is a structured combination of a stylistic meta-frame of tragic apocalyptic dualism merged with narratives built around the components of demonization and scapegoating." So now you know.

www.rense.com Radio host Jeff Rense keeps this continually updated with contentious takes on the news of the day.

www.rotten.com "When Hell is full, the dead will walk the earth." Indeed. Includes a lot of pretty disturbing images of death and mutilation (as well as some hard-core porn), but also worryingly fascinating news updates on the most scurrilous events of the day, and the day before.

www.rumormillnews.com Alternative news website, with pieces written by "agents", usually with a Christian, conservative, conspiracist leaning. The site does not contain any classified information because "Rumor Mill News is a strong supporter of the American Military". There's also a forum area for discussion of news, theories etc.

www.sherryshriner.com Talk show host Sherry Shriner seems to have a thing about aliens, and making the best use of the Bible to smite them. Also includes the New World Order, Illuminati, Jews – all evidence of the work of Satan. But fear not: a donation will help Shriner fight the good fight. More of the same at www.thewatcherfiles.com.

www.skepdic.com This "skeptics' dictionary" is an alphabetically arranged list of links for paranormal, mystical and conspiratorial stories.

www.steamshovelpress.com A real magazine with its own website (which doesn't present much by way of links or news itself), Steamshovel Press mixes full-on conspiracy theories with fascinating articles on the more plausible – but no less dark – methods of how those in power seek to hold onto it, and profit from it. Attracts some good writers, and a fair few crazies to boot. Requires a subscription.

www.theforbiddenknowledge.com Crammed with intricately detailed pieces articulating everything from the perils of Freemasonry to the computer chips that will take over your life.

www.theinsider.org Well-run conspiracy site with regularly updated news headlines, a newsletter, links to sites and forums, and special reports on issues from "Unfair World Trade" and "Oil Running Out" to the "G8 Bible Prophecy".

www.totse.com The bulletin board of the Temple of the Screaming Electron has a distinctly anarchic bent, offering anti-government theories, hackers' tips and unverifiable information on how to make drugs and things that go bang.

www.weirdload.com The coverage of this one-man site ranges from aliens to the New World Order, with a genuinely offbeat take on the world. The presiding theme is anti-Catholicism; as the author puts it: "I was an 'unlucky' altar boy, having been repeatedly sexually and ritualistically abused by my parish priest. As an adult I long ago fled the Church of Rome and became an ordained priest in the Church of Antioch – Malabar Rite."

www2.winchester.ac.uk/ccc The Centre for Conspiracy Culture at Winchester University, UK, has ties with some of the leading academics in the field. Carries possibly the best bibliography on conspiracism, covering both print and online material, and plentiful links to articles.

www.zeitgeistmovie.com Enthralling but glaringly tendentious online film, which explains the world by graphically linked conspiracy theories going back to Ancient Egypt.

Conspiracy blogs and forums

www.abovetopsecret.com A handsomely made website mixing acerbic cut-downs of manipulated news with cover-ups and a few out-and-out fantasies. The site's best aspect, though, is its forum including a dedicated conspiracy-related area that attracts lots of relatively informed commentators following the numerous threads.

alexconstantine.blogspot.com The "anti-fascist research bin", in which Constantine brings together media scannings and his own ruminations, focusing on US political corruption and foreign policy. Has a self-proclaimed "20-year career of reporting while living under intense CIA harassment including torture … with non-lethal weapons that burn and cause sleep deprivation and worse."

www.ctrl.org Eye-wateringly colourful site that allows you to sign up for the email traffic of the Conspiracy Theory Research List. But beware – there can be up to 100 posts a day. The archive section gives you a bit more control, and includes postings of conspiracy-related news items from newspapers, agencies and broadcasters around the world.

www.dailygrail.com Wide-ranging blog whose posts range from "astrobiology" and Yonaguni Underwater Monuments through to Votergate, Masonic influences in the US and conspiratorial chat about the day's news stories.

www.danielpipes.org Articles, comments and spats on Middle Eastern current affairs and conspiracism from a high-profile academic with Republican links. Becomes curiously strident when the subject is Islam (or "the Islamist enemy") and the liberal Left – and when isn't it?

groups.google.com/group/alt.conspiracy/topics Vast list of topics – and an excellent forcing ground for new theories. US-dominated, inevitably.

groups.msn.com/conspiracytheory Popular conspiracy news group, with scores of posts every day. If you can't find someone to argue your pet theory with here, you'll just have to talk it through with the voices in your head.

www.order-order.com "Guido Fawkes' blog of plots, rumours and conspiracy." Named after the infamous would-be bomber of the British Parliament (reputed to be "the only man to enter Parliament with honest intentions"), this UK-based political blog and discussion site uses salacious news and irreverent comment instead of gunpowder.

General resources

www2.gwu.edu/~nsarchiv/index.html Home of the National Security Archive, an NGO and research library based at George Washington University in Washington, DC. A top source for declassified documents acquired through the Freedom of Information Act, and a great resource for conspiracy theorists who do their own research.

www.aarclibrary.org The Assassination Archives and Research Center is a privately run news archive and online library. Thousands of online documents on political assassinations, including John and Robert Kennedy and Martin Luther King, many released from government records under the Freedom of Information Act. Includes facsimiles of the entire Warren Commission hearings.

www.adl.org The Anti-Defamation League's page has an archive of patiently written rebuttals and shootdowns of the more anti-Semitic theories that make the rounds, and takes a few shots at what might be considered fair comment.

www.campus-watch.org Deeply controversial site that "monitors" Middle East-related issues and articles in US universities, and names and shames those it sees as stepping out of line. Opponents would say it conflates anti-Israeli politics with anti-Semitism and attacks free speech. The project says it is aimed at "analytical failures, the mixing of politics with scholarship, intolerance of alternative views, apologetics, and the abuse of power over students".

www.fas.org/irp/hotdocs.htm The nonprofit Federation of American Scientists – originally a group of atomic scientists concerned about the accelerating arms race – makes available all the most topical US government documents in the public sphere, from Justice Department memos and press releases to full downloads of the 9-11 Commission and WMD Commission reports. The hotdocs page includes the most requested documents on this popular site.

www.mufon.com The Mutual UFO Network is "dedicated to the Scientific Study of UFOs for the Benefit of Humanity." One of the best-respected groups of its kind.

www.museumofhoaxes.com Everything from Pope Joan to Milli Vanilli. Also includes a forum and the Hoaxipedia, covering "hoaxes, urban legends, pranks, tall tales, scams, and deceptions of all kinds".

www.religioustolerance.org As the name suggests, this site is dedicated to giving all religions due respect. Features well-written articles on all things religious, including a number aimed at countering conspiracists' misconceptions about Wicca, Masons, Satanism and so on.

www.snopes.com Witty, accurate and utterly browsable analysis of urban myths, covering anything from "racial rumours" to "old wives' tales", taking in lots of conspiracy theories on the way. Explodes most myths, but the fun is in seeing exactly how they grew and finding out the real story. Gives ratings for true, false and "undetermined". Fully searchable, but the hierarchical format is well thought out.

www.ufoevidence.org Relatively serious-minded site compiling research on UFO sightings, including photos etc.

General news media

www.aljazeera.com Not the international Arab news network Al Jazeera, but an online magazine with a superb section dedicated to conspiracy theories with a Middle Eastern angle – lots on Iran, Iraq and Palestine, of course.

www.commondreams.org Breaking news and views for the "progressive community", this hosts a wealth of taut, Left-leaning essays and alternative (as opposed to flatly conspiratorial) takes on political issues worldwide, with some big-name thinkers contributing.

www.consortiumnews.com Serious-minded news/comment website originally set up as "a home for important, well-reported stories that weren't welcome in the O.J. Simpson-obsessed, conventional-wisdom-driven national news media of that time". Run by Robert Parry, an experienced investigative journalist and author with a broadly liberal agenda and a taste for conspiracy.

www.drudgereport.com Compiled and directed by the notorious "Internet news aggregator" Matt Drudge, this site, with its links to a wealth of US news wires, websites and columnists, reports on "alleged" political scandal – yellow journalism in its modern-day format.

www.globalismnews.com Journalistic anti-globalization news and comment site. Click on "who dares call it conspiracy" for lots of good links to classic conspiracy theory articles elsewhere on the Web.

www.indymedia.org A site dedicated to real news stories with a more radical, anti-authority perspective. This is the main hub for the global network of indymedia-affiliated sites, and for the organization's own campaigns.

www.informationclearinghouse.info A left-wing, progressively oriented site of current affairs articles, with links to a host of films and online documentaries, including some rare gems of footage.

www.newsmakingnews.com A rolling news service of mainly US and UK stories with an anti-authoritarian bent, updated daily. The chronological listing gives a somewhat random feel to the site, but it's a good way to gauge which way the wind's blowing.

www.no2id.net Some would say there are no conspiracies here, but it's certainly a good place to find all the news you need to scare yourself about the coming digi-neo-Stasi state.

www.spinwatch.org Founded in 2004, Spinwatch charts and attacks the endemic use of spin, PR and propaganda throughout the news media and parliamentary lobbying.

www.thesmokinggun.com With information gleaned from Freedom of Information requests and court reports, the Smoking Gun carries some truly eye-widening stories from the glittery worlds of politics and entertainment, and others from the cesspits of life.

www.underthecarpet.co.uk Rolling news and current affairs site with mainstream press articles, as well as other links to films and "documents", selected from a somewhat conspiracist perspective.

www.whatreallyhappened.com Less conspiracy, more political controversy. An anti-war site with stacks of links to news sites every day.

INDEX

B

C

D

E

F

G

H

I

J

K

L

M

N

O

P

T

U